The

AMERICAN JOURNEY
A HISTORY OF THE UNITED STATES

Portfolio Edition

VOLUME I

David Goldfield

Carl Abbott

Virginia DeJohn Anderson

Jo Ann E. Argersinger

Peter H. Argersinger

William L. Barney

Robert M. Weir

PEARSON
Prentice
Hall

Upper Saddle River, New Jersey 07458

Library of Congress Cataloging-in-Publication Data

The American Journey: a history of the United States / David Goldfield . . . [et al.].—
  Portfolio ed.
    p. cm.
    "Combined volume."
    Includes bibliographical references and index.
    ISBN 0-13-192098-7 (paperback)
    1. United States—History—Textbooks. I. Goldfield, David R.

  E178.1.A4925 2005b
  973—dc22   2005042970

VP, Editorial Director: Charlyce Jones Owen
Associate Editor: Emsal Hasan
Editorial Assistant: Maureen Diana
Director of Marketing: Heather Shelstad
Marketing Assistant: Cherron Gardner
Managing Editor: Joanne Riker
Production Liaison: Randy Pettit
Prepress and Manufacturing Manager: Nick Sklitsis

Prepress and Manufacturing Buyer: Benjamin
  Smith
Interior Design: Brian Molloy, GGS Book Services
Cover Design: Jayne Conte
Composition/Full-Service Project Management:
  GGS Book Services, Atlantic Highlands
Printer/Binder: R.R. Donnelley

Credits and acknowledgments borrowed from other sources and reproduced, with permission, in this textbook appear on appropriate page within text.

Pearson Education LTD., London
Pearson Education Australia PTY., Limited, Sydney
Pearson Education Singapore, Pte., Ltd.
Pearson Education North Asia Ltd., Hong Kong

Pearson Education, Canada, Ltd., Toronto
Pearson Educación de Mexico, S.A. de C.V.
Pearson Education—Japan, Tokyo
Pearson Education Malaysia, Pte. Ltd.

10 9 8 7 6 5 4 3 2 1

ISBN 0-13-192098-7

CONTENTS

3 The Creation of New Worlds   43

4 Convergence and Conflict, 1660s–1763   61

5 Imperial Breakdown, 1763–1774   85

6 The War for Independence, 1774–1783   104

7 The First Republic, 1776–1789 126

8 A New Republic and the Rise of Parties, 1789–1800

9 The Triumph and Collapse of Jeffersonian Republicanism, 1800–1824

10 The Jacksonian Era, 1824–1845   184

11 Slavery and the Old South, 1800–1860   205

12 The Market Revolution and Social Reform, 1815–1850   223

13 The Way West, 1815–1850 251

14 The Politics of Sectionalism, 1846–1861 270

15 Battle Cries and Freedom Songs: The Civil War, 1861–1865

291

16 Reconstruction, 1865–1877   321

17 A New South: Progress and Social Tradition, 1877–1900   337

18 Industry, Immigrants, and Cities, 1870–1900   360

19 Transforming the West, 1865–1890   386

20 Politics and Government, 1877–1900   403

21 The Progressive Era, 1900–1917   423

22 Creating an Empire, 1865–1917   448

23 America and the Great War, 1914–1920   469

24 Toward a Modern America, The 1920s 491

25 The Great Depression and the New Deal, 1929–1939 510

26 World War II, 1939–1945   534

27 The Cold War at Home and Abroad, 1946–1952 555

28 The Confident Years, 1953–1964   578

31 Complacency and Crisis, 1993–2003   652

PREFACE

The path that led us to *The American Journey* began in the classroom with our students. Our goal is to make American history accessible to students. The key to that goal—the core of the book—is a strong, clear narrative. American history is a compelling story and we seek to tell it in an engaging, forthright way. But we also provide students with an abundance of tools to help them absorb that story and put it in context. We introduce them to the concerns of the participants in America's history with primary source documents. The voices of contemporaries open each chapter, describing their own personal journeys toward fulfilling their dreams, hopes, and ambitions as part of the broader American journey. These voices provide a personal window on our nation's history, and the themes they express resonate throughout the narrative.

But if we wrote this book to appeal to our students, we also wrote it to engage their minds. We wanted to avoid academic trendiness, particularly the restricting categories that have divided the discipline of history over the last twenty years or so. We believe that the distinctions involved in the debates about multiculturalism and identity, between social and political history, between the history of the common people and the history of the elite, are unnecessarily confusing.

What we seek is integration—to combine political and social history, to fit the experience of particular groups into the broader perspective of the American past, to give voice to minor and major players alike because of their role in the story we have to tell.

Approach

In telling our story, we had some definite ideas about what we might include and emphasize that other texts do not—information we felt that the current and next generations of students will need to know about our past to function best in a new society.

Chronological Organization   A strong chronological backbone supports the book. We have found that the jumping back and forth in time characteristic of some American history textbooks confuses students. They abhor dates but need to know the sequence of events in history. A chronological presentation is the best way to be sure they do.

Regional Balance   *The American Journey* presents balanced coverage of all regions of the country. In keeping with this balance, the South and the West receive more coverage in this text than in comparable books.

Point of View   *The American Journey* presents a balanced overview of the American past. But "balanced" does not mean bland. We do not shy away from definite positions on controversial issues, such as the nature of early contacts between Native Americans and Europeans, why the political crisis of the 1850s ended in a bloody Civil War, and how Populism and its followers fit into the American political spectrum. If students and instructors disagree, that's great; discussion and dissent are important catalysts for understanding and learning.

Religion   Nor do we shy away from some topics that play relatively minor roles in other texts, like religion. Historians are often uncomfortable writing about religion and tend to slight its influence. This text stresses the importance of religion in American society both as a source of strength and a reflection of some its more troubling aspects.

Historians mostly write for each other. That's too bad. We need to reach out and expand our audience. An American history text is a good place to start. Our students are not only our future historians, but more important, our future. Let their American journey begin.

Features of the Text

The American Journey Portfolio Edition includes an array of features designed to make American history accessible to students.

- **Voices from the American Journey** opens each chapter. Consisting of letters, diary entries, and other firsthand accounts, these voices highlight the personal dimension of the American journey and show students the wealth and variety of experiences that make up this country's history.

- **Chapter-Opening Questions** ask students to consider carefully the main issues addressed in the narrative.

- **Chapter Chronologies** help students build a framework of key events.

- **Chapter Review Questions**, organized by key subtopics in each chapter, help students review material and relate it to broader themes.

Supplementary Instructional Materials

The American Journey comes with an extensive package of supplementary print and multi-media materials for both instructors and students.

PRINT SUPPLEMENTS

Instructor's Resource Manual with Tests This resource contains chapter outlines, detailed chapter overviews, activities, discussion questions, information on audio-visual resources that are useful for preparing lectures and assignments, and a test item file of multiple-choice, true-false, essay, and map questions organized by chapter.

Prentice Hall Test Generator Suitable for both Windows and Macintosh environments, this commercial-quality, computerized test-management program allows instructors to select items from the test-item file and design their own exams.

HistoryNotes (Volumes I and II) HistoryNotes provides students with practice tests, map exercises, and How? When? Where? Questions for each chapter of *The American Journey*.

American Stories: Biographies in United States History This two-volume collection of sixty-two biographies in United States history is free when packaged with *The American Journey*. Introductions, pre-reading questions, and suggested resources enrich this new supplement.

Prentice Hall and Penguin Bundle Program Prentice Hall is pleased to provide adopters of *The American Journey* with an opportunity to receive significant discounts when copies of the text are bundled with Penguin titles in American history. Contact your local Prentice Hall representative for details.

MULTIMEDIA SUPPLEMENTS

Companion Website   Available at http://www.prenhall.com/goldfield, *The American Journey Companion Website* offers students multiple choice, true-false, essay, identification, map labeling, and document questions based on material from the text, organized by the primary subtopics in each chapter.

U.S. History Documents CD-ROM   Bound in every new copy of *The American Journey*, and organized according to the main periods in American history, the U.S. History Documents CD-ROM contains over 300 primary sources in an easily navigable PDF file. Each document is accompanied by essay questions that allow students to read important sources in U.S. history via the CD-ROM and respond online via a dedicated website.

OneSearch with Research Navigator   This brief guide focuses on developing critical thinking skills necessary to evaluate and use online sources. It also provides an access code and instruction on using *Research Navigator*, a powerful research tool that provides access to three exclusive databases of reliable source material: ContentSelect Academic Journal Database, *The New York Times* Search by Subject Archive, and Link Library.

Acknowledgments

All of us are grateful to our families, friends, and colleagues for their support and encouragement. Jo Ann and Peter Argersinger would like in particular to thank Anna Champe, Linda Hatmaker, and John Willits; William Barney thanks Pamela Fesmire and Rosalie Radcliffe; Virginia Anderson thanks Fred Anderson, Kim Gruenwald, Ruth Helm, Eric Hinderaker, and Chidiebere Nwaubani; and David Goldfield thanks Frances Glenn and Jason Moscato. Jim Miller, Sylvia Mallory, and Sally Constable played key roles in the book's inception and initial development.

Finally, we would like to acknowledge the members of our Prentice Hall family. They are not only highly competent professionals but also pleasant people. We regard them with affection and appreciation. None of us would hesitate to work with this fine group again. We would especially like to thank our editorial team: Charles Cavaliere, executive editor; Charlyce Jones Owen, vice president and editorial director for the Humanities; Heather Shelstad, marketing director; Joanne Riker and Randy Pettit for keeping the production on schedule; Nick Sklitsis, manufacturing manager; Ben Smith, manufacturing buyer; and Yolanda de Rooy, president of Prentice Hall's Humanities and Social Sciences division.

DG, CA, VDJA, JEA, PHA, WLB, RMW

U.S. History Documents CD-ROM

Worlds Apart

What was life like for Native Americans prior to 1492?

What benefits to European princes, merchants, and traders did exploration provide?

How did the French, English, and Spanish fare in their early efforts in the New World?

What were the consequences of contact between the Old and New Worlds?

After a journey of over two hundred miles, the exhausted man arrived in the grand city of Tenochtitlán. He had hurried from the Gulf Coast with news for the Aztec leader, Moctezuma.

Our lord and king, forgive my boldness. I am from Mictlancuauhtla. When I went to the shores of the great sea, there was a mountain range or small mountain floating in the midst of the water, and moving here and there without touching the shore. My lord, we have never seen the like of this, although we guard the coast and are always on watch.

[When Moctezuma sent some officials to check on the messenger's story, they confirmed his report.]

Our lord and king, it is true that strange people have come to the shores of the great sea. They were fishing from a small boat, some with rods and others with a net. They fished until late and then they went back to their two great towers and climbed up into them.... They have very light skin, much lighter than ours. They all have long beards, and their hair comes only to their ears.

Miguel Leon-Portilla, *The Broken Spears: The Aztec Account of the Conquest of Mexico* (Boston, 1962).

MOCTEZUMA RECEIVED NEWS, like the messenger's initial report, filled with foreboding. In Aztec religion, omens and prophecies were thought to foreshadow coming events. Several unusual omens had recently occurred—blazing lights in the sky, one temple struck by lightning and another that spontaneously burst into flames, monstrous beings that appeared and vanished. Now light-skinned strangers were offshore. Magicians warned that trouble lay ahead.

The messenger's journey to Tenochtitlán occurred in 1519. The "mountains" he saw were the sails of European ships, and the strange men were Spanish soldiers under the command of Hernán Cortés. Like Columbus's voyage to the Caribbean in 1492, Cortés's arrival in Mexico is often considered a key episode in the European discovery of the "New World." But we might also view the messenger's entry into the Aztec capital as announcing the native Mexicans' discovery of a New World to the east, from which the strangers must have come. Neither the Aztecs nor the Spaniards could have foreseen the far-reaching consequences of these twin discoveries. Before long, Native Americans, Africans, and Europeans—who had previously lived worlds apart—would come together to create a world that was new to all of them.

Different Worlds

The New World reflected the diverse experiences of the peoples who built it. Improving economic conditions in the fifteenth and early sixteenth centuries propelled Europeans overseas to seek new opportunities for trade and settlement. Spain, Portugal, France, and England competed within Europe, and their conflict carried over into the Americas. Native Americans drew upon their familiarity with the land and its resources, their patterns of political and religious authority, and their systems of trade and warfare to deal with the European newcomers. Africans were brought to the Americas by the Europeans to work as slaves. They too would draw on their cultural heritage to cope with a new land and a harsh life.

NATIVE AMERICAN SOCIETIES BEFORE 1492

Convinced that he had landed in the East Indies in 1492, Columbus called the people he met *indios*. His error is preserved in the word *Indian*, used by Europeans to identify the original inhabitants of the two American continents.

By 1492, the continents of North and South America had been inhabited for a long time—estimates range from 15,000 to 50,000 years. The human population of the two continents may have been as high as 70 million—nearly equal to the population of Europe at that time, most of them south of what is now the border between the United States and Mexico. These people belonged to hundreds of groups, each with its own language or dialect, history, and way of life.

The first Americans were nomadic hunters from Siberia who probably came in several waves across a land bridge that once connected Siberia and Alaska. Some may have arrived from Asia as recently as 8,000 years ago. They and their descendants gradually ranged southward and eastward, spreading throughout North and South America.

The earliest Americans, whom archaeologists call *Paleo-Indians*, traveled in small bands, tracking and killing mammoths, bison, and other large game. Paleo-Indians were resourceful hunters who crafted sharp stone points for their spears. Their efficiency may have led to overhunting for by 9000 B.C. mammoths, mastodons, and other game had become extinct. The world's climate also grew warmer, turning grasslands into deserts and reducing the animals' food supply, hastening their disappearance. This meant that humans had to find other food sources.

Between roughly 8000 B.C. and 1500 B.C.—what archaeologists call the *Archaic* period—Indians adapted to regional environments, learning to use local resources efficiently. Gradually, populations grew, and people began living in larger villages. Men did most of the hunting and fishing. Women remained closer to home, gathering and preparing wild plant foods and caring for children. Each group made the tools it used, with men carving fishhooks and arrowheads and women making bone needles and baskets.

Archaic Indians also collected local nonfood resources, including rocks, shells, and bones. They fashioned goods from these materials and traded them with other peoples, sometimes hundreds of miles away. At Indian Knoll, in western Kentucky, archaeologists have found copper from the Great Lakes area and shells from as far away as the Gulf of Mexico. Ideas as well as goods circulated among Archaic Indian peoples. Across the continent, human burials became more elaborate, suggesting that ideas about death and the afterlife passed between groups. Bodies might be wrapped in woven mats or cloths, and the deceased's personal possessions were often placed in the grave.

Near the end of the Archaic period, some groups began farming. Around 5000 B.C., the people of southern Mexico started raising an ancient type of maize, or corn. At first, farming supplemented a diet still largely dependent on hunting and gathering, but agriculture gradually became more widespread. In addition to maize, the main crop in both South and North America, farmers in Mexico, Central America, and the Peruvian Andes learned to cultivate peppers, beans, pumpkins, squash, avocados, sweet and white potatoes (native to the Peruvian highlands), and tomatoes. Mexican farmers also grew cotton. Maize and bean cultivation spread from Mexico in a wide arc to the north and east. Peoples in what is now the southwestern United States began farming between 1500 and 500 B.C., and by A.D. 200, farmers tilled the soil in present-day Georgia and Florida.

Wherever agriculture took hold, populations grew, since farming produced a more secure food supply than hunting and gathering. Permanent villages appeared as farmers settled near their fields. In central Mexico, agriculture eventually sustained the populations of large cities. Trade in agricultural surpluses flowed through exchange networks. In many Indian societies, women's status improved because of their role as the principal farmers. Specialized craftworkers produced pottery and baskets to store harvested grains. Even religious beliefs and practices reflected the centrality of farming. In describing the origins of their people, Pueblo Indians of the Southwest compared their emergence from the underworld to a maize plant sprouting from the earth.

Despite their diversity, certain generalizations can be made about societies that developed within broad regions, or *culture areas*. Throughout the North and West, Indians did not adopt agriculture. In the challenging environment of the Arctic and Subarctic, small nomadic bands moved seasonally to fish, follow game, and, in the brief summers, gather wild berries. Far to the north, Eskimos and Aleuts hunted whales, seals, and other sea mammals. Further inland, the Crees and other peoples followed migrating herds of caribou and moose. Northern peoples fashioned tools and weapons of bone and ivory, clothing and boats from animal skins, and houses of whalebones and hides or blocks of sod or snow.

Along the Northwest Coast and Columbia River Plateau, abundant resources supported one of the most densely populated areas of North America. With rivers teeming with salmon and other fish and forests full of game and edible plants, people prospered without agriculture. Among groups like the Kwakiutls and Chinooks, extended families lived in large communal houses located in villages of several hundred people.

Farther south, in present-day California, hunter-gatherers lived in smaller villages, several of which might be led by the same chief. These settlements usually adjoined oak groves, where Indians gathered acorns. To protect their access to this important food, chiefs and villagers vigorously defended their territorial claims to the oak groves.

Small nomadic bands in the Great Basin, where the climate was warm and dry, lived in caves and rock shelters. Shoshone hunters captured antelope in corrals and trapped small game, such as squirrels and rabbits. In present-day Utah and western Colorado, Utes hunted elk, bison, and mountain sheep and fished in mountain streams. Women gathered pinyon nuts, seeds, and wild berries. In hard times, people ate rattlesnakes, horned toads, and insects. They celebrated whenever food was plentiful and urged religious leaders to seek supernatural help when starvation loomed.

Mesoamerica, the birthplace of agriculture in North America, extends from central Mexico into Central America. A series of complex, literate, urban cultures emerged in this region, beginning around 1200 B.C. with the Olmecs, who flourished on Mexico's Gulf Coast until 400 B.C. The Olmecs and other early Mesoamerican peoples built cities featuring large pyramids, developed religious practices that included human sacrifice, and devised calendars and writing systems.

Mayan civilization followed, reaching its greatest glory between about A.D. 150 and 900 in the southern Yucatán, creating Mesoamerica's most advanced writing and calendrical systems and developing a sophisticated mathematics that included the concept of zero. The Mayans of the southern Yucatán suffered a decline after 900, but there were still many thriving Mayan centers in the northern Yucatán in 1492. The great city of Teotihuacán dominated central Mexico from the first century to the eighth century A.D. and influenced much of the rest of Mesoamerica through trade and conquest.

Some two hundred years after the fall of Teotihuacán, the Toltecs, a warrior people, rose to prominence, dominating central Mexico from about 900 to 1100. In the wake of the Toltec collapse, the **Aztecs**, another warrior people, migrated from the north into the Valley of Mexico and built a great empire that soon controlled much of Mesoamerica. The Aztec capital, Tenochtitlán, was a city of great plazas, broad avenues, magnificent temples and palaces, ball courts, and busy marketplaces. Built on islands in the middle of Lake Texcoco, it was connected to the mainland by four broad causeways. In 1492, Tenochtitlán was home to some 200,000 people, one of the largest cities in the world at the time.

In the great pyramid in Tenochtitlán, Aztec priests sacrificed human victims—by cutting open their chests and removing their still-beating hearts—to offer to the gods to prevent them from destroying the earth. Hundreds, even thousands, of victims died in ceremonies that sometimes lasted for days.

Aztec culture expanded through continuous military conquest, driven by a quest for sacrificial victims and for wealth in the form of tribute payments of gold, food, and handcrafted goods. Neighboring peoples hated the Aztecs and submitted to them out of fear. With a powerful ally to lead them, they would readily turn on their overlords and bring the empire down.

Native societies emerging north of Mexico shared certain characteristics with those of Mesoamerica. The introduction of a drought-resistant type of maize (probably from Mexico) into the desert Southwest in 400 B.C. enabled a series of cultures to develop. Beginning about 300 B.C., the Hohokams settled in southern Arizona, eventually building permanent villages of several hundred people. Substantial harvests of beans, corn, and squash, watered by a complex system of canals, fed Hohokam villagers. In large communities, inhabitants built ball courts similar to those found in Mexico. Artisans wove cotton cloth and made goods reflecting Mesoamerican artistic styles out of shell, turquoise, and clay. Extensive trade networks linked the Hohokams to places as far away as California and Mexico. Their culture endured for over a thousand years and then disappeared mysteriously by 1450.

Beginning around A.D. 1, the Anasazis (their name is Navaho for "ancient alien ones") settled where the borders of present-day Colorado, Utah, Arizona, and New Mexico meet. They gradually adopted agriculture, first adding maize and later beans and squash to a diet of wild foods. Scarce rainfall, routed through dams and hillside terraces, watered the crops.

The Anasazis originally lived in villages on mesas or canyon floors. Their dwellings included special rooms, or *kivas*, for religious ceremonies. The largest communal dwelling, Pueblo Bonito in New Mexico's Chaco Canyon, covered three acres and contained 650 to 800 rooms, housing about 1,200 people. Pueblo Bonito may have been the center of Anasazi society from about A.D. 900 to 1100.

After around 1200, the Anasazis began carving multistoried houses into canyon walls. These were not easy places in which to live, and they could be reached only by difficult climbs up steep cliffs and along narrow ledges. Archaeologists suggest that warfare and climate change forced the Anasazis into these homes. Around 1200, a colder climate reduced food supplies, and food scarcity may have encouraged violence. The Anasazis may have moved to the cliff dwellings for protection. By 1300, most Anasazi survivors had dispersed to villages along the Rio Grande.

The Pueblo peoples of the Southwest, including the Hopis and Zunis, are descendants of the Anasazis. In 1492, many lived in large communal dwellings in permanent villages (*pueblo* is the Spanish word for "village"). Pueblo men did most of the farming, and in religious rituals all Pueblos prayed to the gods for rain for the all-important harvest.

The Great Plains of the continent's interior were much less densely settled than the desert Southwest. Scattered villages of Mandans, Pawnees, and other groups clung to tree-lined rivers. Women raised crops and gathered wild plants for food and medicine. Men hunted bison, whose skin and bones were used for clothing, shelter, and tools. Plains Indians moved frequently, seeking more fertile land or better hunting.

The spread of agriculture transformed native societies in the Eastern Woodlands, a vast territory extending from the Mississippi Valley to the Atlantic seaboard. Farming first appeared around 2500 B.C. but was not firmly established until about A.D. 700. As agriculture

---

• CHRONOLOGY •

c. 40,000–8000 B.C. Ancestors of Native Americans cross to Americas.

c. 10,000–9000 B.C. Paleo-Indians expand through the Americas.

c. 9000 B.C. Extinction of large land mammals in North America.

c. 8000–1500 B.C. Archaic Indian era.

c. 3000 B.C. Beginnings of agriculture in Mesoamerica.

c. 1500 B.C. Earliest mound-building culture begins.

c. 500 B.C.–400 A.D. Adena-Hopewell mound-building culture.

c. 700–1600 A.D. Rise of West African empires.

c. 900 First mounds built at Cahokia. Anasazi expansion.

c. 1000 Spread of Islam in West Africa.

c. 1000–1500 Last mound-building culture, the Mississippian.

c. 1290s Anasazi dispersal into smaller pueblos.

1400–1600 Renaissance in Europe.

1430s Beginnings of Portuguese slave trade in West Africa.

1492 End of *reconquista* in Spain. Christopher Columbus's first voyage.

1494 Treaty of Tordesillas.

1497 John Cabot visits Nova Scotia and Newfoundland.

1497–1499 Vasco da Gama sails around Africa to reach India.

1517 Protestant Reformation begins in Germany.

1519–1521 Hernán Cortés conquers the Aztec empire.

1532–1533 Francisco Pizarro conquers the Inca empire.

1534–1542 Jacques Cartier explores eastern Canada for France.

1540–1542 Coronado explores southwestern North America.

1542–1543 Roberval's failed colony in Canada.

1558 Elizabeth I becomes queen of England.

1565 Spanish establish outpost at St. Augustine in Florida.

1560s–1580s English renew attempts to conquer Ireland.

1587 Founding of "Lost Colony" of Roanoke.

1598 Spanish found colony at New Mexico.

spread, several "mound-building" societies—named for the large earthworks their members constructed—developed in the Ohio and Mississippi Valleys. The oldest flourished in Louisiana between 1500 and 700 B.C. Members of the Adena-Hopewell culture, which appeared in the Ohio Valley between 500 B.C. and A.D. 400, built hundreds of mounds, often in the shapes of humans, birds, and serpents. Most mounds were grave sites, where people were buried with valuable goods, many obtained through long-distance trade.

The last mound-building culture, the Mississippian, emerged between 1000 and 1500 in the Mississippi Valley. One of the largest cities was *Cahokia*, located on the Mississippi River across from present-day St. Louis. By 1250, Cahokia, the largest city north of Mexico, had perhaps thirty thousand residents, making it about the same size as medieval London. Its central feature was a 100-foot-high mound, the world's largest earthwork. Cahokia dominated the Mississippi Valley, but numerous other towns, some with hundreds or thousands of residents, dotted the Woodlands region, linked by trade networks. Powerful chiefs, thought to be related to the sun, dominated these communities.

Mississippian culture began to decline in the thirteenth century. Food shortages and warfare drove people from the great cities into the countryside. Elements of Mississippian culture survived among dispersed Woodlands people, particularly methods of maize and bean agriculture. By 1492, although the large cities of the Mississippian era had disappeared, Woodlands Indians maintained long-distance trade links throughout the region, with such precious goods as copper, shell beads, and pearls passing among groups.

The Caribbean islanders whom Columbus first encountered descended from ancient cultures. Ancestors of the Tainos probably came from what is now Venezuela. The Guanahatabeys of western Cuba originated in Florida, and the Caribs of the easternmost islands moved from Brazil's Orinoco Valley. Island peoples began farming perhaps in the first century A.D. on clearings made in the tropical forests. Canoes carried trade goods throughout the Caribbean, as well as Mesoamerica and coastal South America.

By 1492, as many as 4 million people may have inhabited the Caribbean islands. Powerful chiefs ruled over villages, conducted war and diplomacy, and distributed food and other goods obtained as tribute from villages. Elite islanders were easily recognized by their fine clothing, bright feather headdresses, and golden ear and nose ornaments—items that eventually attracted European visitors' attention.

Long before 1492, North America had witnessed centuries of dynamic change. Populations grew and spread across thousands of miles of territory. Farmers developed new varieties of essential food plants. Empires rose and fell. Large cities flourished and disappeared. People formed alliances with trading partners and warred with groups who refused to trade. Because their histories have been preserved in oral traditions and archaeological evidence rather than written documents, they are less distinct, but no less real, than the Europeans whom they would soon meet.

CULTURAL PERCEPTIONS AND MISPERCEPTIONS

Misunderstandings inevitably arose between Indians and Europeans when such dissimilar peoples encountered each other for the first time. Even simple transactions had unexpected results. When Columbus showed swords to the Tainos, for example, "they took them by the edge and through ignorance cut themselves" because they had never seen metal weapons. Similarly, French explorers choked when they tried to smoke unfamiliar Iroquois tobacco, which tasted, one of them reported, like "powdered pepper."

Many misunderstandings, however, had far graver consequences for the outcome of the encounter. Each group struggled to understand the strange behavior and customs of the other. Europeans usually decided that native practices were not just different from their own but inferior. Indians doubtless felt the same about European practices but their opinions were rarely recorded.

Religious differences were the hardest to reconcile. Seeing no churches or recognizable religious practices among the Tainos, Columbus wrote, "I do not detect in them any religion." His comment derived from his own Christian background. Christian Europeans worshiped one God in an organized church led by trained priests. They preserved their religious traditions in a written bible. Most Indians, however, believed in a variety of gods. They considered nature itself to be sacred and understood certain beings, including plants, animals, and stars, to possess spiritual powers. Indians living north of Mexico preserved religious beliefs through oral traditions, not in writing. Their religious leaders performed ceremonies that mediated between the human and spiritual worlds. Europeans, however, thought that these men were magicians or even witches. They assumed that Indians worshiped the devil and insisted that they adopt Christianity. In the face of this demand, many native peoples doubtless shared the opinion voiced by some Iroquois: "We do not know that God, we have never seen him, we know not who he is."

Europeans also disapproved of the relative equality of men and women they observed among some Native American peoples. Europeans believed that men were naturally superior to women and should dominate them. But in North America they encountered female rulers among the Wampanoags and Powhatans and learned that among groups such as the Hurons, women helped select chiefs. They found that many Indian societies, including the Pueblos, Hurons, and Iroquois, were *matrilineal;* that is, they traced descent through the mother's family line instead of the father's, as Europeans did.

In most Indian societies, men cleared the fields, but women planted and harvested the crops. Women also prepared food, cared for children, made clothing and baskets, carried burdens, and, in some regions, broke down, transported, and reassembled shelters when villages changed location. Europeans, who came from a society in which men did most agricultural work, thought that Indian women lived "a most slavish life." Misjudging the importance of Indian men's roles as hunters and warriors, Europeans scorned them as lazy husbands. Such confusion worked both ways. Massachusetts Indians ridiculed English husbands "for spoiling good working creatures" because they did not send their wives into the fields.

The ultimate source of conflict between Indians and Europeans was the intention of the Europeans to dominate the land. Within three days of his arrival in America, Columbus announced his intention "not to pass by any island of which I did not take possession" and soon speculated on the possibility of enslaving Indians. Native peoples everywhere challenged European claims to possession of their lands and resisted European attempts at domination.

WEST AFRICAN SOCIETIES

Many Europeans followed Columbus's lead in exploring what they soon realized was not Asia after all. Yet in the three centuries after 1492, fully six out of seven people who crossed the Atlantic to the Americas were not Europeans but Africans, the vast majority of whom arrived as slaves. Most came from West Africa, and like the inhabitants of North America or Europe, they belonged to many different ethnic groups, each with its own language and culture.

In 1492, Timbuktu, with a population of perhaps seventy thousand, was one of the greatest cities in West Africa. Located on the Niger River, the flourishing commercial metropolis was the seat of the powerful Songhai empire ruled by Sunni Ali. The city was a center of trade as well as government. A visitor in 1526 described Timbuktu's busy streets lined with "shops of artificers and merchants, and especially of such as weave linen and cotton cloth," and reported—with some exaggeration—that the inhabitants "are exceeding rich."

The Songhai empire was only the latest in a series of powerful states to develop in western Sudan, the vast plain lying south of the arid Sahara. This large and wealthy empire emerged around 1450, dominating the Sudan until it fell to a Moroccan invasion in 1591. Large empires did not appear in coastal West Africa, although the Asante, Dahomey, Oyo, and Bini kingdoms there grew to be powerful. Other coastal peoples, such as the Mendes and Ibos, lived in autonomous villages where all adult males participated in making decisions.

In the vast grasslands of the Sudan, people raised cattle and cultivated millet and sorghum. In the 1500s, European visitors introduced varieties of Asian rice, which soon became another important crop. On the coast—where rain falls nearly every day—people grew yams, bananas, and various kinds of beans and peas in forest clearings. They also kept sheep, goats, and poultry.

West Africans were skilled artisans and particularly fine metalworkers. Smiths produced intricate bronze sculptures, designed distinctive miniature gold weights, and forged weapons.

Complex trade networks linked inland and coastal states, and long-distance commercial connections tied West Africa to southern Europe and the Middle East. For centuries, mines in the area of present-day Guinea and Mali produced tons of gold each year, which were exchanged for North African salt, a rare commodity in West Africa. North African

Craftsmen from the West African kingdom of Benin were renowned for their remarkable bronze sculptures. This intricate bronze plaque depicts four African warriors in full military dress. The two tiny figures in the background may be Portuguese soldiers, who first arrived in Benin in the late fifteenth century.

Benin bronze plaque. National Museum of African Art, Smithsonian Institution, Washington, D.C., U.S.A. Aldo Turino, Art Resource, N.Y.

merchants also bought pepper, leather, and ivory. The wealth generated by this trans-Saharan trade contributed to the rise of the Songhai and earlier empires.

Most West Africans, however, were farmers, not merchants. West African men and women shared agricultural tasks. Men generally prepared fields for planting, while women cultivated the crops, harvested them, and dried grain for storage. Men also hunted and, in the grassland regions, herded cattle. Women in the coastal areas owned and cared for other livestock, including goats and sheep. West African women regularly traded goods, including their crops, in local markets.

Family connections helped define each person's place in society. West Africans emphasized not only ties between parents and children but also those linking aunts, uncles, cousins, and grandparents. Groups of families formed clans that further extended an individual's kin ties. Most clans were *patrilineal*—tracing descent through the father's line—but some (including the Akans and Ibos) were matrilineal.

Religious beliefs magnified the powerful influence of family on African life. Africans believed that their ancestors acted as mediators between the worlds of the living and the dead. Families held elaborate funerals, which helped keep the memory of ancestors alive for younger generations.

West Africans worshiped a supreme being and several subordinate deities. West Africans, like Native Americans, believed that the gods often sent spirits to speak to people. And like Native American priests who mediated between the human and spirit worlds, West African medicine men and women provided protection against evil spirits and sorcerers. Religious ceremonies took place in sacred places often near water—but not in buildings that Europeans recognized as churches. And like the Indians, West Africans preserved their faith through oral traditions.

Islam began to take root in West Africa around the eleventh century, probably introduced by Muslim traders from North Africa. By the fifteenth century, the cities of Timbuktu and Djenné had become centers of Islamic learning. Even so, most West Africans probably retained traditional religious beliefs and practices.

Before the fifteenth century, Europeans knew little about Africa beyond its Mediterranean coast. Spain, much of which had been subject to Islamic rule before 1492, had stronger ties to North Africa than most of Europe, but Christian merchants from other European lands had also traded for centuries with North Africans. When stories of West African gold reached the ears of European traders, they tried to move deeper into the continent, but they encountered powerful Muslim merchants intent on monopolizing the gold trade.

The kingdom of Portugal, eager to expand its trade, sought in the early fifteenth century to circumvent this Muslim monopoly. In 1415, Portuguese forces conquered Ceuta in Morocco and gained a foothold on the continent. Portuguese mariners gradually explored the West African coast, establishing trading posts along the way to exchange horses, clothing, wine, lead, iron, and steel for African gold, grain, animal skins, cotton, pepper, and camels.

By the 1430s, the Portuguese had discovered perhaps the greatest source of wealth they could extract from Africa—slaves. Slavery had long been a part of West African society. African law made land available to anyone willing to cultivate it—provided that no one else was using the same plot—and the possession of a large labor force to work the land became the principal means to wealth. Some people became slaves as punishment for crime, but most slaves were captured in raids into neighboring territories, a regular feature of African life.

Most slaves worked at a variety of tasks for their owners. Many labored more or less independently as farmers, producing surplus crops for their masters. Some rulers acquired female slaves to serve as wives, concubines, or workers. Powerful Sudanese rulers employed large numbers of slaves as bureaucrats and soldiers, rewarding them for loyal service with good treatment and, occasionally, freedom.

Europeans who observed African slaves' relative freedom and variety of employment often concluded that slaves in Africa were "slaves in name only." Slavery in Africa was not necessarily a permanent status and did not automatically apply to the slaves' children. European purchasers of African slaves generally treated them much more harshly. Slavery became even more oppressive as it developed in the Americas.

WESTERN EUROPE ON THE EVE OF DISCOVERY

When Columbus sailed from Spain in 1492, he left a continent recovering from the devastating disease and warfare of the fourteenth century and about to embark on the devastating religious conflicts of the sixteenth century. Between 1337 and 1453, England and France had exhausted each other in a series of conflicts known as the Hundred Years' War. And between 1347 and 1351, an epidemic known as the *Black Death* (bubonic plague) killed perhaps a third of all Europeans, with results that were felt for more than a century.

The plague left Europe with far fewer workers, but the survivors learned to be more efficient, adopting labor-saving techniques to increase productivity. Metalworkers, for instance, built larger furnaces with huge bellows driven by water power. Shipbuilders redesigned vessels with steering mechanisms that could be managed by smaller crews. Innovations in banking, accounting, and insurance also fostered economic recovery.

By 1500, Europe had a stronger, more productive economy than ever before, but not everyone prospered equally. In parts of England, France, Sweden, and the German states, peasants and workers rebelled against the propertied classes. Protests grew from the workers' desire to protect their improving economic fortunes. They did not want to see their rising wages eaten up by higher rents and taxes.

In some parts of Europe, economic improvement encouraged an extraordinary cultural movement known as the *Renaissance*—a "rebirth" of interest in the classical civilizations of ancient Greece and Rome. The Renaissance originated in the city–states of Italy, where a prosperous and educated urban class promoted learning and artistic expression. Wealthy townspeople joined princes in becoming patrons of the arts, offering financial support to numerous painters, sculptors, architects, writers, and musicians.

European states were hierarchical, with their populations divided into fairly rigid classes. Monarchs stood at the top of society. Just below were the aristocrats, who, along with the royal family, dominated government and owned most of the land. Next came prosperous gentry families, independent landowners, and, at the bottom, landless peasants and laborers.

Most of Europe's people were peasant farmers. Peasant men did most of the heavy field work, while women helped at planting and harvest time and cared for children, livestock, and the household. The economic recovery after the Black Death brought prosperity to some families, but crop failures and disease could often cause great suffering in villages and towns.

European society was *patriarchal,* with men dominating political and economic life. Men also controlled the Catholic Church. Inheritance was patrilineal, and only men could own property.

By the end of the fifteenth century, after more than a hundred years of incessant conflict, a measure of stability had returned to Western Europe. Ferdinand and Isabella of Spain, Louis XI of France, and Henry VII of England successfully asserted royal authority over their previously fragmented realms, creating strong state bureaucracies to control political rivals. They gave special trading privileges to merchants to gain their support, creating links that would later prove important in financing overseas expeditions.

The consolidation of military power went hand in hand with the strengthening of political authority. Portugal developed a strong navy to defend its seaborne merchants. Louis XI of France commanded a standing army, and Ferdinand of Spain created a palace guard to use against potential opponents. Before overseas expansion began, European monarchs exerted military force to extend their authority closer to home. Louis XI and his successors used warfare and intermarriage with ruling families of nearby provinces to expand French influence. In the early sixteenth century, England's Henry VIII sent soldiers to conquer Ireland. And the Spain of 1492 was forged from the successful conclusion of the *reconquista* ("reconquest") of territory from Muslim control.

Even as these rulers sought to unify their realms, religious conflicts began to tear Europe apart. For more than a thousand years, Catholic Christianity had united western Europeans in one faith. By the sixteenth century, the Catholic Church had accumulated enormous wealth and power. The pope wielded influence not only as a spiritual leader but also as the political ruler of parts of Italy. The church owned considerable property throughout Europe. Many Christians, especially in northern Europe, began to criticize the worldliness of the popes and the church itself for corruption, abuse of power, and betrayal of the legacy of Christ.

In 1517, a German monk, Martin Luther, invited open debate on these issues, asserting that the church had become too insistent on the performance of good works, such as charitable donations or other actions intended to please God. He called for a return to what he understood to be the purer practices and beliefs of the early church, emphasizing that salvation came not by good deeds but only by faith in God. With the help of the newly invented printing press, his ideas spread widely, inspiring a challenge to the Catholic Church that has come to be called the **Reformation**.

When the church refused to compromise, Luther and other critics formed their own religious organizations, emphasizing the relationship between God and the individual believer. Luther urged people to take responsibility for their own spiritual growth by reading the Bible, which he translated for the first time into German. What started as a religious movement, however, quickly acquired an important political dimension.

Sixteenth-century Germany was a fragmented region of small kingdoms and principalities that were officially part of the Holy Roman Empire. Many German princes supported Luther for both spiritual and secular reasons. When the Holy Roman Empire under Charles V (who was also king of Spain) tried to silence them, the reformist princes protested. From that point on, these princes—and all Europeans who supported religious reform—became known as **Protestants**.

The Protestant movement took a more radical turn under the influence of the French reformer John Calvin, who emphasized the doctrine of **predestination**. Calvin maintained that an all-powerful and all-knowing God chose at the moment of creation which humans would be saved and which would be damned. Each person's fate is thus foreordained, or predestined, by God, although we cannot know our fate during our lifetimes. Good Calvinists struggled to behave as God's chosen, continually searching their souls for evidence of divine grace.

Calvin founded a religious community consistent with his principles at Geneva, a Swiss city–state near the French border. From Germany and Geneva the Protestant Reformation spread to France, the Netherlands, England, and Hungary. In succeeding years, other Protestant groups formed, split, and split again, increasing Europe's religious fragmentation. The new religious ideas particularly interested literate city dwellers, while peasants adopted the new ideas more slowly.

The Reformation addressed spiritual needs that the Catholic Church had left unfulfilled, but it also fractured the religious unity of western Europe and spawned a century of warfare unprecedented in its bloody destructiveness. Protestants fought Catholics in France and the German states. Popes initiated a "Counter Reformation," intended to strengthen the Catholic Church. Europe thus fragmented into warring camps just at the moment when Europeans were coming to terms with their discovery of America.

Contact

Portugal, Spain, France, and England competed to establish footholds on other continents in an intense scramble for riches and dominance. The success of these early endeavors was a reflection of Europe's prosperity and a series of technological breakthroughs that enabled its mariners to navigate beyond familiar waters. By 1600, Spain had emerged as the apparent winner among the European competitors for New World dominance. Its astonishingly wealthy empire included vast territories in Central and South America.

THE LURE OF DISCOVERY

Most Europeans, busy making a living, cared little about distant lands. But certain princes and merchants anticipated spiritual and material benefits from voyages of discovery. The spiritual advantages included making new Christian converts and blocking Islam's expansion. On the material side, the voyages would contribute to Europe's prosperity by increasing trade.

Merchants especially sought access to Asian spices like pepper, cinnamon, ginger, and nutmeg that added interest to an otherwise monotonous diet and helped preserve certain foods. But the overland spice trade—and the trade in other luxury goods such as silk and furs—spanned thousands of miles, involved many middlemen, and was controlled at key points by Muslim merchants. One critical center was Constantinople, the bastion of Christianity in the eastern Mediterranean. When it fell to the Ottomans—the Muslim rulers of Turkey—in 1453, Europeans feared that caravan routes to Asia would be disrupted. This encouraged merchants to turn westward and seek alternate routes. Mariners ventured farther into ocean waters, hoping to sail around Africa and chart a sea route to Asia.

Ocean voyages required sturdier ships and more reliable navigational tools. In the early fifteenth century, Prince Henry of Portugal, excited by the idea of overseas discovery, sponsored the efforts of shipbuilders, mapmakers, and other workers to solve these practical problems. Iberian shipbuilders perfected the caravel, a ship whose narrow shape and steering rudder suited it for ocean travel. Ship designers combined square sails (good for speed) with triangular "lateen" sails, which increased maneuverability. Two Arab inventions—the magnetic compass and the astrolabe (which allowed mariners to determine their position in relation to a star's known location in the sky)—gained popularity among European navigators. As sailors acquired practical experience on the high seas, mapmakers recorded their observations of landfalls, wind patterns, and ocean currents.

Portugal's Bartolomeu Días reached the southern tip of Africa in 1488. Eleven years later, Vasco da Gama brought a Portuguese fleet around Africa to India, opening a sea route to Asia. These initiatives gave Portugal a virtual monopoly on Far Eastern trade for some time.

The new trade routes gave strategic importance to the islands that lie in the Atlantic off the west coast of Africa and Europe. Spain and Portugal vied for control of the Canary Islands, located 800 miles southwest of the Iberian peninsula. Spain eventually prevailed in 1496 by defeating the islands' inhabitants. Portugal acquired Madeira and the Cape Verde Islands, along with a set of tiny islands off Africa's Guinea Coast.

Sugar, like Asian spices, commanded high prices in Europe, so the conquerors of the Atlantic islands began to cultivate sugar cane on them on large plantations worked by slave labor. In the Canaries, the Spanish first enslaved the native inhabitants. When disease and exhaustion reduced their numbers, the Spanish brought in African slaves, often purchased from Portuguese traders.

These island societies, in which a small European master class dominated a much larger population of native peoples or imported African slaves, were to provide a model for Spain's and Portugal's later exploitation of their American colonies. As early as 1494, Christopher Columbus wrote to Ferdinand and Isabella of Spain to suggest that Caribbean islanders could be sold as slaves in order to cover the costs of exploration.

CHRISTOPHER COLUMBUS

Columbus was not the first European to believe that he could reach Asia by sailing westward. The idea developed logically during the fifteenth century as mariners gained knowledge and experience from their exploits in the Atlantic and around Africa. Columbus himself may have gained valuable experience on a voyage to Iceland. He also read widely in geographical treatises and paid close attention to the stories and rumors that circulated among mariners.

Most Europeans knew that the world was round, but most also scoffed at the idea of a westward voyage to Asia, believing that it would take so long, it would exhaust any ship's supplies. Columbus's confidence that he could make the voyage grew from a mistaken calculation of the earth's circumference as 18,000 (rather than 24,000) miles, which led him to conclude that Asia lay just 3,500 miles west of the Canary Islands. Columbus first sought financial support from the king of Portugal, whose advisers warned him that he would starve at sea before reaching Asia. Undaunted, he turned to Portugal's rival, Spain.

Columbus tried to convince Ferdinand and Isabella that his plan suited Spain's national goals: Spain could grow rich from Asian trade, send Christian missionaries to Asia (a goal in keeping with the religious ideals of the *reconquista*), and perhaps enlist the Great Khan of China as an ally in the long struggle with Islam. If he failed, the "enterprise of the Indies" would cost little. The Spanish monarchs nonetheless kept Columbus waiting nearly seven years—until 1492, when the last Muslim stronghold at Granada fell to Spanish forces—before they gave him their support.

After thirty-three days at sea, Columbus and his men made landfall. Although puzzled not to find the fabled cities of China or Japan, they still believed they had reached Asia. Three more voyages, between 1493 and 1504, however, failed to yield clear evidence of an Asian landfall or substantiate Columbus's reports of "great mines of gold and other metals" and spices in abundance.

Obsessed with the wealth he had promised himself and others, Columbus and his men turned violent, sacking the villages of Tainos and Caribs and demanding tribute in gold. The Spanish forced native gangs to pan rivers for the precious nuggets. Dissatisfied with the meager results, Columbus sought to enslave islanders, a desperate attempt to show that the

Indies could yield a profit. Queen Isabella initially opposed the enslavement of people she considered to be new Spanish subjects. Within thirty years of Columbus's first voyage, however, Spanish exploitation of native labor had brought the populations of many Caribbean islands close to extinction.

Columbus died in Spain in 1506, still convinced he had found Asia. What he had done was to set in motion a process that would transform both sides of the Atlantic. It would eventually bring wealth to many Europeans and immense suffering to Native Americans and Africans.

SPANISH CONQUEST AND COLONIZATION

Of all European nations, Spain was best suited to take advantage of Columbus's discovery. Its experience with the *reconquista* gave it both a religious justification for conquest (bringing Christianity to nonbelievers) and an army of seasoned soldiers—*conquistadores*. In addition, during the *reconquista* and the conquest of the Canary Islands, Spain's rulers had developed efficient techniques for controlling newly conquered lands that could be applied to New World colonies.

The Spanish first established outposts on Cuba, Puerto Rico, and Jamaica (see Map 1–1). The conquistadores, who were more interested in finding gold and slaves than in creating permanent settlements, attacked Taino and Carib villages and killed or captured the inhabitants. By 1524, the Tainos had all but died out; the Caribs survived on more isolated islands until the eighteenth century. Spanish soldiers then ventured to the mainland. Juan Ponce de León led an expedition to Florida in 1513. In that same year, Vasco Núñez de Balboa arrived in Central America, crossing the isthmus of Panama to the Pacific Ocean.

In 1519, Hernán Cortés led a force of six hundred men to the coast of Mexico. "I and my companions," he declared, "suffer from a disease of the heart which can be cured only with gold." By 1521, Cortés and his men had conquered the powerful Aztec empire. The Spanish soldiers also discovered riches beyond their wildest dreams. They "picked up the gold and fingered it like monkeys," reported one Aztec witness. They were "transported by joy, as if their hearts were illuminated and made new."

The swift, decisive Spanish victory over a more numerous enemy depended on several factors. Spanish guns and horses often enabled them to overwhelm larger groups of Aztec foot soldiers armed with spears and wooden swords edged with obsidian. Cortés also benefited from divisions within the Aztec empire, acquiring indispensable allies among subject Indians who resented Aztec domination. Cortés led only six hundred Spanish soldiers but eventually gained 200,000 Indian allies eager to throw off Aztec rule.

An even more significant contribution to this quick victory was the fact that Indians lacked resistance to European diseases. One of Cortés's men was infected with smallpox, which soon devastated the native population. Nearly 40 percent of the inhabitants of central Mexico died of smallpox within a year. Other diseases followed, including typhus, measles, and influenza. By 1600, the population of Mexico may have declined from over 15 million to less than a million people.

Aztec society and culture collapsed in the face of appalling mortality. One survivor recalled, "The sick were so utterly helpless that they could only lie on their beds like corpses, unable to move their limbs or even their heads. . . . If they did move their bodies, they screamed with pain." Early in their bid to gain control of the Aztec empire, the Spanish seized Moctezuma, the Aztec king, and eventually put him to death. His successor died of disease less than three months after gaining the throne.

MAP 1–1

Spanish, English, and French Settlements in North America in the Sixteenth Century

By the end of the sixteenth century, only Spain had established permanent settlements in North America. French outposts in Canada and at Fort Caroline, as well as the English settlement at Roanoke, failed to thrive. European rivalries for North America, however, would intensify after 1600.

BASED ON this map, what factors might help to explain why Spain was more successful in the establishment of permanent settlements before 1600 than either France or England? Do you think geographic location (climate, terrain, etc.) may have played a role?

In 1532, Francisco Pizarro and 180 men discovered the Inca empire high in the Peruvian Andes. Taking advantage of a civil war within the empire following its ruler's death, the Spaniards captured Cuzco, the Inca capital, and established a new one at Lima.

By 1550, Spain's New World empire extended from the Caribbean through Mexico to Peru. It was administered from Spain by the Council of the Indies. The council aimed to project royal authority into every village in New Spain in order to maintain political control and extract as much wealth as possible from the land and its people.

For more than a century, Spanish ships crossed the Atlantic carrying seemingly limitless treasure from the colonies. The colonial rulers subjected the native inhabitants of New Spain to compulsory tribute payments and forced labor. Tens of thousands of Indians toiled in silver mines in Peru and Bolivia and on sugar plantations in the Caribbean. When necessary, Spaniards imported African slaves to supplement a native labor force ravaged by disease and exhaustion.

The desire for gold eventually lured Spaniards farther into North America. In 1528, an expedition to Florida ended in the deaths of nearly all Spanish intruders when they provoked an attack by Apalachee Indians. In 1539, Hernán de Soto led an expedition from Florida to the Mississippi River. Along the way, the Spaniards harassed native peoples, demanding provisions, burning villages, and capturing women to be servants and concubines. They also exposed the Indians to deadly European diseases. The expedition kept up its rampage for three years, turning toward Mexico only after de Soto died in 1542. In these same years, Francisco Vásquez de Coronado led three hundred troops on an equally destructive expedition through present-day Arizona, New Mexico, and Colorado on a futile search for gold and precious stones.

The failure to find gold and silver halted the Spanish attempt to extend their empire to the north. By the end of the sixteenth century, they maintained just two precarious footholds north of Mexico. One was at St. Augustine, on Florida's Atlantic coast. Founded in 1565, this fortified outpost served as a naval base to defend Spanish treasure fleets from raids by English and French privateers. The other settlement was located far to the west in what is now New Mexico. Juan de Oñate, on a futile search for silver mines, claimed the region for Spain in 1598 and proceeded to antagonize the area's inhabitants. Having earned the enmity of the Pueblo people—astonishing even his own superiors with his brutality—Oñate barely managed to keep his tiny colony together.

The conquistadores' bloody tactics aroused protest back in Spain. The Indians' most eloquent advocate was Bartolomé de Las Casas, a Dominican priest shamed by his own role (as a layman) in the conquest of Hispaniola. Las Casas wrote *In Defense of the Indians*, including graphic descriptions of native sufferings. Instead of eliciting Spanish reforms, however, his work inspired Protestant Europeans to create the "Black Legend," an exaggerated story according to which a fanatical Catholic Spain sought to spread its control at any cost.

Meanwhile, between 1500 and 1650, an estimated 181 tons of gold and 16,000 tons of silver were shipped from the New World to Spain, making it the richest and most powerful state in Europe. But this influx of American treasure had unforeseen consequences that would soon undermine Spanish predominance.

In 1492, the Spanish crown expelled from Spain all Jews who refused to become Christians. The refugees included many leading merchants who had contributed significantly to Spain's economy. The remaining Christian merchants, now awash in American riches, saw no reason to invest in new trade or productive enterprises that might have sustained the economy once the flow of New World treasure diminished. As a result, Spain's economy eventually stagnated.

The flood of American gold and silver also inflated prices throughout Europe, hurting workers, whose wages failed to rise as fast, and aristocrats, dependent on fixed rents from their estates. Most damaging, Spain's monarchs wasted their American wealth fighting expensive wars in Europe that ultimately only weakened the nation. By 1600, some disillusioned Spaniards were arguing that the conquest had brought more problems than benefits to their country.

THE COLUMBIAN EXCHANGE

Spain's long-term economic decline was just one of many consequences of the conquest of the New World. In the long run, the biological consequences of contact—what one historian has called the **Columbian exchange**—proved to be the most momentous.

The most catastrophic result of the exchange was the exposure of Native Americans to Old World diseases. Epidemics of smallpox, measles, typhus, and influenza struck Native Americans with great force, killing half, and sometimes as much as 90 percent, of the people in communities exposed to them. The only American disease to infect the Old World was syphilis, which appeared in Spain just after Columbus returned from his first voyage.

The Columbian exchange also introduced Old World livestock to the New World. Columbus brought horses, sheep, cattle, pigs, and goats with him on his second voyage in 1493. Native Americans had few domesticated animals and initially marveled at these large beasts. However, with few natural predators to limit their numbers, livestock populations boomed in the New World, competing with native mammals, such as bison, for good grazing. The use of horses also often gave European soldiers a decisive military advantage in conflicts with Indians.

But the introduction of European livestock created opportunities for Yaquis, Pueblos, and other peoples in the American Southwest, who began to raise cattle and sheep. By the eighteenth century, Plains Indians had not only adopted horses but also become exceptionally skilled riders. The men found it much easier to hunt buffalo on horseback than on foot, and the women valued horses as beasts of burden.

European ships carried unintentional passengers as well, including the black rat and honeybees, both previously unknown in the New World. Ships also brought weeds such as thistles and dandelions, whose seeds were often embedded in hay for animal fodder.

Europeans brought a variety of seeds and plants in order to grow familiar foods. Columbus's men planted wheat, chickpeas, melons, onions, and fruit trees on Caribbean islands. European plants did not always fare well, at least not everywhere in the New World, so Europeans learned to cultivate native foods, such as corn, tomatoes, squash, beans, and potatoes, as well as nonfood plants such as tobacco and cotton. They carried many of these plants back to Europe, enriching Old World diets with new foods.

Competition for a Continent

In 1494, the pope resolved the conflicting claims of Portugal and Spain for New World territory with the **Treaty of Tordesillas**. The treaty drew a north-south line approximately 1,100 miles west of the Cape Verde Islands. Spain received all lands west of the line, while Portugal held sway to the east. This limited Portugal's New World empire to Brazil, where settlers followed the precedent of the Atlantic island colonies and established sugar plantations worked by slave labor. But the treaty also protected Portugal's claims in Africa and Asia, which lay east of the line.

France and England, of course, rejected the papal grant of the Western Hemisphere to Spain and Portugal. Initially, domestic troubles—largely sparked by the Protestant Reformation—distracted the two countries from the pursuit of empire. By the close of the sixteenth century, both France and England insisted on their rights to New World lands, but neither had created a permanent settlement to support its claim.

EARLY FRENCH EFFORTS IN NORTH AMERICA

France was a relative latecomer to New World exploration. Preoccupied with European affairs, France's rulers paid little attention to America until news of Cortés' exploits in Mexico arrived in the 1520s.

In 1524, King Francis I sponsored a voyage by Giovanni de Verrazano, an Italian navigator, who mapped the North American coast from present-day South Carolina to Maine. During the 1530s and 1540s, the French mariner Jacques Cartier made three voyages in search of rich mines to rival those of Mexico and Peru. He explored the St. Lawrence River up to what is now Montreal, hoping to discover a water route through the continent to Asia (what came to be called the Northwest Passage). On his second voyage, in 1535, he and his crew almost froze to death and suffered from scurvy, a disease caused by a lack of Vitamin C. Some of the men survived because the Iroquois showed them how to make a vitamin-rich concoction of boiled white cedar needles and bark.

On his third voyage, in 1541, Cartier was to serve under the command of a nobleman, Jean François de la Rocque, sieur de Roberval, who was commissioned by the king to establish a permanent settlement in Canada. Unable to recruit colonists, he finally set sail in 1542, taking convicts as settlers. Cartier had sailed ahead, gathered samples of what he thought were gold and diamonds, and returned to France without Roberval's permission.

Roberval's expedition was poorly organized, and his cruel treatment of the convicts provoked several uprisings. The Iroquois, suspicious of repeated French intrusions on their lands, saw no reason to help them. A year after they arrived in Canada, Roberval and the surviving colonists were back in France. Their return coincided with news that the gold brought back by Cartier was iron pyrite (fool's gold) and the diamonds were quartz crystals.

Disappointed with their Canadian expeditions, the French made a few brief forays to the south, establishing outposts in what is now South Carolina in 1562 and Florida in 1564. They soon abandoned the Carolina colony (though not before the starving settlers resorted to cannibalism), and Spanish forces captured the Florida fort. Then, back in France, civil war broke out between Catholics and Protestants. Renewed interest in colonization would have to await the return of peace at home.

ENGLISH ATTEMPTS IN THE NEW WORLD

The English were quicker than the French to stake a claim to the New World but no more successful at colonization. In 1497, King Henry VII sent John Cabot, an Italian mariner, to explore eastern Canada on England's behalf, but neither Henry nor his wealthier subjects would invest the funds necessary to follow up on Cabot's discoveries.

The lapse in English activity in the New World stemmed from religious troubles at home. Between 1534 and 1558, England changed its official religion several times. King Henry VIII took up the Protestant cause when the pope refused to annul his marriage to Catherine of Aragon. In 1534, Henry declared himself the head of a separate Church of England and seized the Catholic Church's English property. But in 1553, Mary—daughter of the spurned Catherine of Aragon—became queen and tried to bring England back to Catholicism. She had nearly three hundred Protestants burned at the stake for their beliefs (earning her the nickname "Bloody Mary"), and many others went into exile in Europe.

After Mary's death in 1558, her half-sister Elizabeth, a committed Protestant, became queen, restoring Protestantism as the state religion, bringing stability to the nation, and renewing England's interest in the New World. She and her subjects saw colonization not only as a way to gain wealth and political advantage but also as a Protestant crusade against Catholic domination.

England's first target for colonization, however, was not America but Ireland. Located less than sixty miles west of England and populated by Catholics, Ireland threatened to become a base from which Spain or another Catholic power might invade England. Elizabeth launched a series of brutal expeditions that destroyed Irish villages and slaughtered the inhabitants. Several veterans of these campaigns later took part in New World colonization and drew on their Irish experience for guidance.

The English transferred their assumptions about Irish "savages" to Native Americans. Englishmen in America frequently observed similarities between Indians and the Irish. "The natives of New England," noted one Englishman, "are accustomed to build their houses much like the wild Irish." When Indians resisted conquest, the English recalled the Irish example, claiming that native "savagery" required brutal suppression.

The Irish experience also influenced English ideas about colonial settlement. English conquerors set up "plantations" surrounded by palisades on seized Irish lands, importing Protestant tenants from England and Scotland to farm the land. Native Irish people were excluded. English colonists in America followed this precedent when they established plantations that separated English and native peoples.

Sir Humphrey Gilbert, a notoriously cruel veteran of the Irish campaigns, composed a treatise to convince Queen Elizabeth to support New World colonization. The queen authorized several exploratory voyages, including Martin Frobisher's three trips in 1576–1578 in search of the Northwest Passage to Asia. Frobisher failed to find the elusive passage and sent back shiploads of glittering ore that proved to be fool's gold. Elizabeth had better luck in allowing privateers, such as John Hawkins and Francis Drake, to raid Spanish ships and New World ports for gold and silver.

Meanwhile, Gilbert continued to promote New World settlement, arguing that it would increase England's trade and provide a place for the nation's unemployed people. Like many of his contemporaries, Gilbert believed that England's "surplus" population threatened social order. The population was indeed growing, and economic changes often made it difficult for people to support themselves. Gilbert suggested offering free land in America to English families willing to emigrate.

In 1578, Gilbert received permission to set up a colony along the North American coast. It took him five years to organize an expedition to Newfoundland, which he claimed for England. After sailing southward seeking a more favorable site for a colony, Gilbert headed home, only to be lost at sea during an Atlantic storm. His half-brother, Sir Walter Raleigh (another veteran of the Irish wars), immediately took up the cause of English colonization.

In 1585 Raleigh sent men to build a settlement on Roanoke Island off the Carolina coast. Most colonists were soldiers fresh from Ireland who refused to grow their own food, insisting that the Roanoke Indians should feed them. When the local chief, Wingina, organized native resistance, they killed him. Eventually, the colonists, disappointed not to have found gold or precious stones and exhausted by a harsh winter, returned to England in 1586.

Two members of these early expeditions, however, left a more positive legacy. Thomas Hariot studied the Roanoke and Croatoan Indians and identified plants and animals in the area, hoping that some might prove to be profitable commodities. John White drew maps and painted a series of watercolors depicting the natives and the coastal landscape. When Raleigh tried once more, in 1587, to found a colony, he chose White to be its leader.

This attempt also failed. The ship captain dumped the settlers—who, for the first time, included women and children—on Roanoke Island so that he could pursue Spanish treasure ships. White waited until his granddaughter, Virginia Dare (the first English child born in America), was safely born and then sailed to England for supplies. But the outbreak of war with Spain delayed his return for three years. Spain had gathered an immense fleet to invade England, and all English ships were needed for defense. Although England defeated the Armada in 1588, White could not obtain a relief ship for Roanoke until 1590.

White found the colony deserted. Digging through the ruins of the village, he found "my books torn from the covers, the frames of some of my pictures and Maps rotten and spoiled with rain." He also saw the word *CROATOAN* carved on a post and assumed that the colonists had moved to nearby Croatoan Island. But bad weather prevented him from searching there. For years, English and Spanish mariners reported seeing white people along the coast of Chesapeake Bay. But no Roanoke colonists were ever found.

England's interest in colonization did not wane. In 1584, Richard Hakluyt had aroused enthusiasm for America by writing the "Discourse of Western Planting" for the queen and her advisors. He argued that England would prosper from the expansion of trade and the sale of New World commodities. Once the Indians were civilized, Hakluyt added, they would eagerly purchase English goods. Equally important, England could plant Protestant Christianity in the New World and prevent the power of "the Spanish king from flowing over all the face . . . of America."

Hakluyt's arguments fired the imaginations of many people, and the defeat of the Spanish Armada emboldened England to challenge Spain's New World dominance. The experience of Roanoke should have tempered that enthusiasm. The colony's fate underscored the need for adequate funding, the unsuitability of soldiers as colonists, and the need to maintain good relations with the Indians. But the English were slow to learn these lessons. As it was, the sixteenth century ended with no permanent English settlement in the New World.

Conclusion

After Columbus's first voyage, Europeans, eager for wealth and power, came by the thousands to a continent that just a hundred years earlier they had not dreamed existed. Africans came in even greater numbers to the Caribbean, Mexico, and Brazil, forced to labor for white masters in unfamiliar lands. In many parts of the Americas, native peoples encountered white and black strangers whose presence often destroyed their accustomed ways of life.

In 1600 only Spain had established North American colonies. Though its New World dominance seemed secure, even Spain had struggled to expand north of Mexico. Virtually the entire continent north of the Rio Grande remained firmly in Indian hands. Except in Mexico and the Caribbean, Europeans had merely touched the continent's shores. In 1600, native peoples still greatly outnumbered European and African immigrants. The next century, however, brought powerful challenges both to native control and to the Spanish monopoly of settlement.

REVIEW QUESTIONS

1. How did the Aztecs describe the Spanish ships off the coast of Mexico to Moctezuma? What details most captured their attention?

2. What were the similarities and differences between men's and women's roles in Native American, West African, and European societies? How did differences lead to misunderstandings?

3. Many of the first European colonizers in North America were military veterans. How did this affect their relations with Indian peoples?

4. Why did Spain so quickly become the dominant colonial power in North America? What advantages did it enjoy over France and England?

5. How did religion affect early European overseas colonization? Did religious factors encourage or interfere with European expansion?

CHAPTER 2

Transplantation

1600–1685

What role did the fur trade and fur traders play in the success of French colonies?

How did the English colonies in and around Jamestown of the early seventeenth century differ from those in New England later in that same century?

Why was tobacco so important to the economies of the southern colonies?

What role did religion play in the establishment of the New England colonies?

How were the Dutch able to successfully establish New Netherland along the eastern seaboard of America?

How were the societies of the West Indies and Carolina different from societies in other parts of North America?

Boston in New England
March 28, 1631

To the Right Honorable my very good lady, the Lady Bridget, Countess of Lincoln, Madam:

I have . . . thought fit to commit to memory our present condition and what hath befallen us since our arrival here. . . . [I] must do [so] rudely, having yet no table nor other room to write in than by the fireside upon my knee in this sharp winter. . . .

[In] April 1630 we set sail from old England with four good ships. And in May following, eight more followed, two having gone before in February and March and two more following in June and August, besides another set out by a private merchant. These seventeen ships arrived all safe in New England for the increase of the plantation here this year 1630, but made a long, a troublesome and costly voyage, being all windbound long in England and hindered with contrary winds after they set sail, and so scattered with mists and tempests that few of them arrived together. . . .

[Once we disembarked in mid-June, after more than nine weeks at sea] we began to consult of the place of our sitting down, for Salem, where we landed, pleased us not. And to that purpose some were sent to the Bay to search up the rivers for a convenient place. . . . [We] found a place . . . three leagues up Charles river, and thereupon unshipped our goods into other vessels and with much cost and labor brought them in July to Charlestowne, but there receiving advertisements by some of the late arrived ships from London and Amsterdam of some French preparations against us . . . we were forced to change counsel and for our present shelter to plant dispersedly. . . . This dispersion troubled some of us, but help it we could not. . . . The best counsel we could find out was to build a fort to retire to, in some convenient place, if an enemy pressed thereunto, after we should have fortified ourselves against the injuries of wet and cold.

Everett Emerson, ed., *Letters from New England: The Massachusetts Bay Colony,* 1629–1638 (Amherst, 1976).

THOMAS DUDLEY, the man who wrote this letter, was 54 years old when he moved with his family to New England. Thomas and his wife Dorothy had six children ranging in age from 9 to 25 years old. Dudley had prospered in England by working as a steward for local aristocrats, including the Countess of Lincoln to whom he addressed his letter. A man of talent and education, he had been chosen as deputy governor of the new colony of Massachusetts and worried that it might not survive its first months.

The Countess of Lincoln could not help but sense the contrast between her comfortable situation and the hardships Dudley endured. Neither could she miss this preoccupation with the French, who had established a colony in Canada. Remote as they were from Europe, the English colonists worried more about Old World enemies than about the Indians whose lands they now occupied.

The Dudleys ended up in Newtown (now Cambridge) and prospered. Thomas Dudley served four terms as governor and accumulated a large estate. He died in July 1653 at the age of 76, an unusually long life span for the seventeenth century. But Dudley could not have predicted such a happy outcome in the first difficult months following his voyage to America. His journey took place at a time of increased rivalry among European nations for New World territory. England's greatest adversaries were France and the Netherlands. Each nation scrambled to claim pieces of the North American mainland and islands in the Caribbean, hoping to match Spain's earlier success. As Thomas Dudley's letter suggests, this international race for overseas possessions was never far from colonists' minds.

The French in North America

The economic base of France's New World empire, known as New France, was the fur trade, which depended more on the control of waterways and alliances with Indians than on the occupation of land.

The focus of the French colony was the St. Lawrence River, which provided access to a vast interior populated by an abundance of beavers and by Indian peoples eager for trade. Because of its emphasis on the fur trade rather than extensive settlement, New France's population grew slowly in the seventeenth century. Its few, scattered villages were linked as closely to their Indian neighbors as to each other.

THE DEVELOPMENT OF NEW FRANCE

As we saw in Chapter 1, French efforts to found American colonies in the late sixteenth century ended in failure, but French fishermen continued to visit the Newfoundland coast. Setting up frames onshore to dry their catch, they met Indians with furs to trade for European goods. The already strong market for furs in Europe soon expanded dramatically as broad-brimmed beaver fur hats became fashionable.

Once it was clear that a profit could be made in Canada, France's interest revived. French kings sold exclusive trading rights to merchants willing to set up outposts in Canada. But to succeed, the merchants needed to bring farmers to New France to produce food and other supplies for the traders.

Quebec, organized in 1608 by Samuel de Champlain, was the first permanent French settlement in Canada. It was inhabited for its first two decades by only a few dozen settlers. Thereafter, efforts to recruit colonists to New France intensified, and French Jesuits—members of a Catholic religious order founded during the Counter Reformation—sent missionaries to convert the Indians. In 1642, Montreal was founded as a religious and commercial center, and by the 1650s, the Jesuits claimed thousands of Indian converts, many of whom lived in native Christian communities.

By 1700, New France had about fifteen thousand settlers, less than 7 percent of the number of English colonists in mainland North America that same year. One observer reported that "if they are the least inclined to work," immigrants could prosper in Canada. Colonists generally lived in sturdier houses, enjoyed a better diet, and paid lower taxes than their relatives back home. They acquired land to pass on to their children with an ease that French peasants could only envy. However, few French people moved to North America, and almost three out of four of those who did eventually returned to France.

Accounting for this reluctance to emigrate was Canada's reputation as a distant and inhospitable place. Rumors about frigid winters and surprise Indian attacks circulated among French peasants and villagers. In addition, the government required prospective settlers to be Catholic, reducing the pool from which they could be drawn.

Most settlers were sponsored by the government or by employers who paid their passage in return for three years of labor. Those who completed their terms of service received land. Most settlers were young men eager to marry and raise children to help them farm. But as late as 1666, only one out of three French settlers was female. Some young Frenchmen married Indian women. Others found brides from among the female orphans whom the French government paid to go to Canada in an attempt to remedy the sexual imbalance. Most young men, however, chose to go home to France.

THE FUR TRADE

Fur traders, not settlers, determined the colony's success. Furs were an ideal commodity—light, easy to transport, and very profitable. For the French, at least, the fur trade was also not very hard work. Indians, not Frenchmen, trapped the beavers, prepared the skins, and carried them from the interior to trading posts. French traders paid for the pelts with such goods as axes, knives, metal pots, and glass beads.

The Indians understood trade as part of a broader process of alliance that involved the exchange of gifts and mutual military assistance. When Champlain approached the Hurons for trade, they insisted that the French agree to help them fight the Iroquois. By becoming Huron allies, the French acquired Iroquois enemies. Thereafter the security of the colony depended on the ability of its governors to handle delicate diplomatic relations with the Indians.

Beginning in 1663, the colony was ruled by a governor and an intendant, both royal appointees who in turn appointed several lesser officials. New France's settlers never developed institutions of self-government as English colonists did. The king also insisted on a strong military force to protect the colony from attack by Indian enemies or European rivals. He ordered the construction of forts and sent several companies of professional soldiers.

Yet colonial officials disobeyed orders from France when it suited them. Even though instructions from Paris prohibited westward expansion, the intendant in Quebec allowed explorers to move inland. By the 1670s, French traders and missionaries had reached the Mississippi River, and in 1681–1682, Robert, sieur de La Salle, followed it to the Gulf of Mexico, claiming the entire river valley (which he named Louisiana in honor of King Louis XIV) for France. Scores of independent fur traders, known as *coureurs de bois* ("woods runners"), roamed the forests, living and trading among the Indians there.

English Settlement in the Chesapeake

When the English again attempted to settle in America in 1607, they chose the lower Chesapeake Bay region. The new settlement, Jamestown, eventually developed into the prosperous colony of Virginia. The reason for Virginia's success was an American plant—tobacco—that commanded good prices from European consumers. Tobacco also underlay the economy of a neighboring colony, Maryland, and had a profound influence on the development of Chesapeake society.

THE ORDEAL OF EARLY VIRGINIA

In 1606, several English merchants, convinced that they could succeed where others had failed, petitioned King James I for a charter incorporating two companies, the *Virginia Company* and the *Plymouth Company*, to attempt New World settlement. James I issued a charter granting the companies two tracts of land along the mid-Atlantic coast. These *joint-stock companies* sold shares to investors (who expected a profit in return) to raise money for colonization.

On a peninsula about 50 miles up a river they named the James, in honor of their king, 104 colonists, all men, built a fortified settlement they called Jamestown (see Map 2–1). They immediately began searching for gold and exploring the James in search of the Northwest Passage to Asia. All they found were disappointment and suffering. The swampy region was a perfect breeding area for malarial mosquitoes and parasites carrying other diseases. The settlers neglected to plant crops, and their food supplies dwindled. By January 1608, only thirty-eight of them were still alive.

The colony's governing council turned to Captain John Smith for leadership. Just 28 years old, Smith had fought against Spain in the Netherlands and the Ottomans in Hungary. He imposed military discipline on Jamestown, organizing settlers into work gangs and decreeing that "he that will not worke shall not eate." His high-handed methods revived the colony but antagonized certain settlers. When a gun-powder explosion wounded Smith in 1609 and forced him to return to England, his enemies had him replaced as leader.

Once again, the colony nearly disintegrated. New settlers arrived, only to die of disease and starvation. Of the five hundred people in Jamestown in the autumn of 1609, just sixty remained alive by the spring of 1610—some of whom survived only by eating their dead companions. Facing financial ruin, company officials back in England tried to conceal the state of the colony. They reorganized the company twice and sent more settlers, including glassmakers, wine-growers, and silkmakers, in a desperate effort to find a marketable product. They experimented with harsh military discipline, with a legal code—the *Lawes Divine, Morall and Martiall*—that prescribed the death penalty for offenses as trivial as swearing or killing a chicken. When it became clear that such severity discouraged immigration, the company tried more positive inducements.

The first settlers had been expected to work together in return for food and other necessities. With no profits forthcoming, governors began assigning small plots of land to colonists who finished their terms of service to the company. In 1616, the company instituted the *headright system*, giving 50 acres to anyone who paid his own way to Virginia and an additional 50 for each person (or "head") he brought with him.

In 1619, three other important developments occurred. The company began transporting women to Virginia to become wives for planters and induce them to stay in the colony. It was also the year in which the first Africans arrived in Virginia, and the company created the first legislative body in English America, the *House of Burgesses*, setting a precedent for

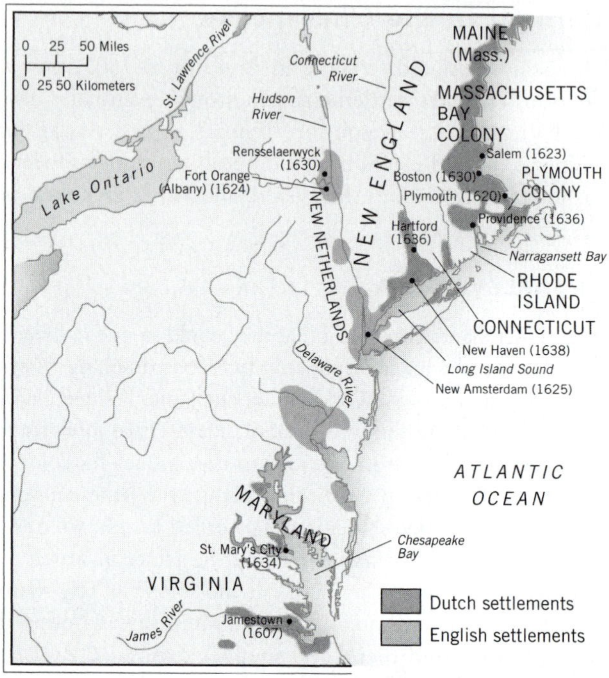

MAP 2–1
English and Dutch Mainland Colonies in North America, c. 1655   Early English colonies clustered in two areas of the Atlantic seaboard—New England and the Chesapeake Bay. Between them lay Dutch New Netherlands, with settlements stretching up the Hudson River. The Dutch also acquired territory at the mouth of the Delaware River in 1655 when they seized a short-lived Swedish colony located there.

ON THE BASIS of this map, what about the geographic location of Dutch colonies was ideal for Dutch colonists? What about their locations might have been problematic?

the establishment of self-government in other English colonies. Landowners elected representatives to the House of Burgesses, which, subject to the approval of the company, made laws for Virginia.

The settlers were still unable to earn the company a profit. To make things worse, the headright system expanded English settlement beyond Jamestown, straining the already tense relations with the Indians.

The English settlement was in the heart of territory ruled by the Indian leader Powhatan, then at the peak of his power and chief of a confederacy of about thirty tribes with some fourteen thousand people. After an initial skirmish with English soldiers, he sent gifts of food, assuming that by accepting the gifts, the colonists acknowledged their dependence on him. Further action against the settlers seemed unnecessary, since they seemed fully capable of destroying themselves.

However, armed colonists began seizing corn from Indian villages whenever the natives refused to supply it. During one raid in 1609, John Smith held a pistol to the chest of Opechancanough, Powhatan's younger brother, until the Indians ransomed him with

• C H R O N O L O G Y •

1603–1625 James I reigns as king of England.

1607 Founding of English colonies at Jamestown and Sagadahoc.

1608 Establishment of French colony at Quebec.

1619 First Africans arrive in Jamestown. Virginia's House of Burgesses meets for the first time.

1620 Founding of Plymouth Colony in New England. Mayflower Compact signed.

1620s Tobacco boom in Virginia.

1624 Dutch found colony of New Netherlands.

1625 Virginia becomes a royal colony. Fort Amsterdam founded.

1625–1649 Charles I reigns as king of England.

1627 English colony at Barbados founded.

1630 Massachusetts Bay Colony founded.

1630–1642 Great Migration to New England.

1634 Lord Baltimore (Cecilius Calvert) founds proprietary colony of Maryland.

1635–1636 Roger Williams banished from Massachusetts, founds Providence, Rhode Island.

1637 Anne Hutchinson banished from Massachusetts.
Pequot War.

1638 New Haven colony founded.

1640s Sugar cultivation and slavery established in West Indies.

1642–1660 English Civil War and Interregnum.

1649 Maryland's Act for Religious Toleration.

1660 Charles II restored to English throne; reigns until 1685.

1663 Founding of Carolina colony.

1664 New Netherlands conquered by the English, becomes New York.
New Jersey established.

1673 French explorers reach the Mississippi River.

1681 Founding of Pennsylvania.

corn. Protesting that the English came "to invade my people and possesse my Country," Powhatan besieged Jamestown and tried to starve the colony to extinction. The colony was saved by reinforcements from England. War with the Indians continued until 1614, when the colonist John Rolfe married Pocahontas, Powhatan's daughter. Pocahontas had briefly been held captive by the English during the war and had been instructed in English manners and religion by Rolfe. Sent to negotiate with Powhatan in the spring of 1614, Rolfe asked him for his daughter's hand. Powhatan gave his consent, and Pocahontas—baptized in the Church of England and renamed Rebecca—became Rolfe's wife.

Pocahontas died on a trip to England in 1617, severing the tie between her family and the English. Powhatan died in 1618, and Opechancanough succeeded him as chief. Still harboring intense resentment against the English, the new chief made plans to retaliate against them. Early in the morning on March 22, 1622, hundreds of Indian men traveled to the scattered English settlements, as if they meant to visit or trade. Instead they attacked the unsuspecting colonists, killing 347 by the end of the day—more than one-fourth of the English population.

The English gathered to plot revenge. They struck at native villages, killing the inhabitants and burning cornfields. At peace talks held in April 1623, the English served poisoned wine to their enemies, killing two hundred more. During nine years of war, the English treated the Indians with a ferocity that recalled their earlier subjugation of the Irish.

Economic activity ceased as settlers retreated to fortified garrisons. The Virginia Company went bankrupt. A royal commission investigating the 1622 surprise attack was shocked to discover that nearly ten times more colonists had died from starvation and disease than at the hands of Indians. King James had little choice but to dissolve the company in 1624 and Virginia became a royal colony the following year. Now the king chose the colony's governor and council, and royal advisors monitored its affairs.

THE IMPORTANCE OF TOBACCO

In their search for a marketable product, settlers had begun growing tobacco after 1610. Initially expensive, it became popular among wealthy European consumers. The first cargo of Virginia-grown tobacco arrived in England in 1617 and sold at a highly profitable 3 shillings per pound.

Settlers immediately planted tobacco everywhere—even in the streets of Jamestown. Company officials, unwilling to base the colony's economy on a single crop, tried to restrict annual production. After company rule ended, tobacco planting surged.

Between 1627 and 1669, annual tobacco exports climbed from 250,000 pounds to more than 15 million pounds. As the supply grew, the price per pound plunged from 13 pence in 1624 to a mere penny in the late 1660s, where it remained for the next half-century. The only way colonists could compensate for falling prices was to grow even more, pushing exports to England to more than 20 million pounds by the late 1670s.

Tobacco shaped nearly every aspect of Virginia society, from patterns of settlement to the recruitment of colonists. Planters scrambled to claim lands near navigable rivers so that ships could easily reach their plantations and carry their crops to market. As a result, the colonists dispersed across the countryside instead of gathering in towns. People settled, one governor wrote, wherever "a choice veine of rich ground invited them, and further from neighbours the better." Colonists competed to produce the biggest and best crop and get it to market the fastest, hoping to enjoy even a small price advantage over everyone else.

The key to success was to control a large labor force. Tobacco kept workers busy nine months of the year. Planters sowed seeds in the early spring, transplanted seedlings a few weeks later, and spent the summer pinching off the tops of the plants (to produce larger leaves) and removing worms. After the harvest, the leaves were "cured"—dried in ventilated sheds—and packed in large barrels. During the winter, planters cleared and fenced more land and made barrels for next year's crop. Working on his own, one planter could tend two thousand plants, which yielded about 500 pounds of cured tobacco.

To make a profit, planters needed help. They turned to England, importing thousands of **indentured servants**, or contract workers, who agreed to a fixed term of labor, usually four to seven years, in exchange for free passage to Virginia. The master provided food, shelter, clothing, and, at the end of the term of service, "freedom dues" paid in corn and clothing. Between 1625 and 1640, an estimated one thousand or more indentured servants arrived each year. Some were orphans; others were condemned criminals given a choice between execution and transportation to Virginia. Most, however, came from the ranks of England's unemployed, who emigrated in hopes of "bettering their condition in a Growing Country."

Most found such hopes quickly dashed. Many servants died from disease, and some, occasionally, from mistreatment. Richard Price beat his servant, Endymion Inleherne, for "being a common runaway and one that did use to feign himself sick" so severely that the young man died. A jury refused to charge Price with murder, reasoning that Inleherne deserved punishment and Price had not intended to kill him. The courts (administered by masters) usually favored masters' authority over servants' rights.

Virginia-grown tobacco found a ready market among European consumers such as this contemplative smoker. As tobacco prices declined during the seventeenth century due to increased production, even people of modest means could take up the habit of smoking.

Arents Collection, The New York Public Library, Astor, Lenox, and Tilden Foundation.

For every ex-servant who became a landholder, dozens died in poverty. Many ex-servants could find farms only in parts of the colony less suitable for tobacco cultivation and more vulnerable to Indian attack.

Because of their labor needs, masters favored young men in their teens and twenties as indentured servants, importing three or four times as many of them as women. As a result, Virginia's population in the seventeenth century was overwhelmingly young and male. Many free male servants found that marriage was as remote a possibility as landownership. John Rolfe's union with Pocahontas was one of only three English-Indian marriages recorded in seventeenth-century Virginia.

Population growth was further slowed because servants could not marry until their indentures were completed. Many men were already in their thirties when they married, usually to women in their early twenties. Older couples had fewer children than younger couples would have had. Few colonists lived past 50, and many of their offspring died young. Children who survived had usually lost one or both parents by the time they reached adulthood.

Surviving spouses often remarried a widow or widower with children, creating complex households with stepparents and half-brothers and half-sisters. Widows controlled property left to them by their husbands, assuming the normally male responsibility of managing estates for their children's benefit. A widow tried to choose a new spouse wisely, for he would manage the property that the children of her first marriage would inherit.

The number of settlers rose from about 2,500 in 1630 to 21,000 in 1660, thanks to the demand for indentured servants. When Opechancanough launched another raid in 1644 that killed nearly five hundred colonists, it had a far less devastating effect than his attack of 1622 because the settler population had grown so much and now outnumbered the Indians.

Some settlers acquired large estates and grew wealthy from the labor of indentured servants tilling their tobacco fields. Others, cultivating small land-holdings or renting plots from more successful colonists, grew just enough food to survive and as much tobacco as they could manage. But even the most successful settlers, investing every penny of profit in labor and land, lived under quite primitive conditions.

Early colonial dwellings were often no larger than 16 by 20 feet, with one or two rooms. Poor settlers slept on the floor on straw mattresses and had few other furnishings. Rich planters owned more goods, though often of poor quality. In 1655, for instance, William Brocas, a prominent colonial official, owned "a parcell of old hangings, very thin and much worn"; seven chairs, "most of them unusefull"; and seven guns, "most unfixt."

MARYLAND: A REFUGE FOR CATHOLICS

Encouraged by Virginia's success, King Charles I in 1632 granted 10 million acres of land north of Chesapeake Bay to the nobleman Cecilius Calvert, Lord Baltimore. Unlike Virginia, which was founded by a joint-stock company, Maryland was a *proprietary colony*—the sole possession of Calvert and his heirs. They owned all the land, which they could divide up as they pleased, and had the right to set up the colony's government.

Calvert, who was Catholic, intended Maryland to be a refuge for others of his faith. English Catholics were a disadvantaged minority. They paid double taxes, could not worship in public, hold political office, or send their children to universities. In Maryland, Calvert wanted Catholic colonists to enjoy economic and political power. He intended to divide the land into manors—large private estates like those of medieval England—and distribute them to wealthy Catholic friends. These manor lords would live on rents collected from tenant farmers, hold the most important governmental offices, and run their own law courts.

Calvert died before settlement began, and his plans unraveled. The majority of colonists, who began arriving in 1634, were Protestants who despised Catholics. Refusing to live as tenants on Catholic estates, they claimed land of their own—a process that accelerated after 1640, when Maryland adopted a headright system like Virginia's as a way to recruit settlers.

Maryland's problems intensified when civil war broke out in England in 1642. Charles I, who became king in 1625, clashed with Protestants who called for further reform of the Church of England. He also antagonized many government leaders by dissolving Parliament in 1629 and ruling on his own for eleven years. Needing funds to suppress a rebellion in Scotland in 1640, however, Charles was forced to recall Parliament, which quickly turned against him. Both king and Parliament recruited armies and went to war in 1642. Parliamentary forces triumphed, and in 1649, they executed Charles. For the next decade, Oliver Cromwell, a general, ruled until his death in 1658. His son, Richard, proved an inept successor, and in 1660 a group of army officers invited Charles's exiled son to accept the throne.

During the 1640s and 1650s, Maryland Protestants took advantage of the upheaval in England, contesting the Calverts' control of the colony. To pacify them, Calvert's son Cecilius established a legislature, assuming that Protestants would dominate the elective lower house while he could appoint Catholics to the upper house. In 1649, Calvert also approved the *Act for Religious Toleration*, the first law in America to call for freedom of worship for all Christians, but the Protestant majority continued to resist Catholic political influence, at one point passing a law that prohibited Catholics from voting.

Instead of the peaceful Catholic refuge Calvert intended, Maryland soon resembled neighboring Virginia. Its settlers raised tobacco and imported as many indentured servants as possible. Because Maryland initially provided former servants with 50 acres of land, more became landholders than in Virginia. As in Virginia, however, economic opportunity diminished after 1660 when the price of tobacco dropped. Maryland's settlers enjoyed more peaceful relations with the Indians among whom they settled than Virginians had, but they fought intensely among themselves.

The Founding of New England

The first English attempt to settle the northeastern coast of North America was a miserable failure. In 1607, the Plymouth Company sent a group of settlers who abandoned their settlement in present-day Maine the next summer. But English explorers and fishermen continued to visit New England, among them John Smith, who in 1616 published his book extolling its virtues as a site for colonization.

Six colonies appeared in the region between 1620 and 1640, settled by thousands of people troubled by religious, political, and economic upheavals in England. The society these settlers created differed markedly from the one developing in the Chesapeake—not least of all in the absence of significant Indian opposition. Between 1616 and 1618 a terrible epidemic swept through coastal New England, killing up to 90 percent of the Indians living there. The devastated survivors were unable to prevent the encroaching English from building towns where their villages had once stood.

THE PILGRIMS AND PLYMOUTH COLONY

Plymouth Colony, the first of the New England settlements, was founded in 1620. Its origins lay in religious disputes that had plagued England since the late sixteenth century. Most of Queen Elizabeth's subjects approved of her efforts to keep England a Protestant nation, but some believed that she had not rid the Church of England of Catholic practices. The enemies of these reformers, ridiculing them for wanting to purify the Church of England (or *Anglican* Church) of all corruption, called them *Puritans*.

Following the doctrine of predestination taught by John Calvin, English Puritans believed in an all-powerful God who, at the moment of Creation, had determined which humans would be saved and which would be damned. The centerpiece of their spiritual life was conversion: the transforming experience that occurred when individuals felt the stirrings of grace in their souls and began to hope that they were among the saved. Those who experienced conversion were considered saints and acquired new strength to live godly lives.

Puritans rejected the *Book of Common Prayer*, which regulated Anglican worship, insisting that ministers should pray from the heart and preach from the Bible. They objected when Anglican clergy wore rich vestments that set them apart from ordinary Christians. And they objected to any church organization above the level of individual congregations, seeing no need for bishops and archbishops. But what they hated most of all about the Anglican Church was that anyone could be a member. Puritans believed that everyone should attend church services, but they wanted church membership—which conferred the right to partake in the Lord's Supper, or communion—to be limited to saints.

Puritans thus insisted on further reform. Elizabeth and the rulers who followed her disagreed and tried to silence them. Some Puritans, known as **separatists**, were convinced that the Church of England would never change and left it to form their own congregations.

One such group, mainly artisans and middling farmers from the village of Scrooby, in Nottinghamshire, left England in 1607–1608, settling for more than a decade in Holland. There they worshiped in peace, but many struggled to make a living and feared that their children were being tempted by the worldly pleasures of Dutch city life. Some Scrooby separatists gained the backing of the Plymouth Company for a move to America. Called **Pilgrims** because they thought of themselves as spiritual wanderers, they were joined by other separatists and by nonseparatist "strangers" hired to help get the colony started. In all, 102 men, women, and children set sail on the *Mayflower* in September 1620.

After a long and miserable voyage, they landed near Massachusetts Bay. Because this was about 200 miles north of the land their charter permitted them to settle, some of the "strangers" claimed that they were no longer legally bound to obey the expedition's separatist leaders. The leaders responded by drafting the *Mayflower Compact*, which became the first document to establish self-government in North America, and urging all adult males to sign it.

The Pilgrims settled at Plymouth, the site of a Wampanoag village recently depopulated by disease, where they found abandoned cornfields, Indian graves, and baskets of corn buried underground. Even with this corn, nearly half of the Pilgrims died of starvation and disease that first winter.

Two English-speaking natives, Squanto and Samoset, emerged from the woods the next spring and approached the Pilgrims on behalf of Massasoit, the Wampanoag leader. The Wampanoags thought the Pilgrims might be useful allies against Wampanoag enemies, such as the Narragansetts, who had escaped the recent epidemics.

In 1621, the Wampanoags and the Pilgrims signed a treaty of alliance. The Pilgrims assumed that Massasoit had submitted to the superior authority of King James, whereas Massasoit assumed that the agreement treated himself and the English king as equal partners. Despite frequent disputes caused by English assertion of authority over the Wampanoags, the two groups enjoyed relatively peaceful relations for nearly half a century.

The Indians taught the English how to plant corn and traded corn with them for manufactured goods. The Pilgrims also exchanged corn with other Indians to the north for furs, which they shipped back to England to help pay off their debts to English investors. In the autumn of 1621, Indians and Pilgrims gathered for a feast celebrating the settlers' first harvest—an event Americans still commemorate as the first Thanksgiving.

Plymouth remained small, poor, and weak. It never had more than seven thousand settlers and never produced more than small shipments of furs, fish, and timber to sell in England. It took the Pilgrims more than twenty years to repay their English creditors. Yet because of the idealistic visions of the founders of Plymouth Colony, who saw in the New

World a chance to escape religious persecution and create peaceful communities and pure churches, it has become an important symbol in American history.

MASSACHUSETTS BAY COLONY AND ITS OFFSHOOTS

The Puritans who settled Massachusetts shared many of the Pilgrims' beliefs, but they insisted that the Anglican Church *could* be reformed and so were not separatists. They went to New England to create godly churches to serve as models for English reform. And England, they believed, was in more desperate need of reformation than ever.

Charles I, who became king in 1625, opposed Puritans more forcefully than his father had and supported changes in Anglican worship that recalled Catholic practices. England at the time also suffered from economic troubles that many Puritans saw as signs of God's displeasure with their country.

In 1629, a group of Puritan merchants received a royal charter for a joint-stock enterprise, the Massachusetts Bay Company, to set up a colony north of Plymouth. They chose John Winthrop, a prosperous Puritan lawyer, as their leader. In the spring of 1630, a fleet of eleven ships carried about a thousand men, women, and children across the Atlantic.

Before Winthrop's ship landed, he preached a lay sermon, called "A Model of Christian Charity," to his fellow passengers, reminding them of their goal "to do more service to the Lord." They should "love one another with a pure heart" and place the good of all above private ambitions. Winthrop argued that the Lord had made them his chosen people, and that as a result, "we shall be as a city upon a hill, the eyes of all people are upon us." If they failed to live up to God's expectations, he would punish them. With this mingled encouragement and threat, the emigrants soon landed and founded Boston and six adjoining towns.

Winthrop described the settlers' mission in New England as a *covenant*, or contract, with God, binding them to meet their religious obligations in return for God's favor. The settlers also created covenants when they founded towns and churches, agreeing to live together in peace. The desire for peace and purity could breed intolerance. Settlers scrutinized their neighbors for signs of unacceptable behavior. But the insistence on convenants and conformity also created a remarkably stable society, far more peaceable than Virginia's.

That stability was enhanced by the development of representative government. The *General Court*, which initially included only the shareholders of the joint-stock company, was transformed into a twohouse legislature. Freemen—adult males who held property and were church members—had the right to elect representatives to the lower house, as well as 18 members (called "assistants") to the upper house. They also chose a governor and a deputy governor.

Between 1630 and 1642, at least thirteen thousand settlers came to New England and established dozens of towns. The progress of settlement was generally untroubled in coastal Massachusetts, but when colonists moved into the Connecticut River Valley, tensions with Indians grew rapidly. These erupted in 1637 in the brief, tragic conflict called the ***Pequot War***.

English settlers from Massachusetts first arrived in the Connecticut Valley in the mid-1630s. Dutch traders already in the region had been dealing exclusively with the Pequot Indians as partners. In 1633, however, they invited other Indian groups to trade with them. The Pequots, suffering terribly from a recent smallpox epidemic, resented losing their special trading rights and began fighting the Dutch. Initially, they saw the English settlers as potential allies against the Dutch. But when the settlers demanded Pequot submission to English authority as the price of an alliance, they turned against them too.

The English settlers formed alliances with the Narragansetts and Mohegans, who were both rivals of the Pequots. In May 1637, English forces surrounded a Pequot village inhabited mainly by women and children, located on the Mystic River. They set it ablaze and shot anyone who tried to escape. Between three hundred and seven hundred Pequots died, a toll that shocked the settlers' Indian allies, who protested that English-style warfare was "too furious, and slays too many men." After the surviving Pequots had fled or been sold into slavery, many more settlers moved to Connecticut, which soon declared itself a separate colony. In 1639, the settlers adopted the *Fundamental Orders*, creating a government similar to that of Massachusetts, and the English government granted them a royal charter in 1662.

Massachusetts spun off other colonies as its population expanded in the 1630s and dissenters ran afoul of its intolerant government. Puritan leaders tried to suppress unorthodox religious opinions whenever they emerged, for fear that God would interpret their failure to do so as a breach of their covenant with him. Some dissenting colonists, however, refused to be silenced.

Roger Williams was one such irrepressible dissenter. Williams was a separatist minister who declared that because Massachusetts churches had not rejected the Church of England, they shared its corruption. He argued for the separation of church and state, and also attacked the Massachusetts charter, insisting that the king had no right to grant Indian lands to English settlers.

Williams was an immensely likable man—even Governor Winthrop remained on friendly terms with him, but the General Court sentenced him to banishment, intending to ship him back to England. In the winter of 1635, Williams slipped away with a few followers and found refuge among the Narragansett Indians, from whom he purchased land for the village of Providence, founded in 1636. More towns soon sprang up nearby when a new religious crisis, provoked by a woman named Anne Hutchinson, sent additional refugees to Rhode Island from Massachusetts.

Anne Hutchinson arrived in Boston from England with her husband and seven children in 1634. Welcomed by the town's women for her talents as a midwife, she also began to hold religious meetings in her house, where she denounced several ministers.

Many people, including prominent Boston merchants, flocked to Hutchinson's meetings. But her critics believed her to be a dangerous *antinomian* (someone who claimed to be free from obedience to moral law) because she seemed to maintain that saints were accountable only to God and not to any worldly authority. Her opponents also objected to her teaching of mixed groups of men and women, a breach of normal gender roles. Colony magistrates arrested her and tried her for sedition—that is, for advocating the overthrow of the government.

During her trial, Hutchinson mounted a lively defense. In the end, however, the court found her guilty and banished her from the colony. With many of her followers, she moved to Rhode Island, where Roger Williams had proclaimed a policy of religious toleration.

At the height of the Hutchinson controversy, a group of zealous Puritan emigrants led by the Reverend John Davenport departed Boston to found New Haven in 1638. Davenport's efforts to impose perfect Puritan conformity in his colony made Massachusetts seem easygoing in comparison. But New Haven failed to thrive, and in 1662, the poor, intolerant, and isolated colony was absorbed into Connecticut.

FAMILIES, FARMS, AND COMMUNITIES IN EARLY NEW ENGLAND

"This plantation and that of Virginia went not forth upon the same reasons," declared one of Massachusetts's founders. Virginians came "for profit," whereas New Englanders emigrated to bear witness to their Puritan faith. Unlike the unmarried young men who moved in great numbers to Virginia, most New Englanders settled with their families.

The average family in early New England had seven or eight children. Because women and men arrived in nearly equal numbers, young adults easily found spouses and produced more children. Thus the population continued to grow rapidly even when immigration slowed after 1642, so that by 1660, New England's settlers numbered more than 33,000.

New Englanders were largely spared from the diseases that ravaged Virginia's settlers and devastated Indian populations. It seemed a "marvelous providence of God" to Plymouth's Governor Bradford that many settlers made it to their seventies and eighties when few of England's adults lived past 60. Longevity strengthened economic security as well as emotional ties. Fathers lived long enough to build prosperous farms to pass along to their sons. And they accumulated herds of livestock and stores of household goods to give to their daughters when they married.

Unlike Chesapeake colonists, who spread out on tobacco lands near navigable rivers, New Englanders clustered in towns. The Massachusetts government strongly encouraged town formation by granting land to groups of families who promised to settle together. The families divided the land among themselves, allotting each family a farm of sufficient size to support all its members. People who had had higher social standing in England received larger farms than those of lower standing. Land that the original families could not yet farm was held "in common" to be distributed to their children as they grew up. Settlers and their children generally remained in their chosen towns for the rest of their lives.

Towns—usually made up of fifty to a hundred families—provided the context for religious, political, and economic activity. The importance Puritans placed on worship with fellow Christians helped promote community feeling. Every Sunday, townspeople gathered at the meetinghouse to listen to the minister preach God's word. At other times, the meetinghouse served as a town hall, where men assembled to discuss matters ranging from local taxes to making sure that everyone's fences were mended. Townsmen tried to reach decisions by consensus in order to preserve harmony. To oversee day-to-day local affairs, men chose five to seven of their most trusted neighbors to serve as selectmen.

Economic life likewise centered on the town. New England's stony soil and short growing season offered few ways to get rich, but most people achieved a modest prosperity. Farmers grew corn and other foods and raised livestock. Their goal was to achieve what they called *competency*—the possession of enough property to ensure their families' economic independence.

Maintaining competency was a family affair. New England farmers relied on their wives and children for labor. Women cared for children, cleaned, cooked, sewed and mended, milked cows, and tended poultry. Many farmwives made butter and cheese, brewed beer, preserved fruits and vegetables, salted meat, spun yarn, and wove cloth. Although they generally did not perform heavy agricultural work, women helped with planting and harvesting crops and tended gardens near their houses. If their husbands worked as merchants or craftsmen, wives might also help out in the shop.

Children began work shortly after their fifth birthday. Older siblings cared for younger ones, fetched tools, and minded cattle. Around age 10, girls began learning more complicated housekeeping skills from their mothers, and boys received instruction from their fathers in such tasks as plowing, cutting hay and wood, and caring for livestock. Many children in their early teens performed tasks little different from adult duties.

No family could produce all the goods that it needed, so New Englanders regularly traded with their neighbors. A skilled carpenter might erect a house in return for barrels of salted beef. Men with several sons sent them to help neighbors whose children were too young to work. Midwives delivered babies in return for cheese or eggs. Women nursed sick neighbors, whom they might one day call on for similar help. These sorts of transactions allowed most New Englanders to enjoy a fairly comfortable life.

Without a staple crop like tobacco, New England prospered by exploiting a variety of resources, developing a diversified economy that was less vulnerable to depression than Virginia's. Farmers sent livestock and meat to merchants to be marketed abroad. Fishermen caught thousands of pounds of cod, haddock, and other fish to be sold in Europe. Some of the region's timber found its way abroad, but most of it ended up in shipyards. New Englanders became such skilled shipbuilders and seafaring merchants that by the 1670s, London merchants complained about competition from them. England itself had little use for the dried fish, livestock, salted meat, and wood products that New England vessels carried, but enterprising merchants found exactly the market they needed in the West Indies.

Competition in the Caribbean

The Spanish claimed all Caribbean islands by right of Columbus's discovery, but during the early seventeenth century, French, Dutch, and English adventurers defied them. France eventually retained Guadaloupe, Martinique, Haiti (which the French called Saint Dominque), and several smaller islands. The Dutch had Aruba, Curaçao, St. Martin, and St. Eustasius. The English occupied Antigua, Barbados, Montserrat, Nevis, and St. Christopher; in 1655, they conquered the Spanish-held island of Jamaica. The West Indies soon became the jewel of England's empire, producing vast wealth from the cultivation of sugar. Caribbean planters created a society totally unlike any of the mainland colonies—not least of all because their prosperity depended on the exploitation of African slaves.

SUGAR AND SLAVES

The first English colonists who came to the West Indies in the 1630s raised tobacco and imported indentured servants to work their fields. By that time, however, tobacco fetched low prices. Moreover, the disease environment of the West Indies proved even harsher than that of the Chesapeake, and settlers died in great numbers.

But by the 1640s, a Barbados planter boasted of "a great change on this island of late from the worse to the better, praised be God." That change was a shift from tobacco to sugar cane. Many sugar planters grew wealthy. In 1646, a 500-acre plantation on Barbados sold for £16,000—more than the whole island had been worth just a few years before. On average, the estate of a Caribbean sugar planter was worth four times as much as a prosperous Chesapeake plantation.

Sugar rapidly transformed the West Indies. Planters deforested whole islands to raise sugar cane. They stopped planting food crops and raising livestock—thereby creating a demand for lumber and provisions that boosted New England's economy.

The sugar boom also led to a scramble for labor. Planters continued to import white indentured servants, including some kidnapped English and Irish youths, but soon turned to African slaves. Africans were already used to agricultural work in a tropical climate. And the English would not have to enslave any Africans themselves; they could simply import people who had already been enslaved by other Africans and sold to Dutch or Portuguese traders. The planters' choice has been called an "unthinking decision," but it had an enormous impact on English colonial life, first in the islands and then on the mainland.

A BIRACIAL SOCIETY

The West Indies had the first biracial plantation society in the English colonial world. By 1700, more than 250,000 slaves had been imported into the region, quickly becoming the most numerous segment of its population. Slaves lived in wretched conditions, underfed, poorly dressed, and housed in rough huts. They labored six days a week from sunrise to sunset—except at harvest time, when they toiled seven days a week in round-the-clock shifts. Masters considered them property, often branding them like livestock and hunting them with bloodhounds when they ran away.

Laws declared slavery to be a lifelong condition that passed from slave parents to their children. Slaves had no legal rights and were under the complete control of their masters. Only rarely would masters who killed slaves face prosecution, and those who did and were found guilty were subject only to fines. Slaves, in contrast, could be whipped, branded, or maimed for stealing food or harboring a runaway compatriot. Serious crimes such as murder or arson brought execution without trial. Slaves who rebelled were burned to death.

When masters began to import African women as well as men—hoping to create a self-reproducing labor force—slaves formed families and preserved at least some African traditions. They gave their children African names (although masters often gave them English names as well). They celebrated with African music and worked to the rhythm of familiar songs. They performed West African funeral rituals, often burying their dead with food and other goods to accompany them on the journey to the afterlife.

Some planters, profiting handsomely from their slaves' toil, lived better than many English gentlemen, dwelling in large houses, with fine furnishings. But sugar production required a heavy investment in land, slaves, mills, and equipment. As great planters took vast amounts of land for themselves, freed servants and small farmers struggled to survive. After 1650, some poorer white colonists headed for the mainland. They were joined by planters looking for a place to expand their operations once most of the good land on the islands had been brought under cultivation.

The Proprietary Colonies

The initial burst of English colonization ended in 1640 when England tottered on the brink of civil war. With the accession of Charles II to the English throne in 1660, however, interest in North American colonies revived. Charles II rewarded the supporters who had remained loyal to him during his long exile in France with huge tracts of American land. Four new colonies—Carolina, Pennsylvania, New Jersey, and New York—resulted from such grants during his reign (1660–1685). All were proprietary colonies, essentially the private property of the people to whom they had been given. Carolina and Pennsylvania, like the earlier proprietary colony of Maryland, provided their owners the chance to test idealistic social visions. The origins of New York and New Jersey as English colonies, in contrast, lay not in proprietary visions of social harmony but in the stern reality of military conquest.

EARLY CAROLINA

In 1663, Charles II granted a group of supporters an enormous tract of land stretching from southern Virginia to northern Florida. The proprietors, who included several Barbados planters, called their colony Carolina, after the Latin form *(Carolus)* of the king's name. They envisioned it growing into a prosperous, orderly society.

One of the proprietors, Anthony Ashley Cooper, working closely with his secretary, John Locke, devised the **Fundamental Constitutions of Carolina**, a plan to ensure the stability of the colony by balancing property ownership and political rights. It called for the creation of a colonial aristocracy, who would own two-fifths of the land and wield extensive political power. Below them, a large class of freeholders would own small farms and elect representatives to an assembly. At the bottom of the social order would be slaves.

This plan never went into effect. People moved in from Virginia and the West Indies and settled where they pleased. They even voted in the assembly to reject the Fundamental Constitutions. When English traders first appeared, eager to buy deerskins, many Indians had welcomed them. But they grew hostile when some traders began selling guns to some tribes in exchange for captives from rival tribes who were sold as slaves to the West Indies. Resentments deepened as settlers moved onto native lands.

The colonists at first raised livestock to be sold to the West Indies. But the introduction of rice in Carolina in the 1690s transformed the settlers' economy, making it, as one planter noted, "as much their staple Commodity, as Sugar is to Barbadoes and Jamaica, or Tobacco to Virginia and Maryland." West African slaves probably introduced rice cultivation in Carolina. Ironically, the profits earned from rice persuaded Carolina planters to invest even more heavily in slave labor.

By 1708, there were more black slaves than white settlers in the colony, and two decades after that, black people outnumbered white people by two to one. Rice farming required a substantial investment in land, labor, and equipment, including dikes and dams for flooding fields. Those who could afford such an investment set themselves up as planters in Carolina's coastal rice district, acquiring large estates and forcing poorer settlers to move elsewhere.

Some of these dislocated men went to the northern part of Carolina, where the land and climate were unsuited to rice. There they raised tobacco and produced pitch, tar, and timber products from the region's pine forests. So different were the two regions that the colony formally split into two provinces—North and South Carolina—in 1729.

South Carolina rice planters became some of the wealthiest colonists on the mainland. But their luxurious style of life came at a price. As Carolina began to look "more like a negro country than like a country settled by white people," planters dreaded the prospect of slave rebellion. To avert this nightmare, they enacted **slave codes** as harsh as those of the sugar islands. Carolina would not be the harmonious colony that John Locke and Cooper had envisioned. It evolved instead into a racially divided society founded on the oppression of a black majority and permeated by fear.

PENNSYLVANIA: THE DREAM OF TOLERANCE AND PEACE

William Penn put his own utopian plans into action in 1681, when Charles II granted him a huge tract of land north of Maryland as payment for a royal debt owed to Penn's father. Penn intended his colony to be a model of justice and peace, as well as a refuge for members of the Society of Friends, or **Quakers**, a persecuted religious sect to which Penn himself belonged.

Like the separatists, Quakers abandoned the Church of England as hopelessly corrupt, but they went even further in their beliefs. Rejecting predestination, they maintained that every soul had a spark of grace and that salvation was possible for all who heeded that "Inner Light." They rejected trained clergy and elaborate church rituals. Instead of formal religious services, Quakers held meetings in silence until someone, inspired by the Inner Light, rose to speak.

Quaker beliefs had disturbing social and political implications. Quakers granted women spiritual equality with men, allowing them to preach, hold separate prayer meetings, and exercise authority over "women's matters." Arguing that social distinctions were not the work of God, Quakers refused to remove their hats in the presence of those of higher social class. And instead of the formal *you*, Quakers addressed superiors with the informal *thee* and *thou*. Because their faith required them to renounce the use of force, Quakers also refused to perform military service.

When English authorities began harassing Quakers, William Penn (who was himself jailed briefly) conceived his plan for a New World "holy experiment," a harmonious society governed by brotherly love. Using his father's connection with the king, he acquired the land that became Pennsylvania ("Penn's Woods") and recruited settlers from among Europe's oppressed peoples and persecuted religious sects. By 1700, about 18,000 emigrants had left England, Wales, Scotland, Ireland, and various German provinces for the new colony.

Many came in families and settled in an area occupied by the Delaware Indians, whose numbers had recently been reduced by disease and warfare. The "holy experiment" required colonists to live "as Neighbours and friends" with the Indians as well as with one another. Penn paid Indians for land and regulated trade. As long as he remained in control of the colony, relations between the settlers and the Indians were generally peaceful—so much so that refugee Indians from nearby colonies moved into Pennsylvania. Relations between Penn and the settlers, however, were less cordial.

In the **Frame of Government**, his constitution for Pennsylvania, Penn remained true to his Quaker principles with a provision allowing for religious freedom. But true to his aristocratic origins, he designed a legislature with limited powers and reserved considerable authority for himself. When Penn returned to England after a brief stay in the colony (1682–1684), the governor and council—both appointed by Penn—fought with elected members of the assembly. Penn's opponents—many of whom were fellow Quakers—objected to his proprietary privileges, including his control of foreign trade and his collection of fees from landholders. Settlers on the lower Delaware River gained autonomy for themselves with their own legislature, in effect creating an unofficial colony that later became Delaware.

Settlers continued to fight among themselves, and with Penn's heirs, after his death. A flood of increasingly aggressive immigrants undermined peaceful relations with the Indians, forcing many natives to abandon their homelands and move west.

By 1720, Pennsylvania's ethnically and religiously diverse population numbered more than thirty thousand. The colony had some of the richest farmland along the Atlantic coast and was widely known as the "best poor man's country in the world." Growing wheat and other crops, the settlers lived mostly on scattered farms rather than in towns. From the busy port of Philadelphia, ships carried much of the harvest to markets in the West Indies and southern Europe. Penn's "holy experiment" in social harmony may have failed, but as a thriving colony, Pennsylvania succeeded handsomely.

The Dutch Overseas Empire

Small but densely populated, the Dutch Republic joined the scramble for empire in the early seventeenth century. The Northern Provinces, sometimes known as Holland, had declared their independence from Spain in 1581. The new republic, dominated by Protestants, was intent on challenging Catholic Spain's power for religious as well as political reasons in the New World as well as the Old. More than any other factor, however, the desire for profit drove the Dutch quest for colonies.

THE WEST INDIA COMPANY AND NEW NETHERLAND

The Dutch Republic served as a major center of world trade. Thousands of Dutch ships plied the world's oceans and the republic's earnings from foreign trade may have surpassed those of the rest of Europe combined. This commercial vitality provided the context for overseas expansion.

The first instrument of colonial dominance was the Dutch East India Company, founded in 1602. Eager to reap profits from spices and other exotic goods, the Company challenged what had until then been a virtual Portuguese monopoly of Asian trade. Its first success was the capture of the Spice Islands (now Indonesia and East Timor), followed by the takeover of Batavia (Jakarta), Ceylon (Sri Lanka), and Sumatra. The Company established trading posts on the Gold Coast of West Africa, where it competed with the Portuguese in the slave trade, and at the Cape of Good Hope on Africa's southern tip. Its far-flung commercial net eventually encompassed parts of India and Formosa (Taiwan). These possessions sealed Dutch trading predominance for decades to come.

The Dutch next set their sights on the Americas, creating the West India Company in 1621. Its claim to the Connecticut, Hudson, and Delaware valleys stemmed from the 1609 voyage of Henry Hudson, an Englishman sailing for the Dutch, who discovered the river that bears his name.

The first permanent Dutch settlers on mainland North America arrived in 1624 to set up a fur-trading post at Fort Orange (now Albany). Two years later, a company of Protestant refugees established New Amsterdam on Manhattan Island. The Hudson River corridor between these two settlements became the heart of the New Netherland colony. Like New France, its economic focus was the fur trade. Dutch merchants forged ties with the Iroquois, who brought furs to exchange for European tools and weapons.

In the 1630s, to help supply colonial traders, the West India Company offered large landed estates (called patroonships) to wealthy Dutchmen who would be responsible for populating them with tenant farmers. The plan never really worked, and at its peak, New Netherland's colonists only numbered about ten thousand.

What they lacked in numbers the colonists made up for in divisiveness. New Netherland became a magnet for religious refugees from Europe, as well as a destination for Africans acquired through the slave trade. Ethnic differences hindered a sense of community. Among the colony's Dutch, German, French, English, Swedish, Portuguese, and African settlers were Calvinists, Lutherans, Quakers, Catholics, Jews, and Muslims.

The West India Company, more interested in making money than keeping order, dispatched inept governors who provoked conflict with Indians. Although colonists maintained good relations with their Iroquois trading partners on the upper Hudson River, they had far less friendly dealings with Algonquian peoples around New Amsterdam. In one gruesome incident in 1645, Governor Willem Kieft ordered a massacre at an encampment of Indian refugees who had refused to pay tribute. A horrified Dutch witness described Indian children being "thrown into the river, and when the fathers and mothers endeavored to save them, the soldiers would not let them come on land, but made both parents and children drown." He saw victims "with their hands, some with their legs cut off, and some holding their entrails in their arms." Ten years later, Governor Peter Stuyvesant antagonized Susquehannock Indians along the Delaware River by seizing a small Swedish colony where the Susquehannocks had traded.

Such actions provoked retaliatory raids by the Indians, further weakening the colony. Though profitable, the fur trade did not generate the riches to be found in other parts of the Dutch empire. By the 1650s and 1660s, New Netherland looked like a poor investment to company officials in Europe.

NEW NETHERLAND BECOMES NEW YORK

The proprietary colonies of New York and New Jersey were carved out of the Dutch colony of New Netherland. Competition between the English and the Dutch had generated two Anglo-Dutch wars, first in 1652–1654, and again in 1665–1667. In the New World, tensions were heightened by the presence of English colonists on Long Island, which the Dutch claimed for themselves.

In 1664, Charles II brought matters to a head by claiming that since the site of New Netherland lay within the bounds of the original charter of Virginia, the land belonged to England. He granted the territory to his brother James, Duke of York, who sent ships to Long Island to back up England's claim. Their arrival provoked a rebellion by the island's English colonists, leading the Dutch governor, Peter Stuyvesant—who commanded just 150 soldiers—to surrender without firing a shot.

The Duke of York became proprietor of this new English possession, which was renamed New York. James immediately created another colony, New Jersey, when he granted some of the land to a group of his supporters.

New York, which James retained for himself, included the port of New York City (the former New Amsterdam) and the Hudson Valley with its fur trade. James, who succeeded his brother to the English throne in 1685, encouraged Dutch colonists to remain and promoted immigration from England. By 1700, the settlers numbered twenty thousand.

Conclusion

During the seventeenth century, France, the Netherlands, and England competed for land and trade in North America, with France and England gaining colonies on the mainland and all three joining Spain in the Caribbean. New France's small and scattered settlements clung to the St. Lawrence River Valley. The profits from the fur trade encouraged the French to maintain friendly relations with their Indian allies and ensured that French kings would monitor the colony's affairs and invest in its defense. English kings granted charters—sometimes to joint-stock companies (Virginia, Plymouth, Massachusetts), sometimes to proprietors (Maryland, Carolina, New York, New Jersey, Pennsylvania)—and let the colonies develop more or less on their own.

English settlers adjusted to different environments, developed different economies and labor systems, and worshiped in different churches. In South Carolina, New York, Pennsylvania, and the West Indies, most settlers were not even of English origin. What held these colonies together was an overlay of common English institutions of government. By the mid–1680s, all the colonies had legislatures that provided for self-government and laws and judicial institutions based on English models.

The planting of French, Dutch, and English colonies not only ended Spain's monopoly of settlement in North America but also challenged the Indians' hold on the continent. Native peoples had to deal with a rising tide of settlers and often to choose sides between European antagonists. Transplanted Europeans adapted too, not only in their dealings with native peoples but also in finding and controlling the supply of laborers they needed to make their colonies prosper. For English colonists this meant the widespread adoption of slavery. For millions of Africans, the result was forced migration to the New World.

REVIEW QUESTIONS

1. Comparing French, Dutch, and English colonies, which ones attracted the most settlers, and which the fewest? How did these differences in emigration affect the various colonies' development?

2. Which English settlements were proprietary colonies? Did they share any common characteristics? What plans did the various proprietors have for their colonies?

3. Religion played a major role as a motive for settlement in both Massachusetts and Pennsylvania. What were the religious beliefs of the settlers in each colony, and how did those beliefs help shape each colony's development?

4. The Chesapeake, the West Indies, and Carolina were all colonies dependent upon staple crops. What were those staple crops? In what ways did staple crop agriculture shape society in each region?

The Creation
of New Worlds

What factors shaped the character of the relationship between
Native Americans and Europeans?

Who were the first slaves in North America and what role did
they play in early America colonies?

What effect did the development of African-American families
and communities have on slaves and slave owners?

What factors motivated European immigrants to make the long
journey to North America during the seventeenth and eighteenth
centuries?

⭐

One day [in 1756], when all our people were gone out to their work as usual, and only I and my
sister were left to mind the house, two men and a woman got over our walls, and in a moment
seized us both; and without giving us time to cry out, or to make any resistance, they stopped our
mouths and ran off with us into the nearest wood. Here they tied our hands, and continued to
carry us as far as they could. . . . Thus I continued to travel, both by land and by water, through
different countries and various nations, till at the end of six or seven months after I had been
kidnapped, I arrived at the sea coast. . . .

The first object that saluted my eyes when I arrived on the coast was the sea, and a slave ship,
which was then riding at anchor, and waiting for its cargo. These filled me with astonishment, that
was soon converted into terror, which I am yet at a loss to describe. . . . I was immediately handled
and tossed up to see if I was sound, by some of the crew; and I was now persuaded that I had got
into a world of bad spirits, and that they were going to kill me. Their complexions too, differing so
much from ours, their long hair, and the language they spoke, which was very different from any
I had ever heard, united to confirm me in this belief. . . . I asked . . . if we were not to be eaten by
those white men with horrible looks, red faces, and long hair. . . .

In a little time after, amongst the poor chained men, I found some of my own nation. . . . They
gave me to understand we were to be carried to these white people's country to work for them. . . .
[Many weeks later] we were landed up a river a good way from the sea, about Virginia county, where
we saw few of our native Africans, and not one soul who could talk to me.

Olaudah Equiano, *The Interesting Narrative of the Life of Olaudah Equiano,* or Gustavus Vassa, the African.

OLAUDAH EQUIANO, born in 1745 in the African kingdom of Benin, was only a boy
when his terrifying journey to America began. The son of an Igbo chief, he was caught in
the web of the expanding transatlantic slave trade. Slavery had spread from England's
Caribbean colonies to dominate the Chesapeake settlements as well.

The freed slave Olaudah Equiano appears in this 1780 portrait by an unknown artist. After purchasing his freedom, Equiano wrote a vivid account of his capture in Africa and his life in slavery. One of the first such accounts to be published (in 1789), this narrative testified to slavery's injustice and Equiano's own fortitude.

"Portrait of a Negro Man, Olaudah Equiano," 1780s (previously attributed to Joshua Reynolds) by English School (18th c.). Royal Albert Memorial Museum, Exeter, Devon, UK. Bridgeman Art Library, London/New York.

At the same time, North American Indian peoples, faced with a flood of immigrants from Europe and Africa, employed adaptation, co-existence, diplomacy, and resistance to assert their claims to land and their right to participate in the events and deliberations that affected their lives as much as those of colonists. The America to which Olaudah Equiano had been forcibly transported remained a place where Indian voices had to be heeded.

Equiano's journey did not end in Virginia. Over the next quarter-century, he visited nearly every part of England's empire and beyond. He worked as the servant of a naval officer, a barber, a laborer, and an overseer until he could purchase his own freedom. His extraordinary career bore witness to the emergence of an international market for laborers, which—like slavery and Indian relations—shaped the development of North America. Thousands of people from England, Scotland, Ireland, and Germany sought their fortunes in America. The interactions of Indians, Africans, and Europeans created not one but many New Worlds.

Indians and Europeans

Although, by 1750, European colonists and African slaves together outnumbered Indians north of the Rio Grande, Native Americans continued to dominate much of the continent. The colonists remained clustered along the coasts and had yet to make significant movement into the interior. Some native peoples had scarcely seen any colonists. Indians living along the northern Pacific coast, for instance, met their first white men—Russian fur traders—only in the 1740s. By this time, the Pueblos of the Southwest, the Hurons of Canada, and the Algonquians of the Atlantic seaboard had more than a century's experience with European colonists.

The character of the relationship between Indians and Europeans depended on more than relative population size and the length of time they had been in contact. It was also shaped by

• C H R O N O L O G Y •

1440s Portuguese enter slave trade in West Africa.

c. 1450 Iroquois form Great League of Peace and Power.

1610–1614 First war between English settlers and Powhatan Indians.

1619 First Africans arrive in Virginia.

1622–1632 Second war between English settlers and Powhatan Indians.

1637 Pequot War in New England.

1640s Slave labor begins to dominate in the West Indies. First phase of the Beaver Wars.

1651 First "praying town" established at Natick, Massachusetts.

1661 Maryland law defines slavery as lifelong, inheritable status.

1670 Virginia law defines status of slaves.

1675–1676 King Philip's War in New England.

1676 Bacon's Rebellion in Virginia.

1680 Pueblo Revolt in New Mexico.

1680s Second phase of Beaver Wars begins.

1690s Shift from white indentured servants to black slaves as principal labor force in the Chesapeake.

1701 Iroquois adopt policy of neutrality toward French and English.

1711–1713 Tuscarora War in Carolina.

1713 Beginnings of substantial Scottish, Scots-Irish, and German immigration to colonies.

1715–1716 Yamasee War in Carolina.

1720s Black population begins to increase naturally in English mainland colonies.

1732 Georgia established.

1739 Stono Rebellion in South Carolina.

1741 Slave conspiracy discovered in New York City.

1750 Slavery legalized in Georgia.

1760–1775 Peak of European and African immigration to English colonies.

---

the intentions of the newcomers—whether they came to extract resources, to trade, to settle, or to gain converts—and the responses of particular Native American groups intent on preserving their cultures. The result was a variety of regionally distinctive New World communities.

INDIAN WORKERS IN THE SPANISH BORDERLANDS

More than any other European colonists, the Spanish sought direct control over Indians. Their ability to marshal Indian workers for Spanish gain depended on the existence of sizable Indian communities and Spanish military force. In North America outside of Mexico itself, these conditions could be found in New Mexico and parts of Florida.

One of the Spaniards' most important methods of labor control was the *encomienda*. *Encomiendas*, granted to influential Spaniards in New Mexico, gave these colonists the right to collect tribute from the native peoples living on a specific piece of land. It was not supposed to include forced labor, but often it did.

The *repartimiento* was another Spanish technique for exploiting Native American labor. This was a mandatory draft of Indian labor for public projects, such as building forts, bridges, and roads. Laws stated that native workers should be paid and limited the length of their service, but the Spanish sometimes compelled Indians to work on private estates. Spaniards also acquired laborers by ransoming captives that Indian groups seized from one another. This practice, called *rescate*, obliged rescued Indians to work for those who had paid their ransom.

Together these Spanish strategies for controlling Indian labor aroused considerable resentment on the part of native peoples. Spanish demands for labor and tribute remained constant, even when Indian populations declined from disease or crops failed in bad weather. Workers who resisted were punished. Resentments simmered until late in the seventeenth century, when native anger burst forth in rebellion.

The Web of Trade

Europeans eager to trade with Indians had to prove their friendship by offering gifts and military aid as well as trading goods. French traders in Canada brought gifts and prepared feasts for their native partners, obliging the Indians to offer the furs that the French wanted. One seventeenth-century observer described the French governor giving the Hurons barrels of hatchets and arrowheads, in part "to waft their canoes gently homewards, [in] part to draw them to us next year." The Indians also got iron tools, kettles, cloth, beads, and—eventually—guns.

Trading with Europeans would gradually destroy the Indians' way of life. Contact with traders exposed Indians to deadly European diseases. The Huron population declined by half in just six years between 1634 and 1640. Indians trading with the Dutch in New Netherlands in the 1650s insisted "their population had been melted down" by smallpox.

Trade also undermined self-sufficiency. Before the French arrived, for instance, the Micmacs in easternmost Canada supported themselves mainly by fishing. After becoming partners of the French around 1610, they trapped beaver year 'round, relying on the French and New England Indians for food. After they had trapped virtually all the beavers on their lands, they were abandoned by the French, who turned instead to the Hurons. The once prosperous Micmacs barely survived.

Other groups would suffer a similar fate. "The Cloaths we wear, we cannot make ourselves," a Carolina Cherokee used to woolen garments observed in 1753. "We cannot make our Guns. . . . Every necessary Thing in Life we must have from the white People."

Before European contact, most Indian bands living north of the Rio Grande made war to seek revenge for violent acts committed against their own people. But after the Europeans arrived, Indians began to fight each other for economic advantage, and the hostilities became far more deadly. Rivalries among French, English, and Dutch traders led to conflicts among their Indian partners. The **Beaver Wars**, a long struggle between the Hurons and the Iroquois, began in the 1640s.

Because the French already traded with the Hurons, Dutch merchants in the Hudson River Valley seeking to break into the fur trade turned to the *Iroquois League*. Composed of five separate Indian nations—the Mohawks, Oneidas, Onondagas, Cayugas, and Senecas—it functioned as a religious organization to preserve peace among the five nations and strengthen them in their conflicts with other Indian peoples. The Iroquois agreed to supply the Dutch with furs in return for trade goods.

By the 1630s, the Hurons and Iroquois had killed nearly all the beavers on their own lands and began to look elsewhere for furs. The Hurons traded corn for furs with Indians living north of the Great Lakes. The Iroquois began to raid Huron trading parties and then to attack Huron villages.

The Iroquois triumphed in the resulting conflict largely because the Dutch readily supplied them with guns while the French did not arm the Hurons. In the end, the Hurons were destroyed. A French traveler reported seeing no Hurons in "districts which, not ten years ago, I reckoned to contain eight or ten thousand men."

The cycle of warfare did not end with the destruction of the Hurons. The Iroquois went on to challenge Indian nations near the Great Lakes and in the Ohio Valley. Seeking iron kettles more durable than earthenware pots, cloth that was lighter and more colorful than animal skins, and guns that were deadlier than bows and arrows, Indians changed their lives in ways that suited their own needs as much as those of European traders.

DISPLACING NATIVE AMERICANS IN THE ENGLISH COLONIES

Trading colonies relied on Indian partners to supply them with furs and so maintained friendly relations with them out of self-interest. The European population of the trading colonies also stayed fairly low. Even after the devastation of disease, Indians outnumbered Europeans in New France and New Netherlands. As late as 1650, there were just 657 French people in Canada (compared to perhaps ten thousand Hurons) and only three thousand Europeans in New Netherlands. The English, in contrast, came mainly to settle. By 1650 there were more than fifty thousand Europeans and two thousand Africans in England's North American colonies.

The influx of settlers into the English colonies, as always, exposed native peoples to European diseases. So swift was the decline in native populations—and so rapid the influx of Europeans—that in coastal Massachusetts and eastern Virginia, colonists outnumbered Indians by 1650.

Largely because of the colonists' desire for land, violence between Europeans and Indians occurred with greater regularity in the English colonies than in New France or New Netherlands. Colonists thrilled at the sight of what they saw as vast unoccupied territory. One New England settler declared that the natives "do but run over the grass, as do also the foxes and wild beasts" and that therefore the "spacious and void" land was free for the taking.

The settlers misunderstood how Indians used their territory. Eastern Algonquian peoples cleared areas for villages and planting fields, which native women farmed until the soil grew less fertile. Then they moved to a new location, allowing the former village site to return to forest. In ten to twenty years, they or their descendants might return to that site to clear and farm it again. Indians often built villages near the seacoast or rivers so they could fish and use reeds and grasses for weaving. In the winter, village communities broke up into small bands to hunt in the forest for deer and other animals.

Thus what the colonists considered "vacant" lands were either being used for non-farming activities or recovering from human occupation in order to be farmed in years to come. Settlers who built towns on abandoned native village sites deprived the Indians of these future planting fields. Competition from the rapidly increasing settlers threatened Indian survival.

Disputes between Europeans and Indians frequently arose from misunderstandings about land ownership and property rights. Indian villages claimed collective sovereignty over a certain territory to be used for farming, fishing, hunting, and gathering. For Europeans, ownership conferred on an individual the exclusive right to use or sell a piece of land.

When Indians transferred land to settlers, the settlers assumed that they had obtained complete rights to the land, whereas the Indians assumed that they had given the settlers not the land itself but only the right to use it, and that no Indian inhabitants would have to leave. It was the English understanding that ultimately prevailed, enforced in the settlers' courts under the settlers' laws.

Settlers' agricultural practices also strained relations with the Indians. Cutting down forests destroyed Indian hunting lands. When colonists dammed rivers, they disrupted Indian fishing. When they surrounded fields with log fences and stone walls, they made trespassers of natives who crossed them. Yet the colonists felt free to let their cattle and pigs loose to graze in the woods and meadows, where they could wander into unfenced Indian cornfields and damage the crops.

The settlers gradually displaced Indian inhabitants, acquiring their lands in various ways. Some colonial leaders, such as Roger Williams in Rhode Island and William Penn of Pennsylvania, insisted on buying it. But sometimes settlers bought collectively owned land from individual Indians who had no right to sell it. Indians frequently misunderstood the terms of sale recorded in English. Even Indian groups who had willingly sold land grew resentful as colonists approached them for more. Finally, native peoples could be forced to sell land to settle debts they had run up with English creditors.

Increasingly, colonists simply settled on Indian lands without permission and appealed to colonial governments for help when the Indians objected. Land speculators amplified this kind of unrest as they sought to acquire land as cheaply as possible and sell it for as much as they could.

Finally, the settlers often seized Indian lands in the aftermath of war, as befell, among others, the Pequots in Connecticut in 1637, and in Carolina the Tuscaroras in 1713 and the Yamasees in 1715. Sometimes colonial leaders contrived for some Indian groups to help them displace others. During the Pequot War, Narragansetts had aided Connecticut settlers' efforts to oust the Pequots. Carolina colonists enlisted the help of the Yamasees against the Tuscaroras and then turned to the Cherokees to help them against the Yamasees.

The English viewed the Indians, as they had the Irish, as savages with whom it would be better not to mix. Colonists built communities on lands bought or taken from natives and then discouraged them from living there. In New France and New Spain, Europeans and Indians mingled more freely and even intermarried, but in the English colonies, separation prevailed.

BRINGING CHRISTIANITY TO NATIVE PEOPLES

In early colonial North America, the three major New World empires—those of Spain, France, and England—competed for Indians' souls as well as their lands and riches.

Catholic missionaries—mainly Franciscan priests—were the driving force behind Spain's efforts to assert control over its colonies of New Mexico and Florida. Spain's bases in Florida helped protect Spanish ships bearing treasure from the mines of Mexico and Peru and discouraged the southward spread of English settlement. New Mexico similarly served as a buffer between the silver mines of northern Mexico and roaming Plains Indians. Neither colony attracted many settlers, however, because neither offered much opportunity for wealth. When Franciscan missionaries proposed to move into New Mexico and Florida in order to convert their inhabitants to Christianity, Spanish officials agreed and even provided financial support.

The priests wore their finest vestments and displayed religious paintings and statues, trying to impress the Indians with European goods and Catholic ceremonies. They gave away bells, knives, cloth, and food. According to one Franciscan in New Mexico, these gifts brought Indians to the missions "like fish to the fish hook." The natives believed that accepting these gifts obliged them to listen to the priests' Christian message and help them build houses and churches.

After brief religious instruction, the missionaries convinced many Indians to accept baptism into the Catholic Church and with it the promise of salvation and a heavenly afterlife. Such conversions often followed epidemics that devastated native villages but spared the Spanish, leading many Indians to wonder if the Christian God might indeed be more powerful than their own gods. In New Mexico, the Spanish offered Pueblo converts protection against Apache raids and access to Franciscan storehouses in times of famine.

Many Indians did not understand that baptism committed them to abandoning native beliefs and adopting Spanish food, clothing, and work routines. Priests in New Mexico, objecting to the ease with which Pueblo marriages could be dissolved, tried to enforce lifelong unions. Punishments for violating the new code were severe and in rare cases led to their victims' deaths.

By the mid-seventeenth century, Spanish missionaries claimed to have baptized tens of thousands of Indians. But many converts blended Christianity with native religion, adding Jesus, Mary, and the Catholic saints to the list of Indian gods and accepting missionaries as counterparts to native priests. Many converts were *mestizos*—people of mixed Indian and Spanish descent—who often practiced native rituals in secret. Some groups, such as the Zuni and Hopi peoples, rejected Christianity altogether. In the end, the spread of Christianity in the Spanish borderlands was not as complete as the Franciscans claimed.

French priests in Canada also tried to convert Indians to Catholicism. Like the Franciscans, they tried to impress potential converts with religious rituals and material objects. Priests amazed Indians with clocks, magnets, and their ability to predict eclipses and to read and write. "All this serves to gain their affections, and to render them more docile when we introduce the admirable and incomprehensible mysteries of our Faith," explained one priest.

French missionaries also resorted to economic pressure, convincing merchants to sell guns only to converted Indians and to offer them other trade goods at a discount. The Jesuits were generally more tolerant than the Franciscans of native ways. "One must be careful before condemning a thousand things among their customs," warned one priest, because to do so would "greatly offend minds brought up and nourished in another world."

The Protestant English were less successful at attracting Native American converts. Puritans frowned on the rituals and religious objects that drew Indian converts to Catholicism. And with its emphasis on the direct study of scripture, Protestantism required that potential converts learn to read.

Beginning in the 1650s, Puritan ministers in New England, such as John Eliot, established several praying towns, communities where Indians lived apart from settlers to learn Protestant Christianity and English ways. By 1674 about 2,300 Indians resided in these towns. Although individual ministers were interested in missionary work, efforts at conversion in the Anglican southern colonies enjoyed little success. English settlers preferred to isolate Indians rather than convert them.

AFTER THE FIRST HUNDRED YEARS: CONFLICT AND WAR

After nearly a century of European settlement, violence between colonists and Indians erupted in all three North American empires, in **King Philip's War** in New England, **Bacon's Rebellion** in Virginia, the **Pueblo Revolt** in New Mexico, and the resumption of the Beaver Wars in New France.

King Philip's War, which broke out in 1675, was sparked by the growing frustration of the Wampanoags—the Indians who had befriended the Pilgrims more than half a century before—with the land-hungry settlers whose towns now surrounded them. Massasoit's younger son, Metacom—called King Philip by the English—led the Wampanoags and struggled to preserve their independence. He had little reason to trust the colonists. His older brother had died mysteriously while being questioned by colonial officials about rumors of an Indian conspiracy. Philip himself had been accused of plotting against the settlers and then forced to sign a treaty submitting to English authority.

In the spring of 1675, a colonial court found three Wampanoags guilty of murdering a Christian Indian who had warned the English of Wampanoag preparations for war. The court sentenced the men to be hanged. The Wampanoags decided to strike back against the English. Only "a small part of the dominion of my ancestors remains," declared Philip. "I am determined not to live until I have no country."

At least a thousand colonists and perhaps three thousand Indians died in King Philip's War. One out of every sixteen male colonists of military age was killed, making this the deadliest conflict in American history in terms of the proportion of casualties to total population. The Indians succeeded in forcing back the line of settlement but lost what remained of their independence in New England. Philip died in an ambush in August 1676, and the war ended soon afterward. The victorious English sold many native survivors, including Philip's wife and young son, into slavery in the West Indies. Philip's head, impaled on a stake, was left for decades on the outskirts of Plymouth as a grisly warning of the price to be paid for resisting colonial expansion.

A bloody conflict erupted in Virginia that had a similarly devastating effect on that colony's native population. Frustrated by shrinking economic opportunities in eastern Virginia, many settlers moved to Virginia's western frontier. In the summer of 1675, a group of frontier settlers attacked the Susquehannocks in order to seize their lands. The Indians struck back, prompting Nathaniel Bacon, a young, wealthy planter who had only recently arrived in Virginia, to lead the settlers in a violent campaign against all Indians, even those at peace with the colonial government. Governor William Berkeley ordered Bacon and his men to stop their attacks. They defied him and marched on Jamestown, turning a war between settlers and Indians into a rebellion of settlers against the colonial authorities.

The rebels believed that Berkeley and the colonial government represented the interests of established tobacco planters. Desperate because of the low price of tobacco, the rebels demanded lower taxes and easier access to land. They also wanted help exterminating the Indians. Rebels captured and burned the colonial capital at Jamestown, forcing Berkeley to flee. They burned Indian villages and massacred the inhabitants. Trying to appease the rebels, the House of Burgesses passed measures allowing them to seize native lands and legalizing the enslavement of Indians.

By the time troops arrived from England to put down the rebellion, Bacon had died of a fever and most of his men had drifted home. Berkeley hanged twenty-three rebels, but the real victims of the rebellion were Virginia's Indians. The remnants of the once-powerful Powhatans lost their remaining lands and either moved west or lived in poverty on the edges of English settlement. Hatred of Indians became a permanent feature of frontier life in Virginia.

In 1680 the Pueblo Revolt erupted against Spain's colony of New Mexico. Nearly twenty thousand Pueblo Indians in New Mexico had grown restless under the harsh rule of only 2,500 Spaniards. During a prolonged drought that began in the 1660s, many people starved. The Apaches, who had once traded with the Pueblos for corn, now raided their storehouses instead, and Spanish soldiers could not stop them.

The spark that ignited the revolt, however, was an act of religious persecution. Spanish officials unwisely chose this troubled time to stamp out Pueblo religion. In 1675, the governor arrested forty-seven native religious leaders on charges of sorcery. The court ordered most of them to be publicly whipped and released but sentenced four of them to death.

Spanish soldiers marched into Pueblo villages and destroyed kivas, the underground chambers that Indians used for religious ceremonies. Led by Popé, one of the freed leaders, the outraged Pueblos organized a network of rebels. By the summer of 1680, Popé commanded an enormous force drawn from twenty Pueblo villages. On August 10, the rebels attacked the Spanish settlements. Popé urged them to "break up and burn the images of the holy Christ, the Virgin Mary and the other saints, the crosses, and everything pertaining to Christianity." Within a few weeks, the rebels had destroyed or damaged every Spanish building and killed more than four hundred Spaniards, including twenty-one of the colony's thirty-three missionaries. By October, all Spaniards had fled New Mexico.

They did not return for thirteen years. By then, internal rivalries had split the victorious Pueblo coalition. Even so, the Spanish understood the folly of pushing the Indians too far. Officials reduced demands for tribute, and the Franciscans eased their attacks on Pueblo religion.

In the last phase of the Beaver Wars, what began as a struggle between the Iroquois and western native peoples for control of the fur trade blossomed into a larger conflict as it was absorbed into the imperial rivalry between England and France.

Looking for new trading partners, the French turned in the 1680s to the Ottawas, Wyandots, and other Indian peoples living near the Great Lakes. But the Iroquois had begun to raid these same peoples for furs and captives, much as they had attacked the Hurons in the first phase of the Beaver Wars in the 1640s. They exchanged the furs with their English allies. The Iroquois objected to French traders' attempt to "have all the Bevers" for themselves.

The French attacked the Iroquois to prevent them and their English allies from extending their influence in the west. In June 1687, a combined force of French and Christian Indian soldiers invaded the lands of the Senecas, the westernmost of the five nations of the Iroquois League. The Iroquois retaliated by besieging a French garrison at Niagara, where nearly two hundred soldiers starved to death, and killing hundreds of colonists in attacks on French villages along the St. Lawrence River.

In 1689, France and England went to war in Europe, and the struggle between them and their Indian allies for control of the fur trade in North America became part of a larger imperial contest between the two countries. The European powers made peace in 1697, but calm did not immediately return to the Great Lakes region.

The conflict was devastating for the Iroquois. Perhaps a quarter of their population died from disease and warfare by 1689. The devastation encouraged Iroquois diplomats to find a way to extricate themselves from future English-French conflicts. In 1701, a pair of treaties, negotiated separately with Albany and Montreal, recognized Iroquois neutrality and, at least for a few decades, prevented either the English or the French from dominating the western lands.

English settlers fought with Wampanoags, Powhatans, and Susquehannocks for control of land, and the losers were the outnumbered Indians. In 1680 a Pueblo revolt drove the Spanish from New Mexico for thirteen years. The Spanish were only able to reestablish control by abolishing the *encomienda system* and relaxing their strictures against Pueblo religious practices. French soldiers battled with the Iroquois over control of the fur trade until both sides agreed to an uneasy truce. In each case, nearly a century of contact culminated in a struggle that revealed how difficult, if not impossible, it was to reconcile European and native interests.

Africans and Europeans

Many more Africans than Europeans came to the New World during the colonial period. Virtually all of them arrived as slaves; thus the history of African experience in America is inseparable from the history of slavery and the slave trade.

LABOR NEEDS AND THE TURN TO SLAVERY

Europeans in the New World thrilled to find that land was abundant and quite cheap by European standards. They were perplexed, however, by the unexpectedly high cost of labor. In Europe, the reverse had been true. There land was expensive but labor cheap because competition for jobs among large numbers of workers pushed wages down.

Colonial workers commanded high wages because there were so few of them compared to the supply of land waiting to be developed. Moreover, few settlers wanted to work for others when they could get farms of their own. The scarcity and high cost of labor led some colonial employers to turn to enslaved Africans as a solution.

Europeans had owned slaves (both white and black) long before the beginning of American colonization. But by 1500 slavery had all but disappeared in northern Europe. It persisted longer in southern Europe and the Middle East. Because neither Christians nor Muslims would hold as slaves members of their own faiths, Arab traders turned to sub-Saharan Africa to find slaves who did not belong to either religion. Eventually the Arabic word for slave—*abd*—became a synonym for "black man." By the fifteenth century, a durable link between slave status and black skin had been forged in European minds.

When Spanish and Portuguese adventurers needed workers to develop newly colonized Atlantic islands and New World lands, they turned to slavery. Masters exercised complete control over slaves and paid them no wages. English colonists later adopted slavery in America even though it was unknown as a system of labor at home.

It was Indians, however, not Africans, whom the Europeans first forced into slavery in the Americas. Spaniards held native slaves in all their New World colonies and English colonists condemned Indian enemies captured in wartime to slavery. In early Carolina, English traders encouraged Indians "to make War amongst themselves to get Slaves" whom the traders could buy and then resell to West Indian and local planters.

Native American slaves, however, could not fill the settlers' labor needs. Disease and harsh working conditions reduced their numbers. Enslaved Indian men refused to perform agricultural labor, which they considered women's work. Because they knew the land better than the colonists, Indians could easily escape and make their way back to their own people. By 1700 the Indian slave trade had given way to a much larger traffic in Africans.

The Spanish and Portuguese first brought Africans to the Americas to supplement the dwindling numbers of Indian slaves toiling in silver mines and on sugar plantations. English colonists adopted slavery more slowly. West Indian planters were the first to do so on a large scale in the 1640s, following the Portuguese example in using black slaves to grow sugar.

Black slaves first arrived in Virginia in 1619 when a Dutch trader sold "20. and odd Negroes" in Jamestown, but they did not form a significant portion of the colony's population until the end of the century. For decades, tobacco planters saw no reason to switch from white indentured servants to slaves. Servants were cheap, available, and familiar; slaves were expensive, difficult to obtain, and exotic.

Beginning in the 1680s, planters in the Chesapeake colonies of Virginia and Maryland began to shift from servants to slaves. White indentured servants became harder to find.

Fewer young English men and women chose to emigrate as servants after 1660 because an improving economy in England provided jobs for them at home. And Virginia's white population tripled between 1650 and 1700, rapidly increasing the competition for a shrinking supply of laborers. Chesapeake planters also faced competition from newer colonies.

As white servants grew scarcer, African slaves became more available, largely due to changes in the slave trade. After 1698, England's Royal African Company lost its monopoly rights and many English merchants—and New Englanders—entered the fiercely competitive trade.

Chesapeake planters eventually came to prefer slaves to servants. Although more expensive than servants, slaves were a better long-term investment. Buying both men and women gave planters a self-reproducing labor force. Runaway black slaves were more easily recaptured than escaped servants, who blended into the white population. And unlike indentured servants, slaves were slaves for life and would not someday compete as planters with their former masters.

Chesapeake planters' view of white servants as possessions, whose labor could be bought and sold like any other commodity, eased the gradual transition in the 1680s and 1690s to the much harsher system of slavery. In Carolina, slaves had arrived right from the start, brought in the 1670s by colony founders accustomed to slavery in Barbados. By 1720, one-third of Virginia's settlers—and nearly three-quarters of South Carolina's—were black people.

Slavery grew rapidly in the South because it answered the labor needs of planters engaged in the commercial production of tobacco and rice. When James Oglethorpe founded Georgia in 1732, however, he intended to keep slavery out. Oglethorpe's idea was to send English debtors to Georgia to produce exotic goods like silk and wine. But when only rice turned a profit in Georgia, its founders reluctantly legalized slavery. By 1770, slaves made up nearly half of the colony's settlers.

In the northern colonies, slaves were too expensive for farmers who mainly produced food for their families, not export crops. The relatively few northern slaves generally worked as domestic servants, craftsmen, and day laborers.

Race relations in the mainland colonies were less rigid in the seventeenth century than they would later become. In the few Chesapeake households that had slaves, white and black people lived and worked in close contact. Black slaves and white servants cooperated during Bacon's Rebellion. In some areas, free black people—often slaves who had bought their own freedom—prospered in an atmosphere of racial tolerance that would be unthinkable by the eighteenth century.

The career of an ambitious black Virginian named Anthony Johnson, for example, resembled that of many white settlers—a remarkable achievement given that he arrived in the colony as a slave in 1621. Once free, Johnson married and raised a family. By 1651, he owned a large plantation, and later he even bought a slave. Johnson belonged to the first or what one historian has called the "charter" generation of American slaves. These people mainly came from African port towns or via the West Indies or New Netherlands. Familiar with European ways and languages, they bargained with their masters in ways their descendants would not be able to replicate, and they often gained their freedom.

But Johnson's descendants, and the generations of slaves who came afterward, encountered harsher conditions. After 1700, slavery became the dominant labor system in the Chesapeake. Tobacco planters feared that free black people might encourage slaves to escape. In 1699, Virginia's assembly passed a law requiring newly freed black people to leave the colony.

The condition of black people swiftly deteriorated. Laws defined slavery as lifelong and hereditary according to the condition of the mother and identified slave status with black skin. Other measures deprived black persons, slave or free, of basic civil rights. They could not testify in court against white people, hold property, congregate in public places, or travel without permission. Interracial marriages, never common, were now prohibited as "shameful Matches."

Colonists resorted to these slave codes—which reduced human beings to the status of property—largely because of fears generated by a rising black population. In 1720, a South Carolina planter predicted that slaves would soon rise up against their masters because black people were "too numerous in proportion to the White Men there." The changing composition of the slave labor force also created tensions.

Unlike the charter generation, slaves who came later usually came from the African interior. Planters commented on the strange appearance and behavior of these slaves, but the colonists' uneasiness scarcely compared to the Africans' harrowing experience.

THE SHOCK OF ENSLAVEMENT

European traders relied on other Africans to capture slaves for them, tapping into a preexisting African slave trade and helping to expand it. Europeans built forts and trading posts on the West African coast and bought slaves from African traders (see Map 3–1). Attracted by European cloth, iron, liquor, guns, and other goods, West Africans fought increasingly among themselves to secure captives and began kidnapping individuals from the interior.

People of all social ranks ended up on the slave ships. Some had been slaves in Africa; others had been village leaders. Even members of African royal families ended up in shackles as slavery reduced all Africans, regardless of their social origins, to the same degraded status.

Once captured, slaves marched in chains to the coast, to be confined in cages called "barracoons" until there were enough to fill a ship. Captains examined them to ensure their fitness and branded them like cattle with a hot iron. The slaves then boarded canoes to be ferried to the ships.

Slaves suffered through a horrendous six- to eight-week-long ocean voyage known as the **Middle Passage**. Captains wedged men below decks into spaces about 6 feet long, 16 inches wide, and 30 inches high. Women and children were packed even tighter. They occasionally came up on deck for fresh air, but spent most of the time below decks, where the air grew foul from the vomit, blood, and excrement in which the terrified victims lay. Sailors sometimes heard a "howling melancholy noise" coming from below. Some slaves tried to commit suicide by jumping overboard or starving themselves. Between 5 and 20 percent of the slaves perished from disease, but captains had usually packed the ships tightly enough to make a profit selling the rest.

Survivors of the dreadful voyage endured the fear and humiliation of sale. Sometimes buyers rushed aboard ship in a scramble to choose slaves. Ship captains also sold slaves at public auctions, where eager purchasers poked them, looking for signs of disease. The terrified Africans often thought they were about to be eaten.

AFRICAN-AMERICAN FAMILIES AND COMMUNITIES

Most Africans brought to the New World went to New Spain, Brazil, or the West Indies. Black communities developed slowly in English America. In the northern colonies, most slaves lived alone or in pairs with their master's family. Only in the cities, where slaves were more numerous, could they have regular contact with other black people. In the South, until the eighteenth

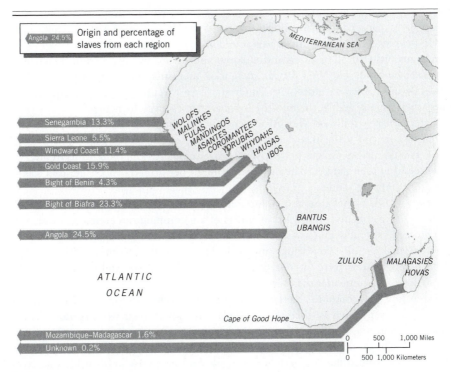

MAP 3–1
African Origins of North American Slaves, 1690–1807   Nearly all slaves in English North America were West Africans. Most had been captured or purchased by African slave traders, who then sold them to European merchants.

WHY MIGHT the Bight of Biafra and Angola together have made up nearly 50 percent of all slave trading out of West Africa?

Source: After Philip Curtin, *The Atlantic Slave Trade: A Census* (1969), tab. 45, p. 157.

century, slaves were dispersed among a much larger white population. Slave numbers grew after 1700, but much of the increase consisted of African immigrants. These people retained African ethnic identities, which delayed their developing a sense of community.

By about 1750, more slaves in the southern colonies were *creoles* (American-born) than African natives. Creoles lived longer than African immigrants, and creole women usually bore twice as many children as African-born mothers. The mainland slave population began to grow by natural increase.

Creole slaves grew up without personal memories of Africa, so African ethnic differences seemed less important to them. Most creoles knew some English and spoke dialects they had created by mixing English and African words and speech patterns. The ability to communicate helped them develop a new identity as African Americans that mingled aspects of their African heritage and a common experience of slavery.

Kinship ties, crucial to West Africans' sense of identity, remained important to American slaves. But slave families were fragile units, subject to the whims of masters who could break up families by sale at any time, and who could take slave women as sexual partners at will. Even so, slaves managed to form families that preserved and modified African traditions.

Households headed by mothers reappeared in America. Slave fathers often belonged to different masters than their wives and children and had to live apart from their families. Some slave husbands, like West African men, took more than one wife (a practice masters allowed because it led to more slave children). Slave parents gave their children African names, often secretly adding them to the "official" names given by masters.

Carolina slaves followed West African practice by building their houses of "tabby," a mixture of lime and seashells, and constructing houses on a circular plan. Potters and basketmakers used African designs in their work. Slaves raised African food plants (millet, yams, sesame seeds) in their gardens. They also made music, performed dances, and told folk tales derived from African models.

Traces of African religion also endured in America. Faith in magic and fortune tellers and the belief that relatives remained members of kin communities even after death, which made funerals extremely important, reflected slaves' West African background. During most of the colonial period Christianity offered little competition to these African religious practices. Few masters were interested in converting their slaves, and most slaves did not adopt Christianity until after the Revolution.

Labor, however, consumed most of a slave's waking hours. On tobacco plantations, slaves toiled in gangs supervised by overseers. Rice planters allowed their workers more flexibility, permitting them free time after they finished assigned tasks. On large plantations, masters selected slaves to be trained as shoemakers, weavers, or tailors. Only a few slave women— nurses, cooks—avoided the drudgery of field work. And after a day in the fields, slave women had to take care of their families, doing the cooking, child care, washing, and housework.

The growth of slave family and community ties made it much more difficult for slaves to risk escape or contemplate rebellion. The master could use his power to break up families as a tool to ensure compliant behavior. In effect, every slave child was his hostage.

Community life offered further opportunities to preserve elements of African heritage. Traces of African religious practices endured in America. Magical charms and amulets have been found buried in slave quarters, indicating that certain spiritual ceremonies may have been conducted out of sight of white masters. Slave conjurors told fortunes, concocted herbal potions, and placed curses on their clients' enemies. Reflecting their West African background, slaves placed great emphasis on funerals, in the belief that relatives remained members of kin communities even after death. Funerals were sometimes divided into two distinct ceremonies. First, the deceased received a somber burial, often with beads or other ceremonial objects placed in the grave; some weeks later, slaves played music and danced at livelier funeral rites.

Christianity offered little competition to African religious practices during most of the colonial period. Few masters showed much interest in converting their slaves. Evangelical ministers, who began to preach to slave audiences around the middle of the eighteenth century, did gain some converts, but the widespread adoption of Christianity by slaves did not occur until after the Revolution.

African influences shaped aspects of slaves' recreational activity and material life. Slave musicians used African-style instruments, including drums and banjos, to accompany traditional songs and dances. In parts of South Carolina, slaves enjoyed *papaw*, an African game with dice. Storytellers entertained audiences with folk tales that may have had African roots. Where slaves were allowed to build their own houses, they often incorporated African elements into the designs, for instance, by using mud walls and roofs thatched with palmetto leaves. Their gardens frequently contained African foods such as millet, yams, peppers, and sesame seeds along with European and Native American crops.

Family and community ties gave a sense of belonging and dignity to people whose masters treated them as outcasts. Working and living together, slaves preserved at least some elements of African culture despite the harrowing conditions of their forced migration. Out of their African past and their American experience, they created new identities as African Americans as they coped with the oppressiveness of slavery.

RESISTANCE AND REBELLION

Slaves on ships anchored off the Guinea Coast waiting to leave for America sometimes mutinied but rarely succeeded. The powerful desire for freedom and the spirit of resistance remained strong among Africans and their descendants in America.

Thousands of slaves ran away from masters. Deciding where to go posed a problem as slavery was legal in every colony. Some runaways went to Florida, where Spanish officials promised them freedom. Others tried to survive on their own in the woods or join the Indians. But South Carolina planters paid Indians to catch escaped slaves, causing distrust between the two peoples. Running away also carried the high emotional cost of separation from loved ones as well as physical danger. Many slaves chose other ways to resist their bondage.

Landon Carter of Virginia, who complained that his slaves "seem to be quite dead hearted and either cannot or will not work," was the target of another form of resistance. Slaves worked slowly, broke tools, and pretended to be ill in order to conserve strength and exert some control over their working lives. When provoked, they also took more direct action, damaging crops, stealing goods, and setting fire to their masters' barns, houses, and fields. Some occasionally tried to poison whites.

South Carolinians and coastal Virginians, who lived in regions where black people outnumbered white people, had a particular dread of slave revolt. No slave rebellion succeeded in the British colonies, however. In Charleston, South Carolina, rumors of a planned uprising in 1740 led to the torture and execution of fifty black suspects. The following year, thirty-five accused rebels (including four white people) were executed in New York City.

Two slave revolts did occur in the colonial period and instilled lasting fear in white colonists. In 1712 in New York City, about twenty slaves set a building on fire and killed nine white men who came to put it out. The revolt was quickly suppressed. The court sentenced twenty-four alleged rebels to death: Thirteen were hanged, three burned at the stake, one starved to death, and one was broken on the wheel. Six committed suicide before execution.

The *Stono Rebellion*, colonial America's largest slave uprising, occurred in South Carolina in 1739. About twenty slaves—including several recently arrived Angolans—broke into a store and armed themselves with stolen guns. As the rebels marched southward along the Stono River, their ranks grew to perhaps a hundred. Heading for freedom in Spanish Florida, they attacked white settlements along the way. White troops (with Indian help) defeated the rebels within a week, but tensions remained high for months. The death toll, in the end, was about two dozen white people and perhaps twice as many black rebels.

In the wake of the Stono Rebellion, South Carolina's assembly passed a law requiring stricter supervision of slave activities. Other measures encouraged more white immigration to offset the colony's black majority. But the colony continued to consider slavery indispensable to economic survival and would not end it.

European Laborers in North America

Slavery was one of several responses to the scarcity of labor in the New World. It took hold mainly in areas where the profits from growing export crops such as sugar, rice, and tobacco offset the high purchase price of slaves and where a warm climate permitted year-round work. Elsewhere, Europeans found other means to acquire and manage laborers.

A SPECTRUM OF CONTROL

Most colonial laborers were, in some measure, unfree. One-half to two-thirds of all white emigrants to the English colonies arrived as indentured servants. Servants were most common in the Chesapeake, and to a lesser extent in Pennsylvania, where they produced export crops valuable enough to enable their masters, to feed, clothe, and shelter them—and still make a profit.

Slaves gradually replaced white indentured servants in Chesapeake tobacco fields. By the middle of the eighteenth century, white servitude was in decline as a dominant labor system throughout the colonies.

Eighteenth-century Chesapeake planters availed themselves of another unfree labor source: transported English convicts, serious criminals who might otherwise have been executed. Between 1718 and 1775, nearly fifty thousand convicts were sent to the colonies, 80 percent of whom ended up in the Chesapeake. Labor-hungry planters eagerly bought them for seven-year terms at relatively low prices and exploited them ruthlessly.

The *redemptioner* system brought many German families to the colonies in the eighteenth century. Instead of negotiating contracts for service before leaving Europe, as indentured servants did, redemptioners promised to redeem, or pay, the costs of passage on arrival in America. They often paid part of the fare themselves before sailing. If they could not raise the rest soon after landing, the ship captain who brought them sold them into servitude. The length of their service depended on how much they still owed. Most Germans went to Pennsylvania, where they hoped to find friends or relatives willing to help them pay off their debt quickly.

Purchasing slaves, servants, or convicts did not make sense for everyone. Colonists who owned undeveloped land faced many tasks—cutting trees, clearing fields, building fences and barns—that brought no immediate profit. These landowners, many of whom lived in Pennsylvania, New Jersey, and New York, rented undeveloped tracts to propertyless families. Both tenants and landlords benefited from this arrangement. Tenants enjoyed greater independence than servants and could save toward the purchase of their own farms. The landlord secured the labor necessary to transform his property into a working farm, which increased the land's value. He also received an annual rent payment, usually a portion of the tenant's crop, and eventually profited from selling the land—often to the tenant family that had rented it.

Merchants eager to develop New England's fisheries devised other means to fill their labor needs. Because it was fairly easy to get a farm, few New Englanders cared to take on the difficult and risky job of fishing. Moreover, few could afford the necessary equipment. New England fish merchants advanced credit to coastal villagers so they could outfit their own boats and become fishermen. To pay off the debt, the fishermen were legally bound to bring their catch to the merchant, who then sold it to Europe and the West Indies.

In the northern colonies, the cost of servants or slaves exceeded whatever small profit could be made on farms that produced no export crops and could not be worked during cold winter months. So northern farmers turned to the cheapest and most dependable workers they could find—their children.

Children as young as 5 or 6 years old began with simple tasks and moved on to more complex work as they grew older. By the time they were in their late teens, girls knew how to run households and boys knew how to farm. Fathers used their ownership of property to prolong the time their sons worked for them. Young men in New England could not marry until they could support a wife and family. Often sons did not actually own any land until their fathers died and left it to them in their wills.

Thus New England's labor shortage produced strong ties of dependency between generations. Fathers kept their sons working for them as long as possible; sons accepted this arrangement as a way to become independent farmers, eventually employing their own children in the same way.

Property owners in all the English colonies found different ways to control laborers. But where property owners saw problems—high wages (often twice what workers in England received) and abundant land (which deterred colonists from working for others when they could have their own farms)—others saw opportunities. For tens of thousands of Europeans, the chance to own or rent a farm or to find steady employment made North America an irresistible magnet, promising a prosperity that was beyond their reach at home.

NEW EUROPEAN IMMIGRANTS

European immigrants flooded into America in the seventeenth and eighteenth centuries. By 1773, the tremendous outflow of Britons—Protestant Scots-Irish, Scots, and Irish Catholics—to America sparked debate in England over whether emigration should be prohibited lest the British Isles be left empty. Continental Europe contributed another stream of emigrants, mostly from the German states. Perhaps 100,000 Protestants left the Rhine Valley, fleeing war, economic hardship, and religious persecution. French Protestants (known as Huguenots) began emigrating after 1685, when their faith was made illegal in France. Swiss Protestants likewise fled religious persecution. Even a few Poles, Greeks, Italians, and Jews reached the colonies in the eighteenth century.

Streams of emigrants flowed to places where land was cheap and labor most in demand. Few went to New England, where descendants of the first settlers already occupied the best land. They also avoided areas where slavery predominated—the Chesapeake tidewater and low-land South Carolina—in favor of the foothills of the Appalachian Mountains from western Pennsylvania to the Carolinas.

Not all emigrants realized their dreams of becoming independent landowners. The scarcity of labor in the colonies led as easily to the exploitation of white workers as of slaves and Indians. Even so, for many people facing bleak prospects in Europe, the chance that emigration might bring prosperity was too tempting to ignore.

Conclusion

By the middle of the eighteenth century, America offered a strikingly diverse mosaic of peoples and communities. Along the St. Lawrence River lay Kahnawake, a village of Mohawks and Abenakis who had adopted Catholicism and French ways under Jesuit instruction. In Andover, Massachusetts, New Englanders tilled fields that their Puritan grandparents had cleared. German immigrants who had forsaken the world in search of spiritual perfection populated the isolated Pennsylvania settlement of Ephrata. The hundred or so slaves on Robert Carter's Virginia plantation at Nomini Hall gathered on Sunday evenings to nurture ties of community with songs and dances, while the master cultivated his very different sense of community with neighboring planters. Near St. Augustine, Florida, runaway slaves farmed and gathered shellfish under the protection of Spanish soldiers. Far to the west, the Spanish, *mestizo*, and Pueblo residents of Santa Fe warily reestablished ties broken during the Pueblo Revolt.

In these and many other communities, peoples from three continents adapted to one another and to American conditions. Indians struggled with the consequences of disease, trade, religious conversion, settlement, and warfare resulting from European immigration. Africans exchanged traditional ethnic connections for a new identity as African Americans. English settlers became landowners in unprecedented numbers and adopted new ways to control laborers, reinventing slavery, unknown in England for centuries. No European settlement in America fully reproduced Old World patterns, and no native village fully preserved the precontact Indian way of life.

REVIEW QUESTIONS

1. Why did English colonists experience more frequent, and more violent, conflicts with the Indians than the settlers of New France?

2. Why were Catholic missionaries more successful than Protestants in converting Indians to Christianity in early America?

3. When did Chesapeake planters switch from servants to slaves? Why did they make this change?

4. By about 1750, more slaves in the mainland British colonies were creoles (American-born) than African-born. What effects did this have on the formation of African-American communities in America?

5. Many European immigrants came to America in the eighteenth century, but they tended to settle only in certain colonial regions. What regions did they favor and why?

Convergence and Conflict

1660s–1763

In what ways was trade regulated between Britain and the colonies?

How did prominent colonists go about developing America's intellectual life?

When did the "Great Awakening" reach the colonies and what effect did it have there?

How did the "Glorious Revolution" affect the colonists?

What geographic area made up the "backcountry" and who settled there?

How did the French and Indian War affect the colonists?

⭐

Virginia
26th April 1763

Mr. Lawrence

Be pleased to send me a genteel sute of Cloaths made of superfine broad Cloth handsomely chosen; I shou[l]d have Inclosed [for] you my measure but in a general way they are so badly taken here that I am convinced it wou[l]d be of very little service; I wou[l]d have you therefore take measure of a Gentleman who wears well made Cloaths of the following size—to wit—Six feet high & proportionably made; if any thing rather Slender than thick for a Person of that highth with pretty long arms & thighs—You will take care to make the Breeches longer than those you sent me last, & I wou[l]d have you keep the measure of the Cloaths you now make by you and if any alteration is required, in my next [letter] it shall be pointed out. Mr Cary will pay your Bill—& I am Sir Yr Very H[um]ble Serv[an]t . . .

—George Washington

W. W. Abbot and Dorothy Twohig, eds., *The Papers of George Washington*, Colonial Series, vol. 7 (Charlottesville, 1990).

GEORGE WASHINGTON, along with a few other privileged Virginians, had traveled to Williamsburg for a visit that mixed politics, business, and pleasure. These men had come to the capital to represent their respective counties in the House of Burgesses. When not engaged in government business, they attended to private affairs. They arranged to ship tobacco from their plantations to England, to pay debts, or to seek credit. Washington was surely not the only one to write to his London tailor and order fashionable clothing. He and his fellow burgesses donned their best coats and breeches to attend evening dinner parties and theater performances.

April 1763 marked the fourth time Washington had gone to Williamsburg to take his seat in the legislature. Just 31 years old in 1763, he had recently married Martha Custis, a wealthy widow, and inherited his older brother's plantation at Mount Vernon. He had served his king during the Seven Years' War; now he was eager to exchange his military uniform for the "genteel" broadcloth suits appropriate to his new station. With land and wealth to support his ambitions, he wanted to live, look, and behave like an English country gentleman, not merely like a Virginia planter.

But Washington could not be sure what an English gentleman wore. He had never been to England and trusted neither his own judgment nor Williamsburg tailors to know how a proper English gentleman should dress. So, while he instructed Mr. Lawrence about measurements and fabric quality, he had to trust his tailor to make him clothing as suitable for the drawing rooms of London as for the parlors of Williamsburg.

Throughout British America, colonists who had achieved wealth and power tried, like Washington, to imitate the English gentry. Prosperity and the demand of a growing population for English products tied the colonies ever more tightly into a trade network centered on the imperial metropolis, London. The flow of goods and information between England and America fueled the desires of Washington and other successful colonists for acceptance as transatlantic members of the English elite. No longer a collection of rough outposts clinging to the Atlantic seaboard, British America was growing in size and sophistication.

These developments in Britain's American colonies brought them to the attention of European statesmen, who increasingly factored North America into their calculations. Parliament devised legislation that would channel tobacco and other colonial goods into England and away from its European competitors. Spain and France viewed the economic growth and expansion of British North America as a threat to their own possessions, and they responded by augmenting their territorial claims. With expansion came conflict and four imperial wars, which themselves became powerful engines of change in the New World.

Economic Development and Imperial Trade in the British Colonies

The greatest assets that Great Britain could call on in its competition with other European nations were a dynamic economy and a sophisticated financial system that put commerce at the service of the state. In the century after 1690, England became the most advanced economic power in Europe.

England's leaders came to see colonies as indispensable to the nation's economic welfare. Colonies supplied raw materials unavailable in the mother country, and settlers provided a healthy market for English manufacturers. As the eighteenth century progressed, colonial economies grew in tandem with England's. Parliament knitted the colonies into an empire with commercial legislation, while British merchants traded with and extended credit to growing numbers of colonial merchants and planters.

THE REGULATION OF TRADE

England, the Netherlands, and France competed vigorously in transatlantic trade. Between 1651 and 1733, Parliament passed laws that regulated trade to ensure that more wealth flowed into England's treasury than out of it. This governmental intervention in the economy for the purpose of increasing national wealth—called *mercantilism*—aimed to draw the colonies into a mutually beneficial relationship with England.

Parliament enacted four types of mercantilist regulations. The first aimed at ending Dutch dominance in England's overseas trade. Beginning with the *Navigation Act of 1651*, all trade in the empire had to be conducted in English or colonial ships, with crews that were at least half Englishmen or colonists. The act stimulated rapid growth in both England's merchant marine and New England's shipping industry. Shipbuilding and earnings from what was called the "carrying trade" soon became the most profitable sector of New England's economy.

The second type of legislation channeled certain colonial goods, called "*enumerated products*," through England or another English colony. These raw materials initially included tobacco, sugar, indigo, and cotton; other products, such as rice, were added later. European goods also had to pass through England before they could be shipped to the colonies. When these goods entered English ports, they were taxed, which made them more expensive and encouraged colonists to buy English-made items.

With the third and fourth sorts of regulation Parliament subsidized certain goods, including linen, gunpowder, and silks, to allow manufacturers to undersell European competitors in the colonies. Other laws protected English manufacturers from colonial competition by prohibiting colonists from manufacturing wool, felt hats, and iron on a large scale.

The colonies prospered under mercantilist legislation. Between 1650 and 1770, the colonial economy grew twice as fast as England's did. Because the trade laws allowed colonial merchants to operate on equal terms with English traders, they could take full advantage of commercial opportunities within the empire.

THE COLONIAL EXPORT TRADE AND THE SPIRIT OF ENTERPRISE

By the mid-eighteenth century, the Atlantic had become a busy thoroughfare of international commerce. Between 1700 and 1770, the number of British merchant ships nearly tripled, from 3,300 to 9,400. At the heart of Anglo-American trade lay the highly profitable commerce in staple crops, most of which were produced by slave labor.

West Indian sugar was the most important colonial product. By the late 1760s, the value of sugar and sugar by-product exports reached almost £4 million per year—nearly 50 percent more than the total value of exports from all the other British American colonies combined. Many West Indian planters joined with the English merchants who marketed their sugar to lobby Parliament for favorable treatment. The "sugar interest" convinced Parliament in 1733 to pass the Molasses Act, which taxed sugar products from foreign sources, especially the French West Indies. Parliament removed sugar from the list of enumerated items in 1739, allowing merchants to ship it directly from the islands to southern Europe.

Tobacco from the Chesapeake colonies was the second most valuable staple crop. Exports worth about £750,000 arrived each year in England during the late 1760s. Nearly 90 percent of the crop was later reexported to continental Europe. But persistent low prices led many tobacco planters, after 1750, to sow some of their land with wheat.

Exports of rice and indigo helped make South Carolina planters some of the richest mainland colonists. Most of the rice went to England and the West Indies. Parliament subsidized indigo production as well as colonial production of naval stores—such as tar, pitch, and turpentine—to reduce England's dependence on Swedish suppliers for materials essential to its navy. The export of these items made up a small but important part of the North and South Carolina economies.

• C H R O N O L O G Y •

1651–1733 Parliament passes series of Navigation Acts to regulate imperial trade.

1660 Charles II becomes king of England.

1662 Halfway Covenant adopted by Massachusetts clergy.

1685 James II becomes king of England.

1686–1689 Dominion of New England.

1688 Glorious Revolution in England; James II loses the throne.

1689 William and Mary become English monarchs; Leisler's Rebellion begins in New York.

1689–1697 King William's War in America.

1691–1692 Witchcraft trials in Salem, Massachusetts.

1698 First French settlements near mouth of Mississippi River.

1701 Iroquois adopt policy of neutrality toward France and Britain.

1702–1713 Queen Anne's War in America.

1718 Establishment of San Antonio, Texas; New Orleans founded.

1734–1735 Jonathan Edwards leads religious revival in Northampton, Massachusetts.

1739 Great Awakening begins in Middle Colonies with George Whitefield's arrival.

1744–1748 King George's War in America.

1754–1763 Seven Years' War in America.

1760s Spanish begin establishing missions in California.

Wheat exports from the Middle Colonies boomed after 1750, when a combination of poor harvests and warfare in Europe created strong overseas demand. Ships traveling from Philadelphia or New York to English ports also carried a variety of goods, including unrefined iron, potash (used in making soap and glass), salted meats, and wood products.

New England had no staple crop and produced little for export to Great Britain except whale products, such as oil. The region's merchants nevertheless developed a thriving transatlantic trade, eventually dominating shipping within the empire. By 1770, New England's earnings from shipping fees, freight charges, and insurance exceeded the total value of its exports.

New England merchants also strengthened trade links to the West Indies. By the mid-eighteenth century, more than half of all New England exports went to the islands: salted meat for planters' dinners, salted fish for slaves, wood for sugar barrels, and other equipment. Merchants accepted molasses and other sugar by-products in payment, bringing them back to New England to be distilled into cheap rum. Enterprising traders then carried rum to Africa to exchange for slaves. Because New Englanders trafficked in slaves and provisioned the West Indies, their commercial economy depended on the institution of slavery, even though few slaves lived in the region.

THE IMPORT TRADE AND TIES OF CREDIT

By the late 1760s, the colonists imported goods worth nearly £4 million each year, almost all of which came from Great Britain. Most imports consisted of manufactured goods, which could not be produced in America. Some of these goods—ironware, sugar, hats—were made of materials that had come from the colonies in the first place.

In terms of value, colonists in fact imported more goods than they exported. Earnings from shipping fees, as well as payments from the British government for colonial military expenses, made up most of the difference between imports and exports. The colonial economy may have run an annual deficit of £40,000 by the late 1760s, but that was only about 1 percent of a transatlantic trade worth over £4 million a year.

Great tobacco planters like Washington virtually lived on the easy credit that British merchants provided. These merchants marketed the planters' tobacco and supplied them with English goods, charging the costs of purchase and transportation against the profits they expected the next year's crop to bring.

Gradually, planters sank into debt. A Virginian noted that no planter would have dared run up a debt of £1,000 in the 1740s, but in the 1760s "Ten times that sum is . . . spoke of with Indifference." When tobacco prices dropped or an international crisis made overseas trading risky, creditors called in the debts owed to them. At such times, colonial debtors realized how much they (like Indians involved in European trade) depended on goods and credit supplied by distant merchants.

BECOMING MORE LIKE ENGLAND

By 1770, Philadelphia's population had reached 30,000, New York's 25,000, Boston's 16,000, and Charleston's 12,000. Baltimore was rapidly developing as the best harbor on Chesapeake Bay. Only about 5 percent of all mainland colonists lived in cities, but the influence of urban centers far outweighed their size.

An English visitor declared in 1759 that Philadelphia "must certainly be the object of every one's wonder and admiration." Less than eighty years old, it already boasted three thousand houses, impressive public buildings, "handsomely built" streets, two libraries, eight or ten churches, and a college (chartered as the College of Philadelphia in 1755, now the University of Pennsylvania). This same visitor judged Boston to be a "most flourishing" place with "much the air of some of our best country towns in England."

All colonial cities (like England's major ones) were seaports. Indeed, in their bustle and cosmopolitan atmosphere, colonial cities resembled English provincial cities more than they did the villages and farms of the American countryside. Cities provided all sorts of amenities, including inns, taverns, coffeehouses, theaters, and social clubs. Their populations were much more diverse in ethnic origin and religion.

Perhaps two out of three adult white males living in cities worked at a craft. Many of them—shipbuilders, ropemakers, sailmakers—labored at trades directly related to overseas commerce. Others produced pottery, furniture, paper, glassware, iron tools, and various household items. Talented colonists such as the Boston silversmith Paul Revere and the Philadelphia furniture maker John Folwell fashioned goods that would have been prized possessions in any English gentleman's home.

Colonial manufacturing took place in workshops often attached to artisans' houses. Artisans managed a work force consisting of their wives and children, along with apprentices, usually teenage boys, who contracted to work for a master for four to seven years in order to learn the craft. Like indentured servants, they worked for food, clothing, shelter, and a small payment at the end of their service. Once an apprentice finished his training, he became a journeyman, working for a master but now earning wages and saving until he could afford to set up his own shop.

Many artisans flourished in colonial cities. Adino Paddock moved from the countryside to Boston in 1736 to learn how to make the light carriages known as chaises. By 1758, he had his own shop, and as his business prospered, Bostonians elected him to important local offices. As a gesture of public spirit, Paddock arranged for the transplanting of elm trees on

Boston Common, to beautify the city where he had made his fortune, which by 1775 amounted to more than £3,000.

Craftwork also offered economic opportunities to city women that were generally unavailable to rural women. Mary Wallace and Clementia Ferguson stitched fashionable hats and dresses for New York customers. Nonetheless, even in cities, women's options were limited. Many employed women were widows striving to maintain a family business until sons grew old enough to take over.

Workers at less skilled crafts often earned only a bare living, and ordinary laborers faced seasonal unemployment. The gap between rich and poor widened during the eighteenth century. In 1687, the richest 10 percent of Boston residents owned 46 percent of the taxable property in the town; by 1771, the top tenth held 63 percent of taxable wealth. Similar changes occurred in Philadelphia, South Carolina, and the Chesapeake, wherever colonists engaged heavily in commerce. Over time, it became extremely difficult for newcomers to enter the ranks of the elite.

Most cities built workhouses and other shelters for people who could not take care of themselves. Towns collected funds for poor relief in greater amounts than ever before. Even so, poverty had not yet become an entrenched problem. Temporary downturns in the economy were more often than not the result of dislocations caused by war.

Even in the worst of times, no more than one out of ten white colonists (mainly city dwellers) depended on public assistance. As much as one-third of England's population regularly received relief, and the numbers swelled during hard times. As long as land was available—even if one had to move to the edges of settlement to get it—colonists could at least eke out a bare subsistence, and many did much better.

The growth of colonial cities mirrored British urban development. The widening gap between rich and poor convinced many colonists that their society had at last matured from its crude beginnings. Eighteenth-century Britons on both sides of the Atlantic believed that societies ought to be organized hierarchically, with people arranged in ranks from rich to poor according to their abilities and God's design. The more America resembled Britain, many colonists assumed, the more stable and prosperous it would be.

The Transformation of Culture

Despite the convergence of English and colonial society, many influential settlers worried that America remained culturally inferior to Great Britain. Just as Washington trusted a London tailor, not a Virginian, to make him a fashionable suit, other colonial gentlemen tended to see American architecture, fashion, manners, and intellectual life as poor imitations of British models. Some colonial gentlemen even reshaped their religious beliefs to reflect European notions that God played only an indirect role in human affairs.

Most colonists, however, had little interest in copying the manners of the English elite, and very few altered their spiritual beliefs to fit European patterns. Indeed, religion flourished in eighteenth-century America and, when a tremendous revival swept through the colonies beginning in the 1730s, it occupied center stage in American life.

GOODS AND HOUSES

Eighteenth-century Americans imported more manufactures from England with every passing year. In the less secure economic climate of the seventeenth century, colonists had limited their purchases of goods, investing instead in land to pass on to their children. But by the eighteenth century, prosperous colonists felt secure enough to buy goods to make their lives more comfortable.

Benjamin Franklin described such changes in his own household. Accustomed to eating his breakfast of bread and milk with a pewter spoon from an earthenware bowl, he found it one morning "in a China Bowl with a Spoon of Silver" that had cost "the enormous Sum of three and twenty Shillings." His wife, Deborah, justified the purchase by declaring "that she thought her Husband deserved a Silver Spoon & China Bowl as well as any of his Neighbors." Many colonists likewise acquired such goods to advertise their refined style of life.

By the 1760s, nearly every item that George Washington ordered from his London agent could have been purchased in Philadelphia, but Washington and many other colonists wanted the latest English styles. One visitor to Maryland declared that he was "almost inclined to believe that a new fashion is adopted earlier by the polished and affluent American than by many opulent persons" in London.

Prosperous colonists built grand houses where they lived in greater comfort than ever before. In the seventeenth century, Virginia's governor lived in a four-room dwelling. His eighteenth-century counterpart, however, resided in Williamsburg in the Governor's Palace, an elegant two-storied mansion designed after British architectural styles. Washington extensively remodeled Mount Vernon, adding a second story and extra wings. In the northern colonies, merchants built the most impressive houses, often following architectural pattern books imported from England.

These houses were different in design from the homes of less affluent colonists. Most settlers cooked, ate, and slept in the same chamber. But the owners of great houses could devote rooms to specialized uses. Cooking and other domestic work took place in back or in separate outbuildings. Private bedrooms were located upstairs. The most distinctive feature of these grand homes was the parlor, an elaborately decorated room used for receiving guests. Prosperous colonists built such homes to emulate the English gentry in their country estates and London townhouses.

SHAPING MINDS AND MANNERS

Colonists knew that the manners of English gentlefolk set them apart from ordinary people. Many Americans imported "courtesy books," which contained the rules of polite behavior. The young George Washington studied such books carefully. At age 13, he copied 110 rules from *Youth's Behaviour, or Decency in Conversation Among Men*, including such advice as "In the Presence of Others Sing not to yourself with a humming Noise, nor Drum with your Fingers or Feet" and "In Company of those of Higher Quality than yourself Speak not till you are ask'd a Question then Stand upright put of[f] your Hat and Answer in few words."

In Charleston, South Carolina, dozens of girls' boarding schools advertised instruction in "the different branches of Polite Education." Female pupils studied reading, writing, and arithmetic but also learned French, music, dancing, and fancy needlework. This curriculum prepared them for married lives as mistresses of great houses, mothers of future gentlemen and ladies, and hostesses of grand entertainments. Invitations to balls, musical performances, and tea parties circulated among well-bred neighbors. Such occasions excluded ordinary settlers and reinforced elite colonists' sense of themselves as a separate—and better—class of people.

Prominent colonists, intent on developing America's intellectual life, began to participate in a transatlantic world of ideas. Literacy rates among white colonists were quite high by eighteenth-century standards. In New England, where settlers placed great emphasis on Bible study, about 70 percent of men and 45 percent of women could read and write. Farther south, literacy rates were lower, but still higher than in England, where only a third of all men and even fewer women could read and write.

Elite colonists, however, were more consumers of British and European ideas than producers of an American intellectual tradition. They imported thousands of books, subscribed to British journals, and established libraries in Philadelphia, Charleston, and New York where borrowing privileges could be purchased for a modest fee. Students at Harvard in Cambridge (founded in 1636) modeled their college newspaper on an English periodical, *The Spectator.* In Virginia, William Byrd—the son of an Indian trader who had risen to the rank of gentleman—composed verse in the style of contemporary English poets, and Thomas Jefferson copied out passages from the English novel *Tristram Shandy.* Benjamin Franklin honed his writing skills by rewriting essays from *The Spectator* and comparing his versions to the originals.

Educated colonists were especially interested in the new ideas that characterized what has been called the ***Age of Enlightenment.*** A group of European thinkers drew inspiration from recent advances in science—such as the English scientist Isaac Newton's explanation of the laws of gravity—that suggested that the universe operated according to natural laws that human reason could discover. They also drew on the work of the English philosopher John Locke, who maintained that God did not dictate human knowledge but rather gave us the power to acquire knowledge through experience and understanding. The hallmark of Enlightenment thought was a belief in the power of human reason to improve the human condition.

Enlightenment thinkers rejected earlier ideas about God's unknowable will and continued intervention in human and natural events. They instead assigned God a less active role as the creator of the universe, who had set the world running according to predictable laws, and then let nature—and human beings—shape events.

Colonial intellectuals sought membership in a growing international community of scholars. A few of them—the Reverend Cotton Mather of Massachusetts, William Byrd, Benjamin Franklin—gained election to the Royal Society of London, the most prestigious learned society in the empire. Most of their scholarly contributions were unimpressive, but Benjamin Franklin achieved genuine intellectual prominence. His experiments with a kite proved that lightning was electricity and gained him an international reputation. Franklin also invented the lightning rod (which prevented fires in wooden buildings by channeling the electrical charge of a lightning bolt into the ground), bifocal spectacles, the iron "Franklin stove" (in which wood burned more efficiently than in fireplaces), and the glass harmonica.

Very few prosperous and educated colonists could afford such intellectual pursuits. Only after retiring from business at age 42 could Franklin purchase the equipment for his electrical discoveries and begin his scientific work, devoting the "leisure during the rest of my life for philosophical studies and amusements." Most colonists remained ignorant of scientific advances and Enlightenment ideas. They had little leisure to devote to literature and polite conversation.

Colonial Religion and the Great Awakening

Church steeples dominated the skylines of colonial cities. Often the largest and finest buildings in town, they bore witness to the thriving—and diverse—condition of religion in America.

In all New England colonies except Rhode Island, the Puritan (or Congregationalist) faith was the established religion. The many Congregational churches in the region, headed by ministers trained at Harvard College and Yale University (founded in 1636 and 1701, respectively), served the majority of the colonists and received financial support from their taxes. Ministers and believers adapted in important ways to changing social and religious conditions.

The principal adaptation consisted of a move away from strict requirements for church membership. New England's founders had required prospective members to give convincing evidence that they had experienced a spiritual conversion. Only members could receive communion and have their children baptized. By the 1660s, however, fewer colonists sought admission under such strict standards, which left them and their unbaptized children outside the church. In 1662 the clergy adopted the *Halfway Covenant*, which allowed adults who had been baptized (because their parents were church members), but who had not themselves experienced conversion, to have their own children baptized. By the 1680s, some ministers made church admission even easier, requiring members only to demonstrate knowledge of the Christian faith and to live godly lives.

The Congregational Church also had to accept a measure of religious toleration in New England. In 1691, Massachusetts received a royal charter granting "liberty of Conscience" to all Protestants, bringing the colony into line with England's religious policy. Anglicans and Baptists eventually won exemptions from paying taxes to support the Congregational Church. At the same time, some Congregationalist preachers began emphasizing personal piety and good works in their sermons, ideas usually associated with Anglicanism.

In the South, the established Church of England consolidated its authority in the early eighteenth century but never succeeded in exerting effective control over spiritual life. Parishes often lacked trained clergy, and those who did emigrate encountered unexpected obstacles.

Anglican clergymen in the southern colonies served parishes that were vast and sparsely settled. One South Carolina parish, for example, contained 10,400 square miles— and only seven hundred white residents. Aware that the planters' taxes paid their salaries, many ministers found it easiest simply to preach and behave in ways that offered the least offense. In frontier regions, dissenting religious groups, such as Presbyterians, Quakers, and Baptists, gained followers among people neglected by the Anglican establishment.

No established church dominated in the Middle Colonies of New York, New Jersey, and Pennsylvania. The region's ethnically diverse population and William Penn's policy of religious toleration guaranteed that a multitude of groups would compete for followers. By the mid-eighteenth century, the region had more congregations per capita than even New England.

Groups such as the Quakers and the Mennonites, who did not believe in having specially trained ministers, easily formed new congregations in response to local demand. Lutheran and German Reformed churches, however, required European-educated clergy, who were always scarce. So pious laymen held worship services in their homes. When more Lutheran and Reformed clergy arrived in the 1740s and 1750s, they sometimes discovered that laymen balked at relinquishing control of the churches. Because so many other religious alternatives were available, these ministers had to compete for their parishioners' allegiance.

Bewildering spiritual diversity, relentless religious competition, and a comparatively weak Anglican Church all distinguished the colonies from England. Yet in one important way, religious developments during the middle third of the eighteenth century drew the colonies closer to England. A transatlantic religious revival, the *Great Awakening*, originated in Scotland and England, and first touched the Middle Colonies in the 1730s.

By 1730, Presbyterians in Pennsylvania had split into factions. One group was led by an immigrant Scottish evangelist, William Tennent Sr., and his four sons. In the 1730s, Tennent set up the Log College in Neshaminy, Pennsylvania, to train his sons and other young men to be evangelical ministers. His challenge to the Presbyterian establishment gained momentum in late 1739, when one of the most charismatic evangelists of the century, George Whitefield, arrived in the colonies from England.

Whitefield, an Anglican priest, had experienced an intense religious conversion while he was still a university student. Famous in Britain as a preacher of great emotional intensity, he embarked on a tour of the colonies. In Pennsylvania and New Jersey, Whitefield's powerful preaching on the experience of conversion lent support to the Presbyterian faction led by the Tennents and sparked local revivals. Whitefield then moved on to New England, where some communities had already experienced small, local awakenings.

Whitefield exhorted his audiences to examine their souls for evidence of the "indwelling of Christ" that would indicate that they were saved. He criticized most ministers for emphasizing good works and "head-knowledge" instead of the emotional side of religion.

Whitefield's sermons scarcely resembled the colonists' structured church services. His sermons were highly dramatic performances. He preached outdoors to thousands of strangers, jostling in crowds that often outnumbered the populations of several villages put together.

In the wake of Whitefield's visits, Benjamin Franklin noted, "it seem'd as if all the World were growing Religious." Revivals and mass conversions often followed his appearances, to the happy astonishment of local clergy. But their approval evaporated when disputes between individuals converted in the revivals—called "*New Lights*"—and those who were not ("Old Lights") split churches. "Formerly the People could bear with each other in Charity when they differ'd in Opinion," lamented one colonist, "but they now break Fellowship and Communion with one another on that Account."

The Awakening came late to the southern colonies, but it was there, in the 1760s, that it produced perhaps its greatest controversy. Many southern converts became Baptists, combining their religious criticism of the Anglicans with a condemnation of the wealthy planters' way of life. Planters, in turn, viewed Baptists as dangerous people who could not "meet a man upon the road, but they must ram a text of Scripture down his throat." Most of all, they hated the Baptists for their willingness to preach to slaves.

The Great Awakening had a lasting impact on colonial society, forging new links between Great Britain and the colonies. Evangelical ministers on both sides of the Atlantic exchanged correspondence. Periodicals such as *The Christian History* informed British and American subscribers of advances in true religion throughout the empire.

In the colonies, the Awakening led to the founding of new colleges. Middle Colony evangelicals founded the College of New Jersey (now Princeton University) in 1746. In the 1760s, New England Baptists established the College of Rhode Island (now Brown University). An evangelical wing of the Dutch Reformed Church founded Queens College (now Rutgers University) in 1766.

Everywhere, the New Light challenge to established ministers and churches undermined habits of deference to authority. Revivalists urged colonists to think for themselves in choosing which church to join and which minister to follow, not just conform to what the rest of the community did. As their churches fractured, Americans—particularly New Englanders—faced more choices than ever before in their religious lives.

The exercise of religious choice also influenced political behavior. Voters took note of whether candidates for office were New or Old Lights and cast their ballots for men on their own side. Tactics first used to mobilize religious groups—organizing committees, writing petitions and letters—proved useful for political activities as well.

The Colonial Political World

The political legacy of the Great Awakening—particularly the emphasis on individual choice and resistance to authority—corresponded to developments in the colonial political world. For most of the seventeenth century, ties within the empire developed from trade rather than governance. But as America grew in wealth and population, king and Parliament sought to manage colonial affairs more directly than ever before.

THE DOMINION OF NEW ENGLAND
AND THE LIMITS OF BRITISH CONTROL

When Charles II became king in 1660, he initially showed little interest in the colonies except as sources of land and government offices with which he could reward his supporters. With the passage of mercantile regulations governing colonial trade, for example, Parliament required customs officers to administer the imperial trading system and thus created a certain number of jobs.

Charles's brother James, the duke of York, envisioned a more tightly controlled empire. He encouraged Charles to appoint military officers, with strong ties of loyalty to him, as royal governors in America. In 1675, James convinced Charles to create the *Lords of Trade*, a committee of the Privy Council (the group of nobles who served as royal advisers), to oversee colonial affairs.

When James became king in 1685, the whole character of the empire abruptly changed. James set out to reorganize it along the lines of Spain's empire, combining the colonies into three or four large provinces. He appointed powerful governors to carry out policies that he himself would formulate.

James began in the north, creating the ***Dominion of New England*** out of eight previously separate colonies stretching from Maine (then part of Massachusetts) to New Jersey. He chose Sir Edmund Andros, a former army officer, to govern the vast region with an appointive council but no elective assembly. Andros moved to Boston and antagonized New Englanders by rigidly enforcing the Navigation Acts, limiting towns to just one annual meeting, remodeling the law courts, challenging property titles, and levying taxes without the colonists' consent. He even compelled Boston Puritans to share a meetinghouse with Anglicans.

Events in England ultimately sealed the fate of the Dominion. For years, English Protestants had worried about James's absolutist governing style and his conversion to Catholicism. Their fears increased in 1688 when the queen bore a son to carry on a Catholic line of succession. Parliament's leaders invited James's Protestant daughter, Mary, and her husband, William of Orange, the Stadtholder of the Netherlands, to take over the throne. In November 1688, William landed in England and gained the support of most of the English army. In December, James fled to France, ending a bloodless coup known as the ***Glorious Revolution***.

Bostonians overthrew Andros the following April, even before they knew for sure that William was king. In 1691, Massachusetts received a new charter. Massachusetts now included within its borders what had formerly been Plymouth Colony as well as Maine. Its colonists no longer elected their governor, who would instead be appointed by the English monarch. Voters no longer had to be church members, and religious toleration was extended to all Protestants.

The new charter ended exclusive Puritan control in Massachusetts but also restored political stability. During the three years between Andros's overthrow and the arrival of a royal governor in 1692, the colony lacked a legally established government. In this atmosphere of uncertainty, a local outbreak of accusations of witchcraft in Salem grew to unprecedented proportions. In the winter of 1691–1692, when several young girls of Salem experienced fits and other strange behavior, hundreds of settlers were accused of witchcraft, and nineteen were hanged. Salem's crisis gathered momentum because the courts, which would normally have intervened to settle matters, were unable to function.

The impact of the Glorious Revolution in other colonies likewise reflected distinctive local conditions. In New York, Jacob Leisler, a rich merchant and militia captain, gained power and ruled in dictatorial fashion. Too slow in relinquishing command to the newly arrived royal governor in 1691, Leisler was arrested for treason and executed. In Maryland, Protestants used the occasion of William and Mary's accession to challenge the Catholic proprietorship. The Calvert family lost its governing powers but retained rights to vast quantities of land. The Anglican Church became the established faith, and Catholics were barred from public office.

The colonists' support of the Glorious Revolution largely reflected powerful anti-Catholic sentiment. William's firm Protestantism reassured them. But the Glorious Revolution in England and the demise of the Dominion had long-lasting effects that shaped political life in England and America for years to come.

THE LEGACY OF THE GLORIOUS REVOLUTION

In England, the Glorious Revolution signaled a return to political stability after years of upheaval. In 1689, Parliament passed the Bill of Rights, which justified James's ouster and bound future monarchs to abide by the rule of law. They could not suspend parliamentary laws, collect taxes or engage in foreign wars without Parliament's consent, or maintain a standing army in peacetime. Parliamentary elections and meetings would follow a regular schedule without royal interference. In sum, Parliament claimed to be the crown's equal partner in governing England.

Colonists believed that their successful resistance to Andros confirmed that their membership in the empire was founded on voluntary allegiance and not forced submission to the mother country. Observing the similarity between Parliament and the colonial assemblies, they concluded that their own legislatures had a critical role in governance and in the protection of their rights. Parliament, however, claimed full authority over the colonies and did not recognize their assemblies as its equal.

William and his immediate successors lacked James's compulsion to control the colonies. In 1696, William replaced the Lords of Trade with the *Board of Trade*, which gathered information from the colonies and recommended policy changes but itself had no executive role. William also approved the *Navigation Act of 1696*, which closed loopholes in earlier laws and created vice-admiralty courts in the colonies similar to those of England. Admiralty judges settled maritime disputes and smuggling cases without using juries.

The mild imperial rule of the early eighteenth century, later called the era of "salutary neglect," allowed the colonies to grow in wealth, population, and self-government. It also encouraged colonial self-confidence, leading colonists to assume equality with the English as members of the empire.

DIVERGING POLITICS IN THE COLONIES AND GREAT BRITAIN

English people on both sides of the Atlantic believed that politics ought to reflect social organization. They often compared the state to a family. Just as fathers headed families, adult men led societies. In particular, adult male property holders, who enjoyed economic independence, claimed the right to vote and hold office. Women (who generally could not own property), propertyless men, and slaves had no political role because they, like children, were subordinate to the authority of others, which rendered them incapable of exercising freedom of choice.

English people believed that rulers ought to govern with the same fairness and benevolence that fathers presumably exercised within their families. When George II became king in 1727, he reassured Parliament of his "constant care" to "secure to All My subjects, the full Enjoyment of their religious and civil Rights." In return for protection, the people owed their rulers the same obedience that children accorded their parents. The House of Commons responded to George II's assurance of goodwill in 1727 with its own promise of "Duty, Zeal and Affection to Your Majesty's Person and Government."

Eighteenth-century people also believed that government should reflect society's hierarchical organization. In England, the crown represented the interests of the royal family. Parliament represented society's two main divisions: the aristocracy in the *House of Lords* and the common people in the *House of Commons*. Americans shared the view that government should mirror social hierarchies but found it much more difficult to put the idea into practice.

American social and political structure never fully mirrored that of England. One of the most obvious differences was that America lacked an aristocracy. In England, the members of this tiny privileged minority were easily recognizable by their great wealth, prestigious family lines, leisured lives, and official titles of nobility. British America had elites but no aristocracy.

In both England and America, land ownership was the prerequisite for political participation. By the mid-eighteenth century, only one-tenth of all English heads of households owned all the country's land, and thus only a tiny portion of men could vote. In America, however, a large majority of white male farmers owned the land they tilled. In most colonies, 50 to 75 percent of white men were eligible to vote.

In England, electoral districts for Parliament often reflected their status in past centuries. Dunwich retained its right to elect a parliamentary representative long after the city itself had washed into the North Sea. Meanwhile, rapidly growing cities, such as Manchester, lacked any representative. Most of the English accepted the idea of *virtual representation*, which held that representatives served the interests of the nation as a whole, not just the locality from which they came. They assumed that since the colonists held interests in common with English people at home, they were virtually represented in Parliament—just like Manchester's residents.

Since the founding of their colonies, however, Americans had experienced *actual representation* and believed that elected representatives should be directly responsive to local interests. They were accustomed to instructing their legislators about how to vote on important issues. Colonial representatives, unlike members of Parliament, resided in their districts. The Americans' experience with actual representation made them extremely skeptical of Parliament's claims to virtual representation.

The most direct political confrontations between England and the colonies focused on the role of colonial governors. In every colony except Connecticut and Rhode Island, either the king or proprietors appointed the governors. Their interests thus lay with their English patrons and not the colonies. Governors exercised greater powers over the colonial assemblies than the king (after the Glorious Revolution) did over Parliament. Governors could veto laws enacted by the assemblies and initiate legislation in consultation with councilors whom they appointed. They could delay legislative sessions, dissolve the assemblies at will, and nominate and dismiss colonial judges as they wished.

Several conditions hampered governors' efforts to exercise their legal authority. Many arrived with detailed instructions on how to govern, which limited their ability to negotiate with colonists over sensitive issues. Governors controlled few offices or other prizes with which to buy the allegiance of their opponents. They struggled to dominate assemblies that grew in size as the colonial population expanded. And in several colonies, including Massachusetts and New York, governors relied on the assemblies to appropriate the money for their salaries—a financial dependence that restrained even the most autocratic executive.

In response to the perceived threat of powerful governors, colonial assemblies asserted themselves as never before. They sent agents (including such prominent figures as Benjamin Franklin) to England to lobby on behalf of colonial interests. Local factions fought for election to the increasingly important legislature, leading to some of the most contentious politics in the British Empire.

Decades of struggles with governors led colonists to exalt the assemblies' role as the guarantors of their liberties. Most colonists, however, believed that as long as Parliament treated the Americans as partners in empire and refrained from ruling by coercion, colonists could celebrate British government as "the most perfect combination of human powers in society . . . for the preservation of liberty and the production of happiness."

Expanding Empires

During the first half of the eighteenth century, England, Spain, and France all enlarged their North American holdings. England's empire continued to expand as a result of the unrelenting growth of its colonial population. Spain and France still relied on missionaries, soldiers, and traders to stake their claims to American territory. In the eighteenth century as in the seventeenth, English settlement generally displaced native peoples. Newly established Spanish and French colonies, however, contained small numbers of Europeans amid much larger populations of Indians. Over time, these empires came into closer contact with one another, intensifying the competition for land, trade, resources, and Indian allies.

BRITISH COLONISTS IN THE BACKCOUNTRY

Black and white settlers in the mainland colonies numbered 265,000 in 1700; by 1770, they had increased to 2.3 million. Benjamin Franklin predicted in 1750 that if the colonial population continued to grow at this rate, within two hundred years "the greatest Number of Englishmen will be on this Side" of the Atlantic Ocean.

Much of this growth stemmed from natural increase. White families, particularly in the northern colonies, often had between five and ten children, most of whom survived to produce many more offspring. When 80-year-old Judith Coffin, the matriarch of an unusually large Massachusetts family, died in 1705, she had a total of 177 children and grandchildren. By the mid-eighteenth century, even the slave population began to reproduce itself, although more slowly than the white population.

Immigration also boosted the population. Thousands of Scots-Irish and German settlers—and many involuntary African immigrants—increased the population of the Lower South at nearly twice the rate of New England, which attracted few immigrants (and therefore remained the most thoroughly English of all colonial regions). By 1770, Pennsylvania had 240,000 settlers—ten times the number it had in 1710. Indeed, extensive German immigration worried Pennsylvania leaders. Like Benjamin Franklin, they feared that the newcomers would "never adopt our Language or Customs" and would soon "be so numerous as to Germanize us."

Most of the coast from Maine to Georgia was settled by 1760, forcing many immigrants and descendants of earlier settlers to move inland. The most dramatic expansion occurred in the foothills and valleys of the Appalachian Mountains from Pennsylvania to Georgia, a region known as the backcountry. Between 1730 and 1770, nearly a quarter of a million German, Scots-Irish, and English colonists entered the backcountry. They mainly raised crops and livestock for subsistence on small, isolated farms. Community life developed slowly, in part because backcountry settlers often moved frequently. In addition, a surplus of men among the first settlers delayed the formation of families.

Contemporary observers derided the crudeness of frontier life. William Byrd, a wealthy planter from Virginia's Tidewater, scornfully described one backcountry house as a "castle containing of one dirty room with a dragging door to it that will neither open or shut." Charles Woodmason, an English-born Anglican missionary, was appalled by the sight of western Carolina settlers who "Live in Logg Cabbins like Hogs." Genteel observers offered what they considered the most damaging insult by referring to such settlers as "white Indians."

Yet many coastal planters—including William Byrd and George Washington—acquired vast tracts of western land with the intent to sell it to these "crude" settlers. During the 1740s and 1750s, scores of Virginia planters, northern merchants, and London investors formed companies whose purpose was to profit from this kind of land speculation. Their interests collided with those of settlers—squatters—who occupied the land without acquiring legal title in the hope that their labor in clearing farms would establish their property rights.

Backcountry settlers often complained that rich eastern planters, who dominated the colonial legislatures, ignored western demands for adequate representation. Many argued that the crudeness of frontier life was only temporary. Perhaps the best measure of their desire to resemble eastern planters was the spread of slaveholding. In one western Virginia county in 1750, only one-fifth of the household heads owned slaves. Just nineteen years later, more than half of them did.

Colonists who moved to the backcountry often displaced native groups. Indians moving to avoid friction with whites, however, frequently encroached on lands claimed by other tribes—particularly those of the Iroquois Confederacy—leading to conflict among native peoples.

Even where English settlers had not yet appeared, English and Scottish traders could often be found, aggressively pursuing trade with the Indians. Spanish and French observers feared this commercial expansion even more than the movement of settlers. Knowing that the Indians viewed trade as a counterpart to military alliance, the Spanish and French expanded their own territorial claims and tried to strengthen relations with Indian peoples.

THE SPANISH IN TEXAS AND CALIFORNIA

Spanish Florida had become the target of English raiders from South Carolina. Years of religious persecution and forced labor under Spanish rule encouraged Florida's Indians to oppose the Spanish, but the natives also liked English trade goods and guns. Spain held on to coastal bases at St. Augustine, San Marcos de Apalachee, and Pensacola, but by the mid-eighteenth century, control of Florida's interior effectively passed to Indian bands allied with the English.

In 1700, Franciscan priests in New Mexico, fearful of sparking another native revolt, eased their labor demands and avoided outright religious persecution, allowing the Pueblos to retain many of their customs and religious practices. New Mexican officials worried about news brought by Apache hunters that Frenchmen who might contest Spanish control had been seen on the plains.

To create a buffer zone around their existing colonies, the Spanish moved into Texas and California. Franciscan priests established several missions in east Texas between 1690 and 1720. San Antonio, founded in 1718, served as a way station between the Rio Grande and east Texas missions; its fortified chapel, San Antonio de Valero, later became famous as the Alamo. The Spanish advance into Texas, however, met with resistance from the French (who also had outposts on the Gulf Coast) and from the Caddos and other Indians armed with French guns. With only 1,800 settlers there as late as 1742, Spain exerted a weak hold on Texas.

Largely through the efforts of two men—José de Gálvez, a royal official, and Junípero Serra, a Franciscan priest—the Spanish constructed a string of forts and missions in California from San Diego north to San Francisco between 1769 and 1776. They initially encountered little opposition from California's Indians, who lived in small, scattered villages and lacked experience with organized warfare. With no European rivals nearby to compete with them, the Spanish erected an extensive mission system designed to convert and educate Indians and set them to work. Thousands of native laborers farmed irrigated fields and tended horses, sheep, and cattle.

The Spanish worked the Indians hard and maintained them in overcrowded, unsanitary dwellings. Native women suffered from sexual exploitation by Spanish soldiers. Epidemics of European diseases reduced the Indian population from 300,000 in 1769 to about 200,000 fifty years later. Signs of native resistance met with quick and cruel punishment—including whipping, burning, and execution—so that the Indians would not (as one official later wrote) "come to know their power" over the vastly outnumbered Spanish. (As late as 1790, California had only 990 Spanish residents.) Despite the gruesome consequences, Indians staged several revolts during the eighteenth century, but Spanish soldiers usually suppressed them quickly.

Spain's empire grew, even as it weakened, during the eighteenth century. From the beginning, Spain's vision of empire had rested not on extensive settlement but on expansive territorial claims backed up by soldiers and missionaries who subjugated native peoples in order to control their labor for Spanish profit. After 1700, however, the Spanish simply could not compete with the vigorous commercial empires of France and England.

THE FRENCH ALONG THE MISSISSIPPI AND IN LOUISIANA

French expansion followed major waterways—the St. Lawrence River, the Great Lakes, the Mississippi—into the heart of North America. Explorers reached the Mississippi Valley in the 1670s. Within twenty years, French outposts appeared along the Gulf Coast. New Orleans, the capital and main port of French Louisiana, was founded in 1718. Soon forts, trading posts, and villages sprang up in the continent's interior—a chain of way stations between Canada and the Gulf of Mexico. Defying official regulators, French colonists settled in six villages along the Mississippi in a place they called the *Pays des Illinois*.

This panel of an eighteenth-century painting by an unknown Mexican artist is representative of a genre of portraits illustrating the categories Spanish colonists developed to designate the offspring of various kinds of mixed marriage. This one, labeled "Español, con India, Mestizo," depicts a Spanish father, an Indian mother, and their mestizo child. The scarcity of European women made mixed marriage common in Spanish colonies. Such unions were exceedingly rare in the English colonies, where cultural preferences and the relative abundance of European women discouraged intermarriage.

Schalkwijlk, Art Resource, N.Y.

The first Illinois settlers were independent fur traders (*coureurs de bois*, or "woods runners") unwilling to return to Canada after the French government tried to prohibit their direct trade with Indians. Many found Christian Indian wives and began farming the rich lands along the river. The settlers and other Canadian emigrants, using the labor of their families and of black and Indian slaves, produced profitable surpluses of wheat, corn, and livestock to feed the growing population of New Orleans and the lower Mississippi Valley.

French Louisiana contained a diverse population of Indian peoples, French soldiers and settlers, German immigrants, and African slaves who, by the 1730s, outnumbered European colonists. Louisiana's economy depended mainly on the combined efforts of Indians, settlers, and slaves, who farmed, herded, fished, and traded deerskins. Due to the lack of profits, however, substantial European emigration to Louisiana essentially ceased after the 1720s.

But the French approach to empire—in Louisiana as in Canada—had always depended more on Indian alliances than on settlement. Louisiana's principal allies, the Choctaws, and other Indians offered trade and military assistance in return for guns, trade goods, French help in fighting English raiders seeking Indian slaves, and occasional French mediation of Indian disputes.

French expansion along the Mississippi Valley drove a wedge between Florida and Spain's other mainland colonies; it also blocked the westward movement of English settlers. But France's enlarged empire was only as strong as the Indian alliances on which it rested. The fear of losing Indian favor preoccupied officials because France's empire in America consisted of two disconnected pieces: New France, centered in the St. Lawrence Valley and the Great Lakes basin, and Louisiana, stretching from New Orleans to the *Pays de Illinois*. Between them lay one thousand miles of wilderness through which only one thoroughfare passed—the Ohio River. For decades, communication between the two parts of France's North American empire posed no problem because Indians in the Ohio Valley allowed the French free passage through their lands. If that policy ended, however, France's New World empire would be dangerously divided.

A Century of Warfare

From the time of the Glorious Revolution, English foreign policy aimed at limiting the expansion of French influence. This resulted in a series of four wars, which increasingly involved their American colonies as well as Spain and its colonies. The conclusion of the final conflict signaled a dramatic shift in North American history.

IMPERIAL CONFLICT AND THE ESTABLISHMENT
OF AN AMERICAN BALANCE OF POWER, 1689–1738

When he became king of England in 1688, the Dutch Protestant William of Orange was already fighting the War of the League of Augsburg against France's Catholic king, Louis XIV. William brought England into the conflict. The war lasted until 1697 and ended—as most eighteenth-century European wars did—in a negotiated peace that reestablished the balance of power. Little territory changed hands, either in this war or in the War of the Spanish Succession (1702–1713), which followed it.

In America, these two wars—known to British colonists as **King William's War** and **Queen Anne's War**, after the monarchs on the throne at the time—ended with equal indecisiveness. New France's Indian allies attacked New England's northern frontier with devastating success. New Englanders struck back at the exposed settlements of Acadia, which ultimately entered the British Empire as Nova Scotia, and tried unsuccessfully to seize Quebec. Neither war caused more than marginal changes for the colonies in North America. Both had profound effects, however, on the English state and on the Iroquois League.

All European states of the eighteenth century financed their wars by borrowing. But the English were the first to realize that wartime debts did not necessarily have to be repaid during the following peace. The government instead created a funded debt. Having borrowed heavily from large joint-stock corporations, the government agreed to use tax revenues to pay interest on those loans but not to pay off the loans themselves. The corporations agreed because the interest payments amounted to a steady form of income that over the long run could amount to more than the original loans. In this way, England became the first European country to harness its national economy efficiently to military ends.

As the debt grew larger, more taxes were necessary to pay interest on it and for a powerful navy and a standing army. When the treasury created a larger and more efficient bureaucracy to collect taxes, many Englishmen's anxiety emerged as a strain of thought known as **Country**, or "**Real Whig**," **ideology**, which stressed the threats that a standing army and a powerful state posed to personal liberty. It also emphasized the dangers of taxation to property rights and the need for property holders to retain their right to consent to taxation. Real Whig politicians publicized their fears but could not stop the growth of the state. In every successive war, the claims of national interest and patriotism—and the prospect of profit for parties rich enough to lend money to the government—overrode the objections of those who feared the expansion of state power.

In America, the first two imperial wars transformed the role of the Iroquois League. By 1700, the League had suffered such horrendous losses—perhaps a quarter of the population had died from causes related to King William's War—that its leaders created the **Grand Settlement of 1701**, a policy of neutrality with regard to the French and British Empires. Their goal was to refrain from alliances with either European power and instead maneuver between them. The Iroquois's strategic location between New France and the English colonies allowed them to serve as a geographical and diplomatic buffer between the two. This neutralist policy ensured that for nearly fifty years neither England nor France could gain ascendancy in North America.

Iroquois neutrality offered benefits to the Europeans as well as the Indians. To smooth relations with the English, the Iroquois sold them land formerly occupied by Delawares and Susquehannocks. This simultaneously helped satisfy the colonists' land hunger and enrich the Iroquois League. Meanwhile, a neutral Iroquois League claiming control over the Ohio Valley and blocking English access across the Appalachian Mountains helped the French protect the strategic corridor of the Ohio and Mississippi Valleys that linked Canada and Louisiana.

If the English ever established a permanent presence on this strategic corridor, however, the Iroquois would cease to be of use to the French. The Iroquois remained reasonably effective at keeping the British out of the Ohio Valley until the late 1740s. The next European war, however, altered these circumstances.

KING GEORGE'S WAR SHIFTS THE BALANCE, 1739–1754

The third confrontation between Britain and France in Europe, the *War of the Austrian Succession* (**King George's War** to the British colonists) began as a small war between Britain and Spain in 1739. Its immediate cause was British attempts to poach on trade to Spain's Caribbean colonies. But in 1744, France joined in the war against Britain and conflict erupted in North America.

New Englanders tried once again to attack Canada. This time, their target was the great fortress of Louisbourg on Cape Breton Island, a naval base that dominated the Gulf of St. Lawrence. An expedition from Massachusetts and Connecticut, supported by a squadron of Royal Navy warships, captured Louisbourg in 1745 and cut Canada off from French reinforcement and resupply. English forces should now have been able to conquer New France.

Instead, politically influential merchants in Albany, New York, continued to trade with the enemy via Lake Champlain, enabling Canada to hold out until the end of the war. When the peace treaty was signed in 1748, Britain, which had fared badly in the European fighting, returned Louisbourg to France. This diplomatic adjustment, routine by European standards, shocked New Englanders. New York's illegal trade with the enemy, unremarkable by previous colonial standards, appalled British administrators.

Even before the war's end, aggressive English traders from Pennsylvania began moving west to buy furs from Indians who had once traded with the French. The movements of these traders, along with the appearance of Virginians in the Ohio Valley after 1748, gravely concerned the French.

In 1749, the governor general of New France set out to assert direct control over the region by building a set of forts from Lake Erie to the Forks of the Ohio. This signaled the end of France's commitment to Iroquois neutrality. The chiefs of the Iroquois League now found themselves trapped between empires edging closer to confrontation in the Ohio Valley.

The appearance of English traders in the valley offering goods on better terms than the French or the Iroquois had ever provided also undermined Iroquois dominance. The Ohio Valley Indians increasingly ignored Iroquois claims of control and pursued their own independent course.

One spur to their disaffection from the Iroquois was the 1744 **Treaty of Lancaster**, by which Iroquois chiefs had sold a group of Virginia land speculators rights to trade at the Forks of the Ohio. The Virginians assumed that these trading rights included the right to acquire land for eventual sale to settlers. The Ohio Valley Indians found this intolerable, as did the French. When in 1754 the government of Virginia sent out a small body of soldiers under Lieutenant Colonel George Washington to protect Virginia's claims to the Forks of the Ohio, the French struck decisively to stop them.

THE FRENCH AND INDIAN WAR, 1754–1760: A DECISIVE VICTORY

In April 1754, French soldiers overwhelmed a group of Virginians who had been building a small fort at the Forks of the Ohio. They then erected a much larger fort of their own on the spot, Fort Duquesne. The French intended to follow up by similarly ousting Washington's weak, untrained troops, who had encamped further up the Monongahela River. However, at the end of May, Washington's men killed or captured all but one of the members of a small French reconnaissance party. The French decided to teach the Virginians a lesson. On July 3, they attacked Washington at his encampment, Fort Necessity. The next day, with a quarter of his troops killed or wounded, Washington surrendered.

British imperial officials worried that the Iroquois might ally with the French. Britain ordered New York's governor to convene an intercolonial meeting in Albany—known as the *Albany Congress*—to discuss matters with the Iroquois. Several prominent colonists, including Governor William Shirley of Massachusetts and Benjamin Franklin, took advantage of the occasion to put forward the **Albany Plan of Union**, which called for an intercolonial union to coordinate colonial defense, levy taxes, and regulate Indian affairs. But the colonies, too suspicious of one another to see their common interests, rejected the Albany Plan.

Meanwhile, the French expulsion of the Virginians left the Indians of the region, Delawares and Shawnees, with no choice but to ally with the French in what came to be called the **French and Indian War**. Soon French and Indian attacks fell like hammer blows on backcountry settlements from Pennsylvania to the Carolinas. Iroquois neutrality no longer mattered. Europeans were at last contending directly for control of the Ohio Country.

The French and Indian War blazed in America for two years before it erupted as a fourth Anglo-French war in Europe in 1756. Known in Europe as the *Seven Years' War* (1756–1763), it involved fighting in the Caribbean, Africa, India, and the Philippine Islands as well as in Europe and North America. It was unlike any other eighteenth-century conflict not only in its immense scope and expense but also in its decisive outcome.

During the first phase of the war, the French enjoyed a string of successes as they followed what had been a proven strategy in previous conflicts, guerrilla war. Relying on Indian allies and Canadian soldiers, the French raided English frontier settlements, killing and capturing hundreds of civilians and forcing tens of thousands more to flee. Then they attacked fortified outposts whenever the opportunity appeared. This style of warfare allowed the Canadians' Indian allies—who came from all over the Northeast and the upper Midwest—to act independently in choosing targets and tactics.

In 1755, Britain dispatched troops to attack Fort Duquesne. Major General Edward Braddock marched to within ten miles of Fort Duquesne, only to have his 1,450-man force surrounded and destroyed by Indians and Canadian militiamen. Braddock's defeat set the tone for virtually every military engagement of the next three years and opened a period of demoralization and internal conflict in the British colonies.

Britain responded by sending a new commander in chief, Lord Loudoun, to set colonial military affairs on a professional footing. He insisted on managing every aspect of the war effort, not only directing the campaigns but also dictating the amount of support, in men and money, that each colony would provide. The colonists grew increasingly stubborn in response to Loudoun's high-handed style. Colonial soldiers objected to Loudoun's command and colonial assemblies refused to cooperate.

Britain's aim had been to "rationalize" the war by making it conform to European professional military standards. This approach to warfare required soldiers to advance in formation in the face of massed musket fire without breaking rank. Such iron discipline was enforced—as in the British army—by savage punishments, including hundreds of lashes at the whipping post. Few colonial volunteers met professional standards, and few colonists thought them necessary. British officers assumed that colonial soldiers were simply lazy cowards. Colonial volunteers, appalled to see men lashed "till the blood came out at the knee" of their breeches, saw British officers as brutal task-masters. They resisted all efforts to impose such discipline on their own units, even to the point of desertion and mutiny.

In 1756, the marquis de Montcalm, a strong proponent of European professional standards of military conduct, assumed command of French forces. In his first battle, the successful siege of Fort Oswego, New York, Montcalm was horrified by the behavior of his Indian allies, which included killing wounded prisoners, taking personal captives, and collecting scalps as trophies. He came to regard the Indians—so essential to the defense of New France—as mere savages.

Following his next victory, the capture of Fort William Henry, New York, Montcalm conformed to European practice by allowing the defeated garrison to go home in return for the promise not to fight again. Montcalm's Indian allies—a thousand or more strong—were not to take prisoners, trophies, or plunder. The tragic result came to be known as the Massacre of Fort William Henry. Feeling betrayed by their French allies, the Indians took captives and trophies anyway, killing as many as 185 defenders and taking about 300 captive. Ironically, Montcalm's efforts to limit the war's violence alienated his Indian allies and helped the British army and its colonial auxiliaries to win an unlimited victory.

At the same time that the Europeanization of the war was weakening the French, the British moderated their policies and reached accommodation with the colonists. William Pitt, who as secretary of state directed the British war effort from late 1757 through 1761, realized that friction between the colonists and the commander in chief arose from the colonists' sense that they were bearing all the financial burdens of the war without having any say in how the war was fought. Pitt's ingenious solutions were to promise reimbursements to the colonies in proportion to their contribution to the war effort, to deemphasize the power of the commander in chief, and to replace the arrogant Loudoun with a less objectionable officer.

Pitt's money and measures restored colonial morale. He sent thousands of British soldiers to America to fight alongside tens of thousands of colonial troops. The Anglo-American forces operated more successfully, seizing Louisbourg again in 1758. Once more, Canada experienced crippling shortages of supplies, weapons, and trade goods. British emissaries persuaded the Delawares and Shawnees to abandon their French alliance, and late in 1758, an Anglo-American force again marched on Fort Duquesne. In command of its lead battalion was Colonel George Washington. The French defenders, abandoned by their native allies and confronted by overwhelming force, blew up the fort and retreated to the Great Lakes.

From this point on, the Anglo-Americans suffered no setbacks and the French won no victories. Montcalm, forced back to Quebec, decided to risk everything in a European-style, open-field battle against a British force led by General James Wolfe. At the Battle of Quebec (September 13, 1759), Montcalm lost the gamble—and his life (as did the victorious General Wolfe).

What finally decided the outcome of the war in America was the Battle of Quiberon Bay in France (November 20, 1759), which cost the French navy its ability to operate on the Atlantic, preventing it from carrying reinforcements and supplies to Canada. The Iroquois decision to enter the war on the side of the Anglo-Americans tipped the balance irrevocably against the French. The last ragged, hungry defenders of Canada, surrounded at Montreal by a vastly superior Anglo-American-Iroquoian force, surrendered on September 8, 1760.

THE TRIUMPH OF THE BRITISH EMPIRE, 1763

The war pitting Britain against France and Spain (which had entered the fighting as a French ally in 1762) concluded with an uninterrupted series of British victories. In the Caribbean, every valuable sugar island the French owned came under British control. Britain's capture of the Philippine capital of Manila on October 5 literally carried British power around the world.

Hostilities ended formally on February 10, 1763, with the conclusion of the *Treaty of Paris*. France regained its West Indian sugar islands—its most valuable colonial possessions—but lost the rest of its North American empire. France ceded to Britain all its claims to lands east of the Mississippi River (except the city of New Orleans) and compensated Spain for the losses it had sustained as an ally by handing over all claims to the Trans-Mississippi West and the port of New Orleans (see Map 4–1). Britain returned Cuba and the Philippines to Spain and in compensation received Florida. Now Great Britain owned everything east of the Mississippi, from the Gulf of Mexico to Hudson's Bay. With France and Spain both humbled and on the verge of financial collapse, Britain seemed preeminent in Europe and ready to dominate in the New World. Never before had Americans felt more pride in being British.

Conclusion

The George Washington who ordered a suit in 1763 was not a revolutionary; on the contrary, he was a man who longed to be part of the elite of the great British Empire. For Washington, as for virtually all other colonial leaders, 1763 was a moment of great promise and patriotic devotion to the British Empire. It was a time to rejoice in the fundamental British identity and liberty and rights that seemed to ensure that life in the colonies would be better and more prosperous than ever.

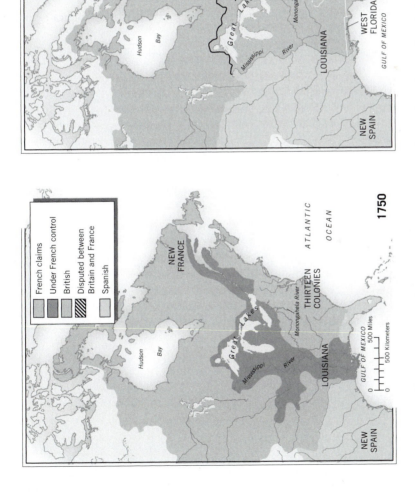

MAP 4-1

European Empires in North America, 1750–1763 Great Britain's victory in the French and Indian War transformed the map of North America. France lost its mainland colonies, England claimed all lands east of the Mississippi, and Spain gained nominal control over the Trans-Mississippi West.

USING THIS map, explain why Great Britain's victory in the French and Indian War was so crucial to its continued dominance of the Western world.

83

REVIEW QUESTIONS

1. Why did George Washington prefer to order a suit from London rather than trust a Virginia tailor to make him one? How does this attitude reflect elite colonists' attitudes about American society and culture in the eighteenth century?

2. How did economic ties between Britain and the colonies grow closer in the century after 1660?

3. What was the Great Awakening, and what impact did it have? How did it affect different groups in colonial society?

4. How were colonial and British political ideas and practices similar? How were they different?

5. Why did England, Spain, and France renew their competition for North America in the eighteenth century?

6. What role did warfare play in North America in the eighteenth century? What role did the Iroquois play?

Imperial Breakdown

1763–1774

How did Great Britain deal with its growing empire at the conclusion of the French and Indian War?

How did conflicts such as the Cherokee War and Pontiac's Rebellion affect relations between Native Americans and colonists?

What effect did the Sugar and Stamp Acts have on colonists' views of Great Britain?

Who were the Regulators, and what were the Regulator movements?

Who made up the first Continental Congress, and what was its purpose?

Philadelphia,
January 1774

My Dear Jack,

Your Uncle wrote the 27 Dec. by Capt. Ayres who brought the Tea. His ship came within four miles of this City on Sunday the 26th where she was stopped, not being suffered to come any farther. . . . The inhabitants sent a Supply of fresh provisions & a Pilot on board [who put them on course for England]. I believe they were glad they came off so well, for at Boston they threw it all into the River, and it would have gone near to have shared the same fate here, but the Capt. had more prudence than to endeavour to force a landing by which means he prevented a great deal of Mischief & Confusion, for they were all determined to oppose it. They think now that the India Company will get the Act which imposes a duty of 3d per pound repealed and then send more over.

Kensington,
September 19, 1774

Dear Jack,

The Congress [The First Continental Congress] are now Setting here & have been a fortnight but nothing Transpires. All is kept a profound Secret. There was a [false] report the other day of the Town of Boston being Bombarded by the Men of War lying off the Town . . . which Occasioned a general consternation along the Continent, and in some parts of the Country they Armed and Marched to the Number of 15,000 & more were getting ready. . . . In Short the Provinces are determined one and all to stand by each other. What the Consequences will be we don't know. To be sure thy [they] may send Men of War and destroy the Towns on the sea shore but its Impossible to take the Country, and the damage they do in destroying the Towns will fall on the English in the end.

Kensington
Nov 1, 1774

My Dear Jack,

Our Congress are broke up and are come to a great Spirited Resolves . . . together with a petition to his Majestie. . . . It is to be published and they have bound themselves to abide by those resolves . . . and if Necessitated to repel force with force. All Importation ceases after the first of December next.

April 28, 1775

Dear Jackey,

The Provinces are all Arming themselves, and the men are almost all for inlisting as fast as they take them so am afraid we shall have Troublesome times. I heartily wish the Authors of all this Mischief may be brought to Justice.

Kensington
June 28, 1775

My Dear Jack,

All the Provinces [are] arming and Training in the same Manner, for they are all determined to die or be Free. It is not the low Idle Fellows that fight only for pay but Men of great property are Common Soldiers who say they are fighting for themselves and Posterity. . . . The People are getting in Manufactures of different sorts, particularly Salt Peter and Gunpowder. The Smiths are almost all turnd Gunsmiths and cannot work fast enough. God knows how it will end but I fear it will be very bad on both sides, and if your drivalish minestry and parliament dont make some concessions and Repeal the Acts, England will lose America for as I said before they are determined to be free.

—Eliza Farmar

Pennsylvania Magazine of History and Biography, vol. 40 (1916): 199–207.

ELIZA FARMAR and her family had recently moved to Kensington, a suburb of Philadelphia, when she wrote these letters, and her ties to relatives in England remained strong. Jack, the recipient of these letters, was her nephew and a clerk in the London office of the East India Company, whose shipment of tea precipitated the Boston Tea Party. Although she hoped that he might come to America, she minced no words in emphasizing the determination of Americans to resist British measures that appeared to infringe upon their freedoms. These letters accordingly chronicle a psychological counterpart to her move to Kensington. She began both journeys as an English subject; she ended them as an American citizen. Her initial reports of political developments, though sympathetic to the colonial point of view, were fairly objective, but by the eve of the Revolution she had disowned the British government by referring to "your minestry and parliament" as "drivalish," a slip of the pen that covered ineffective and devilish.

Like most colonists, she started out proud to be a British subject and part of Britain's powerful empire. Americans had fought the king's enemies as well as their own in a series of imperial wars and had gloried in British successes. But they had also developed a sense of their identity as Americans. Largely governing themselves through their own legislatures, they believed that they enjoyed all the rights of British subjects anywhere.

But after the French and Indian War, British authorities faced a burdensome debt and vastly increased territory to administer. In response, they attempted to change how they governed the colonies and, for the first time, imposed direct taxes on the colonists. Most Americans opposed these measures as violations of their rights, although they disagreed over how far to carry their resistance.

Imperial Reorganization

At the close of the French and Indian War, British officials adopted a new and ultimately disastrous course in dealing with America. Lacking experience, they panicked at the magnitude of the problems confronting them, and led by a young and somewhat naive monarch (George III, who ascended to the English throne in 1760), they tried to fix a relationship between England and the colonies that most Americans would have said was not broken. They did this by adopting measures that worked mostly to the disadvantage of the colonies. As one contemporary critic observed, "A great Empire and little minds go ill together."

BRITISH PROBLEMS

Britain's empire in 1763 was indeed a great one, and the problems its rulers faced were correspondingly large. Its territories in North America stretched from Hudson's Bay in the north to the Caribbean Sea in the south and from the Atlantic Ocean west to the Mississippi River. French territory on the North American mainland had been reduced to two tiny islands in the Gulf of St. Lawrence. But France would be eager for revenge, and French inhabitants in the recently acquired territories might prove disloyal.

Spain was less powerful militarily than France but a more significant presence on the North American mainland. In the territorial settlement at the end of the French and Indian War, it surrendered East and West Florida to Britain but got back its possessions in Cuba and the Philippines and acquired Louisiana from France. Shocked by their inability to defend Cuba and the Philippines, Spanish officials stepped up the pace of reforms that they had begun making earlier in the century. They appointed new officials—who were generally Spaniards rather than colonials—to ensure better tax collection. Spain also expelled the Jesuit order from its dominions because Jesuit priests were too independent of royal control to suit Spanish officials. Spain further strengthened its military forces in much of the empire and began to settle in California and Louisiana.

Protecting and controlling the old and new territories in North America as inexpensively as possible presented British officials with difficult questions. How should they administer the new territories? How should they deal with Indians likely to resist further encroachments on their lands? And perhaps most vexing, how could they rein in the seemingly out-of-control colonists in the old territories?

Permitting most of the new areas to have their own assemblies appeared inadvisable and indeed, for quite some time British authorities had wanted to roll back the power of the old colonial assemblies. Britain had needed the cooperation of the assemblies during the years of war with France, but now, with France vanquished, imperial officials felt they could crack down on the local governments. Some British statesmen, however, realized that with France gone from the continent, Americans would be less dependent on Britain for protection and therefore more inclined to resist unpopular restrictions.

Resentment against American conduct during the war colored British thinking. Some of the colonies failed to enlist their quota of recruits, and for this the British blamed the local assemblies. Worse yet, some Americans continued to smuggle goods to and from the enemy in the French West Indies during the war. Smuggling was so common in New England that it cost Britain more to operate the customs service in America than it collected in duties.

England emerged from the war with what was then an immense national debt of approximately £130 million. Interest payments alone accounted for half the government's annual expenditures after the war. Alarmed by the unprecedented debt, many Britons concluded that Americans should bear more of the financial burden of running the empire. The colonists certainly appeared prosperous to British soldiers who had served in America. Compared to the English, who paid on average perhaps a third of their income in taxes, many Americans normally rendered no more than 5 percent.

DEALING WITH THE NEW TERRITORIES

In 1763, the British government took several important steps to deal with the new territories, protect the old colonies, and maintain peace with the Indians. One was to keep a substantial body of troops stationed in America even in peacetime. Another, accomplished in the **Proclamation of 1763**, was to temporarily forbid white settlement west of the Appalachian Mountains. The purpose of the **Proclamation Line** restricting white settlement was presumably twofold: to keep white settlers and Indians apart, preventing fighting between them, and to keep the colonists closer to the coast where they would be easier to control (see Map 5–1).

Neither the Proclamation Line nor the stationing of troops in America was particularly wise. The Proclamation Line provoked resentment because it threatened to deprive settlers and speculators in the rapidly developing colonies of the land they coveted, and it was often ignored. As for the troops, the British government further provoked American resentment with passage of **Quartering Acts** that required colonial assemblies to provide barracks and certain supplies for the troops.

The presence of troops in peacetime alarmed Americans. Imbued with a traditionally English distrust of standing armies, they wondered whether the soldiers were there to coerce rather than to protect them. Given their wariness, Americans would doubtless have objected to the troops and the taxes necessary to support them even if the troops had done an exemplary job of protecting the frontiers. But conflicts with Indians cast doubt on their ability to do even that.

Indian Affairs

From a Native American standpoint, the problems Britain confronted in America were nothing compared to their own troubles in dealing with the British. Colonial settlers and livestock were displacing Indians from their ancient lands. Free-flowing rum and rampant cheating among traders were making the fur and deerskin trades increasingly violent. Regulation of the Indian traders by the colonists was uncoordinated and generally ineffective.

The British victory over the French and the westward expansion of British territory undermined the Indians' traditional strategies and alignments. British officials no longer

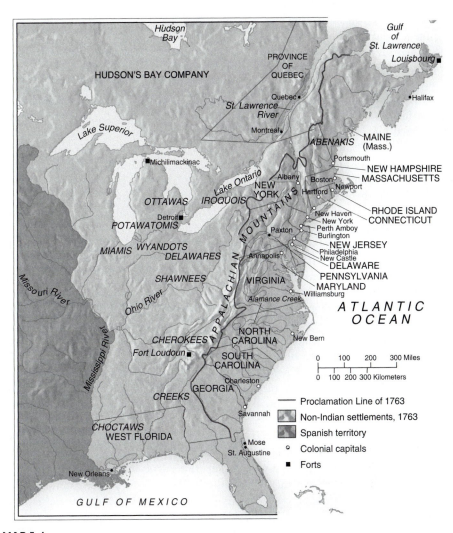

MAP 5–1
Colonial Settlement and the Proclamation Line of 1763 This map depicts the regions claimed and settled by the major groups competing for territory in eastern North America. With the Proclamation Line of 1763, positioned along the crest of the Appalachian Mountains, the British government tried to stop the westward migration of settlers under its jurisdiction and thereby limit conflict with the Indians. The result, however, was frustration and anger on the part of land-hungry settlers.

WHY DO you suppose the Proclamation Line of 1763 was positioned along the crest of the Appalachian Mountains?

found Native American neutrality or military help as important as they once had. Increasingly superfluous as allies and unable to play the European powers off against each other, Native Americans lost much of their former ability to protect themselves by any means short of military resistance. The British took advantage of this increasing vulnerability: Traders exploited the Indians, and settlers encroached on their lands.

Two major Indian wars—one breaking out in the late 1750s during the closing years of the French and Indian War and the other erupting in its aftermath in the early 1760s— challenged British policy toward Native Americans. The first conflict, the **Cherokee War**, took place in the southern Appalachian highlands and resulted in a treaty in 1761 in which the Cherokees agreed to surrender land in the Carolinas and Virginia to the colonists. The second major conflict, **Pontiac's Rebellion**, represented a united effort to resist the British and revitalize Indian cultures. The spiritual catalyst for this movement was a Delaware leader named Neolin, also known as the Delaware Prophet, who began urging Native Americans to reject European goods and ways. The Pontiac Rebellion itself, named for an Ottawa chief who was one of its principal leaders, began when at least eight major groups joined in attacking British forces and American settlers from the Great Lakes to Virginia in 1763. Pontiac's Rebellion raged until 1766. The British eventually forced the Indians to give up portions of their territory in return for compensation and guarantees that traditional hunting grounds in the Ohio Valley would remain theirs.

At one point during the war, a British commander used germ warfare against the Indians, sending them blankets that smallpox victims had used. Settlers in Paxton township (near modern Harrisburg, Pennsylvania) were equally unrestrained. Angered by the Pennsylvania Assembly's lack of aggressive action against the Indians, the settlers lashed out at convenient targets, massacring their peaceful neighbors, the Conestogas. Facing arrest and trial for this outrage, the so-called *Paxton Boys* marched toward Philadelphia, threatening the Pennsylvania Assembly. Benjamin Franklin convinced them to disperse. Despite the government's efforts, the Paxton Boys were never effectively prosecuted.

Pontiac's Rebellion and the Cherokee War were costly for both sides, claiming the lives of hundreds of Indians and white settlers. Hoping to prevent such outbreaks, British officials began experimenting with centralized control of Indian affairs during the 1760s. Following the recommendations of the Albany Congress in 1754 (see Chapter 4), they had already created two districts, northern and southern, for the administration of Indian affairs, each with its own superintendent. The Proclamation of 1763, and the line it established restricting further white settlement, gave these superintendents increased responsibility for protecting the Indians against the encroachments of settlers. But they faced daunting obstacles in their efforts to mediate between Indians and colonists and in 1768 Britain returned supervision of the Indian traders to the individual colonies.

CURBING THE ASSEMBLIES

As an episode in Virginia known as the **Parson's Cause** illustrates, British authorities took advantage of opportunities to curb the American legislatures as early as the 1750s. Anglican ministers in Virginia drew tax-supported salaries computed in pounds of tobacco. As a result, when a drought in the mid-1750s caused a sharp rise in tobacco prices, they expected a windfall. The Virginia House of Burgesses, however, restricted their payment to 2 pennies a pound, below the market value of the tobacco that backed their salaries. Lobbying by the clergy convinced the king to disallow the Two Penny Act, and some Virginia clergymen sued for the unpaid portion of their salaries.

In the most famous of these cases, the Virginia government was defended by Patrick Henry, a previously obscure young lawyer who looked like "a Presbyterian clergyman, used to haranguing the people." Henry gained instant notoriety when he declared that a king who vetoed beneficial acts became a tyrant and thereby forfeited "all right to his subjects'

• CHRONOLOGY •

1759–1761 Cherokee War.

1760 George III becomes king.

1761–1762 Writs of Assistance case in Massachusetts.

1763 Peace of Paris ends French and Indian War.
Spanish accelerate imperial reforms.
British troops remain in America.
Proclamation Line of 1763 limits western expansion of colonial settlement.
Pontiac's Rebellion begins.
Paxton Boys murder peaceful Indians.
Virginia Court decides Parson's Cause.

1764 Sugar Act passed. Currency Act passed.

1765 Quartering Act passed. Stamp Act passed.
Stamp Act Congress meets in New York.

1766 Stamp Act repealed; Declaratory Act passed.

New York Assembly refuses to comply with the Quartering Act.

1767 Townshend duties imposed.
Regulator movements in North and South Carolina.

1770 Boston Massacre.
Tea duty retained, other Townshend duties repealed.

1771 North Carolina Regulator movement defeated.

1772 *Gaspee* burned.
Committees of Correspondence formed.

1773 Boston Tea Party.

1774 Coercive Acts passed.
Quebec Act passed.
First Continental Congress meets and agrees to boycott British imports.

---

obedience." Given Henry's eloquence, the jury found in favor of the suing minister but awarded him only one penny in damages. This pittance reflected the hostility many Virginians of all denominations felt toward the pretensions of the Anglican clergy.

British authorities also sought to restrict the power of colonial legislatures to issue legal tender currency, paper notes that could be used to settle debts. These notes frequently depreciated to only a fraction of their face value in British money. Not surprisingly, British merchants who had to accept them felt cheated and complained. Parliament had responded in 1751 by forbidding further issues of legal tender paper money in New England. In the *Currency Act* of 1764, Parliament extended this restriction to the rest of the colonies, prohibiting all of them from printing their own legal tender paper money. Because the new restrictions came when most colonies were in an economic recession, Americans considered this step an especially burdensome attempt to curtail the assemblies' powers. To deprive them of their paper money was, in the words of one American, "downright Robbery." Worse, however, was yet to come.

THE SUGAR AND STAMP ACTS

In 1764, the British Parliament, under Prime Minister George Grenville, passed the American Revenue Act, commonly known as the *Sugar Act*. The main purpose of this act, as stated in its preamble, was "for improving the revenue of this kingdom." To generate funds, the Sugar Act and its accompanying legislation combined new and revised duties on colonial imports with strict provisions for collecting those duties. To prevent trade with other countries the Sugar Act legislation also lengthened the list of enumerated products—goods that could be sent only to England or within the empire—and required that ships carry elaborate new documents certifying the legality of their cargoes. A ship's captain could have his entire cargo seized if any of the complicated documents were out of order.

To enforce these cumbersome regulations, the British government continued to use the Royal Navy to seize smugglers' ships, a practice begun during the French and Indian War. It also ordered colonial customs collectors to discharge their duties personally, rather than through the use of easily bribed deputies. Responsibility for trying violations would (three years later) eventually rest in vice-admiralty courts in Boston, Philadelphia, and Charleston, which normally operated without a jury and were more likely to enforce trade restrictions.

In the spring of 1765, Parliament enacted another tax on Americans, the **Stamp Act**. This required that all valid legal documents, as well as newspapers, playing cards, and various other papers, bear a government-issued stamp for which there was a charge. The Sugar Act, though intended to raise revenue, appeared to fall within Britain's accepted authority to regulate commerce; the Stamp Act, by contrast, was the first internal tax (as opposed to an external trade duty) that Parliament had imposed on the colonies. Grenville, a lawyer, realized that it raised a constitutional issue: Did Parliament have the right to impose direct taxes on Americans when Americans had no elected representatives in Parliament? Following the principle of virtual representation—that members of Parliament served the interests of the nation as a whole, not just the locality from which they came—Grenville maintained that it did. Americans, he would find, vigorously disagreed. Nor were they without at least some support in Parliament. Colonel Isaac Barré, a member who had served in the colonies, spoke out against the Stamp Act. In one speech he referred to Americans as "Sons of Liberty," a label Americans soon would adopt for themselves.

American Reactions

The measures Britain took to solve its financial and administrative problems first puzzled, then shocked, and eventually outraged Americans. The colonists had emerged from the French and Indian War believing that they had done their fair share and more toward making Great Britain ruler of the greatest empire in the world, and they expected to be respected for their efforts. They were certain that as British-Americans they shared in the glory and enjoyed all the rights of Englishmen in England. The new restrictions and taxes accordingly hit them like a slap in the face.

CONSTITUTIONAL ISSUES

To Americans, it was self-evident that the British measures were unfair. It was difficult to contend, however, that the British authorities had no right to impose them. Then as now, the **British Constitution** was not a single written document. It consisted, rather, of the accumulated body of English law and custom, including acts of Parliament. How, then, could the colonists claim that an act of Parliament was unconstitutional?

Constitutional conflict surfaced early in Massachusetts over the issue of **writs of assistance**. These general search warrants, which gave customs officials in America the power to inspect virtually any building suspected of holding smuggled goods, had to be formally renewed at the accession of a new monarch. When George III became king in 1760, Massachusetts merchants—perhaps out of a fondness for smuggling as well as for liberty—sought to block the reissuance of the writs. Their attorney, James Otis Jr., arguing before the Massachusetts superior court, called the writs "instruments of slavery." Parliament, he maintained, lacked the authority to empower colonial courts to issue them. Otis lost, but "then and there," a future president of the United States, John Adams, would later write, "the child independence was born."

TAXATION AND THE POLITICAL CULTURE

The constitutional issue that most strained the bond between the colonies and the empire was taxation. British measures on other issues annoyed and disturbed Americans, but it was outrage over taxation—the most fundamental issue—that would be the midwife of American independence. Because Parliament had customarily refrained from taxing them, Americans assumed that it could not. To deprive them of the right to be taxed only by their own elected representatives was to deny them one of the most basic rights of Englishmen. If taxes were imposed "without our having a legal Representation where they are laid," one American asked, "are we not reduced from the Character of free Subjects to the miserable State of tributary Slaves?"

American views on taxation and the role of government reflected the influence of country ideology. As mentioned in Chapter 4, this opposition political philosophy emerged in England in the late seventeenth and early eighteenth centuries. Country ideology held that government power, no matter how necessary or to whom entrusted, is inherently aggressive and expansive. According to the English political philosopher John Locke, rulers have the authority to enforce law "only for the public good." When government exceeds this proper function, the people have the right to change it. But only in the last resort does this right justify revolution.

Country ideology stressed that in the English system of government, it was the duty of Parliament, in particular the House of Commons (which represented the people as a whole), to check the executive power of the Crown. The House of Commons' control of taxation enabled it to curb tyrannical rulers. When the Crown did its job properly, the Commons appropriated the necessary funds; when rulers infringed on the liberty of the people, the Commons restrained them by withholding taxes.

Such important responsibilities required that the people's representatives be men of sufficient property and judgment to make independent decisions. A representative should be "virtuous" (meaning public-spirited), and avoid political partisanship. A representative of the appropriate social status who exhibited the proper behavior, many assumed, was more qualified to understand and manage public affairs than his constituents and should accordingly be followed. But if he did not measure up, the people should be able to vote him out.

Country ideology appealed to Americans for a number of reasons. In part, colonists were drawn to it as they were to other English fashions. The works of Alexander Pope, the most widely read English poet of the eighteenth century and a proponent of a version of country ideology, appeared in many colonial libraries. So also did the works of two readable and prolific country ideology publicists, John Trenchard and Thomas Gordon, who collaborated in writing *Cato's Letters* (1720–1724) and the *Independent Whig* (1721). More important, country ideology's suspicion of those in power suited American politics on the local level, where rivalries and factionalism fostered distrust between those with and without power. And it emboldened the many Americans who feared they had no voice in the decisions of the government in London. Finally, with its insistence on the important political role of the propertied elite, country ideology appealed to America's local gentry. These ideas have had an enduring influence on American politics, surfacing even today in the suspicion of Washington and "big government," and they helped inspire the American Revolution.

PROTESTING THE TAXES

Given this ideological background, the initial American response to the Sugar Act was surprisingly mild. This was because not every colonist was equally affected by it. The speaker of the legislature in one southern colony commented that it was "much divided" over the effects of the act and would probably not petition against it. In New England, in contrast, the Sugar Act threatened to cut into the profits of the lucrative smuggling trade with the French West Indies. As a result, people there and in other northern colonies were quicker to recognize the act's implications. The legislative body that imposed it—Parliament—and whose constituents in England stood to gain from it, was not accountable to the people on whom it was imposed, the colonists. As one alarmed colonist noted, if his fellow Americans submitted to any tax imposed by Parliament, they were dumb and docile donkeys.

The size of the burden was less important than the principle involved. To Americans steeped in country ideology, direct taxation by London threatened to undercut the elected representatives' power of the purse and thereby remove the traditional first line of defense against a tyrannical executive. Eventually all the assemblies passed resolutions flatly maintaining that any parliamentary tax on America, including the Sugar Act, was unconstitutional. By the end of 1764, New York merchants had joined the artisans and merchants of Boston in a *nonimportation movement*, an organized boycott of British manufactured goods.

Unlike the Sugar Act, the Stamp Act had an equal impact throughout the colonies, and the response to it was swift and vociferous. Newspapers and pamphlets were filled with denunciations of the supposedly unconstitutional measure, and in taverns everywhere outraged patrons roundly condemned it. "The minds of the freeholders," wrote one observer, "were inflamed . . . by many a hearty damn of the Stamp Act over bottles, bowls and glasses." Parliament, Americans were convinced, did not represent them. The colonial legislatures were also quick to condemn the new measure. Virginia's lower house was the first to act, approving Patrick Henry's strong resolutions against the Stamp Act.

Shared outrage at the Stamp Act inspired the colonies to join in unified political action. The *Sons of Liberty*, a collection of loosely organized protest groups, put pressure on stamp distributors and British authorities. In August 1765, a Boston crowd led by shoemaker Ebenezer MacIntosh demolished property belonging to a revenue agent, and another mob sacked Lieutenant Governor Thomas Hutchinson's house. Later demonstrations organized by the Sons of Liberty in other cities were kept more peaceful with tighter discipline.

Members of the Sons of Liberty included people from all ranks of society. The leaders, however, among them Christopher Gadsden, came mostly from the middle and upper classes. Often pushed by more radical common people, some of them doubtless joined in the hope of protecting their own positions and interests. Indeed, in Charleston, slaves alarmed their masters and other white people when they paraded through the streets crying, "Liberty!"

Movement leaders were also concerned that disorderly behavior could discredit the American cause. Even the fiery Samuel Adams, one of the leading organizers of the protest in Boston, would later claim, "I am no friend to *Riots*." Still, he added, "when the People are oppressed," they will be "discontented, and they are not to be blamed."

Partly as a result of the growing unrest, leaders throughout the colonies determined to meet and agree on a unified response to Britain. As Gadsden observed at the time, "There ought to be no New England men, no New Yorker, etc. known on the Continent, but all of us Americans." Nine colonies eventually sent delegates to the *Stamp Act Congress*, which met in New York City in October 1765. A humorist in the South Carolina legislature, who had opposed sending anyone, observed that the gathering would produce a most unpalatable combination: New England would throw in fish and onions; the middle provinces, flax seed and flour; Virginia and Maryland, tobacco; North Carolina, pitch, turpentine, and tar; South Carolina, indigo and rice—and Georgia would sprinkle the whole with sawdust. "Such an absurd jumble will you make if you attempt to form [a] union among such discordant materials as the thirteen British provinces," he concluded. A quick-witted member of the assembly shot back that he would not choose his colleague for a cook but that the congress would prepare a dish fit for any king.

It did indeed. The congress adopted the ***Declaration of Rights and Grievances***, which denied Parliament's right to tax the colonies, and petitioned unsuccessfully both king and Parliament to repeal the Stamp and Sugar acts. As protests spread, the stamp distributors got the message and resigned, "for the welfare of the people." In some areas, Americans went about their business as usual without using stamped paper. In other places, they avoided activities that required taxed items. They also stepped up the boycott of British goods that had begun in response to the Sugar Act. British merchants, hurt by this economic pressure, petitioned Parliament for repeal of the Stamp Act, and a new ministry obliged them by rescinding it in March 1766.

The Aftermath of the Stamp Act Crisis

At this point, Americans were in no mood to accept any tax imposed by Parliament, and they misunderstood the ***Declaratory Act*** that accompanied the repeal of the Stamp Act. Intended to make Parliament's retreat more acceptable to its members, this act stated that Parliament had the right to "legislate for the colonies in all cases whatsoever." Americans assumed the Declaratory Act was a mere face-saving gesture. Unfortunately, it was more than that. As one colonist later observed, it created a "platform for the Invincible Reasoning from the Mouths of four and twenty pounders [cannons]."

A STRAINED RELATIONSHIP

The aftermath of the Stamp Crisis was growing strain between Parliament and the colonies. Most members of Parliament continued to believe that they represented everyone in the empire and that they could therefore tax people in the colonies as well as in England. Americans believed just as strongly that "in taxing ourselves and making Laws for our own internal government . . . we can by no means allow our Provincial legislatures to be subordinate to any legislative power on earth."

An exchange between British merchants and their American correspondents in the wake of the Stamp Act's repeal illustrates how far apart Englishmen and Americans had become. The British merchants lectured the Americans, enjoining them "to express filial duty and gratitude to your parent country." To which one Virginia planter tartly replied, "We rarely see anything from your side of the water free from the authoritative style of a master to a schoolboy." This, he observed, was more than "a little ridiculous."

Events likewise testified to continuing tensions between the two sides. When British authorities required Massachusetts to compensate those who had suffered damage in the Stamp Act rioting, the legislature complied but pardoned the rioters. In 1767, an irritated Parliament then passed an act suspending the New York legislature because it had not

A satirical British engraving from 1766 showing English politicians burying the Stamp Act, "born 1765 died 1766." The warehouses in the background symbolize the revival of trade with America.
The Granger Collection, N.Y.

complied with the Quartering Act of 1765. The New York legislature finally obeyed before the suspending act went into effect, and it remained in business.

REGULATOR MOVEMENTS

Growing strain was also evident on the local level with the emergence in 1766 of vigilante groups calling themselves *Regulators* in response to official corruption in North Carolina and lawlessness in South Carolina. North Carolina's western farmers were oppressed by high taxes, court costs, and debt resulting from the limited supply of money in circulation after the Currency Act. In South Carolina, outlaws roamed the back country stealing live-stock and raiding isolated houses. In neither colony did representation in the assemblies reflect the growing backcountry population and its pressing needs. As a result, the Regula-tors did by extralegal action what they couldn't do through legal channels—in North Carolina they closed courts and intimidated tax officials and in South Carolina they pur-sued outlaws and whipped people suspected of harboring them.

The activities of the Regulators brought them into conflict with the local elites in North and South Carolina, which were slow in redressing regulator grievances. British offi-cials made matters worse by doing the opposite of what was required. Instead of encourag-ing the assemblies to increase their western representation, they tried to limit their power by forbidding them to increase their size. As for the shortage of currency, they callously dis-missed "any possible local inconvenience" that might result.

Thanks to such help from London, as well as their own mistakes, a crisis confronted local authorities by 1767. In South Carolina, the assembly belatedly reapportioned itself, giving the backcountry some representation, and established courts for the area. But in North Carolina, peace returned only after fighting between the local militia and the Regulators killed twenty-nine men and wounded more than 150 on both sides. The rise of the Regulators demonstrated that while American leaders had to understand and respond to local conditions, British authorities remained inflexible.

The Townshend Crisis

After an unsuccessful attempt by the British to introduce a new collection of taxes, the Townshend duties, in 1767, a relatively quiet period followed until Britain made yet another attempt to enforce compliance with the one duty still on the books, the duty on tea.

TOWNSHEND'S PLAN

Charles Townshend became the leading figure in Britain's government in 1767. The *Townshend Duty Act* was based on Townshend's mistaken assumption that the colonists were willing to accept new duties or external taxes, but no direct, or internal, taxes like the Stamp Tax. The duties covered a number of items the colonists regularly imported—tea, paper, paint, lead, and glass. To make sure that the duties were collected, British authorities added a new board of customs commissioners for America and located its headquarters in Boston, the presumed home of many smugglers. To the alarm of the Americans, the new customs officials were far more diligent than their predecessors, going after wealthy Boston merchants like John Hancock, perhaps because he was so openly contemptuous of them. The officials seized Hancock's appropriately named vessel *Liberty* and accused him of smuggling. Hancock may indeed have violated the acts of trade at times, but in this case the accusations were apparently false. The incident sparked a riot in Boston during which a crowd on the waterfront roughed up members of the customs service. British authorities responded in 1768 by sending troops to Boston and maintaining them there for the next year and a half.

AMERICAN BOYCOTT

The Townshend duties, like the stamp tax, provoked resistance throughout the colonies. Rejecting the argument that duties were somehow different from taxes, John Dickinson, a wealthy lawyer who wrote under the pen name "A Farmer in Pennsylvania," asserted that a tax was a tax, whatever its form.

There was no equivalent to the Stamp Act Congress in response to the Townshend Act because British officials (acting through the colonial governors) barred the assemblies from sending delegates to such a meeting. Even so, Americans gradually organized an effective nonimportation movement. Many Americans signed subscription lists binding them, with the other signers, to buy only goods made in the colonies and nothing made in Great Britain. Handbills, like one urging "the Sons and Daughters of *LIBERTY*" to shun a particular Boston merchant, brought pressure to bear on uncooperative importers. To avoid imported English textiles, American women spun more thread and wove more cloth at home. Wearing homespun became a moral virtue, a sign of self-reliance, personal independence, and the rejection of "corrupting" English luxuries.

The nonimportation movement forged a sense of common purpose among all who participated in it—men and women, southern planters and northern artisans alike—giving them the sense of belonging to a larger community of fellow Americans. Although it was at this point more an imagined community than a political community, it was real enough and large enough to reduce imports from Britain by 40 percent after only one year.

By 1770, Britain was prepared to concede that the Townshend duties had been counterproductive because they interfered with British trade. When Parliament eventually repealed most of the Townshend articles, it left the duty on tea. This symbolic equivalent of the Declaratory Act served to assert Parliament's continuing right to tax the colonies.

THE BOSTON MASSACRE

Ironically, on the same day that the proposal to rescind most of the Townshend duties was introduced to Parliament—March 5, 1770—British troops fired on American civilians in Boston. This incident, which came to be known as the **Boston Massacre**, resulted from months of increasing friction between townspeople and the British troops stationed in the city. The townspeople complained that the soldiers insulted them, leered at women, and competed for scarce jobs. Samuel Adams recounted these real and imagined misdeeds in a column called "A Journal of the Times" that he circulated to other American cities. The hostility was so great, complained a British officer, that "twenty" soldiers could be "knocked down in the Streets" and nothing be heard of it, but if a soldier merely kicked a resident, "the Town is immediately in an Alarm."

The Boston Massacre occurred when angry and frightened British soldiers fired on a crowd that was pelting them with sticks and stones. Five men died, including Crispus Attucks—"that half Indian, half negro and altogether rowdy," as someone once called him—who has since become the most celebrated casualty of the incident. To preserve order, the troops withdrew from the city, but the damage had been done.

THE "QUIET PERIOD"

In the so-called Quiet Period that followed, no general grievance united all Americans. But in almost every colony, issues continued to simmer. Local circumstances produced the most spectacular confrontation in Rhode Island. The crew of a British revenue schooner, the *Gaspee*, had been patrolling Narragansett Bay, seizing smugglers and, it was said, stealing livestock and cutting down farmers' fruit trees for firewood. Thus when the *Gaspee* ran aground while chasing some American ships, Rhode Islanders got even. Led by John Brown, a local merchant, they boarded the vessel, shot its captain in the buttocks, putting him and his crew ashore, and burned the ship. The British government offered a reward for information about the incident but learned nothing. The British attempt to stamp out smuggling in the colonies was so heavy-handed that it offended the innocent more than it frightened the guilty.

Such incidents, and in particular the British threat to send Americans to England for trial, led American leaders to resolve to keep one another informed about British actions. Twelve colonies established **committees of correspondence** for this purpose, and Boston soon became the scene of a showdown between imperial authority and colonial resistance.

THE BOSTON TEA PARTY

During the Quiet Period, Americans drank smuggled (and therefore untaxed) Dutch tea. Partly as a result, the British East India Company, which had the exclusive right to distribute tea in the British Empire, nearly went bankrupt. Lord North, the prime minister, tried to rescue it with the *Tea Act of 1773*. This act permitted the company to ship tea from its warehouses in Britain without paying the duty normally collected there. The idea was to make its tea more competitive in price with the Dutch product and thereby induce Americans to buy it and simultaneously pay the old Townshend duty.

The colonists' response surprised British officials. What outraged most Americans was the attempt to trick them into paying the tax on tea. Thousands decided not to touch the stuff. Newspapers discussed its dangers to the body as well as to the body politic and offered recipes for substitutes. Many women rejected the tea and put pressure on others to do likewise, while schoolboys collected and burned tea leaves.

Thomas Hutchinson, who had been lieutenant governor of Massachusetts during the Stamp Act riots, was now the colony's royal governor. In most other cities, threats from the Sons of Liberty had convinced the captains of the tea ships to return to England without landing their cargo. Hutchinson, however, was determined to have the tea landed in Boston, and he barred the tea ships there from leaving. As a result, violence once again erupted in the city.

When the Sons of Liberty realized they could not force the ships to leave, they decided on dramatic action. On December 16, 1773, Samuel Adams reportedly told a large gathering at Old South Meeting House that it "could do nothing more to preserve the liberties of America." This remark was apparently a prearranged signal for what came to be known as the *Boston Tea Party*. War whoops immediately answered him from the street outside, and a well-organized band of men disguised as Indians raced aboard the tea ship *Dartmouth*, broke open 342 chests of tea, and heaved the contents in the harbor.

THE INTOLERABLE ACTS

The destruction of property in the Boston Tea Party shocked many Americans. British officials reacted even more strongly. The response in Parliament was to pass a series of repressive measures known as the *Coercive Acts*. The first of these, effective June 1, 1774, was the Boston Port Act, which closed the port of Boston to all incoming and outgoing traffic until the East India Company and the crown received payment for the dumped tea and its duties. The Administration of Justice Act, which followed, declared that an official who killed a colonist while performing his duties could be tried in England (where he would almost certainly receive sympathetic treatment) rather than in Massachusetts. The third measure, the Massachusetts Government Act, drastically modified that colony's charter of 1691, providing that the Crown would appoint members to the governor's council and limiting the number of town meetings that could be held without the governor's prior approval. A new Quartering Act declared that the troops under the governor's command could be lodged in virtually any uninhabited building.

On the same day that Parliament enacted these measures, it also passed the *Quebec Act*, which enlarged the boundaries of Quebec south to the Ohio River, provided for trial of civil cases without a jury, and recognized the Catholic Church, giving it the privileges it had enjoyed under the French. The colonists labeled the Quebec and Coercive Acts together as the *Intolerable Acts*.

The Road to Revolution

Americans considered the Intolerable Acts so threatening that they organized the *First Continental Congress* to respond to them. Congress renewed and took measures to enforce the nonimportation movement. These measures further divided those who supported British authorities and those who opposed them.

AMERICAN RESPONSE TO THE INTOLERABLE ACTS

Americans found the territorial, administrative, and religious provisions of the Quebec Act deeply disturbing. By giving Canada jurisdiction over lands north of the Ohio River that were claimed by Virginia, Connecticut, and Massachusetts, the Quebec Act deprived settlers of their hoped-for homesteads and speculators of their hoped-for profits, angering both. The religious provisions of the Quebec Act were ominous reminders of an attempt by Anglican clergymen during the 1760s to have a bishop appointed for America.

The Quebec Act accordingly "gave a General Alarm to all Protestants," whose ministers throughout the continent warned their congregations that they might be "bound by Popish chains."

The Boston Port Act arbitrarily punished innocent and guilty Bostonians alike. The Administration of Justice Act—which some with vivid imaginations dubbed the "Murder Act"—seemed to declare an open season on colonists, allowing crown officials to kill them without fear of punishment. The Massachusetts Government Act raised the more realistic fear that no colonial charter was safe. A Parliament that had stripped the Massachusetts legislature of an important power might equally decide to abolish the lower houses of all the colonies.

Nightmarish scenarios filled the colonial newspapers. One clergyman observed that the terms of the Coercive Acts were such that if someone were to "make water" on the door of the royal customs house, an entire colonial city "might be laid in Ashes." He undoubtedly knew that he exaggerated, but his words embodied real fear and anger. Trying to make an example of Boston, British authorities had taken steps that united Americans as nothing had ever done before.

THE FIRST CONTINENTAL CONGRESS

Leaders in most colonies wanted to organize a coordinated response and called for another meeting like the Stamp Act Congress. The colonies accordingly agreed to send delegates to a meeting in Philadelphia that came to be called the First Continental Congress, and in the end, all the colonies except Georgia were represented.

The First Continental Congress met at Carpenter's Hall in Philadelphia from September 5 to October 26, 1774, with fifty-five delegates present at one time or another. All were leading figures in their home colonies, but only a few knew members from elsewhere. Each colony had one vote, irrespective of the size of its delegation. Those who favored strong measures—like Samuel Adams and his cousin John, Patrick Henry, and Christopher Gadsden—prevailed. They persuaded most of their colleagues to endorse the *Suffolk Resolves*, which had been passed at a meeting held in Suffolk County (the site of Boston). These strongly worded resolves denounced the Coercive Acts as unconstitutional, advised the people to arm, and called for general economic sanctions against Britain. Learning of them, one British official told an American, "If these Resolves of your people are to be depended on, they have declared War against us."

THE CONTINENTAL ASSOCIATION

The Congress created the ***Continental Association*** to organize and enforce sanctions against the British. As a first step, the Association pledged Americans to cut off imports from Britain after December 1, 1774. If the dispute with Britain was not resolved by September 1775, the Association called for barring most exports to Britain and the West Indies. All who violated the terms of the association were to be considered "enemies of American liberty" and ostracized.

Congress also issued a declaration of rights and grievances summarizing its position. The declaration condemned most of the steps taken by British authorities since 1763 but "cheerfully" consented to trade regulations for the good of the whole empire. The Congress sent addresses to the people of America, to the inhabitants of Great Britain, and to the king. The address to the king asked him to use his "royal authority and interposition" to protect his loyal subjects in America.

The proceedings of the First Continental Congress revealed division as well as agreement among its delegates. All of the delegates believed that the Coercive Acts were unconstitutional, but they differed over how to resist them. Only a minority was prepared to take up arms against Britain. Most representatives tried to protect the interests of their own colonies. Some South Carolina delegates, in an early example of the sectional stubbornness that would culminate nearly a century later in the U.S. Civil War, threatened to walk out of the meeting unless the nonexportation agreement omitted rice, most of which went to northern Europe by way of Britain. To placate the Carolinians, northerners agreed to the exemption. But Gadsden was disgusted, feeling that these actions betrayed the spirit of united purpose that Patrick Henry had spoken of so stirringly earlier in the Congress: "The distinctions between Virginians, Pennsylvanians, New Yorkers and New Englanders are no more. I am not a Virginian, but an American."

POLITICAL DIVISIONS

In the wake of the First Continental Congress, Americans were forced to take sides for and against the Continental Association. But even such well-known radicals as Adams and Gadsden were far from advocating independence for the colonies. Throughout the pre-Revolutionary period, most colonists hoped and expected that imperial authorities would change their policy toward America. English history, Americans believed, was full of instances in which the resolute opposition of a free people forced oppressive ministries and tyrannical kings to back down. They were confident that it could happen again.

What Americans were divided over was the extent of Parliament's authority over them and the degree to which they could legitimately challenge its power. As British officials failed, with the passing of time, to accommodate American views of their rights, Americans began in increasing numbers to challenge London's control over them. The experience of James Wilson, a Pennsylvania lawyer, illustrates this shift. In *Considerations on the Nature and Extent of the Legislative Authority of the British Parliament* (published in 1774), Wilson writes that he set out to find a reasonable dividing line between those areas in which Parliament had legitimate authority over the colonies and those in which it did not. But the more he thought, the more he became convinced "that such a line does not exist" and that there can be "no medium between acknowledging and denying that power in all cases." Wilson therefore concluded that Parliament had no authority at all over the colonies.

During 1774 and early 1775, as the British-American confrontation grew more heated, lively debates raged in newspapers and pamphlets, and the colonists became increasingly polarized. In the last months before the outbreak of the American Revolution, the advocates of colonial rights began to call themselves **Whigs** and condemned their opponents as **Tories**. These traditional English party labels dated from the late seventeenth century, when the Tories had supported the accession of the Catholic King James II, and the Whigs had opposed it. By calling themselves Whigs and their opponents Tories (loyalist was a more accurate label), the advocates of colonial rights cast themselves as champions of liberty and their enemies as defenders of religious intolerance and royal absolutism.

Conclusion

All Americans, Whigs and loyalists alike, had considered themselves good British subjects. But Americans were a more diverse and more democratic people than the English. A considerably larger percentage of them could participate in government, and for all practical purposes, had been governing themselves for a long time.

British officials recognized the different character of American society and feared it might lead Americans to reject British controls. But the steps they took to prevent this from happening had the opposite effect.

From Britain's perspective, the measures it took in the wake of the French and Indian War were a reasonable response to its administrative and financial problems in the colonies. Taken one by one from the colonists' perspective, however, they were a rain of blows that finally impelled them to rebel. No wonder that Americans, whose political ideology had already made them wary of governmental power, believed that they were the victims of a conspiracy in London to deprive them of their liberty. That Parliament should be a party to this presumed conspiracy particularly shocked and offended them.

Yet Americans probably should not have been surprised at Parliament's role. Indeed, both Parliament and the colonial assemblies were doing what similar bodies throughout Europe were also doing at roughly the same time—asserting their powers and defending their liberties against encroachments from above and below.

The attempts to protect their accustomed autonomy first brought the colonial assemblies into conflict with Parliament. Asserting their rights led the individual colonies to cooperate more among themselves. This in turn led to increasingly widespread resistance, then to rebellion, and finally to revolution. Moving imperceptibly from one stage to the next, Americans grew conscious of their common interests and their differences from the English. They became aware, as Benjamin Franklin would later write, of the need to break "through the bounds, in which a dependent people had been accustomed to think, and act" so that they might "properly comprehend the character they had assumed."

Review Questions

1. What do Eliza Farmar's letters tell us about the crisis over dutied tea in 1773 and 1774? What makes her increasingly sympathetic to the colonial position?

2. How did the British victory in the French and Indian War affect the relations between Native Americans and white settlers? Between British authorities and Americans?

3. How did the expectations of American and British authorities differ in 1763? Why were new policies offensive to Americans?

4. How was stationing British troops in America related to British taxation of the colonists? Why did the colonists object to taxation by Parliament?

5. How did Americans oppose the new measures? Who participated in the various forms of resistance? How effective were the different kinds of resistance?

6. What led to the meeting of the First Continental Congress? What did the Congress achieve?

The War
for Independence

1774–1783

What developments led to mounting tensions between the colonies and Britain?

What was the mood of the colonists leading up to the Declaration of Independence?

What were some of the key differences between the British and American forces?

What were the major turning points of the war?

What were the terms of the Peace of Paris?

What were the social effects of the war?

★

Headquarters, Valley Forge
January 14, 1778

I barely hinted to you my dearest Father my desire to augment the Continental Forces from an untried Source. . . . I would solicit you to cede me a number of your able bodied men Slaves, instead of leaving me a fortune. I would bring about a twofold good, first I would advance those who are unjustly deprived of the Rights of Mankind to a State which would be a proper Gradation between abject Slavery and perfect Liberty and besides I would reinforce the Defenders of Liberty with a number of gallant Soldiers. . . . If I could obtain authority for the purpose I would have a Corps of such men trained, uniformly clad, equip'd and ready in every respect to act at the opening of the next Campaign.

February 2, 1778

My Dear Father,

The more I reflect upon the difficulties and delays which are likely to attend the completing our Continental Regiments, the more anxiously is my mind bent upon the Scheme which I lately communicated to you. . . . I was aware of having that monster popular Prejudice open-mouthed against me . . . [and] of being obliged to combat the arguments and perhaps the intrigues of interested persons. But zeal for the public Service and an ardent desire to assert the rights of humanity determined me to engage in this arduous business. . . .

You seem to think my dear Father, that men reconciled by long habit to the miseries of their Condition would prefer their ignominious bonds to the untasted Sweets of Liberty, especially when offer'd upon the terms which I propose. I confess indeed the minds of this unhappy species must be debased by a Servitude from which they can hope for no Relief but Death and that every motive to action but Fear must be also nearly extinguished in them. But do you think they are so perfectly moulded to their State as to be insensible that a better exists? Will the galling comparison between themselves and their masters leave them unenlightened in this respect? Can their Self-Love be so totally annihilated as not frequently to induce ardent wishes for a change? ... I am tempted to believe that this trampled people have so much human left in them, as to be capable of aspiring to the rights of men by noble exertions, if some friend to mankind would point the Road, and give them prospect of Success.

I have long deplored the wretched State of these men and considered in their history, the bloody wars excited in Africa to furnish America with Slaves. The Groans of despairing multitudes toiling for the Luxuries of Merciless Tyrants. I have had the pleasure of conversing with you sometimes upon the means of restoring them to their rights. When can it be better done than when their enfranchisement may be made conducive to the Public Good.

—John Laurens

Henry Laurens Papers, vol. 12, pp. 305, 309–392.

JOHN LAURENS wrote these letters to his father, Henry, at one low point of the American Revolution, when victory seemed remote. The letters reveal much about the war and the aspirations and limitations of the Revolutionary generation. Henry, a wealthy slaveholder from South Carolina, was president of the Continental Congress; his son John was an aide to General Washington while the Continental Army wintered at Valley Forge.

John, then 23 years old, had been born in South Carolina but educated for the most part in Geneva and London, where he had been exposed to the progressive currents of the Enlightenment. Among these were compassion for the oppressed and the conviction that slavery should be abolished. The war for independence was a cause that appealed deeply to him. American republicanism combined a New Whig distrust of central authority with a belief in a government rooted in a virtuous citizenry. Clinging to this ideology, Americans at first expected to defeat the British Army with a citizens' militia, but they learned that they needed a professional fighting force of their own. With vital French assistance, the new American army triumphed, but the Continental Army was often critically short of soldiers.

Laurens sought to fill this need by enlisting slaves in the Army. This would also provide blacks with a stepping stone to freedom. However, he failed to convince legislatures in the Deep South to enroll black troops in exchange for their freedom.

His idealistic quest for social justice ended in South Carolina, where he died in one of the last skirmishes of the war.

The Outbreak of War and the Declaration of Independence, 1774–1776

After the Boston Tea Party, both the British and the Americans knew that they were approaching a crisis. A British officer in Massachusetts commented in late 1774 that "it is thought by every body here" that British forces would soon have "to take the field." "The people in general are very enraged," he explained, and some would "defend what they call their Liberties," to the death. Many Americans also expected a military confrontation but continued to hope that the king would not "reason with us only by the roar of his Cannon."

MOUNTING TENSIONS

In May 1774, General Thomas Gage, the commander in chief of the British army in America, replaced Thomas Hutchinson as governor of Massachusetts. After Gage dissolved the Massachusetts legislature, the General Court, it defied him by assembling anyway. Calling itself the Provincial Congress, the legislature in October 1774 appointed an emergency executive body, the **Committee of Safety**, headed by John Hancock, which began stockpiling weapons and organizing militia volunteers. Some localities had already provided for the formation of special companies of **Minute Men**, who were to be ready at "a minute's warning in Case of an alarm."

Enforcing the Continental Association's boycott of British goods, local committees sometimes assaulted suspected loyalists and destroyed their property. The increasingly polarized atmosphere, combined with the drift toward military confrontation, drove a growing wedge between American loyalists and the patriot anti-British American Whigs.

THE LOYALISTS' DILEMMA

Loyalists and Whigs began to part company in earnest during the fall and winter of 1774–1775 as the threat of war mounted. Most loyalists were farmers, officeholders, and professionals, and many were recent immigrants to the colonies, who felt more secure under the protection of the Crown than with more established Americans. Including those who did not actually fight, the loyalists numbered close to half a million men and women—some 20 percent of the colonies' free population.

BRITISH COERCION AND CONCILIATION

The British parliamentary elections in the fall of 1774 strengthened Prime Minister Lord North's hand and enabled Parliament to prohibit the New England (and later other) colonies from trading outside the British Empire or sending their ships to the North Atlantic fishing grounds. Meanwhile, in a gesture of appeasement, Parliament endorsed Lord North's **Conciliatory Proposition** pledging not to tax the colonies if they would voluntarily contribute to the defense of the empire. Had it specified a maximum colonial contribution and had it been offered ten years earlier, the colonists might have found the Conciliatory Proposition acceptable. Now it was too late. North's government, in any case, had already sent orders to General Gage to take decisive action against the Massachusetts rebels. These orders triggered the first clash between British and American forces.

THE BATTLES OF LEXINGTON AND CONCORD

Gage received his orders on April 14, 1775. On the night of April 18, he assembled seven hundred men on the Boston Common and marched them toward the little towns of Lexington and Concord, some 20 miles away (see Map 6–1). Their mission was to arrest rebel leaders Samuel Adams and John Hancock (then staying in Lexington) and to destroy the military supplies the Committee of Safety had assembled at Concord. Patriots in Boston got wind of the troop movements and sent out riders—one of them the silversmith Paul Revere—to warn their fellows. Adams and Hancock escaped.

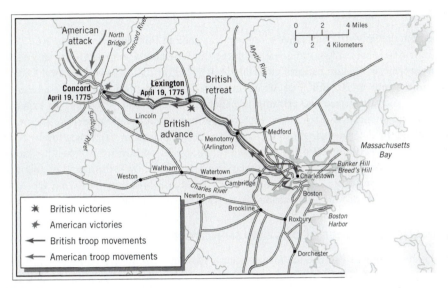

MAP 6–1
The Battles of Lexington and Concord   This map shows the area around Boston, Massachusetts, where in April 1775 British and American forces fought the first military engagements of the Revolution.

WAS BRITAIN'S early strategy against the colonists effective?

When the British soldiers reached Lexington at dawn, they found about seventy armed militiamen drawn up in formation on the village green. Their precise intentions are not clear. Outnumbered ten to one, they probably did not plan to begin a fight. More likely, they were there in a show of defiance.

Months of mounting tension exploded on the Lexington green. A British major ordered the militia to disperse. They were starting to obey when a shot cracked through the dawn stillness. No one now knows who fired. The British responded with a volley that killed or wounded eighteen Americans.

The British troops pressed on to Concord and burned what few supplies the Americans had not been able to hide. When their rear guard came under patriot fire at Concord's North Bridge, the British panicked. As they retreated to Boston, patriot Minute Men and other militia harried them from both sides of the road. By the time the column reached safety, 273 British soldiers were either dead, wounded, or missing. The four thousand Americans who had shot at them along the way suffered nearly one hundred dead, wounded, and missing.

The speed with which distant colonies heard about the outbreak of fighting at the *Battles of Lexington and Concord* suggests both the importance Americans attached to it and the extraordinary efforts patriots made to spread word of it. Everywhere, news of Lexington and Concord spurred Whigs into action. The shots fired that April morning would, in the words of the nineteenth-century Concord philosopher and poet Ralph Waldo Emerson, be "heard round the world." They signaled the start of the American Revolution.

THE SECOND CONTINENTAL CONGRESS, 1775–1776

By the time the Second Continental Congress convened in Philadelphia on May 10, 1775, it had a war on its hands. Assuming leadership of the rebellion, Congress in the succeeding months became, in effect, a national government. It called for the patchwork of local forces to be organized into the Continental Army, authorized the formation of a navy, established a post office, and authorized the printing of paper continental dollars to meet its expenses. Denying Parliament's claim to govern the colonies but not yet ready to declare themselves independent, the delegates sought to preserve their ties to Britain by expressing loyalty to the crown. In the *Olive Branch Petition*, addressed to George III on July 5, they asked the king to protect his American subjects from the military actions ordered by Parliament. The following day, Congress approved the Declaration of the Causes and Necessity of Taking Up Arms, asserting the resolve of American patriots "to die freemen, rather than to live slaves."

COMMANDER IN CHIEF GEORGE WASHINGTON

To take command of the patriot forces around Boston—the newly named Continental Army—Congress turned to George Washington. John Adams, a Whig leader from Massachusetts, selected the Virginian. Realizing that this would help transform a local quarrel in New England into a continental conflict, Adams also expected Washington's leadership to help attract recruits from Virginia, which was then the most populous colony.

Washington was the ideal person for the job. Some of his contemporaries had quicker minds and broader educations; Washington, however, was blessed with good judgment, a profound understanding of both the uses and the limitations of power, and a quiet air of authority. In short, he had the gift of command. He soon also realized that the fate of the patriot cause depended on the survival of the army. The troops revered him. In a crisis, wrote a man who served under him, "his likeness was worth more . . . than the British would have given for his person"—presumably a great deal.

EARLY FIGHTING

General Gage, finding himself besieged in Boston after the fighting at Lexington and Concord, decided to seize and fortify territory south of Boston, where his cannons could command the harbor. But the Americans seized high ground first, entrenching themselves on Breeds Hill north of town. On June 17, 1775, Gage sent 2,200 well-trained soldiers to drive the 1,700 patriot men and boys from their new position. The British succeeded, but at great cost. In three assaults, they suffered more than a thousand casualties. The Americans, who retreated when they ran short of gunpowder, lost just under four hundred dead or wounded. One glum British officer observed afterward that another such victory "would have ruined us." Misnamed for another hill nearby, this encounter has gone down in history as the *Battle of Bunker Hill*.

During the winter of 1775–1776, the Americans dragged some sixty cannons 300 miles through snow and over mountains from Fort Ticonderoga to Boston, mounting them overlooking Boston harbor, and putting the British in an indefensible position. The British then evacuated Boston and moved their troops to Halifax, Nova Scotia. New England was for the moment secure for the patriots. Initial fighting in the South also went well for the patriots, who defeated loyalist forces, who included slaves who had been promised their freedom if they fought for the Loyalist cause, at Great Bridge, near Norfolk, and Moore's

This portrait of George Washington appears in multiple versions depicting the victorious general against different backgrounds, including the battles of Princeton and Yorktown. The painter, Charles Willson Peale, served under Washington at Princeton, and the French commander at Yorktown, the Count de Rochambeau, took an appropriate version home with him in 1783.

Peale, Charles Willson (1741–1827). (after): George Washington after the battle of Princeton, January 3, 1777. 1779. Oil on canvas, 234.5x155 cm. Inv.:MV 4560. Photo: Gerard Blot. Chateaux de Versailles et de Trianon, Versailles, France. Reunion des Musees Nationaux/Art Resource, NY.

Creek Bridge in North Carolina. In June 1776, patriot forces also repulsed a large British expedition sent to capture Charleston, South Carolina.

In contrast, an attempt to win Canada to the patriot side met with disaster. Two American armies attacked in late 1775. One quickly captured Montreal. The other, under Benedict Arnold, approached Quebec through the Maine wilderness in the face of great hardships. Linking up outside heavily fortified Quebec, the American commanders attacked the city on December 31. The assault, followed by the Siege of Quebec, failed. Canada remained a British province.

INDEPENDENCE

The stunning American successes in New England and the South in late 1775 and early 1776 bolstered the patriots' confidence.

In August 1775, King George III rejected Congress's Olive Branch Petition. Instead, he issued a proclamation declaring the colonies in rebellion and denying them his protection. In December, Parliament barred all exports from the American colonies. These aggressive actions, especially the king's, persuaded many colonists to abandon their loyalty to the crown. More and more, Whigs began to think seriously of declaring full independence from Britain.

At this critical moment, a ne'er-do-well Englishman, recently arrived on American soil, gave the cause of independence a powerful boost. Thomas Paine was by trade a corsetmaker— and a twice-fired tax collector. Also a man of radical ideas that he expressed forcefully in the everyday English of ordinary people, he became a powerful polemicist for the American cause. In his pamphlet *Common Sense*, published in Philadelphia in January 1776, Paine denounced King George and made the case for independence. He ridiculed the absurdity of "supposing a continent to be perpetually governed by an island," and described the king as "the Royal Brute" whose tyranny should be thrown off. Simple common sense, Paine concluded, dictated that "'TIS TIME TO PART."

• C H R O N O L O G Y •

1775 April 19: Battles of Lexington and Concord.
May 10: Second Continental Congress meets.
June 17: Battle of Bunker Hill.
December 31: American attack on Quebec.

1776 January 9: Thomas Paine's *Common Sense*.
July 4: Declaration of Independence.
September 15: British take New York City.
December 26: Battle of Trenton.

1777 January 3: Battle of Princeton.
September 11: Battle of Brandywine Creek.
October 17: American victory at Saratoga.
Runaway inflation begins.
Continental Army winters at Valley Forge.

1778 February 6: France and the United States sign an alliance.
June 17: Congress refuses to negotiate with British peace commissioners.
July 4: George Rogers Clark captures British post in the Mississippi Valley.

December 29: British capture Savannah.

1779 June 21: Spain declares war on Britain.
Americans devastate the Iroquois country.
September 23: John Paul Jones captures the British ship *Serapis*.

1780 May 12: Fall of Charleston, South Carolina.
October 7: Americans win Battle of Kings Mountain.
Nathanael Greene takes command in the South.

1781 January 17: Americans defeat British at Battle of Cowpens.
March 15: Battle of Guilford Court House.
October 19: Cornwallis surrenders at Yorktown.

1783 March 15: Washington quells the Newburgh "Conspiracy."
September 3: Peace of Paris signed.
November 21: British begin evacuating New York.

Common Sense, which promptly sold more than 100,000 copies throughout the colonies, helped predispose Americans toward independence. Tactical considerations also led patriot leaders toward a formal separation from Great Britain. Such a move would make it easier for America to gain desperately needed aid from foreign countries, especially from England's ancient enemy, France. Declaring independence would also give the local political elites leading the resistance to British rule a solid legal basis for their newly claimed authority.

On June 7, 1776, Virginian Richard Henry Lee introduced in Congress a resolution stating that the united colonies "are, and of right ought to be, free and independent States." Postponing a vote on the issue, Congress appointed a committee to draw up a declaration of independence. The committee turned to a young Virginian named Thomas Jefferson to compose the first draft. "You can write ten times better than I," John Adams supposedly told Jefferson. When the committee presented the document to Congress and it became clear that the majority favored independence, the Pennsylvania and South Carolina delegations switched sides in favor of it, and the New York delegation decided to abstain. Thus when Congress voted on the resolution for independence on July 2, 1776, it was approved unanimously by all voting delegations. After further tinkering with the wording, Congress officially approved the **Declaration of Independence** on July 4, 1776.

Congress intended the declaration to be a justification for America's secession from the British Empire. Jefferson later maintained that he did not write any more than what everyone was thinking. The political theory that lies behind the declaration is known as the **contract theory of government**. Developed by the late seventeenth-century English philosopher John Locke and others, the contract theory maintains that legitimate government rests on an agreement between the people and their rulers. The people are bound to obey their rulers only so long as the rulers offer them protection. Jefferson's prose, however, transformed what might have been a bland statement into one of history's great assertions of human rights.

The Declaration of Independence consists of a magnificently stated opening assumption, two premises, and a powerful conclusion. The opening assumption is that all men are created equal, that they therefore have equal rights, and that they can neither give up these rights nor allow them to be taken away. The first premise—that people establish governments to protect their fundamental rights to life, liberty, and property—is a restatement of contract theory. (With a wonderful flourish reflecting the Enlightenment's optimism about human potential, Jefferson changed "property" to "the pursuit of happiness.") The second premise is a long list of charges meant to justify the Americans' rejection of their hitherto legitimate ruler. Then follows the dramatic conclusion: Americans can rightfully overthrow King George's rule and replace it with something more satisfactory.

Historians have spilled oceans of ink debating Jefferson's use of the expression "all men." Almost certainly he was thinking in the abstract and meant "humanity in general." In practice, of course, many people were excluded from full participation in eighteenth-century American society. Women, propertyless white men, and free black men had no formal political rights and limited legal rights, and slaves enjoyed no rights at all. (Although himself a slaveowner, Jefferson was deeply troubled by American slavery. He had wanted to include a denunciation of the slave trade among the charges against George III in the Declaration of Independence, but Congress took it out, believing that to blame the king for this inhumane business would appear hypocritical.) But if the words "all men are created equal" had limited practical meaning in 1776, they have ever since confronted Americans with a moral challenge.

REPUBLICANISM

Americans reacted to news of the Declaration of Independence with mixed emotions. There was rejoicing as orators read the declaration to great crowds. But even many who favored independence worried how Americans would govern themselves. Most Whigs, animated by the political ideology known as *republicanism*, thought a republican government was best suited to American society.

Republicanism held that self-government—either directly by the citizens of a country or indirectly by their elected representatives—provided a more reliable foundation for the good society and individual freedom than rule by kings. Thus drawing on contract theory, as in the Declaration of Independence, republicanism called for government by consent of the governed. Drawing on country ideology, it was suspicious of excessively centralized government and insistent on the need for virtuous, public-spirited citizenry. Republicanism therefore helped give the American Revolution a moral dimension.

But other than a state that was not ruled by a hereditary king, what was a republic? Americans had at hand a recent example of a republic in the English Civil War of the mid-seventeenth century, in which English Puritans had for a time replaced the monarchy with a republican "Commonwealth," dedicated to advancing the "common weal," or common good. Some New Englanders, spiritual descendants of the Puritans, considered the Commonwealth to have been a noble experiment and regarded the American Revolution as another chance to establish a republic of the godly. "When the mere Politician weighs the Danger or Safety of his Country," warned one clergyman, "he computes them in Proportion to its Fortresses, Arms, Money, Provisions, Numbers of Fighting Men, and its Enemies." But, the clergyman continued, the "Christian Patriot" calculates them "by its Numbers of Sinful or praying People, and its Degrees of Holiness or Vice." Such language recalled the Great Awakening; it reached beyond the upper classes who had been directing resistance to the British and mobilized ordinary people for what their ministers repeatedly assured them was a just war against sin and despotism.

The Combatants

Republican theory mistrusted professional armies as the instruments of tyrants. A free people, republicans insisted, relied for defense on their own patriotism. When individual or community rights were in danger, free men should grab their muskets from over the fireplace, assemble as the local militia, take care of the problem, and go home. But militiamen, as one American general observed, had trouble coping with "the shocking scenes of war" because they were not "steeled by habit or fortified by military pride." In real battles, they often proved unreliable. Americans therefore faced a hard choice: develop a professional army or lose the war. In the end, they did what they had to do. While state militias continued to offer support, it was the disciplined forces of the *Continental Army* that won the crucial battles.

PROFESSIONAL SOLDIERS

Washington tightened things up in the new Continental Army. Eventually, he prevailed on Congress to adopt stricter regulations and to require enlistments for three years or the duration of the war. Although he used militia effectively, his consistent aim was to turn the Continental Army into a disciplined force that could defeat the British in the large engagements of massed troops characteristic of eighteenth-century European warfare. Guerrilla fighters shooting from behind trees like "savages" had their place in the American war effort, but they could never win a decisive, formal battle. And only such a "civilized" victory would impress the other European powers and establish the legitimacy of the United States.

Many soldiers of fortune, as well as a few idealists, offered their services to American representatives in Europe. France's 19-year-old Marquis de Lafayette was one of the youngest, wealthiest, and most idealistic. Two Poles, Tadeusz Kosciuszko, an engineer, and Kazimierz Pulaski, a cavalry commander mortally wounded at the Battle of Savannah in 1779, also rendered good service. Most useful of all, probably, was Baron von Steuben. His title was new, but he had genuine experience in the Prussian army, continental Europe's best. He knew how to get along with American soldiers by explaining the reasons for his orders. He became the Continental Army's drillmaster, and thanks partly to him, Washington's troops increasingly came to resemble their disciplined European counterparts.

The British troops—and the nearly thirty thousand German mercenaries (Americans called them "Hessians") whom the British government also employed—offered Americans the clearest model of a professional army. Most enlisted men did come from the lower classes and from economically depressed areas, but many also had skills. Most British troops carried the "Brown Bess" musket. With bayonet attached, it was almost 6 feet long and weighed over 16 pounds. In battle, soldiers usually stood close together in lines three deep. They were expected to withstand bombardment without flinching, fire on command in volleys, charge with the bayonet, and use their heavy musket stock (the wooden end) to crush the skulls of any wounded enemy they strode over.

Military life was tough. On the march, seasoned troops carrying 60-pound packs normally covered about 15 miles a day but could go 30 miles in a "forced" march. In all weather conditions, they wore heavy woolen uniforms dyed bright red for visibility on smoke-filled battlefields (hence their nickname "Redcoats"). They were frequently undernourished, however, and many more died of disease than of injury in battle. Medical care was, by modern standards, primitive: Treatments for illness included bleeding and purging (induced vomiting and diarrhea). Serious arm or leg wounds usually meant amputation, without antiseptics or anesthetics, and often proved fatal.

Severe discipline held soldiers in line. Striking an officer or deserting could bring death; lesser offenses usually incurred a beating. Several hundred lashes, "well laid on" with the notorious cat-o'-ninetails (a whip with multiple cords, each ending in a nasty little knot or a metal ball), were not uncommon.

Soldiers amused themselves with gambling (despite regulations against it) and drinking. Perhaps two-thirds of the Redcoats were illiterate, and they all suffered from loneliness and boredom. Camaraderie and a legendary loyalty to their regiments sustained them.

After the winter of 1777–1778, conditions in the Continental Army came to resemble those of the British army. Like British regulars, American recruits tended to be low on the social scale. The chances for talented enlisted men to win an officer's commission were greater in the Continental Army than the British army. And despite their ragged uniforms, they carried themselves like soldiers. Indeed, Continental soldiers frequently had little more than "their ragged shirt flaps to cover their nakedness," and more than once their bare marching feet left bloody tracks in the snow.

Both British and American authorities had trouble supplying their troops. Both sides suffered from bureaucratic inefficiencies, but the fundamental problems of each were different. The British had plenty of hard-coin money with a stable value, which many American merchants and farmers were happy to take in payment for supplies. But the British had to rely mostly on supplies shipped to them from the British Isles. The Continental Army, in contrast, had to pay for supplies in paper money, both Continental dollars and state-issued currency, whose value sank steadily as the war progressed.

Feeling themselves outcasts from an uncaring society, the professional soldiers of the Continental Army developed a community of their own. The soldiers were "as strict a band of brotherhood as Masons," one later wrote, and their spirit kept them together in the face of misery. Attempts at mutiny in Washington's camp were few and largely unsuccessful.

Occasionally, American officers let their disgruntlement get out of hand. The most notorious such case was that of Benedict Arnold, a general who compiled a distinguished record during the first three years of the war but then came to feel himself shabbily treated by Congress and his superiors. Seeking better rewards for his abilities, he offered to surrender the strategic fort at West Point (which he commanded) to the enemy; before he could act, however, his plot was discovered, and he fled to the British, serving with them until the end of the war. Among Americans, his name became a synonym for traitor.

What was perhaps the most serious expression of army discontent—one that threatened the future of republican institutions and civilian government in the United States—occurred near Newburgh, New York, in March 1783, after the fighting was over. During the war, Congress had promised officers a pension of half pay for life (the custom in Great Britain), but now many veterans demanded instead full pay for six years. When Congress failed to grant real assurances that *any* pay would be forthcoming, hotheaded young officers called a meeting that could have led to an armed uprising and military coup. General Washington, in a dramatic speech, subtly warned the men of all that they might lose by insubordination. A military coup would "open the flood Gates of Civil discord" and "deluge" the nation in blood; loyalty now, he said, would be "one more distinguished proof" of their patriotism. With the fate of the Revolution and the honor of the army hanging apparently in the balance, the movement collapsed. The officers and politicians behind the "conspiracy" were only bluffing, using the threat of a discontented army to frighten the states into granting Congress the power (which it then lacked) to levy taxes so it would have the funds to pay the army.

WOMEN IN THE CONTENDING ARMIES

Women accompanied many units on both sides, as was common in eighteenth-century warfare. A few were prostitutes. Most were the married or common-law consorts of ordinary soldiers. These women "camp followers" cooked and washed for the troops, occasionally helped load artillery, and provided most of the nursing care. A certain number in a company were subject to military orders and were authorized to draw rations and pay. The role of these women found its way into American folklore in the legend of Molly Pitcher (perhaps Mary Ludwig Hays, the wife of a Continental artillery sergeant), who heroically carried water to gunners to cool them and their overheated guns at the Battle of Monmouth Court House in 1778.

AFRICAN-AMERICAN AND NATIVE AMERICAN
PARTICIPATION IN THE WAR

On June 30, 1779, the British commander in chief Sir Henry Clinton promised to allow slaves who fled from rebel owners to join the royal troops to "follow . . . any Occupation" they wished. Hedged as this promise of freedom was, news of it spread quickly among the slave communities, and late in the war enough black people flocked to the British army in South Carolina and Georgia to make feeding and housing them a serious problem. The British shared the racial prejudices of many Americans, however, and despite their efforts to recruit African Americans, they were reluctant to arm them. Instead, the British put most of the ex-slaves to work as agricultural or construction workers (many of the free and enslaved black people accompanying American troops were similarly employed). A few relatively well-equipped black British dragoons (mounted troops), however, saw some combat in South Carolina, much to the horror of local Whigs.

Approximately 5,000 African Americans fought against the British and for American independence, hundreds of them in the Continental Army. Many were freemen from Massachusetts and Rhode Island. Several free black men served among the defenders at Bunker Hill, and at least one distinguished himself sufficiently for his commander to commend him as "an experienced officer as well as an excellent soldier." But the idea of arming African Americans was not well received in the South.

Many Indians also favored the British. To Native Americans, the key issue of the American Revolution, as well as in most disputes with white settlers, was about their land. Many Indian peoples, including the Cherokees, decided that it was in their interest to back the British. Their aid mainly took the form of attacks on white frontier settlements. Usually they did not tell the British in advance what they were planning to do. Thus in one notorious incident, an Indian attack in the Hudson River Valley resulted in the mistaken scalping of Jane McCrae, the fiancé of a British officer. Whig propagandists exploited this tragedy to the fullest. Because they could not control the Indians, the British regarded their native allies as a liability as well as an asset and seldom made unrestricted use of them. Other Native Americans, such as the Oneidas and the Tuscaroras, however, joined the Americans.

The War in the North, 1776–1777

The Revolutionary War can be divided into three phases. In the first, from the outbreak of fighting in 1775 to 1778, most of the important battles took place in New England, New York, New Jersey, and Pennsylvania. During these years, the Americans faced the British alone. But in 1778, France entered the war on the American side, opening the second phase of the war. Fighting in the second phase would rage from 1778 to 1781 mainly in the South, at sea, and on the western frontier. The third phase of the war, from late 1781 to 1783, saw little actual fighting. With American victory ensured, attention shifted to the diplomatic maneuvering leading up to the Treaty of Paris (1783), which ended the war and recognized American independence.

THE BRITISH ARMY HESITATES

During the first phase of the war, the British concentrated on subduing New England, the hotbed of what they saw as "rebellious principles." Replacing General Gage, the government appointed Sir William Howe as commander in chief of British forces and his brother, Richard Howe, as admiral of the naval forces in North American waters. New York City had been the headquarters of the British army during the late colonial period, and the Howes decided to make it their base of operations. In August 1776, the Howes landed troops on Long Island, and in the Battle of Brooklyn Heights they quickly drove the American forces deployed there from Brooklyn Heights and back to Manhattan Island.

In the ensuing weeks, British forces overwhelmed Washington's forces, driving them out of Manhattan and then, moving north, clearing them from the area around the city at the Battle of White Plains. But the Howes were hesitant to deal a crushing blow, and the Americans were able to retreat across New Jersey into Pennsylvania. The American cause seemed lost, however; Congress fled from Philadelphia to Baltimore, and the Continental Army almost melted away.

On Christmas night, Washington led his forces back across the icy Delaware from Pennsylvania and, in the Battle of Trenton, launched an unorthodox surprise attack on a garrison of Hessian mercenaries at Trenton, New Jersey, on the morning of December 26. Still in the midst of their Christmas celebrations, the Hessians quickly surrendered. A week later, in the Battle of Princeton, Washington overwhelmed a British force at Princeton, New Jersey. Thereafter, Washington withdrew to winter quarters in Morristown, New Jersey, and the Howes made no further effort to pursue him. Both sides suspended operations until the spring.

The victories at Trenton and Princeton boosted morale and saved the American cause. But why did the Howes not annihilate the Continental Army while they had the chance? Clearly, they wanted to regain loyal subjects, not alienate them. But if they had inflicted a crushing defeat on the Americans, they would have risked making them permanent enemies of British rule. By the time it later became apparent that this cautious strategy was not working and the Howes were replaced with more aggressive commanders, the British had lost their best chance to win the war.

THE YEAR OF THE HANGMAN

Contemporaries called 1777 the Year of the Hangman because the triple sevens suggested a row of gallows. Living up to its ominous name, it was indeed a crucial year for the American cause.

The British began the year by mounting a major effort to end the rebellion. Their strategy was to send a force south from Canada down the Hudson River to link up with the Howes in New York City, separate New England from the rest of the states, and then crush the rebellion in that most recalcitrant region. Unfortunately, there was no effort to coordinate strategy between the forces advancing from Canada and the forces under the command of the Howes in New York. Thus in the end, poorly planned, poorly executed, and unsupported from the South, the campaign ended in disaster for the British.

Some five thousand Redcoats and three thousand German mercenaries assembled in Canada during the winter of 1776–1777 under the command of the jaunty, high-living, and popular "Gentleman Johnny" Burgoyne. The army finally set off in June with 1,500 horses hauling its heavy artillery and ponderous supply train. Crossing Lake Champlain, Burgoyne's army on July 5 recaptured Fort Ticonderoga, but success eluded him after that.

Trouble began as the troops started moving overland through the woods at the southern end of the lake. Forced to clear away huge trees in its path felled by American axmen, the army crawled along at only two or three miles a day. Promised reinforcements never arrived, and a Whig militia force wiped out a force of eight hundred men that Burgoyne had sent into Vermont to round up badly needed horses. By October 1777, Burgoyne's army was down to less than six thousand men and was facing disaster. A force of nearly three thousand Continentals and nine thousand militia, commanded by General Horatio Gates, had now assembled to confront the British. Unable to break through the American lines, Burgoyne surrendered to Gates following the Battle of Saratoga on October 17, 1777. A stunning reversal for the British, Burgoyne's defeat would help convince the French to join the fighting on the American side.

While Burgoyne was meeting disaster, William Howe, rather than moving north to support him, was making plans to destroy Washington's army and capture Philadelphia. In July 1777, Howe's troops sailed from New York to Chesapeake Bay and from there marched on Philadelphia from the south. They met Washington's army on the banks of Brandywine Creek, near the Pennsylvania-Delaware border. The Americans put up a good fight before giving way with a loss of 1,200 killed or captured (twice as many as the British).

Howe occupied Philadelphia, and his men settled down in comfortable winter quarters. Congress fled to York, Pennsylvania, and the Continental Army established its own winter camp outside Philadelphia, at *Valley Forge*. Here Washington was joined by his wife, Martha, in a small stone farmhouse, surrounded by the log huts that his men built for themselves. The Continental Army's miserable winter at Valley Forge has become legendary in American history. Suffering from cold, disease, and starvation, as many as 2,500 soldiers died. Yet the troops managed to transform themselves into a disciplined professional army by drilling endlessly under the watchful eye of General von Steuben, and with the coming of spring, American prospects improved dramatically.

The War Widens, 1778–1781

Foreign intervention would transform the American Revolution into a virtual world war, engaging British forces in heavy fighting not only in North America but also in the West Indies and India. In the end, had it not been for French assistance, the American side probably would not have won the clear-cut victory it did.

THE UNITED STATES GAINS AN ALLY

Since late 1776, Benjamin Franklin and a team of American diplomats had been in Paris negotiating French support for the patriot cause. In the winter of 1777–1778, aware that a Franco-American alliance was close, Parliament belatedly tried to end the rebellion by granting the former colonies full autonomy, including the exclusive right to tax themselves, in return for a resumption of allegiance to the Crown. But France and the United States concluded an alliance on February 6, 1778, and news of it reached America before the British commission arrived. Seeing independence within reach, Congress refused to negotiate.

The agreements the United States signed with France included both a commercial treaty and a military alliance. Both sides promised to fight together until Britain recognized the independence of the United States, and France pledged not to seek the return of lands in North America. In turn, France persuaded Spain to declare war on Britain in June 1779. The Spanish fleet augmented the naval power of the countries arrayed against Great Britain.

Meanwhile, Catherine the Great of Russia suggested that European powers form a League of Armed Neutrality to protect their trade with the United States and other warring countries against British interference. Denmark and Sweden soon joined; Austria, the Netherlands, Portugal, Prussia, and Sicily eventually followed. Britain, however, quickly went to war with Holland, ostensibly over another issue (to avoid war with the League), but really to cut off Dutch trade with the United States.

Great Britain thus found itself nearly completely isolated and even, briefly, threatened with invasion. Accordingly, as early as the spring of 1778, the British replaced the Howes with a tough new commander, Sir Henry Clinton, instructing him to detach some of his troops to attack the French West Indies. Knowing he now faced a serious French threat, Clinton began consolidating his forces. He evacuated Philadelphia and pulled his troops slowly back across New Jersey to New York.

On June 28, 1778, Washington caught up with the British and engaged them at the Battle of Monmouth Court House. The day was hot and the battle hard-fought. For a while, it looked as if the now well-trained Americans might win, but a mix-up in orders cost Washington the victory. This inconclusive battle proved to be the last major engagement in the North for the rest of the war. Clinton withdrew to New York, and Continental troops occupied the hills along the Hudson Valley north of the city. The war shifted to other fronts.

FIGHTING ON THE FRONTIER AND AT SEA

Native Americans called Kentucky "a dark and bloody ground," a designation that took on added meaning when Indians began raiding the territory in 1777 on British instructions. The nerve center for coordinating these attacks was the British post of Detroit, and the Americans accordingly made plans to capture it. After two unsuccessful expeditions, a third, under Virginian George Rogers Clark, captured three key British settlements in the Mississippi Valley (Kaskaskia, Cahokia, and Vincennes) in July 1778. These successes may have strengthened American claims to the West at the end of the war.

Blood also ran on the Pennsylvania and upstate New York frontiers with British and Indian raids on settlers in Pennsylvania's Wyoming Valley and New York's Cherry Valley. Both raids became the stuff of legends and stimulated equally savage reprisals against the Iroquois, destroying forty-one Indian villages in the New York Finger Lakes region.

Anglo-American clashes at sea had begun in 1775, shortly after the Battles of Lexington and Concord and continued until the end of the war as Americans struggled to break the British navy's blockade. Great Britain was the preeminent sea power of the age, and the United States never came close to matching it, in either the number or the size of its ships. But Congress did its best to challenge the British at sea, and the Americans engaged in what was essentially a guerrilla naval war. Their naval flag, appropriately, pictured a rattlesnake and bore the motto "Don't Tread on Me."

The country's first naval hero, Scottish-born John Paul Jones, was primarily a hit-and-run raider. In the colonies by chance when the war broke out, this adventurer offered his services to Congress. Benjamin Franklin helped Jones secure an old French merchant ship, which he outfitted for war and renamed the *Bon Homme Richard*. After capturing seventeen enemy vessels, he encountered the formidable H.M.S. *Serapis* in the North Sea on September 23, 1779. Completely outgunned, Jones brought the *Bon Homme Richard* close enough to make his small arms fire more effective. Asked by the British if he was surrendering, Jones gave the legendary reply, "I have not yet begun to fight." More than four hours later, the *Serapis* surrendered. Jones's crew took possession of the British vessel and left the crippled *Bon Homme Richard* to sink.

Congress and the individual states supplemented America's naval forces by commissioning individual sea captains to outfit their merchant vessels with guns and act as privateers. Some two thousand American privateers captured more than six hundred British ships and forced the British navy to spread itself thin doing convoy duty.

THE LAND WAR MOVES SOUTH

During the first three years of the war, the British had made little effort to mobilize what they believed to be considerable loyalist strength in the South. In 1778, however, facing a threat from France and with their forces in the North concentrated and inactive, they gave Southern loyalists a key role in a new strategy for subduing the rebellion. The British Southern strategy began to unfold in November 1778, when General Clinton dispatched 3,500 troops to take control of Georgia (see Map 6–2). Meeting only light resistance, they quickly seized Savannah and Augusta. Indeed, enough inhabitants seemed happy to have the British back that the old colonial government was restored under civilian control. After their initial success, however, the British did suffer some serious setbacks. The Spanish entered the war and seized British outposts on the Mississippi and Mobile Rivers. And in February 1779, at the Battle of Kettle Creek, South Carolina's Whig militia decimated a loyalist militia contingent.

But the Americans could not beat the British army. In late September and early October 1779, a combined force of 5,500 American and French troops, supported by French warships, unsuccessfully attacked Savannah. The way was now open for the British to attack Charleston, the military key to the Lower South. In December 1779, Clinton sailed through storm-battered seas from New York to the Carolina coast with about nine thousand troops. In the *Battle of Charleston*, he encircled the city, trapping the patriot forces inside. On May 12, 1780, more than five thousand Continentals and militia laid down their arms—the worst American defeat of the war and the largest single loss of United States troops to a foreign army until the surrender of American forces in the Philippines to Japan in 1942.

The British were now poised to sweep all the South before them. So complete did the British success seem that Clinton tried to force the American troops whom he had taken prisoner to resume their duties as British subjects and join the loyalist militia. Thinking that matters were now well in hand, Clinton sailed back to New York, leaving the southern troops under the command of Lord Cornwallis.

Clinton's confidence that the South had returned securely to the loyalist camp was premature. Atrocities like Colonel Banastre Tarleton's slaughter of 350 Virginia Continentals who had already offered to surrender inflamed anti-British feelings. And Clinton's decision to force former rebels into the loyalist militia backfired, infuriating real loyalists—who saw their enemies getting off lightly—as well as Whigs. Atrocities and reprisals mounted on both sides.

AMERICAN COUNTERATTACKS

In 1780, after a complete rout of General Horatio Gates's forces near Camden, South Carolina, American morale revived when "over mountain men" (militia) from Virginia, western North and South Carolina, and what is today eastern Tennessee inflicted a defeat on the British at Kings Mountain, South Carolina, and Nathanael Greene replaced the discredited Gates, bringing competent leadership to the Continentals in the South. The resourceful Greene realized he would need an unorthodox strategy to defeat Cornwallis's larger army of seasoned professional troops. He divided his forces, keeping roughly half with him in northeastern South Carolina and sending the other half westward under General Daniel Morgan. At the Battle of Cowpens on January 17, 1781, Morgan cleverly posted his least reliable troops, the militia, in the front line, telling them to run after firing two volleys. When Tarleton attacked, the militia fired and withdrew. Thinking that the American ranks had broken, the Redcoats charged—straight into devastating fire from Morgan's Continentals. Tarleton escaped, but his reputation for invincibility had been destroyed.

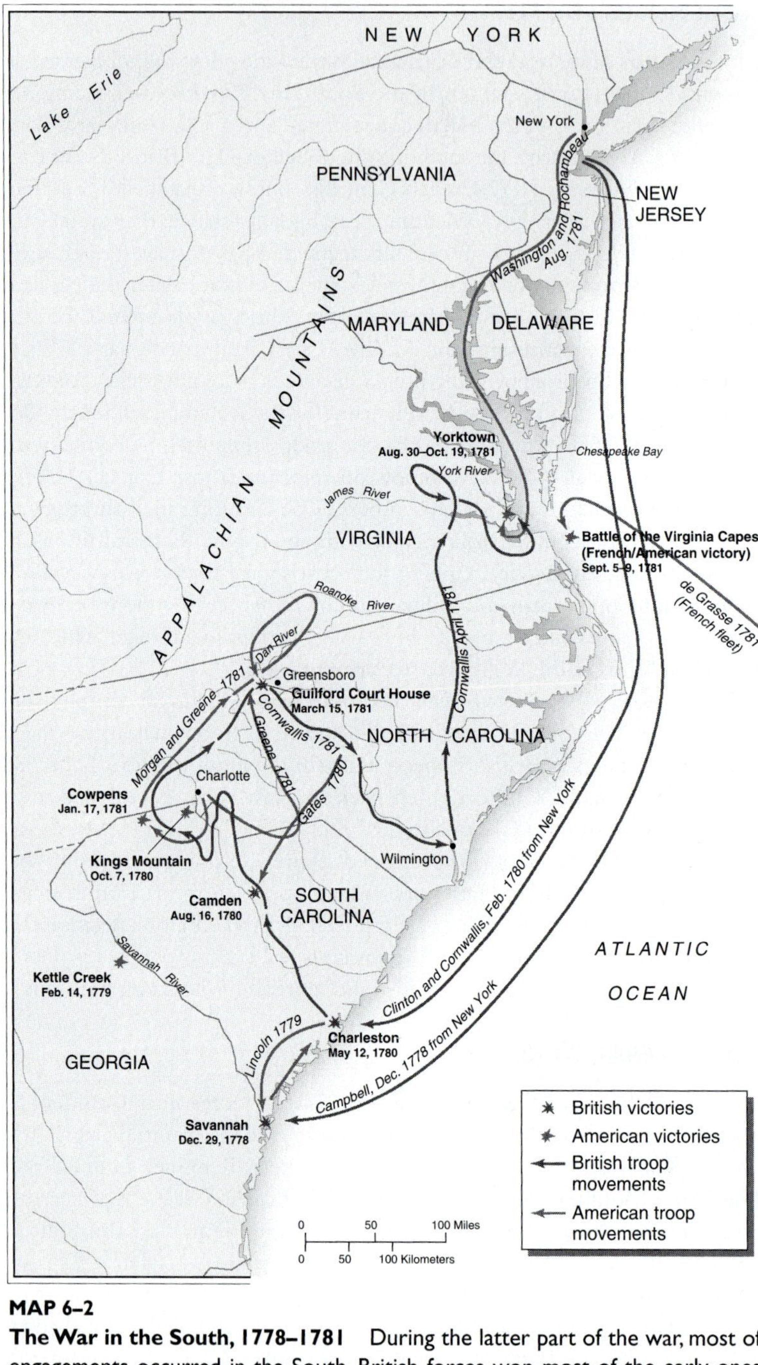

MAP 6–2

The War in the South, 1778–1781   During the latter part of the war, most of the major engagements occurred in the South. British forces won most of the early ones but could not control the immense territory involved and eventually surrendered at Yorktown.

WHY DID the war moved southward as it progressed?

Cornwallis now badly needed a battlefield victory. Burning his army's excess baggage, he set off in hot pursuit of Greene and Morgan, who had rejoined forces. The Continentals had the advantage of knowing the country, which was laced with rain-swollen rivers. Finally, on February 13, 1781, Greene's tired men crossed the Dan River into Virginia, and Cornwallis gave up the chase, marching his equally exhausted Redcoats southward. To his surprise, Cornwallis now found himself pursued—though cautiously, to be sure—by Greene. On March 15, the opposing forces met at Guilford Court House (near present-day Greensboro, North Carolina) in one of the war's bloodiest battles.

By the late summer of 1781, British fortunes were waning in the Lower South. The Redcoats held only the larger towns and the immediately surrounding countryside. With their superior staying power, they won most major engagements, but these victories brought them no lasting gain. As General Greene observed of the Americans, "We fight, get beat, and rise and fight again." Patriot guerrilla forces, led by such colorful figures as "Swamp Fox" Francis Marion, disrupted British communications between their Charleston headquarters and outlying garrisons. The loyalist militias that the British had hoped would pacify the countryside proved unequal to the task. Although Greene never defeated the Redcoats outright, his campaign was a strategic success. The British could not hold what they had taken; the Americans had time on their side. Frustrated, Cornwallis decided to conquer Virginia to cut off Greene's supplies and marched north to Yorktown, Virginia, during the summer of 1781.

The final military showdown of the war was at hand at Yorktown. By now, five thousand French soldiers were in America ready to fight alongside the Continentals, and a large French fleet in the West Indies had orders to support an attack on the British in North America. Faking preparations for an assault on British-occupied New York, the Continentals (commanded by Washington) and the French headed for the Chesapeake. Cornwallis and his six thousand Redcoats soon found themselves besieged behind their fortifications at Yorktown by 8,800 Americans and 7,800 French. A French naval victory gave the allies temporary command of the waters around Yorktown. Cornwallis had nowhere to go, and Clinton—still in New York—could not reinforce him quickly enough. On October 19, 1781, the British army surrendered.

The American Victory, 1782–1783

The British surrender at Yorktown marked the end of major fighting in North America, though skirmishes continued for another year. But the majority in Parliament now felt that enough men and money had been wasted trying to keep the Americans within the empire. In March 1782, the king accepted Lord North's resignation and appointed Lord Rockingham as prime minister, with a mandate to make peace.

THE PEACE OF PARIS

The peace negotiations, which took place in Paris, were lengthy. The Americans demanded independence, handsome territorial concessions—Franklin, the senior American negotiator, asked for all of Canada—and access to the rich, British-controlled fishing grounds in the North Atlantic. The new British prime minister, Lord Shelburne (Rockingham had died in 1782), was inclined to be conciliatory, hoping to help British merchants recover their lost colonial trade.

The American negotiators, Franklin, John Adams, and John Jay, masterfully threaded their way among the conflicting interests of the Americans, British, French, and Spanish. With good reason, they feared that the French and Spanish would strike a bargain with the British at the expense of the United States. As a result, the Americans disregarded Congress's instructions to avoid making peace unilaterally. Instead, they secretly worked out their own arrangements with the British that would meet Shelburne's objective of restoring Anglo-American commercial ties. On November 30, 1782, the negotiators signed a preliminary Anglo-American treaty of peace. Its terms were embodied in the final **Peace of Paris**, signed by all the belligerents on September 3, 1783.

The Peace of Paris gave the United States nearly everything it sought except Canada (which was never really a serious issue). Great Britain acknowledged that the United States was "free, sovereign and independent." The northern boundary of the new nation extended west from the St. Croix River (which separated Maine from Nova Scotia) past the Great Lakes to what were thought to be the headwaters of the Mississippi River. The Mississippi itself—down to just north of New Orleans—formed the western border. Spain acquired the provinces of East and West Florida from Britain. This territory included a substantial chunk of present-day Louisiana, Mississippi, Alabama, and Georgia. The treaty did not, however, provide the United States with access to the Gulf of Mexico, which would be a source of diplomatic friction for years.

Several provisions of the treaty addressed important economic issues. Adams, on behalf of his fellow New Englanders, insisted on a provision granting American fishermen access to the waters off eastern Canada. The treaty also required that British forces, on quitting American soil, were to leave behind all American-owned property, including slaves. Another provision declared existing debts between citizens of Britain and the United States still valid, giving British merchants hope of collecting on their American accounts. Congress was to "recommend" that the states restore rights and property taken from loyalists during the war. Nothing was said about the slave trade, which Jay had hoped to ban.

THE COMPONENTS OF SUCCESS

The War for Independence was over. In December 1783, the last British transports put to sea with troops evacuated from New York. Despite the provisions of the peace treaty and the objections of Southern planters, about three thousand African Americans went with them. Washington's Continental Army had already disbanded in the summer of 1783 (but not, as we have seen, before a dispute over pay came close to provoking a military coup). The American commander said an emotional farewell to his officers at New York City's Fraunces Tavern, resigned his commission to Congress, and like the legendary citizen-soldier Cincinnatus, who after defending the ancient Roman Republic gave up his power and went back to plowing his land, went home to Mount Vernon.

Washington's leadership was only one of the reasons why the Americans won the Revolutionary War. French assistance played a crucial role. Some historians even contend that without the massive infusion of French men and money in 1781, the Revolution would have failed. The British also contributed heavily to their own downfall. Their fatal mistakes included bureaucratic inefficiency, hesitant command, and, worst of all, overconfidence.

Yet it took 175,000 to 200,000 soldiers—Continentals and militia troops—to prevent Great Britain from recovering the colonies. Of these, some seven thousand—like the soldier recalled at the beginning of this chapter—died in battle for their "country and for its just cause." Those who served in the Continental Army, probably more than half of all who fought, served the longest and saw the most action. Their casualty rate—30 to 40 percent—may have been the highest of any war in which the United States has been engaged.

War and Society, 1775–1783

Regular combatants were not the only ones to suffer during the struggle for independence. Eight years of warfare also produced profound dislocations throughout American society. Military service wrenched families apart, and everyone endured economic disruptions. As a forge of nationhood, the Revolution tested all Americans, whatever their standing as citizens.

THE WOMEN'S WAR

Everywhere women had to see their husbands, sons, brothers, and fiancés go off to fight and die. Like Mary Silliman in Connecticut, they waited, trying to stay calm until they knew "what tidings God" had for them. At first, with spirits still running high, Mary's letters to her husband, Selleck, reveal an affectionate lightheartedness. Later the couple's letters grew less playful. Then her husband was captured. The daily round of domestic duties helped to keep her going, but his extended absence increased her burdens and enlarged her responsibilities. Such circumstances elevated women's domestic status. Women also assumed new public roles during the conflict. Some nursed the wounded. More wove cloth for uniforms. The Ladies' Association of Philadelphia was established in 1780 to demonstrate women's patriotism and raise money to buy shirts for the army. Similar associations formed in other states.

Despite their increasing private responsibilities and new public activities, it did not occur to most women to encroach very far on traditional male prerogatives. When John Adams' wife, Abigail, urged him and the Second Continental Congress to "Remember the Ladies," she was not expecting equal political rights. What she wanted, rather, was some legal protections for women and recognition of their value and need for autonomy in the domestic sphere.

Republican ideology, responding to the changing status of women, assigned them a role that was at once exalted and subordinate. It was their job to nurture wise, virtuous, and public-spirited men. It would be this view of women that would prevail in the post-Revolutionary era.

EFFECT OF THE WAR ON AFRICAN AMERICANS AND NATIVE AMERICANS

In the Northern states, where slavery was already economically marginal and where black men were welcome as volunteers in the Continental Army, the Revolutionary War helped bring an end to slavery, although it remained legal there for some time (see Chapter 7). In the South, however, slavery was integral to the economy, and white planters viewed it as crucial to their postwar recovery, so the war ultimately strengthened the institution, especially in the Carolinas and Georgia. Of the African Americans who left with the British at the end of the war, many, both slave and free, went to the West Indies. Others settled in Canada, and some eventually went back to Africa, where Britain established the colony of Sierra Leone for them.

Survivors among the approximately thirteen thousand Native Americans who fought for the British did not have the option of leaving with them at the end of the war. How many died during the war is not known, but certainly many did. Their families and their communities also paid a high price. The Americans repeatedly invaded the Cherokees' homeland in the southern Appalachian Mountains and ravaged the Iroquois country in western New York.

With the peace treaty of 1783, Britain surrendered its territory east of the Mississippi, shocking and infuriating the Native Americans living there. They had not surrendered, and none of them had been at the negotiations in Paris. With the Americans now claiming their country by conquest, the Revolutionary War was a disaster for most Native Americans.

THE PRICE OF VICTORY

The British and American armies both needed enormous quantities of supplies. This heavy demand disrupted the normal distribution of goods and drove up real prices seven- or eightfold. The widespread use of depreciating paper money by the American side amplified this rise in prices and triggered severe inflation. By March 1780, Congress was forced to admit officially that the continental dollar was worthless. (The popular expression "not worth a continental" suggests that the public had long since agreed.)

Necessity, not folly, drove Congress and the states to rely on the printing press. Rather than alienate citizens by immediately raising taxes to pay for the war, the states printed paper money supposedly redeemable by future tax revenues. Because the quantity of this paper money rose faster than the supply of goods and services, prices skyrocketed and the value of the money plunged. Savvy people tried to spend money before its value could drop further, whereas those who had salable commodities like grain tended to hoard them in the hope that the price would go even higher. The rampant inflation was demoralizing and divisive. Lucky speculators and unscrupulous profiteers grew rich while ordinary and patriotic people suffered. These conditions sparked more than thirty protest demonstrations. As usual, war and its deprivations brought out both the best and the worst in human nature.

The successful outcome of the war and the stable peace that followed suggest that most Americans somehow managed to cope. But during the last years of the conflict, their economic and psychological reserves ran low. The total real wealth of private individuals declined by an average of 0.5 percent annually from 1774 to 1805, even with the returning prosperity of the 1790s. Such statistics suggest the true economic cost of the War for Independence. And the atrocities committed on both sides—the burning, plundering, and murdering by regular troops, militias, and civilians acting on their own—provide nearly as accurate an indicator of the conflict's psychological cost.

Conclusion

Despite the devastation and divisiveness of the war, many people in Europe and the United States were convinced that it represented something momentous. The *Annual Register,* an influential British magazine reflecting respectable opinion, commented accurately in 1783 that the American Revolution "has already overturned those favourite systems of policy and commerce, both in the old and in the new world, which the wisdom of the ages, and the power of the greatest nations, had in vain endeavored to render permanent; and it seems to have laid the seeds of still greater revolutions in the history and mutual relations of mankind."

Americans, indeed, had fired a shot heard round the world. Thanks in part to its heavy investment in the American Revolution, France suffered a grave financial crisis in the late 1780s. This in turn ushered in the political crisis that culminated in the French Revolution of 1789.

Once prosperous but distant provinces of a far-flung empire, the North American states had become an independent confederation, a grand experiment in republicanism whose fate mattered to enlightened men and women throughout the Western world. In his written farewell to the rank and file of his troops at the end of October 1783, Washington maintained that "the enlarged prospects of happiness, opened by the confirmation of our independence and sovereignty, almost exceed the power of description." He urged those who had fought with him to maintain their "strong attachments to the union" and "prove themselves not less virtuous and useful as citizens, than they have been persevering and victorious as soldiers." The work of securing the promise of the American Revolution, Washington knew, would now shift from the battlefield to the political arena.

REVIEW QUESTIONS

1. Who were the loyalists and how many of them were there? Why did British and American attempts in 1775 to avert war fail?

2. What actions did the Second Continental Congress take in 1775 and 1776? Why did it choose George Washington to command its army? Why was he a good choice?

3. Why did Congress declare independence in July 1776? How did Americans justify their claim to independence?

4. What was republicanism, and why was the enthusiasm that it inspired insufficient to win the war?

5. Why did the British not crush the Americans immediately? Why did France decide to enter the war as an ally of the United States?

6. Why did the United States ultimately win? What were the immediate results of the American victory?

The First Republic

1776–1789

What were the Articles of Confederation?

What were the weaknesses of the United States after the Revolution?

What was the Constitutional Convention?

What was the struggle over ratification between the Federalists and Antifederalists?

Springfield
Jan. 26, 1787

Sir,

The unhappy time is come in which we have been obliged to shed blood. Shays, who was at the head of about twelve hundred men, marched yesterday afternoon about four o'Clock, towards the public buildings in battle array. He marched his men in an open column by platoons. I sent several times [through aides] to him to know what he was after, or what he wanted. His reply was he wanted barracks, and barracks he would have and stores. The answer returned was he must purchase them dear if he had them. He still proceeded on his march until he approached within two hundred and fifty yards of the arsenal. He then made a halt. I immediately sent Major Lyman, one of my aides, and Capt. Buffington to inform him not to march his troops any nearer to arsenal on his peril, as I was stationed here by order of your Excellency and the secretary at war, for the defence of the public property, in case he did I should surely fire on him and his men. [After rebuffing Lyman and Buffington,] Shays immediately put his troops in motion, and marched on rapidly near one hundred yards. I then ordered Major Stephens, who commanded the artillery to fire upon them. He accordingly did. The two first shott he endeavored to overshoot them, in hopes they would have taken warning without firing among them, but it had no effect on them. Major Stevens then directed his shott thro' the center of his column. The fourth or fifth shot put their whole column into the utmost confusion. Shays made an attempt to display [spread out] the column, but in vain. We had one howitz which was loaded with grape shot, which when fired, gave them great uneasiness. Had I been disposed to destroy them, I might have charged upon their rear and flanks with my Infantry and the two field pieces, and could have killed the greater part of his whole army within twenty five minutes. There was not a single musket fired on either side. I found three men dead on the spol, and one wounded, who is since dead. . . .

I am, Sir, with great respect, Your Excellency's most

Obedient lible Servt
—W. Shepard

General Shepard to Governor Bowdoin, Jan. 26, 1787, in *American Historical Review*, vol. 2 (July 1897): 694.

WILLIAM SHEPARD, the commander of the Hampshire county militia, informed Massachusetts Governor James Bowdoin that the armed insurgents led by Daniel Shays had been routed in their attempt to seize the federal arsenal at Springfield. Shays was a hitherto obscure Revolutionary War captain. Like many of his fellow farmers in western Massachusetts, Shays faced hard times in the 1780s. Falling farm prices, a shortage of money, heavy taxes, and mounting debts produced an economic crisis that threatened many farmers with imprisonment for debt and the loss of their farms. Faced with an unresponsive state legislature, angry farmers protested and shut down the county courts. By 1786 Shays had emerged as one of their key leaders, and the ragtag army of farmers that he marched against the Springfield arsenal now aimed to overthrow the state government.

State leaders and Eastern merchants were horrified. Liberty for them was equated with the right of the individual to pursue wealth and amass property. By contrast, the struggling farmers and artisans defined the liberty won in the Revolution more in terms of the right of communities to defend their interests against moneyed and aristocratic elites.

Driven out of Massachusetts when his army collapsed in 1787, Shays again became an obscure figure. Still, the movement that bears his name dramatized the fragile nature and conflicting values of America's first republic under the Articles of Confederation. Providing for little more than a loose union of the states, the Articles were ratified in 1781. The years that followed were marked by a running debate over the meaning of liberty and the extent of power to be entrusted to a national government. Americans favoring a stronger, more centralized government cited Shays's Rebellion as an example of the chaos that could destroy the republic unless fundamental changes were made. Those changes came with the writing and ratification of the Constitution of the United States in 1788.

The New Order of Republicanism

As royal authority collapsed during the Revolution, various provincial congresses and committees assumed power in each of the former colonies. The Continental Congress, seeking to build support for the war effort, was concerned that these new institutions should have a firm legal and popular foundation. In May 1776, the Congress called on the colonies to form new state governments "under the authority of the people."

This call reflected the political philosophy of republicanism that animated the Revolution (see Chapter 6). To Americans, republicanism meant that legitimate political authority derives from the people. The people are sovereign and should elect the officials who govern them; those officials should represent the people's interests. Another key aspect of republicanism was the revolutionary idea that the people could define and limit governmental power through written constitutions.

DEFINING THE PEOPLE

When news of the peace treaty with Britain reached New Bern, North Carolina, in June 1783, the citizens held a grand celebration. As reported by Francisco de Miranda, a visiting Spanish officer, "There was a barbecue [a roast pig] and a barrel of rum, from which the leading officials and citizens of the region promiscuously drank with the meanest and lowest kind of people, holding hands and drinking from the same cup."

For Miranda, this boisterous mingling of all citizens as seeming equals confirmed the republican belief that the people were sovereign. But republicanism also taught that political rights should be limited to property owners, as informed political judgment required economic self-sufficiency. This precept restricted political participation to propertied white men. Virtually everyone else—propertyless white men, servants legally bound to others, women, slaves, most free black people, and Native Americans—was denied political rights during the Revolutionary era.

Some 60 to 85 percent of adult white men owned property and could participate in politics—a far higher proportion than elsewhere in the world of the eighteenth century. The greatest concentration of the remaining 25 percent or so shut out of the political process were unskilled laborers and mariners living in port cities. In Philadelphia, for example, half the population of taxable adult men and women in the 1780s reported no taxable property. The city's working poor still included indentured servants, bound by contract to give personal service for a fixed time, as well as the walking poor—vagrants and transients.

The Revolution did little to change the traditional patriarchal assumption that politics and public life should be the exclusive domain of men. Women, according to republican beliefs, were dependent under the control of their husbands and fathers. Under common law (the customary, largely unwritten law that Americans had inherited from Britain), women surrendered their property rights at marriage. Legally and economically, husbands had complete control over their wives. As a result, argued Theophilus Parsons of Massachusetts in 1778, women were, as a matter of course, "so situated as to have no wills of their own."

To be sure, some women saw in the political and social enthusiasm of the Revolution an opportunity to protest the most oppressive features of their subordination. "I won't have it thought that because we are the weaker sex as to bodily strength we are capable of nothing more than domestic concerns," wrote Eliza Wilkinson of South Carolina. Men, she lamented, "won't even allow us liberty of thought and that is all I want." But most women accepted the view that their proper place was in the home with their families. Only the New Jersey constitution of 1776 defined *suffrage*—the right to vote—in gender-free terms, extending it to all propertied adults "worth fifty pounds," until 1807, when the state legislature changed its constitution.

The Revolution had a more immediate impact on the lives of many African Americans. Revolutionary principles of liberty and equality and evangelical notions of human fellowship convinced many white people for the first time to challenge black slavery. In 1784,

With the exception of New Jersey, where women meeting the property qualifications were eligible to vote, the state constitutions of the Revolutionary era prohibited women from voting.

Howard Pyle. Corbis/Bettmann.

Virginia Methodists condemned slavery as "contrary to the Golden Law of God on which hang all the Laws and Prophets, and the unalienable Rights of Mankind, as well as every Principle of Revolution." Black people seized opportunities for freedom that emerged from some whites' rejection of slavery, the disruptions of the war, and the needs of both sides for military manpower. As the number of free black people increased from a few thousand at midcentury to 100,000 by 1800, African-American communities and cultures also expanded and developed.

Upward of fifty thousand slaves, or one in ten of those in bondage, gained their freedom as a result of the war. One route was through military service, which generally carried a promise of freedom. When the British began raising black troops, the Americans followed suit. All of the states except Georgia and South Carolina recruited black regiments. Some five thousand black men served in the Continental armies, and they, like their counterparts in British units, were mostly slaves. Most slaves who gained freedom during the war, however, were those who fled their owners and made their way to the port cities of the North.

By making slave property generally less secure, the Revolution encouraged many masters to free their slaves. Once freed, black people tried to break all the bonds of their former servitude. As the number of free black people increased, those still enslaved grew bolder in their efforts to gain freedom. "Henny," warned a Maryland slaveowner in 1783, "will try to pass for a free woman as several have lately been set free in this neighbourhood."

If slavery experienced some strain in the South during the Revolution, in the North, where slaves were only a small percentage of the population, it crumbled. Most Northern states ended slavery between 1777 and 1784. New York followed in 1799 and New Jersey in 1804. Although a majority of white Northerners now agreed that slavery was incompatible with the Revolution's commitment to *natural rights* (the inherent human rights to life and liberty), they refused to sanction an immediate emancipation. The laws ending slavery in most of the Northern states called only for the children of slaves to be freed, and only when they reached adulthood.

Although black men were allowed to vote, most were too poor to meet the property qualifications. They faced discrimination in jobs and housing, were barred from juries, and were denied a fair share of funds for schools. With the help of the small class of property holders among them, they began establishing their own churches and self-help associations.

• C H R O N O L O G Y •

1776 States begin writing the first constitutions.

1777 Articles of Confederation proposed.

1781 Articles ratified.

1783 Americans celebrate independence and the peace treaty with Britain.

1784 Onset of the postwar depression.
Spain closes the Mississippi.
Separatist plots in the West.
Treaty of Fort Stanwix.

1785 Land Ordinance of 1785.
States begin to issue more paper money.
Treaty of Fort McIntosh.

1786 Shays's Rebellion breaks out.
Jay-Gardoqui Treaty defeated.
Annapolis Convention.

1787 Constitutional Convention at Philadelphia.
Northwest Ordinance.

1788 Constitution ratified and goes into effect.
Publication of *The Federalist*.

The impact of the Revolution on Native Americans was almost entirely negative (see Chapter 6). Most stayed neutral during the war or fought for the British. Just as the Americans sought to shake off British control, so the Indians—especially the western tribes and most of the Iroquois Confederation—sought to free themselves from American dominance. Thus British defeat deprived the Indians of a valuable ally and exposed them to the wrath of the victorious patriots. "The minds of these people appear as much agitated as those of the unhappy Loyalists," observed a British officer late in the war of the pro-British southern Indians; "they have very seriously proposed to abandon their country and accompany us [in an evacuation], having made all the world their enemies by their attachment to us."

The state governments and the Confederation Congress treated Indian lands after the Revolution as a prize of war to be distributed to white settlers. Even the few tribes that had furnished troops for the American cause lost control over most of their homelands. White Americans did not consider Native Americans to be part of their republican society. With the exception of Massachusetts, the states denied voting and legal rights to the Indians.

THE STATE CONSTITUTIONS

"Oppose everything that leans to aristocracy, of power in the hands of the rich and chief men exercised to the oppression of the poor." So the voters of Mecklenburg County, North Carolina, instructed their delegates to the state's constitutional convention in 1776.

New state constitutions, ten of which were in place by 1777, were written documents, a striking departure from the English practice of treating a constitution as a collection of customary rights and practices that had evolved over time. In the American view, a constitution was a codification of the powers of government and the rights of citizenship that functioned as a fundamental law to which all public authority was held accountable. Annual elections were now the norm for governors, who were also made subject to *impeachment*—charges of misconduct, resolved at a public trial—and limited in the number of terms they could serve. Most important, for it struck at what patriots felt was the main source of executive domination and corruption, governors lost control over patronage, the power to appoint executive and judicial officials.

As the new constitutions curbed the power of governors, they increased that of the legislatures, making them the focal point of government. Colonial assemblies had been in the forefront of popular opposition to British authority; and the state legislatures that succeeded them were now seen as the most trustworthy defenders of individual liberty. The new constitutions expanded the power of the legislatures to appoint officials and to oversee military and financial matters. To make the legislatures more expressive of the popular will, the new constitutions included provisions that lowered property requirements for voting and officeholding, mandated annual elections, increased the number of seats in the legislatures, and made representation more proportional to the geographical distribution of population. Upper houses, whose members were previously appointed by the colonial governors, were made independent of the executive and opened to popular election.

Americans knew that legislatures, too, could act tyrannically. So in a final check on arbitrary power, each state constitution eventually included some form of a **bill of rights** that set explicit limits on the power of government to interfere in the lives of citizens. The Virginia Declaration of Rights, written by the planter George Mason and adopted in June 1776, set the precedent for this notable republican feature. By 1784, the constitutions of all thirteen states had provisions guaranteeing religious liberty, freedom of the press, and a citizen's right to such fair legal practices as trial by jury.

The new constitutions weakened but did not always sever the traditional tie between church and state. Many Americans held, as the Massachusetts Constitution of 1780 put it, that "the happiness of a people, and the good order and preservation of civil government, essentially depend upon piety, religion, and morality." Many states, notably in New England, levied taxes for the support of religion. The states of New England also continued to maintain Congregationalism as the state-supported religion while allowing dissenting Baptists and Methodists access to funds from the compulsory religious taxes.

The Mid-Atlantic states lacked the religious uniformity of New England. The region had several prominent denominations—Quaker, Episcopalian, Presbyterian, Dutch Reformed, and Lutheran—and this pluralism checked legislative efforts to impose religious taxes or designate any denomination as the established church. In the South, where many Anglican (or Episcopalian) clergymen had been Tories, the Anglican Church lost its former established status.

Although in general the executive lost power and the legislative gained power under the new state constitutions, the actual structure of each state government reflected the outcome of political struggles between radical and conservative republicans. The radicals wanted to open government to all male citizens. The conservatives, though they agreed that government had to be derived from the people, feared "mob rule" and wanted to limit government to an educated elite of substantial property holders. Most conservatives, like Jeremy Belknap of New Hampshire, thought that the people had to be "taught . . . that they are not able to govern themselves."

In South Carolina, where conservative planters gained the upper hand, the constitution mandated property qualifications that barred 90 percent of the state's white males from holding elective public office. In contrast, Pennsylvania's Scots-Irish farmers and Philadelphia artisans took charge and gave the vote to all free males who paid taxes and eliminated property qualifications for officeholding. In addition, the constitution concentrated power in a unicameral (single-house) legislature, eliminating both the office of governor and the more elite upper legislative house. The constitution's framers also required legislators to stand for election annually and barred them from serving more than four years out of seven.

The constitutions of the other states, although not as bold in their democratic reforms as Pennsylvania's, typically enhanced the political influence of ordinary citizens more than the constitution of South Carolina did. Unlike the colonial assemblies, the new bicameral (two-house) legislatures included many artisans and small farmers. This growing political equality was accompanied by demands that those in government be more responsive to the people. Summing up the prevailing American view, William Hooper of North Carolina wrote in 1776, "Rulers must be conceived as the creatures of the people, made for their use, accountable to them, and subject to removal as soon as they act inconsistent with the purposes for which they were formed."

THE ARTICLES OF CONFEDERATION

Once the Continental Congress decided on independence in 1776, it needed to create a legal basis for a permanent union of the states. According to the key provision of the *Articles of Confederation* that Congress submitted to the states in November 1777, "Each State retains its sovereignty, freedom and independence, and every power, jurisdiction and right, which is not by this confederation expressly delegated to the United States, in Congress assembled." The effect was to create a loose confederation of autonomous states.

The powers the Articles of Confederation delegated to the central government were extremely limited. There were no provisions for a national judiciary or a separate executive branch of government. The Articles made Congress the sole instrument of national authority but restricted it with constitutional safeguards that kept it from theatening the interests of the states. Each state had one vote in Congress, making each politically equal regardless of size or population. State legislatures were to choose congressional delegations in annual elections, and delegates could serve only three years out of six. Delegates were to follow the instructions of their state legislatures and could be recalled at any time. Important measures, such as those dealing with finances or war and peace, required approval from a majority of nine states. Amendments to the Articles of Confederation, including the levying of national taxes, required the unanimous consent of the states.

Congress had authority primarily in the areas of foreign policy and national defense. It could declare war, make peace, conduct foreign affairs, negotiate with Native Americans, and settle disputes between states. But it had no authority to raise troops or impose taxes. It could only ask the states to supply troops and money.

The central principle behind the Articles was the fear of oppressive, centralized power. Edward Rutledge, a delegate from South Carolina to the Continental Congress, argued that the new Confederation Congress was vested "with no more Power than is absolutely necessary." Residents of West Springfield, Massachusetts, in instructions to their congressional representatives in 1778 resolved: "It is *freedom*, & not a choice of the *forms of servitude* for which we contend."

Most states quickly ratified the Articles of Confederation, but because they needed the approval of all thirteen states, it was not until Maryland ratified the articles in 1781 that they officially took effect. What caused the delay was the demand of some states to give Congress a power not included in the Articles submitted for ratification in 1777.

The issue here concerned the unsettled lands in the West between the Appalachian Mountains and the Mississippi River. Some states claimed these lands by virtue of their colonial charter rights. The so-called landless states—those with no claim to the West— insisted that it be set aside as a reserve of public land. Land speculators, many of them leading politicians, who had purchased huge tracts of land from the Indians before the Revolution, sided with the landless states. They expected Congress would be more likely to honor their land titles than the individual states.

The British threat to the Chesapeake area in early 1781 finally broke the impasse. Though retaining control of Kentucky, Virginia gave up its claim in the West to a vast area extending north of the Ohio River. In turn, Maryland, now desperate for military aid from Congress, agreed to ratify the Articles.

Problems at Home

Neither prosperity nor political stability accompanied the return of peace in 1783. The national government struggled to avoid bankruptcy, and in 1784, an economic depression struck the country. As fiscal problems deepened, creditor and debtor groups clashed angrily in state legislatures. The only solid accomplishment of the Confederation Congress during this troubled period was to formulate an orderly and democratic plan for the settlement of the West.

THE FISCAL CRISIS

The Continental Congress and the states incurred heavy debts to finance the Revolutionary War. Unable to impose and collect sufficient taxes to cover the debts and without reserves of gold or silver, they had to borrow funds and issue certificates or bonds pledging repayment. Congress had the largest responsibility for war debts. To do so it printed close to $250 million in paper notes backed only by its good faith. By the end of the war in 1781, these Continental dollars were nearly worthless, and the national debt stood at $11 million. As Congress issued new securities to settle claims by soldiers and civilians, this sum rose to $28 million in just a few years.

Congress never did put its tottering finances on a sound footing. Its fiscal problems ultimately discredited the Articles of Confederation to the *nationalists*, a loose bloc of congressmen, army officers, and public creditors who wanted to strengthen the Confederation at the expense of the states. The nationalists first began to organize in the dark days of 1780 and 1781 when inflation was rampant, the army was going unpaid, Congress had ceased paying interest on the public debt, and the war effort itself seemed in danger of collapsing. Galvanized by this crisis, the nationalists rallied behind Robert Morris, a Philadelphia merchant appointed as superintendent of finance for the Confederation government.

Morris sought to enhance national authority through a bold program of financial and political reform. He began by securing a charter from Congress in 1781 for the Bank of North America, the nation's first commercial bank. Morris wanted it to serve as a national institution, and he used it to hold government funds, make loans to the government, and issue bank notes—paper money that could be used to settle debts and pay taxes owed to the United States.

Morris temporarily stabilized the nation's finances. Nonetheless, he was blocked in his efforts to gain the taxing power needed to restore the shattered credit of the Confederation government.

Morris's central nationalist objective was to create a "bond of union" by having Congress assume payment of the entire national debt. Once paid back, the people who had financed the war would identify their economic self-interest with the effective exercise of power by the national government.

To achieve this political goal, Morris had to gain for Congress what it had always lacked: the power to tax. In 1781, he proposed a national impost, or tariff, of 5 percent on imported goods. Because this was a national tax, it required an amendment to the Articles of Confederation and the consent of all thirteen states. Rhode Island—critically dependent on its own import duties to finance its war debt—was the only state to reject it. When a revised impost plan was considered two years later, New York blocked its passage. These failures doomed Morris's financial reforms. He left office in 1784.

The failure of the impost tax was one of many setbacks that put the nationalists temporarily on the defensive. With the conclusion of peace in 1783, confidence in state government returned. The states continued to balk at paying Congress and denied it even limited authority to regulate foreign commerce. Most ominously for the nationalist cause, the states began to assume responsibility for part of the national debt. By 1786, New Jersey, Pennsylvania, Maryland, and New York had absorbed one-third of the debt by issuing state bonds to their citizens in exchange for national securities. As Morris had warned in 1781, such a policy entailed "a principle of disunion . . . which must be ruinous."

Without the power to tax, Congress was a hostage to the sovereignty of the individual states with no real authority over the nation's economic affairs. When the economy plunged into a severe depression in 1784, it could only look on helplessly.

ECONOMIC DEPRESSION

During the Revolutionary War, Britain closed its markets to American goods. After the war, the British continued this policy, hoping to keep the United States weak and dependent. In the summer of 1783, they excluded Americans from the lucrative trade with the British West Indies that before the Revolution had been the colonists' primary source for the credits they needed to offset their imports from Britain.

Meanwhile, British merchants were happy to satisfy America's pent-up demand for consumer goods. A flood of cheap British imports inundated the American market, and coastal merchants sold them to inland traders and shopkeepers by extending easy credit terms. In turn, these local businessmen sold the goods to farmers and artisans in the interior. Ultimately, however, the British merchants required payment in hard currency, gold and silver coins. By now, America's only source of hard currency was foreign loans obtained by Congress and what money the French army had spent during the war. This was soon exhausted as America's trade deficit with Britain—the excess of imports over exports—ballooned in the early 1780s to £5 million.

The result was an immense bubble of credit that finally burst in 1784, triggering a depression that would linger for most of the rest of the decade. As merchants began to press debtors for immediate payment, prices collapsed (they fell more than 25 percent between 1784 and 1786), and debtors were unable to pay.

Small farmers everywhere had trouble paying their taxes. In 1786, James Swan of Massachusetts wrote of farmers in his state: "There is no family that does not want some money for some purposes, and the little which the farmer carries home from market, must be applied to other uses, besides paying off the [tax] collector's bills." Rural shopkeepers often could not move goods unless they agreed to barter them for farm produce. Western Massachusetts storeowner Abigail Dwight reported in 1785 that "most of these People sell on credit for To-Morrow at large—for very little Cash stirring this way—to be pay'd for in old Horses—cows some Boards—cabbages—turnips—Potatoes etc."

Wages fell 25 percent between 1785 and 1789, and workers began to organize. They called for tariffs on British imports and for legislative measures to promote American manufacturers. Farmers faced a wave of lawsuits for the collection of debts and the dread possibility of losing their land. "To be tenants to landlords, we know not who," protested the farmers of Conway, Massachusetts, "and pay rent for lands, purchased with our money, and converted from howling wilderness, into fruitful fields, by the sweat of our brows, seems . . . truly shocking."

With insufficient money in circulation to raise prices and reverse the downturn, the depression fed on itself. Congress was powerless to raise cash and was unable to pay off its old debts, including what it owed to the Revolutionary soldiers. Many state governments made things worse by imposing heavy taxes payable in the paper money they had issued during the Revolution. The result was further to reduce the amount of money in circulation, forcing prices still lower.

No longer protected under the old Navigation Acts as British vessels, American ships were now barred from most ports in the British Empire. Cargoes from the West Indies to

New England fell off sharply, and the market for whale oil and fish, two of New England's major exports, dried up.

The economy of the Mid-Atlantic region was stronger, but even there the loss of the provisioning trade to the British West Indies in grains, livestock, and dairy products cut into the income of merchants and farmers and forced layoffs among artisans who serviced the shipping trade.

In the Southern states, British policies compounded the problem of recovering from the physical damage and social disruptions of the war. Some 10 percent of the region's slaves had fled, and production levels on plantations fell. Chesapeake planters needed a full decade to restore tobacco production to its prewar levels. And a collapse in tobacco prices in 1785 left most of them in the same chronic state of indebtedness that had plagued them on the eve of the Revolution. Rice production in the Carolina lowcountry was similarly slow to recover, despite the debts planters piled up to purchase additional slaves and repair their war-damaged plantations and dikes. Burdened by new British duties on American rice, planters saw rice exports fall by 50 percent. Small farmers in the pine barrens of North Carolina likewise had to adjust to the loss of their formerly protected British market for naval stores—tar, pitch, and turpentine.

By the late 1780s, an economic upturn was under way in the Mid-Atlantic states. Food exports to continental Europe were on the rise, and American merchants were developing new trading ties with India and China. Commercial treaties with the Dutch, Swedes, and Prussians also opened up markets that had been closed to the colonists. Nonetheless, a full recovery had to await the 1790s.

A stagnant economy and burdensome debt combined with a growing population (there were 50 percent more Americans in 1787 than there had been in 1775) to reduce living standards. With more losers than winners, economic conflict dominated the politics of the Confederation period.

THE ECONOMIC POLICIES OF THE STATES

Britain was an obvious target of popular anger over the economic depression. Merchants poorly positioned to adjust to the postwar dislocations of trade led a campaign to retaliate with duties on British ships and special taxes on their goods. Artisans and workers, especially in the North, pushed for tariffs on British goods to encourage domestic manufacturing and protect jobs and wages.

Shippers evaded high tariffs by bringing their cargoes in through states with no tariffs or less restrictive ones. States without ports, like New Jersey and North Carolina, complained of economic discrimination. When they purchased foreign goods from a neighboring shipping state, they were forced to pay part of the tariff cost, but all the revenue from the tariff accrued only to the importing state. James Madison neatly summarized the plight of these states: "New Jersey, placed between Philadelphia and New York, was likened to a cask tapped at both ends; And North Carolina, between Virginia and South Carolina, to a patient bleeding at both Arms."

Tariff policies also undermined efforts to confer on Congress the power to regulate commerce. The agrarian states of the South had different interests from the states of the North. With the exception of Virginia, they favored free trade policies that encouraged British imports. Southern planters took advantage of the low rates charged by British ships for transporting their crops to Europe, putting pressure on Northern shippers to reduce their rates.

The bitterest divisions, however, were between debtors and creditors within states. As the value of debt securities dropped during the Revolutionary War, speculators bought them up for a fraction of their face value and then put pressure on the states to raise taxes and repay the debts in full in hard currency. Wealthy landowners and merchants likewise supported higher taxes and the rapid repayment of debts in hard currency. Arrayed against these creditor groups by the mid-1780s was a broad coalition of debtors comprised of middling farmers, small shopkeepers, artisans, laborers, and people who had overextended themselves speculating in Western land. The debtors wanted the states to issue paper money that they could use instead of hard money—gold and silver—to pay their debts. The paper money would have an inflationary effect, raising wages and the prices of farm commodities and reducing the value of debts contracted in hard currency.

This was the economic context in which **Shays's Rebellion** exploded in the fall of 1786. Farm foreclosures and imprisonments for failure to pay debts increased sharply in western Massachusetts. Farmers petitioned the state legislators for economic relief. They demanded legislation that would temporarily prohibit creditors from seizing farms and processing suits for debt. When the creditor and seaboard interests in the legislature refused to pass any relief measures, some two thousand farmers took up arms against the state government. They shut down the courts and hence the legal machinery for collecting debts in three counties in western Massachusetts. When they marched on the state arsenal in Springfield, alarmed state officials raised troops to crush the uprising.

Outside of western Massachusetts, discontented debtors generally were successful in changing the monetary policy of their states. In 1785 and 1786, seven states enacted laws for new paper money issues. In most cases, combined with laws that prevented or delayed creditors from seizing property from debtors to satisfy debts, the currency issues helped keep a lid on popular discontent.

Rhode Island was an exception to this pattern of fiscal responsibility. A rural party that gained control of the Rhode Island legislature in 1786 pushed through a currency law that flooded the state with paper money that could be used to pay all debts. Creditors who balked at accepting the new money at face value were subject to heavy penalties. Shocked, they went into hiding or left the state entirely, and merchants denounced the law as outright fraud.

The actions of the debtor party in Rhode Island alarmed conservatives everywhere. Now they were convinced that state legislatures dominated by farmers and artisans were dangerous. One South Carolina conservative declared that he could see nothing but an "open and outrageous . . . violation of every principle of justice" in paper money and debt relief laws. Conservatives, creditors, and nationalists alike now spoke of a democratic tyranny that would have to be checked if the republic were to survive and protect its property holders.

CONGRESS AND THE WEST

The Treaty of Paris and the surrender of charter claims by the states gave Congress control of a magnificent expanse of land between the Appalachian Mountains and the Mississippi River. Congress set forth a series of effective provisions for the settlement and governance of this first American West and its eventual absorption into the Union.

Asserting for the national government the right to formulate Indian policy, Congress negotiated a series of treaties with the Indians beginning in 1784 for the abandonment of their land claims in the West. By threatening to use military force, congressional commissioners in 1784 coerced the Iroquois Confederation of New York to cede half of its territory to the United States in the Treaty of Fort Stanwix. Similar tactics in 1785 resulted in the Treaty of Fort McIntosh in which the northwestern tribes ceded much of their land in Ohio. In opposition to states intent on grabbing Indian lands for themselves, Congress resolved in 1787 that its treaties were binding on all the states. Anxious for revenue, Congress insisted on payment from squatters who had filtered into the West before provisions for the land sales.

The most pressing political challenge was to secure the loyalty of the West to the new and fragile Union. To satisfy the demands of settlers for self-government, Congress resolved as early as 1779 that new states would be carved out of the western domain with all the rights of the original states. In the Ordinance of 1784, Thomas Jefferson proposed to create ten districts or territories, each of which could apply for admission as a state when its population equaled that of the free inhabitants in the least populous of the existing states. Jefferson also proposed that settlers be permitted to choose their own officials, and he called for the prohibition of slavery in the West after 1800. Shorn of its no-slavery features, the ordinance passed Congress but was never put into practice.

If it couldn't regulate land sales and pass on clear titles, Congress would, in effect, have surrendered its claim to govern. Congress had to act on national land policy, warned a western Pennsylvanian, or else "lose the only opportunity they ever will have of extending their power and influence over this new region." One way or another, settlers were going to get their land, but a pell-mell process of private acquisitions in widely scattered settlements threatened to touch off costly Indian wars, deprive the national government of vitally needed revenue, and encourage separatist movements.

Congress responded with the ***Land Ordinance of 1785***. The crucial feature of this seminal legislation was its stipulation that public lands be surveyed in a rectangular grid pattern before being offered for sale. By requiring that land first be plotted into townships of thirty-six uniform sections of 640 acres each, the ordinance adopted the New England system of land settlement, an approach that promoted compact settlements and produced undisputed land titles.

Congress offered the plots of 640 acres at the then hefty sum of no less than $640, or $1 per acre, payable in hard currency or its equivalent. The goal here was to keep out the shiftless poor and reserve the West for enterprising and presumably law-abiding farm families who could afford the entry cost. Congress also set aside the income from the sale of the sixteenth section in each township for the support of public schools. Support for education, as a congressional report of 1783 put it, would help provide for "security against the increase of feeble, disorderly and dispersed settlements in those remote and extended territories [and] against the depravity of manners which they have a tendency to produce."

Before any land sales occurred under the Ordinance of 1785, impatient settlers continued to push north of the Ohio River and claim homesteads as squatters. They clashed both with local Indian tribes and the troops sent by Congress to evict them. Impatient itself with the slow process of surveying, Congress sold off a million and a half acres to a group of New England speculators organized as the Ohio Company. The speculators bought the land with greatly depreciated loan office certificates that had been issued to Revolutionary War veterans, and their cost per acre averaged less than 10 cents in hard money. They now pressed their allies in Congress to establish a governmental structure for the West that would protect their investment by bringing the unruly elements in the West under control. The ***Northwest Ordinance of 1787***, the most significant legislative act of the Confederation Congress, filled this need, creating a political structure for the territories and a phased process for achieving statehood that neatly blended public and private interests.

According to the ordinance, controls on a new territory were to be strictest in the early stage of settlement, when Congress would appoint a territorial government consisting of a governor, a secretary, and three judges. When a territory reached a population of five thousand adult males, those with 50 acres of land or more could elect a legislature. The actions of the legislature, however, were subject to an absolute veto by the governor. Once a territory had a population of sixty thousand, the settlers could draft a constitution and apply for statehood "on an equal footing with the original states in all respects whatsoever."

The Northwest Ordinance of 1787 stipulated that only three to five states were to be formed out of the Northwest. This was because the admission of new states would weaken the original thirteen states' control over Congress. Although less democratic in many respects than Jefferson's plan in mandating a period of outside control by Congress, the 1787 ordinance did provide greater protection for property rights as well as a bill of rights guaranteeing individual freedoms. Most significant, it prohibited slavery.

Southern congressmen agreed to the slavery ban in part because they feared that planters in the new states would compete with them in the production of slave-produced staples such as tobacco. More important, however, they expected slavery to be permitted in the region south of the Ohio River that was still under the administrative authority of Virginia, North Carolina, and Georgia in the 1780s. Indeed, slavery was allowed in this region when the **Southwest Ordinance of 1790** brought it under national control, a decision that would have grave consequences in the future sectionalization of the United States.

Although the Northwest Ordinance applied only to the national domain north of the Ohio River, it provided the organizational blueprint by which all future territory was brought into the Union. It went into effect immediately and set the original Union on a course of dynamic expansion through the addition of new states.

Diplomatic Weaknesses

In the international arena of the 1780s, the United States was a weak and often ridiculed nation. Under the Articles of Confederation, Congress had the authority to negotiate foreign treaties but no economic or military power to enforce their terms. Unable to regulate commerce or set tariffs, it had no leverage with which to pry open the restricted trading empires of France, Spain, and most important, Britain.

France and the United States remained on friendly terms. The United States even had a favorable trade balance with France, selling more there than it bought. Both Britain and Spain, however, sought to block American expansion into the trans-Appalachian West. And a dispute with Spain over the West produced the most serious diplomatic crisis of the period, one that spilled over into domestic politics, increasing tensions between Northern and Southern states and jeopardizing the country's chances of survival.

IMPASSE WITH BRITAIN

Key among those issues that poisoned Anglo-American relations in the 1780s were provisions in the peace treaty of 1783 that concerned prewar American debts to the British and the treatment of Loyalists by the patriots. To justify its own violations of the treaty, Britain claimed that America had failed to satisfy those provisions. The result was a diplomatic deadlock that hurt American interests in the West and in foreign trade.

The peace treaty called for the payment of all prewar debts at their "full value in sterling money"—that is, in hard currency. Many tobacco planters in the Chesapeake region of Virginia and Maryland had outstanding debts to British creditors. During the Revolution, the British army had carried off and freed many of the region's slaves without compensating the planters. Still angry, the planters were in no mood to repay their debts and agreed only to pay the face value of their debts to their state treasuries in state or Continental paper money, which was practically worthless.

During the Revolution, all the states had passed anti-Loyalist legislation. Many state governments had seized Loyalists' lands and goods, selling them to raise revenue for the war effort. Upward of 100,000 Loyalists fled to Canada and England, and their property losses ran into millions of dollars. The peace treaty pledged Congress to "recommend" to the states that they stop persecuting Loyalists and restore Loyalist property, but wartime animosities remained high. Despite the pleadings of John Jay, the secretary for foreign affairs in the Confederation government, the states were slow to rescind their punitive legislation or allow the recovery of confiscated property.

Unpaid debts and the continued failure of the states to make restitution to the Loyalists gave the British a convenient pretext to hold on to the forts in the West that they had promised to give up in the Treaty of Paris. Refusal to abandon the forts, from Lake Champlain in upstate New York and westward along the Great Lakes was part of a strategy to keep the United States weak, divided, and small. The continued British presence in the region shut Americans out of the fur trade with the Indians, insulted the sovereignty of the United States, and threatened the security of its northern frontier. In 1784, exasperated New Yorkers warned Congress that unless the British were forced to leave, New York would "be compelled to consider herself as left to pursue her own Councils, destitute of the Protection of the United States." Spurred on by Canadian officials, the British also encouraged secessionist movements in the Northwest and sought out Indian allies to fight for a possible buffer state south of the Great Lakes that would keep Americans hemmed in along the Atlantic seaboard.

In Vermont, politicians led by brothers Ethan, Ira, and Levi Allen offered the British a treaty of friendship in exchange for recognition of Vermont's independence and trading privileges within the British Empire. The British declined for fear of unduly antagonizing the United States. In 1791, Vermont joined the Union as the fourteenth state.

American officials viewed Britain's retaliatory trade policies as the gravest threat to American security and prosperity. John Adams, the American minister to London, sought in vain to counter Britain's anti-American economic policies. "I may reason till I die to no purpose," Adams reported to Jay in June 1785, and he complained that he was treated as a complete "cypher."

Adams soon concluded that the British would never lift their trading and shipping restrictions until forced to do so by a uniform American system of discriminatory duties on British goods. However, a uniform policy was impossible to achieve under the Articles of Confederation.

SPAIN AND THE MISSISSIPPI RIVER

At the close of the Revolutionary War, Spain reimposed barriers on American commerce within its empire. Spain also refused to recognize the southern and western boundaries of the United States as specified in the treaty with Britain in 1783, holding out instead for a more northerly border. And of greatest consequence, it denied the claim of the United States to free navigation of the entire length of the Mississippi River. Only with access to the Mississippi and the commercial right of deposit at New Orleans—that is, the right to transfer cargoes to oceangoing vessels—could the region's farmers, then mostly in what would become Tennessee and Kentucky, profitably reach national and international markets.

In the wake of the Revolution, the settlers of Kentucky, which was still part of Virginia, and Tennessee, which was still part of North Carolina, flirted with the idea of secession. Spain sought to trade on the divided loyalties of American speculators and frontier settlers to its advantage, employing some of them as spies and informers. Spain likewise sought to exploit divisions among Indian groups.

Spain stepped up pressure on the West in the summer of 1784 when it closed the Mississippi River within Spanish territory to American trade. Hoping now to benefit from American weakness, Spain also opened negotiations for a long-term settlement with the United States. The Spanish negotiator, Don Diego de Gardoqui, offered John Jay, negotiating for the Americans, a deal that cleverly played the interests of the North against those of the South and West. In exchange for an American agreement to surrender claims to navigate the Mississippi for thirty years, Gardoqui proposed to grant the United States significant trading concessions in the Spanish Empire that would benefit the financially pressed merchants of the northeastern states. Jay reluctantly accepted the offer.

When Jay released the terms of the proposed treaty with Spain in 1786, Congress erupted in angry debate. Southerners, who had taken the lead in the settlement of the West, accused Jay of selling out their interests. The treaty threatened the agrarian alliance they hoped to forge with the West, and increased the odds that the West would break from the East and go its own way. Vowing that they would not surrender the West, Southern congressmen united to defeat ratification of the treaty.

The regional antagonisms exposed by the Jay-Gardoqui talks heightened the alarm over the future of the republic provoked by Shays's Rebellion earlier in 1786. The Union had never appeared more fragile or Congress under the Articles of Confederation so powerless to resolve its differences. As the sense of crisis deepened in 1786, the nationalists, led by Alexander Hamilton of New York and James Madison of Virginia, grew in influence and numbers.

Toward a New Union

In June 1786, a worried John Jay wrote to George Washington that he was "uneasy and apprehensive; more so than during the war. Then we had a fixed object. . . . The case is now altered; we are going and doing wrong, and therefore I look forward to evils and calamities, but without being able to guess at the instrument, nature, or measure of them." Other nationalists fully shared Jay's pessimism. Everywhere they saw unsolved problems and portents of disaster: unpaid debts, social unrest, squabbling states, sectional hostilities, the uncertain status of the West, blocked channels of trade, foreign intrigues, and a paralyzing lack of centralized authority.

In September 1786, delegates from several states met at the ***Annapolis Convention***, in Annapolis, Maryland, seeking to devise a uniform system of commercial regulation for the country. While there, a group of nationalist leaders called on all the states to send delegates to a convention at Philadelphia "to devise such further provisions as shall appear to them necessary to render the constitution of the Federal Government adequate to the exigencies of the Union." The leaders who met at the ***Constitutional Convention*** in Philadelphia forged an entirely new framework of governance, the **Constitution of the United States**, that called for a federal republic with a powerful and effective national government. In 1788, after a close struggle in state ratifying conventions, the Constitution was adopted.

THE ROAD TO PHILADELPHIA

The timing of the call for the Philadelphia Convention could not have been better. During the fall and winter of 1786, the agrarian protests unleashed by Shays's Rebellion in Massachusetts spilled over into other states. Coupled with talk of a dismemberment of the Union in the wake of the Jay-Gardoqui negotiations, the agrarian unrest strengthened the case of the nationalists for more centralized authority.

All the states except Rhode Island sent delegates to Philadelphia. The fifty-five men who attended the convention were chiefly lawyers by training or profession, most of them had served in the Confederation Congress, and more than one-third had fought in the Revolution. The delegates were members of an intellectual and political elite and were far wealthier than the average American. Most had investments in land and the public securities of the United States. At least nineteen owned slaves. Their greatest asset as a working body was their common commitment to a nationalist solution to the crisis of confidence they saw gripping the republic. Strong supporters of the Articles of Confederation mostly refused to attend, perhaps because, as Patrick Henry of Virginia remarked, they "smelt a rat."

THE CONVENTION AT WORK

Congress authorized only a revision of the Articles of Confederation. Almost from the start, however, the delegates at the Philadelphia Convention set about replacing the Articles altogether. Their first action was to elect George Washington unanimously as the convention's presiding officer, gaining credibility for their deliberations from his prestige. The most ardent nationalists then immediately seized the initiative by presenting the **Virginia Plan**. Drafted by James Madison, this plan replaced the Confederation Congress with a truly national government organized like most state governments, with a bicameral legislature, an executive, and a judiciary.

Two features of the Virginia Plan stood out. First, it granted the national Congress power to legislate "in all cases in which the separate states are incompetent" and to nullify any state laws that in its judgment were contrary to the "articles of Union." Second, it made representation in both houses of Congress proportional to population. This meant that the most populous states would have more votes in Congress than the less populous states, giving them effective control of the government. In short, Madison sought to all but eliminate the independent authority of the states while also forcing the smaller states to defer to the more populous ones in national affairs.

Delegates from the small states countered with the **New Jersey Plan**, introduced on June 15 by William Paterson. This plan kept intact the basic structure of the Confederation Congress—one state, one vote—but otherwise amended the Articles by giving the national government the explicit power to tax and to regulate domestic and foreign commerce. In addition, it gave acts of Congress precedence over state legislation.

The New Jersey Plan was quickly voted down, and the convention remained deadlocked for another month. The issue was finally resolved on July 16 with the so-called **Great Compromise**. Based on a proposal by Roger Sherman of Connecticut, the compromise split the differences between the small and large states. Small states were given equal footing with large states in the Senate, or upper house, where each would have two votes. In the lower house, the House of Representatives, the number of seats was made proportional to population, giving larger states the advantage. The Great Compromise also settled a sectional dispute over representation between the free (or about to be free) states and slave states. The Southern states wanted slaves counted for apportioning representation in the House but excluded from direct tax assessments. The Northern states wanted slaves counted for tax assessments but excluded for apportioning representation. The Great Compromise settled on an expedient, if morally troubling, formula: Free residents were to be counted precisely; to that count would be added three-fifths "of all other persons," excluding Indians not taxed. Thus the slave states gained additional political representation while the states in the North received assurances that the owners of nonvoting slaves would have to bear part of the cost of any direct taxes levied by the new government.

Next the convention debated the specific powers to be delegated to the new government. It was at this point that the sectional cleavage between North and South came to a head. As Madison had warned in late June, "the great division of interests" in the United States would arise from the effect of states "having or not having slaves."

The sectional clash first erupted over the power of Congress to regulate commerce. To prevent a northern majority from passing navigation acts favoring Northern shippers, delegates from the Lower South demanded that a two-thirds majority be required to enact trade legislation. Suddenly, the central plank in the nationalists' program—the unified power to force trading concessions from Britain—was endangered. A frustrated Madison urged his fellow southerners to remember that "as we are laying the foundation of a great empire, we ought to take a permanent view of the subject."

In the end, Madison had his way; the delegates agreed that enacting trade legislation would require only a simple majority. In return, however, Southerners exacted concessions on the slavery issue. The convention abandoned a proposal to ban the foreign slave trade. Instead, antislavery New Englanders reached a compromise with the delegates from the Lower South: Congress would be barred from acting against the slave trade for twenty years. In addition, bowing to the fears of planters that Congress could use its taxing power to undermine slavery, the convention denied Congress the right to tax exports from any state. And to alleviate Southern concerns that slaves might escape to freedom in the North, the new Constitution included an explicit provision calling on any state to return "persons held to Service or Labour" in another.

After settling the slavery question in late August, the convention had one last significant hurdle to clear: the question of the national executive. But in early September, the delegates moved quickly to fashion a chief executive office with broad discretionary powers. The prerogatives of the president included the rank of commander in chief of the armed forces, the authority to conduct foreign affairs and negotiate treaties, the right to appoint diplomatic and judicial officers, and the power to veto congressional legislation. The president's term of office was set at four years, with no limits on how often an individual could be reelected. Nearly everyone expected Washington to be the first president.

The delegates envisioned a forceful, energetic, and independent executive insulated from the whims of an uninformed public and the intrigues of the legislature. They rejected both popular election and election by Congress. The solution they hit upon was the convoluted system of an "electoral college." Each state was left free to determine how it would choose presidential electors equal to the number of its representatives and senators. These electors would then cast votes to select a president. If no candidate received a majority of the electoral votes, the election would be turned over to the House of Representatives, where each state would have one vote.

After a style committee polished the wording in the final draft of the Constitution, thirty-nine of the forty-two delegates still in attendance signed the document on September 17. The Preamble, which originally began with a list of the states, was reworded at the last minute to begin simply: "We the people of the United States, in order to form a more perfect Union. . . ." This subtle change had significant implications. By identifying the people, and not a collection of states, as the source of authority, it emphasized the national vision of the framers and their desire to create a government quite different from a confederation of states.

OVERVIEW OF THE CONSTITUTION

The central government outlined in the Constitution was to have far more powers than those entrusted to Congress under the Articles of Confederation. The Constitution's provision for a strong, single-person executive had no precedent in the Articles. Nor did the provision for a Supreme Court. The Constitution vested this Court, as well as the lower courts that Congress was empowered to establish, with the judicial power of the United States. In addition, the Constitution specifically delegated to Congress the powers to tax, borrow and coin money, regulate commerce, and raise armed forces that the Confederation government had lacked.

Most of the economic powers of Congress came at the expense of the states, which were prohibited from passing tariffs, issuing money, or—in an obvious reference to the debtor relief legislation in the 1780s—enacting any law that infringed on the contractual rights of creditors to collect money from debtors. Also included was a clause stipulating that the Constitution and all national legislation and treaties were to be "the supreme law of the land," in effect giving the central government the power to declare state laws unconstitutional.

The Constitution's underlying political philosophy was that, in Madison's wonderful phrase, "ambition must be made to counter ambition." Madison and the other members of the national elite who met at Philadelphia were convinced that self-interest motivated political behavior. Accepting interest group politics as inevitable and seeking to prevent a tyrannical majority from forming at the national level, the architects of the Constitution designed a central government in which competing blocs of power counterbalanced one another.

The Constitution placed both internal and external restraints on the powers of the central government. The division of the government into executive, legislative, and judicial branches, each with ways to limit the powers of the others, created an internal system of checks and balances. For example, the Senate's authority to approve or reject presidential appointments and to ratify or reject treaties curbed the powers of the executive. The president commanded the armed forces, but only Congress could declare war. The president could veto congressional legislation, but Congress could override that veto with a two-thirds vote. To pass in the first place, legislation had to be approved by both the House of Representatives, which, with its membership proportional to population, represented the interests of the people at large, and the Senate, which represented the interests of the states. As an ultimate check against executive abuse of power, Congress could impeach, convict, and remove a president from office for "Treason, bribary, or other high crimes and misdemeanors."

Although the Constitution did not explicitly grant it, the Supreme Court soon claimed the right to invalidate acts of Congress and the president that it found to be unconstitutional. This power of *judicial review* provided another check against legislative and executive authority. To guard against an arbitrary federal judiciary, the Constitution empowered Congress to determine the size of the Supreme Court and to indict and remove federal judges appointed by the president.

The external restraints on the central government were to be found in the nature of its relationship to the state governments. This relationship was based on *federalism*, the division of power between local and central authorities. By listing specific powers for Congress, the Constitution implied that all other powers were to be retained by the states. Thus while strengthening the national government, the Constitution did not obliterate the sovereign rights of the states, leaving them free to curb the potential power of the national government in the ambiguous areas between national and state sovereignty.

This ambiguity in the federalism of the Constitution was both its greatest strength and its greatest weakness. It allowed both nationalists and advocates of states' rights to support the Constitution. But the issue of slavery, left unresolved in the gray area between state and national sovereignty, would continue to fester, sparking sectional conflict over the extent of national sovereignty that would plunge the republic into civil war three-quarters of a century later.

THE STRUGGLE OVER RATIFICATION

The Philadelphia delegates knew that they had exceeded their instructions by proposing an entirely new government, not an amended version of the Articles. Also aware that the Articles' requirement of unanimous consent by the state legislatures to any amendment would result in certain defeat, the delegates boldly bypassed both Congress and the state legislatures.

The last article of the Constitution stipulated that it would go into effect when it had been ratified by at least nine of the states acting through specially elected popular conventions. Influenced by the nationalist sentiments of many of its members, one-third of whom had attended the Philadelphia Convention, and perhaps weary of its own impotence, Congress accepted this drastic and not clearly legal procedure, submitting the Constitution to the states in late September 1787.

The publication of the text of the Constitution touched off a great political debate. Those who favored the Constitution now referred to themselves as *Federalists*, a term that helped deflect charges that they favored an excessive centralization of political authority. By default, the opponents of the Constitution were known as *Antifederalists*, a negative-sounding label that obscured their support of the state-centered sovereignty that most Americans associated with federalism. Initially outmaneuvered in this way, the Antifederalists never did mount an effective campaign to counter the Federalists' output of pamphlets, speeches, and newspaper editorials.

The Antifederalists did attract some men of wealth and social standing. Three of them—Elbridge Gerry of Massachusetts and George Mason and Edmund Randolph of Virginia—had been delegates at Philadelphia. But most Antifederalists were backcountry farmers, men with mud on their boots who lived far from centers of communication and market outlets for their produce. They argued that a large republic, such as the one framed by the Constitution, would inevitably become tyrannical because it was too distant and removed from the interests of common citizen-farmers.

The Antifederalists attacked the Constitution as a danger to the individual liberties and local independence they believed the Revolution had been fought to safeguard, but they lacked the social connections, access to newspapers, and self-confidence of the more cosmopolitan and better-educated Federalists. The Federalists could also more easily mobilize their supporters, who were concentrated in the port cities and commercial farming areas along the coast.

The Federalists skillfully built on the momentum for change that had developed out of the crisis atmosphere of 1786. They successfully portrayed the Constitution as the best opportunity to erect a governing structure capable of preserving and extending the gains of the Revolution.

Conservatives shaken by Shays's Rebellion lined up behind the Constitution. So too did groups like creditors, merchants, manufacturers, urban artisans, and commercial farmers. A stronger national government, they believed, would promote economic development by protecting the home market from British imports, enlarging foreign markets for American exports, promoting a stable and uniform currency, and raising revenues to pay off the Revolutionary War debt.

In the early stages, the Federalists scored a string of easy victories. Delaware ratified the Constitution on December 7, 1787, and within a month, so too had Pennsylvania, New Jersey, Georgia, and Connecticut. Except for Pennsylvania, these were small, sparsely populated states that stood to benefit economically or militarily from a stronger central government. The Constitution carried in the larger state of Pennsylvania because of the Federalists' strength in the commercial center of Philadelphia.

The Federalists faced their toughest challenge in the large states that had generally been more successful in going it alone during the 1780s. One of the most telling arguments of the Antifederalists in these and other states was the absence of a bill of rights in the Constitution. The framers had felt it unnecessary to include such an explicit protection of individual rights in a document intended to specify the powers of a national government and had barely discussed the issue. Responding to this challenge, the Federalists promised to recommend amending the Constitution with a bill of rights once it was ratified. By doing so, they split the ranks of the Antifederalists in Massachusetts. After the Federalists gained the support of two venerable heroes of the Revolution, John Hancock and Sam Adams, the Massachusetts convention approved the Constitution by a close vote in February 1788.

The major hurdles remaining for the Federalists were Virginia, the most populous state, and the strategically located New York. Technically, the Constitution could have gone into effect without them once Maryland, South Carolina, and New Hampshire had ratified it, bringing the total number of states to ratify to the required nine. But without Virginia and New York, the new Union would have been weak and the Federalist victory far from ensured.

As in Massachusetts, the Federalists were helped in these two crucial states by their promise of a bill of rights. And for the New York campaign, Madison, Jay, and Hamilton wrote an eloquent series of eighty-five essays known collectively as *The Federalist* to allay fears that the Constitution would so consolidate national power as to menace individual liberties. In the two most original and brilliant essays in *The Federalist*, essays 10 and 51, Madison turned traditional republican doctrine on its head. A large, diverse republic like the one envisaged by the Constitution, he reasoned, not a small and homogeneous one, offered the best hope for safeguarding the rights of all citizens. This was because a large republic would include a multitude of contending interest groups, making it difficult for any combination of them to coalesce into a tyrannical majority that could oppose minority rights. With this argument Madison had developed a political rationale by which Americans could have both an empire and personal freedom.

New York ratified on June 25, and Virginia followed the next day. North Carolina and Rhode Island did not ratify until after the new government was functioning. North Carolina joined the Union in 1789 once Congress submitted the amendments that comprised the Bill of Rights. The obstinate Rhode Islanders stayed out until 1790, when Congress forced them in with a threat of commercial reprisal.

Conclusion

Between 1776 and 1780, Americans developed a unique system of constitutionalism. They proclaimed the supremacy of constitutions over ordinary legislation; detailed the powers of government in a written document; provided protection for individual freedoms in bills of rights; and fashioned a process for framing governments through the election of delegates to a special constitutional convention and the popular ratification of the work of that convention. In all of these areas, Americans were pioneers in demonstrating how common citizens could create their own governments.

The curbs on centralized power that characterized the state constitutions also applied to what amounted to the first national constitution, the Articles of Confederation. Indeed, the inability of the Confederation Congress to exercise effective power in the areas of taxation and foreign trade was a crippling flaw that thoroughly discredited the Articles in the eyes of the nationalist-minded leaders who had emerged during the Revolution. These leaders overthrew the Articles at the Constitutional Convention in 1787 and engineered a peaceful revolution in securing the ratification of the Constitution. Their victory in creating a new central government with real national powers was built on the foundation of constitutional concepts and mechanisms that Americans had laid down in their states. The new Constitution did rest on the consent of the governed, and it endured because it could be amended to reflect shifts in popular will and to widen the circle of Americans granted the rights of political citizenship.

Accepting as a given that self-interest drove political action, the framers of the Constitution designed the new national government to turn ambition against itself. They created rival centers of power that forced selfish factions to compete in a constant struggle to form a workable majority. The Constitution thus set the stage for an entirely new kind of national politics.

REVIEW QUESTIONS

1. How would you assess the decision made by Shepard and Shays that resulted in the clash at the Springfield arsenal?

2. How would you define republicanism? Do you think Americans still believe in the basic tenets of republicanism?

3. What was so unprecedented about the new state constitutions? What new ideas of government did they use?

4. What were the problems of the economy in the 1780s? Could economic recovery have been achieved under the Articles of Confederation? Why or why not?

5. Were the diplomatic weaknesses of the United States under the Articles as serious as its internal problems? What were the sources of those weaknesses, and how did they threaten national unity?

6. What sorts of men drafted the Constitution in 1787, and how representative were they of all Americans? How widespread was popular backing of the Constitution, and why was it ratified?

7. What explains the differences between the Federalists and Antifederalists? Did they share the same vision of what they wanted America to become?

A New Republic and the Rise of Parties

1789–1800

What were the differences among the four major regions in the United States in 1789?

What is the Bill of Rights?

What reaction or opposition was there to Hamilton's financial policies?

What were the first two major parties in U.S. politics, and how did their ideologies differ?

Why was Adams defeated in the election of 1800?

April 30, 1789

New York City

This is the great important day. Goddess of Etiquette assist me while I describe it. . . . The President was conducted out of the middle window into the gallery [of Federal Hall] and the Oath administered by the Chancellor [Robert R. Livingston, Chancellor of New York]. Notice that the Business was done, was communicated to the Croud by Proclamation. . . . who gave three Cheers. . . . As the Company returned into the Senate Chamber, the president took the Chair, and the Senate and representatives their Seats. He rose & all arose also and [he] addressed them [in his inaugural address]. This great Man was agitated and embarrassed more than ever he was by the levelled Cannon or pointed Musket. He trembled and, several times could scarce make out to read, tho it must be supposed he had often read it before. He put part of the fingers of his left hand, into the side, of what I think the Taylors call the fall, of his Breetches. Changing the paper into his left hand, after some time, he then did the same with some of the fingers of his right hand. When he came to the Words all the World, he made a flourish with his right hand, which left rather an ungainly impression. . . . He was dressed in deep brown, with Metal buttons, with an Eagle on them, White Stockings a Bag and Sword—from the Hall there was a grand Procession to St. Pauls Church where prayers were said by the Bishop. The procession was well conducted and without accident, as far as I have heard. The Militias were all under Arms. [They] lined the Street near the Church, made a good figure and behaved well. The Senate returned to their Chamber after Service, formed & took up the Address. . . . In the Evening there were grand fire Works. . . . and after this the People went to bed.

[William Maclay]

Kenneth R. Bowling and Helen E. Veit, eds., *The Diary of William Maclay and Other Notes on Senate Debates,* March 4, 1789–March 3, 1791 (Baltimore: The Johns Hopkins University Press, 1988), pp. 11–13.

SENATOR WILLIAM MACLAY of Pennsylvania wrote this account of the inauguration of George Washington as the first president of the United States at Federal Hall in New York City on April 30, 1789. Born in Pennsylvania in 1737, he was selected by the Pennsylvania legislature in September 1788 as one of the state's first two U.S. senators. The Constitution had created the framework for a national government, but pressing problems demanded the fleshing out of that framework. The government urgently needed revenue to begin paying off the immense debt incurred during the Revolution. It also had to address unstable conditions in the West. Ultimately, the key to solving these and other problems was to establish the new republic's legitimacy. Washington and his supporters had to inspire popular backing for the government's right to exercise authority even though most Americans feared centralized authority.

The realities of governing would soon shatter the nonpartisan ideal that had prevailed when the Constitution was ratified. By the end of Washington's first term, two political parties had begun to form. The Federalist party (the name came from that used by the original backers of the Constitution), which included Washington and his successor John Adams, favored a strong central government. The opposition party, the Jeffersonian Republicans, which Senator Maclay came to support, took shape as a result of differences over financial policy and the American response to the French Revolution. Led by Thomas Jefferson, the Republicans distrusted excessive central power.

The Federalists, who governed through 1800, showed a doubting world ruled by kings and queens that the American experiment in republican government could work. But as inheritors of a political tradition that equated parties with factions—temporary coalitions of selfish private interests—the Federalists doubted the loyalty of the Republicans. When the Federalists under President Adams attempted to suppress the Republicans, the stage was set for the critical election of 1800. Jefferson's victory in that election ended both federalist rule and the republic's first major internal crisis.

Washington's America

Who were the Americans whom Washington was called on to lead? There is no easy answer. In 1789, as now, Americans identified and grouped themselves according to many factors, including race, gender, class, ethnicity, religion, and degree of personal freedom. Variations in climate and soil further divided them into regions and sections. The resulting hodgepodge sorely tested the assumption that a single national government could govern Americans as a whole.

THE UNIFORMITY OF NEW ENGLAND

The national census of 1790 counted nearly 4 million Americans, one in four of whom lived in New England. It alone of the nation's formative regions had largely shut itself off from outsiders. New England's poor soils and long, cold winters made it an impractical place to cultivate cash crops like the tobacco and rice of the South. As a result, New England farmers had little need of imported white indentured servants or black slaves. Puritan values and a harsh environment thus combined to make New England the most religiously and ethnically uniform region in the United States. Most of the people living there were descended from English immigrants who had arrived in the seventeenth century. Small pockets of Quakers, Baptists, and Catholics had gained the legal right of worship by the 1720s, but Congregationalism remained the official, state-supported religion in Connecticut and

Massachusetts. Black people and Indians together barely constituted 3 percent of New England's population. The few remaining Indians lived on reservations of inferior land, which they usually left only to find work as servants or day laborers.

New Englanders found slavery incompatible with the natural rights philosophy that had emerged during the Revolution and abolished it in the 1780s. Slavery had, in any case, always been marginal in its economy. Women outnumbered men in parts of New England in 1789. This pattern—not found in other parts of the country—was the result of the pressure of an expanding population and the practice of dividing family farms among male heirs that left young men to migrate west in search of cheap, arable land. Thus by 1789, women formed a slight majority in Connecticut, Massachusetts, and Rhode Island. Yet despite their superior numbers, women in New England, as elsewhere, remained subordinate to men. Republican ideology, emphasizing the need of women to be intellectually prepared to raise virtuous, public-spirited children, led reformers in New England to seek equal access for women to education. In 1789, Massachusetts became the first state to allocate funds specifically for girls' elementary education. Liberalized divorce laws in New England also allowed a woman to seek legal separation from an abusive or unfaithful spouse.

In other respects, politics in New England remained rooted in the Puritan past. Age, property, and reputation determined one's standing in a culture that valued a clearly defined social order. The moral code that governed town life promoted curbs on individual behavior for the benefit of the community as a whole. With their notions of collective liberty, New Englanders subscribed to a version of republicanism that favored strong government, setting themselves apart from most other Americans, who embraced a more individualistic idea of liberty and a republicanism suspicious of government power.

MID-ATLANTIC PLURALISM

The states of the Mid-Atlantic region—New York, New Jersey, and Pennsylvania—were the most diverse in the nation. People of English descent comprised somewhat less than 40 percent of the population. Other major ethnic groups included the Dutch and Scots-Irish in New York and Germans and Scots-Irish in New Jersey and Pennsylvania. With ethnic diversity came religious diversity. In contrast to Puritan New England, the Middle Colonies had offered freedom of worship to attract settlers. In addition, economic opportunities for newcomers were much greater than in New England. The soil was better, the climate was milder, and market outlets for agricultural products were more abundant. These conditions made the Mid-Atlantic region the nation's first breadbasket.

The demand for labor had also been met by importing African slaves. But despite its considerable strength in the port cities and adjacent rural areas, slavery was never an economically vital institution in most of the Mid-Atlantic region. The region's major cash crop, wheat, required seasonal labor, which did not warrant tying up capital in slaves.

Consequently, Pennsylvania in 1780, New York in 1799, and New Jersey in 1804 each passed laws of gradual emancipation. These laws did not free adult slaves but provided that children born of a slave mother were to be freed at ages ranging between 18 and 28. Nevertheless, African Americans had to confront enduring white racism. The comments of one white New Yorker suggest what they were up against. "We may sincerely advocate the freedom of black men," he wrote, "and yet assert their moral and physical inferiority."

The diversity of the Mid-Atlantic region created a complex political environment. Some Mid-Atlantic groups, including mercantile and financial leaders and commercial farmers, favored a strong central government to foster economic development and maintain traditional authority. Others, coming principally from the middle and lower classes, wanted to keep government weak so as to foster a republican equality that would promote individual freedom.

THE SLAVE SOUTH AND ITS BACKCOUNTRY

In the South—the region from Maryland and Delaware to Georgia—climate and soil conditions favored the production of cash staples for world markets. Cultivating these crops required backbreaking labor and Southern planters relied on the coerced labor of African slaves, whose numbers made the South the most populous region in the country. Just under 40 percent of all Southerners were slaves, but their concentration varied within each region.

The free black population in the South had grown rapidly during the 1780s. Thousands of slaves fled behind British lines to win their freedom, and patriots freed others as a reward for enlisting in their forces. The Revolutionary values of liberty and equality also led many slave owners to question the morality of slavery. Legislatures in the Upper South passed laws making it financially easier than before for masters to manumit (free) their slaves. In Virginia alone, ten thousand slaves were manumitted in the 1780s. Slavery, however, remained the foundation of the southern economy. As a result, no southern state embarked on a general program of emancipation, and slavery survived the turbulence of the Revolutionary era.

Economic conditions in the South, where the raw poverty of the backcountry offset the great wealth of the lowcountry, stamped the region's politics and culture. Tidewater planters were predominantly Anglican and of English descent. Piedmont farmers were more likely to be Scots-Irish Presbyterians and Baptists. More evangelical in their religion, and with simpler habits and tastes, the backcountry Baptists denounced the lowcountry planters for their luxury and arrogance.

Planters understood liberty to mean the power of white males, unchecked by any outside authority, to rule over others. The only acknowledged check on this power was the planter's sense of duty, his obligation to adhere to an idealized code of conduct befitting a gentleman and a man of honor. Backcountry farmers also jealously guarded their liberties.

THE GROWING WEST

Between the Appalachian Mountains and the Mississippi River stretched the most rapidly growing region of the new nation, the West. During the 1780s, the white population of the West exploded from less than 10,000 to 200,000. The region's Native American population was, in contrast, about 150,000.

Although Indians and white settlers struck many friendships and mutually advantageous ties, their relations were more generally marked by tension and sporadic violence. For example, when James Boone, the eldest son of the fabled Daniel Boone, who had blazed the first trail for white settlers into Kentucky, was captured, tortured, and killed by a band of Indians, a group of white settlers sought vengeance. They lured some Mingo Indians into their camp, got them drunk, and then killed and scalped them. According to one account, they strung up a pregnant Mingo woman, "sliced open her belly with a tomahawk, and impaled her unborn child on a stake." Indians had every reason to oppose the white intrusion, and they strongly resisted white claims on their lands.

Most white migrants in Kentucky and Tennessee were the young, rural poor from the seaboard slave states. The West offered them the opportunity to claim their own farms and gain economic independence free from the dominance of planters and the economic

---

• C H R O N O L O G Y •

1789 Inauguration of Washington.
Congress establishes the first federal departments.
French Revolution begins.

1790 Hamilton submits the first of his financial reports to Congress.

1791 Bill of Rights ratified.Congress charters the Bank of the United States.

1792 St. Clair's defeat along the Wabash.
Reelection of Washington.

1793 France goes to war against Britain, Spain, and Holland.
Genêt Mission.
Washington issues Proclamation of Neutrality.

1794 Ohio is opened with the victory of General Anthony Wayne at the Battle of Fallen Timbers.

Suppression of the Whiskey Rebellion in western Pennsylvania.

1795 Jay's Treaty with Britain ratified.
Treaty of Greenville with Ohio Indians.

1796 Pinckney's Treaty with Spain ratified.
Washington's Farewell Address.
John Adams elected president.

1797 Beginning of the Quasi-War with France.

1798 XYZ Affair.
Alien and Sedition Acts.
Provisional army and direct tax.
Virginia and Kentucky Resolutions.

1799 Fries's Rebellion in Pennsylvania.

1800 Franco-American Accord.
Thomas Jefferson elected president.

---

competition of slave labor. But planters also saw the West as a land of opportunity, speculating in vast tracts of western land.

Life in the Western settlements was harsh and often cruel. Mortality was high, especially among infants. Travelers from the East described settlers living in crudely built log cabins with squalid, filthy interiors infested with fleas and lice. Many were *squatters*, occupying land in the hopes of someday gaining title to it. Easterners also found an appallingly casual acceptance of violence in the West. Men commonly settled disputes in knife-slashing, eye-gouging brawls.

In Kentucky, squatters, aligned with a small class of middling landowners, spearheaded the movement for political separation from Virginia that gained statehood for the territory in 1792. But despite the statehood movement, the ultimate political allegiance of the West was uncertain in 1790. Westerners wanted the freedom to control their own affairs and outlets for their crops. Apparently, they were willing to strike a deal with any outside power including the British and the Spanish offering to meet these needs.

Forging a New Government

The Congress that assembled in New York from 1789 to 1791 faced a challenge scarcely less daunting than that of the Constitutional Convention of 1787. It had to give form and substance to the framework of the new national government outlined in the Constitution. Executive departments had to be established, a federal judiciary organized, sources of revenue found, terms of international trade and foreign policy worked out, and a commitment to add a bill of rights to the Constitution honored.

Staunch supporters of the new government had easily carried the first national elections in 1788 and enjoyed large majorities in both houses of Congress. These people brought superb administrative talents to the task of governing. Many, however, were clumsy politicians and unsympathetic to the egalitarian sensibilities of the electorate. By 1792, they faced growing political opposition.

"MR. PRESIDENT" AND THE BILL OF RIGHTS

The first problem for Washington and Congress was to decide just how the chief executive of the new republic should be addressed. In a debate that tied up Congress for a month, the more democratically inclined members of the House argued that a title like "His Highness" smacked of a longing for monarchical rule; Adams and the others grudgingly agreed to accept "Mr. President." Whatever his title, Washington was intent on surrounding the presidency in a halo of respectability and he set down guidelines for presidential etiquette. He established strict rules for his interactions with the public. He met with visitors twice a week for an hour and bowed with republican deference to the people but refused to shake hands. He traveled outside New York in a luxurious coach pulled by six horses, and at all times he carried himself with stern reserve.

Meanwhile Congress got down to business. James Madison, now a representative from Virginia, early emerged as the most forceful leader in the House. To allay the fears of Antifederalists that the Constitution granted too much power to the national government, the Federalists had promised to consider amendments that protected both individual rights and liberties and the rights of states. But Madison, concerned not to have the new government immediately hobbled by concessions to states, astutely kept the focus of the amendments on personal liberties. He submitted nineteen amendments, and Congress soon settled on twelve. Ten of these amendments, known collectively as the *Bill of Rights*, were ratified by the states and became part of the Constitution as of December 15, 1791.

The Bill of Rights has been one of the most enduring legacies of the first Congress. The first eight amendments are concerned mostly with individual rights. They guarantee religious freedom, freedom of expression, and the safeguarding of individuals and their property against arbitrary legal proceedings. Only three amendments speak of state interests. Citing the necessity of a "well regulated militia" for "the security of a free State," the Second Amendment guarantees "the right of the people to keep and bear Arms." The Ninth and Tenth Amendments stipulate that the powers not granted to the national government in the Constitution are retained by the people and the states.

The Bill of Rights broadened the government's base of popular support. Once Congress submitted the amendments to the states for ratification, North Carolina (1789) and Rhode Island (1790) overcame their lingering objections and joined the Union. The Bill of Rights also assured Americans that the central government would not try to impose on them a uniform national culture.

DEPARTMENTS AND COURTS

In the summer of 1789, Congress authorized the first executive departments: the State Department for foreign affairs, the Treasury for finances, and the War Department for the nation's defense. These departments already existed under the Articles of Confederation, and the only debate about them concerned the extent of presidential control over the officials who would head them. The Constitution was silent on whether or not the president could dismiss an official without the Senate's consent. Congress decided that the president could do so, setting an important precedent that bolstered presidential power. Department heads would now be closely bound to the president. As a group, they would evolve into the *cabinet*, the president's chief advisory body.

Greater controversy attended the creation of the federal judiciary. The Constitution called for "one Supreme Court" but left it up to Congress to authorize lower federal courts.

The framers were deliberately vague about the federal judiciary because Antifederalists and proponents of states' rights did not want national courts enforcing a uniform judicial system.

The *Judiciary Act of 1789* represented an artful compromise that balanced the concerns of the Antifederalists and states' rights advocates with the concerns of nationalists who strongly opposed leaving matters of national law up to state courts. It created a hierarchical national judiciary based on thirteen federal district courts, one for each state. Appeals from these courts were to be heard in one of three circuit courts, and the Supreme Court was to have the final say in contested cases. In a major concession to the Antifederalists, however, the act limited jurisdiction in federal courts to legal issues stemming from the Constitution and the laws and treaties of the national government. The distinctive legal systems and customs of the states remained intact. State courts would continue to hear and rule on the vast majority of civil and criminal cases.

REVENUE AND TRADE

The government's most pressing need was for revenue, and Madison acted to put the finances of the new federal government on a firm footing. Nearly everyone agreed that the government's chief source of income should be a tariff on imported goods and tonnage duties (fees based on cargo capacity) on ships entering American ports. The United States imported most of its manufactured goods, as well as many raw materials, and foreign-owned ships accounted for nearly half of entering tonnage.

The *Tariff Act of 1789* levied a duty of 5 percent on most imported goods but imposed tariffs as high as 50 percent on items such as steel, salt, cloth, and tobacco. The debate on the Tariff Act provoked some sectional sparring. In general, manufacturers, who were concentrated in the North, wanted high tariffs for protection against foreign competition. In contrast, farmers and Southern planters wanted low tariffs to keep down the cost of the manufactured goods they purchased.

Madison originally hoped to use tonnage duties not only to raise revenue but also to strike at foreign nations like Great Britain that had not signed a commercial treaty with the United States. The duties Madison would impose on British ships entering American ports were in effect a declaration of economic warfare against Britain, and they failed to pass Congress, defeated by an unlikely coalition of sectional interests. Southerners voted against them because they feared their result would be to give New England merchants a monopoly on the carrying trade and raise the cost of shipping tobacco to Europe. Northern merchants, presumably the beneficiaries of the duties, also opposed them, leery of disrupting their profitable trade with Britain, especially with the economic slump of the 1780s abating. The *Tonnage Act of 1789*, as finally passed, treated all foreign ships equally.

HAMILTON AND THE PUBLIC CREDIT

The Treasury was the largest and most important new department. To its head, Alexander Hamilton of New York, fell the task of bringing order out of the nation's ramshackle finances. The basic problem was the huge debt left over from the Revolution. With interest going unpaid, the debt was growing, and by 1789, it had reached $52 million.

More than any other individual, Hamilton imparted energy and purpose to the Washington administration. Coming from humble beginnings, he was ambitious, egotistical, and overbearing. When he spoke of the people, he usually did so with a sneer. But he also had a brilliant financial mind and a sweeping vision of national greatness. He was convinced that the economic self-interests of the wealthy and well-born offered the only sound foundation for the success of the new government.

At the request of Congress, Hamilton prepared a series of four reports on the nation's finances and economic condition. In the first, issued in January 1790, Hamilton proposed a bold plan to address the Revolutionary War debt. The federal government, he maintained, should fund the national debt at full face value. To do this, he proposed exchanging the old debt, including accrued interest, for new government bonds bearing interest at about 4 percent. In addition, Hamilton maintained that the federal government should assume the remaining war debt of the state governments. The intent of this plan was to give the nation's creditors an economic stake in the stability of the new nation.

In his second report, Hamilton called for an excise tax (a tax on the production, sale, or consumption of a commodity) on distilled whiskey produced within the United States to raise additional revenue for interest payments on the national debt and establish the government's authority to levy internal taxes on its citizens.

The third report recommended the chartering of a national bank, the Bank of the United States. Hamilton patterned his proposed bank after the Bank of England and intended it to meet a variety of needs. Jointly owned by the federal government and private investors, it would serve as the fiscal (financial) and depository agent of the government and make loans to businesses. Through a provision that permitted up to three-fourths of the value of bank stock to be purchased with government bonds, the bank would create a market for public securities and hence raise their value. Most important, the bank would provide the nation with a stable currency.

Hamilton's final report, issued in December 1791, recommended government actions to promote industry. Looking, as always, to the British model of economic development, he argued that the United States would never become a great power as long as it imported most of its manufactured goods. Hamilton advocated aid in the form of protective tariffs (high tariffs meant to make imported goods more expensive than domestic goods) for such industries as iron, steel, and shoemaking—which had already begun to establish themselves—and direct subsidies to assist with start-up costs for other industries. He believed that such "patronage," as he called it, would ultimately foster interregional economic dependence.

REACTION AND OPPOSITION

The breadth and boldness of Hamilton's program invited opposition. About half of the members of Congress owned some of the nation's debt, and nearly all of them agreed with Hamilton that it should be paid off. Some opponents, however, were concerned that Hamilton's plan was unfair. Hard times had forced most of the original holders of the debt—by and large, ordinary citizens—to sell their certificates to speculators at a fraction of their face value. Others objected on republican grounds that Hamilton had no intention of actually eliminating the government's debt. He envisioned instead a permanent debt, with the government making regular interest payments as they came due. The debt, in the form of government securities, would serve as a vital prop for the support of moneyed groups.

Opposition to Hamilton's proposal to have the federal government assume state debts reflected sectional differences. With the exception of South Carolina, the Southern states had already paid back a good share of their war debts. Thus Hamilton's plan stood to benefit the Northern states disproportionately.

A compromise was reached in July 1790. Southerners agreed to accept funding in its original form because, as Hamilton correctly noted, it would be impractical, if not impossible, to distinguish between the original and current holders of the national debt. Assumption passed after Hamilton cut a deal with Virginians James Madison and Thomas Jefferson. In exchange for Southern support of assumption, Hamilton agreed to line up Northern votes for locating the nation's permanent capital on the banks of the Potomac River, where it would be surrounded by the slave states of Maryland and Virginia.

The bank bill passed Congress on a vote that divided on sectional lines. Madison objected that the Constitution did not explicitly authorize Congress to charter a bank or any other corporation. Washington sought the cabinet's opinion, provoking the first great debate over how the Constitution should be interpreted. Thomas Jefferson, the secretary of state, sided with Madison and for the first time openly clashed with Hamilton. Taking a strict constructionist position, he argued that all powers the Constitution had not expressly delegated to the national government were reserved to the states under the Tenth amendment. Hamilton, in a brilliant rejoinder, argued that Article 1, Section 8 of the Constitution, which declares that Congress has the right "to make all laws which shall be necessary and proper" to exercise its powers and those of the federal government, gives Congress implicit authority beyond its explicitly enumerated powers. With this broad constructionist position, he won Washington to his side.

With Washington's signature on the bill, Hamilton's bank was chartered for twenty years and a hefty 25 percent tax on distilled liquor was also passed. However, little of Hamilton's plan to promote manufacturing survived.

The Emergence of Parties

By the end of Washington's first term, Americans were dividing into two camps. On one side stood those who still called themselves *Federalists*. These were the supporters of Hamilton's program—speculators, creditors, merchants, manufacturers, and commercial farmers. They were the Americans most fully integrated into the market economy and were concentrated in the North. In both economic and cultural terms, the Federalists were drawn from the more privileged segments of society.

Jefferson and Madison shrewdly gave the name *Republican* to the party that formed in opposition to the Federalists, thus identifying it with individual liberties and the heritage of the Revolution. The Republicans accused Hamilton and the Federalists of attempting to impose a British system of economic privilege and social exploitation. The Republicans were committed to an agrarian America in which power remained in the hands of farmers and planters.

In 1792, parties were still in a formative stage. Washington remained aloof from the political infighting and was still seen as a great unifier. Unopposed, he was reelected in 1792. However, a series of crises in his second term deepened and broadened the incipient party divisions. By 1796, rival parties were contesting the presidency and vying for the support of an increasingly politically organized electorate.

THE FRENCH REVOLUTION

The French Revolution began in 1789, and in its early phase, most Americans applauded it. By 1792, however, the Revolution had turned violent and radical. Its supporters confiscated the property of aristocrats and the church, slaughtered suspected enemies, and executed the king, Louis XVI.

These excesses touched off a bitter debate in America. Federalists drew back in horror, arguing in the Federalist *Gazette of the United States* that "The American Revolution, it ought to be repeated, was not accomplished as the French has been, by massacres, assassinations, or proscriptions." For the Republicans, the French remained the standard-bearers of the cause of liberty for common people everywhere. Jefferson admitted that the French Revolution was tarnished by the loss of innocent lives but was convinced that its cause was just.

When the new French ambassador Edmond Genêt arrived in the United States in April 1793—just as the debate in America over the French Revolution was heating up—Franco-American relations reached a turning point. Genêt, it soon became clear, hoped to embroil the United States in the French war against the British. He commissioned American privateers to attack British shipping and tried to enlist an army of frontiersmen to attack Spanish possessions in Louisiana and Florida.

The president feared that Genêt would stampede Americans into the European war, with disastrous results for the nation's finances. The bulk of America's foreign trade was with the British, and tariff duties on British imports were the main source of revenue to pay for Hamilton's assumption and funding programs. Hamilton urged Washington to declare American neutrality in the European war, maintaining that the president could commit the nation to neutrality on his own authority when Congress, as was then the case, was not in session. Jefferson, although he too wanted to avoid war, disputed Washington's power to act on his own, maintaining that the war-making powers of Congress reserved for it alone the right to issue a declaration of neutrality.

Washington accepted Hamilton's argument on his authority to declare neutrality and issued a proclamation on April 22, 1793, stating that the United States would be "friendly and impartial toward the belligerent powers."

After Genêt's visit, American politics became more open and aggressive. Pro-French enthusiasm lived on in a host of grass-roots political organizations known as the Democratic-Republican societies. As their name suggests, these societies reflected a belief that democracy and republicanism were one and the same. This was a new concept in American politics. As a letter writer to the Newark *Gazette* put it:

> It must be the mechanics and farmers, or the poorer class of people (as they are generally called), that must support the freedom which they and their fathers purchased with their blood—the nobility will never do it—they will be always striving to get the reins of government into their own hands, and then they can ride the people at pleasure.

The Democratic-Republican societies attacked the Washington administration for failing to assist France, and they expressed the popular feeling that Hamilton's program favored the rich over the poor. For the first time, Washington himself was personally assailed in the press.

SECURING THE FRONTIER

Control of the West remained an elusive goal throughout Washington's first term. Indian resistance in the Northwest Territory prevented whites from pushing north of the Ohio River. The powerful Miami Confederacy routed two ill-trained American armies in 1790 and 1791 and inflicted the worst defeat an American army ever suffered in frontier fighting.

By 1793, many western settlers felt abandoned by the national government. They believed that the government had broken a promise to protect them against Indians and foreigners. Much of the popularity of the Democratic-Republican societies in the West fed off these frustrations. Westerners also demanded free and open navigation on the Mississippi River.

The Federalists, on the other hand, wanted submission to national authority from both the Indians and the Western settlers. The War Department was reorganized, and it sent into the Ohio region a force built around veterans from the regular (or professional) army under General Anthony Wayne, a savvy, battle-hardened war hero.

On August 4, 1794, at the Battle of Fallen Timbers, near present-day Toledo, Wayne's army dealt a decisive blow to the Ohio Indians. In the *Treaty of Greenville*, signed in August 1795, twelve tribes ceded most of the present state of Ohio to the U.S. government in return for an annual payment of $9,500. The Ohio country was now open to white settlement.

THE WHISKEY REBELLION

Within a few months of Wayne's victory at Fallen Timbers, another American army was on the move. The target this time was the so-called whiskey rebels of western Pennsylvania, who were openly resisting Hamilton's excise tax on whiskey. Hamilton was determined to enforce the tax and assert the supremacy of national laws. Although resistance to the tax was widespread, he singled out the Pennsylvania rebels. Washington was convinced that the Democratic-Republican societies of western Pennsylvania were behind the defiance of federal authority there and welcomed the opportunity to chastise these organizations, which he identified with the dangerous doctrines of the French Revolution.

Washington called on the governors of the Mid-Atlantic states to supply militia forces to crush the *Whiskey Rebellion*. The 13,000-man army that assembled at Harrisburg and marched into western Pennsylvania in October 1794 was larger than any Washington had

This painting by an officer on General Wayne's staff shows Little Turtle, a Miami chief, speaking through an interpreter to General Wayne (with one hand behind his back) during the negotiations that led to the Treaty of Greenville.

Painting; P & S–1914.0001; "The Treaty of Fort Greenville, Ohio," 1795. Artist unknown. Member of Gen. Anthony Wayne's Staff.

commanded during the Revolution. But the rebellion, as Jefferson sardonically noted, "could never be found." The army met no resistance and expended considerable effort rounding up twenty prisoners. Still, the Federalists had made their point: When its authority was openly challenged, this national government was prepared to use military force to compel obedience.

The Whiskey Rebellion starkly revealed the conflicting visions of local liberty and national order that divided Americans of the early republic. The non-English majority on the Pennsylvania frontier—Irish, Scots-Irish, German, and Welsh—justified resistance to the whiskey tax with the same republican ideology that had fueled the American Revolution. In putting down the Pennsylvania rebels, Washington and Hamilton acted on behalf of more English and cosmopolitan groups in the East who valued central power as a check on any local resistance movement that might begin unraveling the still fragile republic.

TREATIES WITH BRITAIN AND SPAIN

Washington's government had the resources to suppress Indians and frontier dissidents but lacked sufficient armed might to push Spain and especially Britain out of the West. Meanwhile, on the high seas, the British began seizing American ships in an effort to prevent them from trading with the French. Desperate to avert a war, Washington sent John Jay, the chief justice of the United States, to London to negotiate an accord.

From the American point of view, the resulting agreement, known as *Jay's Treaty*, was flawed but acceptable. Jay had to abandon the right of the United States to continue trading with France without British harassment. He also had to grant Britain "most favored nation" status, giving up the American right to discriminate against British shipping and merchandise. And he had to reconfirm the American commitment that pre-Revolutionary debts owed by Americans to the British would be repaid in full. In return for these major concessions, Britain pledged to compensate American merchants for the ships and cargoes it had seized in 1793 and 1794, to abandon the six forts it still held in the American Northwest, and to grant the United States limited trading rights in India and the British West Indies. Signed in November 1794, Jay's Treaty caused an uproar in the United States when its terms became known in March 1795. Southerners saw in it another sellout of their interests. The Senate ratified the treaty in June 1795, but only because Washington backed it.

Jay's Treaty helped convince Spain to adopt a more conciliatory attitude toward the United States. In the *Treaty of San Lorenzo* (also known as *Pinckney's Treaty*) of 1795, Spain accepted the American position on the 31st parallel as the northern boundary of Spanish Florida and granted American farmers the right of free transit through the port of New Orleans.

THE FIRST PARTISAN ELECTION

Two terms in office were more than enough for Washington. The partisan politics that emerged during his second term—and its expression in an increasingly partisan press—disgusted him. He announced his decision to retire from public life in his Farewell Address of September 1796, less than two months before the presidential election. He intentionally delayed the announcement to minimize the time the Republicans would have to prepare for the campaign. Washington devoted most of his address to a denunciation of partisanship. He invoked the republican ideal of disinterested, independent statesmanship as the only sure and virtuous guide for the nation. He warned against any permanent foreign alliances and cautioned that the Union itself would be endangered if parties continued to be characterized "by geographical discriminations—*Northern* and *Southern, Atlantic* and *Western.*"

Confirming Washington's fears, the election of 1796 was the first openly partisan election in American history. John Adams was the Federalist candidate and Thomas Jefferson the Republican candidate. Each was selected at a party caucus, a meeting of party leaders.

Adams won despite Alexander Hamilton's interference, which inadvertently almost threw the election to Jefferson. Now a private citizen in New York, Hamilton wanted to be the power behind the throne in any new Federalist administration. Uncomfortable with Adams, he connived to have Thomas Pinckney of South Carolina, the other Federalist running with Adams, win the election. The Constitution did not originally call for electors to cast separate ballots for president and vice president. The Constitution was written with absolutely no thought of organized partisan competition for the presidency. Taking advantage of this weakness, Hamilton convinced some of the South Carolina electors to drop Adams from their ballots. He expected that with the solid support of the New England electors for both Adams and Pinckney, Pinckney would be elected president and Adams vice president. But the scheme backfired. When New Englanders learned of it, they refused to vote for Pinckney. As a result, Adams came in first with seventy-one votes, but Jefferson came in second with sixty-eight. Thanks to Hamilton, Adams entered office with his chief rival as vice president and a politically divided administration. Adams received all the northern electoral votes, with the exception of Pennsylvania's. Jefferson was the overwhelming favorite in the South.

The Last Federalist Administration

The Adams administration got off to a rocky start from which it never recovered. Adams had been a lawyer before the Revolution; he was a veteran of both Continental Congresses, had been a diplomat in Europe for a decade, and had served as Washington's vice president for eight years. But despite this extraordinarily rich background in public affairs, he was politically naive. Scrupulously honest but quick to take offense, he lacked the politician's touch for inspiring personal loyalty and crafting compromises based on a realistic recognition of mutual self-interest. But putting the interests of the country before those of his party, he almost single-handedly prevented a nearly certain war with France and a possible civil war at home. The price he paid was a badly split Federalist party that refused to unite behind him when he sought reelection in 1800.

THE FRENCH CRISIS AND THE XYZ AFFAIR

An aggressive coalition known as the Directory gained control of revolutionary France in 1795 and denounced the Jay treaty as evidence of an Anglo-American alliance against France. The French annulled the commercial treaty of 1778 with the United States; ordered the seizure of American ships carrying goods to the British; and declared that any American sailors found on British ships, including those forcibly pressed into service, would be summarily executed.

In the fall of 1797, Adams sent three commissioners to Paris in an effort to avoid war. The French treated the three with contempt. Having just conquered the Netherlands and detached Spain from its British alliance, France was in no mood to compromise. Through three intermediaries—identified by Adams only as X,Y, and Z when he informed Congress of the negotiations—the French foreign minister demanded a large bribe to initiate talks and an American loan of $12 million.

In April 1798, the Senate published a full account of the insulting behavior of the French in what came to be called the *XYZ Affair*. The public was indignant, and war fever swept the country. By the fall of 1798, American ships were waging an undeclared war against the French in Caribbean waters, a conflict that came to be known as the *Quasi-War*. The Federalists, who had always warned against the French, enjoyed greater popularity than they ever had or ever would again. Congress acted to upgrade the navy and the army dramatically and adopted Washington's suggestion that Hamilton be appointed second in command. To pay for both the expanded army and the naval rearmament, the Federalists pushed through the Direct Tax of 1798, a levy on the value of land, slaves, and dwellings.

CRISIS AT HOME

The thought of Hamilton in charge of a huge army convinced many Republicans that their worst nightmares were about to materialize. The Federalists then passed four laws in the summer of 1798, known collectively as the *Alien and Sedition Acts*, that confirmed the Republicans' fears. The most dangerous of the four acts in the minds of Republicans was the *Sedition Act*, a measure that made it a federal crime to engage in any combination or conspiracy against the government or to utter or print anything "false, scandalous and malicious" against the government. Federalist judges were blatantly partisan in their enforcement of the Sedition Act. Twenty-five individuals, mostly Republican editors, were indicted under the act, and ten were convicted.

Facing a Congress and a Supreme Court dominated by the Federalists, Jefferson and Madison turned to the safely Republican legislatures of Kentucky and Virginia for resolution that attacked the constitutionality of the Alien and Sedition Acts, and they produced the first significant articulation of the southern stand on *states' rights*. The resolutions—adopted in the fall of 1798—proposed a compact theory of the Constitution. They asserted that the states had delegated specific powers to the national government for their common benefit. It followed that the states reserved the right to rule whether the national government had unconstitutionally assumed power not granted to it. If a state decided that the national government had exceeded its powers, it could "interpose" its authority to shield its citizens from a tyrannical law. In a second set of resolutions, the Kentucky legislature introduced the doctrine of *nullification*, the right of a state to render null and void a national law it deemed unconstitutional.

Jefferson and Madison hoped that these resolutions would rally voters to the Republican party as the defender of threatened American liberties, yet not a single additional state seconded them. In the end, what aroused popular rage against the Federalists was not legislation directed against aliens and subversives but the high cost of Federalist taxes.

The Direct Tax of 1798 fell on all owners of land, dwellings, or slaves and provoked widespread resentment. Enforcing it required an army of bureaucrats—more than five hundred for the state of Pennsylvania alone. In February 1799, in the heavily German southeastern counties of Pennsylvania, a group of men led by an auctioneer named John Fries released tax evaders from prison in Bethlehem. President Adams responded to Fries's Rebellion with a show of force, but the fiercest resistance the soldiers he sent to Pennsylvania encountered was from irate farm wives, who doused them with hot water. The Federalists had now lost much of their support in Pennsylvania.

THE END OF THE FEDERALISTS

The events in Pennsylvania reflected an air of menace that gripped the country as the campaign of 1800 approached. The army was chasing private citizens whose only crime in the eyes of many was that they were honoring their Revolutionary heritage by resisting hateful taxes. Federal soldiers also roughed up Republican voters at polling places. Southern Republicans talked in private of the possible need to resist Federalist tyranny by force and, failing in that, to secede from the Union. Hamilton and his backers, known as the High Federalists, saw in the Kentucky and Virginia resolutions "a regular conspiracy to overturn the government."

No one did more to defuse this charged atmosphere than President Adams. The Federalists depended for their popular support on the expectation of a war with France, which as late as 1798 had swept them to victory in the congressional elections. Still, Adams refrained from asking for a declaration of war. Adams recognized that war with France could trigger a civil war at home. Hamilton and the High Federalists, he feared, would use war as an excuse to crush the Republican opposition in Virginia. Fearful of Hamilton's intentions and unwilling to run the risk of militarizing the government, Adams broke with his party and decided to reopen negotiations with France in February 1799.

The *Franco-American Accord of 1800* that resulted from Adams's initiative released the United States from its 1778 alliance with France and in return the United States surrendered all claims against the French for damages done to American shipping. The prospect of peace with France deprived the Hamilton Federalists of their trump card in the election. The Republicans could no longer be branded as the traitorous friends of an enemy state. The enlarged army, with no foe to fight, became a political embarrassment, and the Federalists dismantled it. Although rumors of possible violence continued to circulate, the Republicans grew increasingly confident that they could peacefully gain control of the government.

The Federalists, hampered by party disunity, could not counter the Republicans' aggressive organizational tactics. They found it distasteful to appeal to common people. Wherever the Republicans organized, they attacked the Federalists as monarchists plotting to undo the gains of the Revolution. The Federalists responded with emotional appeals that depicted Jefferson as a godless revolutionary whose election would usher in a reign of terror. "The effect," intoned the Reverend William Linn, "would be to destroy religion, introduce immorality, and loosen all bonds of society."

Attacks like Linn's reflected the fears of Calvinist preachers that a tide of disbelief was about to submerge Christianity in the United States. *Deism*, an Enlightenment religious philosophy popular among the leaders of the Revolutionary era, was making inroads among common citizens as well. Deists viewed God as a kind of master clockmaker who created the laws by which the universe runs but otherwise leaves it alone. They rejected revelation for reason, maintaining that the workings of nature alone reveal God's design. These developments convinced Calvinist ministers, nearly all of them Federalists, that the atheism of the French Revolution was infecting American republicanism.

The Republicans won the election by mobilizing voters through strong party organizations. Voter turnout in 1800 was twice what it had been in the early 1790s, and most of the new voters were Republicans. The Direct Tax of 1798 cost the Federalists the support of commercial farmers in the Mid-Atlantic states. Artisans in port cities had already switched to the Republicans in protest over Jay's Treaty, which they feared left them exposed to a flood of cheap British imports. Adams carried New England and had a smattering of support

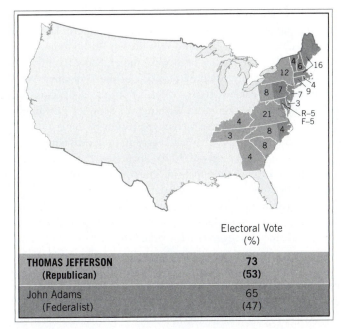

Electoral Vote
(%)

THOMAS JEFFERSON (Republican)	**73** **(53)**
John Adams (Federalist)	65 (47)

MAP 8–1
The Election of 1800 The sharp erosion of Federalist strength in New York and Pennsylvania after 1798 swung the election of 1800 to the Republicans.

WHAT DOES this map show you about the interests of Jeffersonian Republicans versus those of the Federalists? Based on geographic regions, which party was more likely to represent farmers?

elsewhere. With New York added to their solid base in the South and the backcountry, the Jeffersonians gained an electoral majority (see Map 8–1).

Party unity among Republican electors was so strong that Jefferson and Burr each received seventy-three electoral votes. Consequently the election was thrown into the House of Representatives, which, until the newly elected Congress was seated, was still dominated by Federalists. Hoping to deny Jefferson the presidency, the Federalists in the House backed Burr. The result was a deadlock that persisted into the early months of 1801 when the Federalists yielded. Informed through intermediaries that Jefferson would not dismantle Hamilton's fiscal system, enough Federalists cast blank ballots to give Jefferson the majority he needed for election. The Twelfth Amendment to the Constitution, ratified in 1804, prevented a similar impasse from arising again by requiring electors to cast separate ballots for president and vice president.

Conclusion

In 1789, the American republic was little more than an experiment in self-government. The Federalists provided a firm foundation for that experiment. Hamilton's financial program, neutrality in the wars of the French Revolution, and the diplomatic settlement with Britain in Jay's Treaty bequeathed the young nation a decade of peace and prosperity.

Federalist policies, however, provoked strong opposition rooted in conflicting economic interests and contrasting regional views over the meaning of liberty and government in the new republic. The Federalist coalition split during Washington's second term when Southern planters joined urban artisans and backcountry Scots-Irish farmers in opposing Jay's Treaty and the commercially oriented program of the Federalists. When Quaker and German farmers in the Mid-Atlantic states defected from the Federalists over the tax legislation of 1798, three of the four regions in Washington's America now lined up behind the Republicans in the belief that measures such as expansion of the army and passage of the Alien and Sedition Acts threatened individual liberty and regional autonomy.

The openly partisan politics of the 1790s surprised the country's founders, who equated parties with the evils of factionalism. They had not foreseen that parties would forge a necessary link between the rulers and the ruled and create a mechanism by which group values and regional interests could be given a political voice. To the credit of the Federalists, they relinquished control of the national government peacefully. The importance of this precedent can scarcely be exaggerated. It marked the first time in modern political history that a party in power handed over the government to its opposition.

Party formation climaxed in the election of 1800, when the Republicans ended the Federalists' rule. The Republicans won by embracing the popular demand for a more egalitarian social and political order.

It now remained to be seen what the Republicans would do with their newfound power.

REVIEW QUESTIONS

1. What role did the "people" play in Washington's inauguration in 1789? What was the purpose of the grand procession, and why were the militia present?

2. What was distinctive about the four regions of the United States in 1790? What were the common values and goals that brought white Americans together?

3. How were the major problems confronting the Washington administration resolved?

4. How did the Federalists and the Republicans differ over the meaning of liberty and the power of the national government?

5. Why did Jefferson call his election of 1800 the "revolution of 1800"?

The Triumph and Collapse of Jeffersonian Republicanism

1800–1824

What did Thomas Jefferson achieve as president?

What challenges did James Madison face as president?

What were the consequences of the War of 1812?

How did nationalism increase during the Era of Good Feelings?

What was the Missouri Compromise?

Riversdale,
30 August 1814

My dear Sister,

Since I started this letter [on Aug. 9] we have been in a state of continual alarm, and now I have time to write only two or three lines to ask you to tell Papa that we are alive, in good health, and I hope safe from danger. I am sure that you have heard the news of the battle of Bladensburg where the English defeated the American troops with Madison 'not at their head, but at their rear.'

From there they went to Washington where they burned the Capitol, the President's House, all the public offices, etc. During the battle I saw several cannonballs with my own eyes, and I will write all the details to your husband. At the moment the English ships are at Alexandria which is also in their possession.

I don't know how all this will end, but I fear very badly for us. It is probable that it will also bring about a dissolution of the union of the states, and in that case, farewell to the public debt. You know I have predicted this outcome for a long time. Wouldn't it be wise to send your husband here without delay, in order to plan with me the best course to pursue for Papa's interests as well as yours?

This letter will go, I think, by a Dutch ship. If I have time with the confusion we are in, I will write again in a few days, perhaps by the same vessel. At present my house is full of people every day and at night my bedroom is full of rifles, pistols, sabers, etc. Many thanks to your husband for the information in his letter of 27 April, and tell him that I invested all his money in the May loan [of the U.S. Treasury]. Please give many greetings to my dear Father and to Charles [her brother]. Embrace your children for me and believe me.

Your affectionate sister,

—Rosalie E. Calvert

Margaret Law Callcott, ed., *Mistress of Riversdale: The Plantation Letters of Rosalie Steir Calvert, 1795–1821* (Baltimore: The Johns Hopkins University Press, 1991), pp. 271–272.

ROSALIE CALVERT, from her plantation home in Maryland, wrote to her sister about the British attack on Washington, D.C., in August 1814, the low point of the American cause in the War of 1812.

The Calverts lived at Riversdale and managed three plantations worked by slave labor. Rosalie's wealth and elite social standing deepened her political conservatism. In her eyes, Jefferson and his followers were demagogues who catered to the poor and threatened to infect America with the political radicalism of the French Revolution. She blamed the War of 1812 on ill-conceived Republican policies and feared that the war would unleash massive unrest within the United States.

Her fears were overblown. The United States weathered the War of 1812 and the Calverts were spared any property damage at their Riversdale estate. Rosalie, however, survived the war by only six years. The strain of having nine children and suffering one miscarriage in twenty-one years of marriage may have contributed to her death at the age of 43 from congestive heart failure.

Despite her denunciations of the Republicans, Jefferson and his Republican successors, James Madison and James Monroe, promoted the growth and independence of the United States. Expansionist policies to the south and west more than doubled the size of the republic and fueled the westward spread of slavery. The war against Britain from 1812 to 1815, if less than a military triumph, freed Americans to look inward for economic development.

At the height of Republican success during the Era of Good Feelings just after the War of 1812, the Federalist party collapsed. Without an organized opposition to enforce party discipline among themselves, the Republicans followed the Federalists into political oblivion. A financial panic and a battle over slavery in Missouri shattered Republican unity. By the mid-1820s, a new party system was emerging.

Jefferson's Presidency

Thomas Jefferson believed that a true revolution had occurred in 1800, a peaceful overthrow of the Federalist party and its hated principles of government consolidation and military force. In his eyes, the defeat of the monarchical Federalists reconfirmed the true political legacy of the Revolution by restoring the Republican majority to its rightful control of the government.

Unlike the Hamiltonian Federalists, whose commercial vision of America accepted social and economic inequalities as inevitable, the Jeffersonians wanted a predominantly agrarian republic based on widespread economic equality for white yeomen families to counter any threat posed by the privileged few to the people's liberties. Jefferson's first administration was a solid success. A unified Republican party reduced the size and scope of the federal govern-ment, allowed the Alien and Sedition Acts to lapse, and celebrated the Louisiana Purchase. His second term, however, was a bitter disappointment, marked by the failure of his unpopular embargo on American foreign trade. As a result, Jefferson left his successor, James Madison, a divided party, a temporarily revived Federalism, and an unresolved crisis in foreign affairs.

REFORM AT HOME

Jefferson set the style and tone of his administration from the beginning. He was the first president to be inaugurated in Washington, D.C., and his inauguration was as unpretentious as the raw and primitive capital city itself. He walked from his lodgings to the Capitol building to be sworn in. His dress was neat but shorn of gentlemanly refinements such as a wig. After giving notice that an unadorned style of republican egalitarianism would now replace the aristocratic formalities of the Federalists, Jefferson emphasized in his inaugural address the overwhelming commitment of Americans to the "republican form" of govern-ment and affirmed his own support of civil liberties as an American principle.

A poor public speaker, Jefferson sent written messages to Congress to avoid having to read them in person. This change from Federalist policy both eliminated the impression of a monarch addressing his subjects and played to Jefferson's formidable skills as a writer. He replaced the stiff formalism and aristocratic etiquette of receptions for presidential visitors with more relaxed weekly meetings around a circular table at which fine food and wine were nevertheless served.

The cornerstone of Republican domestic policy was retrenchment, a return to the fru-gal, simple federal establishment the Jeffersonians believed was the original intent of the Constitution. The Republicans began with fiscal policy. Jefferson's secretary of the treasury was Albert Gallatin, who convinced Jefferson that the Bank of the United States was essen-tial for financial stability and yet succeeded in reducing the national debt from $83 million in 1800 to $57 million by 1809. Gallatin's conservative fiscal policies shrank both the spending and taxes of the national government. The Republicans eliminated all internal taxes, including the despised tax on whiskey. Slashes in the military budget enabled govern-ment expenditures to stay below the level of 1800. The cuts in military spending combined with soaring revenues from customs collections left Gallatin with a surplus in the budget that he could devote to debt repayment.

Jeffersonian reform targeted the political character, as well as the size, of the national government. He moved to break the Federalist stranglehold on federal offices and appoint officials with sound Republican principles, replacing those deemed guilty of misusing their offices for political gain. By the time Jefferson left the presidency in 1809, Republicans held nearly all the appointive offices.

Jefferson moved most aggressively against the Federalists in the judiciary. Just days before they relinquished power, the Federalists enraged the Jeffersonians by passing the Judiciary Act of 1801, legislation that both enlarged the judiciary and packed it with more Federalists appointed by Adams, the outgoing president.

The Republicans fought back. Now dominant in Congress, they quickly repealed the Judiciary Act of 1801. Frustrated Federalists now turned to John Marshall, a staunch Federalist chief justice of the United States appointed by President Adams in 1801, in the hope that he would rule that Congress had acted unconstitutionally in removing the recently appointed federal judges. Marshall moved carefully, aware that the Republicans contended that Congress and the president had at least a coequal right with the Supreme Court to decide constitutional questions.

The issue came to a head in the case of **Marbury v. Madison** (1803), which centered on Secretary of State James Madison's refusal to deliver a commission to William Marbury, one of Adams's "midnight appointments." Marshall held that although Marbury had a legal right to his commission, the Court had no jurisdiction in the case. The Court ruled that the section of the Judiciary Act of 1789 granting it the power to order the delivery of Marbury's commission was unconstitutional because it conferred on the Court a power not specified in Article 3 of the Constitution on cases of original jurisdiction. Marshall created the precedent of judicial review, the power of the Supreme Court to rule on the constitutionality of federal law. This doctrine was of pivotal importance for the future of the Court. Marshall had brilliantly turned a threatening situation into a success for the judiciary.

THE LOUISIANA PURCHASE

In foreign affairs, fortune smiled on Jefferson during his first term. The European war that had almost sucked in the United States in the 1790s subsided. Jefferson, despite his distaste for a strong navy, ordered a show of force in the Mediterranean to punish the Barbary pirates who were preying on American shipping.

For years, the North African states of Morocco, Algeria, Tunis, and Tripoli had demanded cash tribute from foreigners as the price for allowing trade in the Mediterranean. Jefferson stopped the payments in 1801, and when the attacks on American shipping resumed, he retaliated by sending warships to the Mediterranean. The tribute system continued until 1815, but on much more favorable terms for the United States.

The Anglo–French peace was a mixed blessing for the United States. Although it removed any immediate threat of war, the return of peace also enabled Spain and France to reclaim their colonial trade in the Western Hemisphere. The new military ruler of France, Napoleon Bonaparte, in a secret treaty with Spain in 1800, reacquired for France the Louisiana Territory, a vast, vaguely defined area stretching between the Mississippi River and the Rocky Mountains. Sketchy, unconfirmed reports of the treaty in the spring of 1801 alarmed Jefferson. France, for its part, was a formidable opponent whose control of the Mississippi Valley, combined with the British presence in Canada, threatened to hem in the United States. Jefferson was prepared to reverse the traditional foreign policy of his party and opened exploratory talks with the British on an Anglo-American alliance to drive the French out of Louisiana. He also strengthened American forces in the Mississippi Valley and secured congressional approval for an exploring expedition through upper Louisiana led by Meriwether Lewis and William Clark. This was initially intended to be more of a military than a scientific mission.

Jefferson then sought to acquire New Orleans and control the mouth of the Mississippi River, outlet to world markets. He persuaded Congress to pass resolutions threatening an attack on New Orleans (see Map 9–1).

Meanwhile, Napoleon had envisioned the rich sugar island of St. Domingue (today divided between Haiti and the Dominican Republic) as the jewel of his new empire and he intended to use the Louisiana Territory as a granary to supply the island. But he failed to recover St. Domingue from the slaves on the island, led by Touissant L'Ouverture, who had captured it in a bloody and successful bid for independence. Without firm French control of St. Domingue, Louisiana was of little use to Napoleon and a renewed war against Britain was looming. To Jefferson's surprise, Napoleon sold Louisiana to the United States for $15 million

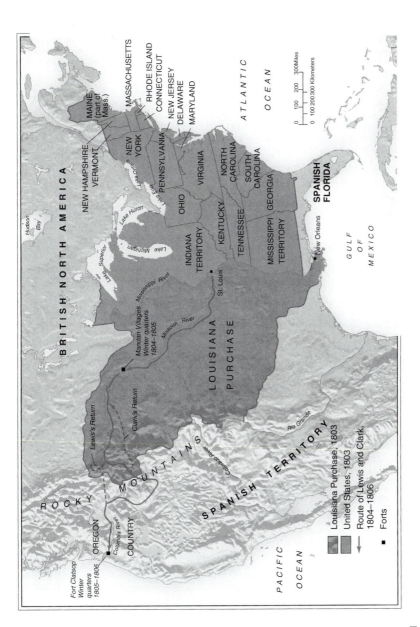

MAP 9–1

The Louisiana Purchase and the Lewis and Clark Expedition The vast expanse of the Louisiana Purchase was virtually unknown territory to Americans before the Lewis and Clark expedition gathered a mass of scientific information about it.

BASED ON this map, how did the Louisiana Purchase impact United States trade and trade routes?

• CHRONOLOGY •

1801 Thomas Jefferson is inaugurated, the first Republican president.
John Marshall becomes chief justice.

1802 Congress repeals the Judiciary Act of 1801.

1803 *Marbury* v. *Madison* sets the precedent of judicial review by the Supreme Court.
Louisiana Purchase.

1804 Vice President Aaron Burr kills Alexander Hamilton in a duel.
Judges John Pickering and Samuel Chase impeached by Republicans.
Jefferson is reelected.

1806 Britain and France issue orders restricting neutral shipping.
Betrayal of the Burr conspiracy.

1807 *Chesapeake* affair.
Congress passes the Embargo Act.

1808 Congress prohibits the African slave trade.
James Madison elected president.

1809 Repeal of the Embargo Act.
Passage of the Nonintercourse Act.

1810 Macon's Bill No. 2 reopens trade with Britain and France.
United States annexes part of West Florida.
Georgia state law invalidated by the Supreme Court in *Fletcher* v. *Peck*.

1811 Battle of Tippecanoe and defeat of the Indian confederation.
Charter of the Bank of the United States expires.

1812 Congress declares war on Britain.
American loss of Detroit.
Madison reelected.

1813 Perry's victory at Battle of Put-in-Bay.
Battle of the Thames and death of Tecumseh.

1814 Jackson crushes the Creeks at the Battle of Horseshoe Bend.
British burn Washington, D.C., and attack Baltimore.
Macdonough's naval victory on Lake Champlain turns back a British invasion.
Hartford Convention meets.
Treaty of Ghent signed.

1815 Jackson routs British at the Battle of New Orleans.

1816 Congress charters the Second Bank of the United States and passes a protective tariff.
James Monroe elected president.

1817 Rush–Bagot Treaty demilitarizes the Great Lakes.

1818 Anglo-American Accords on trade and boundaries.
Jackson's border campaign in Spanish East Florida.

1819 Trans-Continental Treaty between United States and Spain.
Beginning of the Missouri controversy.
Financial panic sends economy into a depression.
Dartmouth College v. *Woodward* upholds the charter rights of corporations.
McCulloch v. *Maryland* upholds constitutionality of the Bank of the United States.

1820 Missouri Compromise on slavery in the Louisiana Purchase.
Monroe reelected.

1823 Monroe Doctrine proclaims Western Hemisphere closed to further European colonization.

1825 John Quincy Adams elected president by the House of Representatives.

(the cost to the United States was about 3 1/2 cents per acre). Jefferson, the strict constructionist, now turned pragmatist. Despite the lack of any specific authorization in the Constitution for the acquisition of foreign territory, he accepted Napoleon's deal and doubled the size of the United States with the *Louisiana Purchase*. Jefferson was willing, as the Federalists had been when they were in power, to stretch the Constitution to support his definition of the national good. Ironically, it was now the Federalists, fearful of a further decline in their political power, who relied on a narrow reading of the Constitution.

FLORIDA AND WESTERN SCHEMES

The magnificent prize of Louisiana did not satisfy Republican territorial ambitions. Still to be gained were river outlets on the Gulf Coast essential for the development of plantation agriculture in Alabama and Mississippi. The boundaries of the Louisiana Purchase were so vague that Jefferson felt justified in claiming Spanish-held Texas and the Gulf Coast eastward from New Orleans to Mobile Bay, including the Spanish province of West Florida. This provoked the first challenge to his leadership of the party.

Once it was clear that Spain did not want to sell West Florida to the United States, Jefferson covertly accepted Napoleon's offer to act as a middleman in the acquisition. Former Republican stalwarts in Congress staged a party revolt against the president's devious tactics.

Jefferson's failed bid for West Florida emboldened Westerners to demand that Americans seize the territory by force. In 1805 and 1806, Aaron Burr, Jefferson's first vice president, apparently became entangled in an attempt at just such a land grab. Republicans had been suspicious of Burr since his dalliance with the Federalists in their bid to make him president rather than Jefferson in 1800. A minority of die-hard Federalists, fearing that incorporation of the vast territory of the Louisiana Purchase into the United States would reduce New England's power, backed Burr in the New York gubernatorial race of 1804. Burr lost, largely because Hamilton denounced his character. The enmity between the two men reached a tragic climax in July 1804, when Burr killed Hamilton in a duel. Facing murder charges, Burr fled to the West and lined up followers for a separatist plot.

The Burr conspiracy remains mysterious. Burr may have been thinking of carving out a separate western confederacy in the lower Mississippi Valley. Whatever he had in mind, he blundered in relying on General James Wilkinson as a coconspirator. Wilkinson, the military governor of the Louisiana Territory and also a double agent for Spain, betrayed Burr. Jefferson made extraordinary efforts to secure a conviction, but Burr was acquitted when the government failed to prove its case for treason in 1807.

EMBARGO AND A CRIPPLED PRESIDENCY

Concern about a possible war against Britain in 1807 soon quieted the uproar over Burr's trial. After Britain and France resumed their war in 1803, the United States became enmeshed in the same thicket of neutral rights, blockades, ship seizures, and impressment of American sailors that had almost dragged the country into war in the 1790s. Caught in the middle, but eager to supply both sides, was the American merchant marine, the world's largest carrier of neutral goods. American merchants and shippers had taken full advantage of the magnificent opportunities opened up by the European war. The flush years from 1793 to 1807 witnessed a tripling of American ship tonnage, and the value of exports soared five times over. American merchants dominated trade not only between Britain and the United States but also between the European continent and the French and Spanish colonies in the West Indies.

The **Chesapeake Incident** in June 1807 nearly triggered an Anglo-American war. When the commander of the U.S. frigate *Chesapeake* refused to submit to a British search in coastal waters off Norfolk, the British ship *Leopard* opened fire, and three Americans were killed. Jefferson resisted the popular outcry for revenge. Instead, he barred American ports to British warships and called for monetary compensation and an end to impressment, not only because the country was woefully unprepared for war but also because he passionately believed that international law should resolve disputes between nations. In a last burst of the idealism that had animated the republicanism of the Revolution, Jefferson resorted to a trade embargo as a substitute for war. The **Embargo Act of 1807** prohibited American ships from clearing port to any nation until Britain and France repealed their trading restrictions on neutral shippers.

The basic premise of the embargo, that Europe was completely dependent on American-supplied foodstuffs and raw materials, was not so much wrong as unrealistic. The embargo did hurt Europe, but the people who first felt the pain were British textile workers and slaves in the colonies, hardly those who wielded the levers of power. Meanwhile, the American export trade and its profits dried up, and nearly all economic groups suffered. Especially hard hit were New England shippers and merchants, who accused the Republicans of near-criminal irresponsibility for forcing a depression on the country. Jefferson responded with a series of enforcement acts that consolidated executive powers far beyond what the Federalists themselves had been able to achieve while in power. As the embargo tightened and the 1808 election approached, Federalism revived. The Federalist Charles C. Pinckney of South Carolina tripled his electoral vote over that of 1804, but Secretary of State Madison carried the South and the West, the heartland of Republican support. Before Madison took office, the Republicans abandoned Jefferson's embargo in 1809, replacing it with the **Nonintercourse Act**, a measure that prohibited American trade only with Britain and France.

Madison and the Coming of War

Frail-looking and short, Madison struck most contemporaries as an indecisive and weaker version of Jefferson. Yet in intellectual toughness and resourcefulness he was at least Jefferson's equal. He failed because of an inherited foreign policy that was partly of his own making as Jefferson's secretary of state. The Republicans' idealistic stand on neutral rights was ultimately untenable unless backed up by military and political force. Madison concluded as much when he decided on war against Britain in the spring of 1812. Thus did the Republicans push for a war they were eager to fight but unprepared to wage.

THE FAILURE OF ECONOMIC SANCTIONS

Early in his administration, Madison became convinced that the impasse in Anglo-American relations was about to be broken. Britain benefited from the Nonintercourse Act at the expense of France. Once at sea, American ships were kept away from France and steered to England by the strong British navy. Perhaps in recognition of this unintended consequence of the new American policy, the British began to relax their restrictions on neutral shipping, known as the Orders in Council, in favor of U.S. commerce. At the same time, the British minister in Washington, David Erskine, reached an agreement with Madison that called for completely rescinding the Orders in Council as they applied to the United States. Unfortunately, Erskine had exceeded his instructions, and the Madison-Erskine agreement was later disavowed in London. Although Madison reimposed sanctions on Britain in August, he was left looking the fool.

Congress stepped in with its own policy in 1810. Macon's Bill No. 2 threw open American trade to everyone but stipulated that if either France or England lifted its restrictions, the president would resume trading sanctions against the other. Madison now looked even more foolish when he accepted Napoleon's duplicitous promises in 1810 to withdraw his decrees against American shipping on the condition that if Britain did not follow suit,

Madison would force the British to respect American rights. French seizures of American ships continued, and by the time Napoleon's duplicity became clear, he had already succeeded in worsening Anglo-American tensions to the point that in November 1810, Madison reimposed nonintercourse against Britain, putting the two nations on a collision course.

THE FRONTIER AND INDIAN RESISTANCE

Mounting frustrations in the South and West also pushed Madison toward a war against Britain. Farm prices, including those for the Southern staples of cotton and tobacco, plunged when Jefferson's embargo shut off exports and stayed low after the embargo was lifted. Blame for the persistent agricultural depression focused on the British and their stranglehold on overseas trade after 1808.

Western settlers also accused the British of inciting Indian resistance. After the *Chesapeake* incident, the British did seek alliances with Indians in the Old Northwest, reviving the strategy of using them as a buffer against any American move on Canada. It was the unceasing demand of Americans for ever more Indian land, however, not any British incitements, that triggered the **pan-Indian resistance movement** that so frightened western settlers on the eve of the War of 1812.

In the Treaty of Greenville (1795), the American government had promised that any future acquisitions of Indian land would have to be approved by all native peoples in the region. Nonetheless, government agents continued their former tactics of playing one group against another and of dividing groups from within. By such means, William Henry Harrison, the governor of the Indiana Territory, procured most of southern Indiana in the *Treaty of Vincennes* of 1804. Two extraordinary leaders, the Shawnee chief Tecumseh and his brother, the Prophet Tenskwatawa, channeled Indian outrage over this treaty into a movement to unify tribes throughout the West for a stand against the white invaders. As preached by Tecumseh and the Prophet, Indian land could be saved and self-respect regained only through racial solidarity and a spiritual rebirth. With the assistance of Tecumseh,

The Prophet Tenskwatawa was the spiritual leader of the pan-Indian movement that sought to revitalize native culture and block the spread of white settlement in the Old Northwest.

Tenskwatawa established the Prophet's Town in 1808, at the confluence of the Wabash and Tippecanoe Rivers in north-central Indiana, as headquarters of an intertribal confederation. As he tried to explain to the worried Governor Harrison, his goals were peaceful. He admonished his followers, "[Do] not take up the tomahawk, . . . do not meddle with any thing that does not belong to you, but mind your own business, and cultivate the ground, that your women and your children have enough to live on."

That ground, of course, was the very reason the Indians could not live in peace and dignity. The white settlers wanted it and would do anything to get it. In November 1811, Harrison marched an army to Prophet's Town and provoked the *Battle of Tippecanoe*. While Tecumseh was absent on a recruiting mission among the southern tribes, impetuous young braves attacked Harrison's army. Harrison's victory came at a high cost, for Tecumseh now joined forces with the British.

While Harrison's aggressiveness was converting fears of a British-Indian alliance into a self-fulfilling prophecy, expansionist-minded Southerners struck at Britain through Spain, now its ally against Napoleon. With the covert support of President Madison, American adventurers staged a bloodless revolt in Spanish West Florida between Louisiana and the Pearl River. Hatred of Native Americans, expansionist pressures, the lingering agricultural depression, and impatience with the administration's policy of economic coercion all pointed in the same direction—a war against Britain coupled with an American takeover of British Canada and Spanish Florida. This was the rallying cry of the *War Hawks*, the forty or so prowar congressmen swept into office in 1810. Generally younger men from the South and West, the War Hawks were led by Henry Clay of Kentucky. Along with other outspoken nationalists such as John C. Calhoun of South Carolina, Clay played a key role in building congressional support for Madison's growing aggressiveness on the British issue.

DECISION FOR WAR

In July 1811, deceived by Napoleon and dismissed by the British as the head of a second-rate power, Madison had run out of diplomatic options and was losing control of his party. When Congress met in November, Madison tried to lay the groundwork for war. But the Republican-controlled Congress balked at strengthening the military or raising taxes to pay for a war that seemed ever more likely, citing their party's traditional view of high taxes and a strong military as the tools of despots. Madison secretly asked Congress on April 1 for a sixty-day embargo, a move designed to give American merchant ships time to return safely to their home ports. On June 1, he sent a war message to Congress in which he laid out the stark alternative of submission or resistance to the British control of American commerce. For Madison and most other Republicans, the impending conflict was a second war for independence. Free and open access to world markets was certainly at stake, but so was national pride. The arrogant British policy of impressment was a humiliating affront to American honor and headed the list of grievances in Madison's war message.

A divided Congress declared war on Britain. Support for the war was strongest in regions like the South and the West, whose economies had been damaged the most by the British blockades and control of Atlantic commerce. The votes that carried the war declaration came from northern Republicans, who saw the impending struggle as a defense of America's experiment in self-government. Nine-tenths of the congressional Republicans voted for war, but not a single Federalist did so. For the Federalists, the real enemy was

France, which had actually seized more American ships than the British. The Federalists' anger increased when they learned that the British had been prepared to revoke for one year the Orders in Council against the United States. A poor harvest and the ongoing economic pressure exerted by Madison had finally caused hard times in England and produced a policy reversal intended to placate the Americans. This concession, however, did not address impressment or monetary compensation, and news of it reached America too late to avert a war.

The War of 1812

The Republicans led the nation into a war it was unprepared to fight (see Map 9–2). The bungled American invasions verged on tragicomedy, and for much of the war, Britain was preoccupied with Napoleon in Europe. When free to concentrate on the American sideshow in 1814, the British failed to secure naval control of the Great Lakes, their minimal strategic objective. By the fall of 1814, both sides were eager for an end to the military stalemate.

Internal dissent endangered the Union almost as much as the British. The war exacerbated Federalist disenchantment with southern dominance of national affairs. A minority of Federalists, convinced that New England could never regain its rightful place in shaping national policy, prepared to lead a secession movement. Although blocked by party moderates at the Hartford Convention in 1814, the secessionists tarred Federalism with the brush of treason. Consequently, the Republicans, the party that brought the country to the brink of a military disaster, emerged from the war more powerful than ever.

SETBACKS IN CANADA

The outbreak of the *War of 1812* unleashed deep emotions that often divided along religious lines, with Federalist Congregationalists (mostly) opposing the war and the Baptists and Methodists favoring the war as "just, necessary, and indispensable." Fiercely loyal to Madison, who had championed religious freedom in Virginia, these Methodists and Baptists harbored old grudges against the established churches of both Britain and New England for suppressing their religious rights.

Madison hoped to channel this Christian, anti-British patriotism into the conquest of Canada. Assuming the Canadians would welcome the U.S. Army with open arms, Madison expected American militia troops to overpower the small British force of five thousand soldiers that was initially stationed in Canada. By seizing Canada, Madison also hoped to weaken Britain's navy and undercut its navigation system by cutting off American foodstuffs and provisions from the British West Indies.

Madison's strategic vision was clear, but its execution was pathetic. Three offensives against Canada in 1812 were embarrassing failures. In the first, in July, General William Hull surrendered to a smaller British-Indian force.

The loss of Detroit and the abandonment of Fort Dearborn (present-day Chicago) exposed western settlements to the full fury of frontier warfare. Americans in the Indiana Territory fled outlying areas for the safety of forts in the interior. By the end of the year, the British controlled half of the Old Northwest.

Farther east, the Americans botched two offensives in 1812. In October, an American thrust across the Niagara River was defeated when a New York state militia refused to cross the river to join the regular army troops on the Canadian side. This left the isolated forces

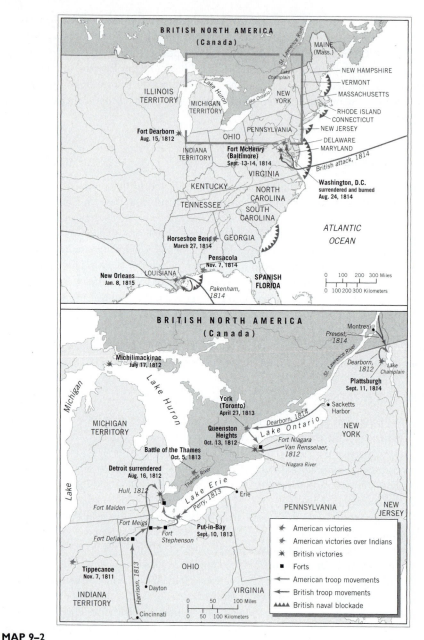

MAP 9–2

The War of 1812   Most of the battles of the War of 1812 were fought along the Canadian-American border, where American armies repeatedly tried to invade Canada. Despite the effectiveness of the British naval blockade, the American navy was successful in denying the British strategic control of the Great Lakes. Andrew Jackson's smashing victory at the Battle of New Orleans convinced Americans that they had won the war.

WHY WAS the successful British naval blockade not enough to secure a victory in the War of 1812?

under General Stephen Van Rensselaer an easy prey for the British at the Battle of Queenston Heights. Then the long-delayed third offensive aimed at Montreal, the center of British operations in Canada, ended in a bloodless fiasco.

All the Republicans had to show for the first year of the war were morale-boosting but otherwise insignificant naval victories. The small American navy acquitted itself superbly in individual ship-to-ship combat.

Military setbacks and antiwar feelings in much of the Northeast hurt the Republicans in the election of 1812. Madison won only narrowly. The now familiar regional pattern in voting repeated itself with Madison sweeping the electoral vote of the South and West. He ran poorly in the Northeast and won only because his party held on to Pennsylvania.

WESTERN VICTORIES AND BRITISH OFFENSIVES

American forces fared better in 1813. In September, the navy won a major engagement on Lake Erie that opened up a supply line in the western theater. Commodore Oliver Hazard Perry attacked the British fleet in the *Battle of Put-in-Bay*, on the southwestern shore of the lake, and forced the surrender of all six British ships.

With the loss of Lake Erie, the British were forced to abandon Detroit. Demonstrating bold leadership and relying on battle-tested western militias, General William Henry Harrison won a decisive victory on the banks of the Thames River in Ontario. Tecumseh, the most visionary of the Indian warriors, was killed, and the backbone of the Indian resistance broken. The Old Northwest was again safe for American settlement.

A coalition of European powers forced Napoleon to abdicate in April 1814, thus freeing Britain to focus on the American war. British strategy in 1814 called for two major offensives, an invasion south from Montreal down Lake Champlain in upstate New York and an attack on Louisiana aimed at seizing New Orleans with a task force out of Jamaica. The overall objective was nothing less than a reversal of America's post-1783 expansion.

The British attacks could hardly have come at a worse time for the Madison administration. The Treasury was nearly bankrupt. Against the wishes of Treasury Secretary Gallatin, Congress had refused to preserve the Bank of the United States when its charter expired in 1811. Lacking both a centralized means of directing wartime finances and any significant increase in taxes, the Treasury was forced to rely on makeshift loans. As the country's finances tottered toward collapse, political dissent in New England was reaching a climax. There was even talk of secession.

The darkest hour came in August 1814. A British amphibious force occupied and torched Washington, D.C., in retaliation for an American raid on York (now Toronto), the capital of Upper Canada. The defense of Washington was slipshod at best. Baltimore's defenses held, stirring Francis Scott Key, a young lawyer who viewed the bombardment from a British prisoner-of-war ship, to write "The Star Spangled Banner." Fittingly in this strange war, the future national anthem was set to the tune of a British drinking song.

The Chesapeake campaign was designed to divert American attention from the major offensive General George Prevost was leading down the shores of Lake Champlain. Prevost commanded the largest and best-equipped army the British had yet assembled, but he was forced to turn back when Commodore Thomas Macdonough defeated a British fleet on September 11 at the Battle of Plattsburgh. The British were now ready for peace, but one of their trump cards had yet to be played—the Southern offensive against New Orleans.

THE TREATY OF GHENT AND THE BATTLE OF NEW ORLEANS

Although the British signed the *Treaty of Ghent* in December 1814, they were not irrevocably committed to the as yet nonratified peace settlement. The showdown between British and American forces at the *Battle of New Orleans* in January 1815 had immense strategic significance for the United States. The hero of New Orleans, in song and legend, was Andrew Jackson. A planter-politician from Tennessee, Jackson rose to prominence during the war as a ferocious Indian fighter. As a general in the Tennessee militia, Jackson crushed Indian resistance in the Old Southwest at the Battle of Horseshoe Bend in March 1814 and forced the vanquished Creeks to cede two-thirds of their territory to the United States. After his Indian conquests, Jackson was promoted to general in the regular army and given command of the defense of the Gulf Coast. In November 1814, he seized Pensacola in Spanish Florida and then hurried to defend New Orleans. The overconfident British frontally attacked Jackson's lines on January 8, 1815. The result was a massacre. More than two thousand British soldiers were killed or wounded while American casualties totaled twenty-one.

Strategically, Jackson's smashing victory at New Orleans ended any possibility of a British sphere of influence in Louisiana. Politically, it was a deathblow to Federalism. As Americans were rejoicing with revived nationalism over the Treaty of Ghent and Jackson's routing of the British, the Federalists now seemed to be parochial sulkers who put regional interests above the national good.

The Era of Good Feelings

In 1817, on the occasion of a presidential visit by James Monroe, a Boston newspaper proclaimed the *Era of Good Feelings*, an expression that nicely captured the spirit of political harmony and sectional unity that washed over the republic in the immediate postwar years. National pride surged with the humbling of the British at New Orleans, the demise of the Federalists lessened political tensions, and the economy boomed. The Republicans had been vindicated, and for a short time they enjoyed de facto status as the only governing party.

In 1819, however, an economic depression and a bitter controversy over slavery shattered the harmony, and the Republicans divided on sectional and economic issues.

ECONOMIC NATIONALISM

The War of 1812 had taught the Republicans to appreciate old Federalist doctrines on centralized national power. For Henry Clay and John Calhoun, leaders of a new generation of young nationalist Republicans, the first order of business was creating a new national bank. Introduced by Calhoun, the Bank bill passed Congress in 1816. Modeled after Hamilton's original Bank and also headquartered in Philadelphia, the *Second Bank of the United States* was capitalized at $35 million, making it by far the nation's largest bank. Its size and official status as the depository and dispenser of the government's funds gave the Bank tremendous power over the economy.

After moving to repair the fiscal damage of the war, the Republicans then acted to protect what the war had fostered. In 1815 and again in 1816, the British inundated the American market with cheap imports to strangle American industry in its infancy. Responding to this challenge to the nation's economic independence, the Republicans passed the Tariff of 1816, the first protective tariff in American history. The act levied duties of 20 to 25 percent on manufactured goods that could be produced in the United States.

Revenue from the tariff and $1.5 million from the Bank of the United States were earmarked for internal improvements (roads and canals). The push for federal subsidies for transportation projects came from the War Department and the West. In early 1817, an internal improvements bill passed Congress. Despite the soaring rhetoric of John Calhoun, the bill's sponsor, seeking to "bind the republic together with a perfect system of roads and canals," President Madison remained unmoved. Though in agreement with the bill's objectives, he was convinced that the Constitution did not permit federal financing of primarily local projects. He vetoed the bill just before he left office.

Congressional passage of Calhoun's internal improvements bill marked the pinnacle of the Republicans' economic nationalism. Frightened by the sectional disunity of the war years, Republicans jettisoned many of the ideological trappings of Jefferson's original agrarian party. Their program was a call for economic, and therefore political, unity. Such unity was to be achieved through a generous program of national subsidies consisting of tariffs for manufacturers in the Northeast and transportation funds for planters and farmers in the South and West.

Support for this program was strongest in the Mid-Atlantic and Western states, the regions that stood to gain the most economically. Opposition centered in the Southeast and took on an increasingly hard edge in the South as the Supreme Court outlined an ever more nationalist interpretation of the Constitution.

JUDICIAL NATIONALISM

Under Chief Justice John Marshall, the Supreme Court had long supported the nationalist perspective that Republicans began to champion after its war. A Virginia Federalist whose nationalism was forged during his service in the Revolutionary War, Marshall dominated the Court throughout his tenure (1801–1835) by his forceful personality and the logical power of his nationalist convictions. The defining principles of Marshall's jurisprudence were the authority of the Supreme Court in all matters of constitutional interpretation and the sanctity of contractual property rights. In *Fletcher v. Peck* (1810), the Court overturned a Georgia law by ruling that it violated the prohibition in the federal Constitution against any state "impairing the obligation of contracts."

In *Dartmouth College v. Woodward* (1819), the Court ruled that Dartmouth's original royal charter of 1769 was a contract protected by the Constitution. The ruling prohibited states from interfering with the rights and privileges they had bestowed on private corporations.

In *McCulloch* v. *Maryland* (1819), a unanimous Court, in language similar to but even more sweeping than that used by Alexander Hamilton in the 1790s, upheld the constitutional authority of Congress to charter a national bank and thereby regulate the nation's currency and finances. As long as the end was legitimate "within the scope of the Constitution," Congress had full power to use any means not expressly forbidden by the Constitution to achieve that end. Here was the boldest statement to date of the loose or "implied powers" interpretation of the Constitution.

TOWARD A CONTINENTAL EMPIRE

Marshall's legal nationalism paralleled the diplomatic nationalism of John Quincy Adams, secretary of state from 1817 to 1825. A former Federalist and the son of the second president, Adams broke with the Federalist party over its refusal to support an expansionist policy. Adams made few friends as a negotiator but he was an effective diplomat, using whatever tactics were necessary to realize his vision of an America that stretched from the Atlantic to the Pacific.

Adams shrewdly exploited the British desire for friendly and profitable relations after the War of 1812. The **Rush–Bagot Agreement** of 1817 signaled the new pattern of Anglo-American cooperation. The agreement strictly limited naval armaments on the Great Lakes, thus effectively demilitarizing the border. The **Anglo–American Accords** of the following year resolved a number of issues left hanging after the war. Of great importance to New England, the British once again recognized American fishing rights off Labrador and Newfoundland. The boundary of the Louisiana Territory abutting Canada was set at the 49th parallel.

Having secured the northern flank of the United States, Adams was now free to deal with the South and West. Adams wanted all of Florida and an undisputed American window on the Pacific. The adversary here was Spain. In March 1818, Jackson led his troops across the border into Spanish Florida in an attempt to stop Indian raids in the Alabama-Georgia frontier. He destroyed the encampments of the Seminole Indians, seized two Spanish forts, and executed two British subjects. Despite later protestations to the contrary, Jackson had probably exceeded his orders. He might well have been censured by the Monroe administration had Adams not taken the offensive by lecturing Spain that Jackson was acting in the defense of American interests and warning that he might be unleashed again.

Spain yielded to the American threat in the **Trans-Continental Treaty of 1819**. The United States annexed East Florida, and Spain recognized the prior American seizures of West Florida in 1810 and 1813. Adams secured an American hold on the Pacific Coast by drawing a boundary between the Louisiana Purchase and the Spanish Southwest.

Adams's success in the Spanish negotiations turned on the British refusal to threaten war or assist Spain in the wake of Jackson's highhanded actions in Florida. Spanish possessions and the lives of two British subjects were worth little when weighed against the economic advantages of retaining close trading ties with the United States. Moreover, Britain had a vested interest in the Latin American market opened by the loss of Spain's monopoly.

Adams was confident that within a generation, the United States would acquire California, Texas, and perhaps Cuba as well. He wanted to maintain the maximum freedom of action for future U.S. policy and avoid any impression that America was beholden to Britain. Thus originated the most famous diplomatic statement in early American history, the **Monroe Doctrine**. In his annual message to Congress in December 1823, Monroe declared that the Americas "are henceforth not to be considered as subjects for future colonization by any European power." In turn, Monroe pledged that the United States would not interfere in the internal affairs of European states.

The Breakdown of Unity

For all the intensity with which he pursued his continental vision, John Quincy Adams worried in early 1819 that "the greatest danger of this union was in the overgrown extent of its territory, combining with the slavery question." His words were prophetic. A sectional crisis flared up in 1819 over slavery and its expansion when the territory of Missouri sought admission to the Union as a slave state. Simultaneously, a financial panic ended post-war prosperity and crystallized regional discontent over banking and tariff policies. Party unity cracked under these pressures, and each region backed its own presidential candidate in the wide-open election of 1824.

THE PANIC OF 1819

From 1815 to 1818, Americans enjoyed a wave of postwar prosperity. European markets were starved for American goods after a generation of war and trade restrictions, and farmers and planters met that demand by expanding production and bringing new land into cultivation. Before the bubble burst, cotton prices doubled to 30 cents a pound, real estate values became wildly inflated, and the money Westerners owed the federal government for the purchase of public lands rose to $21 million, an amount greater than the value of all Western farm goods.

European markets for American cotton and food supplies returned to normal by late 1818. In January 1819, cotton prices sank in England, and the Panic of 1819 was on. The fall in cotton prices triggered a credit contraction that soon engulfed the overextended American economy. A sudden shift in policy by the Bank of the United States virtually guaranteed that the economic downturn would settle into a depression as the Bank stopped all loans, called in all debts, and refused to honor drafts drawn on its branches in the South and West. Hardest hit by these policies were farmers and businessmen in the West, who had mortgaged their economic futures. Bankruptcies mushroomed as creditors forced the liquidation of farms and real estate.

In addition to resenting the hard times brought on by low cotton prices, Southerners saw an ominous pattern of unchecked and unconstitutional federal power emerging in the form of high tariffs, the judicial nationalism of the Supreme Court, and Northern efforts to interfere with slavery in Missouri. If Northerners, they asked, could stretch the Constitution to incorporate a bank or impose a protective tariff, what could prevent them from emancipating the slaves?

THE MISSOURI COMPROMISE

Until 1819, slavery had not been a major divisive issue in American politics. The Northwest Ordinance of 1787, which banned slavery in federal territories north of the Ohio River, and the Southwest Ordinance of 1790, which permitted slavery south of the Ohio, represented a compromise that had allowed slavery in areas where climate and soil conditions favored slave-based agriculture. What was unforeseen in the 1780s, however, was the explosive demand for slave-produced cotton generated by the English textile industry in the early nineteenth century. By 1819, Kentucky, Tennessee, Louisiana, Mississippi, and Alabama had all been added to the Union as slave states. Florida was expected to be another slave state, and even Missouri, a portion of the Louisiana Purchase, had fallen under the political control of slaveholders.

The Missouri issue increased long-simmering Northern resentment with the spread of slavery and the Southern dominance of national affairs under the Virginia presidents. In February 1819, James Tallmadge, a Republican congressman from New York, introduced an amendment in the House mandating a ban on future slave importations and a program of gradual emancipation as preconditions for the admission of Missouri as a state. Missourians, as well as Southerners in general, rejected the Tallmadge Amendment as completely unacceptable, arguing that any attempt by Congress to set conditions for statehood was unconstitutional. Without a two-party system in which each of the parties had to compromise to protect its intersectional interests, voting followed sectional lines. The Northern-controlled House passed the amendment, but it was repeatedly blocked in the Senate, where there were eleven free and eleven slave states.

The stalemate persisted into the next session of Congress. Finally, Speaker of the House Henry Clay engineered a compromise in March 1820. Congress put no restrictions on slavery in Missouri, and the admission of Missouri as a slave state was balanced by admitting Maine (formerly part of Massachusetts) as a free state. In return for their concession on Missouri, Northern congressmen obtained a prohibition on slavery in the remainder of the Louisiana Purchase north of the 36°30′ parallel, the southern boundary of Missouri.

The compromise almost unraveled when Missouri submitted a constitution the next November that required the state legislature to bar the entry of free black people. This mandate violated the guarantee in the U.S. Constitution that "the citizens of each State shall be entitled to all privileges and immunities of citizens in the several States." The nearly universal acceptance of white Americans of second-class citizenship for free black Americans permitted Clay to dodge the issue. Missouri's constitution was accepted with the proviso that it "shall never be construed" to discriminate against citizens in other states. In short, with meaningless words that begged the issue of Missouri's defiance of the federal Constitution, the **Missouri Compromise** was salvaged. At the cost of ignoring the claims of free black people for equal treatment as citizens, the Union survived its first great sectional crisis over slavery.

The Missouri crisis made white Southerners realize that they were now a distinct political minority within the Union. More rapid population growth in the North had reduced Southern representation in the House to just over 40 percent. Of greater concern was the crystallization in Congress of a Northern majority arraigned against the expansion of slavery.

THE ELECTION OF 1824

The election of 1820 made Monroe, like both his Republican predecessors, a two-term president. Voters had no choice in 1820, and without two-party competition, no outlets existed for expressing popular dissatisfaction with the Republicans. Instead, the Republicans split into factions as they began jockeying almost immediately for the election of 1824.

The politics of personality dominated Monroe's second administration. Monroe had no obvious successor, and five candidates competed to replace him. All of them (Secretary of War Calhoun, Secretary of the Treasury William Crawford, Secretary of State John Quincy Adams, Henry Clay, and Andrew Jackson) were nominal Republicans, and three were members of his cabinet.

None of the candidates ran on a platform, but Crawford was identified with states' rights and Clay and Adams with centralized government. Clay in particular was associated with the national bank, protective tariffs, and federally funded internal improvements, a package of federal subsidies he called the **American System**. Jackson took no stand on any of the issues.

Jackson's noncommittal stance turned out to be a great asset. It helped him project the image of a military hero fresh from the people who was unsullied by any connection with Washington politicians, whom the public associated with hard times and sectional controversies. He was the highest vote getter (43 percent of the popular vote), but none of the four candidates had a majority in the electoral college.

As in 1800, the election was thrown into the House of Representatives. Anxious to undercut Jackson, his chief rival in the West, Clay used his influence as speaker of the House to line up support for Adams, a fellow advocate of a strong centralized government.

Adams won the election, and he immediately named Clay as his secretary of state, the office traditionally viewed as a steppingstone to the presidency. Jackson and his followers were outraged. They smelled a "corrupt bargain" in which Clay had bargained away the presidency to the highest bidder. Vowing revenge, they began building a new party that would usher in a more democratic era of mass-based politics.

Conclusion

In 1800, the Republicans were an untested party whose coming to power frightened many Federalists into predicting the end of the Union and constitutional government. The Federalists were correct in sensing that their days of power had passed, but they underestimated the ideological flexibility the Republicans would reveal once in office and the imaginative ways in which Jefferson and his successors would wield executive power to expand the size of the original Union. Far from being anarchists and demagogues, the Republicans were shrewd empire builders astute enough to add to their base of political support in the South and West. They also paved the way for the nation to evolve as a democratic republic rather than the more aristocratic republic preferred by the Federalists.

By the mid-1820s, with no Federalist threat to enforce party discipline, the Republicans lost their organizational strength. Embracing economic nationalism after the war made the party's original focus on states' rights all but meaningless. But the party left as its most enduring legacy the foundations of a continental empire.

REVIEW QUESTIONS

1. What changes did the Republicans bring to the federal government? How did their policies differ from those of their Federalist predecessors?

2. Why did the United States go to war against Britain? Could this war have been avoided?

3. Why was the war widely viewed as a great American victory despite several defeats? How did the war lead to increased diplomatic cooperation between the United States and Britain?

4. Why did nationalism increase in the Era of Good Feelings? Why did Republican party unity collapse after 1819?

The Jacksonian Era

1824–1845

What made Andrew Jackson so popular among ordinary Americans?

How were free black people and women disenfranchised in the 1820s and 1830s?

What social, political, and economic events led to the creation of the Whig party?

How did the Whigs come to dominate American politics?

What did the Whigs achieve while in power?

Newport, New Hampshire
September, 1828

Wherever a person may chance to be in company, he will hear nothing but politicks discussed. In the ballroom, or at the dinner table, in the Stagecoach & in the tavern; even the social chitchat of the tea table must yield up to the everlasting subject.

How many friendships are broken up! With what rancor the political war is carried on between the editorial corps! To what meanness[,] vulgarity & abuse is that champion of liberty, in proper hands, the press prostituted! With what lies and scandal does the columns of almost every political paper abound! I blush for my country when I see such things, & I often tremble with apprehension that our Constitution will not long withstand the current which threatens to overwhelm it. Our government is so based that an honest difference between American citizens must always exist. But the rancorous excitement which now threatens our civil liberties and a dissolution of this Union does not emanate from an honest difference of opinion, but from a determination of an unholy league to trample down an Administration, be it ever so pure, & be its acts ever so just. It must not be. There is a kind Providence that overlooks the destinies of this Nation and will not suffer it to be overthrown by a party of aspiring office seekers & political demagogues.

—Benjamin B. French

Donald B. Cole and John J. McDonough, eds., *Witness to the Young Republic: A Yankee's Journal*, 1828–1870 (Hanover, N. H.: University Press of New England, 1989), pp. 15–16.

BENJAMIN BROWN FRENCH, a young editor and county clerk in Newport, New Hampshire, penned these words in his journal in September 1828. Like most other Americans, he was amazed by the intense partisanship stirred up in the presidential election of 1828 between Andrew Jackson and John Quincy Adams. Whether measured by the vulgar personal attacks launched by a partisan press, the amount of whiskey and beef consumed at political barbecues, or the huge increase in voter turnout, this election marked the entrance of ordinary Americans onto the political stage.

The partisanship that French found so disturbing in 1828 quickly became the basis of his livelihood. After joining the Democrats in 1831, he held a variety of appointive jobs in Washington, first as a Democratic and then, after breaking with the Democrats in the 1850s over slavery, in Republican administrations until his death in 1870.

What had made possible French's career was the democratization of American politics. The number and potential power of the voters expanded, and party success depended on reaching and organizing this enlarged electorate. Men like French, working for the party, could help them do this. The "Jacksonian Democrats," named for their leader Andrew Jackson, were the first party to learn this fundamental lesson. They won a landslide victory in 1828 and held national power through the 1830s. The Jacksonians promised to protect farmers and workers from the monied elite.

The Whig party, formed in opposition to the Jacksonians in the mid-1830s, offered an ordered vision of American progress and liberty, anchored in the use of governmental power to expand economic opportunities and promote morality. Their capture of the presidency in 1840s heralded a new party system based on massive voter turnouts and two-party competition in every state.

However, the Whigs' newly elected president, William Henry Harrison, died shortly after entering office, and Vice President John Tyler, his successor, blocked their economic program. Spurned by the Whigs as a traitor, Tyler then reopened the explosive question of slavery and territorial expansion by pushing to annex Texas, where slavery was legal.

The Democrats regained power in 1844 by exploiting the Texas issue, but debates over the expansion of slavery became embedded in the political system, and the mass-based parties' ability to tap and unleash popular emotions now became their greatest weakness. Party leaders lost control of the slavery issue. The seeds of the Civil War were being sown.

The Egalitarian Impulse

Political democracy, defined as the majority rule of white males, was far from complete in early-nineteenth-century America. Legal barriers prevented the full expression of majority sentiments. Property requirements for voting and officeholding, the prevalence of appointed over elected offices, and the overrepresentation of older and wealthier regions in state legislatures came under increasing attack after 1800 and were all but eliminated by the 1820s.

As politics opened to mass participation, popular styles of religious leadership and worship erupted in a broad reaction against the formalism and elitism of the dominant Protestant churches. The same egalitarian impulse drove these twin democratic revolutions, and both movements represented an empowerment of the common man. (Women would have to wait longer.)

THE EXTENSION OF WHITE MALE DEMOCRACY

In 1816, Congress voted itself a hefty pay raise, which seemed prudent and justified. The public thought otherwise. The citizens of Saratoga, New York, resolved that Congress was guilty of "wanton extravagance" and "a daring and profligate trespass against . . . the *morals* of the *Republic.*"

So sharp was the reaction against the Salary Act of 1816 that 70 percent of the members of Congress were turned out of office at the next election. Congress quickly repealed the salary increase, but not before John C. Calhoun spoke for many in Congress when he plaintively asked, "Are we bound in all cases to do what is popular?" The answer was apparently yes. As Richard M. Johnson of Kentucky noted, "The presumption is, that the people are always right." The uproar over the Salary Act marked a turning point in the transition from the deferential politics of the Federalist-Republican period to the egalitarianism of the Jacksonian era. The public would no longer passively accept decisions handed down by local elites or established national figures.

Individual states, not the federal government, defined who could vote. Six states— Indiana, Mississippi, Illinois, Alabama, Missouri, and Maine—entered the Union between 1816 and 1821, and none of them required white male voters to own property. Constitutional conventions in Connecticut in 1818 and Massachusetts and New York in 1821 eliminated longstanding property requirements for voting. By the end of the 1820s, universal white male suffrage was the norm everywhere except Rhode Island, Virginia, and Louisiana.

Representation in most state legislatures was made more equal by giving more seats to newer, rapidly growing regions in the backcountry. States removed or reduced property qualifications for officeholding. The selection of local officials and, in many cases, judges was taken out of the hands of governors and executive councils and given to the voters in popular elections. With the end of oral or "stand-up" voting, the act of casting a ballot became more private and freer from the intimidation of influential neighbors. Written ballots were the norm by the 1820s. Most significant for national politics, voters acquired the power to choose presidential electors. In 1800, only two states had provided for a statewide popular vote in presidential elections; by 1832 only South Carolina still clung to the practice of having the state legislature choose the electors.

Several currents swelled the movement for democratic reform. Limiting voting rights to those who owned landed property seemed increasingly elitist when economic changes were producing new classes—workers, clerks, and small tradesmen—whose livelihoods were not tied directly to the land. Propertyless laborers in Richmond argued in an 1829 petition that "virtue [and] intelligence are not among the products of the soil. Attachment to property, often a sordid sentiment, is not to be confounded with the sacred flame of patriotism."

Of greatest importance, however, was the incessant demand that all white men be treated equally. Seth Luther, an advocate for workers' rights, insisted that "we wish nothing, but those equal rights, which were designed for us all." This demand for equality was the logical extension of the ideology of the American Revolution. Only the will of the majority could be the measure of a republican government.

As political opportunities expanded for white males, they shrank for women and free black people. New Jersey's constitution of 1776 was exceptional in also granting the suffrage to single women and widows who owned property. By the early 1800s, race and gender began to replace wealth and status as the basis for defining the limits of political participation. Thus when New Jersey's new constitution in 1807 broadened suffrage by requiring only a simple taxpaying qualification to vote, it specifically denied the ballot to women and free black men. None of the ten states that entered the Union from 1821 to 1861 allowed black suffrage. African Americans protested in vain. "Foreigners and aliens to the government and laws," complained New York blacks in 1837, "strangers to our institutions, are permitted to flock to this land and in a few years are endowed with all the privileges of citizens; but we *native* born Americans . . . are most of us shut out." By the 1850s, black males could vote only in certain New England states.

Advocates of greater democratization explicitly argued that only white males had the rational intelligence and love of liberty necessary to be entrusted with political rights.

Women were too weak and emotional, black people too lazy and lascivious. The white egalitarians simultaneously erected new distinctions based on race and gender that were supposedly natural and hence immutable. Thus personal liberties were now to be guarded by all white men, whose equality ultimately rested on assumptions of their shared political superiority over women and nonwhites.

THE POPULAR RELIGIOUS REVOLT

In a blaze of fervor known as the *Second Great Awakening*, evangelical sects led by the Methodists and Baptists radically transformed the religious landscape between 1800 and 1840. A more popularly rooted Christianity moved outward and downward as it spread across frontier areas and converted marginalized and common folk. By 1850, one in three Americans was a regular churchgoer, a dramatic increase since 1800.

The Baptists and Methodists were the largest religious denominations by the 1820s. The key to their success was their ability to give a religious expression to the same popular impulse behind democratic reform. Especially in the backcountry of the South and West, where the first revivals occurred, itinerant preachers reshaped religion to fit the needs and values of ordinary Americans.

Evangelical Christianity emphasized personal, heartfelt experience that would produce a spiritual rebirth. Preaching became a form of theater in which scenes of damnation and salvation were acted out by both preacher and audience. "The scene that then presented itself to my mind was indescribable," recalled James Finley of the camp meeting at Cane Ridge, Kentucky, in 1801. "At one time I saw at least five hundred swept down in a moment, as if a battery of a thousand guns had been opened upon them, and then immediately followed shrieks and shouts that rent the very heavens."

Salvation no longer passively depended on an implacable God as taught by the Calvinist doctrine of individual predestination. Ordinary people could now actively choose salvation, and this possibility was exhilarating. "Why, then, I can be saved!" exclaimed Jesse Lee upon hearing a Methodist preacher in Massachusetts. "I have been taught that only a part of the race could be saved, but if this man's singing be true, all may be saved." Evangelical churches bound the faithful into tightly knit communities that expressed and enforced local values and standards of conduct. Their hymns borrowed melodies from popular music and were accompanied by fiddles and other folk instruments.

The revivals converted about twice as many women as men. Church membership offered them, as the wife of a Connecticut minister explained, a welcome release from "being treated like beasts of burden [and] drudges of domineering masters." In the first flush of evangelical excitement, female itinerant preachers spread the gospel up and down the East Coast. Other women organized their own institutions within denominations still formally controlled by men. Women activists founded and largely directed hundreds of church-affiliated charitable societies and missionary associations.

Evangelicalism also empowered black Americans. Baptists and Methodists welcomed slaves at their revivals, encouraged preaching by blacks, and, above all else, advocated secular and spiritual equality. Many of the early Baptist and Methodist preachers directly challenged slavery. In converting to Methodism, one slave stated that "from the sermon I heard, I felt that God had made all men free and equal, and that I ought not be a slave."

But for all its liberating appeal to women and African Americans, evangelicalism was eventually limited by race and gender in much the same way as the democratic reform movement. Denied positions of authority in white-dominated churches and resentful of white opposition to integrated worship, free black Northerners founded their own independent churches. Southern evangelical attacks on slavery were replaced by a full-blown religious defense of it. Just as southern Protestant ministers rested their proslavery case on the biblical sanctioning of human bondage, they also used the Old Testament patriarchs to shore up the position of fathers as the unquestioned authority figures in their households, the masters of slaves, women, and children. Many popular religious sects in the North also used a particular reading of the Bible in the same way.

In religion as well as politics, white men still held the power in Jacksonian America. Still, the Second Great Awakening removed a major intellectual barrier to political democracy. Traditional Protestant theology—whether Calvinist, Anglican, or Lutheran—viewed the mass of humanity as sinners predestined to damnation. In rejecting this theology, ordinary Americans made a fundamental breakthrough in intellectual thought. "Salvation open to all" powerfully reinforced the legitimacy of "one man, one vote."

THE RISE OF THE JACKSONIANS

At the core of the Jacksonian appeal was the same rejection of established authority that was the hallmark of the secular and religious populists. By tapping into the hopes and fears of ordinary Americans the Jacksonians built the first mass-based party in American history.

In Andrew Jackson the new **Democratic party** that formed between 1824 and 1828 had the perfect candidate for the increasingly democratic temperament of the 1820s. Born of Scots-Irish ancestry on the Carolina frontier in 1767, Jackson was a self-made product of the southern backcountry. Lacking any formal education, family connections, or inherited wealth to ease his way, he relied on his own wits and raw courage to carve out a career as a frontier lawyer and planter in Tennessee. He won fame as the military savior of the republic with his victory at the Battle of New Orleans. Conqueror of the British, the Spanish, and the Indians, all of whom had blocked frontier expansion, he achieved incredible popularity in his native South. His strengths and prejudices were those most valued by the restless, mobile Americans to whom he became a folk hero.

Jackson lost the election of 1824, but his defeat turned out to be a blessing in disguise. The wheeling and dealing in Congress that gave the presidency to John Quincy Adams enveloped that administration in a cloud of suspicion from the start. It also enhanced Jackson's appeal as the honest tribune of the people. His supporters now claimed that the people, as well as Jackson, had been swindled by the "corrupt bargain" between Adams and Clay.

The ill-fated Adams presidency virtually destroyed itself. Though the same age as Jackson, Adams seemed frozen in an eighteenth-century past in which gentlemanly statesmen were aloof from the people.

Adams revealed how out of touch he was when he delivered his first annual message to Congress in 1825. He presented a bold vision of an activist federal government promoting economic growth, social advancement, and scientific progress. The Jacksonians charged that an administration born in corruption now wanted to waste the people's money by promoting more corruption and greed. They also pounced on Adams's political gaffe of urging Americans not to "proclaim to the world that we are palsied by the will of our constituents." Besides being depicted as the tool of the Northeastern monied interests, Adams was attacked as an arrogant aristocrat contemptuous of the common man.

Little of Adams's program passed Congress, and his nationalist vision drove his opponents into the Jackson camp. Southern planters jumped onto the Jackson bandwagon out of fear that Adams might use federal power against slavery; more Westerners joined because Adams revived their suspicions of the East. The most important addition came from New York, where Martin Van Buren had built the **Albany Regency**, a tightly disciplined state political machine.

Van Buren was a new breed of politician. The son of a tavern keeper, he became a professional who made a business out of politics. The discipline and regularity of strict party organization gave him a winning edge in competition against his social betters. In battling against the system of family-centered wealth and prestige on which politics had previously been based, Van Buren redefined parties as indispensable instruments for the successful expression of the popular will against the dominance of elites.

State leaders such as Van Buren organized the first national campaign that relied extensively on new techniques of mass mobilization. In rallying support for Jackson against Adams in 1828, they put together chains of party-subsidized newspapers and coordinated a frantic schedule of meetings and rallies. Grass-roots Jackson committees reached out to the voters by knocking on their doors, pressing party literature into their hands, dispensing mass-produced medals and buttons with a likeness of Jackson, and lavishly entertaining all who would give them a hearing.

The election of 1828 centered on personalities, not issues. This in itself was a victory for Jackson's campaign managers, who proved far more skillful in image making.

Jackson carried every state south and west of Pennsylvania in 1828 and polled 56 percent of the popular vote. Voter turnout shot up to 55 percent from the apathetic 25 percent

---

• C H R O N O L O G Y •

1826 Disappearance of William Morgan.

1827 Emergence of the Anti-Masons, the first third party.

1828 Andrew Jackson elected president.
John Calhoun writes *The South Carolina Exposition and Protest*.

1830 Congress passes the Indian Removal Act.

1831 William Lloyd Garrison starts publication of *The Liberator*.
Nat Turner leads a slave uprising in Virginia.

1832 Jackson vetoes bill for rechartering the Second Bank of the United States;
Bank War begins.
South Carolina nullifies the Tariffs of 1828 and 1832.
Jackson reelected.

1833 Congress passes the Force Act and the Compromise Tariff.
American Anti-Slavery Society established.

1834 Whig party begins to organize.

1836 Texas War of Independence and establishment of the Republic of Texas.
Congress passes first gag rule on abolitionist petitions.
Van Buren elected president.

1837 Panic of 1837 sets off a depression.

1840 Independent Treasury Act passes.
William Henry Harrison elected as first Whig president.

1841 John Tyler succeeds to presidency on death of Harrison.

1842 United States and Britain sign the Webster-Ashburton Treaty.

1844 Polk elected president.
Gag rule repealed.

1845 Texas admitted to the Union.

of 1824. Adams ran well only in New England and in commercialized areas producing goods for outside markets. Aside from the South, where he was virtually untouchable, Jackson's appeal was strongest among ordinary Americans who valued their local independence and felt threatened by outside centers of power beyond their control. He rolled up heavy majorities from Scots-Irish farmers in the Baptist-Methodist evangelical belt of the backcountry and unskilled workers with an Irish Catholic background.

Jackson's Presidency

Once in office, Jackson tolerated no interference from his subordinates. At one time or another, his administration angered Southern planters, frightened Eastern bankers and commercial interests, and outraged New England reformers. Nonetheless, Jackson remained popular because he portrayed himself as the embodiment of the people's will.

The Jacksonians had no particular program in 1828. Two political struggles that came to a head in 1832–1833—the **Bank War** and the **nullification crisis**—stamped the Jacksonians with a lasting party identity. By destroying the Second Bank of the United States and rejecting the attempt of South Carolina to nullify (or annul) a national tariff, Jackson firmly established the Democrats as the enemy of special privilege, the friend of the common man, and the defender of the Union.

THE JACKSONIAN APPEAL

Jackson's inauguration struck many conservatives as ushering in a vulgar new order in national affairs. A vast crowd poured into Washington to applaud their hero. They cheered loudly when Jackson took his oath of office and then rushed to the White House for a postinauguration reception. Bowls of liquor-laced punch went flying, and glass and china crashed to the floor as a seeming mob surged through the White House. "But it was the People's day," reported one conservative onlooker, "and the People's President and the People would rule. God grant that one day or other, the People do not put down all rule and rulers."

Jackson proclaimed his task as one of restoring the federal government to the ideal of Jeffersonian republicanism, in which farmers and artisans could pursue their individual liberty free of any government intervention that favored the rich and powerful. Jackson began his assault on special privilege by proclaiming a reform of the appointment process for federal officeholders. Accusing his predecessors, especially Adams, of having created a social elite of self-serving bureaucrats, he vowed to make government service more responsive to the popular will. He insisted that federal jobs required no special expertise or training and proposed to rotate honest, hard-working citizens in and out of the civil service.

In reality, Jackson removed only about one-fifth of the officeholders he inherited, and most of his appointees came from the same relatively high status groups as the Adams people, but he opened the way for future presidents to move more aggressively against incumbents by providing a democratic rationale for government service. Thus emerged the **spoils system**, in which the victorious party gave government jobs to its supporters and removed the appointees of the defeated party, tying party loyalty to the reward of a federal appointment.

When Jackson railed against economic privilege, he had in mind Henry Clay's American System, which called for a protective tariff, a national bank, and federal subsidies for internal improvements. Clay's goal was to bind Americans together in an integrated national market. To the Democrats, Clay's system represented government favoritism at its worst, a set of costly benefits at the public's expense for special-interest groups. In 1830, Jackson struck a blow for the Democratic conception of the limited federal role in economic development. He vetoed the Maysville Road Bill, which would have provided federal money for a road to be built entirely within Kentucky. The bill was unconstitutional, he claimed, because it benefited only the citizens of Kentucky and not the American people as a whole. Moreover, since the Maysville project was within Clay's congressional district, Jackson also embarrassed his most prominent political enemy.

Jackson's Maysville veto did not rule out congressional appropriations for projects deemed beneficial to the general public. This pragmatic loophole allowed Democrats to pass more internal improvement projects during Jackson's presidency than during all of the previous administrations together.

Jackson's strongest base of support was in the West and South. By driving Native Americans from these regions, he enhanced his appeal as the friend of the common (white) man.

INDIAN REMOVAL

Some 125,000 Indians lived east of the Mississippi when Jackson became president. Five Indian confederations—the Cherokees, Creeks, Choctaws, Chickasaws, and Seminoles—controlled millions of acres of land in the Southeast that white farmers coveted for their own economic gain.

Pressure from the states to remove the Indians had been building since the end of the War of 1812. It was most intense in Georgia. In early 1825, Georgia authorities finalized a fraudulent treaty that ceded most of the Creek Indians' land to the state. When Adams tried to obtain fairer terms for the Creeks in a new treaty, he was brazenly denounced in Georgia. Not willing to risk an armed confrontation between federal and state authorities, Adams backed down.

In 1828, Georgia moved against the Cherokees. By now a prosperous society of small farmers with their own written alphabet and schools for their children, the Cherokees wanted to avoid the fate of their Creek neighbors. In 1827, they adopted a constitution declaring themselves an independent nation with complete sovereignty over their land. The Georgia legislature reacted by placing the Cherokees directly under state law, annulling Cherokee laws and even their right to make laws, and legally defining the Cherokees as tenants on land belonging to the state of Georgia. By also prohibiting Indian testimony in cases against white people, the legislature stripped the Cherokees of any legal rights. They were now easy prey for white settlers, who scrambled onto Cherokee land after gold was discovered in northern Georgia in 1829. Alabama and Mississippi followed Georgia's lead in denying Indians legal rights.

The stage was set for what Jackson always considered the most important measure of his first administration, the *Indian Removal Act*. Jackson allowed state officials to override federal protection of Native Americans. In his first annual message, Jackson sided with state authorities in the South and advised the Indians "to emigrate beyond the Mississippi or submit to the laws of those States." This advice enabled Jackson to pose as the friend of the Indians, the wise father who would lead them out of harm's way and save them from rapacious white people. Congress acted on Jackson's recommendation in the Indian Removal Act of 1830. The act appropriated $500,000 for the negotiation of new treaties under which the Southern Indians would surrender their territory and be removed to land in the Trans-Mississippi area (primarily present-day Oklahoma). Although force was not authorized and Jackson stressed that

For the Cherokees, the *Trail of Tears* stretched 1,200 miles from the homeland in the East to what became the Indian Territory in Oklahoma.

The Granger Collection, New York.

removal should be voluntary, no federal protection was provided for Indians harassed into leaving by land-hungry settlers. Ultimately, Jackson did deploy the U.S. Army, but only to round up and push out Indians who refused to comply with the new removal treaties.

And so most of the Indians were forced out of the Eastern United States—the Choctaws in 1830, the Creeks and Chickasaws in 1832, and the Cherokees in 1838 (see Map 10–1). The private groups who won the federal contracts for transporting and provisioning the Indians were a shady lot interested only in making a quick buck. Thousands of Indians, perhaps as many as one-fourth of those who started the trek, died on the way to Oklahoma, the victims of cold, hunger, disease, and the general callousness of whites they met along the way. "It is impossible to conceive the frightful sufferings that attend these forced migrations," noted a Frenchman who observed the Choctaw removal. It was indeed, as recalled in the collective memory of the Cherokees, a *Trail of Tears*.

Federal troops joined local militias in 1832 in suppressing the Sauk and Fox Indians of Illinois and Wisconsin in what was called **Black Hawk's War**. This affair ended in the slaughter of five hundred Indian men, women, and children by white troops and their Sioux allies. The Seminoles held out in the swamps of Florida for seven years between 1835 and 1842 in what became the longest Indian war in American history. Their resistance continued even after their leader, Osceola, was captured while negotiating under a flag of truce.

Aligned with conservatives concerned by Jackson's cavalier disregard of federal treaty obligations, eastern reformers and Protestant missionaries came within three votes of defeating the removal bill in the House of Representatives. Jackson ignored their protests as well as the legal rulings of the Supreme Court. In *Cherokee Nation* v. *Georgia* (1831) and

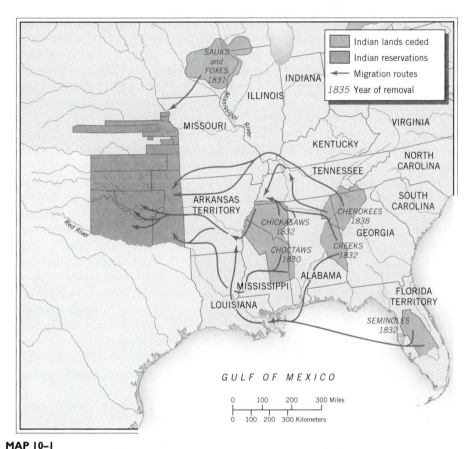

MAP 10–1
Indian Removals The fixed policy of the Jackson administration and pressure from the states forced Native Americans in the 1830s to migrate from their Eastern homelands to a special Indian reserve west of the Mississippi River.

WHY DO you think the Indian reservations are located west of the Mississippi?

Worcester v. *Georgia* (1832), the Court ruled that Georgia had violated the U.S. Constitution in extending its jurisdiction over the Cherokees. Chief Justice Marshall defined Indian tribes as "dependent domestic nations subject only to the authority of the federal government." But Marshall was powerless to enforce his decisions without Jackson's cooperation. Jackson ignored the Supreme Court rulings and pushed Indian removal to its tragic conclusion.

THE NULLIFICATION CRISIS

Jackson's stand on Indian removal confirmed the impression of many of his followers that on issues of centralized power, Jackson could be trusted to take the states' rights position. The most sensitive issue involving the power of the national government concerned tariffs. States' rights forces in South Carolina directly challenged Jackson in the early 1830s over tariff policy. After the first protective tariff in 1816, rates increased further in 1824 and then jumped to 50 percent in 1828 in what was denounced as the "Tariff of Abominations." Southerners were especially angry over the last tariff because it had been contrived by Northern Democrats to win additional Northern support for Jackson's presidential campaign. What fueled antitariff sentiment was not just the economic argument that high tariffs worsened the agricultural depression in the state. Protective tariffs were also denounced as an unconstitutional extension of national power over the states; many Southern planters feared that it was only a prelude to forced emancipation.

South Carolina was the only state where African Americans made up the majority of the population. In the marshes and tidal flats south of Charleston, South Carolina, the lowcountry district of huge rice plantations, blacks outnumbered whites ten to one in the summer months. Nat Turner's Rebellion, a bloody slave uprising in Virginia in 1831, and earlier aborted rebellions in the 1820s (see Chapter 13) left fearful planters convinced that growing antislavery agitation in the North and in England was feeding slave unrest. Turner's revolt and renewed talk of emancipation would be "nothing to what we shall see," warned the South Carolina planter James Hamilton Jr., "if we do not stand manfully at the Safety Valve of Nullification."

Led by the lowcountry planters, the antitariff forces in South Carolina controlled state politics by 1832. They called themselves the nullifiers, a name derived from the constitutional theory developed by Calhoun in an anonymous tract of 1828 entitled *The South Carolina Exposition and Protest*. Calhoun argued that a state, acting through a popularly elected convention, had the sovereign power to declare an act of the national government null and inoperative. Once a state nullified a law, it was to remain unenforceable within that state's borders unless three-fourths of all the states approved a constitutional amendment delegating to the national government the power that was challenged. If such an amendment passed, the nullifying state had the right to leave the Union.

Calhoun, who had been elected Jackson's vice president in 1828, openly embraced nullification only after he had broken with the president. Jackson felt betrayed by Calhoun and vowed political revenge. With Calhoun's approval, a South Carolina convention in November 1832 nullified the tariffs of 1828 and 1832 and decreed that customs duties were not to be collected in South Carolina after February 1, 1833.

Calhoun always insisted that nullification was not secession. He defended his doctrine as a constitutional means of protecting minority rights within a Union dominated by a tyrannical national majority. Jackson rejected such reasoning as the talk of a scheming disunionist and vowed to crush any attempt to block the enforcement of federal laws. He told a congressman from South Carolina that "if a single drop of blood shall be shed there in opposition to the laws of the United States, I will hang the first man I can lay my hand on engaged in such treasonable conduct, upon the first tree I can reach."

In January 1833, Jackson received full Congressional authorization in the Force Act to put down nullification by military force. Simultaneously, he worked to defuse nullification by supporting a new tariff that would cut duties by half within two years. Because Jackson's opponents in Congress did not want him to get political credit for brokering a compromise, they pushed through their own tariff measure. The Compromise Tariff of 1833 lowered duties to 20 percent but extended the reductions over a ten-year period. Up against this combination of the carrot and the stick, the nullifiers backed down.

Jackson's stand established the principle of national supremacy grounded in the will of the majority. Despite his victory, however, states' rights doctrines remained popular both in the South and among many Northern Democrats. Many Southerners, and especially slaveholders, agreed that the powers of the national government had to be strictly limited. By dramatically affirming his right to use force against a state in defense of the Union, Jackson drove many planters out of the Democratic party. In the shock waves set off by the nullification crisis, a new anti-Jackson coalition began to form in the South.

THE BANK WAR

What amounted to a war declared by Jackson against the Bank of the United States became the centerpiece of his presidency and a defining event for the shaping of the Democratic party. Like most Westerners, Jackson distrusted banks. As a result of the scarcity of gold and silver coins and the absence of any paper currency issued and regulated by the national government, money consisted primarily of notes issued as loans by private and state banks. These bank notes fluctuated in value in accordance with the reputation and credit worthiness of the issuing banks. In the credit-starved West, many banks were "wildcat" operations that made a quick profit by issuing notes without the gold or silver reserves to redeem them and then skipping town when they were on the verge of being found out. Even when issued by honest bankers, notes often could not be redeemed at face value because of market conditions. All of this struck many Americans, and especially farmers and workers, as inherently dishonest. They wanted to be paid in "real" money, gold or silver coin, and they viewed bankers suspiciously.

The largest and most powerful bank was the Bank of the United States, and citizens who were wiped out or forced to retrench drastically by the Panic of 1819 never forgave the Bank for saving itself at the expense of its debtors. Still, prosperous times had returned, and the Bank underwrote the economic expansion with its healthy credit reserves and stable banknotes.

Beginning with his first annual message, Jackson had been making noise about not rechartering the Bank. In the presidential campaign of 1832, Clay then forced Jackson's hand and convinced Bank president Nicholas Biddle to apply to Congress for a new charter. Clay reasoned that he had Jackson trapped. If Jackson went along with the new charter, Clay could take credit for the measure. If he vetoed it, Clay could attack Jackson as the enemy of a sound banking system.

Clay's clever strategy backfired. Jackson turned on Clay and the Bank with a vengeance. As he told his heir apparent, "The bank, Mr. Van Buren, is trying to kill me, *but I will kill it!*" On July 10, 1832, Jackson vetoed the rechartering bill for the Bank in a message that appealed both to state bankers and to foes of all banks. He took a ringing "stand against all new grants of monopolies and exclusive privileges, against any prostitution of our Government to the advancement of the few at the expense of the many."

The business community and Eastern elites in general lashed out at Jackson's veto as the demagogic ravings of an economic fool. For Biddle, the veto message had "all the fury of a chained panther, biting the bars of his cage." But Jackson won the political battle, and he went to the people in the election of 1832 as their champion against the banking aristocracy. Although his support was no stronger than in 1828, he easily defeated Clay, the candidate of the short-lived National Republican party that had also backed Adams in 1828.

Having blocked the rechartering of the Bank when Congress failed to override his veto, Jackson then set out to destroy it. He claimed that the people had given him a mandate to do so by reelecting him in 1832. He finally found a secretary of the treasury (his first two choices refused) who agreed to sign the order removing federal deposits from the Bank in 1833. The government's monies were deposited in "pet banks," state banks controlled by loyal Democrats.

Jackson won the Bank War, but he left the impression that the Democrats had played fast and loose with the nation's credit system. In his second term, high commodity prices and abundant credit, both at home and abroad, propelled a buying frenzy of western lands. Prices soared, and inevitably the speculative bubble had to burst. Jackson was out of office when the Panic of 1837 hit; Van Buren, his successor, paid the political price for Jackson's economic policies.

Van Buren and Hard Times

Like John Adams and James Madison, Martin Van Buren followed a forceful president who commanded a strong popular following. Where Jackson forged ahead regardless of consequences, Van Buren tended to hang back, carefully calculating all the political angles. Facing a sharp economic downturn, Van Buren appeared indecisive and unwilling to advance a bold program. When the rise of a radical abolitionist movement in the North revived sectional tensions over slavery, he awkwardly straddled the middle of the divisive issue. In the end, he undermined himself by failing to offer a compelling vision of just what he wanted his presidency to be.

THE PANIC OF 1837

Van Buren was barely settled into the White House when the nation was rocked by a financial panic. For over a decade, the economy had benefited from easy credit and the availability of Western territories opened up by Jackson's Indian removal policy. Government land sales ballooned from under 4 million acres in 1833 to 20 million acres by 1836. As in 1817 and 1818, Americans piled up debt. A banking crisis in 1837 painfully reintroduced economic reality.

Even as it expanded, the American economy had remained vulnerable to disruptions in the supply of foreign capital and the sale of agricultural exports. The key foreign nation was Britain, a major source of credit and demand for exports. In late 1836, the Bank of England tightened its credit policies. Concerned with the large outflow of specie to the United States, it raised interest rates and reduced the credit lines of British merchants heavily involved in the American trade. Consequently, the British demand for cotton fell and with it the price of cotton. Because cotton, as the leading export, was the main security for most loans issued by American banks and mercantile firms, its drop in value set off a chain reaction of contracting credit and falling prices. When panic-stricken investors rushed to the banks to redeem their notes in specie, the hard-pressed banks suspended specie payments.

The shock waves hit New Orleans in March 1837 and spread to the major New York banks by May. What began as a bank panic soon dragged down the entire economy. Bankruptcies multiplied, investment capital dried up, and business stagnated. State governments slashed their budgets and halted all construction projects. Nine states in the South and West defaulted (stopped making payments) on their bonds. Workers in the shoe, textile, mining, and construction industries suddenly found themselves without jobs. "Workmen thrown out of employ by the hundreds daily," nervously noted a wealthy merchant in New York City in May 1837. He half expected that "we shall have a revolution here."

After a brief recovery in 1838, another round of credit contraction drove the economy into a depression that did not bottom out until 1843. In the manufacturing and commercial centers of the Northeast, unemployment reached an unheard-of 20 percent. The persistence of depressed agricultural prices meant that farmers and planters who had incurred debts in the 1830s faced the constant threat of losing their land or their slaves. Many fled west to avoid their creditors.

THE INDEPENDENT TREASURY

Although the Democrats bore no direct responsibility for the economic downturn, their political opponents, now coalescing as the ***Whig party***, pinned the blame on Jackson's destruction of the Bank of the United States. In their view, Jackson had then compounded his error by trying to force a hard-money policy on the state banks that had received federal deposits.

Jackson had taken his boldest step against paper money when he issued the ***Specie Circular*** of 1836, which stipulated that henceforth large blocks of public land could be bought only with specie. The Specie Circular likely contributed to the Panic of 1837 by requiring the transfer of specie to the West for land transactions just when Eastern banks were strapped for specie reserves to meet demands on their own bank notes. Bankers and speculators denounced Jackson for unwarranted government interference with the natural workings of the economy and blundering into a monetary disaster.

By dramatically politicizing the banking issue and removing federal monies from the national bank, the Democrats had in effect assumed the burden of protecting the people from the paper aristocrats in the banking and business community. Once they shifted treasury receipts to selected state banks, they had to try to regulate these banks. But even the "pet banks" joined in the general suspension of specie payments when the Panic of 1837 hit. Thus the banks favored by the Democrats proved themselves unworthy of the people's trust.

Van Buren reestablished the Democrats' tarnished image as the party of limited government when he came out for the ***Independent Treasury System***. Under this plan, the government would dispense with banks entirely. The Treasury would conduct its business only in gold and silver coin and would store its specie in regional vaults or subtreasuries.

The Independent Treasury System passed Congress in 1840 and restored the ideological purity of the Democrats as the friends of honest money, but it prolonged the depression. Specie locked up in government vaults was unavailable for loans in the private banking system that could expand the credit needed to revive the economy. The end result was to reduce the money supply and put even more downward pressure on prices.

UPROAR OVER SLAVERY

In 1831, the year that Nat Turner led a slave uprising in Virginia, William Lloyd Garrison of Boston inaugurated a radical new phase in Northern attacks on slavery with the publication of his abolitionist paper *The Liberator*. The abolitionists embraced the doctrine of *immediatism*, an immediate moral commitment to begin the work of emancipation. Inspired by the wave of religious revivals sweeping the North in the late 1820s, they called upon all Americans to recognize their Christian duty of ending a system of human bondage that deprived the enslaved of their God-given right to be free moral beings. (For more on the abolitionists, see Chapter 14.)

Most white Southerners ignored the abolitionists until 1835, the year that the abolitionists produced over a million pieces of antislavery literature, much of which was sent to the South through the U.S. mails. Alarmed whites vilified the abolitionists as fanatics intent on enticing the slaves to revolt. Abolitionist tracts were burned, and, with the open approval of Jackson, Southern postmasters violated federal law by censoring the mails to keep out antislavery materials.

Beginning in 1836 and continuing through Van Buren's presidency, hundreds of thousands of antislavery petitions, some of them with thousands of signatures, flooded into Congress. Most of them called for the abolition of slavery in the District of Columbia. Southern congressmen responded by demanding that free speech be repressed with the *gag rule*, a procedural device whereby antislavery petitions were automatically tabled with no discussion.

The gag rule first passed in 1836. With Van Buren's reluctant support, it became a Democratic party measure, and it identified the Democrats as a prosouthern party in the minds of many Northerners. Ironically, while Van Buren was attacked in the North as a lackey of the slave interests, he was damned in the South as a nonslaveholder from the North. His fate was to be cast as a vacillating president fully trusted by neither section.

The Rise of the Whig Party

The Bank War and Jackson's reaction to nullification shook loose pro-Bank Democrats and many Southern states' righters from the original Jacksonian coalition, and these groups joined the opposition to Jackson. By 1834, the anti-Jacksonians started to call themselves Whigs, a name associated with the eighteenth-century American and British opponents of monarchical tyranny.

By 1840, the Whigs had mastered the techniques of political organization and mobilization pioneered by the Democrats in the late 1820s. They ran William Henry Harrison, their own version of a military hero, and swept to victory. The *second party system* of intense national competition between Whigs and Democrats was now in place. It would dominate politics until the rise of the antislavery Republican party in the 1850s.

THE PARTY TAKING SHAPE

The Whig party was born in the congressional reaction to Jackson's Bank veto and his subsequent attacks on the national bank. Led by the unlikely trio of Henry Clay and Daniel Webster, nationalists from the West and New England, and John C. Calhoun, a states' righter from the South, the congressional opposition accused Jackson of demagogic appeals to the poor against the rich. What upset them was the way Jackson wielded his executive power like a bludgeon. Whereas all earlier presidents together had used the veto only ten times, Jackson did so a dozen times. He openly defied the Supreme Court and Congress. To his opponents, Jackson was threatening to undermine the constitutional system of checks and balances.

Local and state coalitions of the Whigs sent an anti-Jackson majority to the House of Representatives in 1835. The most powerful of these coalitions was in New York, where a third party, the *Anti-Masons*, joined the Whigs. The party had originated in western New York in the late 1820s as a grass-roots response to the sudden disappearance and presumed murder of William Morgan, an itinerant artisan who threatened to expose the secrets of the Order of Freemasons. An all-male order steeped in ritual and ceremony, the Masons united urban and small-town elites into a tightly knit brotherhood of personal contacts and mutual aid. Rumors spread that the Masons constituted a vast conspiracy that conferred special privileges and legal protection on its exclusive members. Farmers and townspeople flocked to the new Anti-Masonic party, seeking, in the words of an 1831 Anti-Masonic address, "equal rights and equal privileges among the freemen of the country."

Despite spreading into New England and the neighboring Mid-Atlantic states, the Anti-Masons were unable to sustain themselves as a separate party. Shrewd politicians, led by Thurlow Weed and William Seward of New York, took up the movement and absorbed most of it into the anti-Jackson coalition. They thus broadened the Whigs' mass base and added an egalitarian message to their appeal.

By 1836, the Whigs were strong enough to mount a serious challenge for the presidency. They ran three candidates—Webster of Massachusetts, William Henry Harrison of Ohio, and Hugh Lawson White of Tennessee—and some Whigs hoped that the regional popularity of these candidates would siphon off enough votes from Van Buren to throw the election into the House of Representatives. But Van Buren won an electoral majority by holding on to the populous Mid-Atlantic states and improving on Jackson's showing in New England. Still, the Whigs were encouraged by the results. Compared to Jackson, Van Buren did poorly in what had been the overwhelmingly Democratic South, which was now open to further Whig inroads.

WHIG PERSUASION

The Whigs, like the Democrats, based their mass appeal on the claim that they could best defend the republican liberties of the people. They attributed the threat to those liberties to the expansive powers of the presidency as wielded by Jackson and in the party organization that put Jackson and Van Buren into office. In 1836, the Whigs called for the election of "a president of the *nation*, not a president of party." Underlying this call was the persistent Whig belief that parties fostered and rewarded the selfish interests of the party faithful. The Whigs always insisted that Congress should be the locus of power in the federal system.

The Whigs were quicker than the Democrats to embrace economic change in the form of banks and manufacturing corporations. Most Whigs viewed governmental power as a positive force to promote economic development. They favored encouraging the spread of banking and paper money, chartering corporations, passing protective tariffs to support American manufacturers, and opening up new markets for farmers through government-subsidized transportation projects.

The Whigs drew heavily from commercial and planting interests in the South. They were also the party of bankers, manufacturers, small-town entrepreneurs, farmers prospering from the market outlets of canals and railroads, and skilled workers who valued a high tariff as protection from the competition of goods produced by cheap foreign labor. These Whig groups also tended to be native-born Protestants of New England or Yankee ancestry, particularly those caught up in the religious revivals of the 1820s and 1830s. The strongest Whig constituencies comprised an arc of Yankee settlement stretching from rural New England through central New York and around the southern shores of the Great Lakes.

Whigs believed in promoting social progress and harmony through an interventionist government. The Whigs favored such social reforms as prohibiting the consumption of alcohol; preserving the sanctity of the Protestant Sabbath through bans on business activities on Sundays; caring for orphans, the physically disabled, and the mentally ill in state-run asylums and hospitals; and teaching virtuous behavior and basic knowledge through a centralized system of public education.

Much of the Whigs' reform impulse was directed against non-English and Catholic immigrants, those Americans whom the Whigs believed most needed to be taught the virtues of self-control and disciplined work habits. Not coincidentally, these groups—the Scots-Irish in the backcountry, the Reformed Dutch, and Irish and German Catholics—were the most loyal Democrats. They resented the aggressive moralism of the Whigs. These Democrats were typically subsistence farmers on the periphery of market change or unskilled workers who equated an activist government with special privileges for the economically and culturally powerful and identified with the Democrats' demand for keeping the government out of the economy and individual religious practices.

THE ELECTION OF 1840

Aside from the Independent Treasury Act and legislation establishing a ten-hour workday for federal employees, the Van Buren administration had no program to combat the Whig charge of helplessness in the face of economic adversity. The natural choice for the Whigs against Van Buren in 1840 was seemingly Henry Clay running on his American System to revive the economy with government aid. Yet the party dumped Clay for their version of a military hero popular with the people, William Henry Harrison of Ohio.

Harrison had run surprisingly well as one of the Whigs' regional candidates in 1836 and had revealed a common touch with the voters that the Whigs generally lacked. Unlike Clay, he was untainted by any association with the Bank of the United States, the Masonic Order, or slaveholding. As the victor at the Battle of Tippecanoe and a military hero in the War of 1812, he enabled Whigs to cast him in Jackson's former role as the honest, patriotic soldier worthy of the people's trust. In a decision that came back to haunt them the Whigs geographically balanced their ticket by selecting John Tyler, a planter from Virginia, as

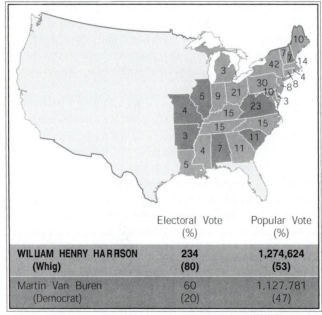

	Electoral Vote (%)	Popular Vote (%)
WILLIAM HENRY HARRISON (Whig)	234 (80)	1,274,624 (53)
Martin Van Buren (Democrat)	60 (20)	1,127,781 (47)

MAP 10–2
The Election of 1840   Building upon their strength in the commercializing North, the Whigs attracted enough rural voters in the South and West to win the election of 1840.

WHY WERE Southerners not unified in their support for a party in the election of 1840?

Harrison's running mate. Tyler was an advocate of states' rights and a former Democrat who had broken with Jackson over the Force Bill.

When a Democratic editor wisecracked that "Old Granny" Harrison (he was 67) was such a simpleton that he would like nothing better than to retire to a log cabin with a government pension and a barrel of hard cider, the Whigs created a Harrison who never was—a yeoman farmer of humble origins and homespun tastes whose rise to prominence was a democratic model of success for other Americans to follow. Thus Harrison, who was descended from the Virginia slaveholding aristocracy, became a Whig symbol of the common man. Indeed, the Whigs pinned the label of the dandified and elitist aristocrat on Van Buren whom they called "Martin Van Ruin."

The Whigs beat the Democrats at their own game of mass politics in 1840. They reversed the roles and symbolism of the Jackson-Adams election of 1828 and seized the high ground as the party of the people. In a further adaptation of earlier Democratic initiatives, Whig politics became a carnival in which voters were shamelessly wooed with food, drink, and music in huge rallies complete with live animals and gigantic buckskin balls that were triumphantly rolled from one rally to another.

The Whigs gained control of both Congress and the presidency in 1840. Harrison won 53 percent of the popular vote, and for the first time the Whigs carried the South (see Map 10–2). Voter turnout surged to an unprecedented 78 percent, a whopping increase over the average of 55 percent in the three preceding presidential elections (see Figure 10–1). As the new majority party, they finally had the opportunity, or so they thought, to implement their economic program.

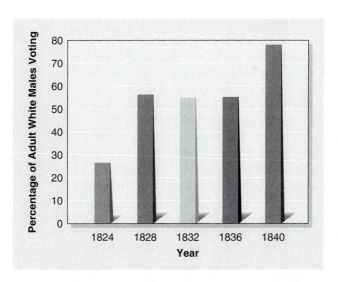

FIGURE 10–1

Voter Turnout in Presidential Elections, 1824–1840   The creation of mass-based political parties dramatically increased voter turnout in presidential elections. Voting surged in 1828 with the emergence of the Jacksonian Democratic party, and again in 1840 when the Whig party learned to appeal to the mass electorate.

Source: Richard P. McCormick, "New Perspectives on Jacksonian Politics" in *The Nature of Jacksonian America,* ed. Douglas T. Miller (1972), p. 103.

The Whigs in Power

The Whigs expected that Clay would move quickly on Whig economic policies by marshaling his forces in Congress and trying to dominate a pliant Harrison. Harrison's death from pneumonia in April 1841, barely a month after his inauguration, ruined Clay's plans.

HARRISON AND TYLER

As president, Harrison fumed that "I am bothered almost to death with visitors. I have not time to attend to my person, not even to change my shirt, much less to attend to the public business." He had pledged to follow the dictates of party leaders in Congress and defer to the judgment of his cabinet. Bowing to Clay's demands, he agreed to call Congress into special session to act on Whig party measures. Thus his death was a real blow to Whig hopes of establishing the credibility of their party as an effective agent for positive change.

The first vice president to succeed on the death of a president, Tyler was cut from quite different cloth than Harrison. This stiff, unbending planter subscribed to a states' rights agrarian philosophy that put him at odds with the urban and commercial elements of the Whig party even in his home state of Virginia. Clay's economic nationalism struck him as a program of rank corruption that surrendered the constitutional rights of the South to power-hungry politicians and manufacturers in the North. Clay forged ahead with the party agenda—the repeal of the Independent Treasury System and its replacement by a new national bank, a protective tariff, and the distribution of the proceeds of the government's public land sales to the states as funds for internal improvements.

Tyler used the negative power of presidential vetoes to stymie the Whig program. He twice vetoed bills to reestablish a national bank. The second veto led to the resignation of the cabinet he had inherited from Harrison, save for Secretary of State Daniel Webster, who was in the midst of negotiations with the British. Enraged congressional Whigs then expelled Tyler from the party.

A now desperate Clay sought to salvage what was left of his American System. He lined up Southern votes for the distribution of federal funds to the states by agreeing to a ceiling of 20 percent on tariff rates. Westerners were won over by Clay's support for the Preemption Act of 1841, a measure that allowed squatters—settlers on public land that had not yet been surveyed and put on the market—to purchase with noncompetitive bids up to 160 acres of land at the minimum government price of $1.25 per acre.

Clay's legislative wizardry got him nowhere. When the Whigs passed a higher tariff in 1842 with a provision for distribution, Tyler vetoed it and forced them to settle for a protective tariff with no distribution. In the end, Clay had no national bank, no funds for internal improvements, and only a slightly higher tariff. Although Clay's leadership of the Whigs was strengthened, Tyler had deprived that leadership of meaning by denying the Whigs the legislature fruits of their victory in 1840.

THE TEXAS ISSUE

In 1842, Webster wrapped up his negotiations with the British. The **Webster-Ashburton Treaty** of that year settled a long-standing dispute over the boundary between British Canada and Maine and parts of the Upper Midwest. An agreement was also reached to cooperate in suppressing the African slave trade. Webster now resigned from the cabinet to join his fellow Whigs, allowing Tyler to follow a prosouthern policy of expansion that he hoped would gain him the Democratic nomination for the presidency in 1844. His goal was the annexation of Texas.

Texas had been a slaveholding republic since 1836, when rebellious Americans, joined by some *tejanos* (Texans of Mexican descent), declared their independence from Mexico. Jackson extended diplomatic recognition before leaving office, but he refused the new nation's request to be annexed to the United States out of fear of provoking a war with Mexico. But he was also aware that the addition of Texas, a potentially huge area for the expansion of plantation slavery, would inflame sectional tensions and endanger Van Buren's chances in the upcoming presidential election. In private, however, he urged Texans to seize harbors on the Pacific Coast from Mexican control and thus make annexation more attractive to the commercial interests of the Northeast.

Party leaders sidestepped the Texas issue after 1836. Spurned by the Whigs and anxious to return to the Democrats, Tyler renewed the issue in 1843 to curry favor among Southern and Western Democrats. He replaced Webster as secretary of state with a proannexationist Virginian, Abel P. Upshur, and secretly opened negotiations with the Texans. After Upshur's death, Calhoun, his successor, completed the negotiations and dramatically politicized the slavery issue. Calhoun made public his correspondence with Richard Pakenham, the British minister in Washington. He accused the British of seeking to force emancipation on Texas to block American expansion and destroy slavery in the South. Calhoun concluded that the security and preservation of the Union demanded the annexation of Texas.

The Pakenham letter hit the Senate like a bombshell, and antislavery Northerners were now convinced that the annexation of Texas was a slaveholders' conspiracy to extend slavery and swell the political power of the South. In June 1844, the Senate rejected Calhoun's treaty of annexation by a two-to-one margin. Still, the issue was hardly dead.

THE ELECTION OF 1844

The Whig and Democratic National Conventions met in the spring of 1844. Both Clay, who had the Whig nomination locked up, and Van Buren, who was the strong favorite for the Democratic one, came out against immediate annexation. Clay's stand was consistent with Whig fears that territorial expansion would disrupt the party's plans for ordered economic development, but Van Buren's anti-Texas stand cost him his party's nomination. In a carefully devised strategy, Western and Southern Democrats united to deny him the necessary two-thirds vote of convention delegates. A deadlocked convention turned to James K. Polk of Tennessee, a confirmed expansionist who had received the blessing of Jackson, the party's patriarch.

To counter the charge that they were a prosouthern party, the Democrats ran in 1844 on a platform that linked Oregon to Texas as territorial objectives. Glowing reports from Protestant missionaries of the boundless fertility of Oregon's Willamette Valley triggered a migration by Midwestern farm families still reeling from the Panic of 1837. The report of a naval expedition sent to explore the Pacific aroused the interest of New England merchants in using Oregon for expanded trade with China.

Some six thousand Americans were in Oregon by the mid-1840s, and demands mounted, especially from Northern Democrats, that the United States abandon its 1818 agreement of joint occupation with the British and lay exclusive claim to Oregon far to the north of the area of American settlement. The Polk Democrats seemed to endorse them when they asserted an American claim "to the whole of the Territory of Oregon."

Polk's expansionist program united the Democrats and enabled them to campaign with much more enthusiasm than in 1840. Acquiring Texas and Oregon not only held out the economic hope of cheap, abundant land to debt-burdened farmers in the North and planters in the South but also played on the anti-British sentiments of many voters. In contrast, the Whig campaign was out of focus. Clay began to waver on the issue of annexation of Texas but he failed to stem the defection of proslavery southern Whigs to the Democrats and lost support among antislavery Whigs in the North. Clay lost to Polk by less than 2 percent of the popular vote.

Tyler claimed Polk's victory as a mandate for the immediate annexation of Texas. He knew that it would still be impossible to gain the two-thirds majority in the Senate necessary for the approval of a treaty. Thus he resorted to the constitutionally unprecedented expedient of a joint resolution in Congress inviting Texas to join the Union. By the narrow margin of twenty-seven to twenty-five, the Senate concurred with the House in favor of annexation. Tyler signed the joint resolution on March 1, 1845.

Although Tyler had failed to secure the Democratic nomination in 1844, he had gained Texas. He also had the satisfaction of getting revenge against the Whigs, the party that had disowned him. Texas, more than any other issue, defeated Clay and the Whigs in 1844.

Conclusion

The Jacksonian era ushered in a revolution in American political life. Politicians learned how to appeal to a mass electorate and to build disciplined parties that channeled popular desires into distinctive party positions. Voter participation in national elections tripled, and Democrats and Whigs competed on nearly equal terms in every region.

Politics did not fully enter the mainstream of American life until the rise of the second party system of Democrats and Whigs. The election of 1824 revived interest in presidential politics, and Jackson's forceful style of leadership highlighted the presidency as the focal point of American politics. Voters in favor of government aid for economic development and a social order based on Protestant moral controls turned to the Whigs' program of economic and moral activism. Conversely, those who saw an activist government as a threat to their economic and cultural equality turned to the Democrats.

The national issues around which the Democrats and Whigs organized and battled down to 1844 were primarily economic. Slavery in the form of the Texas question replaced the economy as the decisive issue in the election of 1844. Once this shift occurred and party appeals began to focus on the place of slavery in American society, an escalating politics of sectionalization was set into motion.

REVIEW QUESTIONS

1. What role did race and gender play in the democratic movements of the nineteenth century?

2. How did Jackson redefine the role of the president?

3. Why did American politics change between 1824 and 1840?

4. In terms of ideology and voter appeal, how did the Democrats and Whigs differ? How did each party represent a distinctive response to economic and social change?

Slavery and the Old South

1800–1860

How did the increasing demand for cotton make slavery highly profitable in the Lower South?

What caused the decline of slavery after 1800 in the Upper South?

What were the living and working conditions of most slaves?

What were the divisions in free white society regarding slavery?

What were Southern defenses of slavery?

Had Mrs. Wheeler condemned me to the severest corporal punishment, or exposed me to be sold in the public slave market in Wilmington [N.C.] I should probably have resigned myself with apparent composure to her cruel behests. But when she sought to force me into a compulsory union with a man whom I could only hate and despise it seemed that rebellion would be a virtue, that duty to myself and my God actually required it, and that whatever accidents or misfortunes might attend my flight nothing could he worse than what threatened my stay.

Marriage like many other blessings I considered to be especially designed for the free, and something that all the victims of slavery should avoid as tending essentially to perpetuate that system. Hence to all overtures of that kind from whatever quarter they might come I had invariably turned a deaf ear. I had spurned domestic ties not because my heart was hard, but because it was my unalterable resolution never to entail slavery on any human being. And now when I had voluntarily renounced the society of those I might have learned to love should I be compelled to accept one, whose person, and speech, and manner could not fail to be ever regarded by me with loathing and disgust. Then to be driven in to the fields beneath the eye and lash of the brutal overseer, and those miserable huts, with their promiscuous crowds of dirty, obscene and degraded objects, for my home I could not, I would not bear it.

—Hannah Crafts

Henry Louis Gates Jr., ed., *The Bondwoman's Narrative* (New York: Warner Books, 2002), pp. 206–207.

HANNAH CRAFTS was the name adopted by an African-American woman after escaping from slavery in the late 1850s. This passage is from *The Bondwoman's Narrative*, the only known novel written by a female black slave. Crafts was probably a house slave of John Hill Wheeler of North Carolina who fled North in the spring of 1857, and merged into the black middle class of southern New Jersey. As a fugitive slave in the North, Crafts risked recapture at any time prior to the outbreak of the Civil War. Her decision not to publish her autobiographical slave narrative might well have been based on the fear that it would reveal her whereabouts to an owner intent on reclaiming her. Among other details the novel reveals the brutal living conditions that field slaves had to endure.

Knowing that masters frequently violated the sanctity of slave marriages and could keep any resulting children as slaves, she believed that all slaves should remain celibate: "Marriage can only be filled with profit, and honor, and advantage by the free." Triggering her decision to flee was Mrs. Wheeler's demand that she "marry" the field hand Bill—that is, submit to being raped by a man she despised and to living in the squalor of the slave quarter.

Only the system of slavery that Crafts described with revulsion makes it possible to speak of the antebellum South as a single region despite its geographical and cultural diversity. Black slavery created a bond among white Southerners and cast them in a common mold.

Slavery was also the source of the South's immense agricultural wealth, and the means by which white people controlled a large black minority. Slavery also frightened white Southerners with a vision of what might happen to them should they not protect their own personal liberties, including, paradoxically, the liberty to enslave African Americans. Because slavery was so embedded in Southern life and customs, white leadership reacted to mounting attacks on slavery after 1830 with an ever more defiant defense of the institution, which reinforced a growing sense among white Southerners that their values divided them from their fellow citizens in the Union.

The South of 1860 was much larger and more diverse than it had been in 1800, but it was also more uniformly committed to a single cash crop, cotton. King cotton provided the economic basis for Southern sectionalism. During its reign, however, regional differences emerged between the Lower South, where the linkage between cotton and slavery was strong, and the Upper South, where slavery was relatively less important and the economy more diversified.

The Lower South

South and west of South Carolina in 1800 stretched some of the best cotton land in the world. A long growing season, adequate rainfall, navigable rivers, and untapped fertility gave the Lower South—consisting in 1850 of South Carolina, Georgia, Florida, Alabama, Mississippi, Louisiana, and Texas—incomparable natural advantages for growing cotton. Ambitious white Southerners exploited these advantages by extending slavery after 1800 to the newer cotton lands that opened up in the Lower South. Cotton production and slavery thus went hand in hand.

COTTON AND SLAVES

Once the cotton gin removed the technical barrier to its commercial production, upland, or short-staple, cotton could be planted far inland, and small farmers could grow it profitably because it required no additional costs for machinery. As a result, after the 1790s, the production of short-staple cotton boomed. Moreover, like the South's other cash crops, upland cotton required fairly continuous tending throughout most of the year. Once the harvest was in—a time when Northern agricultural workers were laid off—the slaves cleared land, cut wood, and made repairs. The long workyear maximized the return on capital invested in slave labor.

The cultivation of cotton left plenty of time for slaves to grow food. The major grain in the Southern diet was corn, which needed little attention while cotton was being harvested and could be planted earlier or later than cotton during the long growing season.

Surplus corn could be fed to hogs and converted into pork. Because almost all cotton farms and plantations also raised corn and hogs, the South virtually fed itself.

From its original base in South Carolina and Georgia, the cotton kingdom moved into the Old Southwest and then into Texas and Arkansas. As wasteful agricultural practices exhausted new lands, planters moved to the next cotton frontier farther west. Cotton output exploded from 73,000 bales (each bale weighed close to 500 pounds) in 1800 to over 2 million bales by midcentury, thanks to the fertility of virgin land and technological changes, such as improved seed varieties and steam-powered cotton gins. Slave labor accounted for more than 90 percent of cotton production.

Plantations, large productive units specializing in a cash crop and employing at least twenty slaves, were the leading economic institution in the Lower South. Planters were the most prestigious social group, and, though less than 5 percent of white families were in the planter class, they controlled more than 40 percent of the slaves, cotton output, and total agricultural wealth. Most had inherited or married into their wealth, but they could stay at the top of the South's class structure only by continuing to profit from slave labor.

Planters had the best land. The ownership of twenty or more slaves enabled planters to use gangs to do both routine and specialized agricultural work. This *gang system*, a cruder version of the division of labor that was being introduced in Northern factories, permitted a regimented pace of work that would have been impossible to impose on free agricultural workers. Teams of field hands, made up of women as well as men, had to work at a steady pace or else feel the lash. They were supervised by white overseers and black drivers, slaves selected for their management skills and agricultural knowledge.

"During two days' sail on the Alabama River from Mobile to Montgomery," noted a traveler in 1860, "I did not see so many houses standing together in any one spot as could be dignified with the appellation of village." The plantation districts of the Lower South stifled the growth of towns and the economic enterprise they fostered. Planters, as well as ordinary farmers, strove to be self-sufficient. The most significant economic exchange— exporting cotton—took place in international markets and was handled by specialized commission merchants in Charleston, Mobile, and New Orleans. The Lower South had amassed great wealth, but most outsiders saw no signs of progress there.

THE PROFITS OF SLAVERY

The average rate of return on capital invested in a slave was about 10 percent a year, a rate that at least equaled what was available in alternative investments in the South or the North. The newer regions of the cotton kingdom in the Lower South, with the most productive land and the greatest commitment to plantation agriculture, consistently led the nation in per capita income.

The profitability of slavery ultimately rested on the enormous demand for cotton outside the South. This demand grew at about 5 percent a year in the first half of the nineteenth century. Demand was so strong that prices held steady at around 10 cents a pound in the 1850s even as Southern production of cotton doubled. Textile mills in Britain were always the largest market, but demand in continental Europe and the United States grew even faster after 1840.

Prices for a male field hand rose from $250 in 1815 to $900 by 1860. The steady appreciation of prices meant that owners could sell some of their slaves and realize a profit over and above what they had already earned from the slaves' labor. Slave women of childbearing age were therefore valued nearly as much as male field hands. More than 800,000 slaves were moved between regions in the South from 1790 to 1860, and professional slave traders transported at least 60 percent of them. Drawing on lines of credit from banks, the traders paid cash for slaves, most of whom they bought from plantations in the Upper South. By selling these slaves in regional markets where demand had driven up the price, they turned a tidy profit. About half of all slave sales separated family members. Slave children born in the Upper South after 1820 stood a one-in-three chance of being sold during their lifetime.

As long as slaves employed in growing cash staples returned 10 percent a year, slave owners had little economic incentive to shift their capital resources into manufacturing or urban development. The South had one-third of the nation's population in 1860 but produced by value only 10 percent of the nation's manufacturing output. Fewer than one in ten Southerners lived in a city, compared to more than one in three Northeasterners and one in seven Midwesterners.

The Lower South had the smallest urban population and the fewest factories. Planters here were not opposed to economic innovations, but they feared social changes that might undermine the stability of slavery. Urbanization and industrialization both entailed such risks.

An editorial in the New Orleans *Crescent* charged that slaves in the city were "demoralized to a deplorable extent, all owing to the indiscriminate license and indulgence extended them by masters, mistresses, and guardians, and to the practice of *forging passes*, which has now become a regular business in New Orleans." Urban slaves, though scarcely free, enjoyed a degree of personal and economic independence that blurred the line between freedom and servitude.

Urban slaves were artisans, semi-skilled laborers, and domestics, and unlike their rural counterparts, they usually lived apart from their owners. They had much more freedom than field hands to move around and interact with white people and other black people. If they had a marketable skill, such as carpentry or tailoring, they could hire out their labor and retain some wages for themselves after reimbursing their owners. In short, the direct authority of the slave owner was less clear-cut in the town than in the country.

• C H R O N O L O G Y •

1790s Large-scale conversions of slaves to Christianity begin.

1793 Eli Whitney patents the cotton gin.

1800 Gabriel Prosser leads a rebellion in Richmond, Virginia.

1808 Congress prohibits the African slave trade.

1811 Slaves rebel in Louisiana.

1816–1819 First cotton boom in the South.

1822 Denmark Vesey's Conspiracy fails in Charleston, South Carolina.

1831 Nat Turner leads a rebellion in Southampton County, Virginia.

1831–1832 Virginia legislature debates and rejects gradual emancipation.

1832 Thomas R. Dew publishes the first full-scale defense of slavery.

1837–1845 Slavery issue divides Presbyterians, Methodists, and Baptists into separate sectional churches.

1845 Florida and Texas, the last two slave states, are admitted to the Union.

1850s Cotton production doubles.

1857 Hinton R. Helper publishes *The Impending Crisis of the South*.

From 1820 to 1860 slaves decreased from 22 percent to 10 percent of the urban population. This decline reflected both doubts about the stability of slavery in an urban setting and the large profits that slave labor earned for slave owners in the rural cotton economy.

The ambivalence of planters toward urban slavery also characterized their attitudes toward industrialization itself. Many planters considered free workers potential abolitionists.

But the use of slaves as factory operatives threatened slave discipline because an efficient level of production required special incentives. "Whenever a slave is made a mechanic, he is more than half freed," complained James Hammond, a South Carolina planter. Elaborating on Hammond's fears, a Virginian noted of slaves that he had hired out for industrial work: "They were worked hard, and had too much liberty, and were acquiring bad habits. They earned money by overwork, and spent it for whisky, and got a habit of roaming about and *taking care of themselves;* because, when they were not at work in the furnace, nobody looked out for them."

The anxieties of planters over industrialization and their refusal to shift capital from plantation agriculture to finance it ensured that manufacturing played only a minor economic role in the Lower South. Planters did invest in railroads and factories, but their holdings remained concentrated in land and slaves. They augmented their income by renting slaves to manufacturers and railroad contractors but were quick to recall these slaves to work on the plantations when needed.

The Upper South

Climate and geography distinguished the Upper South from the Lower South. The eight slave states of the Upper South lay north of the best growing zones for cotton. The northernmost of these states—Delaware, Maryland, Kentucky, and Missouri—bordered on free states and were known as the Border South. The four states south of them—Virginia, North Carolina, Tennessee, and Arkansas—constituted a middle zone. Slavery was entrenched in all these states, but it was less dominant than in the cotton South.

The key difference from which others followed was the suitability of the Lower South for growing cotton with gangs of slave labor. For the most part, the Upper South lacked the fertile soil and long growing season necessary for the commercial production of cotton, rice, or sugar. Consequently, the demand for slaves was less than in the Lower South. Percentages of slave ownership and of slaves in the overall population were roughly half those in the cotton South.

While the Lower South was undergoing a cotton boom after the War of 1812, the Upper South was mired in a long economic slump from which it did not emerge until the 1850s. The improved economy of the Upper South in the late antebellum period increasingly relied on free labor, a development that many cotton planters feared would splinter Southern unity in defense of slavery.

A PERIOD OF ECONOMIC ADJUSTMENT

Upper South land values fell as farmers dumped their property and headed west. "Emigration is here raging with all the strength of fanaticism," wrote a Virginian in 1837, "and nothing else can be talked of but selling estates, at a great sacrifice, and '*packing off*' for the '*far west.*'"

Agricultural reform emerged in the 1830s as one proposed solution to the economic crisis. Its leading advocate was Edmund Ruffin, a Virginia planter who tirelessly promoted the use of marl (shell deposits) to neutralize the overly acidic and worn-out soils of the

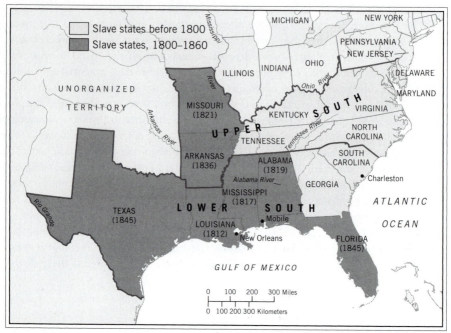

MAP 11-1

The Spread of Slavery: New Slave States Entering the Union, 1800–1850   Seven slave states entered the Union after 1800 as cotton production shifted westward.

WHY WAS cotton production especially suited to slave labor?

Upper South. He also called for deeper plowing, systematic rotation of crops, and upgrading the breeding stock for animal husbandry.

Ruffin's efforts, and reform programs pushed in agricultural societies and fairs, met with some success but only a minority of farmers ever embraced reform. These were generally the well-educated planters who read the agricultural press and could afford to change their farming practices. The landscape of Ruffin's beloved Virginia Tidewater still provoked travelers to remark, as one did in the early 1850s, "I've heard 'em say out West that old Virginny was the mother of statesmen—reckon she must be about done, eh? This 'ere's about the *barrenest* look for a mother ever I see."

Although soil exhaustion and wasteful farming persisted, agriculture in the Upper South had revived by the 1850s. A rebound in the tobacco market accounted for part of this revival, but the growing profitability of general farming was responsible for most of it.

Particularly in the Border South, farmers and planters lessened their dependence on slave labor or on a single cash crop and practiced a thrifty, efficient agriculture geared to producing grain and livestock for urban markets. Western Maryland and the Shenandoah Valley and northern sections of Virginia grew wheat, and in the former tobacco districts of the Virginia and North Carolina Tidewater, wheat, corn, and garden vegetables became major cash crops.

African-American field hands return from a South Carolina cotton field in the 1860s. The economy of the prewar South was based on the production of cotton by a large enslaved labor force.

Collection of The New York Historical Society, negative number 47843.

Expanding urban markets and a network of internal improvements facilitated this transition to general farming. Although not far advanced by Northern standards, urbanization and industrialization in the Upper South were considerably greater than in the Lower South. By 1860, the Upper South accounted for three-fourths of the South's manufacturing capital and output and nearly all of its heavy industry. Canals and railroads linked cities and countryside in a denser transportation grid than in the Lower South.

The Upper South at midcentury was gradually becoming less tied to plantation agriculture and slave labor. The rural majority increasingly prospered by growing foodstuffs for city dwellers and factory workers. The labor market for railroad construction and manufacturing work was strong enough to attract Northern immigrants and help reduce the loss of the native-born population that had migrated to other states.

The economic adjustment in the Upper South converted the labor surplus of the 1820s into a labor scarcity by the 1850s. "It is a fact," noted Edmund Ruffin in 1859, "that labor is greatly deficient in all Virginia, and especially in the rich western counties, which, for want of labor, scarcely yet yield in the proportion of one tenth of their capacity." Like many planters in the cotton states, Ruffin feared that free labor was about to replace scarce and expensive slave labor in Virginia and much of the Upper South.

THE DECLINE OF SLAVERY

Slavery was clearly growing weaker in the Upper South by the 1850s. The decline was most evident along the northern tier of the Upper South. By 1860, slaves in the Border South had dropped to 2 percent of the population in Delaware, 13 percent in Maryland, 19 percent in Kentucky, and 10 percent in Missouri. In Virginia from 1830 to 1860, slaves fell from 39 to 31 percent of the population.

Elsewhere in the Upper South, slavery was more or less holding its own by the 1850s. Only in Arkansas, whose alluvial lands along the Mississippi River offered a new frontier for plantation agriculture, was slavery growing rapidly. Still, slaves made up only 25 percent of the population of Arkansas in 1860 and were confined mainly to the southeastern corner of the state.

In every decade after 1820, the internal slave trade drained off about 10 percent of the slaves in the Upper South, virtually the entire natural increase. The sale of surplus slaves was a windfall for planters whose slaves had become an economic burden. This same windfall gave planters the capital to embark on agricultural reform and shift out of tobacco production. Investment capital in the Upper South was not flowing into slave property but into economic diversification that expanded urban manufacturing. Both of these structural changes increasingly put slavery at a competitive disadvantage against free labor.

The wheat, small grains, and fodder crops that replaced tobacco in much of the Upper South did not require the nearly continuous attention of a work force. As planters abandoned tobacco, they kept fewer slaves and relied on seasonal and cheap agricultural workers to meet peak labor demand.

Cheapness and flexibility were also what urban manufacturers wanted in their labor supply—workers who could be hired and fired at a moment's notice. Immigrant workers displaced slaves in most of the factories in the Border South. By 1860, slaves made up just 1 percent of the population in St. Louis and Baltimore, the South's major industrial cities.

After 1830, there were still plantation districts with large concentrations of slaves, and slave owners retained enough political power to defeat all challenges to their property interests. Nevertheless, the gradual turn to free labor was unmistakable. Agitation for emancipation had begun in the cities of the Border South. As Alfred Iveson, a Georgia planter, noted with alarm in 1860: "Those border States can get along without slavery. Their soil and climate are appropriate to white labor; they can live and flourish without African slavery; but the cotton States cannot."

Slave Life and Culture

Nearly 4 million slaves lived in the South by 1860, more than a fivefold increase since the ratification of the Constitution. Although some slaves were smuggled in after the African slave trade was banned in 1808, an excess of births over deaths accounted for nearly all of this population increase.

Almost all Southern slaves were thus native-born by the mid-nineteenth century. They were not Africans but African Americans, and they shared the common fate of bondage. In their family life and religious beliefs, slaves found the strength to sustain themselves under nearly intolerable circumstances.

WORK ROUTINES AND LIVING CONDITIONS

Each southern state had its own *slave codes*, laws defining the status of slaves and the rights of masters; the codes gave slave owners near-absolute power over their human property.

"The right of personal liberty in the slave is utterly inconsistent with the idea of slavery," wrote Thomas R. R. Cobb of Georgia in a legal treatise on slavery. Slaves could not own property, make contracts, possess guns or alcohol, legally marry (except in Louisiana), leave plantations without the owner's written permission, or testify against their masters or any other white person in a court of law. Many states also prohibited teaching a slave to read or write. The murder of a slave by a master was illegal, but in practice the law and community standards looked the other way if a disobedient slave was killed while being disciplined.

Whippings were the most common authorized punishment for slaves' infractions of plantation rules: twenty lashes on the bare back for leaving a plantation without a pass, one hundred lashes for writing a pass for another slave, and so on. Striking a master, committing arson, or conspiring to rebel were punishable by death.

The owner, as expressed in the Alabama Slave Code of 1852, had "the right to the time, labor and services of the slave." Most masters recognized that it was good business sense to feed, clothe, and house their slaves well enough to ensure productive labor and to encourage a family life that would enable the slave population to reproduce itself. However, planters rarely provided more than the bare necessities. The slaves lived mainly on rations of cornmeal, salt pork, vegetables they grew on small garden plots, and occasional catches of game and fish. This diet was often insufficient in vitamins and nutrients. As a result, diseases such as beriberi and pellagra were common. Slaves also faced frequent outbreaks of dysentery and cholera. According to one study, the life expectancy for slaves at birth was twenty-one to twenty-two years, roughly half that for whites.

Planters furnished slaves with two sets of coarse clothing, one for summer and one for winter. Their housing, typically a 15-by-15-foot one-room cabin for five or six occupants, provided little more than basic shelter against the elements. "They were built of logs," a traveler noted of slave cabins in South Carolina, "with no windows—no opening at all, except the doorway, with a chimney of sticks and mud; with no trees about them, no porches, or shades, of any kind. Except for the chimney . . . I should have conjectured that it had been built for a powder-house, or perhaps an ice-house—never for an animal to sleep in." Large planters placed these cabins in a row, an arrangement that projected precision and undifferentiated order.

The diet and housing of most slaves may have been no worse than that of the poorest whites in both the North and the South, but their workload was undoubtedly heavier. Just over half of the slave population at midcentury was concentrated on plantation units with twenty or more slaves, and most of these slaves worked as field hands in gang labor. Overseers freely admitted that they relied on whippings to make slaves work in these gangs.

The fear of the whip on a bare back set the work pace. At daybreak, recalled Solomon Northrup of his enslavement on a Louisiana plantation, "the fears and labors of another day begin; and until its close there is no such thing as rest. [The slave] fears he will be caught lagging through the day; he fears to approach the gin-house with his basket-load of cotton at night; he fears, when he lies down, that he will over-sleep himself in the morning."

Some 15 to 20 percent of plantation slaves were house servants or skilled artisans who had lighter and less regimented workloads than field hands. Some planters used the prospect of transfer to these relatively privileged positions as an incentive to field hands to work harder. Extra rations, time off on weekends, passes to visit a spouse on a nearby plantation, and the right to have a garden plot were among the other incentives planters used to keep labor productivity high.

Nearly three-fourths of the slaves worked on plantations and medium-sized farms. Most of the remainder—those in units with fewer than ten slaves—worked on small farms in close contact with the master's family. Slave couples in small holdings were more likely to live on separate farms, and the owners of only a few slaves were more vulnerable than planters to market downturns that could force them to sell their slaves and thus further divide families.

Ten percent of slaves were not attached to the land. Instead, they labored at jobs that most white workers shunned. Every Southern industry—but most particularly extractive industries like mining and lumbering—relied heavily on slaves. The Tredegar Iron Works in Richmond, the largest iron foundry in the South, used slaves as its main work force after 1847, partly to curb strikes by its white workers. Racial tensions often flared in Southern industry. When the races worked together, skilled white laborers typically insisted on being placed in supervisory positions over the slaves.

Compared to plantation slaves, industrial slaves had more independence off the job and greater opportunities to earn money of their own. By undertaking extra factory work, known as "overwork," industrial slaves could earn $50 or more a month, money that could be used to buy goods for their families or, in rare cases, to purchase their freedom.

FAMILIES AND RELIGION

The core institution of slave life was the family. Despite all the obstacles arrayed against them, many slave marriages produced enduring commitments and a supportive moral code for family members. Most slave unions remained intact until death or, more likely, the sale of a spouse ended the partnership. Close to one-third of slave marriages were broken up by sales or forced removals. A slave bitterly recalled that "the separation of slaves in this way is little thought of. A few masters regard their union as sacred, but where one does, a hundred care nothing about it."

Both parents were present in about two-thirds of slave families, the same ratio as in contemporary peasant families in Western Europe. Most slave fathers struggled to help feed their families by hunting and fishing, and they risked beating and death to defend their wives from sexual abuse by the overseer or master. Besides their field labor, slave mothers had all the burdens of pregnancy, caring for children, laundering, and preparing meals. After escaping from slavery, Sojourner Truth told how she placed her babies in a basket hanging from a tree while she worked in the field and had older children care for them.

No anguish under slavery was more heartrending than that of a mother whose child was sold away from her. "Oh, my heart was too full!" recalled Charity Bowery on being told that her boy Richard was sold. "[My mistress] had sent me away on an errand, because she didn't want to be troubled with our cries. I hadn't any chance to see my poor boy. I shall never see my poor boy. I shall never see him again in this world. My heart felt as if it was under a great load."

Most parents could only teach their children the skills of survival in a world in which white people had a legal monopoly on violence. The most valuable of these skills was the art of hiding one's true feelings from white people and telling them what they wanted to hear. As a perceptive traveler noted: "When therefore a white man approaches [the slaves] with inquiries concerning their condition, they are at once put upon their guard, and either make indefinite and vague replies, or directly contradict their real sentiments."

Extensive kinship ties provided a support network for the vulnerable slave family. These networks included both blood relatives and other significant people. Children were taught to address elders as "Aunt" and "Uncle" and fellow slaves as "sister" and "brother." If separated from a parent, a child could turn to relatives or the larger slave community for care and assistance.

The ancestors of nineteenth-century slaves brought no common religion with them when they were taken to the New World. However, beliefs common to a variety of African religions survived. In keeping with African traditions, the religion of the slaves fused the natural and spiritual worlds, accepted the power of ghosts over the living, and relied on an expressive form of worship in which the participants shouted and swayed in rhythm with the beat of drums and other instruments. Associated with reverence for ancestors, dance was sacred in Africa. Spirituals, the religious songs of the slaves, were sung in a dance known in America as the "ring shout." Moving counterclockwise and stamping their feet to establish a beat for the music, slaves blended dance and song in a religious ceremony that helped them endure oppression and sustain their self-confidence.

By most estimates, no more than 20 percent of the slaves ever converted to Christianity. Those who did convert found in Christianity a message of deliverance rooted in the liberation of Moses's people from bondage in Egypt. The Jesus of the New Testament spoke to them as a compassionate God who had shared their burden of suffering so that all peoples could hope to find the Promised Land of love and justice. By blending biblical imagery into their spirituals, the slaves expressed their yearning for freedom: "Didn't my Lord deliver Daniel/Then why not every man?"

The initial exposure of slaves to Christianity usually came from evangelical revivalists. The evangelical message of universal spiritual equality confirmed the slaves' sense of personal worth. Less formal in both their doctrines and organization than the Presbyterians and Episcopalians, the evangelical sects allowed the slaves more leeway to choose their own preachers and engage in the physical activism and the call-and-response pattern that characterized slave religion. Perhaps because they baptized by total immersion, which evoked the purifying power of water so common in African religions, the Baptists gained the most slave converts.

Most planters favored Christianity among their slaves only if they could control it. Worried that abolitionist propaganda might attract the slaves to Christianity as a religion of secular liberation, some planters invited white ministers to their plantations to preach a gospel of passivity and obedience centered on Paul's call for servants to "obey in all things your Masters."

Slaves often feigned acceptance of the religious wishes of their masters at the special slave chapels on some plantations or in the segregated galleries of white churches on Sunday mornings. But in the evening, out of sight of the master or overseer, they held their own services in the woods and listened to their own preachers. As much as they could, the slaves hid their religious life from white people. Many slaves experienced religion as a rebirth that gave them the inner strength to endure their bondage. As one of them recalled, "I was born a slave and lived through some hard times. If it had not been for *my God*, I don't know what I would have done."

RESISTANCE

Open resistance to slavery was futile. The fate of Richard, Charity Bowery's boy who was sold away from her, typified that of the openly defiant slave. He resisted the efforts of his new owner in Alabama to break his will. When the owner threatened to shoot him if he did not consent to being whipped, Richard replied, "Shoot away, I won't come to be flogged." The master shot and killed him.

Although the odds of succeeding were infinitesimal, four major uprisings occurred in the nineteenth century. The first, **Gabriel Prosser's Rebellion** in 1800, involved about fifty armed slaves around Richmond. State authorities executed Prosser and twenty-five of his followers before the rebellion got under way.

A decade later, in what seems to have been a spontaneous bid for freedom, several hundred slaves in the river parishes (counties) above New Orleans marched on the city. Poorly armed, they were no match for the U.S. Army troops and militiamen who stopped them. More than sixty slaves died, and the heads of the leading rebels were posted on poles along the Mississippi River to warn others of the fate that awaited rebellious slaves.

The most carefully planned slave revolt, **Denmark Vesey's Conspiracy**, like Prosser's, failed before it got started. Vesey, a literate carpenter and lay preacher in Charleston who had purchased his freedom with the money he had won in a lottery, planned the revolt in the summer of 1822. Vesey assigned teams of rebels specific targets, such as the municipal guardhouse and arsenal. Once Charleston was secured, the rebels apparently planned to flee to Haiti. The plot collapsed when two domestic servants betrayed it. White authorities hanged thirty-five conspirators, including Vesey, and banished thirty-seven others. After destroying the African Methodist Episcopal Church where Vesey had preached, they also passed the Negro Seamen's Act, which mandated the imprisonment of black sailors while their ships were berthed in Charleston.

Nat Turner's Rebellion in Southampton County, Virginia, did erupt before it could be suppressed. Turner was a literate field hand driven by prophetic visions of black vengeance against white oppressors, who led a small band of followers on a murderous rampage in late August 1831. The first white man to be killed was Joseph Travis, Turner's owner. In the next two days, sixty other white people were also killed. An enraged posse, aided by slaves, captured or killed most of Turner's party. Turner hid for two months before being apprehended. He and more than thirty other slaves were executed, and panicky white people killed more than a hundred other slaves.

Slaves well understood that the odds against a successful rebellion were insurmountable. They could see who had all the guns. White people were also more numerous. Mounted patrols of whites were part of the police apparatus of slavery, and their surveillance limited organized rebellion by slaves to small, local affairs that were quickly suppressed.

Nor could many slaves escape to freedom. The **Underground Railroad**, a secret network of stations and safe houses organized by Quakers and other antislavery whites and blacks, provided some assistance. However, out of more than 3 million slaves in the 1850s, only about a thousand a year permanently escaped.

The few who made it to the North did so by running at night and hiding during the day. The most ingenious resorted to clever stratagems. Henry "Box" Brown arranged to have himself shipped in a box from Richmond to Philadelphia. Ellen Craft, a light-skinned slave who could pass as white, disguised herself as a male slaveholder accompanied by his dark-skinned servant (her husband, William). What could have been a fatal flaw in their plan as they traveled from Savannah to Philadelphia—their inability to write and hence sign their names or document their assumed identities—was overcome by having Ellen pose as a sickly, rheumatic master whose right hand had to be kept bandaged.

Running away was common, but most runaways fled no farther than to nearby swamps and woods. Most voluntarily returned or were tracked down by bloodhounds within a week.

Slaves resisted complete domination by their masters in less overt ways. They mocked white people in folktales like those about Brer Rabbit, for example, in which weak but wily animals cunningly outsmart their stronger enemies. Slave owners routinely complained of slaves malingering at work, abusing farm animals, losing tools, stealing food, and committing arson. These subversive acts of protest never challenged the system of slavery itself, but they did help slaves maintain a sense of dignity and self-respect.

Free Society

Southern cities, though small by Northern standards, provided jobs for a growing class of free workers who increasingly clashed with planters over the use of slave labor. These same cities, notably in the Upper South, were also home to the nation's largest concentration of free blacks. Though restricted in their freedom, these blacks competed with white workers for jobs. Pressure was mounting on them by the 1850s to leave the South or be enslaved. Overriding racism bonded most white people together to defend the prerogatives of white supremacy.

THE SLAVEHOLDING MINORITY

The white-columned plantation estate approached from a stately avenue of shade trees and framed by luxuriant gardens remains the most popular image of the slave South. In fact, only the wealthiest planters could live in such splendor, and they comprised less than 1 percent of Southern white families in 1860. Yet displayed in their homes and grounds, their wealth and status were so imposing that they created an idealized image of grace and grandeur that has obscured the cruder realities of the slave regime.

Families of the planter class—defined as those who held a minimum of twenty slaves—constituted only around 3 percent of all Southern families in 1860. Most planters lived in drab log cabins. "The planter's home is generally a rude ungainly structure, made of logs, rough hewn from the forest; rail fences and rickety gates guard its enclosures," complained a speaker to the Alabama horticultural society in 1851. "We murder our soil with wasteful culture because there is plenty of fresh land West—and we live in tents and huts when we might live in rural palaces."

Most planters were acquisitive and restless. The sheer drive and penny-pinching materialism of these planters on the make impressed Tyrone Power, an Irish actor who visited the South in the 1830s. The slaveholders he saw carving plantations out of the wilderness were "hardy, indefatigable, and enterprising to a degree; despising and condemning luxury and refinement, courting labour, and even making a pride of the privations which they, without any necessity, continue to endure with their families."

Besides raising her own children, the plantation mistress managed the household staff, oversaw the cooking and cleaning, gardened, dispensed medicine and clothing to the slaves, and often assisted in their religious instruction. When guests or relatives came for an extended visit, the wife had to make all the special arrangements that this entailed. On the occasions when the master was called off on a business or political trip, she kept the plantation accounts. In many respects, she worked harder than her husband.

Planter wives often complained in their journals and letters of their social isolation from other white women and the physical and mental toil of managing slaves. Still, they only rarely questioned the institution of slavery. Their deepest anger stemmed from their humiliation by husbands who kept slave mistresses or sexually abused slave women. "Sometimes white mistresses will surmise that there is an intimacy between a slave woman & the master," recalled a former slave, "and perhaps she will make a great fuss & have her whipped, & perhaps there will be no peace until she is sold."

Generally younger than the planters, small slaveholders were a diverse lot. About 10 percent were women, and another 20 percent or so were merchants, businessmen, artisans, and urban professionals. Most were farmers trying to acquire enough land and slaves to enter the ranks of planters.

Small slaveholders enjoyed scant economic security. A deadly outbreak of disease among their slaves or a single bad crop could destroy their credit and force them to sell their slaves to clear their debts. Owners of fewer than ten slaves stood a fifty-fifty chance within a decade of dropping out of the slaveholding class. In any given area suitable for plantations, small holders were gradually pushed out as planters bought up land to raise livestock or more crops.

Especially in the Lower South, owning slaves was a necessary precondition for upward mobility, but it was hardly a sufficient one. As a Baptist opponent of slavery put it, "Without slaves a man's children stand but poor chance to marry in reputation." Aside from confer- ring status, owning a few slaves could relieve a white household of much hard domestic labor. "I wish to God every head of a family in the United States had one [slave] to take the drudgery and menial service off his family," proclaimed Andrew Johnson of Tennessee in the U.S. Senate.

THE WHITE MAJORITY

Three-fourths of Southern white families owned no slaves in 1860. Nonslaveholders predominated wherever the soil and climate were not suitable for plantation agriculture. Most of them were yeoman farmers who worked their own land with family labor.

These farmers were quick to move when times were bad and their land was used up, but once settled in an area, they formed intensely localized societies. The community extended 5 to 10 miles around the nearest country store or county courthouse. Networks of kin and friends provided labor services when needed, fellowship in evangelical churches, and staple goods that an individual farm could not produce. The yeomanry aimed to be self-sufficient and limited market involvement to the sale of livestock and an occasional cotton crop that could bring in needed cash.

Yeoman farmers prized their independence. They tried to avoid debt and wanted to limit government authority. Rather than risk financial ruin by buying slaves on credit to grow cotton, they grew food crops and depended on their sons and, when needed, their wives and daughters to work the fields. Far longer than most Northern farmers, they con- tinued to make their own clothes, shoes, soap, and other consumer items.

In areas where there were both small farms and scattered plantations, the interests of the yeomen and the planters were often complementary. Planters provided local markets for the surplus grain and livestock of nonslaveholders and, for a small fee, access to grist mills and gins for grinding corn and cleaning cotton. They lent small sums to poorer neighbors in emergencies or to pay taxes. The yeomen staffed the slave patrols and became overseers on the plantations. Both groups sought to protect property rights from outside interference and to maintain a system of racial control in which white liberties rested on black degradation.

When yeomen and planters did clash, it was usually over economic issues. Large slave- holders needing better credit and marketing facilities gravitated toward the Whig party, which called for banks and internal improvements. Nonslaveholding farmers, especially in the Lower South, tended to be Democrats who opposed banks and state-funded economic projects. But as long as planters deferred to the egalitarian sensibilities of the yeomen by courting them at election time and promising to safeguard their liberties, the planters were able to maintain broad support for slavery across class lines.

Around 15 percent of rural white families owned neither land nor slaves. These were the so-called poor whites, stigmatized by both abolitionists and planters as lazy and shiftless. The abolitionists considered them a kind of underclass who proved that slavery so degraded the dignity of labor that it led people to shun work and lapse into wretched poverty. Planters habitually complained that poor whites demoralized the slaves by showing that a person could survive without steady labor.

Most landless white people were resourceful and enterprising enough to squat on a few acres of land, put up crude cabins for shelter, plant some corn, and graze livestock in the surrounding woods. Although poor by most standards, they were also defiantly self-reliant.

Nonslaveholders were a growing majority in Southern cities, and their numbers were growing fastest among the working classes. These urban workers shared no agricultural interests or ties with the planters. Nor were most of them, especially in the unskilled ranks, southern-born. Northerners and immigrants dominated the urban work force.

Free workers, especially Irish and German immigrants, increasingly replaced slaves in urban labor markets. These white workers bitterly resented competition from black slaves, and their demands to exclude slaves from the urban workplace reinforced planters' belief that cities bred abolitionism.

FREE BLACK PEOPLE

A few Southern black people—6 percent of the total in 1860—were "free persons of color" and constituted 3 percent of the free population in the South. White intimidation and special legal provisions known as *black codes* (found throughout the North as well) denied them nearly all the rights of citizenship. Because of the legal presumption in the South that all black people were slaves, they had to carry freedom papers, official certificates of their freedom. Many occupations, especially those involved in the communication of ideas, such as the printing trades, were closed to them.

Every slave state forbade the entry of free black people, and every municipality had its own rules and regulations that forced them to live as an inferior caste. In Charleston, for example, a free black person could not smoke a cigar or carry a cane in public. White people had the right of way, and a free black person who bumped into a white person on the street was likely to be flogged.

More than four-fifths of the Southern free black population lived in the Upper South. Most of them were the offspring of slaves freed by private manumissions between 1780 and 1800 when a slump in tobacco markets and the Revolutionary War creed of natural rights had loosened slavery in the Chesapeake region.

As in the North, legal barriers and white prejudice generally confined free black people to the poorest paying and most menial work. In rural areas, most were farm laborers or tenants. The best economic opportunities came in the cities, where some found factory jobs and positions in the skilled trades. The percentage of black people in the skilled trades was generally higher in the South than in the North. Talented artisans, such as Thomas Day, widely recognized as the finest cabinet-maker in North Carolina, could command a premium in wages from white employers.

Cities offered free black people not only jobs but also enough social space to found their own churches and mutual-aid associations. Especially after 1840, urban African-American churches proliferated to become the center of black community life. These churches sponsored Sunday schools and day schools that were about the only means of education open to black people. Despite white opposition to black schools, the demand for schooling persisted. A "good education," declared a black schoolmaster in Baltimore, "is the *sine qua non* as regards the elevation of our people."

Less than 2 percent of the black people in the Lower South were free in 1860. Most of them descended from black emigrants who fled the revolutionary unrest in Haiti in the 1790s. Able to secure a solid economic footing, they left their descendants wealthier than any other free black people in the United States. Free black people in the Lower South were more likely than those in the Upper South to have a marketable skill, and two-thirds of them lived in cities.

A light skin also enhanced the social standing of free black people among color-conscious whites in the Lower South. Nearly 70 percent of free black people in 1860 were mulattoes, and from their ranks came nearly all of the very small number of black planters. A mulatto elite emerged in Charleston, Mobile, and New Orleans that carefully distanced itself from most black people, slave or free. In New Orleans, where the tradition of racially mixed unions dated back to French and Spanish rule, mulattoes put on lavish "octoroon balls" attended by free women of color and white men. Even here, however, the mulatto elite remained suspended between black and white worlds that never fully accepted them.

Despite the tendency toward a three-tiered racial hierarchy in the port cities of the Lower South, white people still insisted on making a racial dichotomy between white and black the overriding social division in the South. As the racial defense of slavery intensified in the 1850s, more calls were made for laws to banish or enslave free black people.

Despised and feared by white people as a subversive element in a slave society, free black Southerners were daily reminded that their freedom rested on the whims of the white majority. As white attitudes turned uglier in the late antebellum period, that freedom was less secure than ever.

The Proslavery Argument

In the early nineteenth century, most Southern whites would have called slavery a necessary evil, an unfortunate legacy from earlier generations that was needed to maintain racial peace. The 1830s marked a turning point. After the twin shocks of Nat Turner's Rebellion and the onset of the abolitionist crusade, white mobs emerged to stifle any open criticism of slavery in the Lower South. White Southerners also began to develop a defense of slavery. By the 1850s, politicians, intellectuals, and evangelical ministers were arguing that it was a positive good, an institution ordained by God as the foundation of southern prosperity, white democracy, and Christian instruction for heathen Africans. Slavery, they insisted, was a mild, paternalistic, and even caring institution.

Evangelical Protestantism dominated Southern religious expression by the 1830s, and its ministers took the lead in combating abolitionist charges that slavery was a moral and religious abomination. Most of the Southern churches had always supported slavery. This support grew more pronounced and articulate once the abolitionists stepped up their attacks on slavery in the mid-1830s. Through a selective reading of the Bible, the proslavery ideologues found abundant evidence to proclaim slavery fully in accord with God's moral dictates.

Southern evangelicals also turned to the Bible to support their argument that patriarchal authority—the unquestioned power of the father—was the basis of all Christian communities. Slavery thus became a matter of family governance, a domestic institution in which Christian masters of slaves accepted responsibility for caring for their workers in sickness and old age. Slavery was part of God's plan to Christianize an inferior race and teach its people how to produce raw materials that benefited the world's masses.

The growing commitment of Southern evangelicals to slavery clashed with the anti-slavery position and the generally more liberal theology of Northern evangelicals. In 1837, the Presbyterians split along sectional lines because of differences over slavery. In 1844, and as a direct result of the slavery issue, the Methodist Episcopal Church, the nation's largest, divided into Northern and Southern churches. The Baptists did the same a year later. These religious schisms foreshadowed the sectionalized political divisions of the 1850s; they also severed one of the main emotional bonds between white Northerners and Southerners.

The religious defense of slavery was central to the slaveholding ethic of paternalism that developed after 1830. By the 1850s, planters commonly described slaves as members of an extended family who were treated better than free workers in the North. Led by Charles Colcock Jones, a minister and planter in the Georgia lowcountry, a group of evangelical masters founded religious missions to the slaves and sought reforms, such as legal measures that would prevent the separation of slave families. Such efforts to reform slavery failed largely because most masters would accept no limits on their power to control and work their slaves as they saw fit.

More common than the biblical defense of slavery was the racial argument that black people were unfit for freedom among white people. The racial defense alleged that black people were naturally lazy and inherently inferior to white people. If freed, so went the argument, they would turn to crime and sexually assault white women.

Slavery as a necessary means of racial control was a central theme in Thomas R. Dew's *Review of the Debates in the Virginia Legislature of 1831 and 1832*, the first major justification of slavery by a Southerner. Concerned by the efforts of nonslaveholders in Virginia to enact a program of gradual emancipation, Dew, a tidewater planter, tried to unite white people behind slavery by stressing the issue of race.

The racial argument resonated powerfully among white people. The attitude of a Tennessee farmer, as recorded by a northern traveler in the 1850s, was typical: "He said he'd always wished there hadn't been any niggers here . . . , but he wouldn't like to have them free." Most white Southerners could see no middle ground between slavery and the presumed social chaos of emancipation.

Despite its apparent success in forging white solidarity, the racial argument could be turned on its head and used to weaken slavery. Most white Northerners were about as racist as their Southern counterparts, but they were increasingly willing to end slavery on the grounds that the stronger white race should help black people improve themselves as free persons. Some white Southerners challenged the economic prerogatives of slaveholders. Why, for example, should any white people, as members of the master race, be forced into economic competition against skilled slave artisans? Why should not all nonagricultural jobs be legally reserved for white people? Doctrines of black inferiority could not prevent white unity from cracking when the economic interests of nonslaveholders clashed with those of planters.

Conclusion

The spread of plantation agriculture across the Lower South after 1830 deepened the involvement of white Southerners in cotton and slavery. At the same time, an abolitionist movement in the North morally attacked slavery and demanded that it be abolished. As Southern interests became more enmeshed in an institution that outsiders condemned, religious and intellectual leaders portrayed slavery as a Christian institution and a positive good necessary for white democracy and harmonious race relations. Proslavery ideologues stridently described the South as separate from and superior to the rest of the nation.

The proslavery argument depicted a nearly ideal society blessed by class and racial harmony. In reality, social conditions in the slave South were far more contradictory and conflict ridden. Slaves were not content in their bondage. They dreamed of freedom and sustained that dream through their own forms of Christianity and the support of family and kin. Relations between masters and their slaves were antagonistic, not affectionate, and wherever the system of control slackened, slaves resisted their owners. The publication in 1857 of Hinton Rowan Helper's *Impending Crisis of the South*, a scathing indictment by a white North Carolinian of how slavery stunted economic opportunities for average white people, vividly showed that not all were convinced by the proslavery argument.

Planters were not fooled by the public rhetoric of white unity. They knew that slavery was increasingly confined to the Lower South, and that elsewhere in the South white support for it was gradually eroding. They feared the double-edged challenge to their privileged positions from outside interference with slavery and internal white disloyalty. By the 1850s, many of them were concluding that the only way to resolve their dilemma was to make the South a separate nation.

REVIEW QUESTIONS

1. Why did cotton production expand in the South? How was this expansion linked to slavery and westward movement?

2. How was the Upper South different from the Lower South? What role did slavery play in each region after 1815?

3. How would you characterize the life of a plantation slave?

4. How did most nonslaveholding white Southerners live?

5. How did white Southerners defend slavery and reconcile it with Christianity?

The Market Revolution and Social Reform

1815–1850

What marked the increasing industrialization in the U.S. economy between 1815 and 1850?

How and why did inequalities increase among the rich, the middle class, and the working classes?

What role did women play in the reform movement that followed the War of 1812?

Why did the abolitionist agitation and sentiment in the North grow?

East Boylston, Mass.
10th mo. 2d, 1837.

Dear Friend: . . .

The investigation of the rights of the slave has led me to a better understanding of my own. I have found the Anti-Slavery cause to be the high school of morals in our land—the school in which *human rights* are more fully investigated, and better understood and taught, than in any other. Here a great fundamental principle is uplifted and illuminated, and from this central light, rays innumerable stream all around. Human beings have *rights*, because they are *moral* beings: the rights of all men grow out of their moral nature; and as all men have the same moral nature, they have essentially the same rights. These rights may be wrested from the slave, but they cannot be alienated; his title to himself is as perfect now, as is that of Lyman Beecher [a prominent minister]: it is stamped on his moral being, and is, like it, imperishable. Now if rights are founded on the nature of our moral being, then the *mere circumstance of sex* does not give to man higher rights and responsibilities, than to woman. To suppose that it does, would be to deny the self-evident truth, that the "physical constitution is the mere instrument of the moral nature." To suppose that it does, would be to break up utterly the relations, of the two natures, and to reverse their functions, exalting the animal nature into a monarch, and humbling the moral into a slave; making the former a proprietor, and the latter its property. When human beings are regarded as moral beings, sex, instead of being enthroned upon the summit, . . . sinks into insignificance and nothing-ness. My doctrine then is, that whatever it is morally right for man to do, it is morally right for woman to do. Our duties originate, not from difference of sex, but from the diversity of our

223

relations in life, the various gifts and talents committed to our care, and the different eras in which we live.

—Angelina Emily Grimké

Aileen S. Kraditor, ed., *Up from the Pedestal: Selected Writings in the History of American Feminism* (New York: Quadrangle, 1968), pp. 62–63.

ANGELINA GRIMKÉ wrote the above as part of a public letter to Catherine Beecher, a pioneer in women's education and the daughter of the evangelical preacher Lyman Beecher mentioned in the letter. In 1837, on an abolitionist lecture tour in New England, Angelina had become the first American woman to defy the social taboo against women speaking in public to a mixed audience of men and women. Catherine Beecher was among her many critics, and Angelina publicly responded to her attacks.

Born in 1805 to a wealthy slaveholding family in Charleston, Angelina nonetheless rejected slavery and joined the abolitionist movement in 1835. As she made clear in her letter to Beecher, her commitment to women's rights flowed out of her exposure to abolitionism.

Soon after her marriage in 1838 to the abolitionist Theodore Weld, Angelina compiled much of the firsthand documentation on slavery for his *American Slavery As It Is*, a popular antislavery tract that appeared in 1839. Her marriage also coincided with her withdrawal from public life for a dozen years. Although she worked for the emancipation of the slaves during the Civil War, she spoke only rarely in public.

Although Angelina's commitment to radical reform was hardly typical of antebellum American women, her social activism speaks to the radicalizing potential of the reform impulse that swept over the nation after the War of 1812.

This reform impulse was strongest in the North, where traditional social and economic relations were undergoing wrenching changes as a market revolution accelerated the spread of cities, factories, and commercialized farms. Urbanization also brought new production patterns and increasingly separated one's home from one's place of work. New middle and working classes evolved in response to such changes. The North was also the area where the emotional fires of evangelical revivals burned the hottest.

The religious message of the Second Great Awakening that began in the early 1800s provided a framework for responding to the changes that accompanied the market revolution. Through Christian activism, individuals could strive toward moral perfectibility. Social evils, and the sinful consequences of economic and social changes, could be cleansed if good Christians helped others find the path of righteousness.

The first wave of reform after the War of 1812 focused on individual behavior, targeting drinking, gambling, sexual misconduct, and Sabbath-breaking. A second phase of reform turned to institutional solutions for crime, poverty, and social delinquency. The third phase of the reform cycle rejected the social beliefs and practices that prescribed fixed and subordinate positions to certain Americans based on race and gender. This radical phase culminated in the abolitionist and women's right's movements.

Industrial Change and Urbanization

In 1820, four in five of the free labor force worked in agriculture, and manufacturing played a minor role in economic activity. Over the next three decades, however, the United States joined England as a world leader in industrialization. By 1850, manufacturing

TABLE 12-1
Impact of the Transportation Revolution on Traveling Time

Route	1800	1830	1860
New York to Philadelphia	2 days	1 day	Less than 1 day
New York to Charleston	More than 1 week	5 days	2 days
New York to Chicago	6 weeks	3 weeks	2 days
New York to New Orleans	4 weeks	2 weeks	6 days

accounted for one-third of total commodity output, and nonfarm employment had more than doubled to 45 percent of the labor force.

The most direct cause of this surge in manufacturing was the increasing consumption within the United States of the goods the country was producing. The *transportation revolution* dramatically reduced transportation costs and shipping times, opened up new markets for farmers and manufacturers alike, and provided an ongoing incentive for expanding production (see Table 12–1). As agricultural and manufactured goods were exchanged more efficiently, a growing home market stimulated the development of American manufacturing.

THE TRANSPORTATION REVOLUTION

In 1815 the cost of moving goods by land transportation was prohibitively high. It cost as much to haul heavy goods by horse-drawn wagons 30 miles into the interior as to ship them 3,000 miles across the Atlantic Ocean. Water transportation was much cheaper, but it was limited to the coast or navigable rivers. Only farmers located near a city or a river could grow surplus crops for sale in an outside market. Western farm surpluses followed the southerly flow of the Ohio and Mississippi river systems to market outlets in New Orleans.

Steamboats provided the first transportation breakthrough. In 1807, Robert Fulton demonstrated their commercial practicality when he sent the *Clermont* 150 miles up the Hudson River from New York City to Albany. By the 1820s, steamboats had reduced the cost and the time of up-river shipments by 90 percent. More and more farmers could now export corn, pork, and other regional foodstuffs.

Western trade did not start to flow eastward until the completion of the Erie Canal in 1825, the first and most successful of the artificial waterways designed to link eastern seaboard cities with Western markets. Funded by the New York legislature, the Erie Canal stretched 364 miles from Albany to Buffalo. Its construction by Irish immigrants was the greatest engineering feat of its era. The Erie Canal reduced the cost of sending freight from Buffalo to New York City by more than 90 percent, and by the 1840s, it was pulling in more Western trade than was being sent to New Orleans on the Mississippi River.

Before the Panic of 1837 abruptly ended the canal boom, three broad networks of canals had been built. One set linked seaboard cities on the Atlantic with their agricultural hinterlands, another connected the Mid-Atlantic states with the Ohio River Valley, and a third funneled Western grain to ports on the Great Lakes.

Railroads were the most important link in the transportation improvements that spurred economic development in Jacksonian America. Moving at 15 to 20 miles per hour—four times as fast as a canal boat and twice the speed of a stagecoach—the railroads of the 1830s were a radically new technology that overturned traditional notions of time and space. "I cannot describe the strange sensation produced on seeing the train of cars come up. And when I started in them . . . it seemed like a dream," exclaimed Christopher Columbus Baldwin of Massachusetts when he saw his first railroad car in 1835.

In 1825, the same year the Erie Canal was completed, the world's first general-purpose railroad, the Stockton and Darlington, opened in England. The construction of the first American railroads began in the late 1820s, and they all pushed outward from seaboard cities eager to connect to the Western market. The Baltimore and Ohio crossed the

---

• C H R O N O L O G Y •

1790 Samuel Slater opens the first permanent cotton mill in Rhode Island.

1793 Eli Whitney patents the first cotton gin.

1807 Robert Fulton's steamboat, the *Clermont*, makes its pioneering voyage up the Hudson River.

1814 The Boston Associates opens its Waltham mill, the first textile factory to mechanize all phases of production.

1817 Construction on the Erie Canal begins. American Colonization Society is founded.

1819–1823 Economic depression.

1824 In *Gibbons* v. *Ogden*, the Supreme Court strikes down a state monopoly over steamboat navigation.

1825 Erie Canal is completed.

1826 American Temperance Society launches its crusade.

1828 The Baltimore and Ohio, the most important of the early railroads, is chartered.

1829 David Walker publishes *Appeal to the Colored Citizens of the World*.

1830 Joseph Smith founds the Church of Jesus Christ of Latter-day Saints.

1830–1831 Evangelical revivals are held in Northern cities.

1831 William Lloyd Garrison begins publishing *The Liberator*.

1833 Slaves in the British Empire are emancipated. American Anti-Slavery Society is organized.

1834 New York Female Reform Society is founded.
Female workers at the Lowell Mills stage their first strike.

1836 Congress passes gag rule.

1837 Horace Mann begins campaign for school reform in Massachusetts.
Antiabolitionist mob kills Elijah P. Lovejoy.
In *Charles River Bridge* v. *Warren Bridge*, the Supreme Court encourages economic competition by ruling that presumed rights of monopolistic privileges could not be used to block new economic enterprises.

1839–1843 Economic depression.

1840 Abolitionists split into Garrisonian and anti-Garrisonian societies.
Political abolitionists launch the Liberty party.

1841 Brook Farm is established.

1842 Massachusetts Supreme Court in *Commonwealth* v. *Hunt* strengthens the legal right of workers to organize trade unions.

1845 Potato famine in Ireland sets off a mass migration of Irish to the United States.

1846–1848 Mormons migrate to the West.

1847 John Humphrey Noyes establishes the Oneida Community.

1848 Seneca Falls Convention outlines a program for women's rights.

Appalachians and connected Baltimore with Wheeling, Virginia, on the Ohio River. The Boston and Worcester linked New England and the eastern terminus of the Erie Canal at Albany. By 1840, U.S. rails had become the most dynamic booster of interregional trade. Whereas the canal network stopped expanding after 1840, the railroads tripled their mileage in the 1840s. By 1849, trunk lines from Atlantic Coast cities had reached the Great Lakes and the Ohio Valley and were about to enter the Mississippi Valley.

The rail network in place by midcentury was already altering the North-South sectional balance. Western trade was mostly shipped to the East, and Northern-born settlers, manufactured goods, and cultural values increasingly unified the free states east of the Mississippi into a common economic and cultural unit. The Northeast and the Old Northwest were becoming just the North. No direct rail connection linked the North and the South.

Both national and state government promoted the transportation revolution. High construction costs and the uncertainty of profits made private investors leery of risking their capital in long-term transportation projects. State legislatures furnished some 70 percent of the funding for canals and about half of all railroad capital. By the 1830s, the states were also making it easier for private businesses, and especially those in transportation, to receive the legal privileges of incorporation, which included the protection of limited liability—that is, the limiting of an investor's liability to one's direct financial stake in the company—and the power of eminent domain—the legal right to purchase land for rights-of-way. The federal government provided engineers for railroad surveys, lowered tariff duties on iron used in rail construction, and subsidized the railroads in the form of public land. Two decisions of the Supreme Court helped open up the economy to competition. In *Gibbons v. Ogden* (1824), the Court overturned a New York law that had given Aaron Ogden a monopoly on steamboat service between New York and New Jersey. Thomas Gibbons, Ogden's competitor, had a federal license for the coastal trade. The right to compete under the national license, the Court ruled, took legal precedence over Ogden's monopoly. The decision affirmed the supremacy of the national government to regulate interstate commerce.

A new Court, presided over by Roger B. Taney, who became chief justice when John Marshall died in 1835, struck a bolder blow against monopoly in the case of *Charles River Bridge v. Warren Bridge* in 1837. Taney ruled that the older Charles River Bridge Company had not received a monopoly from Massachusetts to collect tolls across the Charles River. Any uncertainties in the charter rights of corporations, reasoned Taney, should be resolved in favor of the broader community interests that free and open competition would serve.

CITIES AND IMMIGRANTS

At midcentury, more than one in seven Americans was a city dweller, and the nation had ten cities whose population exceeded fifty thousand. The transportation revolution triggered this surge in urban growth. The cities that prospered were those with access to the expanding network of cheap transport on steamboats, canals, and railroads. This network opened up the rural interior for the purchase of farm commodities by city merchants and the sale of finished goods by urban importers and manufacturers. A huge influx of immigrants after the mid-1840s and advances in steam engines provided the cheap labor and power that made cities manufacturing centers.

America's largest cities in the early nineteenth century were its Atlantic ports: New York, Philadelphia, Baltimore, and Boston. These seaports all benefited from the transportation revolution, but only New York experienced phenomenal growth. By 1810, it had become the largest American city, and its population exceeded 800,000 by the 1850s. One-third of the nation's exports and more than three-fifths of its imports passed through New York between 1820 and 1860. No wonder poet Walt Whitman trumpeted this metropolis as "the great place of the Western Continent, the heart, the brain, the focus, the main spring, the pinnacle, the extremity, the no more beyond of the new world."

New York's harbor gave oceangoing ships direct, protected access to Manhattan Island, and from there the Hudson River provided a navigable highway flowing 150 miles north to Albany, deep in the state's agricultural interior. No other port was so ideally situated for trade. New York City merchants established the Black Ball Line in 1817, the first line of packet ships that ran on a regular schedule for moving cargoes, passengers, and mail across the Atlantic. The city's merchants also convinced the state legislature to finance the Erie Canal, which guaranteed the ongoing commercial preeminence of the port of New York.

New York City also benefited from the swelling flow of finished goods shipped out of New York for sale in the West. Western families with access to the Erie Canal became increasingly specialized economically. New markets encouraged them to concentrate on cash crops, and profits were spent on finished goods. The rise in the disposable income of farmers generated a demand for the consumer goods that the Erie Canal brought in. These goods came out of New York, but most were not manufactured in the city. Nonetheless, the jobs created by handling these goods and the profits derived from supplying the western market solidified the city's position as the nation's most dynamic economic center.

New Yorkers plowed the profits of this commerce into local real estate and into financial institutions such as the New York Stock Exchange, founded in 1817. The city's banks brought together the capital that made New York the country's chief financial center. Agents for the city's mercantile and financial interests used this capital to offer advantageous terms to capture much of the Southern trade and dominate commerce with South America.

Commercial rivals in other port cities launched their own canal and railroad ventures to penetrate the West, but none developed a hinterland as rich or extensive as New York's. Still, Boston, Baltimore, and Philadelphia at midcentury remained the nation's largest cities behind New York.

As they grew, the Atlantic ports pioneered new forms of city transportation. Omnibuses (horse-drawn coaches carrying up to twenty passengers) and steam ferries were in common use by the 1820s. The first commuter railroad, the Boston and Worcester, began service in 1838. Horse-drawn street railway lines in the 1850s moved at speeds of about 6 miles an hour, overcoming some of the limitations of the "walking cities" of the early nineteenth century. Cities began to spread outward as cheaper, faster ways of traveling to work became available.

The first slums also appeared. Small, flimsy wooden structures, often crammed into a back alley, housed the working poor in cramped, fetid conditions. Backyard privies, supplemented by chamber pots, were the standard means of disposing of human wastes. These outhouses overflowed in heavy rain and often contaminated private wells, the source of drinking water. Garbage and animal wastes accumulated on streets, scavenged by roving packs of hogs.

A densely packed population in a poorly drained, garbage-strewn setting made cities unhealthy. Mortality rates were much higher than in rural areas, and the death rate in New York City was double that of London. Stagnant pools of water bred mosquitoes that carried yellow fever, and contaminated water supplies produced frequent epidemics of cholera and typhus. But the cities continued to grow.

The fastest-growing cities were in the interior. Their share of the urban population quadrupled from 1800 to 1840. Pittsburgh, at the head of the Ohio River, was the first

Western city to develop a manufacturing sector to complement its exchange function. With access to the extensive coalfields of western Pennsylvania, Pittsburgh had a cheap fuel that provided the high heat needed to manufacture iron and glass. It emerged as America's best-known and most polluted manufacturing city. "It is surrounded," noted the French traveler Michel Chevalier in the 1830s, "with a dense, black smoke which, bursting forth in volumes from the foundries, forges, glass-houses, and the chimneys of all the factories and houses, falls in flakes of soot upon the dwellings and persons of the inhabitants. It is, therefore, the dirtiest town in the United States."

Cincinnati, downstream on the Ohio, soon became famous for its hogs. "Porkopolis," as it was called, was the West's first meatpacking center. Industries in animal by-products, such as soap, candles, shoes, and boots, gave the city a diversified manufacturing base that kept it in the forefront of Western urban growth.

By the 1840s, St. Louis and the Great Lakes ports of Buffalo, Cleveland, Detroit, Milwaukee, and Chicago were the dynamic centers of Western urbanization. St. Louis, just below the merger of the Missouri and the Mississippi Rivers, serviced American trade with the Trans-Mississippi West. The city was also the eastern end of the Santa Fe Trail, a corridor of Anglo-Mexican trade that stretched across the southern plains to Santa Fe, New Mexico. St. Louis tripled in population in the 1830s, and by midcentury, it was developing rail connections that linked it to the Great Lakes cities.

The Great Lakes served as an extension of the Erie Canal, and cities on the lakes where incoming and outgoing goods had to be unloaded for transshipment benefited enormously. They soon evolved into regional economic centers serving the surrounding agricultural communities. They also promoted themselves into major rail hubs and thus reaped the economic advantages of being at the juncture of both water and rail transport.

The combined populations of Cleveland, Detroit, Milwaukee, and Chicago increased twenty-five-fold between 1830 and 1850. The only other cities experiencing such phenomenal rates of growth were the new industrial towns. The densest cluster of these was in rural New England along the fall line of rivers, where the rapidly falling water provided cheap power to drive the industrial machinery of factories and machine shops. Each town was tied to a transportation network that brought in raw cotton for the textile mills from the mercantile centers of Boston and Providence and shipped out the finished goods.

Lowell, Massachusetts, was America's first large-scale, planned manufacturing city. Founded in 1822 by Boston businessmen, Lowell was built around the falls of the Merrimack River. Within a decade, rural fields had been transformed into a city of eighteen thousand people. Lowell's success became a model for others to follow, and by 1840, New England led the North in both urbanization and industrialization.

A surge of immigrants swelled the size of the cities after the 1830s. At midcentury, most of the population in New York was foreign-born, and in all the port cities of the Northeast, immigrants dominated the manufacturing work force. Most of these immigrants were Irish and Germans who settled in the Northeast.

In the 1840s, economic and political upheavals in Europe spurred mass migration, mostly to America. Catholic peasants of Ireland, dominated by their Protestant English landlords, eked out a subsistence as tenants on tiny plots of land. A potato blight wiped out the crop in 1845 and 1846, and in the next five years about 1 million Irish died of malnutrition and disease. Another 1.5 million fled, many to America.

Without marketable skills, the Irish had to take the worst and lowest paying jobs: rag-pickers, porters, day laborers, and unskilled factory hands. Wives and daughters became laundresses and maids for the urban middle class. Packed into dark cellars, unventilated attics, and rank tenements, they suffered from high mortality rates.

German immigrants came to America to escape poor harvests and political turmoil. Far more Germans than Irish had the capital to purchase land in the West and the skills to join the ranks of small businesspeople in the cities. They were also more likely than the Irish to have entered the country through Baltimore or New Orleans, Southern ports engaged in the tobacco and cotton trade with continental Europe. From there they fanned out into the Mississippi and Ohio Valleys. With the Irish, they made up over half of the population of St. Louis by the 1850s and were close to a majority in the other large cities of the Midwest and Northeast. With their diversified skills, the Germans found ample economic opportunities in the fast-growing cities and a setting in which to build neighborhoods of German-speaking shops, churches, schools, and benevolent societies.

About four in five of the 4.2 million immigrants from all nations who arrived from 1840 to 1860 settled in the New England and Mid-Atlantic states. Their sheer numbers transformed the size and ethnic composition of the working class, especially in the cities of the Northeast. And their cheap labor provided the final ingredient in the expansion of industrialization that began after the War of 1812.

THE INDUSTRIAL REVOLUTION

The Northeast led America's industrial revolution. In 1815, this region had the largest cities, the most developed capital markets, the readiest access to the technological skills of artisans, and the greatest supply of available labor. For the next thirty years, the United States had the most rapidly developing industrial economy in the world.

The household and the small workshop were the sites of manufacturing in Jefferson's America. Wider markets for household manufactures began to develop in the late eighteenth century with the coming of the *putting-out system*. Local merchants furnished ("put out") raw materials to rural households and paid at a piece rate for the labor that converted those raw materials into manufactured products. The supplying merchant then marketed and sold these goods.

In the cities and larger towns, most manufacturing was done by artisans, skilled craftsmen who were also known as mechanics. Working in their own shops and with their own tools, they produced small batches of finished goods. Close to half of the population in the seaport cities, artisans and their families fed, clothed, and housed the urban population. Each artisan had a skill that set him above common laborers. These skills came from hands-on experience and craft traditions that were handed down from one generation to the next.

The "mysteries of the craft" were taught by master craftsmen to the journeymen and apprentices who lived with them and worked in their shops. Journeymen had learned the skills of their craft but lacked the capital to open their own shops. Before establishing their own businesses, they saved their earnings and honed their skills while working for a wage under a master. Apprentices were adolescent boys sent by their fathers to live with and obey a master craftsman in return for being taught a trade. By the terms of the contract, known as an indenture, the master also provided for the apprentice's schooling and moral upbringing. An apprentice could expect to be promoted to journeyman in his late teens and begin advancement toward his competency, a secure income from an independent trade that would support a family.

Artisans controlled entry into their trades and the process of production from start to finish. They set their own work rules and were their own bosses. "The Mechanics are a class

Shown here working at power looms under the supervision of a male overseer, young single women comprised the bulk of the labor force in the first textile factories of New England.
Corbis.

[of] men," proudly wrote "Peter Single" in the *Mechanic's Free Press* of Philadelphia, "who compose that proportion of the population of our country, on whom depends its present and future welfare; from them emanates her glory, her greatness and her power."

The factory system of production that undercut both household and artisanal manufacturing could produce goods far more quickly and cheaply per worker than artisans or rural households. Factories subdivided the specialized skills of the artisan into a series of semiskilled tasks. Factories also put workers under systematic controls, and in the final stage of industrialization, they boosted workers' productivity through the use of power-driven machinery.

Britain pioneered the technological advances that drove early industrialization. The secrets of this technology, especially the designs for the machines that mechanized textile production, were closely guarded by the British government. Despite attempts to prohibit the emigration of artisans who knew how this machinery worked, some British mechanics got to the United States. Samuel Slater was one of them, and he took over the operation of a fledging mill in Providence, Rhode Island. With his knowledge of how to build water-powered spinning machinery, Slater made the mill the nation's first permanent cotton factory.

Slater's factory, and those modeled after it, manufactured yarn that was put out to rural housewives to be woven into cloth. The first factory to mechanize the operations of spinning and weaving and turn out finished cloth was incorporated in Waltham, Massachusetts, in 1813 by the Boston Associates, a group of wealthy merchants. The Waltham factory was heavily capitalized, relied on the latest technology, and recruited its work force from rural farm families.

The first real spurt of factory building came with the closing off of British imports during the Embargo and the War of 1812. Hundreds of new cotton and woolen mills were established from 1808 to 1815. But the great test of American manufacturing came after 1815 when peace with Britain brought a flood of cheap British manufactured goods. If factories were to continue to grow, American manufacturers had to reach more consumers in their home market and overcome the British advantage of lower labor costs.

Industrial labor was more expensive in America than in England, where the high cost of land forced the peasantry into the cities to find work. In contrast, land was cheap and plentiful in the United States, and Americans preferred the independence of farm work to the dependence of factory labor. Consequently, the first mill workers were predominantly children. The owners set up the father on a plot of company-owned land, provided piece-work for the mother, and put the children to work in the mills.

But this so-called Rhode Island system of family employment was inadequate for the larger, more mechanized factories that were built in New England after the War of 1812. These mill owners recruited single, adolescent daughters of farmers from across New England as their laborers in the **Waltham system**.

Throughout the 1820s and 1830s, most mill hands in New England were young farm daughters. Factory wages (a little over a dollar per week after deductions for room and board) were more than these young women could earn doing piecework in the home or as domestics. The wages also brought a liberating degree of financial independence. "When they felt the jingle of silver in their pockets," recalled Harriet Hanson Robinson of her fellow workers at Lowell in the 1830s, "there for the first time, their heads became erect and they walked as if on air."

Based on what they had heard of conditions in British factories, most Americans associated mill towns with morally depraved, impoverished workers. To overcome these fears New England manufacturers set up paternalistic moral controls. Single female workers had to live in boardinghouses owned by the company. Curfews were imposed, visitors were screened, and church attendance was mandatory.

The mill women still worked six days a week from dawn to dusk for low wages. The operatives tended clattering, fast-moving machinery in a work environment kept humid to minimize the snapping of threads in the machines. In 1834 and 1836, the female hands at Lowell "turned out" to protest wage reductions in demonstrations that were the largest strikes in American history up to that time.

After the economic downturn of the late 1830s, conditions in the mills got worse. By the mid-1840s, however, the Irish, desperate for work, sent their children into the mills at an earlier age than Yankee farm families had. These workers did not leave after two or three years of building up a small dowry for marriage, as many New Englanders did. By the early 1850s more than half of the textile operatives in New England were Irish women.

The rise in immigration after the 1820s was crucial for urban manufacturing. By drawing on this cheap pool of immigrant labor, manufacturers could increase production while driving down the cost. Urban manufacturing became labor-intensive, depending more heavily on workers than on investment in machines and other capital. New York and Philadelphia, followed by Boston in the 1840s, thus built up a diversified manufacturing sector in consumer goods.

Except in New England textile factories and the smaller factories and shops in the seaboard cities, native-born males were the largest group of early manufacturing workers. As late as 1840, women, including those working at home, made up about half of the manufacturing work force and one-quarter of the factory hands. Regardless of their gender, few of these workers brought skills to their jobs. Economic necessity forced them to accept low wages and harsh working conditions. The sheer increase in their numbers, as opposed to productivity gains from technological innovations, accounted by 1850 for two-thirds of the gains in manufacturing output.

After 1815 American manufacturers began to close the technological gap with Britain by drawing on the skills of American mechanics. Mechanics experimented with and improved designs and patented inventions that had new industrial applications.

The most famous early American invention was the cotton gin. Eli Whitney, a Massachusetts Yankee, built the first prototype in 1793 while working as a tutor on a Georgia plantation. By cheaply and mechanically removing the seeds from cotton fibers, the cotton gin spurred the cultivation of cotton across the South.

Whitney also pushed the idea of basing production on interchangeable parts. After receiving a federal contract to manufacture muskets, he designed new milling machines and turret lathes that transformed the technology of machine tool production. The federal arsenal at Harpers Ferry, Virginia, developed machine tools that could manufacture standardized, interchangeable parts. The new techniques were first applied in 1815 to the manufacture of wooden clocks and by the 1840s to sewing machines, farm machinery, and watch parts. The ***American system of manufacturing***—low-cost, standardized mass production, built around interchangeable parts stamped out by machines—was America's unique contribution to the industrial revolution.

The 1840s registered the highest rate of expansion in the manufacturing sector of the economy in the nineteenth century. The adoption of the stationary steam engine in urban manufacturing fueled much of this expansion.

In the 1840s, high-pressure steam engines enabled power-driven industry to locate in the port cities of the Northeast and the booming cities on the Great Lakes. The West became the center of the farm machinery industry, and the region produced 20 percent of the nation's manufacturing output by the 1850s.

Steam power was beginning to transform the American landscape by the mid-nineteenth century. However, most of the change evident in the countryside by 1850 was the product of preindustrial technologies and the aftermath of impounding water for factory use.

About one-fifth of the original forest cover in the United States east of the Mississippi was gone by 1850. Most of this loss resulted from agricultural use. Wood that was not needed for farmhouses, fences, and fuel found a ready market in the cities and factories, where it was both the primary energy source and the basic building material.

As the land was being cleared and carved into private farms, the lakes and streams became dumping grounds for agricultural and industrial wastes. By 1840, the woolens industry alone was discarding some 18,000 tons of grease into rivers and streams.

To provide their mills with a steady, reliable source of water, one that would not be affected by the whims of nature, the Boston Associates constructed a series of dams and canals that extended to the headwaters of the Merrimack River in northern New Hampshire. Inevitably, the ecology of the region changed. Farmers protested when their fields and pastures were submerged, but lawyers for the Boston Associates argued that water, like any other natural resource, should be treated as a commodity that could contribute to economic progress. Increasingly, the law treated nature as an economic resource to be engineered, bought, and sold.

Growing Inequality and New Classes

As the economy expanded after 1815 and the industrial revolution began to take hold, per capita income doubled in the first half of the century. Living standards for most Americans improved. Houses, for those who could afford them, became larger, better furnished, and heated. Food was more plentiful and varied, and factory-made consumer goods made domestic life easier and more comfortable.

There was a price to be paid, however, for the benefits of economic growth. Half of the adult white males were now propertyless. Wealth had become more concentrated, and extremes of wealth and poverty eroded the Jeffersonian ideal of a republic of independent proprietors who valued liberty because they were economically free.

The gap between the rich and the poor widened considerably in the early phases of industrialization. In 1800, the richest 10 percent of Americans owned 40 to 50 percent of the national wealth. By the 1850s, that share was about 70 percent. The most glaring discrepancies in wealth appeared in the large cities. In all American cities by the 1840s, the top 10 percent of the population owned over 80 percent of urban wealth.

Most of the urban rich at midcentury had been born wealthy, the offspring of old-money families who had married and invested wisely. They belonged to exclusive clubs, attended lavish balls and dinners, were waited on by a retinue of servants in their mansions, and recoiled from what they considered the "mob government" ushered in by the Jacksonian Democrats.

The faster pace of economic growth also created opportunities for an expanding new middle class. This class grew as the number of nonmanual jobs increased. Most of these jobs were in Northern cities and bustling market towns, where the need was greatest for office and store clerks, managerial personnel, sales agents, and independent retailers. The result by midcentury was a new middle class superimposed on the older one of independent farmers, artisans, shopkeepers, and professionals.

The apparent separation of work and home constituted the first step in an evolving sense of class consciousness. As the market revolution advanced, the workplace increasingly became a specialized location of production or selling. Middle-class fathers left for their jobs in the morning, while mothers governed households that were primarily residential units.

Homes became places of material comfort for the rising middle class. Growing quantities of consumer goods—pianos, carpets, draperies, mirrors, oil lamps, and ornate furniture—filled their homes. Stoves replaced open fireplaces as the main source of heat, and plumbing eliminated outdoor privies.

Having servants, the single largest field of employment in the cities, became a status symbol. Shunned as degrading by most native-born white women, these low-paying jobs were filled by African-American and young immigrant (especially Irish) women. Work had not left the middle-class home; instead, it was disguised as the "domestic duties" of middle-class wives who supervised servants.

Besides seeking guidance from etiquette books on proper manners, the middle class also tried to shape its behavior by the tenets of evangelical religion. Revivals swept Northern cities in the late 1820s. Charles G. Finney led the most dramatic and successful ones in the cities along the Erie Canal in upstate New York. Finney preached that salvation was available to those who willed it.

He also stressed that economic and moral success depended on the virtues of sobriety, self-restraint, and hard work. Aggressiveness and ambition were not necessarily sinful as long as businessmen led moral lives and helped others do the same. This message reassured the urban middle class, for it confirmed and sanctified their pursuit of economic self-interest. It also provided them with a religious inspiration for attempting to exert moral control over their communities and employees. *Temperance*—the prohibition of alcoholic beverages—was the greatest of the evangelically inspired reforms, and abstinence from alcohol became the most telling evidence of middle-class respectability.

In a reversal of traditional Calvinist doctrine, the evangelical ministers of the Northern middle class enshrined women as the moral superiors of men. Held to be uniquely pure and pious, women were now responsible for converting their homes into loving, prayerful centers of domesticity. "There is a ministry that is older and deeper and more potent than ours," wrote a liberal Presbyterian clergyman; "it is the ministry that presides over the crib and impresses the first gospel influence on the infant soul."

This sanctified notion of motherhood reflected and reinforced shifting patterns of family life. Families became smaller as the birthrate fell by 25 percent in the first half of the nineteenth century. The decline was greatest in the urban middle class after 1820. Children were no longer an economic asset as they had been as workers on a family farm. Middle-class couples limited the size of their families, and women stopped having children at a younger age.

Beginning in the 1820s, ministers and female writers elevated the family role of middle-class women into a *cult of domesticity*. This idealized conception of womanhood insisted that the biological differences of God's natural order determined separate social roles for men and women. Characterized as strong, aggressive, and ambitious, men naturally belonged in the competitive world of business and politics. Women's providential task was to preserve religion and morality in the home and family. Only they possessed the moral purity necessary for rearing virtuous children and preserving the home as a refuge from the outside world.

Parents could now devote more care and resources to child rearing. Middle-class children lived at home longer than children had in the past and received more schooling than working-class children.

Unlike the wealthy, whose riches were inherited, members of the middle class believed that their property was the product of hard work and self-denial. They also saw themselves as the industrious Americans whose moral fortitude and discipline enabled them to escape the clutches of poverty, the fate of those who were presumed to be lazy and undisciplined.

The economic changes that produced a new middle class also transformed the working class. In preindustrial America, the working class was predominantly native-born and of artisan origins. By midcentury, most urban workers were immigrants or the children of immigrants and had never been artisans in a skilled craft.

Job skills, gender, race, and ethnicity all divided workers after 1840. Master craftsmen were the most highly skilled and best-paid members of the labor force. Industrialization splintered the unity of the old artisan class. Ambitious master craftsmen with access to capital ignored craft traditions to rise into the ranks of small businessmen and manufacturers. They expanded output and drove down the cost of production by contracting out work at piece wages and hiring the cheapest workers they could find. The result was to transform the apprentice system into a system of exploited child labor.

By the 1830s, most journeymen were becoming a class of permanent wage earners with little prospect of opening their own shops. They denounced the new industrial relations as a "system of mental and physical slavery." To protect their liberties from what they considered a new aristocracy of manufacturers, they organized workingmen's political parties in the 1830s. At the top of these parties' list of reforms were free public education, the abolition of imprisonment for debt, and a ten-hour workday. But the depression of 1839–1843 forced mechanics to concentrate on their economic survival, and the Democrats siphoned off many of their political leaders.

Journeymen also turned to trade union activity in the 1820s and 1830s to gain better wages, shorter hours, and enhanced job security. Locals from various trades formed the

National Trades Union, the first national union, in 1834. The new labor movement launched more than 150 strikes in the mid-1830s.

Although the Panic of 1837 decimated union membership, the early labor movement achieved two notable victories. First, by the late 1830s, it had forced employers to accept the ten-hour day as the standard for most skilled workers. Second, in a landmark decision handed down in 1842, the Massachusetts Supreme Court ruled in *Commonwealth v. Hunt* that a trade union was not necessarily subject to laws against criminal conspiracies and that a strike could be used to force employers to hire only union members.

The unions were the defenders of artisanal rights and virtues, and they ignored workers whose jobs had never had craft status. As massive immigration merged with industrialization after 1840, this basic division between workers widened. On one side was the male, Protestant, and native-born class of skilled artisans. On the other side was the working-class majority of factory laborers and the unskilled. These workers were predominantly immigrants and women who worked for a wage as domestic or factory hands. On average, they earned less than $500 a year, about half what skilled workers earned. Their financial survival rested on a family economy in which all members contributed whatever they could earn.

Increasingly fearing these workers as a threat to their job security and Protestant values, American-born artisans joined **nativist organizations** in the 1840s, which sought to curb mass immigration from Europe and limit the political rights of Catholic immigrants. Ethnic workers viewed temperance as business-class meddling in their lives, while successful native-born workers tended to embrace the evangelical, middle-class ideology of temperance and self-help. The greatest unity achieved by labor was the nearly universal insistence of white workers that black workers be confined to the most menial jobs.

Gender also divided workers. Working-class men shared the dominant ideology of female dependence. They measured their own status as husbands by their ability to keep their wives and daughters from having to work. Male workers also argued that their wages would be higher if women were barred from the work force. A report of the National Trades Union in 1836 cited women's "ruinous competition to male labor." It insisted that a woman's "efforts to sustain herself and family are actually the same as tying a stone around the neck of her natural protector, Man, and destroying him with the weight she has brought to his assistance."

With these views, male workers helped lock wage-earning women into the lowest-paying and most exploited jobs. Of the 25,000 women in 1860 working in manufacturing in New York City, two-thirds were in the clothing trades. Many were seamstresses working at home fifteen to eighteen hours a day for starvation wages of less than $100 a year. Over half of them were the sole breadwinners in their households.

"If we do not come forth in our defence, what will become of us?" asked Sarah Monroe of New York City in the midst of a strike by seamstresses in 1831. Women tried to organize as workers, but the male labor movement refused to lend much support. The men tried to channel the discontent of women workers into "proper female behavior" and generally restricted their assistance to pushing for legislation that would limit the hours worked by women and children, a stand that enhanced their male image as protectors of the family.

Reform and Moral Order

The rapidity and extent of the social and economic changes that accompanied the market revolution were disorienting, even frightening, to many Americans, particularly religious leaders and wealthy businessmen in the East. Alarmed by what they perceived as a breakdown in moral authority, they sought to impose moral discipline on Americans.

These Eastern elites, with the indispensable support of their wives and daughters, created a network of voluntary church-affiliated reform organizations known collectively as the *benevolent empire*. Revivals in the 1820s and 1830s then broadened the base of reform to include the newly evangelicalized middle class in Northern cities and towns.

THE BENEVOLENT EMPIRE

For the Reverend Lyman Beecher, the American condition in 1814 presented "a scene of destitution and wretchedness." He believed that only religion, as preached by "pious, intelligent, enterprising ministers through the nation," could provide the order that would preserve the Union and place it under "the moral government of God."

Evangelical businessmen in the seaboard cities backed Beecher's call to restore moral order. Worried by the increasing number of urban poor, wealthy merchants financed a network of reform associations that grew to include the American Board of Commissioners for Foreign Missions (1810), the American Bible Society (1816), the American Sunday School Union (1824), the American Tract Society (1825), and the American Home Missionary Society (1826).

The reform societies built on the Second Great Awakening's techniques of organization and communication. The Christian reformers sent out speakers on regular schedules along prescribed routes. They developed organizations that maintained a constant pressure for reform. National and local boards of directors supervised the work of salaried managers, who inspired volunteers to combat sin among the unconverted.

When steam presses and stereotype plates halved the cost of printing and dramatically increased its speed, the American Bible Society was the first to exploit this revolution in the print media. By 1830 religious presses were churning out more than 1 million Bibles and 6 million tracts a year. These publications were mass distributed by traveling agents and heavily promoted in national advertising campaigns. As the *Christian Herald* editorialized in 1823, "Preaching of the gospel is a Divine institution—'printing' is no less so. . . . The PULPIT AND THE PRESS are inseparably connected."

A host of local societies were more concerned with stamping out individual vices. Their purpose, as summed up by a Massachusetts group, the Andover South Parish Society for the Reformation of Morals, was "to discountenance [discourage] immorality, particularly Sabbath-breaking, intemperance, and profanity, and to promote industry, order, piety, and good morals." These goals linked social and moral discipline in a way that appealed both to pious churchgoers concerned about godlessness and profit-oriented businessmen eager to curb their workers' unruly behavior.

With volunteers drawn largely from the teenage daughters of evangelical businessmen, Sunday interdenominational schools combined elementary education with the teaching of the Bible and Christian principles. The American Sunday School Union was both a coordinating agency for local efforts and a publishing house for books and periodicals. By 1832, nearly 10 percent of all American children aged 5 to 14 were attending one of eight thousand Sunday schools.

The boldest expression of the drive to enhance Christian power was the *Sabbatarian movement*. In 1828, evangelicals led by Lyman Beecher formed the General Union for Promoting the Observance of the Christian Sabbath whose immediate goal was the repeal of a law passed by Congress in 1810 directing post offices to deliver mail on Sunday. This law symbolized to Christian reformers the moral degeneracy into which the republic had fallen. Its broader mission was to enforce local statutes that shut down business and leisure activities on Sundays. The Sabbatarians considered such statutes no less "necessary to the welfare of the state" than "laws against murder and polygamy." To their opponents, such statutes were "repugnant to the rights of private property and irreconcilable with the free exercise of civil liberty."

In 1829, insisting on the separation of church and state, the Democratic Congress upheld the postal law of 1810. Businessmen, workingmen, Southern evangelicals, and religious conservatives in New England all felt that the Sabbath purists had gone too far.

The General Union disbanded in 1832, but it left an important legacy for future reform movements. On the one hand, it developed techniques that converted the reform impulse into direct political action. In raising funds, training speakers, holding rallies, disseminating literature, lobbying for local Sunday regulations, and coordinating a petition to Congress, the Sabbatarians created an organizational model for other reformers to follow in mobilizing public opinion and influencing politicians. On the other hand, the failure of the Sabbatarians revealed that heavy-handed attempts to force the "unconverted" to follow Christian standards of conduct were self-defeating. A new approach was needed that encouraged individuals to reform themselves without coercive controls. It soon emerged in the temperance movement.

THE TEMPERANCE MOVEMENT

Temperance—the drive against the consumption of alcohol—had the greatest immediate impact on the most people of any reform movement. Its success rested on what Lyman Beecher called "a new moral power." Dismayed by popular resistance to the coercive moralism of the first wave of Christian reform, evangelicals like the Reverend John Chester concluded in 1821 that "you cannot coerce a free people that are jealous to fastidiousness of their rights." Therefore, reform had to rest on persuasion, and it had to begin with the voluntary decision of individuals to free themselves from sin. For these evangelicals, the self-control to renounce alcohol became the key to creating a harmonious Christian society of self-regulating citizens.

In 1826, evangelicals founded the American Temperance Society in Boston and took control of the movement. They were inspired by Beecher's *Six Sermons on Temperance*, a stirring call for voluntary associations dedicated to the belief that "the daily use of ardent spirits, in any form, or in any degree" was a sin. They now sought a radical change in American attitudes toward alcohol and its role in social life.

American consumption of alcohol reached an all-time high by 1830 of 7.1 gallons of pure alcohol per year for every American aged 14 and over (about three times present-day levels). Alcoholic beverages were plentiful and cheaper than tea or coffee. Alcohol was used to pay both common laborers and the itinerant preachers on the early Methodist circuit. Masters and journeymen shared a drink as a customary way of taking a break from work. No wedding, funeral, or meeting of friends was complete without alcohol.

For the temperance crusade to succeed, the reformers had to finance a massive propaganda campaign and link it to an organization that could energize thousands of people. They built such a mass movement by merging temperance into the network of churches and lay volunteers that the benevolent empire had developed and by adopting the techniques of revivals to win new converts.

Evangelical reformers denounced intemperance as the greatest sin of the land. Alcohol represented all that was wrong in America—crime, poverty, insanity, broken families, boisterous politicking, Sabbath-breaking.

This message was thundered from the pulpit and the public lectern. It was also broadcast in millions of tracts printed on the latest high-speed presses. As in the revivals, temperance rallies combined emotionally charged sermons with large, tearful prayer meetings to evoke guilt among sinners, who would then take the pledge of abstinence.

Within a decade, the American Temperance Society had more than five thousand local chapters and statewide affiliates. A million members had pledged abstinence by 1833. New England and New York alone claimed 72 percent of all temperance societies in the mid-1830s. Most of the converts came from the upper and middle classes. Businessmen welcomed temperance as a model of self-discipline in their efforts to regiment factory work. Young, upwardly mobile professionals and petty entrepreneurs learned in temperance how to be thrifty, self-controlled, and more respectable and creditworthy. Many of them presumably agreed with the *Temperance Recorder* that "the enterprise of this country is so great, and competition so eager in every branch of business . . . , that profit can only result from . . . *temperance.*"

Women were indispensable to the temperance movement. As the moral protectors of the family, they pressured their husbands to take the teetotaler's pledge and stick by it, raised sons to shun alcohol, and banished liquor from their homes. By the 1840s, temperance and middle-class domesticity had become synonymous.

Temperance made its first significant inroads among the working classes during the economic depression of 1839–1843. Joining together in what they called Washington Temperance Societies, small businessmen and artisans, many of them reformed drunkards, carried temperance into working-class districts. The Washingtonians gained a considerable following by insisting that workers could survive the depression only if they stopped drinking and adopted the temperance ethic of frugality and self-help. Their wives organized auxiliary societies and pledged to enforce sobriety and economic restraint at home.

By 1845, per capita consumption of alcohol had fallen to less than two gallons. In 1851, Maine passed the first statewide prohibition law. Other Northern states followed suit, but antitemperance coalitions soon overturned most of these laws outside New England. Nonetheless, alcohol consumption remained at the low level set in the 1840s.

WOMEN'S ROLES IN REFORM

The first phase of women's reform activities represented an extension of the Cult of Domesticity. Assumptions about their unique moral qualities encouraged women to assume the role of "social mother" inspired by the revivalist call of the 1820s. They founded maternal associations, sponsored revivals, visited the poor, established Sunday Schools, and distributed Bibles and religious tracts. These reformers widened the public role of women, but their efforts also reinforced cultural stereotypes of women as nurturing helpmates who deferred to males.

A second phase in the reform efforts by women developed in the 1830s. Unlike their benevolent counterparts, the reformers now began to challenge male prerogatives and move beyond moral suasion. The crusade against prostitution exemplified the new militancy. Women seized leadership of the movement in 1834 with the founding of the New York Female Moral Reform Society. In the pages of their journal, *Advocate for Moral Reform,* members identified male greed and licentiousness as the causes for the fallen state of women. Identified, too, were the male patrons of the city's brothels. The society blamed businessmen for the low wages that forced some women to resort to prostitution and denounced lustful men for engaging in "a regular crusade against [our] sex."

In 1839, this attack on the sexual double standard became a national movement with the establishment of the American Female Moral Reform Society. With 555 affiliates throughout the evangelical heartland of the North, female activists mounted a lobbying campaign that reached out to a mass audience for signatures. By the 1840s, such unprecedented political involvement enabled women to secure the first state laws criminalizing seduction and adultery.

Other women's groups developed a more radical critique of American society and its male leadership. The Boston Seamen's Aid Society, founded in 1833 by Sarah Josepha Hale, a widow with five children, soon rejected the benevolent tradition of distinguishing between the "respectable" and the "unworthy" poor. Hale discovered that her efforts to guide poor women toward self-sufficiency flew in the face of the low wages and substandard housing that trapped her clients in poverty. She concluded in 1838 that "it is hardly possible for the hopeless poor to avoid being vicious." Hale attacked male employers for exploiting the poor. "Combinations of selfish men are formed to beat down the price of female labor," she wrote in her 1836 annual report, "and then they call the diminished rate the market price."

BACKLASH AGAINST BENEVOLENCE

Some of the benevolent empire's harshest critics came out of the populist revivals of the early 1800s. They considered the Christian reformers' program a conspiracy of orthodox Calvinists to impose social and moral control on behalf of a religious and economic elite. The goal of the "orthodox party," warned the Universalist *Christian Intelligencer*, was the power of "governing the nation."

These criticisms revealed a profound mistrust of the emerging market society. In contrast to the evangelical reformers, drawn from the well-educated business and middle classes who were benefiting from economic change, most evangelical members of the grass-roots sects and followers of the itinerant preachers were unschooled, poor, and hurt by market fluctuations that they could not control. Often they were farmers forced by debt to move west or artisans and tradesmen displaced by new forms of factory production and new commercial outlets. Socially uprooted and economically stranded, they found a sense of community in their local churches and resisted control by wealthier, better-educated outsiders. Above all, they clung to beliefs that shored up the threatened authority of the father over his household.

With the elevation of women to the status of moral guardians of the family and agents of benevolent reform outside the household, middle-class evangelicalism in the Northeast was becoming feminized. This new social role for women was especially threatening— indeed, galling—for men who were the casualties of the more competitive economy. Raised on farms where the father had been the unquestioned lawgiver and provider, these men attacked feminized evangelicalism for undermining their paternal authority. They found in Scripture an affirmation of patriarchal power for any man, no matter how poor.

The ***Church of Jesus Christ of Latter-day Saints*** (also known as the ***Mormon Church***) represented the most enduring religious backlash of economically struggling men against the aggressive efforts of reforming middle-class evangelicals. Joseph Smith, who established the church in upstate New York in 1830, came from a New England farm family uprooted and impoverished by market speculations gone sour. He and his followers were alienated, not only from the new market economy but also from what they saw as the religious and social anarchy around them.

Based on Smith's divine revelations as set forth in *The Book of Mormon* (1830), their new faith offered converts to Mormonism both a sanctuary as a biblical people and a release from social and religious uncertainties. Mormonism assigned complete spiritual and secular authority to men. Only through subordination and obedience to their husbands could women hope to gain salvation.

To be a Mormon was to join a large extended family that was part of a shared enterprise. Men bonded their labor in a communal economy to benefit all the faithful. Driven by a strong sense of social obligation, the Mormons forged the most successful alternative vision in antebellum America to the individualistic Protestant republic of the benevolent reformers. (For the Mormons' role in the westward movement, see Chapter 13.)

Institutions and Social Improvement

Although evangelical Protestantism was its main-spring, antebellum reform also had its roots in the European Enlightenment. Enlightenment thinkers, like the evangelicals inspired by religious optimism, had unbounded faith in social improvement.

Studies published in the 1820s that documented increasing urban poverty, crime, and teenage delinquency created a sense of urgency for many reformers. Guided by the Enlightenment belief that environmental conditions shaped human character, reformers created a new system of public schooling in the North. They also prodded state legislatures to fund penitentiaries for criminals, asylums for the mentally ill, reformatories for the delinquent, and almshouses for the poor.

As reformers were implementing new institutional techniques for shaping individual character after 1820, a host of utopian communities also tapped into an impulse for human betterment. They typically rejected either private property or families based on monogamous marriage and offered a communitarian life designed to help a person reach perfection. Most of these communities were short-lived.

SCHOOL REFORM

Before the 1820s, schooling in America was an informal, haphazard affair that nonetheless met the basic needs for reading, writing, and arithmetic skills of an overwhelmingly rural population. Private tutors and academies for the wealthy, a few charitable schools for the urban poor, and rural one-room schoolhouses open for a few months a year comprised formal education at the primary level.

The first political demands for free tax-supported schools originated with the Workingmen's movement in Eastern cities in the 1820s. Decrying what the Philadelphia Working Men's Committee in 1830 described as "a monopoly of talent, which consigns the multitude to comparative ignorance, and secures the balance of knowledge on the side of the rich and the rulers," workers called for free public schooling. In pushing for what they called "equal republican education," they were also seeking to guarantee that all citizens, no matter how poor, could achieve meaningful liberty and equality. Wealthier property holders, however, refused to be taxed to pay for the education of working-class children.

The breakthrough in school reform came in New England. Increasing economic inequality, growing numbers of Irish Catholic immigrants, and the emergence of a mass democracy based on nearly universal white male suffrage convinced reformers of the need for state-supported schools.

In 1837, the Massachusetts legislature established the nation's first state board of education. The head of the board for the next twelve years was Horace Mann, a former Whig politician and temperance advocate who now tirelessly championed educational reform. Mann demanded that the state government assume centralized control over Massachusetts schools. All schools should have the same standards of compulsory attendance, strict discipline, common textbooks, professionally trained teachers, and graded, competitive classes of age-segregated students.

Once this system was in place, Mann promised, poverty would no longer threaten social disruption because the ignorant would have the knowledge to acquire property and wealth. Trained in self-control and punctuality, youths would be able to take advantage of economic opportunities and become intelligent voters concerned with the rights of property.

Democrats in the Massachusetts legislature denounced Mann's program as "a system of centralization and of monopoly of power in a few hands, contrary in every respect, to the true spirit of our democratical institutions." The laboring poor, who depended on the wages their children could earn, resisted compulsory attendance laws and a longer school year. Farmers fought to maintain local control over schooling and to block the higher taxes needed for a more comprehensive and professionalized system. The Catholic Church protested the attempts of the reformers to indoctrinate students in the moral strictures of middle-class Protestantism. Catholics began building their own parochial schools.

Mann and his allies prevailed in most of the industrializing states with strong support from the professional and business constituencies of the Whig party. School reform appealed to the growing Northern urban middle class. Schools would instill the moral and economic discipline that the middle class deemed essential for a progressive and ordered society. Teaching morality and national pride was central to the educational curriculum, and from the popular McGuffey Readers students learned that "God gives a great deal of money to some persons, in order that they may assist those [who] are poor."

Out of the Northern middle class also came the young female teachers who increasingly staffed elementary schools. Presumed by their nature to be more nurturing than men, women now had an entry into teaching, the first profession open to them. Besides, women could also be paid far less than men; school boards assumed that they would accept low wages while waiting to be married.

By 1850 just over 50 percent of the white children between 5 and 19 years of age in the United States were enrolled in school—the highest percentage in the world at the time, although the slave states, especially in the Lower South, lagged behind the rest of the nation in public education.

PRISONS, WORKHOUSES, AND ASYLUMS

Up to this time, Americans had depended on voluntary efforts to cope with crime, poverty, and social deviance. Reformers now turned to public authorities to establish a host of new institutions—penitentiaries, workhouses, mental hospitals, orphanages, and reformatories—to deal with social problems.

Eighteenth-century Americans never thought of rehabilitating criminals, but the institutional reformers of the Jacksonian era believed that criminals, the poor, and other deviants, could be morally redeemed. In the properly ordered environment of new institutions, discipline and moral character would be instilled in those who lacked the self-control to resist the corrupting vices and temptations that pervaded society.

As two French observers noted in the early 1830s, "The penitentiary system . . . to them seems the remedy for all the evils of society." Unlike earlier prisons, the penitentiaries were huge, imposing structures that isolated the prisoners from each other and the outside world. No longer were criminals to be brutally punished or thrown together under inhumane conditions that perpetuated a cycle of moral depravity. Now, cut off from all corrupting influences, forced to learn that hard work teaches moral discipline, and uplifted by religious literature, criminals would be guided toward becoming law-abiding, productive citizens.

The same philosophy of reform provided the rationale for asylums to house the poor and the insane. The number of transient poor and the size of urban slums increased as commercial capitalism uprooted farmers from the land and undercut the security of craft trades. Believing that the poor, much like criminals, had only themselves to blame, public officials and their evangelical allies prescribed a therapeutic regimen of discipline and physical labor to cure the poor of their moral defects. The structured setting for that regimen was the workhouse.

The custodians of the workhouses banished drinking, gambling, and idleness. Inmates lived in a tightly scheduled daily routine built around manual labor. Once purged of their laziness and filled with self-esteem as the result of work discipline, the poor would be released to become useful members of society.

Public insane asylums offered a similar order for the mentally ill. Reformers believed that too many choices in a highly mobile, materialistic, and competitive society drove some people insane. By 1860, twenty-eight states had established mental hospitals. These facilities set rigid rules and work assignments to teach patients how to order their lives.

While the reformers did provide social deviants with cleaner and safer living conditions, their penitentiaries and asylums succeeded more in classifying and segregating their inmates than in reforming them. Submission to routine turned out not to be the best builder of character. Witnessing the rigorous control of every movement of the isolated prisoners at the Eastern State Penitentiary in Philadelphia, English novelist Charles Dickens declared "this slow and daily tampering with the mysteries of the brain to be immeasurably worse than any torture of the body."

Penitentiaries, reformatories, and workhouses failed to eliminate or noticeably check poverty, crime, and vice. By midcentury, reformers were defining deviants and dependents as permanent misfits who suffered from ingrained character defects. Stripped of their earlier optimism, the asylums became little more than holding pens for the outcasts of society.

UTOPIAN ALTERNATIVES

Unlike the reformers, who aimed to improve the existing order by guiding individuals to greater self-discipline, the utopians sought perfection by withdrawing from society. A radically new social order, not an improved old one, was their goal.

Though following different religious and secular philosophies of communitarian living, all the utopians wanted to fashion a more rational and personally satisfying alternative to the competitive materialism of antebellum America. Nearly all the communities sought to transform the organization and rewards of work, thus challenging the prevailing dogmas about private property.

The most successful utopian communities were religious sects whose reordering of both sexual and economic relations departed most sharply from middle-class norms.

The *Shakers*, at their height in the 1830s, attracted some six thousand followers. Named for the convulsive dancing that was part of their religious ceremonies, the Shakers traced their origins to the teachings of Ann Lee ("Mother Ann"). An illiterate factory laborer in mid-eighteenth-century England, Lee had a revelation in 1770 that the Second Coming of Christ was to be fulfilled in her own womanly form, the embodiment of the female side of God. Fired by another vision in 1774, Lee led eight of her followers to America, where, after her death in 1784, her disciples established the first Shaker community in New Lebanon, New York.

Organized around a doctrine of celibate *communism*, Shaker communities held all property in common. The genders worked and lived apart from each other. Dancing during religious worship brought men and women together and provided an emotional release from enforced sexual denial. As an early Shaker leader explained, "There is evidently no labor which so fully absorbs all the faculties of soul and body, as real spiritual devotion and energetic exercise in sacred worship." In worldly as well as spiritual terms, women enjoyed an equality in Shaker life that the outside world denied them. For this reason, twice as many women as men joined the Shakers.

The Shakers gradually dwindled. Their rule of celibacy meant, of course, that they could propagate themselves only by recruiting new members and few new converts joined the movement after 1850. The Shakers today are best remembered for the beautiful simplicity of the furniture they made in their workshops.

John Humphrey Noyes established the *Oneida Community* in upstate New York in 1847. He attracted over two hundred followers with his perfectionist vision of plural marriage, community nurseries, group discipline, and common ownership of property. Charged with adultery, Noyes fled to Canada in 1879, but the Oneida Community, reorganized in 1881 as a joint-stock company in the United States and committed thereafter to conventional sexual mores, survived into the twentieth century.

Secular utopians aspired to perfect social relations through the rational design of planned communities. Bitter critics of the social evils of industrialization, they tried to construct models for a social order free from poverty, unemployment, and inequality. They envisioned cooperative communities that balanced agricultural and industrial pursuits in a mixed economy that recycled earnings to the laborers who actually produced the wealth.

Despite their high expectations, nearly all the planned communities ran into financial difficulties and collapsed. The pattern was set by the first of the controversial socialist experiments, *New Harmony* in Indiana, the brainchild of the wealthy, Scottish industrialist and philanthropist Robert Owen who was a proponent of utopian *socialism*. But within two years of its founding in 1825, New Harmony fell victim to inadequate financing and internal bickering.

Brook Farm, established in 1841 in West Roxbury, Massachusetts (today part of Boston), was a showcase for the transcendentalist philosophy of Ralph Waldo Emerson. A former Unitarian minister in Boston, Emerson taught that intuition and emotion could grasp a truer ("transcendent") reality than the senses alone could. Boston intellectuals saw Brook Farm as a refuge from the pressures and coarseness of commercial society, a place where they could realize the Emersonian ideal of spontaneous creativity. Although disbanded after six years as an economic failure, Brook Farm inspired intellectuals such as Nathaniel Hawthorne. His writings and those of others influenced by *transcendentalism* flowed into the great renaissance of American literature in the mid-nineteenth century.

In an 1837 address at Harvard, Emerson had called for a national literature devoted to the democratic possibilities of American life. "The literature of the poor, the feelings of the child, the philosophy of the street, the meaning of household life, are the topics of the time," he proclaimed. Writers soon responded to Emerson's call.

Walt Whitman, whose *Leaves of Grass* (1855) foreshadowed modern poetry in its use of free verse, shared Emerson's faith in the possibilities of individual fulfillment, and his poems celebrated the democratic variety of the American people. Henry David Thoreau, Emerson's friend and neighbor, embodied the transcendentalist fascination with nature and self-discovery by living in relative isolation for sixteen months at Walden Pond, near Concord, Massachusetts. His *Walden, or Life in the Woods* (1854) became an American classic. "I went to the woods," he wrote, "because I wished to . . . confront only the essential facts of life, and see if I could not learn what it had to teach, and not, when I came to die, discover that I had not lived."

Novelists Nathaniel Hawthorne and Herman Melville focused on the existence of evil and the human need for community. In *The Scarlet Letter* (1850) and *The House of the Seven Gables* (1851), Hawthorne probed themes of egoism and pride to reveal the underside of the human soul. Melville's *Moby Dick* (1851) depicted the consequences of a competitive individualism unchecked by a social conscience.

Much of the appeal of the utopian communities flowed from the same concern about the splintering and selfishness of antebellum society that animated Hawthorne and Melville. The works of these novelists have endured, but the utopian experiments quickly collapsed. Promising economic security and social harmony to buttress a threatened sense of community, the utopians failed to lure all but a few Americans from the acquisitiveness and competitive demands of the larger society.

Abolitionism and Women's Rights

Abolitionism emerged from the same religious impulse that energized reform throughout the North. Like other reformers, the abolitionists came predominantly from evangelical, middle-class families, particularly those of New England stock. What distinguished the abolitionists was their insistence that slavery was *the* great national sin, mocking American ideals of liberty and Christian morality.

Under the early leadership of William Lloyd Garrison, the abolitionists attacked slaveholders and those whose moral apathy helped support slavery. After provoking a storm of protest in both North and South, the abolitionist movement split in 1840. Crucial in this division was Garrison's support of women's rights. Most abolitionists broke with him and founded their own antislavery organization. Female abolitionists organized a separate women's rights movement.

REJECTING COLONIZATION

In the early nineteenth century, when slavery was expanding westward, almost all white Americans regardless of class or region were convinced that emancipation would lead to a race war or the debasement of their superior status through racial interbreeding. This paralyzing fear, rooted in racism, long shielded slavery from sustained attack.

In 1817, antislavery reformers from the North and South founded the ***American Colonization Society***. Slaveholding politicians from the Upper South, notably Henry Clay,

James Madison, and President James Monroe, were its leading organizers. Gradual emancipation followed by the removal of black people from America to Africa was the only solution that white reformers could imagine for ridding the nation of slavery and avoiding a racial bloodbath. Their goal was to make America all free and all white.

The American Colonization Society had no chance of success. No form of emancipation could appeal to slave owners who could profit from the demand for their slaves in the Lower South. Black people already free accounted for nearly all of those the society transported to its West African colony, Liberia. At the height of its popularity in the 1820s, the society sent only fourteen hundred colonists to Africa. During that same decade, the American slave population increased by 700,000.

Free African Americans bitterly attacked the colonizers' assumption that free black people were unfit to live as free citizens in America. Most free African Americans were native-born, and they considered themselves Americans with every right to enjoy the blessings of republican liberty. As a black petition in 1817 stated, banishment from America "would not only be cruel, but in direct violation of the principles, which have been the boast of this republic."

Organizing through their own churches in northern cities, free African Americans founded some fifty abolitionist societies, offered refuge to fugitive slaves, and launched the first African-American newspaper in 1827, *Freedom's Journal*. David Walker, a free black man who had moved from North Carolina to Massachusetts, published his ***Appeal to the Colored Citizens of the World*** in 1829. Rejecting colonization, Walker insisted that "America is more our country, than it is the whites'—we have enriched it with our *blood and tears*," and he warned white Americans that "wo, wo, will be to you if we have to obtain our freedom by fighting."

As if in response to his call for revolutionary resistance by the enslaved, Nat Turner's Rebellion exploded in the summer of 1831 (see Chapter 11). Both alarmed and inspired by the increased tempo of black militancy, a small group of antislavery white people abandoned all illusions about colonization and embarked on a radically new approach for eradicating slavery.

ABOLITIONISM

The leading figure in early abolitionism was William Lloyd Garrison, a Massachusetts printer, who became coeditor of an antislavery newspaper in Baltimore in 1829. Before the year was out, Garrison was convicted of criminal libel for his editorials against a Massachusetts merchant engaged in the domestic slave trade and spent seven weeks in jail. Garrison emerged with an unquenchable hatred for slavery. Returning to Boston, he launched his own antislavery newspaper, *The Liberator*, in 1831. A year later, he was instrumental in founding the New England Anti-Slavery Society.

As militant as the free African Americans who comprised the bulk of the early subscribers to *The Liberator*, Garrison thundered, "If we would not see our land deluged in blood, we must instantly burst asunder the shackles of the slaves." He committed abolitionism to the twin goals of immediatism—an immediate moral commitment to end slavery—and racial equality. Only by striving toward these goals, he insisted, could white America ever hope to end slavery without massive violence.

The demand of the abolitionists for the legal equality of black people was as unsettling to public opinion as their call for immediate, uncompensated emancipation. Discriminatory laws, aptly described by abolitionist Lydia Maria Child as "this legalized contempt of color," restricted the political and civil liberties of free African Americans in every state. Denied the vote outside New England, segregated in all public facilities, prohibited from moving into several Western states, and excluded from most jobs save menial labor, free black people everywhere were walled off as an inferior caste unfit for equality.

Garrison was uncompromising in denouncing slavery and advocating black rights. But without the organizational and financial resources of a national society, the message of the early Garrisonians rarely extended beyond free black communities in the North. The success of British abolitionists in 1833 when gradual, compensated emancipation was enacted for Britain's West Indian colonies, inspired white and black abolitionists to gather at Philadelphia in December 1833 and form the ***American Anti-Slavery Society***.

Arthur and Lewis Tappan, two wealthy merchants from New York City, provided financial backing, and Theodore Dwight Weld, a young evangelical minister, fused abolitionism with the moral passion of religious revivalism. Weld brought abolitionism to the West in 1834 with the revivals he preached at Lane Theological Seminary in Cincinnati. The "Lane rebels," students gathered by Weld, fanned out as itinerant agents to seek converts for abolitionism throughout the Yankee districts of the rural North. Weld's *American Slavery As It Is: Testimony of a Thousand Witnesses*, a massively documented indictment of slavery, became a bestseller in 1839. Abolitionist women, notably Angelina Grimké, Weld's wife and the daughter of a South Carolina planter, contributed much of the research.

Revivalistic exhortations were just one technique the abolitionists exploited to mobilize public opinion against slavery. They spread their message through rallies, paid lecturers, children's games and toys, and the printed word. Drawing on the experience of reformers in Bible and tract societies, the abolitionists harnessed steam printing to the cause of moral suasion. They distributed millions of antislavery tracts, and by the late 1830s, abolitionist sayings appeared on posters, emblems, song sheets, and even candy wrappers.

To change public opinion, the abolitionists described slavery in terms of moral and physical degradation. By 1840, nearly 200,000 Northerners belonged to the American Anti-Slavery Society. Most whites, however, remained unmoved, and some violently opposed the abolitionists.

In the mid-1830s antiabolitionist mobs in the North disrupted antislavery meetings, beat and stoned speakers, destroyed printing presses, burned the homes of the wealthy benefactors of the movement, and vandalized free black neighborhoods in a wave of terror that drove black people from several Northern cities. Elijah P. Lovejoy, an abolitionist editor in Illinois, was killed by a mob in 1837. The mobs' fury expressed the anxieties of semi-skilled and common laborers who thought they might lose their jobs if freed slaves moved North.

In the South, the hostility to abolitionism took the form of burning and censoring antislavery literature, offering rewards for the capture of leading abolitionists to stand trial for inciting slave revolts, and tightening up slave codes and the surveillance of free black people. Meanwhile, Democrats in Congress passed a gag rule that automatically tabled antislavery petitions.

In 1838, Garrison helped found the New England Non-Resistant Society, dedicated to the belief that a complete moral regeneration, based on renouncing force in all human relationships, was necessary if America were ever to live up to its Christian and republican ideals. The Garrisonian nonresistants rejected all coercive authority, whether expressed in human bondage, clerical support of slavery, male dominance in the patriarchical family, the racial oppression of black people, or the police power of government. The logic of their stand as Christian **anarchists** drove them to denounce all formal political activities and even the legitimacy of the Union, based as it was on a pact with slaveholders.

Garrison's support for the growing demand of antislavery women to be treated as equals in the movement split the American Anti-Slavery Society in 1840. In turn, the opposition of most male abolitionists to the public activities of their female counterparts provoked a militant faction of these women into founding their own movement to achieve equality in American society.

THE WOMEN'S RIGHTS MOVEMENT

Feminism grew out of abolitionism because of the parallels many women drew between the exploited lives of the slaves and their own subordinate status in Northern society. Considered biologically inferior to men, women were denied the vote, deprived of property or control of any wages after marriage, and barred from most occupations and advanced education. "In striving to cut [the slave's] irons off, we found most surely that *we* were manacled *ourselves*," argued Abby Kelley, a Quaker abolitionist.

Antislavery women now demanded an equal voice in the abolitionist movement. Despite strong opposition from male abolitionists, Garrison helped Abby Kelley win a seat on the business committee of the American Anti-Slavery Society at its convention in 1840. The anti-Garrisonians walked out of the convention and formed a separate organization in 1840, the American and Foreign Anti-Slavery Society.

The "woman question" also disrupted the 1840 World Anti-Slavery Convention in London. The refusal of the convention to seat the American female delegates was the final indignity that transformed the discontent of women into a self-conscious movement for women's equality. Two of the excluded delegates, Lucretia Mott and Elizabeth Cady Stanton, vowed to build an organization to "speak out for *oppressed* women."

Their work went slowly. Early feminists were dependent on the abolitionists for most of their followers. Many women sympathetic to the feminist movement held back lest they be shunned in their communities. A minister's wife in Portsmouth, New Hampshire, spoke for many of these women when she wrote to a feminist friend, "There are but few here who think of women as anything more than slave or a plaything, and they think I am different from most women."

In 1848, Stanton and Mott were finally able to call the first national convention ever devoted to women's rights at Seneca Falls, in upstate New York. The **Seneca Falls Convention** issued the **Declaration of Sentiments**, a call for full female equality. It identified male patriarchy as the source of women's oppression and demanded the vote for women as a sacred and inalienable right of republican citizenship.

The Seneca Falls agenda defined the goals of the women's movement for the rest of the century. The call for the vote met the stiffest opposition. The feminists' few successes before the Civil War came in economic rights. By 1860, fourteen states had granted women greater control over their property and wages—most significantly under New York's Married Women's Property Act of 1860. Largely the result of the intense lobbying of Susan B. Anthony, the act established women's legal right to their own wage income and to sue fathers and husbands who tried to deprive them of their wages.

The feminist movement did not attract broad support. Most women found in the doctrine of separate spheres a reassuring feminine identity that they could express either at home or in benevolent and reform societies. Within the reform movement as a whole, women's rights were always of minor concern.

POLITICAL ANTISLAVERY

Most abolitionists who had broken with Garrison in 1840 believed that emancipation could best be achieved by moving abolitionism into the mainstream of American politics. Political abolitionism had its roots in the petition campaign of the late 1830s. Congressional efforts to suppress the discussion of slavery backfired when John Quincy Adams, the former president who had become a Massachusetts congressman, resorted to an unending series of parliamentary ploys to get around the gag rule. Adams became a champion of the constitutional right to petition Congress for redress of grievances. White Northerners who had shown no interest in abolitionism as a moral crusade for black people now began to take a stand against slavery when the issue involved the civil liberties of whites and the political power of the South. By the hundreds of thousands, they signed abolitionist petitions in 1837 and 1838 to protest the gag rule and block the admission of Texas as a slave state.

In 1840, anti-Garrison abolitionists formed the **Liberty party** and elected several antislavery congressmen in antislavery districts dominated by evangelical New Englanders. The Liberty party condemned racial discrimination in the North, as well as slavery in the South, and won the support of most black abolitionists.

Frederick Douglass was the black abolitionists' most dynamic spokesman. After escaping from slavery in 1838, Douglass became a spellbinding lecturer for abolitionism and in 1845 published his classic autobiography, *Narrative of the Life of Frederick Douglass, an American Slave*. Dissatisfied with Garrison's Christian pacifism and his stand against political action, Douglass broke with Garrison in 1847 and founded a black abolitionist newspaper, *The North Star*. The break became irreparable in 1851 when Douglass publicly denied the Garrisonian position that the Constitution was a proslavery document. If properly interpreted, Douglass insisted, "the Constitution is a *glorious liberty document*," and he called for a political war against slavery.

That war had started in the 1840s with the Liberty party, which kept slavery in the limelight of national politics. Led by Joshua R. Giddings, a small but vocal bloc of antislavery politicians began to popularize the frightening concept of "the Slave Power"—a vast conspiracy of planters and their Northern lackeys who had seized control of the federal government and was plotting to spread slavery and subvert any free institutions that opposed it. As proof, they cited the gag rule shutting off debate on slavery and the campaign of the Tyler administration to annex slaveholding Texas. The Michigan Liberty party in 1843 claimed that slavery was "not only a monstrous legalized system of wickedness . . . but an overwhelming political monopoly . . . which has thus tyrannically subverted the constitutional liberties of more than 12,000,000 of nominal American freemen." The Liberty party blamed the depression of 1839–1843 on the "withering and impoverishing effect of slavery on the free States." Planters, it was charged, had reneged on their debts to Northern creditors and manipulated federal policies on banking and tariffs to the advantage of the South.

The specter of the Slave Power made white liberties and not black bondage central to Northern concerns about slavery. White people who had earlier been apathetic now began to view slavery as a threat to their rights of free speech and self-improvement through free labor untainted by the degrading competition of slave labor.

The image of the Slave Power predisposed many Northerners to see the expansionist program of the incoming Polk administration as part of a Southern plot to secure more territory for slaveholders at the expense of Northern farmers. Northern fears that free labor would be shut out of the new territories won in the Mexican War provided the rallying cry for the Free-Soil Party of 1848 that foreshadowed the more powerful Republican party of the late 1850s.

Conclusion

After 1815, transportation improvements, technological innovations, and expanding markets drove the economy toward industrialization. Wealth inequality increased, old classes were reshaped, and new ones formed. These changes were most evident in the Northeast, where capital, labor, and growing urban markets spurred the acceleration of manufacturing. The reform impulse that both reflected and shaped these changes was also strongest in the Northeast.

The new evangelical Protestantism promised that human perfectibility was possible if individuals strove to free themselves from sin. Influenced by this promise, the Northern middle class embraced reform causes that sought to improve human character. Temperance established sobriety as the cultural standard for respectable male behavior. Middle-class reform also emphasized institutional solutions for what were now defined as the social problems of ignorance, crime, and poverty.

The most radical reform movements focused on women's equality and the elimination of slavery. The women's rights movement emerged out of women's involvement in reform, especially in abolitionism. Feminism and abolitionism triggered a backlash from the conservative majority. That prevented women from gaining legal and political equality, and convinced most abolitionists that they had to switch from moral agitation to political persuasion. Political abolitionists found that the most effective approach was their charge that a Slave Power conspiracy threatened the freedoms of white Northerners.

REVIEW QUESTIONS

1. Why were improvements in transportation essential to the growth of the economy after 1815?

2. What is an industrial revolution? Why did manufacturing surge in the United States from 1815 to 1850?

3. What drew women into reform?

4. Why was abolitionism the most radical reform of all?

5. Why was Angelina Grimké's journey from social privilege to social activism so exceptional?

The Way West

1815–1850

How did economic and demographic pressures in the East
spur Western migration?

How did Westward expansion affect the life of Plains Indians?

How was the United States able to annex Texas from Mexico?

Which peoples lived in the Southwest?

⭐

"On an occasion when I had interrogated a Sioux chief, on the upper Missouri, about their Government—their punishments and tortures of prisoners, for which I had freely condemned them for the cruelty of the practice, he took occasion, when I had got through, to ask me some questions relative to modes in the *civilized* world, which, with his comments upon them, were nearly as follows: and struck me, as I think they must every one, with great force.

He . . . told me he had often heard that white people hung their criminals by the neck, and choked them to death like dogs, and those their own people to which I answered, "yes." He then told me he had learned that they shut each other up in prisons, where they keep them a great part of their lives because *they can't pay money.* I replied in the affirmative to this, which occasioned great surprise and excessive laughter, even among the women. . . . He said . . . that he had been along the Frontier, and a good deal amongst the white people, and he had seen them whip their little children—a thing that is very cruel—he had heard also, from several white *medicine-men,* that the Great Spirit of the white people was the child of a white woman, and that he was at the last put to death by the white people! This seemed to be a thing that he had not been able to comprehend, and he concluded by saying, "the Indians. Great Spirit got no mother—the Indians no kill him, he never die." He put me a chapter of other questions as to the trespasses of the white people on their lands—their continual corruption of the morals of their women—and digging open the Indians graves to get their bones, & c. To all of which I was compelled to reply in the affirmative, and quite glad to close my note-book, and quietly to escape from the throng that had collected around me, and saying (though to myself and silently), that these and an hundred other vices belong to the civilized world, and are practiced upon (but certainly, in no instance, reciprocated by) the "cruel and relentless savage."

—George Catlin

Virgil J. Vogel, ed., *A Documentary History of the American Indian* (New York: Harper and Row, 1972), pp. 138–139.

GEORGE CATLIN, one of the great illustrators of the West of the American Indians, recorded these words in the 1830s when he traveled over the Trans-Mississippi West painting and sketching, in his words, "the looks and customs of the vanishing races of native man in America." Unlike most white people of his generation, he approached Indian cultures with respect, and he realized that native peoples had a valid critique of white America.

251

Born in 1796, he was raised among memories of Indians and their warfare. After briefly practicing law, he turned to painting as a career in the 1820s, and was so taken with the grace and dignity of Indians that he set out to record Indian history and customs before their way of life was engulfed by a surging tide of white settlement.

Some 300,000 Americans traveled the Oregon Trail in the 1840s and 1850s in a trek that eventually made the United States a nation that spanned the continent. They were part of a tide of white migration that eventually saw more than fifty thousand Americans a year migrate west of the Appalachians after the War of 1812.

In the 1840s, the edge of settlement pushed into the Louisiana Purchase territory and across a huge area of plains, desert, mountains, and ocean coast that had seen few American settlers before then.

The broad expanse of the Trans-Mississippi region (stretching from the Mississippi Valley to the Pacific Coast) became a meeting ground of people from diverse cultures as Anglo-Americans came into contact and conflict with the Indians of the Plains and the Mexicans of the Southwest. Convinced of their own superiority, Anglo-Americans asserted a God-given right to spread across the continent and impose their notions of liberty and democracy on peoples whose land they coveted. In the process, they defeated and subjugated those who stood in their way.

Manifest Destiny, the label for this presumed providential right, provided a justification for the expansionist Democratic administration of James K. Polk that came to power in 1845. The most dramatic result of these policies was the Mexican War of 1846–1848, which made California and the present-day Southwest part of the American continental empire.

The Agricultural Frontier

The U.S. population ballooned from 5.3 million in 1800 to more than 23 million by 1850. Four-fifths of this extraordinary gain was from natural increase—the surplus of births over deaths. As the population expanded, it shifted westward. Fewer than one in ten Americans lived west of the Appalachians in 1800; by 1850, about half did.

Through purchase and conquest, the land area of the United States more than tripled in the first half of the nineteenth century. Here was space where Americans could raise the large families of a rural society in which, on average, six to eight children survived to adolescence.

Declining soil fertility and rising population pressure in the rural East propelled these migrations. A common desire for greater economic opportunity, however, resulted in two distinct Western societies by the 1840s. North of the Ohio River, in the Old Northwest, free labor and family farms defined the social order. South of the Ohio was the Old Southwest, a society dominated by slave labor and the plantation.

THE CROWDED EAST

Looking back at his rural youth, Omar H. Morse recalled, "My Parents were in very limited circumstances financially yet blessed with a large family of children which is a poor man's capital though capital of this kind is not considered very available in case of financial Depression." Born in 1824 in the upstate New York village of Hastings, Morse had no prospect of inheriting land from his father and was tired of taking orders as a farm hand for temporary wages. He moved in the 1840s to Wisconsin, but he lost three farms and eventually settled in Minnesota, where he worked at odd jobs and built houses. Heading west did not guarantee economic success, but it was the best option open to land-starved Easterners who dreamed of leaving a productive farm to their children.

By the early nineteenth century, land was scarce in the East, especially in New England. Most New England communities no longer had enough arable land to satisfy all the young men who wanted their own farms. Even recently opened areas such as Vermont felt the pressure of rural overpopulation.

Land was more productive and expensive farther south, in the Mid-Atlantic states. Keyed to the major export crop of wheat, agriculture was more commercialized than in New England, and economic inequality was thus higher. One-third to one-half of the young men in the commercialized agricultural districts of New Jersey and Pennsylvania were landless by the end of the eighteenth century. These men and their families, many of whom were recently arrived Scots-Irish and German immigrants, led the western migration from Pennsylvania.

The pressure to move west was greatest in the slave states along the Eastern Seaboard. Although population density here was just two-thirds of that in New England, landholdings were more concentrated and the soil more exhausted than in the Northeast. Tenants who wanted their own land and small farmers tired of competing against slave labor were forced west across the mountains. They were joined by the sons of planters. Despite marriages arranged to keep land within the wealthy families, there was no longer enough good land left to carve out plantations for all the younger sons.

By the early 1800s, the young and the poor in the rural East had every incentive to head west, where fertile land was abundant, accessible, and, at $2 to $3 per acre, far cheaper than in the East. Land was the basis of wealth and social standing, and its ownership separated the independent from the dependent, the rooted from the rootless. "Those who labor in the earth," Jefferson wrote in 1785, "are the chosen people of God . . . whose breasts He has made his peculiar deposit for substantial and genuine virtue."

The Western settler, observed a traveler on the Missouri frontier in the 1820s, wanted "to be a freeholder, to have plenty of rich land, and to be able to settle his children around him." Public policy and private aspirations merged in the belief that access to land was the key to preserving American freedom.

When Jefferson took office in 1801, the minimum price for public land was $2 per acre, and a block of 320 acres had to be purchased at one time. By the 1830s, the price was down to $1.25 per acre, and the minimum purchase was only 80 acres. Congress also protected squatters, who had settled on public land before it was surveyed, from being outbid by speculators at a land sale. The Preemption Act of 1841 guaranteed the right to purchase up to 160 acres at the minimum price of $1.25 when the public auction was held.

THE OLD NORTHWEST

The number of Americans who settled in the heartland of the Old Northwest—Ohio, Indiana, and Illinois—rose tenfold from 1810 to 1840. Ohio had already entered the Union in 1803; Indiana joined in 1816, Illinois in 1818. The end of the War of 1812 and the abandonment by the British of their former Indian allies opened up the region to a flood of migrants.

Two streams of migrants, one predominantly northern and the other southern, met in the lower Midwest and viewed each other as strangers. Lucy Maynard, a New Englander living in south-central Illinois, noted that her neighbors were "principally from Indiana and

Kentucky, some from Virginia, all friendly but very different from our people in their manners and language and every other way."

The Old Northwest was less a melting pot in which regional cultures merged than a mosaic of settlements in which the different values and folkways of regional cultures from throughout the East took root and expanded. Belts of migration generally ran along a line from east to west as settlers sought out soil types and ecological conditions similar to those they had left behind. Thus a transplanted Yankee culture from New England and upstate New York spread over the upper Midwest—northern Ohio, Indiana, and Illinois, as well as Michigan and Wisconsin. These Westerners were Whiggish in their politics, tended to be antislavery, and valued a communal sense of responsibility that regulated moral behavior and promoted self-improvement. The highland Southerners who settled the lower Midwest—southern Ohio, Indiana, and Illinois, as well as Kentucky—were Democrats: They fiercely distrusted any centralized authority, political or moral, and considered Yankees intolerant do-gooders. Holding the balance of cultural and political power were the migrants from Pennsylvania and New Jersey, who were accustomed to ethnic diversity and the politics of competing economic groups. They settled principally in central Ohio, Indiana, and Illinois. By emphasizing economic growth and downplaying the cultural politics that pitted Yankees against Southerners, they built a consensus around community development.

It took about ten years of backbreaking labor to create an 80-acre farm in heavily wooded sections. Wives and daughters helped tend the field crops, milked cows and churned butter, and produced the homespun cloth that, along with their dairy goods, found

Cyrus McCormick pioneered the development of horse-drawn mechanical reapers. Shown here demonstrating his reaper to potential customers, McCormick helped revolutionize American agriculture with labor-saving machinery that made possible far larger harvests of grain drops.

The Old Print Shop.

a market in the first country stores on the frontier. Charlotte Webb Jacobs, from the Sugar Creek community on the Illinois prairie, proudly recalled, "I made everything that we wore; I even made my towels and table cloths, sheets and everything in the clothing line."

Communities pooled their efforts for such tasks as raising a cabin. Groups of settlers also acted as a cooperative unit at public land auctions. Members of local *claims clubs* physically intimidated speculators who refused to step aside until local settlers had acquired the land they wanted.

Surplus goods were sold to newcomers moving into the area or bartered with local storekeepers for essentials such as salt, sugar, and metalwares. This initial economy, however, soon gave way to a more commercially oriented agriculture when steamboats, canals, and railroads opened up vast new markets (see Chapter 11).

The first large market was in the South, down the corridor of the Ohio and Mississippi Rivers, and the major staples were corn and hogs. By the 1830s, the Erie Canal and its feeder waterways in the upper Midwest began to reorient much of the Western farm trade to the Northeast.

Wheat production skyrocketed when settlers overcame their initial reluctance to farming in a treeless terrain and moved into the prairies of Indiana and Illinois in the 1840s. New plows—a cast-iron one patented by Jethro Wood in 1819 and a steel version developed by John Deere in 1837—helped break the thick prairie sod. The plows were followed in the 1840s by horse-drawn mechanical harvesters equipped with a self-rake reaper that enabled family farmers to harvest vastly more wheat. Using traditional harvesting methods, a scythe with a cradle frame, an experienced worker could cut no more than 2 acres a day. With the new machinery the same worker could harvest 12 acres a day. Once railroads provided direct access to Eastern markets, the Midwest became the nation's breadbasket.

The commercialization of agriculture in the West also contributed to the growth of Eastern manufacturing. Western farms supplied Eastern manufacturers with inexpensive

---

• C H R O N O L O G Y •

1803–1806 Lewis and Clark travel up the Missouri River in search of a water route to the Pacific.

1816 Settlers surge into the Trans-Appalachian region.

1821 Mexico gains its independence from Spain. Santa Fe Trail opens.
Stephen F. Austin establishes the first American colony in Texas.

1824 Rocky Mountain Fur Company begins the rendezvous system.

1830 Congress creates the Indian Territory.

1834 Protestant missions are established in Oregon.
Santa Anna seizes power in Mexico.

1836 Texas wins its independence from Mexico.

1837 Smallpox epidemic hits the Plains Indians.

1842 First large parties of migrants set out on the Oregon Trail.

1845 United States annexes Texas.
Democrats embrace Manifest Destiny.

1846 Mexican War breaks out.
United States and Britain reach an agreement on Oregon.

1847 Mormons begin settlement of Utah.

1848 Oregon Territory is organized.
Treaty of Guadalupe Hidalgo ends the Mexican War.

1851 Fort Laramie Treaty with the Plains Indians is signed.

raw materials for processing into finished goods. Western corn and wheat not only supplied Eastern workers with cheap food but also forced noncompetitive Eastern farmers either to move west or to work in factories in Eastern cities. In turn, the West itself became an ever-growing market for Eastern factory goods. For example, nearly half of the nation's iron production in the 1830s was fashioned into farm implements. At midcentury, the Old Northwest had become part of a larger Midwest whose economy was increasingly integrated with that of the Northeast. Settlers continued to pour into the region, and three additional states—Michigan (1837), Iowa (1846), and Wisconsin (1848)—joined the Union.

The combination of favorable farm prices and steadily decreasing transportation costs generated a rise in disposable income that was spent on outside goods or invested in internal economic development. Manufacturing cities grew out of towns that were favorably situated by water or rail transport. The West north of the Ohio was now economically specialized and socially diverse.

THE OLD SOUTHWEST

"The *Alabama Feaver* rages here with great violence and has *carried off* vast numbers of our Citizens," wrote a North Carolina planter in 1817 about the westward migration from his state. "I am apprehensive, if it continues to spread as it has done, it will almost depopulate the country." By 1850, more than 600,000 white settlers from Maryland, Virginia, and the Carolinas lived in slave states to the south and west, and many of them had brought their slaves with them. Indeed, from 1790 to 1860, more than 800,000 slaves were moved from the South Atlantic region into the Old Southwest. Soaring cotton prices after the War of 1812 and the smashing of Indian confederations during the war, which opened new lands to white settlement, propelled the first surge of migration into western Tennessee and the Black Belt, a crescent-shaped band of rich, black loamy soil arcing westward from Georgia through central Alabama and Mississippi.

Migration surged anew in the 1830s when cotton prices were again high and the Chickasaws and Choctaws had been forced out of the incredibly fertile Delta country between the Yazoo and Mississippi Rivers (see Chapter 10). In less than thirty years, six new slave states—Mississippi (1817), Alabama (1819), Missouri (1821), Arkansas (1836), Florida (1845), and Texas (1845)—joined the Union.

The Southwestern frontier attracted both slaveholding planters and small independent farmers. The planters, though a minority, had the capital or the credit to acquire the best lands and the slave labor to make those lands productive. These slaveholders were responding both to the need for fresh land and to the extraordinary demand for short-staple cotton. As one North Carolina planter put it, Alabama would be a "garden of plenty" compared to the "old-fields and empty corn-houses" of his native state.

Short-staple cotton could be grown anywhere with a minimum of 210 consecutive frost-free days. Eli Whitney's gin, which eliminated the problem of removing the sticky, green seeds from the fiber, was fifty times faster than hand separation. Meanwhile, the mechanization of the British textile industry had created a seemingly unquenchable demand for raw cotton. With new fertile land and a slave labor force, the South increased its share of world cotton production from 9 percent in 1800 to 68 percent in 1850.

More typical settlers on the Southern frontier were small independent yeomen farmers, who generally owned no slaves. Many of them shared the belief of the yeoman farmer Gideon Lincecum "in the pleasure of frequent change of country."

The yeomanry moved onto the frontier in two waves. The first consisted of stockmen-hunters, a restless, transient group who spread from the pine barrens in the Carolina back-country to the coastal plain of eastern Texas. They prized unfettered independence and measured their wealth in the livestock left to roam and fatten on the sweet grasses of uncleared forests. They were quick to move on when farmers, the second wave, started to clear the land for crops.

Like the stock herders, the yeoman farmers valued self-sufficiency and the leisure to hunt and fish. They practiced a diversified agriculture aimed at feeding their families. Corn and pork were the mainstays of their diet, and both could readily be produced as long as there was room for the open-range herding of swine and growing patches of corn and small grains. The yeoman's chief source of labor was his immediate family.

Measured by per capita income, and as a direct result of the profits from slave-produced cotton on virgin soils, the Old Southwest was a wealthier society than the Old Northwest in 1850. The settlement of the Old Southwest was also more significant for national economic development. More than any other commodity, cotton paid for American imports and underpinned national credit.

The Southwest Ordinance, enacted by Congress in 1790, opened all territories south of the Ohio River to slavery. Slaves, land, and cotton were the keys to wealth on the Southern frontier, and agricultural profits were continually plowed back into these assets. In contrast, prosperous farmers in the Old Northwest were much more likely to invest their earnings in promotional schemes designed to attract settlers whose presence would raise land values and increase business for local entrepreneurs. As early as the 1840s, rural communities in the Old Northwest were supporting bustling towns that offered jobs in trade and manufacturing on a scale far surpassing anything in the slave West. By the 1850s, the Midwest was almost as urbanized as the Northeast had been in 1830, and nearly half the labor force no longer worked on farms.

The Old Southwest remained overwhelmingly agricultural. Once the land was settled, the children of the first generation of slaveholders and yeomen moved west to the next frontier. Relatively few newcomers took their place. By the 1850s, Kentucky, Tennessee, Alabama, and Mississippi were all losing more migrants than they were gaining.

The Frontier of the Plains Indians

Few white Americans had ventured west of the Mississippi by 1840. What scanty knowledge there was of this huge inland expanse was the result of government-sponsored expeditions. Reports of explorations led by Zebulon Pike in 1806 and Stephen Long in 1819 dismissed much of the area as the Great American Desert, an arid, treeless landscape with little agricultural potential.

Beyond Texas and the boundary line drawn by the Trans-Continental Treaty of 1819 lay the northern possessions of Mexico, where horse-mounted Indian tribes dominated by the Sioux were a formidable power. Before the 1840s, only fur trappers and traders, who worked with and not against the powerful Sioux, had pushed across the Great Plains and into the Rockies. The 1840s brought a sudden change, a large migration westward that radically altered the ecology of the Great Plains. Farm families trapped in an agricultural depression and enticed by Oregon's bounty turned the trails blazed by the fur traders into ruts on the *Oregon Trail*, the route that led to the first large settlement of Americans on the Pacific Coast.

TRIBAL LANDS

At least 350,000 Native Americans lived in the plains and mountains of the Trans-Mississippi West in 1840. The point where the prairies of the Midwest gave way to the higher, drier plains marked a rough division between predominantly agricultural tribes to the east and nomadic, hunting tribes to the west. The Kansas, Osages, and Omahas in what is now Kansas and Iowa and the Arikaras, Mandans, and Hidatsas along the upper Missouri River grew corn, beans, and squash and lived in semipermanent villages, much as woodland Indians had in the East. On the open plains were hunting and raiding peoples, such as the western Sioux, Crows, Cheyennes, and Arapahos.

In the 1830s, the U.S. government set aside a broad stretch of country between the Platte River to the north and the Red River to the south (most of present-day Oklahoma and eastern Kansas) exclusively for tribes resettled from the East under the Indian Removal Act of 1830 and for village-living groups native to the area. Many government officials envisioned this territory as a permanent sanctuary that would separate Indians from whites and allow them to live in peace on allotments of land granted as compensation for the territory they had ceded to the federal government. However, the pressure exerted on native peoples in the Mississippi Valley both from raiding parties of Plains Indians and the incessant demands of white farmers and speculators for more land was rendering a stable Indian-white boundary meaningless.

On the eve of Indian removal in the East, the defeat of the Sauks and Foxes in what white Americans called Black Hawk's War of 1832 opened Iowa to white settlement and forced tribes to cede land. In 1838, Congress created the Territory of Iowa, which encompassed all the land between the Mississippi and Missouri Rivers north of the state of Missouri. The Indians were now on the verge of being pushed completely out of Iowa. Throughout the upper Mississippi Valley in the 1830s, other groups suffered a similar fate.

Farming peoples whose villages straddled the woodlands to the east and the open plains to the west were caught in a vise between the loss of their land to advancing white settlers and the seizure of their horses and agricultural provisions by Indian raiders from the plains. The Pawnees were among the hardest hit.

By the 1830s, the Pawnees were primarily an agricultural people who embarked on seasonal hunts for game in the Platte River Valley. In 1833, they signed a treaty with the U.S. government, agreeing to withdraw from south of the Platte in return for subsidies and military protection from the hostile Indians on the plains. Once they moved north of the Platte, the Pawnees were attacked by Sioux who seized control of the prime hunting grounds. Sioux raiders seeking provisions and horses also harassed Pawnee agricultural villages. When the desperate Pawnees filtered back south of the Platte, they were constantly harassed by white settlers. In vain Pawnee leaders cited the provisions of the treaty that promised them protection from the Sioux. Forced back north of the Platte by the U.S. government, the Pawnees were eventually driven out of their Nebraska homeland by the Sioux.

The Sioux were more than able to hold their own against white Americans in the first half of the nineteenth century. In the eighteenth century, the western Sioux, armed with guns they had acquired from the French, dominated the prairies east of the Missouri.

The Sioux learned to use the horse from the Plains Indians. Horses made buffalo hunting vastly more productive, they made it easier to transport bulky possessions, and they made possible an aggressive, highly mobile form of warfare. The Sioux were the most successful of all the tribes in melding two facets of white culture, the gun and the horse, into an Indian culture of warrior-hunters.

Although the Sioux frequently fought other tribes, casualties from these encounters were light. The Sioux and other Plains Indians fought not to kill the greatest number of the enemy but rather to dominate hunting grounds and to win individual honor by "counting coup" (touching a live foe). When an Army officer in 1819 urged the Sioux to make peace with the Chippewas, Little Crow, a Santee Sioux, explained why war was preferable: "Why, then, should we give up such an extensive country to save the life of a man or two annually?"

When the United States acquired title to the Great Plains in the Louisiana Purchase of 1803, the western Sioux economy was based on hunting buffalo on horse in summer and trapping beaver in winter. In spring, great trading fairs were held in which the western Sioux exchanged their buffalo robes and beaver pelts for goods acquired by the Santee Sioux from European traders.

As the supply of beaver dwindled and the demand for buffalo hides from American and European traders increased in the early 1800s, the Sioux extended their buffalo hunts. Sioux war parties pushed aside or subjugated weaker tribes to the south and west of the Missouri River basin.

Epidemic diseases brought to the plains by white traders helped Sioux expansion. The nomadic Sioux were less susceptible to these epidemics than the more sedentary village peoples. The Sioux were also one of the first tribes to be vaccinated against smallpox by doctors sent by the Bureau of Indian Affairs in the early 1830s. A major smallpox epidemic in 1837 probably halved the region's Indian population. Sioux losses were relatively light and, unlike the other tribes, their population grew.

Some 25,000 strong by 1850, the western Sioux had increased in power and numbers since they first encountered American officials during the Lewis and Clark Expedition in 1804 and 1805. Even then, Jefferson had cautioned Lewis to cultivate good relations with the Sioux "because of their immense power." "These are the vilest miscreants of the savage race," wrote Lewis and Clark of the Sioux, "and must ever remain the pirates of the Missouri, until such measures are pursued by our government as will make them feel a dependence on its will for their supply of merchandise."

Americans could vilify the Sioux, but they could not force them into dependence in the first half of the nineteenth century.

THE FUR TRADERS

"Curiosity, a love of wild adventure, and perhaps also a hope of profit—for times *are* hard, and my best coat has a sort of sheepish hang-dog hesitation to encounter fashionable folk— combined to make me look upon the project with an eye of favour." These were the motives that induced Warren A. Ferris, a New York civil engineer, to join the American Fur Company in 1829 at the age of 19 and go west as a fur trapper and mountain man. During their golden age in the 1820s and 1830s, the trappers blazed the trails that far greater numbers of white settlers would follow in the 1840s.

Until the early 1820s, the Hudson's Bay Company, a well-capitalized British concern, dominated the Trans-Mississippi fur trade. A breakthrough for American interests came in 1824 when two St. Louis businessmen, William Henry Ashley and Andrew Henry of the Rocky Mountain Fur Company, developed the rendezvous system, which, in keeping with Indian traditions of periodic intertribal meetings, brought together trappers, Indians, and traders in a grand annual fair at a designated site in the high mountain country of Wyoming. White trappers and Indians exchanged the animal skins they had gathered in the seasonal hunt for the guns, traps, tobacco, whiskey, textiles, and other trading goods that agents of the fur companies in St. Louis brought to the fair.

The trappers' closest relations were with Indians, and about 40 percent of the trappers married Indian women, unions that often linked them economically and diplomatically to their bride's tribe. Living conditions in the wilderness were primitive, even brutal. Mortality rates among trappers ran as high as 80 percent a year. Death could result from an accidental gunshot wound, an encounter with a grizzly, or an Indian arrow. "Peg-Leg" Smith became a legend for amputating his own leg after it was shattered by a bullet.

For all its dangers, the life of a trapper appealed to unattached young men like Warren Ferris fleeing the confinements, as well as the comforts, of white civilization. "Fancy to yourself," Ferris asked readers of his published journals, "three thousand horses of every variety of size and colour, with trappings almost as varied as their appearance . . . ridden by a thousand souls . . . their persons fantastically ornamented. . . . Listen to the rattle of num-berless lodgepoles [trailed] by pack-horses. . . . Yonder see a hundred horsemen pursuing a herd of antelopes." He was describing the color, bustle, and motion at the start of a hunt with the Salish Indians of Montana in the 1830s, played out on "a beautiful level prairie, with dark blue snow-capped mountains in the distance for the *locale*."

Such spectacles were increasingly rare after 1840, the year of the last mountain men's rendezvous on the Green River in Wyoming. The most exploitive phase of the fur trade in the 1830s had ravaged the fur-bearing animals and accelerated the spread of smallpox among the tribes. Whiskey, the most profitable item among the white man's trading goods, had corrupted countless Indians and undermined the vitality of tribal cultures.

The main trading corridor of the fur trade—up the lower Missouri to the North Platte and across the plains to the South Pass, a wide plateau crossing the Continental Divide, and into the Wyoming basin—became the main overland route to the West that migrating farm families followed in the 1840s. The mountain men had removed the mystery of western geography, and in so doing they hastened the end of the frontier conditions that had made their unique way of life possible.

THE OREGON TRAIL

The ruts are still there. One can follow them to the horizon in the Platte River Valley of Nebraska and the dry tablelands of Wyoming, Idaho, and Nevada. They were put there by the wheels of wagons hauled by oxen on a jolting 2,000-mile journey across plains, moun-tains, and deserts from Missouri to Oregon, Utah, and California (see Map 13–1). Some 150,000 Americans made this overland trek in the heyday of the Oregon Trail in the 1840s and early 1850s. Most of them walked alongside their wagons. They covered up to 15 miles a day on a trip that lasted close to six months.

Under an agreement reached in 1818, the Oregon Country was still jointly adminis-tered by the United States and Great Britain. Furs—whether beaver pelts or the skins of the Pacific sea otter—had attracted a few American trappers and merchants, but the British-controlled Hudson's Bay Company dominated the region. Protestant missionaries estab-lished the first permanent white settlements in the 1830s. Under the leadership of Jason Lee, they set up their missions in the fertile Willamette Valley, south of the Columbia River.

The missionaries repeatedly failed to convert the Indians to Christianity. Unlike the trap-pers, the missionaries sought to change the entire structure of Indian life and beliefs. With their numbers already thinned by the diseases brought in by the trappers, Oregon tribes such

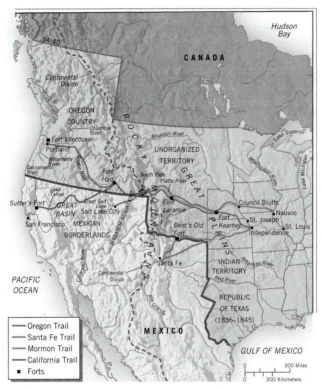

MAP 13–1
Western Overland Trails   The great overland trails to the West began at the Missouri River. The Oregon Trail crossed South Pass in Wyoming and then branched off to Oregon, California, or Utah. The Santa Fe Trail carried American goods and traders to the Mexican Southwest.

WHAT ROLE did geography play in determining overland trails?

as the Cayuses refused to abandon their traditional culture based on hunting and fishing and become farm laborers for whites. During a measles epidemic in 1847, the Cayuses killed two of the most prominent missionaries, Marcus and Narcissa Whitman. In retaliation, white Americans, who now numbered more than five thousand, virtually exterminated the Cayuses.

The first large party of overlanders on the Oregon Trail left Independence, Missouri, in 1842 for the Willamette Valley. Independence and St. Joseph in Missouri and, by the 1850s, Council Bluffs in Iowa competed to capture the lucrative trade of outfitting the migrants. Merchants profited from supplying, usually at inflated prices, wagons, mules, oxen, guns, ammunition, and staples like flour, bacon, and sugar.

Most overlanders were young farm families from the Midwest, who restlessly searched for the perfect farm that would keep them out of debt. Medorum Crawford said of one family that made the journey to Oregon with him in 1842 and then quickly left for California: "They had practically lived in the wagon for more than twenty years, only remaining in one locality long enough to make a crop, which they had done in every State and Territory in the Mississippi Valley."

Usually the male head of a household made the decision to move. Besides their usual work of minding the children and cooking and cleaning, women would now have to help drive wagons and tend livestock. Still, many women were also optimistic about the journey. "Ho—for California—at last we are on the way," exclaimed Helen Carpenter in 1857, "and with good luck may some day reach the 'promised land.'" A study of 159 women's trail diaries indicates that about one-third of the women strongly favored the move. Margaret Frink, for example, recalled that she "never had occasion to regret the prolonged hardships of the toilsome journey."

In the 1840s, some five thousand of the ninety thousand men, women, and children who set out on the Oregon Trail died along the way. Few died from Indian attacks. Indians killed only 115 migrants in the 1840s, and trigger-happy white migrants provoked most clashes. Disease, especially cholera, was the great killer. Second to disease were accidents, especially drownings when drivers tried to force overloaded wagons across swollen rivers.

Cooperation among families was the key to a successful overland crossing. The men often drew up a formal, written constitution at the start of the trip spelling out the assignments and work responsibilities of each wagon. The wagon train had to leave late enough in the spring to get good grass in Nebraska for the oxen and mules. A wagon train that departed too early risked getting bogged down in spring mud; one that left late risked the danger in the Pacific coastal ranges of being trapped in the mountain snows.

Before "Oregon fever" had run its course, the flow of white settlers across the continent radically changed the economy and ecology of the Great Plains. Pressure mounted on plants and animals, reducing the land's ability to support all the Native American tribes accustomed to living off it. Far from being separated from white people by a permanent line of division, the Plains Indians now stood astride the main path of white migration to the Pacific.

In response, officials in the Bureau of Indian Affairs organized a great gathering of the tribes in 1851 to push through the Fort Laramie Treaty, the first U.S. government attempt to draw boundaries within which to contain the Plains Indians. In exchange for accepting limitations on their movement and for the loss of game, the tribes were to receive annual compensation of $50,000 a year for fifty years (later reduced by the U.S. Senate to ten years). When American negotiators tried to restrict Sioux hunting to north of the Platte, the Sioux demanded and received treaty rights to lands south of the Platte as well. "These lands once belonged to the Kiowas and the Crows," argued a western Sioux, "but we whipped those nations out of them, and in this we did what the white men do when they want the lands of the Indians." The Americans conceded the point.

The Fort Laramie Treaty represented a standoff between the Sioux and the U.S. government, the two great powers on the Plains. If neither yielded its claims to the region, war was inevitable.

The Mexican Borderlands

By the mid-1840s, parties of emigrant Americans were beginning to branch off the main Oregon Trail on their way to Utah and California. These areas were then part of the northern borderlands of Mexico. Mostly a semiarid and thinly populated land of high plateaus, dry basins, and desert bisected north to south by mountain ranges, the borderlands had been part of the Spanish empire in North America. Mexico inherited this territory when it won independence from Spain in 1821. Mexico's hold on this region was always weak.

It lost Texas in 1837, and in the next decade, the American penetration of Utah and California set the stage for the American seizure of most of the rest in the Mexican War.

THE PEOPLES OF THE SOUTHWEST

Imperial Spain had divided the population of the Southwest into four main groupings: Indians, full-blooded Native Americans who retained their own languages and customs; *mestizos*, those of racially mixed ancestry, usually Spanish and Indian; *criollos*, American-born whites of Spanish ancestry; and Spaniards.

By far the smallest group were the Spaniards. Despite their small numbers, the Spanish, along with the *criollos*, monopolized economic and political power. This wealthy elite controlled the labor of the *mestizos* in the predominantly ranching economy of the borderlands.

The largest single group in the borderlands were the Indians, about half the population in the 1820s. Most had not come under direct Spanish or Mexican control. Those who had were part of the mission system. This instrument of Spanish imperial policy forced Indians to live in a fixed area, to convert to Catholicism, and to work as agricultural laborers.

Spanish missions, most of them established by the Franciscan order, aimed both to Christianize and to "civilize" the Indians. Mission Indians were forced to abandon their native economies and culture and accept a European definition of civilization that demanded that they live in settled agricultural communities and work under the tight supervision of the friars. Spanish soldiers and royal officials, who lived in military garrisons known as *presidios*, accompanied the friars.

The largest concentration of Indians—some 300,000 when the Spanish friars arrived in the 1760s—was in California. The Paiutes in the Owens Valley perfected an intricate system for irrigating wild grasses, but only the Yumans along the Colorado River in southeastern California practiced full-scale agriculture. The Spanish marveled at their lush fields of wheat, maize, beans, tobacco, and melons. The Yumans also had an elaborate religion based on an oral tradition of dream songs. (Dream songs remain a distinctive feature of Native American culture.)

The major farming Indians east of California were the Pueblo peoples of Arizona and New Mexico. Formally a part of the Spanish mission system, they had incorporated the Catholic God and Catholic rituals into their own polytheistic religion, which stressed the harmony of all living things with the forces of nature. They continued to worship in their underground sanctuaries known as *kivas*.

Once the Pueblos made their peace with the Spaniards after their great revolt in 1680 (see Chapter 3), their major enemies were the nomadic tribes that lived by hunting and raiding. These tribes outnumbered the Pueblos four to one and controlled most of the Southwest until the 1850s. Horses enabled them to gain the means of ranging far and wide for the economic resources that sustained their transformation into societies of mounted warriors.

Other tribes in the Mexican borderlands included the Navajos, the Apaches, the Comanches, and the Kiowas. The Comanches, a branch of the mountain Shoshonis who moved to the plains when horses became available, were the most feared of the nomadic peoples. They took to the horse as few other people ever had. They were utterly fearless, confident, and masterful horsemen. Their stature as mounted warriors reached mythic proportions. For food and clothing, they relied on the immense buffalo herds of the southern plains. For guns, horses, and other trading goods, they lived off their predatory raids. When the Santa Fe Trail opened in the early 1820s, their shrewdness as traders gave them a new source of firearms that strengthened their raiding prowess.

The three focal points of white settlement in the northern borderlands of Mexico—Texas, New Mexico, and Alta California (as distinguished from Lower, or Baja, California)—were never linked by an effective network of communications or transportation. Travel was limited to tortuous journeys along Indian and Spanish trails that barely indented the dry and largely barren landscape. Each of these settlements was an isolated offshoot of Hispanic culture with a semiautonomous economy based on ranching and a mostly illegal trade with French, British, and American merchants that brought in a trickle of needed goods.

Mexico's most pressing problem in the 1820s was protecting its northern states from the Comanches. To serve as a buffer against the Comanches, the Mexican government in 1821 invited Americans into Texas, opening the way to the eventual American takeover of the territory.

THE AMERICANIZATION OF TEXAS

The Mexicans faced the same problems governing Texas that the Spanish had. Sparsely populated and economically struggling, Mexican Texas shared a border with the United States along the Sabine River in Louisiana and the Red River in the Arkansas Territory. As one Mexican official noted with alarm: "If we do not take the present opportunity to people Texas, day by day the strength of the United States will grow until it will annex Texas, Coahuila, Saltillo, and Nuevo León like the Goths, Visigoths, and the other tribes that assailed the Roman Empire." However, attempts to promote immigration into Texas from other parts of Mexico failed. Reasoning that the Americans were going to come in any event, and anxious to build up the population of Texas against Indian attacks, the Mexican government encouraged Americans to settle in Texas by offering huge grants of land in return for promises to accept Mexican citizenship, convert to Catholicism, and obey the authorities in Mexico City.

The first American *empresario*—the recipient of a large grant in return for a promise to bring in settlers—was Stephen F. Austin, who founded the first American colony in Texas. The Austin grant encompassed 18,000 square miles. The *empresarios* stood to grow wealthy by leasing out land, selling parcels to settlers, and organizing the rest into large-scale farms that produced cotton with slave labor in the bottomlands of the Sabine, Colorado, and Brazos Rivers. For the Americans who followed in their wake, Texas offered the chance to acquire good land that was so cheap it was almost free. As early as 1830, eastern and south-central Texas were becoming an extension of the plantation economy of the Gulf coastal plain. More than 25,000 white settlers, with around a thousand slaves, had poured into the region.

Many settlers simply ignored Mexican laws, especially the Emancipation Proclamation of 1829 that forbade slavery in the Republic of Mexico. In 1830, the Mexican government levied the first taxes on the Americans, prohibited the further importation of slaves, and closed the international border to additional immigration. Still, another ten thousand Americans spilled in during the early 1830s, and they continued to bring in slaves.

Unlike the *empresarios*, many of whom became Catholic and married into elite **Tejano** families, these newcomers lived apart from Mexicans and rejected Mexican citizenship. Cultural tensions escalated. Most of these new arrivals sneered at the Mexicans as a mongrelized race of black people, Indians, and Spaniards and resented having to submit to their rule. As Protestants, Americans considered Catholicism a despotic, superstitious religion and ignored legal requirements that they accept the Catholic faith.

When General Santa Anna, elected president of Mexico in 1833, overturned the liberal Mexican constitution of 1824, his dictatorial centralist rule ended any hope that Texas might become an autonomous state within a federated Mexico. Skirmishing between Mexican troops and rebellious Texans began in the fall of 1835.

At first, the Anglo-Tejano leadership sought to overthrow Santa Anna, restore the constitution of 1824, and win separate statehood for Texas within a liberal Mexican republic. When Santa Anna raised a large army to crush the uprising, he radicalized the rebellion and pushed it to declare complete independence on March 2, 1836. Four days later, a Mexican army of four thousand annihilated the 187 defenders of the *Alamo*, an abandoned mission in San Antonio. A few weeks later at Goliad, another three hundred Texans were killed after they had agreed to surrender.

"Remember the Alamo!" and "Remember Goliad!" were powerful rallying cries for the beleaguered Texans. Volunteers from the American South rushed to the aid of the main Texan army, commanded by Sam Houston. A product of the Tennessee frontier and a close friend of Andrew Jackson's, Houston's victory in April 1836 at the Battle of San Jacinto established the independence of Texas. Captured while trying to flee, Santa Anna signed a treaty in May 1836, recognizing Texas as an independent republic with a boundary on the south and west at the Rio Grande. However, the Nueces River to the north of the Rio Grande had been the administrative border of Texas under Mexican rule. The Mexican Congress rejected the treaty, and the boundary remained in dispute.

In part because Mexico refused to recognize the Texas Republic, Anglos feared Tejanos as a subversive element. Pressure mounted on them to leave, especially after Santa Anna launched a major counterattack in 1842, capturing San Antonio. Those who stayed lost much of their land and economic power as Anglos used their knowledge of American legal codes or just plain chicanery to reduce the Tejanos to second-class citizens.

More difficult to subordinate were the Comanches. By the early 1840s, Texans and Comanches were in a state of nearly permanent war. Only the force of the federal army after the Civil War ended the Comanches' long reign as the effective rulers of the high, dry plains of northern and western Texas.

THE PUSH INTO CALIFORNIA AND THE SOUTHWEST

Mexican rule in California was always weak. The Sonoran desert and the resistance of the Yuman Indians in southeastern California cut off Mexico from any direct land contact with Alta California. Only irregular communications were maintained over a long sea route. For *Californios*, Californians of Spanish descent, Mexico was literally *la otra banda*, "the other shore." In trying to strengthen its hold on this remote and thinly populated region, the Mexican government relied on a program of economic development. The centerpiece of the Mexican program was the secularization of the missions, opening up the landholdings of the Catholic Church to private ownership and releasing the mission Indians from paternalistic bondage. Small allotments of land were set aside for the Indians, but most returned to their homelands. Those who remained became a source of cheap labor for the *rancheros* who carved up the mission lands into huge cattle ranches. Thus by the 1830s, California entered its *rancho* era. The main beneficiaries of this process, however, were not Mexican authorities but the American traders who responded to the economic opportunities presented by the privatization of the California economy.

New England merchants shipped out hides and tallow, a trade fed by the immense cattle resources of the rancheros, for processing into shoes and candles. Ships from New England and New York sailed around Cape Horn to California ports, where they unloaded trading goods. Servicing this trade in California was a resident colony of American agents, some three hundred strong by the mid-1840s.

Whereas Yankees dominated the American colonies in coastal California, it was mostly Midwestern farm families who filtered into the inner valleys of California from the Oregon Trail in the 1830s and 1840s. About one in ten of the overland parties ended up in the fertile Sacramento River Valley. Nearly a thousand Americans had arrived by 1846.

California belonged to Mexico in name only by the early 1840s. The program of economic development had strengthened California's ties to the outside world at the expense of Mexico. American merchants and California rancheros ran the economy, and both groups had joined separatist movements against Mexican rule.

Except for Utah, the American push into the interior of the Mexican Southwest followed the California pattern of trade preceding settlement. When Mexico liberalized the formerly restrictive trading policies of Spain, American merchants opened up the 900-mile-long **Santa Fe Trail** from Independence, Missouri, to Santa Fe, New Mexico. Starved for mercantile goods, the New Mexicans were a small but highly profitable market. They paid for their American imports with gold, silver, and furs.

Brent's Old Fort, on the Arkansas River at the point where the Santa Fe Trail turned to the Southwest and Taos, enabled the Brent brothers from Missouri to control a flourishing and almost monopolistic trade with Indians, trappers, caravans on the Santa Fe Trail, and the large landowners and merchants of New Mexico. This trade pulled New Mexico into the cultural and economic orbit of the United States and undermined what little sovereign power Mexico held in the region.

Ties of blood and common economic interests linked a small group of American businessmen with an influential faction of the local elite. After thwarting an 1841 Texan attempt to occupy Santa Fe, the leaders of New Mexico increasingly looked to the United States to protect their local autonomy. They quickly decided to cooperate with the American army of invasion when the Mexican War got under way. Over the opposition of the clergy and ranchers still loyal to Mexico, this group was instrumental in the American takeover of New Mexico.

At the extreme northern and inner reaches of the Mexican borderlands lay Utah. Dominated by an intermountain depression called the Great Basin, Utah was home to the Bannocks, Utes, Navajos, Hopis, and small bands of other Indians. Mexico had largely ignored this remote region. Its isolation made Utah appealing to the leaders of the Mormons, the Church of Jesus Christ of Latter-day Saints.

Founded by Joseph Smith in upstate New York in the 1820s, Mormonism grew rapidly within a communitarian framework that stressed hard work and economic cooperation under the leadership of patriarchal leaders. Harassed out of New York, Ohio, and Missouri, the Mormons thought they had found a permanent home by the late 1830s in Nauvoo, Illinois, but the murder of Joseph Smith and his brother by a mob in 1844 convinced the beleaguered Mormons that they had to leave the settled East. Under the leadership of Brigham Young, they established a new community in 1847 at the Great Salt Lake on the western slopes of the Wasatch Mountains. Ten thousand Mormons joined them.

The Mormons' intense communitarianism was ideally suited to dispensing land and organizing an irrigation system that coordinated water rights with the amount of land under production. To their dismay, however, they learned in 1848 that the United States had acquired Utah, along with the rest of the northern borderlands of Mexico, as a result of the Mexican War. (For more on the Mormons, see Chapter 14.)

Politics, Expansion, and War

In 1844, James K. Polk, the new Democratic president, fully shared the expansionist vision of his party. The greatest prize in his eyes was California. Although silent in public on California for fear of further antagonizing the Mexicans, who had never accepted the loss of Texas, Polk made the acquisition of California the cornerstone of his foreign policy. When he was stymied in his efforts to purchase California and New Mexico, he tried to force concessions from the Mexican government by ordering American troops to the mouth of the Rio Grande, far within the territory claimed by Mexico. When the virtually inevitable clash of arms occurred in late April 1846, war broke out between the United States and Mexico.

Victory resulted in the ***Mexican Cession of 1848***, which added half a million square miles to the United States. Polk's administration also finalized the acquisition of Texas and reached a compromise with the British on the Oregon Territory that recognized American sovereignty in the Pacific Northwest up to the 49th parallel. The United States was now a nation that spanned a continent.

MANIFEST DESTINY

With a phrase that soon entered the nation's vocabulary, John L. O'Sullivan, editor and Democratic politician, proclaimed in 1845 America's "manifest destiny to overspread and to possess the whole of the continent which Providence has given us for the development of the great experiment of Liberty and federated self-government entrusted to us." Central to Manifest Destiny was the assumption that white Americans were a special people, a view that dated back to the Puritans' belief that God had appointed them to establish a New Israel cleansed of the corruption of the Old World. Evangelical revivals in the early nineteenth century then added an aggressive sense of urgency to America's presumed mission to spread the benefits of Christian civilization. Protestant missionaries, as in Oregon, were often in the vanguard of American expansion.

What distinguished Manifest Destiny was its explicitly racial component. Caucasian Anglo-Saxon Americans, as the descendants of ancient Germanic tribes that purportedly brought the seeds of free institutions to England, were now said to be the foremost race in the world. This superior racial pedigree gave white Americans the natural right as a chosen people to expand westward, carrying the blessings of democracy and progress.

Advocates of Manifest Destiny were not warmongers calling for conquest. Still, the doctrine was undeniably a self-serving justification for what other peoples would see as territorial aggrandizement. Manifest Destiny and popular stereotypes lumped Indians and Mexicans together as inferior peoples. An emigrant guide of 1845 spoke of the Mexican Californians as "scarcely a visible grade in the scale of intelligence, above the barbarous tribes by whom they are surrounded." For Waddy Thompson, an American minister to Mexico in the early 1840s, the Mexicans in general were "lazy, ignorant, and, of course, vicious and dishonest." This alleged Mexican inferiority was attributed to racial intermixture with the Indians, who, it was said, were hopelessly unfit for civilization.

Manifest Destiny was closely associated with the Democratic party. For Democrats, expansionism would counterbalance the debilitating effects of industrialization and urbanization. As good Jeffersonians, they stressed the need for more land to realize the ideal of a democratic republic rooted in the virtues and rough equality of independent farmers. For their working-class Irish constituency, the Democrats touted the broad expanses of the West as the surest means to escape the misery of wage slavery.

Manifest Destiny captured the popular imagination when the country was still mired in a depression after the Panic of 1837. The way out of the depression, according to many Democrats, was to revive the export trade. Thomas Hart Benton, a Democratic senator from Missouri, promoted American trade with India and China, to be secured by American possession of the harbors on the Pacific Coast.

THE MEXICAN WAR

Once in office, Polk was willing to compromise on Oregon because he dreaded the possibility of a two-front war against both the Mexicans and the British.

In the spring of 1846, after Polk had abrogated the agreement on the joint occupation of Oregon, the British agreed to a boundary at the 49th parallel if they were allowed to retain Vancouver Island in Puget Sound. The Senate quickly approved the offer in June 1846. British-American trade continued to flourish, Mexico lost a potential ally, and most important, Polk could now concentrate on the Mexican War that had erupted a month earlier.

Polk refused to budge on the American claim (inherited from the Texans, when the United States annexed Texas in 1845) that the Rio Grande was the border between Texas and Mexico. The Mexicans insisted that the Nueces River, 100 miles to the north of the Rio Grande, was the border, as it had been when Texas was part of Mexico. A boundary on the Rio Grande would more than double the size of Texas.

Polk sent 3,500 troops under General Zachary Taylor to the Nueces River in the summer of 1845. Polk also stepped up his efforts to acquire California, instructing Thomas Larkin, the American consul in Monterey, California, to inform the *Californios* and Americans that the United States would support them if they revolted against Mexican rule. Polk also secretly ordered the U.S. Pacific naval squadron to seize California ports if war broke out with Mexico. Polk's final effort at peaceful expansion was to send John L. Slidell to Mexico City to offer $30 million to purchase California and New Mexico and to secure the Rio Grande boundary.

When Polk learned that the Mexican government had refused to receive Slidell, he set out to draw Mexico into a war that would result in the American acquisition of California. In early 1846, Taylor blockaded the mouth of the Rio Grande (an aggressive act even if the river had been an international boundary) and built a fort on the northern bank across from the Mexican town of Matamoros. The Mexicans attacked and were repulsed on April 24.

Even before the news reached Washington, Polk had decided on war. Informed of the clash between Mexican and American troops in early May (it took ten days for the news to reach Washington), he sent a redrafted war message to Congress on May 9 asserting that Mexico "has invaded our territory, and shed American blood on American soil." Congress declared war on May 13, 1846.

The Mexicans fought bravely, but they lacked the leadership, modern artillery, and naval capacity to check the American advances. An army sent west under Colonel Stephen W. Kearny occupied New Mexico. The conquest was relatively bloodless because most of the local elite cooperated with the American authorities. Sporadic resistance was largely confined to poorer Mexicans and the Pueblo Indians, who feared that their land would be confiscated. The largest uprising, one that was ruthlessly suppressed, was the **Taos Revolt** in January 1847, led by Jesús Trujillo and Tomasito, a Pueblo chieftain. A sympathetic observer described the rebels as "those who defend to the last their country and their homes."

Kearny's army then moved to Tucson and eventually linked up in southern California with pro-American rebels and U.S. forces sent ashore by the Pacific squadron. Despite the loss of its northern provinces, Mexico refused to concede defeat. Taylor established a secure defensive line in northeastern Mexico with a victory at Monterrey in September 1846 and repulsed a Mexican counterattack at Buena Vista in February 1847. Polk then directed General Winfield Scott to invade central Mexico. Following an amphibious assault on Vera Cruz in March 1847, Scott captured Mexico City in September.

Peace talks finally got under way and concluded in the Treaty of Guadalupe Hidalgo, signed on February 2, 1848. Mexico surrendered its claim to Texas north of the Rio Grande and ceded Alta California and New Mexico (including present-day Arizona, Utah, and Nevada). The United States paid $15 million, assumed over $3 million in claims of American citizens against Mexico, and agreed to grant U.S. citizenship to Mexicans resident in its new territories.

Polk had gained his strategic goals, but the cost was thirteen thousand American lives (most from diseases such as measles and dysentery), fifty thousand Mexican lives, and the poisoning of Mexican-American relations for generations. The war also, as will be seen in Chapter 14, heightened sectional tensions over slavery and weakened the political structure that was vital to preserving the Union.

Conclusion

Population pressure on overworked farms in the East impelled much of the westward migration, but by the 1840s, expansion had seemingly acquired a momentum all its own, one that increasingly rejected the claims of other peoples to the land.

Far from being a process of peaceful, evolutionary, and democratic change, as was once thought, expansion involved the spread of slavery, violent confrontations, and the uprooting and displacement of native peoples. By 1850, the earlier notion of reserving the Trans-Mississippi West as a permanent Indian country had been abandoned. The Sioux and Comanches were still feared by whites, but their final subjugation was not far off. The derogatory stereotypes of Mexican Americans that were a staple of both popular thought and expansionist ideology showed clearly that American control after the Mexican War would relegate Spanish-speaking people to second-class status.

However misleading and false much of it was, the rhetoric of Manifest Destiny did highlight a central truth. A broad, popular base existed for expanding across the continent. As the Mexican War made clear, the United States was now unquestionably the dominant power in North America. The only serious threat to its dominance in the near future would come from inside, not outside, its continental domain.

REVIEW QUESTIONS

1. Why did Americans move westward? How did slavery affect the development of new settlements?

2. How did migration transform the West of the Plains Indians after 1830?

3. Who lived in the Mexican borderlands of the Southwest? Why was it difficult for Mexican authorities to control the region?

4. What did Americans mean by Manifest Destiny?

5. Who was responsible for the outbreak of the Mexican War? Were Mexicans the victims of American aggression?

The Politics of Sectionalism

1846–1861

Why did the issue of slavery in the territories cause so much controversy?

What were the causes and consequences of political realignment in the 1850s?

Why was Lincoln elected in 1860?

Why could the political system not fix the secession crisis?

⭐

December 16, 1852

My Dear Madam,

So you want to know what sort of woman I am! Well, if this is any object, you shall have statistics free of charge. To begin, then, I am a little bit of a woman—somewhat more than forty, about as thin and dry as a pinch of snuff—never very much to look at in my best days and looking like a used up article now.

I was married when I was twenty-five years old to a man rich in Greek and Hebrew and Latin and Arabic, and alas, rich in nothing else. . . . But then I was abundantly furnished with wealth of another sort. I had two little curly headed twin daughters to begin with and my stock in this line has gradually increased, till I have been the mother of seven children, the most beautiful and the most loved of whom lies buried near my Cincinnati residence. It was at his dying bed and at his grave that I learned what a poor slave mother may feel when her child is torn away from her. In those depths of sorrow which seemed to me immeasurable, it was my only prayer to God that such anguish might not be suffered in vain. There were circumstances about his death of such peculiar bitterness, of what seemed almost cruel suffering that I felt that I could never be consoled for it unless this crushing of my own heart might enable me to work out some great good to others.

I allude to this here because I have often felt that much that is in that book had its root in the awful scenes and bitter sorrow of that summer. It has left now, I trust, no trace on my mind except a deep compassion for the sorrowful, especially for mothers who are separated from their children. . . .

This horror, this nightmare abomination! Can it be in my country! It lies like lead on my heart, it shadows my life with sorrow; the more so that I feel, as for my own brothers, for the South, and am pained by every horror I am obliged to write, as one who is forced by some awful oath to disclose in court some family disgrace. . . .

Yours affectionately,

—H. B. Stowe

Harriet Beecher Stowe to Eliza Cabot Follen, December 16, 1852; from Jeanne Boydston, Mary Kelley, Anne Margolis, *The Limit of Sisterhood* (Chapel Hill: University of North Carolina Press, 1988), 178–180.

HARRIET BEECHER STOWE, while writing to poet and fellow abolitionist Eliza Cabot Follen in the year that *Uncle Tom's Cabin* became an international bestseller, revealed how being a wife and a mother influenced her perception of slavery and inspired her writing. The deep piety and self-effacement expressed in the letter, as well as her transparent grief over the loss of her son, typified mid-nineteenth-century correspondence between women. Her beloved son had died of cholera in 1849; that wrenching event, coupled with the passage of the Fugitive Slave Act a year later, galvanized Stowe to pour her grief and indignation into a novel about plantation slavery.

Stowe personalized slavery in a way that made white Northerners see it as an institution that oppressed black people, destroyed families, and debased Christian masters. The book changed people's moral perceptions about slavery.

Stowe's father, Lyman Beecher, was a prominent evangelical reformer. He believed that personal and societal salvation were closely connected, a principle that is apparent in Harriet's letter.

Stowe's personal journey transformed awareness into a moral crusade for the millions who read her book; the political became personal. Yet, the anguish she expressed in her writing and the outrage it generated among her readers were hardly prefigured when a congressman from Pennsylvania stepped forward in 1846 with a modest proposal that not only placed slavery front and center as a national issue, but would also shake the Union to its very core.

Slavery was not a new political issue, but after 1846, the clashes between Northern and Southern congressmen over slavery became more frequent and more difficult to resolve. In the coming years, several developments—including white Southerners' growing consciousness of themselves as a minority, the mixture of political issues with religious questions, and the rise of the Republican party—would aggravate sectional antagonism. But the flash point that first brought slavery to the fore was the issue of slavery in the territories acquired from Mexico.

Slavery in the Territories

Whatever its boundaries over the years, the West symbolized the hopes and dreams of white Americans. It was the region of fresh starts, of possibilities. For white Southerners, to exclude slavery from the Western territories was to exclude them from pursuing their vision of the American dream. Northern politicians, on the other hand, argued that exclusion preserved equality—the equality of all white men and women to live and work without competition from slave labor or rule by despotic slaveholders. From the late 1840s until 1861, four proposals dominated the debate:

- Outright exclusion
- Extension of the Missouri Compromise line to the Pacific
- Popular sovereignty—allowing the residents of a territory to decide the issue
- Protection of the property of slaveholders (meaning their right to own slaves) even if few lived in the territory

The first major debate on these proposals occurred during the early days of the Mexican War and culminated with the Compromise of 1850.

THE WILMOT PROVISO

In August 1846, David Wilmot, a Pennsylvania Democrat, offered an amendment to an appropriations bill for the Mexican War called the **Wilmot Proviso**, which stipulated that "as an express and fundamental condition to the acquisition of any territory from the Republic of Mexico . . . neither slavery nor involuntary servitude shall ever exist in any part of said territory." This language deliberately reflected Thomas Jefferson's Northwest Ordinance of 1787, which had prohibited slavery in the Old Northwest. Wilmot had, he explained, no "morbid sympathy for the slave" but by linking the exclusion of slavery to freedom for white people, he hoped to generate support across the North and even some areas of the Upper South regardless of party.

Linking freedom for white people to the exclusion of slaves infuriated Southerners by implying that the mere proximity of slavery degraded white people and that Southerners were a degraded people, unfit to join other Americans in the territories. Georgia's Whig senator, Robert Toombs, issued a warning that reflected the feelings of many Southerners: "I do not hesitate to avow before this House and the Country, that if, by your legislation, you seek to drive us from territories of California and New Mexico, purchased by the common blood and treasure of the whole people . . . , thereby attempting to fix a national degradation upon half the states of this Confederacy, *I am for disunion.*" An Ohio congressman responded, "We [the North] will establish a cordon of free states that will surround you; and then we will light up the fires of liberty on every side until they melt your present chains and render all your people free."

This disagreement was reflected in Congress, where Northern congressmen, now a majority in the House of Representatives, passed more than fifty versions of the proviso between 1846 and 1850. In the Senate, where each state had equal representation, the proviso was consistently rejected.

The proviso debate sowed distrust and suspicion between Northerners and Southerners. Congress had divided along sectional lines before, but seldom had divisions become so personal. The leaders of both the Democratic and Whig parties, disturbed that the issue of slavery in the territories could so monopolize Congress and poison sectional relations, sought to defuse the issue as the presidential election of 1848 approached.

THE ELECTION OF 1848

Both Democrats and Whigs wanted to avoid identification with either side of the Wilmot Proviso controversy, and they selected their presidential candidates accordingly. The Democrats nominated Michigan senator Lewis Cass, a veteran party stalwart whose public career stretched back to the War of 1812. Cass understood the destructive potential of the slavery issue and suggested that territorial residents, not Congress, should decide slavery's fate. This solution, **popular sovereignty**, had a do-it-yourself charm: Keep the politicians out of it and let the people decide. Cass was deliberately ambiguous, however, on *when* the people should decide. If residents could decide only when applying for statehood, slavery would be legal up to that point. The ambiguity aroused more fears than it allayed.

The Whigs were silent on the slavery issue. Reverting to their winning 1840 formula of nominating a war hero, they selected General Zachary Taylor of Mexican War fame. Taylor belonged to no party and had never voted. He was also inarticulate to the point of unintended humor. If one had to guess his views, it may have been significant that he lived in Louisiana in the Lower South, owned a one-hundred-slave plantation, and he was related by marriage to Jefferson Davis, currently Mississippi's staunch proslavery senator.

Taylor's background disturbed many antislavery Northern Whigs. These *Conscience Whigs* along with remnants of the old Liberty party and a scattering of Northern Democrats bolted their parties and formed the *Free-Soil party.* Its slogan—"Free soil, free speech, free labor, free men"—was a catalog of white liberties that the South had allegedly violated. The Free-Soilers nominated former president Martin Van Buren, the old New Yorker, who had little hope of winning but might cause the election to be thrown into the House of Representatives. Van Buren ran strongly enough in eleven of the fifteen Northern states to deny the winning candidate in those states a majority of the votes cast, but he could not overcome Taylor's strength in the South. Taylor was elected, giving the nation its first president from the Lower South.

The Compromise of 1850

Taylor had little time to savor his victory. Gold had been discovered in California in January 1848, and in little more than a year, eighty thousand people, most of them from the North, had rushed into the territory. These *Forty-Niners,* as they were called, included free black people as well as slaves brought into the gold fields by their Southern masters. Open hostility flared between white prospectors and their black competitors. The territory's residents drafted a state constitution that contained no provision for slavery, reflecting antiblack rather than antislavery sentiment. Keeping California white shielded residents against social and economic interaction with black people. "Free" in the context of territorial politics became a synonym for "whites only."

If Congress accepted the residents' request for statehood, California would enter the Union as a free state, tipping the balance between the fifteen free and fifteen slave states in the Senate. New Mexico (which then included most of present-day New Mexico, Arizona, part of Nevada, and Colorado) appeared poised to follow suit and enter the Union as the seventeenth free state. Southerners saw their political power slipping away.

When Congress confronted the issue of California statehood in December 1849, partisans on both sides began marshaling forces for what promised to be a long and bitter struggle. South Carolina senator John C. Calhoun understood that only a politically unified South could protect its interests.

No one, at first, knew where Taylor stood. Later it became apparent that he favored allowing California and the other territories acquired from Mexico to decide the slavery issue for themselves. Since California already easily exceeded the population threshold for statehood, Taylor proposed bypassing the territorial stage—and congressional involvement in it—and having California and New Mexico admitted as states directly. The result would be to bring both into the Union as free states. Taylor did not oppose slavery, but he abhorred the slavery issue because it threatened his vision of a continental empire. He was thus willing to forgo the extension of slavery into the territories. "Whatever dangers may threaten [the Union] I shall stand by it and maintain it in its integrity."

Southerners resisted Taylor's plan, and Congress deadlocked on the territorial issue. Henry Clay then stepped forward with his last great compromise. To break the impasse, Clay urged that Congress should take four steps:

- Admit California as a free state, as its residents clearly preferred
- Allow the residents of the New Mexico and Utah territories to decide the slavery issue for themselves too

---

• CHRONOLOGY •

1846 Wilmot Proviso is submitted to Congress but is defeated.

1848 Gold is discovered in California.
Whig party candidate Zachary Taylor defeats Democrat Lewis Cass and Free-Soiler Martin Van Buren for the presidency.

1850 California applies for statehood.
President Taylor dies; Vice President Millard Fillmore succeeds him.
Compromise of 1850 is passed.

1851 Harriet Beecher Stowe publishes *Uncle Tom's Cabin*.

1852 Democrat Franklin Pierce is elected president in a landslide over Whig candidate Winfield Scott.
Whig party disintegrates.

1853 National Black Convention called in Rochester, New York, to demand repeal of the Fugitive Slave Act.

1854 Ostend Manifesto is issued.
Kansas-Nebraska Act repeals the Missouri Compromise.
Know-Nothing and Republican parties are formed.

1855 Civil war erupts in "Bleeding Kansas."
William Walker attempts a takeover of Nicaragua.

1856 "Sack of Lawrence" occurs in Kansas; John Brown makes a retaliatory raid at Pottawatomie Creek.
Democratic congressman Preston Brooks of South Carolina canes Massachusetts senator

Charles Sumner in the U.S. Senate.
Democrat James Buchanan is elected president over Republican John C. Frémont and American (Know-Nothing) candidate Millard Fillmore.

1857 Supreme Court issues *Dred Scott* decision.
Kansas territorial legislature passes the proslavery Lecompton Constitution.
Panic of 1857 begins.

1858 Senatorial candidates Abraham Lincoln and Stephen A. Douglas hold series of debates in Illinois.

1859 John Brown's Raid fails at Harpers Ferry, Virginia.

1860 Constitutional Union party forms.
Democratic party divides into northern and southern factions.
Republican candidate Abraham Lincoln is elected president over Southern Democratic candidate John C. Breckinridge, Northern Democratic candidate Stephen A. Douglas, and Constitutional Unionist candidate John Bell.
South Carolina secedes from the Union.

1861 The rest of the Lower South secedes from the Union.
Crittenden Plan and Tyler's Washington peace conference fail.
Jefferson Davis assumes presidency of the Confederate States of America.
Lincoln is inaugurated.
Fort Sumter is bombarded; Civil War begins.
Several Upper South states secede.

- End the slave trade in the District of Columbia
- Pass a new fugitive slave law to enforce the constitutional provision stating that a person "held to Service or Labor in one state . . . escaping into another . . . shall be delivered upon Claim of the party to whom such Service or Labor may be due."

Clay's proposal provoked a historic Senate debate in February 1850, featuring America's three most prominent elder statesmen—Clay, Calhoun, and Daniel Webster, all of whom would be dead in the next two years. After a tumultuous six-month debate that lasted into the summer of 1850, the Senate rejected the compromise. President Taylor, who had vowed to veto any compromise, died unexpectedly of a stomach ailment after overindulging in cherries and milk in the hot sun at a July 4 celebration in Washington. Vice President Millard Fillmore, a pro-Clay New Yorker, assumed the presidency after Taylor's death. A back-room man, quiet, at home with the cigar-and-brandy crowd, and effective with the deal, Fillmore let it be known that he favored Clay's package and would sign it if passed.

Although the Senate had rejected the compromise, Illinois senator Stephen A. Douglas kept it alive. A small man with a large head that made him mushroomlike in appearance, Douglas epitomized the promise of American life for men of his generation. He envisioned an urban, industrial West linked to the East by a vast railroad network eventually extending to the Pacific. Like Webster, Douglas feared for the Union if the compromise failed. Realizing that it would never pass as a package, he proposed to break it up into its components and hold a separate vote on each. With a handful of senators voting for all parts, and with different sectional blocs supporting one provision or another, Douglas engineered a majority for the compromise, and Fillmore signed it.

The *Compromise of 1850* was not a compromise in the sense of opposing sides consenting to certain terms desired by the other. Southern leaders looked to the West and saw no slave territories awaiting statehood. They gained the *Fugitive Slave Act*, which reinforced their right to seize and return to bondage slaves who had fled to free territory, but it was slight consolation. Few slave owners from the Lower South would bear the expense and uncertainty of chasing an escaped slave into free territory. And the North's hostile reception to the law made Southerners doubt their commitment to the compromise.

RESPONSE TO THE FUGITIVE SLAVE ACT

The effect of the Fugitive Slave Act on public opinion, however, was to polarize North and South even further. The strongest reaction to the act was in the black communities of the urban North. Previously, black abolitionists in the North had focused on freeing slaves in the South. The Fugitive Slave Act brought the danger of slavery much closer to home. Black Northerners formed associations to protect each other and repel—violently, if necessary—any attempt to capture and reenslave fellow black people. Boston's black leaders created the League of Freedom. Black Chicagoans organized the Liberty Association, with teams assigned to "patrol the city, spying for possible slave-hunters." Similar associations appeared in Cleveland and Cincinnati. Black leader Frederick Douglass, an escaped slave himself, explained the need for such organizations: "We must be prepared . . . to see the streets . . . running with blood . . . should this law be put into operation."

During the early 1850s, black people across the North gathered in conventions to demand the repeal of the Fugitive Slave Act. Frederick Douglass convened the National Black Convention in Rochester, New York, in July 1853, at which he established a national council of black leaders to address issues of political and civil rights. Although the council was short-lived, it reflected a growing militancy among black Northerners.

How much of this militancy filtered down to slaves in the South is difficult to say. Slaveholders noted an increase in black resistance during the early 1850s. A white Virginian observed in 1852 that "it is useless to disguise the fact, that a greater degree of insubordination has been manifested by the negro population within the last few months, than at any previous period in our history as a state."

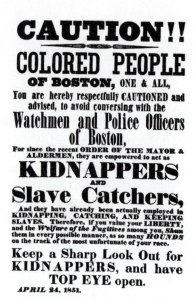

The Fugitive Slave Act threatened the freedom of escaped slaves living in the North, and even of free black Northerners. This notice, typical of warnings posted in northern cities, urged Boston's African-American population to take precautions.

Courtesy of Library of Congress.

UNCLE TOM'S CABIN

Sectional controversy over the Fugitive Slave Act was relatively modest compared to the firestorm abolitionist writer Harriet Beecher Stowe ignited with the publication of a novel about Southern slavery. *Uncle Tom's Cabin*, which first appeared in serial form in 1851, moved many white Northerners from the sidelines of the sectional conflict to more active participation.

Stowe was the daughter of Lyman Beecher, a prominent evangelical reformer, and an active opponent of slavery. What first drew Harriet Beecher Stowe to the subject of slavery was her concern about its impact on family life in the South. It was not until the passage of the Fugitive Slave Act that abolition became a major focus in her life. Even then, her views on black people remained ambivalent. She did not, like William Lloyd Garrison, advocate racial equality. She supported abolition, but she also believed America should be a white person's country, and favored repatriating the former slaves to Africa. Slavery was an abstract concept to most white Northerners. Stowe's challenge was to personalize it in a way that would make them see it as an institution that not just oppressed black people but also destroyed families and debased well-meaning Christian masters as well.

At the beginning of *Uncle Tom's Cabin*, a Kentucky slave owner is reluctantly forced by financial ruin to sell some of his slaves. Among them are the son of two mulatto slaves, George and Eliza Harris, and an older slave, Tom. Eliza escapes across the ice-choked Ohio River, clutching her son to her breast as slavecatchers and their bloodhounds pursue them. Tom submits to sale to a New Orleans master. When that master dies, Tom is sold to Simon Legree, a Vermonter who owns a plantation on the Red River in Louisiana. Legree is vicious and sadistic—the only major slaveholding character in the book whom Stowe portrays in this manner. Tom, a devout Christian, remains loyal and obedient until Legree asks him to whip another slave. When Tom refuses, Legree beats him to death.

Stowe offered not abstractions but characters who seemed real. She aimed to evoke strong emotions in the reader. The broken family, the denial of freedom, and the Christian martyr were emotional themes. The presence of mulattoes in the book testified to widespread interracial and extramarital sex, which Northerners, then in the midst of a religious revival, viewed as an abhorrent sin destructive to family life. And the depiction of Southern masters struggling unsuccessfully with their consciences focused public attention on how slavery subverted Christianity.

Uncle Tom's Cabin created a sensation in the United States and abroad. By the time of the Civil War, the book had sold an unprecedented 3 million copies in the United States and tens of thousands more in Europe. Stowe's book gave slavery a face. Black Northerners embraced *Uncle Tom's Cabin*. Frederick Douglass's National Black Convention resolved that the book was "a work plainly marked by the finger of God" on behalf of black people. Some black people hoped that the popularity of *Uncle Tom's Cabin* would highlight the hypocrisy of white Northerners who were quick to perceive evil in the South but were often blind to discrimination against African Americans in the North. For Southerners, *Uncle Tom's Cabin* was a damnable lie, a political tract disguised as literature.

THE ELECTION OF 1852

While the nation read and reacted to *Uncle Tom's Cabin*, a presidential election campaign took place. The Compromise of 1850 had divided the Whigs deeply. The Democratic party entered the campaign more united. Despite reservations, both northern and southern wings of the party announced their support for the Compromise of 1850. Southern Democrats viewed the party's nominee, Franklin Pierce of New Hampshire, as safe on the slavery issue despite his New England heritage. Pierce satisfied Northerners as a nationalist devoted to the idea of Manifest Destiny. He belonged to *Young America*, a mostly Democratic group that advocated extending American influence into Central and South America and the Caribbean with an aggressive foreign policy. His service in the Mexican War and his good looks and charm won over doubters from both sections, winning him the election.

But Pierce's landslide victory could not obscure the deep fissures in the American party system. The Whigs were ultimately finished as a national party. And the Democrats, despite their electoral success, emerged frayed from the election. In the Lower South, conflicts within the party between supporters and opponents of the Compromise of 1850 had overshadowed the contests between Democrats and Whigs.

As Franklin Pierce took office in March 1853, it seemed that the only thing holding Democrats together was the thirst for political patronage. The low voter turnout in the 1852 election—Whig participation declined by 10 percent and Democratic participation by 17 percent, mostly in the Lower South—reflected public apathy and disgust at the prevailing party system. As the slavery issue confronted the nation with the most serious challenge it had faced since its inception, American voters were losing faith in their parties' ability to govern and in each other.

Political Realignment

Franklin Pierce, only 48 when he took office, was one of the youngest presidents in American history. He hoped to duck the slavery issue by focusing on Young America's dreams of empire. Americans were still susceptible to nationalist fervor. For all their sectional, religious, ethnic, and racial differences, they shared a common language and political institutions. New technologies like the railroad and the telegraph were working to bind them together physically as well. As Florida senator Stephen R. Mallory claimed, "It is no more possible for this country to pause in its career, than for the free and untrammeled eagle to cease to soar." But President Pierce's attempts to forge national sentiment around an aggressive foreign policy failed. And his administration's inept handling of a new territorial controversy in Kansas forced him to confront the slavery debate.

No matter what policies a president pursued, Congress and the American people interpreted them in the light of their impact, real or potential, on slavery. The issue, said Missouri senator Thomas Hart Benton, was like the plague of frogs that God had inflicted on the Egyptians to convince them to release the Hebrews from bondage. So it was with "this black question, forever on the table, on the nuptial couch, everywhere!"

Franklin Pierce lacked the skilled leadership the times demanded. Troubled by alcoholism, worried about his chronically ill wife, and grief-stricken over the death of three young sons, Pierce presided weakly over the nation and increasingly deferred to proslavery interests in his policies.

YOUNG AMERICA'S FOREIGN MISADVENTURES

Pierce's first missteps occurred in pursuit of Young America's foreign ambitions. The administration turned a greedy eye toward Spanish-ruled Cuba, just 90 miles off the coast of Florida. Southerners supported an aggressive Cuba policy, seeing the island as a possible new slave state. And nationalists saw great virtue in replacing what they perceived as a despotic colonial regime with a democratic government under the guidance of the United States.

In October 1854, three American diplomats met in Ostend, Belgium, to compose a document on Cuba called the *Ostend Manifesto* that claimed that the island belonged "naturally to the great family of states of which the Union is the Providential Nursery." The implication was that if Spain wouldn't sell, the United States could wrest control of Cuba. The Ostend Manifesto caused an uproar and embarrassed the Pierce administration when it became public. In the polite world of nineteenth-century diplomacy, it was a significant breach of etiquette. It also provoked a reaction in the United States, raising suspicions in the North that the South was willing to provoke a war with Spain to expand the number of slaveholding states. The Pierce administration also suffered from the greedy and ultimately unsuccessful exploits of self-styled "General" William Walker, who invaded Mexican-owned Baja California and later temporarily gained control of Nicaragua.

STEPHEN DOUGLAS'S RAILROAD PROPOSAL

As Pierce was fumbling in foreign policy, Senator Stephen A. Douglas of Illinois was developing another national project that promised to draw the country together—the construction of a transcontinental railroad and the settling of the land it traversed. Douglas had in mind a transcontinental route extending westward from Chicago through the Nebraska Territory. Unfortunately for his plans, Indians already occupied this region, many of them on land the U.S. government had set aside as Indian Territory and barred to white settlement. Once again, and not for the last time, the federal government responded by reneging on earlier promises and forcing Indians to move. With the Indian "obstacle" removed, Douglas sought congressional approval to establish a government for the Nebraska Territory. As he predicted, the new bill did "raise a hell of a storm."

THE KANSAS-NEBRASKA ACT

Douglas's Kansas-Nebraska Bill split the Nebraska Territory into two territories, Kansas and Nebraska, with the implicit understanding that Kansas would become a slave state and Nebraska a free state. Consistent with Douglas's belief in popular sovereignty, it left the actual decision on slavery to the residents of the territories. But because it allowed Southerners to bring slaves into an area formerly closed to slavery, it repealed the Missouri Compromise.

Northerners of all parties were outraged, using language indicative of the way religious and conspiratorial imagery had infected political debate. Transforming it into a contest of good against evil, of liberty against oppression, they said it was "a gross violation of a sacred pledge," "a criminal betrayal of precious rights," and "part and parcel of an atrocious plot" to make a free territory a "dreary region of despotism, inhabited by masters and slaves." President Pierce, however, backed the bill, ensuring the support of enough Northern Democrats to secure it a narrow margin of victory. The *Kansas-Nebraska Act* was law, but dissatisfaction with it continued to fester.

In August 1854, shortly after Congress adjourned, Douglas left Washington for his home in Chicago, to rest and mend political fences. He did not enjoy a pleasant journey home. "I could travel," he later recalled, ". . . by the light of my own effigy on every tree we passed." Arriving in Chicago, he addressed a large, hostile crowd outside his hotel balcony. As he departed, he lost his temper and blurted. "It is now Sunday morning. I'll go to church; you can go to hell."

"BLEEDING KANSAS"

Because of its fertile soil, favorable climate, and location adjacent to the slave state of Missouri, Kansas was the most likely of the new territories to support slavery. As a result, both Southerners and antislavery Northerners began an intensive drive to recruit settlers and establish a majority there.

After much legislative maneuvering by both sides, a sporadic civil war erupted in Kansas in November 1855 and reached a climax in the spring of 1856. Journalists dubbed the conflict "*Bleeding Kansas*," for it was characterized by an unprecedented level of personal hatred and hostility including a proslavery attack on the town of Lawrence, which the Northern press inflated into the "*sack of Lawrence*" and a bloody retaliatory raid by antislavery agitator John Brown.

KNOW-NOTHINGS AND REPUBLICANS: RELIGION AND POLITICS

The conflict in Kansas reflected deepening divisions throughout the nation that altered the political landscape and sharpened sectional conflict. From 1854 to 1856, Northerners moved into new political parties. Although the slavery issue was mainly responsible for party realignment in the North, other factors played a role as well. Nearly 3.5 million immigrants entered the United States between 1848 and 1860, the greatest influx in American history in proportion to the total population. Some of these newcomers, especially the Germans, were escaping failed democratic revolutions in Europe. They were predominantly middle-class Protestants who, along with fewer German Catholics and Jews, settled mostly in the cities, where they established shops and other businesses. More than 1 million of the immigrants, however, were poor Irish Roman Catholics fleeing their homeland to avoid starvation.

The Irish immigrants made their homes in Northern cities, at the time in the midst of Protestant revivals and reform. They also competed for jobs with native-born Protestant workers. Because the Irish would work for lower wages, the job competition bred animosity and sometimes violence. But it was their Roman Catholic religion that most concerned some urban Protestants. Democrats wooed the Irish newcomers. The champions of individual rights against intrusive government and meddling reformers, they supported the strict separation of church and state. Evangelical Protestants, especially those who were not Democrats, took a different view. As a Boston minister wrote during the debate on the Wilmot Proviso, "The great problem for the Christian world now to accomplish is to effect a closer union between religion and politics. . . . We must make men do good and be good."

New parties emerged from this cauldron of religious, ethnic, and sectional strife. Anti-immigrant, anti-Catholic sentiment gave rise to the **Know-Nothing party**, which began as a secret organization in July 1854. Its name derived from the reply that members gave when asked about the party: "I know nothing." In addition to their biases against Catholics and foreigners, the Know-Nothings shared a fear that the slavery issue could destroy the Union. Know-Nothing candidates fared surprisingly well in local and congressional elections during the fall of 1854, carrying 63 percent of the statewide vote in Massachusetts and making strong showings in New York and Pennsylvania. In office, Know-Nothings achieved some notable reforms. In Massachusetts, where they pursued an agenda similar to that of the Whigs in earlier years, they secured administrative reforms and supported public health and public education programs.

The Know-Nothings' anti-Catholicism, however, overshadowed their reform agenda. Ethnic and religious bigotry were weak links to hold together a national party. Southern and Northern Know-Nothings fell to quarreling among themselves over slavery, despite their vow to avoid it, and the party split. Many Northern Know-Nothings soon found a congenial home in the new **Republican party**.

The Republican party formed in the summer of 1854 from a coalition of antislavery Conscience Whigs and Democrats disgusted with the Pierce administration's Kansas policy. The Republicans supported many of the same kinds of reforms as the Know-Nothings, and like them, the Republicans also supported strong state and national governments to promote those reforms. The overriding bond among Republicans was their opposition to the extension of slavery in the territories. Unlike the Know-Nothings, the Republicans confronted the slavery issue head on.

Reflecting its opposition to slavery, the Republican party was an anti-Southern sectional party. The overwhelming majority of its members were Northerners. Northern Whig merchants and entrepreneurs who joined the party were impatient with Southern obstruction in Congress of federal programs for economic development, such as a transcontinental railroad, harbor and river improvements, and high tariffs to protect American industries (located mostly in the North) from foreign competition. In a bid to keep slavery out of the territories, the Republicans favored limiting homesteads in the West to 160 acres. Not incidentally, populating the territories with white Northerners would ensure a western base for the new party.

Heightened sectional animosity laced with religious and ethnic prejudice fueled the emergence of new parties and the weakening of old political affiliations in the early 1850s and the Republican party was becoming an important political force in the North and, to Southerners, the embodiment of evil.

THE ELECTION OF 1856

The presidential election of 1856 proved one of the strangest in American history. The Know-Nothings and the Republicans faced a national electorate for the first time. The Democrats were deeply divided over the Kansas issue. Rejecting both Pierce and Douglas, they turned instead to a longtime insider, James Buchanan, whose major asset was that he had been absent from the country the previous three years as ambassador to Great Britain and was thus untainted by the Kansas controversy. The Republicans passed over their most likely candidate, the New York senator and former Whig William H. Seward. Instead, they followed a tried-and-true Whig precedent and nominated a military hero, John C. Frémont, a handsome, dark-haired soldier of medium height and medium intelligence. His wife, Jessie Benton, the daughter of Missouri senator Thomas Hart Benton, was his greatest asset. In effect, she ran the campaign and wisely encouraged her husband to remain silent. The Know-Nothings nominated former president Millard Fillmore.

Openly reviling what they called the "Black Republican party," Southerners threatened disunion if Frémont won. Buchanan claimed to be the only national candidate on the ballot. Voters agreed, for Buchanan bested Frémont in the North and Fillmore in the South to win the presidency.

The overall result pleased Southerners, but the details left them uncomfortable. Buchanan won by carrying every Southern state and the Lower North—Pennsylvania, New Jersey, Illinois, Indiana, and California. But Frémont, a political novice running on his party's first national ticket, carried eleven free states, and the rest he lost by scant margins to Buchanan. It was a remarkable showing for a two-year-old party. In the South and border states, Fillmore managed more than 40 percent of the vote and carried Maryland, despite bearing the standard of a fragmented party.

Buchanan, who brought more than a generation of political experience to the presidency, would need every bit and more. He had scarcely settled into office when two major crises confronted him: a Supreme Court decision that challenged the right of Congress to regulate slavery in the territories, and renewed conflict over Kansas.

THE *DRED SCOTT* CASE

Dred Scott was a slave owned by an army surgeon based in Missouri. In the 1830s and early 1840s, he had traveled with his master to the state of Illinois and the Wisconsin Territory before returning to Missouri. In 1846, Scott sued his master's widow for freedom on the grounds that the laws of Illinois and the Wisconsin Territory barred slavery. After a series of appeals, the case reached the Supreme Court.

Chief Justice Roger Taney of Maryland, joined by five other justices of the nine-member Supreme Court (five of whom came from slave states), dismissed Scott's suit two days after Buchanan's inauguration in March 1857. Taney's opinion contained two bombshells. First, using dubious logic and failing to take into account the status of black people in several Northern states, he argued that black people were not citizens of the United States. Because Scott was not a citizen, he could not sue. In reaching this conclusion, Taney noted that the framers of the Constitution had never intended citizenship for slaves.

Second, Taney held that even if Scott had standing in court, his residence in the Wisconsin Territory did not make him a free man. This was because the Missouri Compromise, which was still in effect in the 1840s, was, in Taney's view, unconstitutional. The compromise, the chief justice explained, deprived citizens of their property (slaves) without the due process of law granted by the Fifth Amendment to the U.S. Constitution. In effect, Taney ruled that Congress could not bar slavery from the territories.

Black Americans reacted bitterly to the **Dred Scott** *decision*. Throughout the struggle of black abolitionists to free their compatriots in the South, they had appealed to the basic American ideals of freedom, liberty, and self-determination. Now Taney was saying that these ideals did not apply to black people. Throughout the urban North, black people held meetings to denounce the decision.

The decision also shocked Republicans. The right of Congress to ban slavery from the territories, which Taney had apparently voided, was one of the party's central tenets. Republicans responded by ignoring the implications of the decision for the territories while promising to abide by it so far as it affected Dred Scott himself. Once in office, Republicans vowed, they would seek a reversal. This position allowed them to attack the decision without appearing to defy the law.

The *Dred Scott* decision boosted Republican fortunes in the North even as it seemed to undercut the party. Fears of a Southern Slave Power conspiracy, which some had dismissed as fanciful and politically motivated, now seemed justified.

THE LECOMPTON CONSTITUTION

Establishing a legitimate government in Kansas was the second major issue to bedevil the Buchanan administration. The president made a good start, sending Mississippi resident Robert Walker, a man of integrity, to Kansas as territorial governor to oversee the election of a constitutional convention in June 1857.

But free-staters, fearing that the slavery forces planned to stuff the ballot box with fraudulent votes, announced a boycott of the June election. As a result, proslavery forces dominated the constitutional convention, which was held in Lecompton. And Walker, although a slaveholder, let it be known that he thought Kansas would never be a slave state and thereby put himself at odds with proslavery residents.

Walker convinced the free-staters to vote in October to elect a new territorial legislature. The returns gave the proslavery forces a narrow victory, but Walker discovered irregularities. Undeterred, the proslavery forces drafted a proslavery constitution at the constitutional convention in Lecompton. Buchanan, who had promised Southerners a proslavery government in Kansas, dismissed Walker before he could rule on the **Lecompton Constitution** and submitted the constitution to the Senate for approval even though it clearly sidestepped the popular sovereignty requirement of the Kansas-Nebraska Act.

As with the Kansas-Nebraska Act, many Northerners were outraged by the Lecompton Constitution. The proslavery Kansans behind the constitution had a record of fraud. Northern Democrats, among them Stephen A. Douglas, killed the constitution in Congress. Douglas knew that the *Dred Scott* decision and Buchanan's support of the Lecompton Constitution would help the Republicans and hurt him and his fellow Northern Democrats in the 1858 congressional elections.

The **Panic of 1857**, a severe economic recession that lingered into 1858, also worked to the advantage of the Republicans. The Democratic administration did nothing as unemployment rose, starvation stalked the streets of Northern cities, and homeless women and children begged for food and shelter.

The panic had scarcely touched the South. Cotton seemed indeed to be king. The financial crisis in the North reinforced the Southern belief that Northern society was corrupt and greedy. The Republicans' proposed legislative remedies, in their view, would enrich the North and beggar the South.

Such were the issues confronting Douglas as he returned home to Illinois in the summer of 1858 to begin his reelection campaign.

THE LINCOLN-DOUGLAS DEBATES

Douglas faced a forceful opponent. The Republicans had nominated Abraham Lincoln, a 49-year-old lawyer and former Whig congressman. The Kentucky-born Lincoln had risen from modest circumstances to become a prosperous lawyer in the Illinois state capital of Springfield. His marriage to wealthy and well-connected Mary Todd helped both his law practice and his pocketbook. Strongly opposed to the extension of slavery into the territories, Lincoln had developed a reputation as an excellent stump speaker with a homespun sense of humor, a quick wit, and a self-deprecating style that fit well with the small-town residents and farmers who composed the majority of the Illinois electorate.

But substance counted more than style with Illinois voters. Most of them opposed the extension of slavery into the territories, not out of concern for the slaves, but to keep the territories free for white people. Little known beyond the Springfield area, Lincoln also had to find a way to gain greater exposure. So in July 1858, he challenged Douglas to a series of debates across the state.

The *Lincoln-Douglas debates* were defining events in American politics that put the differences between Lincoln and Douglas, Republicans and Democrats, and North and South into sharp focus. In the debates, Lincoln asked Douglas to reconcile popular sovereignty, which Douglas had long championed, with the *Dred Scott* decision, which seemed to outlaw it by prohibiting a territorial legislature from excluding slavery before statehood. Douglas replied with what became known as the *Freeport Doctrine*. Slavery, he argued, could exist in a territory only if residents passed a law to protect it. Without such a law, no slaveholders would move in, and the territory would be free. Thus if residents did nothing, there could be no slavery in the territory.

For Douglas, slavery was not a moral issue. What mattered was what white people wanted. For Lincoln and many Republicans, slavery *was* a moral issue. As such, it was independent of what the residents of a territory wanted. In the final Lincoln-Douglas debate, Lincoln turned to his rival and explained, "The real issue in this controversy . . . is the sentiment on the part of one class that looks upon the institution of slavery *as a wrong*, and of another class that *does not* look upon it as a wrong. . . ."

Lincoln tempered his moralism with practical politics. He took care to distance himself from abolitionists, asserting that he abided by the Constitution and did not seek to interfere where slavery existed. Privately, however, he prayed for its demise. Nor did he agree, publicly at least, with abolitionist calls for racial equality. At the Springfield debate, he echoed the wishes of most white Illinoisans when he declared, "What I would most desire would be the separation of the white and black races." The Republican party was antislavery, but it did not advocate racial equality. Lincoln lost the senatorial contest but won national respect and recognition.

Despite Lincoln's defeat in Illinois, the Republicans made a strong showing in the 1858 congressional elections across the North. The increased Republican presence and the sharpening sectional divisions among Democrats portended a bitter debate over slavery in the new Congress. *Northern* and *Southern* took on meanings that expressed a great deal more than geography.

The Road to Disunion

The unsatisfying Compromise of 1850, the various misadventures in the Caribbean and Central America, the controversies over Kansas and the *Dred Scott* case, and abolitionist John Brown's failed attempt to spark a slave revolt in 1859 drove a wedge between the North and South.

The presidential election campaign of 1860 began before the uproar over Brown's raid had subsided. In the course of that contest, one of the last nationally unifying institutions, the Democratic party, broke apart. The election of Abraham Lincoln, an avowedly sectional candidate, as president in 1860 triggered a crisis that defied peaceful resolution.

Although the crisis spiraled into a civil war, this outcome did not signal the triumph of sectionalism over nationalism. Ironically, in defending their stands, both sides appealed to time-honored nationalist and democratic sentiments.

NORTH-SOUTH DIFFERENCES

Behind the ideological divide that separated North and South lay real and growing social and economic differences. As the North became increasingly urban and industrial, the South remained primarily rural and agricultural. The demand for farm machinery in the North reflected growing demand for manufactured products in general. The need of city-dwellers for ready-to-wear shoes and clothing, household iron products, processed foods, homes, workplaces, and public amenities boosted industrial production in the North. In contrast, in the South, the slower rate of urbanization, the lower proportion of immigrants, and the region's labor-intensive agriculture kept industrial development modest.

More subtle distinctions in culture and values between North and South became evident as well by midcentury. Southerners tended to be more violent than Northerners. Southern values stressed courtesy, honor, and courage. Southerners were more inclined to military service than Northerners. The South had a high illiteracy rate, nearly three times greater than the North—eight times greater if black Southerners are included.

Evangelical Protestantism attracted increasing numbers in both North and South, but its character differed in the two regions. The Methodist Church divided along sectional lines over slavery in 1844, and the Baptists split the following year. The Presbyterians splintered in 1837 over mainly doctrinal issues, but the rupture became complete in 1861. In the North, evangelical Protestants viewed social reform as a prerequisite for the Second Coming of Christ. As a result, they were in the forefront of most reform movements. Just as Southern politics stressed individual rights, Southern religion emphasized individual salvation over social reform and defended slavery. Northern churches hunted sinners outside their congregations (and often found them in Southerners) and sermonized on political issues; Southern churches confined their preaching to their members and their message to the Gospel.

Slavery accounted for many of the differences between the North and the South. Investment in land and slaves limited investment in manufacturing. The availability of a large slave labor force reduced the need for farm machinery and limited the demand for manufactured products. Slavery contributed to the South's martial tradition and its luke-warm attitude toward public education. Fully 95 percent of the nation's black population lived in the South in 1860, 90 percent of them slaves.

The South's defense of slavery and the North's attack on it fostered an array of stereotypes that exaggerated the real differences between the sections. Like all stereotypes, these reduced individuals to dehumanized categories. They encouraged the people of each section to view those of the other less as fellow Americans than as aliens in their midst.

Ironically, although slavery increasingly defined the character of the South in the 1850s, a growing majority of white Southerners did not own slaves. Slavery nonetheless implicated nonslaveholders in ways that assured their support for it. By satisfying the demand for labor on large plantations, it relieved many rural white people from serving as farm hands and enabled them to work their own land. Slaveholders also recruited nonslave-holders to suppress slave violence or rebellion. Finally, regardless of a white man's social or economic status, he shared an important feature with the largest slaveholder: As long as racial slavery existed, the color of his skin made him a member of a privileged class that could never be enslaved.

While white Southerners were more united on slavery than on other issues, their defense of slavery presented them with a major dilemma: It left them vulnerable to moral condemnation because in the end, slavery was morally indefensible.

JOHN BROWN'S RAID

Ever intent on igniting a revolution among the slaves, abolitionist John Brown proposed in 1859 to attack and capture the federal arsenal at Harpers Ferry, Virginia, a small town near the Maryland border. The assault, Brown imagined, would spark a slave uprising in the area, eventually spreading to the rest of the state. With funds from his New England friends, he equipped a few dozen men and hired an English army officer to train them. When Brown outlined his scheme to Frederick Douglass, the noted black abolitionist warned him against it. But his white New England friends were less cautious, and a group of six prominent abolitionists (the "*Secret Six*") gave Brown additional funds for his project. On the night of October 16, 1859, Brown and twenty-two followers captured the federal arsenal at Harpers Ferry and waited for the slaves to rally to his banner. Meanwhile, the townspeople alerted outside authorities. The Virginia militia and a detachment of United States Marines under the command of Colonel Robert E. Lee arrived and put a quick end to *John Brown's Raid*. They wounded Brown and killed or captured most of his force.

Brown had launched the ill-conceived operation without provisions and at a site from which escape was impossible. Although the primary goal of the attack had been to inspire a slave insurrection, no one had bothered to inform the local slaves. Was Brown crazy? As the *Boston Post* editorialized after the raid, "John Brown may be a lunatic, [but if so] then one-fourth of the people of Massachusetts are madmen."

The raid, though foolish and unsuccessful, played on Southerners' worst fears of slave rebellion, adding a new dimension: Here was an attack engineered not from within the South but from the North. Some white Southerners may have dismissed the ability or even the desire of slaves to mount revolts on their own, but they less easily dismissed the poten-tial impact of outside white agitators.

The state of Virginia tried Brown on the charge of treason to the state, and the jury sentenced him to hang. Throughout his brief imprisonment and trial, Brown maintained a quiet dignity that impressed even his jailers. The governor of Virginia spoke admirably of him as "a man of clear head, of courage, fortitude, and simple ingenuousness." Some Northerners compared Brown's execution with the death of a religious martyr. Abolitionist William Lloyd Garrison asked readers of *The Liberator* to "let the day of [Brown's] execution . . . be the occasion of such a public moral demonstration against the bloody and merciless slave system as the land has never witnessed." When the state of Virginia hanged Brown, church bells tolled across the North. Thoreau compared Brown with Jesus and called the abolitionist "an angel of light." Emerson observed that Brown would "make the gallows glorious like the cross." Condemning Brown's deed, these Northerners nevertheless embraced the cause.

The outpouring of Northern grief over Brown's death convinced white Southerners that the threat to their security was not over. John Brown's Raid significantly changed Southern public opinion. It was one thing to condemn slavery in the territories but another to attack it violently where it was long established. Southerners now saw in the Republican party the embodiment of John Brown's ideals and actions. So in their view, the election of a Republican president would be a death sentence for the South.

The impact of this shifting sentiment was immediately apparent in Congress when it reconvened three days after Virginia hanged Brown. Debate quickly turned tense and ugly. South Carolina senator James H. Hammond captured the mood well, remarking of his colleagues on the Senate floor that "the only persons who do not have a revolver and a knife are those who have two revolvers."

THE ELECTION OF 1860

An atmosphere of mutual sectional distrust and animosity characterized the campaign for the presidential election of 1860. The Democrats disintegrated into two sectional factions united respectively behind Stephen A. Douglas and John C. Breckinridge. Former Whigs from the upper South who could not support Southern Democrat Breckinridge and Northern Whigs who had not defected to the Republicans or to Douglas formed the **Constitutional Union** party and nominated John Bell of Tennessee for president. Sensing victory, the Republicans convened in Chicago. If they could hold the states won by Frémont in 1856, add Minnesota (a new Republican-leaning state), and win Pennsylvania and one of three other Lower North states—Illinois, Indiana, or New Jersey—their candidate would win. These calculations dictated a platform and a candidate who could appeal to the four Lower North swing states where antislavery sentiment was not so strong. Along with the issue of slavery in the territories, the Republicans now embraced a tariff plank calling for the protection of American industry.

In selecting an appropriate presidential nominee, the Republicans faced a dilemma. Senator William H. Seward came to Chicago as the leading Republican candidate, but his immoderate condemnation of Southerners and slavery made moderate northern voters wary of him. Reservations about Seward benefited Abraham Lincoln. A year after his losing 1858 Senate campaign, he had embarked on a speaking tour of the East at the invitation of influential newspaper editor Horace Greeley. Lincoln's lieutenants at the convention stressed their candidate's moderation and morality, distancing him from both the abolitionists and Seward. When Seward faltered, Lincoln rose and won the Republican nomination.

The presidential campaign of 1860 actually comprised two campaigns. In the South, the contest was between Breckinridge and Bell; in the North, it was Lincoln against Douglas. Lincoln did not even appear on the ballot in most southern states.

Lincoln's strategy was to say practically nothing. He spent the entire campaign in Springfield, Illinois. When he did speak, it was to a reporter or friends but not in a public forum. He discounted Southern threats of disunion if he were to become president.

States in those days held gubernatorial elections on different days, even in different months, from the national presidential election. When, in mid-October, Republicans had swept the statehouses in two crucial states, Pennsylvania and Indiana, Douglas made an extraordinary decision, but one consistent with his ardent nationalism. He abandoned his campaign and headed south at great personal peril to urge Southerners to remain in the Union now that Lincoln's election was inevitable.

Lincoln became the nation's sixteenth president with 40 percent of the popular vote (see Map 14–1). He took most Northern states by significant margins and won all the region's electoral votes except three in New Jersey. This gave him a substantial majority of 180 electoral votes.

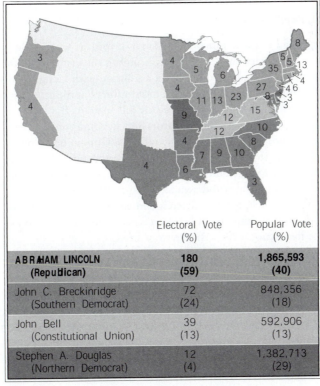

	Electoral Vote (%)	Popular Vote (%)
ABRAHAM LINCOLN (Republican)	**180** **(59)**	**1,865,593** **(40)**
John C. Breckinridge (Southern Democrat)	72 (24)	848,356 (18)
John Bell (Constitutional Union)	39 (13)	592,906 (13)
Stephen A. Douglas (Northern Democrat)	12 (4)	1,382,713 (29)

MAP 14–1
The Election of 1860   The election returns from 1860 vividly illustrate the geography of sectionalism.

BASED ON the geographic sectionalism shown in this map, what issues were important to voters in the election of 1860?

SECESSION BEGINS

The events following Lincoln's election demonstrated how wildly mistaken were those who dismissed Southern threats of secession. Four days after Lincoln's victory, the South Carolina legislature called on the state's citizens to elect delegates to a convention to consider secession. Meeting on December 20, the delegates voted unanimously to leave the Union. By February 1, six other states—Mississippi, Florida, Alabama, Georgia, Louisiana, and Texas—had all held similar conventions and decided to leave the Union. Representatives from the seven seceding states met to form a separate country, the **Confederate States of America**. On February 18, Jefferson Davis was sworn in as its president.

Secessionists mounted an effective propaganda campaign, deftly using the press to convince voters to elect their delegates to the state conventions. Framing the issue as a personal challenge to every Southern citizen, they argued that it would be cowardly to remain in the Union, a submission to despotism and enslavement. Southerners, they maintained, were the true heirs to the spirit of 1776. Lincoln and the Republicans were like King George III and the British—they meant to deny Southerners the right to life, liberty, and the pursuit of happiness. Unionists, in response, could only offer voters a wait-and-see strategy.

PRESIDENTIAL INACTION

Because Lincoln would not take office until March 4, 1861, it was the Buchanan administration that had to cope with the secession crisis during the critical months of December and January. The president's failure to work out a solution with Congress as secession fever swept the Lower South further undermined Unionist forces in the seceding states.

Thereafter, Buchanan's administration quickly fell apart. As the Lower South states left the Union, their representatives and senators left Washington, and with them went Buchanan's closest advisers and key cabinet officials. Commenting on the emotionally charged atmosphere in the Senate as prominent Southerners gave their farewells and departed, one observer wrote, "There was everywhere a feeling of suspense, as if, visibly, the pillars of the temple were being withdrawn and the great Government structure was tottering." Buchanan, a lame duck, bereft of friends and advisers, did little more than condemn secession. He hoped that waiting might bring an isolated Lower South to its senses and give efforts to mediate the sectional rift a chance to succeed.

PEACE PROPOSALS

Kentucky senator John J. Crittenden in January 1861 and later ex-President John Tyler in February proposed similar packages of constitutional amendments designed to solve the sectional crisis. The central feature of the *Crittenden Plan* was the extension of the Missouri Compromise line through the territories all the way to the state of California. The plan was of marginal interest to the South, however, because it was unlikely to result in any new slave states. Neither plan got anywhere in Congress.

LINCOLN'S VIEWS ON SECESSION

President-elect Lincoln monitored the secession of the Lower South states and the attempts to reach a compromise from his home in Springfield. Although he said nothing publicly, he made it known that he did not favor compromises such as those proposed by Crittenden and Tyler. Lincoln counted on Unionist sentiment to keep the Upper South from seceding.

Like Buchanan, he felt that the longer the Lower South states remained isolated, the more likely they would be to return to the fold. For a while, events seemed to bear him out. In North Carolina, the *Wilmington Herald* responded to South Carolina's secession by asking readers, "Will you suffer yourself to be spit upon in this way? Are you *submissionists* to the dictation of South Carolina . . . ?" One by one, Upper South states registered their support for the Union. A closer look, however, reveals that there were limits to the Upper South's Unionism. Most voters in the region went to the polls assuming that Congress would eventually reach a compromise based on Crittenden's or Tyler's proposals, or some other remedy. Leaders in the Upper South saw themselves as peacemakers, but it was unlikely that the Upper South would ever abide the use of federal force against its Southern neighbors.

Lincoln believed that the slavery issue had to come to a crisis before the nation could solve it. Although he said in public that he would never interfere with slavery in the slave states, the deep moral revulsion he felt toward the institution left him more ambivalent in private. As he confided to a colleague in 1860, "The tug has to come, and better now, than any time hereafter."

FORT SUMTER: THE TUG COMES

In his inaugural address on March 4, 1861, Abraham Lincoln denounced secession and vowed to uphold federal law but tempered his firmness with a conciliatory conclusion. Addressing Southerners specifically, he assured them, "We are not enemies but friends. . . . Though passion may have strained, it must not break our bonds of affection. The mystic chords of memory, stretching from every battlefield, and patriot grave, to every living heart and hearthstone, all over this broad land, will yet swell the chorus of the Union, when again touched, as surely they will be, by the better angels of our nature."

Southerners wanted concessions, not conciliation, however. The new president said nothing about slavery in the territories, nothing about constitutional amendments proposed by Crittenden and Tyler, and nothing about the release of federal property in the South to the Confederacy. Even some Northerners hoping for an olive branch were disappointed.

One day after Lincoln's inauguration, Major Robert Anderson (like Lincoln, a native Kentuckian), the commander of ***Fort Sumter*** in Charleston harbor, informed the administration that he had only four to six weeks' worth of provisions left. Sumter was one of three Southern forts still under federal control. Anderson assumed that Lincoln would understand the hopeless military situation and order him to evacuate Fort Sumter.

News of Anderson's plight changed the mood in the North. The Slave Power, some said, was holding him and his men hostage. Frustration grew over Lincoln's silence and inaction. The Confederacy's bold resolve seemed to contrast sharply with the federal government's confusion and inertia. By the end of March, nearly a month after Anderson had informed Lincoln of the situation at Fort Sumter, the president finally made an effort to provision Major Anderson.

The president still hoped to avoid a confrontation. He did not send the troops that Anderson had requested. Instead he ordered unarmed boats to proceed to the fort, deliver the provisions, and leave. Only if the Confederates fired on them were they to force their way into the fort with the help of armed reinforcements.

President Davis wanted to take Sumter before the provisions arrived to avoid fighting Anderson and the reinforcements at the same time. He also realized that the outbreak of fighting could compel the Upper South to join the Confederacy, but his impatience to force the issue placed the Confederacy in the position of firing, unprovoked, on the American flag.

On April 10, Davis ordered Beauregard to demand the immediate evacuation of Fort Sumter. Anderson did not yield, and before dawn on April 12, 1861, the first Confederate shell whistled down on the fort. After more than a day of shelling, during which more than five thousand artillery rounds struck Fort Sumter, Anderson surrendered. Remarkably, neither side suffered any casualties, a deceptive beginning to an exceptionally bloody war.

When the verdict of Fort Sumter reached President Lincoln, he called on the Southern states still in the Union to send troops to put down the rebellion. Refusing to make war on South Carolina, the Upper South states of Virginia, North Carolina, Tennessee, and Arkansas seceded, and the Confederacy expanded to eleven states.

Conclusion

When David Wilmot had submitted his amendment to ban slavery from the territories gained from Mexico, he could not have foreseen that the debate he unleashed would end in civil war just fifteen years later. By the 1850s the slavery issue had become weighted with so much moral and political freight that it defied easy resolution. Northerners and Southerners eventually interpreted any incident or piece of legislation as an attempt by one side to gain moral and political advantage at the other's expense.

By 1861, the national political parties that had muted sectional animosities were gone, and so were national church organizations and fraternal associations. The ideals that had inspired the American Revolution remained in place, especially the importance of securing individual liberty against encroachment by government. But with each side interpreting them differently, these ideals served more to divide than to unite.

Ironically, as Americans in both sections talked of freedom and self-determination, the black men and women in their midst had little of either. Lincoln went to war to preserve the Union, Davis, to defend a new nation. Slavery was the spark that ignited the conflict, but white Americans seemed more comfortable embracing abstract ideals than real people. Northerners and Southerners would confront this irony during the bloodiest war in American history—but they would not resolve it.

REVIEW QUESTIONS

1. Why was Harriet Beecher Stowe's *Uncle Tom's Cabin* such a great success?

2. If you were a Democratic representative to the U.S. Congress in 1854, would you have supported or opposed the Kansas-Nebraska Bill? Why?

3. How did evangelical religion affect the sectional conflict between North and South?

4. Between the time he was elected president in November and his inauguration in March, how might Abraham Lincoln have resolved the sectional crisis?

5. Could Northerners and Southerners both have been correct in their positions?

Battle Cries and Freedom Songs: The Civil War

1861–1865

What were the resource advantages of the North at the outcome of the war?

What were the Confederate and Union military strategies?

What was the Emancipation Proclamation?

What impact did the war have on Northern political, economic, and social life?

How did military reversals affect Confederate political and economic life and civilian morale?

What did the Civil War and its outcome mean for the nation and its citizens?

★

July 14, 1861
Camp Clark, Washington, DC

My very dear Sarah:

The indications are very strong that we shall move in a few days—perhaps tomorrow. And lest I should not be able to write you again I feel impelled to write a few lines that may fall under your eye when I am no more. Our movement may be one of a few days' duration and be full of pleasure. And it may be one of severe conflict and death to me. "Not my will but thine o God be done." If it is necessary that I should fall on the battle-field for my Country I am ready. I have no misgivings about, or lack of confidence in the cause in which I am engaged, and my courage does not halt or falter. I know how American Civilization now leans upon the triumph of the government and how great a debt we owe to those who went before us through the blood and suffering of the Revolution. And I am willing—perfectly willing—to lay down all my joys in this life, to help maintain this government, and to pay that debt. But my dear wife, when I know that with my own joys I lay down nearly all of yours, and replace them in this life with cares and sorrows, when after having eaten for long years the bitter fruit of orphanage myself, I must offer it as the only sustenance to my dear little children, is it weak or dishonorable that while the banner of my purpose floats calmly and proudly in the breeze, underneath, my unbounded love for you my darling wife and children should struggle in fierce though useless contest with my love of country? . . .

Sarah, my love for you is deathless, it seems to bind me with mighty cables that nothing but omnipotence can break; and yet my love of Country comes over me like a strong wind and bears me irresistibly with all those chains to the battle-field.

The memories of the blissful moments I have enjoyed with you come crowding over me, and I feel most deeply grateful to God and you, that I have enjoyed them for so long. And how hard it is for me to give them up and burn to ashes and hopes and future years, when, God willing, we might still have lived and loved together, and see our boys grown up to honorable manhood around us. . . . If I do not [return], my dear Sarah, never forget how much I loved you, nor that when my last breath escapes me on the battle-field, it will whisper your name.

Forgive my many faults, and the many pains I have caused you. How thoughtless, how foolish I have sometimes been! . . .

But, O Sarah, if the dead can come back to this earth and flit unseen around those they love, I shall be with you, in the gladdest days and the darkest nights . . . always, always, and if there be a soft breeze upon your cheek, it shall be my breath[;] as the cool air fans your throbbing temple, it shall be my spirit passing by. Sarah do not mourn me dead; think I am gone and wait for thee, for we shall meet again . . .

—Sullivan

Sullivan Ballou to Sarah Ballou, July 14, 1861. Geoffrey C. Ward, et al., *The Civil War: An Illustrated History* (New York: Alfred A. Knopf, 1990), 82–83.

SULLIVAN BALLOU'S letter to his wife on the eve of the First Battle of Bull Run typified the sentiments of the civilian armies raised by both North and South: a clear purpose of the importance of their mission, a sense of foreboding, an acknowledgment of the guiding hand of God, and words of love for family. He wrote this letter from his camp. A few days later, on July 21, Ballou was killed at the First Battle of Bull Run.

The Civil War preserved the Union, abolished slavery, and killed at least 620,000 soldiers—more than in all other wars the country fought, from the Revolution to the Korean conflict, combined. Union and freedom came at a dear price, we are still paying off its legacy.

When the war began, few Northerners linked the preservation of the Union with the abolition of slavery, but by 1863, Union and freedom had become inseparable Federal objectives. The Confederacy fought for independence and the preservation of slavery. The Confederate objectives dictated a defensive military strategy; the Union objectives dictated an offensive strategy.

At the end of the war's first year, the Confederacy's strong position east of the Appalachians belied its numerical and economic inferiority. By the end of 1862, however, Union officers had begun to expose Southern military shortcomings, and within a year, the Trans-Mississippi portion of the Confederacy capitulated as dissent and despair mounted on the home front. Victory at Gettysburg, Sherman's demoralizing march through Georgia, and the relentless assaults of Ulysses S. Grant overwhelmed Confederate resistance and civilian hope.

Black Southerners seized the initiative in the war against slavery, especially after the Emancipation Proclamation, eventually joining Union forces in combat against their former masters. Soon, another war to secure the fruits of freedom would begin.

Mobilization, North and South

Neither side was prepared for a major war. The Confederacy lacked a national army and navy. Each Southern state had a militia, but by the 1850s, these companies had become more social clubs than fighting units. The Union had a regular army of only sixteen thousand men, most of whom were stationed west of the Mississippi River.

Each government augmented these meager military reserves with thousands of new recruits and developed a bureaucracy to mount a war effort. At the same time, the administrations of Presidents Lincoln and Davis secured the loyalty of their civilian populations and devised military strategies for a war of indeterminate duration. How North and South went about these tasks reflected both the different objectives of the two sides and the distinctive personalities of their leaders, Abraham Lincoln and Jefferson Davis.

WAR FEVER

The day after Major Robert Anderson surrendered Fort Sumter, President Lincoln moved to enlarge his small army by mobilizing state militias for ninety days. Despite the defection of Virginia, Arkansas, North Carolina, and Tennessee and about one-third of the officer corps in the regular army, Lincoln seemed likely to meet his target of 75,000 troops. Both North and South believed that the war would end quickly. William T. Sherman, however, who would become one of the Union's few great commanders, wrote in April 1861, "I think it is to be a long war—very long—much longer than any politician thinks."

Northerners closed ranks behind the president after the Confederacy's attack on Fort Sumter. Leading Democrat Stephen A. Douglas said. "There can be no neutrals in this war *"only patriot—or traitors."* American flags flew everywhere. The *New York Daily Tribune*, an abolitionist paper, made the objective of this patriotic fervor clear: "We mean to conquer [the Southern people]—not merely to defeat, but to conquer, to SUBJUGATE them. . . . They must find poverty at their firesides, and see privation in the anxious eyes of mothers and rags of children."

Southerners were equally eager to support their new nation. Enlistment rallies, wild send-offs at train stations, and auctions and balls to raise money for the troops were staged throughout the Confederacy during the war's early months. As in the North, war fever fired hatred of the enemy. A Louisiana plantation overseer wrote:

> My prayer Sincerely to God is that Every Black Republican . . . that is opposed to negro slavery . . . shal be trubled with pestilences & calamitys of all kinds . . . and O God I pray the to Direct a bullet or a bayonet to pirce the art of every northern Soldier that invades southern Soil.

Volunteers on both sides filled the quotas of both armies. Most soldiers were motivated by patriotism, a desire to defend their homes and loved ones, and a craving for glory and adventure. The initial enthusiasm, however, wore off quickly. After four months of war, a young Confederate soldier admitted, "I have seen quite enough of a Soldier's life to satisfy me that it is not what it is cracked up to be."

The South in particular faced a contradiction between its ideology and the demands of full-scale war. Southern leaders had been fighting for decades to defend states' rights against national authority. Now they had to forge the states of the Confederacy into a nation. By early spring 1862, the Confederate government was compelled to order the first general draft in U.S. history, but the law allowed one white man on any plantation with more than

• C H R O N O L O G Y •

1861 April: Confederates fire on Fort Sumter; Civil War begins.

July: First Battle of Bull Run.

1862 February: Forts Henry and Donelson fall to Union Forces.

March: Peninsula Campaign begins.
Battle of Glorieta Pass, New Mexico.

April: Battle of Shiloh.
New Orleans falls to Federal forces.

May: Union captures Corinth, Mississippi.

July: Seven Days' Battles end.
Congress passes the Confiscation Act.

August: Second Battle of Bull Run.

September: Battle of Antietam.

December: Battle of Fredericksburg.

1863 January: Emancipation Proclamation takes effect.

May: Battle of Chancellorsville; Stonewall Jackson is mortally wounded.

July: Battle of Gettysburg.
Vicksburg falls to Union forces.

New York Draft Riot occurs.
Black Troops of the 54th Massachusetts Volunteer Infantry Regiment assault Fort Wagner outside Charleston.

September: Battle of Chickamauga.

November: Battle of Chattanooga.

1864 May: Battle of the Wilderness.

June: Battle of Cold Harbor.

September: Sherman captures Atlanta.

November: President Lincoln is reelected.
Sherman begins his march to the sea.

1865 January: Congress passes Thirteenth Amendment to the Constitution, outlawing slavery (ratified December 1865).

February: Charleston surrenders.

March: Confederate Congress authorizes enlistment of black soldiers.

April: Federal troops enter Richmond.
Lee surrenders to Grant at Appomattox Court House.
Lincoln is assassinated.

twenty slaves to be excused from service to ensure the security and productivity of large plantations. It led some Southerners to conclude that the struggle had become "a rich man's war but a poor man's fight."

The initial enthusiasm also faded in the North. In March 1863, Congress passed a draft law that allowed a draftee to hire a substitute. This aroused resentment among working-class Northerners, but the North was less dependent on conscription than the South.

The armies of both sides included men from all walks of life. An undetermined number of women, typically disguised as men, also served in both armies. They joined for the same reasons as men: adventure, patriotism, and glory.

THE NORTH'S ADVANTAGE IN RESOURCES

The resources of the North—including its population, industrial and agricultural capacity, and transportation network—greatly exceeded those of the South (see Figure 15–1). The 2.1 million men who fought for the Union represented roughly half the men of military age in the North. The 900,000 men who fought for the Confederacy, in contrast, represented 90 percent of its eligible population. Nearly 200,000 black men, most of them ex-slaves from the South, also took up arms for the Union.

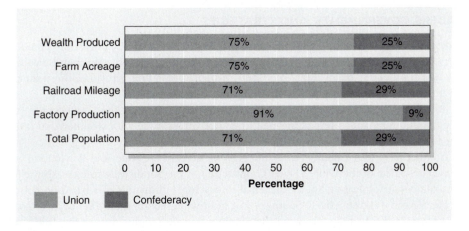

FIGURE 15–1
A Comparison of the Union and Confederate Control of Key Resources at the Outset of the Civil War.

The Union's greater numbers left the South vulnerable to a war of attrition. At the beginning of the war, the North controlled 90 percent of the nation's industrial capacity and had dozens of facilities for producing the tools to make war materiel. The South had no such factories and only one munitions plant, the Tredegar Iron Works in Richmond. The North's railroad system was more than twice the size of the South's.

Thanks to the North's abundance of resources, no soldier in any previous army had ever been outfitted as well as the blue-uniformed Union trooper. The official color of the Confederate uniform was gray, but most Southern soldiers did not wear distinguishable uniforms, especially toward the end of the war. They also often lacked proper shoes or any footwear at all. Still, the South never lost a battle because of insufficient supplies or inadequate weaponry. New foundries and manufacturing enterprises kept the Confederate armies equipped with the supplies they needed to keep fighting.

Unstable finances proved more of a handicap to the Confederacy than low industrial capacity. The Confederate economy—and its treasury—depended heavily on cotton exports, but a Union naval blockade and the ability of textile manufacturers in Europe to find new sources of supply restricted this crucial source of revenue. Because Southerners resisted taxation, the government sold interest-bearing bonds to raise money, but as Confederate fortunes declined, so did bond sales. The Confederacy financed more than 60 percent of the $1.5 billion it spent on the war with printing-press money, and inflation spiraled out of control.

The Federal government was more successful than the Confederate government at developing innovative ways to meet the great cost of the war. Its interest-bearing bonds and treasury notes accounted for 66 percent of the $4 billion that the Union raised to wage the war. Like the Confederacy, the Federal government issued paper money—derisively called "greenbacks"—that was not backed by gold or silver and it also levied the country's first income tax, which citizens could pay in greenbacks, a move that bolstered the value and credibility of the paper currency. Ruinous inflation was thereby averted in the North.

LEADERS, GOVERNMENTS, AND STRATEGIES

Leadership ability, like resources, played an important role in the war. Confederate president Jefferson Davis had to build a government from scratch during the war. Abraham Lincoln at least had the benefit of an established government, a standing army, healthy financial resources, and diplomatic relations with the nations of Europe.

Although Davis's career qualified him for the task of running the Confederacy, colleagues found him aloof. He was inclined to equate compromise with weakness and interpreted any opposition as a personal attack.

Southerners viewed themselves as the genuine heirs of the American Revolution and the true defenders of the United States Constitution. If the South were to establish itself as a separate country, however, Southerners had to develop a distinctive idea based on Southern life. Slavery was distinctively Southern, but most white Southerners did not own slaves. Southerners had forcefully advanced the ideology of states' rights during the 1840s and 1850s, but the primacy of state sovereignty over central authority was too a weak foundation on which to build a national consciousness. Although Southerners sought to protect their home and families, Davis found it difficult to build a loyal base of support.

Northerners also needed a convincing reason to fight. Lincoln and other Northern leaders secured support by convincing their compatriots of the importance of preserving the Union. The president viewed the conflict in global terms, its results affecting the hopes for democratic government around the world.

Lincoln handled disagreement better than Davis did. He defused tense situations with folksy humor, and his simple eloquence captured the imagination of ordinary people. Lincoln viewed himself as a man of the people and was not aloof, like Davis. But even if Jefferson Davis had been a more effective leader than Lincoln, it is unlikely that he could have overcome the odds against him. The key to Southern independence lay with its forces on the battlefield.

The secession of Virginia, Arkansas, North Carolina, and Tennessee left four border slave states—Maryland, Delaware, Kentucky, and Missouri—hanging in the balance. Maryland's strategic location north of Washington, D.C., rendered its loyalty to the Union vital. Although a majority of its citizens opposed secession, pro-Southern sentiment was strong. Lincoln therefore sent Federal troops in a show of force that saved Maryland for the Union. Delaware, although nominally a slave state, remained staunchly for the Union. Missourians settled their indecision in fighting that culminated with a Union victory in March 1862 although pro-Confederate Missourians waged an unsuccessful guerrilla war over the next two years. Kentucky attempted to remain neutral but became a battleground in September 1861, when Confederate forces invaded the state and Union forces moved to expel them. Although Virginia went with the Confederacy, counties in the western part of the state opposed secession and became the separate state of West Virginia, the nation's thirty-fifth state in June 1863.

The political objectives of each side largely determined its military strategy. Southerners wanted independence; Northerners fought to preserve the Union. The North's goal required conquest. The Confederacy had only to fight a defensive battle in its own territory until growing Northern opposition to the war or a decisive Northern military mistake convinced the Union to give up.

But the South's strategy had two weaknesses. First, it demanded more patience than the South had shown in impulsively attacking Fort Sumter. Second, Southern resources might give out before Northern public opinion demanded peace. The question was what would break first: Northern support for the war or Southern ability to wage it?

The Early War, 1861–1862

The North's offensive strategy dictated the course of the war for the first two years. In the West, the Federal army's objectives were to hold Missouri, Kentucky, and Tennessee for the Union, to control the Mississippi River, and eventually to detach the area west of the Appalachians from the rest of the Confederacy. In the East, Union forces sought to capture Richmond, the Confederate capital. The U.S. Navy blockaded the Confederate coast and pushed into inland waterways to capture Southern ports. The Confederates defended strategic locations throughout their territory or abandoned them when prudence required. By the end of 1862, the result remained in the balance.

FIRST BULL RUN

By July 1861, when the border states appeared more secure for the Union, President Lincoln ordered Union general Irvin McDowell to take Richmond. Confronting McDowell 20 miles southwest of Washington at Manassas was a Confederate army under General P. G. T. Beauregard. McDowell and Beauregard's armies clashed on July 21 at the First Battle of Bull Run (known to the Confederacy as the First Battle of Manassas). The Union forces seemed on the verge of winning, but Beauregard's forces repulsed the assault. At the height of the battle, General Barnard Bee of South Carolina in exasperation called out to Colonel Thomas J. Jackson for assistance, shouting, "There stands Jackson—like a damned stone wall!" Somehow the rebuke became a shorthand for courage and steadfastness. Jackson's men henceforth called him "Stonewall."

Bull Run boosted Southerners' confidence and destroyed the widespread belief in the North that the war would be over quickly.

THE WAR IN THE WEST

While Federal forces retreated in Virginia, they advanced in the West. Two Confederate forts, Fort Henry on the Tennessee River and Fort Donelson on the Cumberland River, guarded the strategic waterways that linked Tennessee and Kentucky to the Mississippi Valley. The forts also defended Nashville, the Tennessee state capital (see Map 15–1). In February 1862, Union general Ulysses S. Grant coordinated a land and river campaign against the forts that caught the Southerners unprepared and outflanked. By February 16, both forts had fallen. The Union victory drove a wedge into Southern territory and closed the Confederacy's quickest path to the West from Virginia and the Carolinas. The Confederacy never recovered the strategic advantage in the West.

Grant next moved his main army south to prepare for an assault on the key Mississippi River port and rail center of Vicksburg. After blunting a surprise Confederate attack at Shiloh Church, Grant pushed the Southerners back to Corinth, Mississippi. Another important Federal success came when Admiral David G. Farragut captured New Orleans in April 1862. Two hundred miles of the Mississippi River, the nation's most vital commercial waterway, were now open to Union traffic. After Memphis fell to Union forces in June, Vicksburg remained the only major river town still in Confederate hands. The fall of

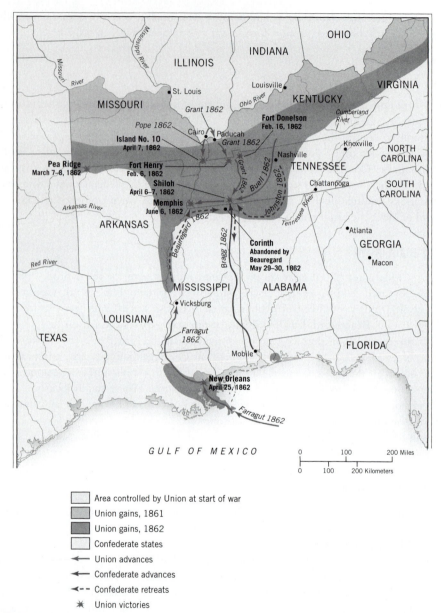

MAP 15–1

The War in the West, 1861–1862   Because of the early Union emphasis on capturing Richmond, the war in the West seemed less important to Northerners. But, from a strategic standpoint, the victories at Forts Henry and Donelson, which drove a wedge into Southern territory and closed the Confederacy's quickest path to the West from Virginia and the Carolinas, and the capture of New Orleans and its Mississippi River port, were crucial and set the stage for greater Federal success in the West in 1863.

BASED ON this map, what was the Union's overall strategy in these campaigns?

New Orleans and Memphis underscored a major problem with the Confederates' defensive strategy: Their military reserves were stretched too thin to defend their vast territory.

REASSESSING THE WAR: THE HUMAN TOLL

More American soldiers were lost at Shiloh than in all of the nation's wars combined up to that time. Each side suffered more than ten thousand casualties. By the time the smoke had cleared, the soldiers' initial bravado was replaced by the realization that death or capture was a likely outcome and that heroism, courage, and piety did not guarantee survival. A hunger for peace replaced the thirst for battle.

Kate Cumming, the nurse at the Confederate hospital in Corinth, wrote of soldiers brought from the battle "mutilated in every imaginable way." Piercing the air were the screams of men undergoing amputations, often with little or no anesthetic. Some pleaded with physicians to kill them and end their misery. Others bore the pain stoically and entrusted last words and letters to nurses, dying with the word "Mother" on their lips.

Women on both sides cared for the wounded and sick. In the North, members of the U.S. Sanitary Commission, a voluntary organization formed in 1861 and staffed mainly by women, attempted to upgrade hospital and medical care. But in the months after Shiloh and with the resumption of fighting in the East, the extent of casualties often overwhelmed the volunteers. And the bloodiest fighting lay ahead.

Even if a soldier escaped death on the battlefield and survived a hospital stay, he often died from disease. Roughly twice as many men died from disease than on the battlefield during the Civil War. Typhoid, appropriately known as camp fever, claimed the most lives.

Many soldiers turned to religion for consolation. Camp prayer meetings and revivals increased after Shiloh. Soldiers often gathered to sing hymns before retiring for the night. Stories circulated of a Bible that stopped a bullet. But veterans knew that a deck of cards did just as well, and neither Bibles nor cards offered protection against artillery.

Soldiers responded in various ways to constant danger and fear. Some talked or yelled loudly. (The Confederate rebel yell probably relieved some of the tension of battle as well as frightened the enemy.) Others shook uncontrollably. A few soldiers could not wake up in the morning without being doused with cold water. Soldiers suffered from strained relations between officers and enlisted men, heavy chores, incessant drills and boredom. Women camp followers cooked, did laundry, and provided sexual services for a price. Venereal disease was rampant.

By 1862, the war's carnage and brutality had dispelled any lingering notions of war as a chivalrous enterprise. The reluctance of some commanders to pursue retreating armies or to initiate campaigns resulted in part from their recognition of how awful the war really was.

THE WAR IN THE EAST

With Grant and Farragut squeezing the Confederacy in the West, Lincoln ordered a new offensive against Richmond. After the defeat at Bull Run, he had appointed General George B. McClellan to lead what was now called the Army of the Potomac. A superb organizer, McClellan would prove overly cautious on the field of battle.

In March 1862, at the outset of the Peninsula Campaign, McClellan moved his 112,000–man army down the Potomac River and Chesapeake Bay to the peninsula between the York and James Rivers southeast of the Confederate capital.

A career army officer who resigned his commission to serve his state and new country, Confederate General Robert E. Lee's quiet courage and sense of duty inspired his men.
Corbis/Bettman.

Moving ponderously up the peninsula, McClellan clashed with General Joseph E. Johnston's army at Seven Pines in late May 1862. Johnston was badly wounded in the clash, and President Davis replaced him with General Robert E. Lee, who renamed his forces the Army of Northern Virginia. Under his daring leadership, the Confederacy's defensive strategy underwent an important shift.

Lee seized the initiative on June 25, 1862, attacking McClellan's right flank. The nervous McClellan took up a defensive position. For a week, the armies sparred in a series of fierce engagements known as the Seven Days' Battles. More than thirty thousand men were killed or wounded on both sides. Although McClellan prevailed in these contests, the carnage so shocked him that he withdrew down the peninsula and away from Richmond. The exasperated Lincoln replaced McClellan with John Pope.

Although Lee had lost one-fourth of his eighty thousand–man army, he remained convinced of the wisdom of his offensive-defensive strategy. Better coordination between his staff and field commanders, he believed, would have reduced his casualties and inflicted greater damage on the enemy.

Lee went to work to vindicate these tactics. After a series of inconclusive skirmishes, Union and Confederate armies gathered once more near Manassas Junction. The Second Battle of Bull Run was another disaster for the Union. Lee's generalship completely befuddled Pope and again saved Richmond. Lee and the Army of Northern Virginia were developing a reputation for invincibility.

Turning Points, 1862–1863

The Confederate victories in the East masked the delicate condition of Southern fortunes. The longer the Confederacy held off Union offensives, the greater the likelihood of securing the South's independence. But the longer the war continued, the higher the probability that the Confederacy's shortcomings in men and resources would erode its ability to keep fighting. The Union was also choking the South's commercial link to Europe to which Davis looked for diplomatic recognition as well as trade.

But the most important arena of the war remained the battlefield. Having stymied the Union war machine, Lee contemplated a thrust into Northern territory to stoke Northerners' hostility to the war. President Lincoln also harbored a bold plan. During the spring and summer of 1862, he had concluded that emancipation of the Confederacy's slaves was essential for preserving the Union, but Lincoln was reluctant to take this step before the Union's fortunes on the battlefield improved. As the fall of 1862 approached, both Union and Confederate governments prepared for the most significant conflicts of the war to date.

THE NAVAL WAR AND THE DIPLOMATIC WAR

The Union's naval strategy was to blockade the Southern coast and capture its key seaports and river towns. The intention was to prevent supplies from reaching the Confederacy and cash crops from leaving. Destroying the South's ability to carry on trade would also prevent the Confederacy from raising money to purchase goods to wage war.

With more than 3,000 miles of Confederate coastline to cover, the Union blockade was weak at first. As time passed and the number of ships in the Union navy grew, the blockade tightened. The skyrocketing prices of Southern staples on world markets by 1862 attested to the effectiveness of the Union strategy.

The Confederate naval strategy was to break the blockade and defend the South's rivers and seaports. Confederate blockade runners and privateers attacked Union merchant ships and disrupted Federal operations. Historians disagree about the effectiveness of the Union naval blockade, but any restriction to the flow of trade hurt the Southern cause.

Southerners, remembering the crucial role that French assistance had played in the American Revolution, thought that the recognition of their independence by overseas governments would legitimize their cause in the eyes of the world. Britain had no great love of the United States. If the country divided, it would pose less of a threat to British interests. The aristocratic pretensions of some Southerners also appealed to their British counterparts. British foreign policy, however, had been antislavery for half a century, and the slavery issue turned many Britons against the South. The Union cause had support in high ruling circles, especially the Royal Family, as well as from middle-class and working-class Britons.

Emperor Napoleon III of France, who had imperial designs on Mexico, favored the Confederacy. A restored Union, he thought, would pose a greater threat to his ambitions than a divided one. But Napoleon would not intervene in the Confederate cause without British support. He did, however, invade Mexico in 1863 and install Archduke Maximillian of Austria as emperor. This Mexican empire was short-lived. American pressure and foreign policy reverses in Europe forced the French to withdraw their troops in 1867. Insurgents led by Benito Juarez then captured and executed Maximillian and restored the Mexican republic.

The Russians were probably the staunchest supporters of the Union abroad. Tsar Alexander II saw the United States as a counterweight to British power.

Southerners were convinced that they could use cotton as a diplomatic bargaining chip. "You dare not to make war on cotton. . . . Cotton is King," declared South Carolina senator James H. Hammond in 1858. But King Cotton was no more successful at coercing the British—who had large cotton reserves and an alternate source of supply in Egypt— into granting recognition to the Confederacy than it was at stopping the North from going to war against the South.

Great Britain and France, however, did declare themselves neutral and allowed their merchants to sell arms and supplies to both sides. This policy benefited the Confederacy, with its limited arsenal, but the Confederacy's hopes for diplomatic recognition depended on its ability to win its independence on the battlefield. After Lee's victories in Virginia in the spring of 1862 and his subsequent decision to invade the North, British intervention in the war grew more likely.

ANTIETAM

Lee was convinced that the South could not sustain a prolonged conflict. If possible his army had to destroy Union forces quickly. He established camp at Frederick, Maryland, in September 1862, scattering his army at various sites, convinced that McClellan and the Army of the Potomac would not attack him.

At this point, luck intervened for the North when a Union corporal found a copy of Lee's orders for the disposition of his army. But "Little Mac" still moved so cautiously that Lee had time to retreat to defensive positions at Sharpsburg, Maryland, along Antietam Creek. There Lee's army of 50,000 men came to blows with McClellan's army of 75,000.

The Battle of Antietam saw the bloodiest single day of fighting in American history. About 2,100 Union soldiers and 2,700 Confederates died on the battlefield, and another 18,500, equally divided, were wounded. McClellan squandered his numerical superiority with timid attacks. The armies fought to a tactical draw, but the battle was a strategic defeat for the Confederacy.

Antietam marked a major turning point in the war. It kept Lee from directly threatening Northern industry and financial institutions. It prompted Britain and France to abandon plans to grant recognition to the Confederacy. And it provided Lincoln with the victory he needed to announce the abolition of slavery.

EMANCIPATION

President Lincoln despised slavery, but he had always maintained that preserving the Union was his primary war goal. Lincoln realized that he had to stress union to keep the Northern public united in support of the war, but from the war's outset, pressure grew to declare emancipation.

Lincoln said in his inaugural address that he had "no purpose, directly or indirectly, to interfere with the institution of slavery in the states where it exists." But pressure from Northern civilians, Union soldiers, and Congress for some form of emancipation mounted in the spring of 1862. In response, the Republican Congress prohibited slavery in the territories and abolished slavery in the District of Columbia. The act emancipating the district's slaves called for compensating slave owners and colonizing the freed slaves in black republics such as Haiti and Liberia. Then in July 1862, the **Confiscation Act** ordered the seizure of land from disloyal Southerners and the emancipation of their slaves.

Although support for emancipation had grown, it was still not favored by a majority in the North, especially not in the border states. But freeing the slaves would gain support for the Union cause abroad and it would weaken the Confederacy's ability to wage war by removing a crucial source of labor.

By mid-1862, Lincoln had resolved to act on his moral convictions and proclaim emancipation. Taking the advice of Secretary of State Seward, however, he decided to wait for a battlefield victory so that the measure would not appear an act of desperation. Antietam gave the president his opening, and on September 22, 1862, he announced his intention to issue the **Emancipation Proclamation**, to take effect January 1, 1863, in all states still in rebellion. The proclamation exempted slaves in the border states loyal to the Union and in areas under Federal occupation.

Even before the Emancipation Proclamation, slaves throughout the South "stole" their freedom. After the Proclamation, the trickle of black slaves abandoning their masters became a flood, as they sought freedom behind Union lines.

Theo Kaufman, "On to Liberty," 1887, oil on canvas. 36" × 56". The Metropolitan Museum of Art, Gift of Erving and Joyce Wolf, 1982. (1982, 443.3) Photograph © 1982. The Metropolitan Museum of Art.

Southerners reacted with outrage, while Northerners generally approved. But the Emancipation Proclamation represented far more than its qualified words and phrases expressed. "A mighty *act*," Massachusetts governor John Andrew called it. Lincoln and the Union war effort were now tied to the cause of freedom. The war had became a holy war of deliverance. Freedom and Union entwined in the public consciousness of the North. Emancipation also unified the Republican party and strengthened the president's hand in conducting the war.

As word of the Emancipation Proclamation raced through the slave grapevine, slaves rejoiced that their long-awaited day of jubilee had arrived. Southern masters fought to deter their slaves by punishing the families of black men who fled to Union lines and employing slavecatchers to reclaim runaways. But slaveholders could not stem the tide of slaves fleeing toward the Union lines and freedom. The 1862 Confiscation Act included slaves with other Confederate property as the "contraband" of war and subject to confisca-tion, a term Union general Benjamin Butler had applied to escaped slaves as early as May 1861. As they helped the Union cause, contrabands also sought to help fellow slaves "steal" their freedom. The former slaves who arrived at Federal camps after emancipation often encountered poor conditions but relished their freedom nonetheless. After 1863, ex-slaves served in increasing numbers in the Union army.

More than 80 percent of the roughly 180,000 black soldiers and 20,000 black sailors who fought for the Union were slaves and free black men from the South. For the typical black Southerner who joined the army, the passage from bondage to freedom came quickly. Making his escape from his master, he perhaps "stole" his family as well. He typically expe-rienced his first days of freedom behind Union lines, where he may have learned to read and write. Finally, he put on the Federal uniform, experiencing as one Southern black vol-unteer commented, "the biggest thing that ever happened in my life."

Although black troops fought as ably as their white comrades, they received lower pay than white soldiers and performed the most menial duties in camp. Abolitionists and black leaders in the North pressured President Lincoln for more equitable treatment of African-American recruits. When Frederick Douglass complained to Lincoln about the lower pay that black troops received, the president defended the practice. Despite discrimi-nation, black soldiers fought valiantly at Port Hudson, Louisiana; near Charleston; and, late in the war, at the siege of Petersburg, Virginia. The most celebrated black encounter with Confederate troops occurred in July 1863 during a futile assault by the 54th Massachusetts Regiment on Fort Wagner outside Charleston. The Northern press, previously lukewarm toward black troops, heaped praise on the effort.

FROM FREDERICKSBURG TO GETTYSBURG

In late 1862, after Antietam, the president replaced McClellan with General Ambrose E. Burnside. Moving swiftly against Lee's dispersed army in northern Virginia, Burnside reached the Rappahannock River opposite Fredericksburg in November 1862. On December 13, the Union forces launched a foolish frontal assault that the Confederates repelled, inflicting heavy Federal casualties. Burnside was relieved of his command, and Major General Joseph Hooker was installed in his place.

Hooker was as incompetent as Burnside. Between May 1 and May 4, Lee's army deliv-ered a series of crushing attacks on Hooker's forces at Chancellorsville. Outnumbered two

These Union and Confederate dead at Gettysburg represent the cost of the war, the price of freedom. President Lincoln transformed the battleground from a killing field to a noble symbol of sacrifice for American ideals. Gettysburg continues to occupy a special place in our nation's history and in the memory of its citizens.

Corbis/Bettmann.

to one, Lee had pulled off another stunning victory but he had lost some thirteen thousand men and Stonewall Jackson. Nervous Confederate sentries mistakenly shot and wounded him as he returned from a reconnoitering mission, and he died a few days later. Jackson had helped Lee win some of the Confederacy's most stunning victories. Lee recognized the tragedy of Jackson's loss for himself and his country.

Chancellorsville thrust Lincoln into another bout of despair. "My God!" he exclaimed in agony, "What will the country say! What will the country say!" Meanwhile, Lee headed north once again.

President Lincoln sent the Union Army of the Potomac after Lee. But General Hooker dallied, and Lincoln replaced him with George Gordon Meade who set out after the Confederate army, which was encamped at Cashtown, Pennsylvania, 45 miles from Harrisburg. That the greatest battle of the war erupted at nearby Gettysburg was pure chance (see Map 15–2). During the first day of battle, July 1, the Confederates forced Union forces back from the town to a new position on Cemetery Hill. On the second day, they took several key locations along Cemetery Ridge before Federal forces pushed them back to the previous day's positions. On July 3, Lee made a fateful error. Believing that the center of Meade's line was weak, he ordered an all-out assault against it by General George Pickett. Meade was prepared for Lee's assault. As the Confederate infantry marched out with battle colors flying, the Union artillery and Federal riflemen tore apart the charging Southerners and half of Pickett's thirteen thousand–man division lay dead or wounded.

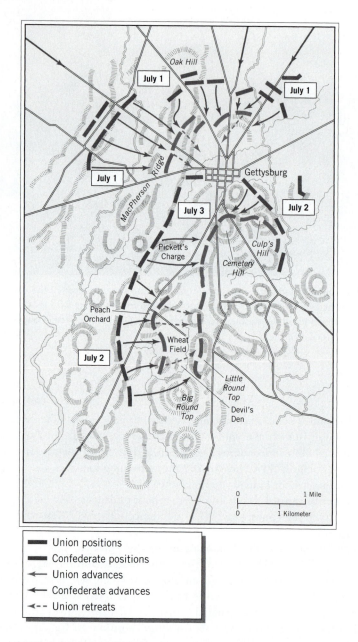

- ▬ Union positions
- ▬ Confederate positions
- ◄— Union advances
- ◄— Confederate advances
- ◄-- Union retreats

MAP 15–2

The Battle of Gettysburg, July 1–3, 1863   In a war that lasted four years, it is difficult to point to the decisive battle, but clearly the outcome during those hot July days at Gettysburg set the tone for the rest of the war. The result was unclear until the final day of battle and, even then, it might have gone either way. Winning by a whisker was enough to propel Union armies to a string of victories over the next year, and throw Confederate forces back on their defenses among an increasingly despairing population. Gettysburg marked the last major Southern invasion of the North.

WHY WAS the Battle of Gettysburg so crucial?

After the battle, Lee explained, "I believed my men were invincible." Meade allowed Lee to withdraw to Virginia. Gettysburg was the bloodiest battle of the war. The Union suffered 23,000 casualties; the Confederacy, 28,000.

VICKSBURG, CHATTANOOGA, AND THE WEST

On July 4, one day after Pickett's charge at Gettysburg, Vicksburg, the last major Confederate strong-hold on the Mississippi, surrendered to Ulysses S. Grant. Grant is often perceived, incorrectly, as a general who ground out victories through superior numbers, with little finesse or concern for his troops' safety. But in his campaigns in the West, he used his forces creatively, swiftly, and with a minimum loss of life.

Grant had devised a brilliant plan to take Vicksburg that called for rapid maneuvering and expert coordination. Grant had his twenty thousand Union troops ferried across the Mississippi from the Louisiana side south of Vicksburg. Then they moved northeastward, captured the Mississippi state capital at Jackson, and turned west toward Vicksburg. On May 22, 1863, Grant settled down in front of the city and cut it off completely. Their situation hopeless, General John Pemberton and his thirty thousand–man garrison surrendered on July 4.

As Grant was besieging Vicksburg in June 1863, Union general William S. Rosecrans advanced on Confederate general Braxton Bragg, whose army held Chattanooga, a "doorway" on the railroad that linked Richmond to the Lower South. The capture of the city would complete the uncoupling of the West from the eastern Confederacy.

At Rosecrans's approach, Bragg abandoned Chattanooga and took up positions at nearby Chickamauga Creek. When the two armies clashed at Chickamauga on September 19, Bragg pushed Rosecrans back and bottled up Rosecrans in Chattanooga much as Grant had confined Pemberton at Vicksburg. Suddenly, the Union's strategy for the conquest of the western Confederacy seemed in jeopardy.

The Confederate position on the heights overlooking Chattanooga appeared impregnable. But Union generals Grant, Sherman, and Hooker broke the siege and forced Bragg's army to retreat into Georgia. The Union now dominated most of the West and faced an open road to the East.

The Confederacy's reverses at Vicksburg and Chattanooga mirrored its misfortunes beyond the Mississippi River. Texas was critical to Confederate fortunes, both as a source of supply for the East and as a base for the conquest of the Far West, but it was far from secure. Texas suffered from internal dissent and violence on its borders. For a time, it maintained commercial contact with the rest of the Confederacy through Matamoros, Mexico. But by 1864, with the Union in control of the Mississippi, Texas had lost its strategic importance. The Confederacy's transcontinental aspirations died early in the war. In March 1862, a Confederate army seeking to conquer the Southwest was overwhelmed by Union forces at the Battle of Glorieta Pass in New Mexico. The Southwest from New Mexico to California would remain firmly in Union hands.

Native American tribes in the Trans-Mississippi West spent much of the Civil War battling Federal troops for territory and resources. Three regiments of Cherokee Indians, however, fought for the South at the Battle of Pea Ridge in 1862. The Union won the battle and with it control of Missouri and northern Arkansas. Most battles between pro-Union and pro-Southern Native Americans occurred in the Indian Territory (now Oklahoma).

War Transforms the North

Union successes by 1863 profoundly affected both sides. For the North, hopes of victory and reunion increased. The Federal government expanded its bureaucracy to wage war efficiently, and a Republican-dominated Congress broadened Federal power. The Lincoln administration successfully weathered dissent thanks to the president's political skill, the desire of the Republicans to remain in power, and the Union's improving military fortunes. Boosted by Federal economic legislation and wartime demand, the Northern economy boomed. Women entered the work force in growing numbers, but labor unrest and class and racial tensions suggested that prosperity had a price.

WARTIME LEGISLATION AND POLITICS

Before the Civil War, the Federal government rarely affected citizens' lives directly. But mobilizing for war required a strong central government. With the departure of the South from the Union, Republicans dominated all branches of the Federal administration. This left them in a position to test the constitutional limits of federal authority.

President Lincoln began almost immediately to use executive authority to suppress opposition to the war effort in the North. Within the first few weeks of the conflict, he ordered the seizure of telegrams to intercept seditious messages to the South. He also suspended the writ of habeas corpus, the constitutional requirement that protects a defendant against illegal imprisonment. Suspending it allowed authorities to hold suspects indefinitely and was permitted by the Constitution "when in cases of Rebellion or Invasion the public Safety" required it.

Executive sanctions fell particularly hard on the Democratic party. "Disloyalty" was difficult to define in the midst of war. Though many Democrats opposed secession and supported the Union, they challenged the president on the conduct of the war, on emancipation, and on Lincoln's coolness toward peace initiatives. A few had ties with Confederate agents. Republicans called these dissenters "*Copper-heads*," after the poisonous snake.

Despite the suspension of habeas corpus, Lincoln compiled a fairly good record for upholding basic American civil liberties. The administration made no attempt to control the news or subvert the electoral process. In the off-year election in 1862, Republicans retained control of Congress but lost several seats to Democrats. In the presidential election of 1864, Lincoln won reelection in a hard-fought contest.

While fellow Republicans sometimes chastised the president for violating civil liberties, mismanaging military assignments, or moving too slowly on emancipation, they rarely threatened to disrupt the party. Lincoln also found support from Republican governors and state governments.

But dissent in the Republican party did affect national policy. **Radical Republicans** hounded Lincoln, establishing the Joint Committee on the Conduct of the War to examine and monitor military policy. They also pressed Lincoln for quicker action on emancipation, but they supported the president on most crucial matters.

Lincoln likewise supported his party on an array of initiatives in Congress. Turning to the settlement of the West, they passed the **Homestead Act** in May 1862, which granted 160 acres of land free to any settler in the territories who agreed to improve the land within five years of the grant. The act was a boon for railroad companies.

Other legislation to boost the nation's economy and the fortunes of individual manufacturers and farmers included the **Land Grant College Act** of 1862, a protective tariff that same year, and the National Banking Act of 1863. The Land Grant Act awarded the proceeds from the sale of public lands to the states for the establishment of colleges offering instruction in "agriculture and mechanical arts." The tariff legislation protected Northern industry from foreign competition while raising revenue for the Union. The National Banking Act of 1863 replaced the bank notes of individual states, which were often backed by flimsy reserves and subject to wild fluctuations in value, with a uniform national currency and brought order to a chaotic monetary system.

However, the expansion of government into some quarters, such as the draft laws, was not welcomed.

CONSCRIPTION AND THE DRAFT RIOTS

Congress passed the first national conscription law in 1863. Almost immediately, evasion, obstruction, and weak enforcement threatened to undermine it. As military authorities began arresting draft dodgers and deserters, secret societies formed to harbor draftees and instruct them on evasion. Conflicts between citizens and federal officials over the draft sometimes erupted in violence. The worst draft riot occurred in New York City in July 1863, when a mostly Irish mob protesting conscription burned the federal marshal's headquarters. Racial and class antagonisms quickly joined antidraft anger as the mob went on a rampage through the city's streets, fighting police, plundering houses of the wealthy, and crying, "Down with the rich!" Racial antagonisms contributed to the violence. The mob lynched two black men and burned the Colored Orphan Asylum. More than one hundred lives were lost in the riot, which was finally quelled by army units fresh from Gettysburg, and the draft resumed a month later.

THE NORTHERN ECONOMY

"The North," one historian has said, "was fighting the South with one hand and getting rich with the other behind its back." After an initial downturn during the uncertain months preceding the war, the Northern economy picked up quickly. High tariffs and massive federal spending soon made up for the loss of Southern markets and the closing of the Mississippi River. Profits skyrocketed for some businesses like the railroads. New industries boomed, and new inventions increased manufacturing efficiency as in the sewing machine industry, which was first commercialized in the 1850s. Technological advances greatly increased the output of the North's garment factories.

Despite the loss of manpower to the demands of industry and the military, the productivity of Northern agriculture grew during the war. As machines replaced men on the farm, the manufacturers of farm machinery became wealthy. Crop failures in Europe dramatically increased the demand for American grain.

Working people should have benefited from wartime prosperity, with men off to war, immigration down, and labor in short supply. Although wages increased, prices rose more. Declining real wages led to exploitation, especially of women in garment factories. The trade union movement, which suffered a serious setback in the depression of 1857, revived. Local unions of shoemakers, carpenters, and miners emerged in 1862 across the North, and so did a few national organizations. By 1865, more than 200,000 Northern workers belonged to a labor union.

Employers struck back at union organizing by hiring strikebreakers, usually black workers. Labor conflicts between striking white workers and black strikebreakers sparked riots in New York City and Cincinnati. The racial antagonism accounted in part for workers' opposition to Lincoln's Emancipation Proclamation and for the continued strength of the Democratic party in Northern cities.

The promise of enormous profits bred greed and corruption as well as exploitation. Illicit trade between North and South was inevitable when cotton could be bought at 20 cents a pound in New Orleans and sold for $1.90 a pound at Boston. Profiteers not only defied the government to trade with the enemy but also sometimes swindled the government outright, supplying defective clothing to soldiers at inflated prices.

Some Northerners viewed the spending spree uneasily. They were disturbed to see older men flaunting their wealth while young men were dying on the battlefield. "The lavish profusion in which the old southern cotton aristocracy used to indulge," wrote an indignant reporter for the *New York World*, "is completely eclipsed by the dash, parade, and magnificence of the new northern shoddy aristocracy. . . ." Exploited workers likewise resented the "shoddy aristocracy."

Comments like these hinted at the deep social and ethical problems that were emerging in Northern society and would become more pronounced in the decades after the Civil War. For the time being, the benefits of economic development for the Union cause outweighed its negative consequences. The thriving Northern economy fed, clothed, and armed the Union's soldiers and kept most civilians employed, providing Northern women with unprecedented opportunities.

NORTHERN WOMEN AND THE WAR

More than 100,000 Northern women took jobs in factories, sewing rooms, and arsenals during the Civil War. They often performed tasks previously reserved for men, but at lower pay.

Women also served the war effort directly in another profession previously dominated by men—nursing. Physicians and officers, however, although they tolerated women nurses as nurturing morale boosters, thought little of their ability to provide medical care. Women sometimes challenged this condescending view, braving dismissal to confront the medical-military establishment head-on. Clara Barton, among the most notable nurses of the war, treated soldiers on the battlefield at great peril and to the consternation of officers.

But the war also left tens of thousands of women widowed and devastated. In a society that assumed that men supported women, the death of a husband could be a financial and psychological disaster. Many women were left to survive on meager pensions.

The new economic opportunities the war created for women left Northern society more open to a broader view of women's roles. One indication of this change was the admission of women to eight previously all-male state universities after the war. Like the class and racial tensions that surfaced in Northern cities, the shifting role of women during the Civil War hinted at the promises and problems of postwar life. The changing scale and nature of the American economy, the expanded role of government, and the shift in class, racial, and gender relations are all trends that signaled what historians call the "modernization" of American society.

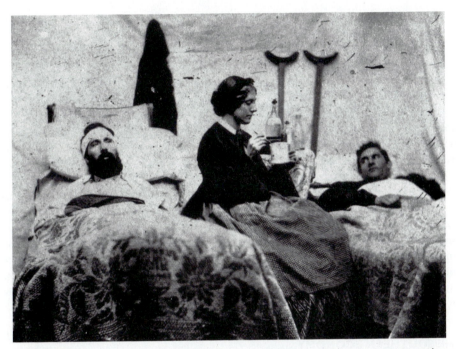

Nurse Ann Bell tends a fallen Union soldier. Although medical practices were primitive and many young men died from poorly treated wounds or disease, the U.S. Sanitary Commission attempted to improve care in Union hospitals during the war. The war helped open nursing as a respectable occupation for women.

Corbis/Bettmann.

The Confederacy Disintegrates

As battlefield losses mounted, the Confederacy disintegrated. Defeat dissolves the bonds that hold a small society like the Confederacy together and exposes the large and small divisions within it. After 1863, defeat infected Confederate politics, ruined the Southern economy, and eventually invaded the hearts and minds of the Southern people. The South pinned its waning hopes on its defensive military strategy. If it could prolong the conflict a little longer, perhaps a war-weary North would replace Lincoln and the Republicans in the 1864 elections with Democrats inclined to make peace.

SOUTHERN POLITICS

Dissent plagued Southern politics. Residents of western Virginia declared themselves for the Union and formed the new state of West Virginia. Counties in north Alabama, in German-speaking districts in Texas, and throughout the mountains of Tennessee and North Carolina contemplated similar action.

As the war turned against the Confederacy, Southerners increasingly turned against each other. States' rights, a major principle of the seceding states, proved an obstacle to the Davis administration's efforts to exert central authority. The governors of Georgia and

North Carolina hoarded munitions, soldiers, supplies, food, and money. Even cooperative governors refused to allow state agents to collect taxes for the Confederacy.

Unlike Abraham Lincoln, Jefferson Davis could not appeal to party loyalty to control dissent because the Confederacy had no parties. Davis's frigid personality, his insistence on attending to minute details, and his inability to accept even constructive criticism gracefully worsened political tensions within the Confederacy.

Parts of the South began clamoring for peace during the fateful summer of 1863. In North Carolina, Jonathan Worth heard calls for the overthrow of the Davis administration and a separate peace with the North. "Every man [I] met," he concluded "was for reconstruction on the basis of the old [U.S.] constitution." By November 1864, the Confederacy suffered as much from internal disaffection as from the attacks of Union armies.

Davis and other Confederate leaders might have averted some of these problems had they succeeded in building a strong sense of Confederate nationalism. Despite several strategies to do so—identifying the Confederacy's fight for independence with the American Revolution of 1776, for example, and casting the Confederacy as a bastion of freedom standing up to Lincoln's despotic abuse of executive authority, they failed. The diaries of Southern soldiers seldom reveal devotion to the Confederacy. In a devout society convinced it was fighting a holy war, some Southerners sought some moral failing to account for their mounting losses. Some identified slavery as the culprit.

THE SOUTHERN ECONOMY

The South lost, according to one historian, "not because the government failed to mobilize the South's resources" but "because there was virtually nothing left to mobilize." By 1863, the Confederacy was having a difficult time feeding itself. Destruction of farms and growing Union control of waterways and rail lines restricted the distribution of food. Speculators made shortages worse. People ate rats and mules to supplement their meager diets. More than one-quarter of Alabama's population was receiving public welfare by the end of the war. "Deaths from starvation have absolutely occurred," a Confederate official in the state informed President Davis in 1864.

Wartime food shortages, skyrocketing inflation, and rumors of hoarding and price-gouging drove women in several Southern cities to protest violently. Demonstrations like the 1863 food riot shown here reflected a larger rending of Southern society as Confederate losses and casualties mounted on the battlefield. Some Southern women placed survival and providing for their families ahead of boosting morale and silently supporting a war effort that had taken their men away. Their defection hurt the Confederate cause.

Corbis/Bettmann.

Southern soldiers had marched off to war in neat uniforms, many leaving behind self-sustaining families. But during the winter of 1863–1864, women lined their clothes with rags and newspapers to keep warm. The women and children left alone on farms and plantations were vulnerable to stragglers and deserters from both armies. Southerners also feared that slaves would rise up against their masters. Most slaves, however, were more intent on escape than revenge. Some felt genuine affection for the families they served and stayed on with them even after the war.

As Confederate casualties mounted, more and more Southern women and children, like their Northern counterparts, faced the pain of grief. With little food, worthless money, and a husband or father gone forever, the future looked bleak.

SOUTHERN WOMEN AND THE WAR

In the early days of the Civil War, Southern white women continued to live according to antebellum conventions. Magazine articles urged them to preserve themselves as models of purity for men debased by the violence of war. Women flooded newspapers and periodicals with patriotic verses and songs that stressed the need to suppress grief and fear for the good of the men at the front.

By the time of the Civil War, such emotional concealment had become second nature to Southern white women. They had long had to endure their anguish over their husbands' nocturnal visits to the slave quarters. They were used to the condescension of men who assumed them to be intellectually inferior. And they accepted in bitter, self-sacrificing silence the contradiction between the myth of the pampered leisure they were presumed to enjoy and the hard demands their lives actually entailed.

But as Confederate manpower and materiel needs became acute, some Southern women took on new productive responsibilities and began to fill positions vacated by men. They managed plantations. They worked in the fields alongside slaves and in factories to make uniforms and munitions. They taught school. A few, like Belle Boyd and Rose O'Neal Greenhow, spied for the Confederacy. And many, like their Northern counterparts, served as nurses. Eventually, battlefield reverses and economic collapse left women and men alike struggling simply to survive.

As the war dragged on and the Southern economy and the social order deteriorated, even the patriots suffered from resentment and doubt. By 1864, many women were helping their deserting husbands or relatives elude Confederate authorities. A North Carolina official explained that "desertion takes place because desertion is encouraged. . . . And though the ladies may not be willing to concede the fact, they are nevertheless responsible. . . ." Some religious women concluded that it was God, not the Yankees, who had destroyed the South for its failure to live up to its responsibilities to women and children.

The Union Prevails, 1864–1865

Despite the Union's dominant position after Vicksburg and Gettysburg and the Confederacy's mounting problems, three obstacles to Union victory remained. Federal troops under General William T. Sherman controlled Chattanooga and the gateway to Georgia, but the Confederate Army of Tennessee, commanded by Joseph E. Johnston, still blocked Sherman's path to Atlanta. Robert E. Lee's formidable Army of Northern Virginia still protected

Richmond. And the Confederacy still controlled the Shenandoah Valley, which fed Lee's armies and supplied his cavalry with horses. In March 1864, Lincoln appointed General Ulysses S. Grant commander of all Union armies. Grant set about devising a strategy to overcome these obstacles.

GRANT'S PLAN TO END THE WAR

Grant brought two innovations to the final campaign. First, he coordinated the Union war effort, directing the Union's armies in Virginia and the Lower South to attack at the same time, keeping steady pressure on all fronts. Second, Grant waged nonstop warfare, eliminating the long periods of rest that had intervened between battles.

Although Grant's strategy ultimately worked, several problems and miscalculations undermined its effectiveness. With Sherman advancing in Georgia, Grant's major focus was Lee's army in Virginia. But Grant underestimated Lee. The Confederate general thwarted him for almost a year and inflicted horrendous casualties on his army. Confederate forces under Jubal Early drove off Union forces from the Shenandoah Valley in June 1864, allowing the Confederates to maintain their supply lines. The incompetence of General Benjamin Butler, charged with advancing up the James River to Richmond in May 1864, further eroded Grant's plan. Grant also had to contend with disaffection in his officer corps. Many officers were loyal to General George McClellan, whom Lincoln had dismissed in 1862, and considered Grant a mediocrity who had triumphed in the West only because his opposition there had been third-rate.

Lee's only hope was to make the campaign so costly that Grant would abandon it before the Southerners ran out of supplies and troops. But Grant kept relentless pressure on Lee.

Grant and General George Meade began their campaign against Lee in May 1864, crossing the Rapidan River near Fredericksburg, Virginia, and marching toward an area known as the Wilderness. Lee attacked the Army of the Potomac, which outnumbered his 118,000 to 60,000, in the Battle of the Wilderness on May 5 and 6 before it could reach open ground. Much of the fighting involved hand-to-hand combat. Gunfire set the dry underbrush ablaze. Wounded soldiers burned to death. The toll was frightful—eighteen thousand casualties on the Union side, ten thousand on the Confederate side.

In the past, Union commanders would have pulled back after such an encounter, but Grant pushed on. Attacking the entrenched Confederate Army at Spotsylvania, his army suffered another eighteen thousand casualties to the Confederates' eleven thousand. Undeterred, Grant moved on toward Cold Harbor, where Lee's troops again awaited him in entrenched positions. Flinging his army against withering Confederate fire on June 3, Grant lost seven thousand men in eight minutes. In less than a month of fighting, the Army of the Potomac had lost 55,000 men. The slaughter undermined Grant's support in Northern public opinion and led peace advocates to renew their quest for a cease-fire.

Abandoning his march on Richmond from the north, Grant shifted his army south of the James River to approach the Confederate capital from the rear. On June 17, 1864, he surprised the Confederates with an attack on Petersburg, a critical rail junction 23 miles south of Richmond. It was a brilliant maneuver, but hesitant Union corps commanders gave Lee time to reinforce the town's defenders. Both armies dug in for a lengthy siege.

While Grant advanced on Lee in Virginia, Union forces under William T. Sherman in Georgia engaged in a deadly dance with the Army of Tennessee under the command of

Union generals (Ulysses Grant, George Meade) conduct a council of war near Massaponax Church, Virginia, May 21, 1864. General Grant is bending over a bench looking over General Meade's shoulder. They are surrounded by military officers.

Source: Library of Congress. Artist: Mathew Brady.

Joseph E. Johnston as they began the Atlanta Campaign, a scheme to take Atlanta, Georgia. Johnston shared Lee's belief that the Confederacy's best hope lay in a defensive strategy. Hoping to lure Sherman into a frontal assault, Johnston settled his forces early in May at Dalton, an important railroad junction in Georgia 25 miles south of Chattanooga and 75 miles north of Atlanta. Instead Sherman made a wide swing around the Confederates, prompting Johnston to abandon Dalton, rush south, and dig in again at Resaca to prevent Sherman from cutting the railroad. Again Sherman swung around without an assault, and again Johnston rushed south to cut him off, this time at Cassville.

This waltz continued for two months until Johnston had retreated to a strong defensive position on Kennesaw Mountain, barely 20 miles north of Atlanta. At this point, early in July, Sherman attacked with disastrous consequences. He resumed his maneuvering and by mid-July had forced Johnston into defensive positions on Peachtree Creek just north of Atlanta. President Davis then replaced Johnston with John Bell Hood of Texas.

In late July, Hood began a series of attacks on Sherman and was thrown back each time with heavy losses. Sherman's flanking maneuvers around the city in late August then left Hood with no choice but to abandon Atlanta and save his army. On the night of September 1, Hood evacuated the city, burning everything of military value.

The loss of Atlanta was a severe blow to the Confederacy and revived the morale of the war-weary North, helping assure Lincoln's reelection in November. The last hope of the Confederacy—that a peace candidate would replace Lincoln and end the war—had faded.

THE ELECTION OF 1864 AND SHERMAN'S MARCH

Northern dismay over Grant's enormous losses and his failure to take Richmond raised the prospect of a Democratic election victory. Nominating George B. McClellan, former commander of the Union's armies, as their presidential candidate, the Democrats appealed to the voters as the party of peace. But the fall of Atlanta and the Union's suddenly improved military fortunes undermined Democratic prospects. In the voting on November 8, Lincoln captured 55 percent of the popular vote, losing only New Jersey, Delaware, and Kentucky. Republicans also retained control of the Senate and the House of Representatives.

The Republican victory reinforced the Union commitment to emancipation. A proposed constitutional amendment outlawing slavery everywhere in the United States, not just those areas still in rebellion, passed Congress and was ratified as the **Thirteenth Amendment** to the U.S. Constitution in 1865.

After Sherman took Atlanta, he proposed to break Confederate resistance once and for all by marching his army to the sea and destroying everything in its path. Sherman's March got under way on November 15. His force of sixty thousand men encountered little resistance, prompting North Carolina's governor, Zebulon Vance, to comment, "It shows what I have always believed, that the great *popular heart* is not now and never had been in this war!" Sherman entered Savannah on December 22, 1864. Just a few weeks earlier, Union forces in Tennessee had routed Hood's army at the Battle of Franklin and then crushed it entirely at the Battle of Nashville. Hood's defeat removed any threat to Sherman's rear.

In February 1865 Sherman headed for South Carolina where the Civil War had begun. "The truth is," Sherman wrote "the whole army is burning with an insatiable desire to wreak vengeance on South Carolina." Sherman's troops wreaked greater destruction in South Carolina than they had in Georgia and burned the state capitol at Columbia. Sherman ordered black troops to be the first to take possession of Charleston.

Sherman ended his march in Goldsboro, North Carolina, in March 1865. Behind the Union army lay a barren swath 425 miles long from Savannah to Goldsboro.

In a move reflecting their desperation in March 1865, Confederate leaders revived a proposal that they had previously rejected to arm and free slaves. The issue divided Confederate leaders. Confederate general Howell Cobb argued that "if slaves will make good soldiers, our whole theory of slavery is wrong." Others thought it was preferable to abandon slavery than to lose independence. Slaves themselves greeted the proposal with little enthusiasm.

On March 13, 1865, the Confederate Congress passed a bill to enlist black soldiers without a provision offering them freedom but President Davis and the War Office promised immediate freedom to slaves who enlisted. The war ended before the order could have any effect. The irony was that in the summer of 1864, a majority of Northerners probably would have accepted reunion without emancipation had the Confederacy abandoned its fight.

THE ROAD TO APPOMATTOX AND THE DEATH OF LINCOLN

Lee's army remained the last obstacle to Union victory. On April 1, Lee was forced to abandon Petersburg and the defense of Richmond. He tried a daring run westward hoping to secure much-needed supplies and join Johnston's Army of Tennessee in North Carolina to

This photograph of Abraham Lincoln was taken four days before John Wilkes Booth assassinated him in Ford's Theater.

continue the fight. While President Davis fled Richmond with his cabinet and headed toward North Carolina, Grant cut off Lee's escape at Appomattox Court House Virginia, on April 7. Convinced that further resistance was futile, he surrendered on April 9. Grant allowed Lee's men to go home unmolested and to take with them horses or mules "to put in a crop." Grant reported feeling "sad and depressed" at "the downfall of a foe who had fought so long and valiantly."

The fleeing Davis met Joseph E. Johnston at Greensboro, North Carolina, hoping to convince him to continue fighting, but Johnston surrendered to Sherman near Durham, North Carolina, on April 26. On May 10, Union cavalry captured Davis and his companions and within two weeks the Civil War came to an end.

Washington greeted the Confederate surrender at Appomattox with raucous rejoicing. On April 11, President Lincoln spoke briefly of his plans to reconstruct the South with the help of persons loyal to the Union, including recently freed slaves. At least one listener found the speech disappointing. Sometime actor and full-time Confederate patriot John Wilkes Booth muttered to a friend in the throng, "That means nigger citizenship. Now, by God . . . That is the last speech he will ever make."

On the evening of April 14, Good Friday, the president went to Ford's Theater in Washington to view a comedy, *Our American Cousin*. During the performance, Booth shot the president, wounding him mortally, then jumped from Lincoln's box to the stage shouting "Sic semper tyrannis" ("Thus ever to tyrants") and fled the theater. Union troops tracked him down to a barn in northern Virginia and killed him.

Southerners reacted to Lincoln's assassination with mixed emotions. Many saw in the death of the man they had regarded as their bitterest enemy for four years some slight hope of relief for the South's otherwise bleak prospects. But General Johnston and others like him understood Lincoln's influence with the radical elements in the Republican party who were pressing for harsh terms against the South. The president's death, Johnston wrote, was "the greatest possible calamity to the South."

Conclusion

Just before the war, William Sherman had warned a friend from Virginia, "You people of the South don't know what you are doing. This country will be drenched in blood. . . ." He was right. More than 365,000 Union soldiers died during the war, 110,000 in battle, and more than 256,000 Confederate soldiers, 94,000 of them in battle. Total casualties on both sides, including wounded, were more than 1 million. Compounding the suffering of the individuals behind these gruesome statistics was the incalculable suffering—in terms of grief, fatherless children, women who never married, families never made whole—of the people close to them.

The war devastated the South. The region lost one-fourth of its white male population between the ages of 20 and 40, two-fifths of its livestock, and half its farm machinery. Union armies destroyed many of the South's railroads and shattered its industry. Between 1860 and 1870, the wealth of the South declined by 60 percent, and its share of the nation's total wealth dropped from more than 30 percent to 12 percent. The wealth of the North, in contrast, increased by half in the same period.

For black Southerners, emancipation was the war's most significant achievement. The issue that dominated the prewar sectional debate had vanished.

The Civil War stimulated other significant changes. It taught the effectiveness of centralized management, new financial techniques, and the coordination of production, marketing, and distribution. Entrepreneurs would apply these lessons to create the expanding corporations of the postwar American economy. By opening new opportunities to women in fields such as nursing and teaching, the war also helped lay the foundation for the woman suffrage movement of the 1870s and 1880s.

The war was not responsible for every postwar change in American society, and it left many features of American life intact. For example, the war did not soften class antagonisms. Capitalism, not labor, triumphed during the war, and industrialists and entrepreneurs, not working people, most benefited from its bonanza. Lincoln brutally suppressed strikes at defense plants and threw labor leaders into military prisons.

The war to end slavery did change some American racial attitudes, especially in the North. When Lincoln broadened the war's objectives to include the abolition of slavery, he connected the success of the Union to freedom for the slave. By the end of the war, perhaps a majority of Northerners supported granting freedmen the right to vote and to equal protection under the law, even if they believed (as many did) that black people were inferior to white people. The courage of black troops and the efforts of African-American leaders to link the causes of reunion and freedom were influential in bringing about this shift.

Most white Southerners did not experience a similar enlightenment. They greeted the end of slavery with fear, anger, and regret. The freed slaves were living reminders of the South's defeat and the end of a way of life grounded in white supremacy.

If the Civil War resolved the sectional dispute of the 1850s by ending slavery and denying the right of the Southern states to secede, it created two new equally troubling problems: how to reunite South and North and how to deal with the legacy of slavery.

In November 1863, President Lincoln was asked to say a few words at the dedication of the federal cemetery at Gettysburg. There, surrounded by fresh graves, Lincoln bound the cause of the Union to that of the country's founders: "Fourscore and seven years ago our fathers brought forth upon this continent a new nation, conceived in liberty and dedicated to the proposition that all men are created equal. Now we are engaged in a great civil war, testing whether that nation, or any nation so conceived and so dedicated can long endure." A Union victory, Lincoln hoped, would not only honor the past but also call forth a new nation, cleansed of its sins, to inspire oppressed peoples around the world. He called on the nation to resolve "that the nation shall, under God, have a new birth of freedom; and that government of the people, by the people, for the people, shall not perish from the earth." The two-minute Gettysburg Address captured what Union supporters were fighting for and connected their sacrifices to the noble causes of freedom and democratic government. That would be both the hope and the challenge of the peace that followed a hard war.

REVIEW QUESTIONS

1. How did the Union and the Confederacy compare in terms of resources, leadership, and military strategies? How did these factors affect the course of the war?

2. Why were the battles of Antietam and Gettysburg turning points in the war?

3. How did the Emancipation Proclamation affect the Union and Confederate causes?

4. What roles did women play in the North and in the South during the Civil War?

5. What changes resulted from the Civil War?

6. Why did Sullivan Ballou fight?

Reconstruction

1865–1877

Why did Southerners remember the Civil War as a Lost Cause?

What were African-American aspirations in 1865?

How did Presidential Reconstruction differ from Congressional Reconstruction?

What role did the Ku Klux Klan play in Counter-Reconstruction?

What were the effects of the Civil Rights Act of 1875 and the Compromise of 1877?

Why and how did Reconstruction end, and what were its failed promises?

✖

Marianna, Florida 1866

The white academy opened about the same time the church opened the school for the Negro children. As the colored children had to pass the academy to reach the church it was easy for the white children to annoy them with taunts and jeers. The war passed from words to stones which the white children began to hurl at the colored. Several colored children were hurt and, as they had not resented the rock-throwing in kind because they were timid about going that far, the white children became more aggressive and abusive.

One morning the colored children armed themselves with stones and determined to fight their way past the academy to their school. [They] approached the academy in formation whereas in the past they had been going in pairs or small groups. When they reached hailing distance, a half dozen white boys rushed out and hurled their missiles. Instead of scampering away, the colored children not only stood their ground and hurled their missiles but maintained a solemn silence. The white children, seeing there was no backing down as they expected, came rushing out of the academy and charged the colored children.

During some fifteen minutes it was a real tug of war. In the close fighting the colored children got the advantage gradually and began to shove the white children back. As they pressed the advantage the white children broke away and ran for the academy. The colored fighters did not follow them but made it hot for the laggards until they also took to their heels. There were many bruises on both sides, but it taught the white youngsters to leave the colored ones alone thereafter.

—T. Thomas Fortune,
Norfolk Journal and Guide

T. Thomas Fortune, "Norfolk Journal and Guide," August 20, 1927, reprinted in Dorothy Sterling, ed., *The Trouble They Seen: Black People Tell the Story of Reconstruction* (Garden City, NY: Doubleday & Co., 1976), pp. 22–24.

T. THOMAS FORTUNE, a New York newspaper editor, recalled this battle between black and white schoolchildren sixty years earlier, at the beginning of the Reconstruction era. In the scheme of things, it did not amount to much. However, for ten-year-old Thomas, born a slave in Marianna, the incident encapsulated the dilemma of Reconstruction. In the journey from slavery to freedom, education was an important element of full citizenship for African Americans. The eagerness with which black children (and adults) flooded schools was matched by the hostility of the white community who resented any pretense of equality that education implied.

Reconstruction was not merely a series of white aggressions against African-American aspirations, followed by black retreats. The violence and disorder that punctuated Southern society after the Civil War was due in part to the refusal of black people to relinquish their dreams of equal citizenship, including the right to a decent education.

Young Thomas did not back down, though by 1878 he felt that the journey from slavery to freedom would always be incomplete in the South. Together with his young bride, Carrie Smiley of Jacksonville, Florida, Thomas left for New York City, where he obtained a job as a printer for the *New York Sun*. He died there in 1928. New York's gain was the South's loss, a process repeated many times over after the Civil War as talented young black men and women left the region of their birth and their ancestors. It was a double tragedy for the South: losing people who could have rebuilt a shattered region, and missing the opportunity to create a society based on racial equality.

White Southerners and the Ghosts of the Confederacy, 1865

Confederate soldiers—generals and troops alike—returned to devastated homes they could scarcely recognize. Their cause lost and their society reviled, white Southerners lived through the summer and fall of 1865 surrounded by ghosts—the ghosts of lost loved ones, joyful times, bountiful harvests, self-assurance, and slavery. Defeat shook the basic tenets of their religious beliefs. But many other white Southerners refused to accept their defeat as a divine judgment. Instead, they insisted, God had spared the South for a greater purpose. Robert E. Lee became the patron saint of this cause, his poignant nobility a contrast to the crassness of the Yankee warlords. Some white Southerners would not allow the memory of the bloody struggle to die, transforming it into the ***Lost Cause***, a symbol of courage against great odds. The Old South was transformed into a stainless civilization, worth fighting and dying for, and the Civil War became not a savage conflict, but a romantic and chivalrous contest.

Fifteen years after the war, Mark Twain traveled the length of the East Coast. After visiting a gentlemen's club in Boston, he recalled that the conversation had covered a variety of topics, none of which included the Civil War. Northerners had relegated that conflict to history books and moved on. In the South, on the other hand, defeat and destruction demanded rationalization and remembrance.

Most white Southerners approached the great issues of freedom and reunification with unyielding views. They saw African Americans as a direct challenge to white people's beliefs in their own racial superiority.

More than Freedom: African-American Aspirations in 1865

If black people could have peered into the minds of white Southerners, they would have been stunned. The former slaves did not initially even dream of social equality; far less did they plot the kind of vengeful murder and mayhem white people feared. They did harbor two potentially contradictory aspirations. The first was to be left alone, free of white supervision. The second was land, voting and civil rights, and education. To secure these, they needed the intervention and support of the white power structure.

The first step Congress took beyond emancipation was to establish the Bureau of Refugees, Freedmen, and Abandoned Lands in March 1865. Congress envisioned the *Freedmen's Bureau*, as it came to be called, as a multipurpose agency to provide social, educational, and economic services, advice, and protection to former slaves and destitute whites. The Bureau marked the federal government's first foray into social welfare legislation. Congress also authorized the bureau to rent confiscated and abandoned farmland to freedmen in 40-acre plots with an option to buy.

EDUCATION

The greatest success of the Freedmen's Bureau was in education. The Bureau coordinated more than fifty Northern philanthropic and religious groups, which in turn established three thousand freedmen's schools in the South serving 150,000 men, women, and children.

Initially, single young women from the Northeast comprised much of the teaching force. One of them, a 26-year-old Quaker named Martha Schofield, came to Aiken, South Carolina, from rural Pennsylvania in 1865. The school she founded has been part of Aiken's public school system since 1953.

By the time Schofield opened her own school in 1871, black teachers outnumbered white teachers in the "colored" schools. Support for them came from black churches, especially the African Methodist Episcopal (AME) Church. The former slaves crowded into basements, shacks, and churches to attend school. At the end of the Civil War, only about 10 percent of black Southerners were literate, compared with more than 70 percent of the white Southerners. Within a decade, the freedmen's schools had reduced illiteracy among the former slaves to below 70 percent.

Some black Southerners went on to one of the thirteen colleges established by the American Missionary Association and black and white churches. Between 1860 and 1880 more than one thousand black Southerners earned college degrees at institutions still serving students today such as Howard University in Washington, D.C., Fisk University in Nashville, and Biddle Institute (now Johnson C. Smith University) in Charlotte.

"FORTY ACRES AND A MULE"

Although education was important to the freed slaves in their quest for civic equality, land ownership offered them the promise of economic independence.

Even before the war's end, rumors circulated through black communities in the South that the government would provide each black family with 40 acres and a mule. These rumors were fueled by General William T. Sherman's *Field Order No. 15* in January 1865, which set aside a vast swath of abandoned land along the South Atlantic coast from the Charleston area to northern Florida for grants of up to 40 acres. The Freedmen's Bureau likewise raised expectations when it was initially authorized to rent 40-acre plots of confiscated or abandoned land to freedmen.

By June 1865, about forty thousand former slaves had settled on "Sherman land" along the southeastern coast. In 1866, Congress passed the *Southern Homestead Act*, giving black people preferential access to public lands in five southern states. By the late 1870s, more than fourteen thousand African-American families had taken advantage of a program to finance land purchases with state-funded, long-term, low-interest loans.

Land ownership did not ensure financial success. Most black-owned farms were small and on marginal land. Black farmers also had trouble obtaining credit to purchase or expand their holdings. A lifetime of field work left some freedmen without the managerial skills to operate a farm.

The vast majority of former slaves, especially those in the Lower South, never fulfilled their dreams of land ownership. Rumors to the contrary, the federal government never intended to implement a land redistribution program in the South. General Sherman viewed his field order as a temporary measure to support freedmen for the remainder of the war. President Andrew Johnson nullified the order in September 1865, returning confiscated lands to their former owners. Even Republican supporters of black land ownership questioned the constitutionality of seizing privately owned real estate. They envisioned former slaves assuming the status of free laborers, not necessarily of independent landowners.

MIGRATION TO CITIES

While some black Southerners asserted their rights as workers on Southern farms, others affirmed their freedom by moving to towns and cities. Even before the war, the city had offered slaves and free black people a measure of freedom unknown in the rural South. After the war, African Americans moved to cities to find families, seek work, escape the tedium and supervision of farm life, or simply test their right to move about. Between 1860 and 1870, the official African-American population in every major Southern city rose significantly.

Once in the city, freedmen had to find a home and a job. They usually settled for the cheapest accommodations in low-lying areas or on the outskirts of town where building codes did not apply. Rather than developing one large ghetto, as in many Northern cities, black Southerners lived in several concentrations in and around cities.

Sometimes armed with a letter of reference from their former masters, black people went door to door to seek employment. Many found work serving white families—as guards, laundresses, maids—for very low wages. Both skilled and unskilled laborers found work rebuilding war-torn cities like Atlanta.

FAITH AND FREEDOM

Religious faith framed and inspired the efforts of African Americans to test their freedom on the farm and in the city. White Southerners used religion to transform the Lost Cause from a shattering defeat to a premonition of a greater destiny. Black Southerners, in contrast, saw emancipation in biblical terms as the beginning of an exodus from bondage to the Promised Land.

Some black churches in the postwar South originated in the slavery era, but most split from white-dominated congregations after the war. The church became a primary focus of African-American life. It gave black people the opportunity to hone skills in self-government and administration that white-dominated society denied them. Within the supportive confines of the congregation, they could assume leadership positions, render important decisions, deal with financial matters, and engage in politics. The church also operated as an educational institution.

The church spawned other organizations that served the black community over the next century. Burial societies, Masonic lodges, temperance groups, trade unions, and drama clubs originated in churches. By the 1870s, African Americans in Memphis had more than two hundred such organizations.

· C H R O N O L O G Y ·

1863 Lincoln proposes his Ten Percent Plan.

1864 Congress proposes the Wade Davis Bill.

1865 Sherman issues Field Order No. 15.
Freedmen's Bureau is established.
Andrew Johnson succeeds to the presidency, unveils his Reconstruction plan.
Massachusetts desegregates all public facilities.
Black people in several Southern cities organize Union Leagues.
Former Confederate states begin to pass black codes.

1866 Congress passes Southern Homestead Act, Civil Rights Act of 1866.
Ku Klux Klan is founded.
Fourteenth Amendment to the Constitution is passed (ratified in 1868).
President Johnson goes on a speaking tour.

1867 Congress passes Military Reconstruction Acts, Tenure of Office Act.

1868 President Johnson is impeached and tried in the Senate for defying the Tenure of Office Act.
Republican Ulysses S. Grant is elected president.

1869 Fifteenth Amendment passed (ratified 1870).

1870 Congress passes Enforcement Act.
Republican regimes topple in North Carolina and Georgia.

1871 Congress passes Ku Klux Klan Act.

1872 Freedmen's Bureau closes down.
Liberal Republicans emerge as a separate party.
Ulysses S. Grant is reelected.

1873 Severe depression begins.
Colfax Massacre occurs.
U.S. Supreme Court's decision in the *Slaughterhouse* cases weakens the intent of the Fourteenth Amendment.
Texas falls to the Democrats in the fall elections.

1874 White Leaguers attempt a coup against the Republican government of New Orleans.
Democrats win off year elections across the South amid widespread fraud and violence.

1875 Congress passes Civil Rights Act of 1875.

1876 Supreme Court's decision in *United States* v. *Cruikshank* nullifies Enforcement Act of 1870.
Outcome of the presidential election between Republican Rutherford B. Hayes and Democrat Samuel J. Tilden is contested.

1877 Compromise of 1877 makes Hayes president and ends Reconstruction.

The church and the congregation were a cohesive force in black communities. They supported families under stress from discrimination and poverty. Most black churches looked inward to strengthen their members against the harsh realities of postbellum Southern society. Few ministers dared to engage in or even support protest activities. Some, especially those in the Colored Methodist Episcopal Church, counseled congregants to abide by the rules of second-class citizenship and to trust in God's will to right the wrongs of racism.

Northern-based denominations, however, notably the AME Church, were more aggressive advocates of black rights. AME ministers stressed the responsibility of individual black people to realize God's will of racial equality. Henry McNeal Turner, probably the most influential AME minister of his day, helped expand the denomination into the South from its small, primarily Northern base at the end of the Civil War. His church elevated him to bishop in 1880.

Turner's career and the efforts of former slaves in the classroom, on the farm, in cities, and in the churches reflect the enthusiasm and expectations with which black Southerners greeted freedom. But the majority of white Southerners were unwilling to see those expectations fulfilled.

Federal Reconstruction, 1865–1870

When the Civil War ended in 1865, no acceptable blueprint existed for reconstituting the Union. In 1863, Lincoln proposed to readmit a seceding state if 10 percent of its prewar voters took an oath of loyalty to the Union and it prohibited slavery in a new state constitution. But this Ten Percent Plan did not require states to grant equal civil and political rights to former slaves, and many Republicans in Congress thought it was not stringent enough. In 1864, a group of them responded with the Wade-Davis Bill, which required a *majority* of a state's prewar voters to pledge their loyalty to the Union and demanded guarantees of black equality before the law. The bill was passed, but Lincoln kept it from becoming law by refusing to sign it (an action known as a pocket veto).

The controversy over these plans reflected two obstacles to Reconstruction that would continue to plague the ruling Republicans after the war. First, neither the Constitution nor legal precedent offered any guidance on whether the president or Congress should take the lead on Reconstruction policy. Second, there was no agreement on what that policy should be.

President Andrew Johnson, some conservative Republicans, and most Democrats believed that because the Constitution made no mention of secession, the Southern states never left the Union, so there was no need for a formal process to readmit them. Moderate and radical Republicans disagreed, arguing that the defeated states had forfeited their rights. Moderates and radicals parted company, however, on the conditions necessary for readmission to the Union. No group held a majority in Congress, and legislators sometimes changed their positions.

PRESIDENTIAL RECONSTRUCTION, 1865–1867

When the Civil War ended in April 1865, Congress was not in session and would not reconvene until December. Thus the responsibility for developing a Reconstruction policy initially fell on Andrew Johnson, who succeeded to the presidency upon Lincoln's assassination. Johnson seemed well suited to the difficult task. Johnson was the only Southern senator to remain in the U.S. Senate after secession. This defiant Unionism won him popular acclaim in the North and credibility among Republican leaders.

Most Northerners and many Republicans approved Johnson's Reconstruction plan when he unveiled it in May 1865. Johnson extended pardons and restored property rights, except in slaves, to Southerners who swore an oath of allegiance to the Union and the Constitution. The plan had nothing to say about the voting rights and civil rights of former slaves.

Northern Democrats applauded the plan's silence on these issues and its promise of a quick restoration of the Southern states to the Union. They expected the Southern states to favor their party and expand its political power. White Southerners, however, were not so favorably impressed, and their response turned Northern public opinion against the president. On the two great issues of freedom and reunion, white Southerners quickly demonstrated their eagerness to reverse the results of the Civil War. Although most states accepted President Johnson's modest requirements, several objected to one or more provisions. Mississippi and Texas refused to ratify the Thirteenth Amendment, which abolished slavery. South Carolina declined to nullify its secession ordinance. No Southern state authorized black voting. When Johnson ordered special congressional elections in the South in the fall of 1865, the all-white electorate returned many prominent Confederate leaders to office.

In late 1865, the newly elected Southern state legislatures revised their antebellum slave codes. The updated and renamed **black codes** allowed local officials to arrest black people who could not document employment and residence, or who were "disorderly," and sentence them to forced labor on farms or road construction crews. The codes also restricted black people to certain occupations, barred them from jury duty, and forbade them to possess firearms. President Johnson did not seem perturbed about this turn of events.

The Republican-dominated Congress reconvened in December 1865 in a belligerent mood. A consensus formed among radical Republicans, who comprised nearly half of the party's strength in Congress, that to gain readmission, a state would have to extend suffrage to black citizens, protect freedmen's civil rights, and have its white citizens officially acknowledge these rights. Some radicals also supported the redistribution of land to former slaves, but few pressed for social equality.

Thaddeus Stevens of Pennsylvania led the radical forces in the House of Representatives, while abolitionist veteran Charles Sumner of Massachusetts rallied radicals in the Senate. Stevens dreamed of a South populated by white and black yeoman farmers. With no large plantations and few landless farmers, the South would become an ideal republic, a boon to the rest of the nation instead of a burden. Few shared his vision, and when he died in 1868, a reporter noted that "no man was oftener outvoted."

Charles Sumner was among the foremost abolitionist politicians before the Civil War. His combative nature won him few friends, even within his own party. As fierce as Stevens was in the promotion of black civil and political rights after the war, he also believed that the Reconstruction era offered a "golden moment" to remake the South into an egalitarian region. Sumner died in 1874 as his dream was fading.

But the radicals could not unite behind a program, and it fell to their moderate colleagues to take the first steps toward a Congressional Reconstruction plan. The moderates shared the radicals' desire to protect the former slaves' civil and voting rights, but they would not support land redistribution schemes or punitive measures against prominent Confederates. The Civil Rights Act of 1866 was a direct response to the black codes. The act specified the civil rights to which all U.S. citizens were entitled. In creating a category of national citizenship with rights that superseded state laws restricting them, the act changed federal–state relations (and in the process overturned the *Dred Scott* decision). President Johnson vetoed the act, but it became law when Congress mustered a two-thirds majority to override his veto, the first time in American history that Congress passed major legislation over a president's veto.

Andrew Johnson's position reflected both his view of government and his racial attitudes. The Republican president remained a Democrat in spirit. Like most Democrats, he favored a balance between federal and state power. He also shared with many of his white Southern neighbors a belief in black inferiority.

To keep freedmen's rights safe from presidential vetoes, state legislatures, and federal courts, the Republican-dominated Congress moved to incorporate some of the provisions of the 1866 Civil Rights Act into the Constitution with an amendment. The **Fourteenth Amendment**, which Congress passed in June 1866, addressed the issues of civil and voting rights. It guaranteed every citizen equality before the law. The two key sections of the amendment prohibited states from violating the civil rights of their citizens, thus outlawing the black codes, and gave states the choice of enfranchising black people or losing representation in Congress.

The amendment disappointed advocates of woman suffrage, because for the first time the word *male* in the Constitution was used to define who could vote. Susan B. Anthony, who had campaigned for the abolition of slavery before the war and helped mount a petition drive that collected 400,000 signatures for the Thirteenth Amendment, formed the American Equal Rights Association in 1866 with her colleagues to push for woman suffrage at the state level.

The amendment had little immediate impact on the South. Although enforcement of black codes diminished, white violence against blacks increased. In the 1870s, several decisions by the U.S. Supreme Court would weaken the amendment's provisions. Eventually, however, the Fourteenth Amendment would play a major role in securing the civil rights of African Americans when the issue reemerged in the 1950s.

President Johnson seemed to encourage white intransigence by openly denouncing the Fourteenth Amendment. The president's diatribes against the Republican Congress won him followers in those Northern states with a reservoir of opposition to black suffrage. But the tone and manner of his campaign offended many as undignified.

CONGRESSIONAL RECONSTRUCTION, 1867–1870

The radicals' first salvo in their attempt to take control over Reconstruction occurred with the passage over President Johnson's veto of the Military Reconstruction Acts. The measures, passed in March 1867, inaugurated a period known as *Congressional Reconstruction* or Radical Reconstruction. They generally divided the ex-Confederate states into five military districts and provided for elections to a state constitutional convention guaranteeing universal manhood suffrage.

The Reconstruction Acts fulfilled the radicals' three major objectives. First, they secured the freedmen's right to vote. Second, they made it likely that Southern states would be run by Republican regimes that would enforce the new constitutions, protect former slaves' rights, and maintain the Republican majority in Congress. Finally, the acts set standards for readmission that required the South to accept the consequences of defeat: the preeminence of the federal government and the end of involuntary servitude.

To limit presidential interference with their policies, Republicans passed the Tenure of Office Act, prohibiting the president from removing certain officeholders without the Senate's consent. Johnson, angered at what he believed was an unconstitutional attack on presidential authority, deliberately violated the act in February 1868. He fired Secretary of War Edwin M. Stanton, a leading radical. The House responded to this defiance of congressional authority by approving, for the first time in American history, articles of impeachment against the president. The Senate voted thirty-five to nineteen to convict, one vote short of the two-thirds necessary to remove Johnson. The outcome weakened the radicals' clout in Congress and eased the way for moderate Republican Ulysses S. Grant to gain the party's nomination for president in 1868.

The Republicans viewed the 1868 presidential election as a referendum on Congressional Reconstruction. Grant won the election, but his margin of victory was uncomfortably narrow.

The Republicans retained a strong majority in both houses of Congress and managed to pass another major piece of Reconstruction legislation, the *Fifteenth Amendment*, in February 1869. In response to growing concerns about voter fraud and violence against freedmen, the amendment guaranteed the right of American men to vote, regardless of race. Although the amendment provided a loophole allowing states to impose restrictions on the right to vote based on literacy requirements or property qualifications, it was nonetheless a milestone. It made the right to vote perhaps the most distinguishing characteristic of American citizenship.

The Fifteenth Amendment allowed states to keep the franchise a male prerogative. Susan B. Anthony now broke with her abolitionist colleagues and opposed the amendment. Fellow abolitionist and woman suffragist Elizabeth Cady Stanton warned that "if you do not wish the lower orders of Chinese, African, Germans and Irish, with their low ideas of womanhood to make laws for you and your daughters . . . awake to the danger . . . and demand that woman, too, shall be represented in the government!" Such ethnic and racial animosity created a major rift in the nascent women's movement. Women who supported the amendment formed the New England Woman Suffrage Association, challenging Anthony's American Equal Rights Association.

SOUTHERN REPUBLICAN GOVERNMENTS, 1867–1870

Away from Washington, the first order of business was to draft state constitutions. The documents embodied progressive principles new to the former Confederacy. They mandated the election of numerous local and state offices. Self-perpetuating local elites could no longer appoint themselves or cronies to powerful positions. The constitutions committed Southern states, many for the first time, to public education. Lawmakers enacted a variety of reforms, including social welfare, penal reform, legislative reapportionment, and universal manhood suffrage.

The Republican regimes that gained control in Southern states promoted vigorous state government and the protection of civil and voting rights. Three diverse Republican constituencies supported these governments. One consisted of white natives, most of them yeomen farmers, who resided mainly in the upland regions of the South and long ignored by lowland planters and merchants in state government. The conflict had left many of them devastated. They struggled to keep their land and hoped for an easing of credit and for debt-stay laws to help them escape foreclosure. They wanted public schools for their children and good roads to get their crops to market. Collectively, these native white Southerners were called *scalawags*, a derogatory term derived from the name of the district of Scalloway, on Scotland's Shetland Islands, known for its scraggly livestock. The term was first applied in western New York before the Civil War to an idle person and then to a mischievous one. Although their opponents may have perceived them as a unified group, scalawags in fact held a variety of views.

Northern transplants, or *carpetbaggers*, as their opponents called them, constituted a second group of Southern Republicans. The term also had antebellum origins, referring to a suspicious stranger. Cartoonists depicted carpetbaggers as shoddily dressed and poorly groomed men, their worldly possessions in a ratty cloth satchel, slinking into a town and swindling the locals before departing with their ill-gotten gains. The reality was far different from the caricature. Many were Union soldiers who simply enjoyed the climate and perhaps married a local woman. Most were drawn by economic opportunity. Land was cheap and the price of cotton high. Some also hoped to aid the freedmen.

Carpetbaggers never comprised more than 2 percent of any state's population. Most white Southerners viewed them as an alien presence, instruments of a hated occupying force. They provoked resentment because they seemed to prosper while most Southerners struggled in poverty.

African Americans constituted the Republican party's largest Southern constituency. In three states—South Carolina, Mississippi, and Louisiana—they also formed the majority of eligible voters. They viewed the franchise as the key to civic equality and economic opportunity and demanded an active role in party and government affairs. In February 1865, black people in Norfolk, Virginia, gathered to demand a say in the new government that Union supporters were forming in that portion of the state. In April, they created the Colored Monitor Union club, modeled after Republican party organizations in Northern cities, called **Union Leagues**. They demanded "the right of *universal* suffrage" for "*all* loyal men, without distinction of color." Despite white threats, black people thronged to Union League meetings in 1867, even forging interracial alliances in states such as North Carolina and Alabama. Focusing on political education and recruitment, the leagues successfully mobilized black voters.

Black Southerners were not content just to vote; they also demanded political office. The number of Southern black congressmen in the U.S. House of Representatives increased from two in 1869 to seven in 1873, and more than six hundred African Americans, most of them former slaves from plantation counties, were elected to Southern state legislatures between 1867 and 1877.

White fears that black officeholders would enact vengeful legislation proved unfounded. African Americans generally did not promote race-specific legislation. Rather, they supported measures such as debt relief and state funding for education that benefited all poor and working-class people. Like all politicians, however, black officials in Southern cities sought to enact measures beneficial to their constituents.

Republicans gained support by expanding the role of state government to a degree unprecedented in the South. Southern Republican administrations appealed to hard-pressed upland whites by prohibiting foreclosure and passing stay laws that allowed farm owners extra time to repay debts. They undertook building programs that benefited both blacks and whites, erecting hospitals, schools, and orphanages. Stepping further into social policy than most Northern states at the time, Republican governments in the South expanded women's property rights, enacted legislation against child abuse, and required child support from fathers of mulatto children. In South Carolina, the Republican government provided medical care for the poor; in Alabama, it provided free legal aid for needy defendants.

Counter-Reconstruction, 1870–1874

Republicans might have survived battles over patronage, differences over policy, and the resentment provoked by extravagant expenditures and high taxes; but they could not overcome racism. Racism killed Republican rule in the South because it deepened divisions within the party, encouraged white violence, and eroded support in the North. Southern Democrats discovered that they could use race baiting and racial violence to create racial solidarity among white people that overrode their economic and class differences. Unity translated into election victories.

Northerners responded to the persistent violence in the South not with outrage but with a growing sense of tedium. Racism became respectable. Noted intellectuals and journalists espoused "scientific" theories that claimed to demonstrate the natural superiority of white people over black people. These theories influenced the Liberal Republicans, followers of a new political movement that splintered the Republican party, further weakening its will to pursue Reconstruction policy.

THE USES OF VIOLENCE

Racial violence preceded Republican rule. As African Americans moved about, attempted to vote, haggled over labor contracts, and carried arms as part of occupying Union forces, they tested the patience of white Southerners.

Cities, where black and white people competed for jobs and where black political influence was most visible, became flashpoints for interracial violence.

White paramilitary groups flourished in the South during the Reconstruction era and were responsible for much of the violence directed against African Americans. Probably the best known of these groups was the ***Ku Klux Klan***. Founded in Tennessee by six Confederate veterans in 1866, the Klan was initially a social club that soon assumed a political purpose. Klan night riders in ghostlike disguises intimidated black communities. The Klan directed much of its violence toward subverting the electoral process. One historian has estimated that roughly 10 percent of all black delegates to the 1867 state constitutional conventions in the South became victims of political violence during the next decade. The most serious example of political violence occurred in Colfax, Louisiana, in 1873 when a white Democratic mob attempted to wrest control of local government from Republicans. For three weeks, black defenders held the town against the white onslaught. When the white mob finally broke through, they massacred the remaining black people, including those who had surrendered and laid down their weapons.

Racial violence and the combative reaction it provoked both among black people and Republican administrations energized white voters. Democrats regained power in North Carolina during the election of 1870, and that same year, the Republican regime in Georgia fell as well.

The federal government responded with a variety of legislation. One example was the Fifteenth Amendment, ratified in 1869, which guaranteed the right to vote. Another was the Enforcement Act of 1870, which enabled the federal government to appoint supervisors in states that failed to protect citizens' voting rights. A more sweeping measure was the Ku Klux Klan Act of 1871, which permitted federal authorities, with military assistance, if necessary, to arrest and prosecute members of groups that denied a citizen's civil rights if state authorities failed to do so and established a new precedent in federal–state relations.

THE FAILURE OF NORTHERN WILL

The success of political violence after 1871 reflected less the inadequacy of congressional legislation than the failure of will on the part of Northern Republicans to follow through on commitments to Southern Republican administrations. The commitment to voting rights for black Southerners, widespread among Republicans in 1865 and affirmed in the Fifteenth Amendment passed in 1869, faded as well. American politics in the 1870s seemed increasingly corrupt and irresponsible. Scandal abounded. Democratic boss William M. Tweed and his associates transformed Tammany Hall, a Democratic club, into a full-fledged political machine that robbed New York City of an astounding $100 million. Federal officials allowed private individuals to manipulate the stock market for spectacular gains. Several members of Congress and President Grant's vice president exchanged government favors for railroad stock.

Racism gained an aura of scientific respectability in the late nineteenth century. Science was held in high esteem at the time, helping ensure public acceptance of the putatively scientific views of the racial theorists. According to those views, some peoples are inherently inferior to others, a natural state of affairs that no government interference can change.

Concerns about the quality of the electorate, also tinged with racism, reflected the rising stakes of public office in post–Civil War America. The urban industrial economy boomed in the five years after the war. Engineers flung railroads across the continent. Steam propelled factories to unprecedented levels of productivity and ships to new speed records.

Discoveries of rich natural resources such as oil and iron presaged a new age of industrial might. Republicans promoted and benefited from the boom, and it influenced their priorities. Railroad, mining, and lumber lobbyists crowded Washington and state capitals begging for financial subsidies and favorable legislation. In an era before conflict-of-interest laws, leading Republicans sat on the boards of railroads, land development companies, and industrial corporations. While the federal government denied land to the freedmen, it doled out millions of acres to corporations.

Not all Republicans approved the party's promotion of economic development. Some questioned the prudence of government intervention in the "natural" operation of the nation's economy. The emerging scandals of the Grant administration led to calls for reform. Republican governments, North and South, were condemned for their lavish spending and high taxes. The time had come to restore good government.

LIBERAL REPUBLICANS AND THE ELECTION OF 1872

Liberal Republicans put forward an array of suggestions to improve government and save the Republican party. They advocated civil service reform to reduce reliance on patronage and the abuses that accompanied office seeking. To limit government and reduce artificial economic stimuli, the reformers called for tariff reduction and an end to federal land grants to railroads. For the South, they recommended a general amnesty for white people and a return to "local self-government" by men of "property and enterprise."

When the Liberals failed to convince other Republicans to adopt their program, they broke with the party. Taking advantage of this split, the Democrats forged an alliance with the Liberals. Together, the Democrats and Liberals nominated journalist Horace Greeley to challenge Ulysses S. Grant for the presidency in the election of 1872. Grant won resoundingly, helped by high turnout among black voters in the South. The election suggested that the excesses of the Grant administration had not yet exceeded public tolerance and that the Republican experiment in the South retained some public support. But within a year, an economic depression, continued violence in the South, and the persistent corruption of the Grant administration would turn public opinion against the Republicans. With this shift, support for Reconstruction and black rights would also fade.

Redemption, 1874–1877

For Southern Democrats, the Republican victory in 1872 underscored the importance of turning out larger numbers of white voters and restricting the black vote. They accomplished these goals over the next four years with a surge in political violence. Preoccupied with corruption and economic crisis and increasingly indifferent, if not hostile, to African-American aspirations, most Americans looked the other way. The elections of 1876—on the local, state, and national levels—affirmed the triumph of white Southerners. Reconstruction did not end; it was overthrown. Southern Democrats called their victory "Redemption," and this interpretation of the Reconstruction era would affect race relations for nearly a century.

THE DEMOCRATS' VIOLENT RESURGENCE

The violence between 1874 and 1876 differed in several respects from earlier attempts to restore white government by force. Attackers operated more openly and more closely identified themselves with the Democratic party. Mounted, gray-clad ex-Confederate soldiers flanked Democratic candidates at campaign rallies and "visited" black neighborhoods afterward to discourage black people from voting. With black people intimidated and white people already prepared to vote, election days were typically quiet.

Democrats swept to victory across the South in the 1874 elections. "A perfect reign of terror" redeemed Alabama for the Democrats. In Louisiana, a group of elite Democrats in New Orleans organized a military organization known as the *White League* in 1874 to challenge the state's Republican government. In September 1874, more than eight thousand White Leaguers staged a coup to overthrow the Republican government of New Orleans.

THE WEAK FEDERAL RESPONSE

Unrest like that in Louisiana also plagued Mississippi and South Carolina. When South Carolina governor Daniel H. Chamberlain could no longer contain the violence in his state in 1876, he asked the president for help. Although President Grant acknowledged the gravity of Chamberlain's situation, the president would only offer the governor the lame hope that South Carolinians would exercise "better judgment and cooperation" and assist the governor in bringing offenders to justice "without aid from the federal Government."

Congress responded to the violence with the Civil Rights Act of 1875. Introduced by Charles Sumner, the bill finally passed in a watered-down version after Sumner's death. The act prohibited discrimination against black people in public accommodations such as theaters, parks, and trains and guaranteed freedmen's rights to serve on juries. It had no provision for voting rights, which Congress presumed the Fifteenth Amendment protected. The only way to enforce the law was for individuals to bring grievances related to it before federal courts in the South.

When black people tested the law by trying to make free use of public accommodations, they were almost always turned away. In 1883, the U.S. Supreme Court overturned the act declaring that only the states, not Congress, could redress "a private wrong, or a crime of the individual."

THE ELECTION OF 1876 AND THE COMPROMISE OF 1877

Reconstruction officially ended with the presidential election of 1876 in which Democrat Samuel J. Tilden ran against Republican Rutherford B. Hayes. When the ballots were counted, it appeared that Tilden, a conservative New Yorker respectable enough for Northern voters and Democratic enough for white Southerners, had won. But despite a majority in the popular vote, disputed returns in three Southern states left him with 184 of the 185 electoral votes needed to win. The three states—Florida, South Carolina, and Louisiana—were the last in the South still to have Republican administrations.

Both camps maneuvered intensively in the months following the election to claim the disputed votes. Congress appointed a fifteen-member commission to settle the issue. Eventually the so-called *Compromise of 1877* installed Hayes in the White House and gave Democrats control of all state governments in the South.

Southern Democrats emerged the major winners of the Compromise of 1877. President Hayes and his successors into the next century left the South alone. In practical terms, the Compromise of 1877 signaled the revocation of civil rights and voting rights for black Southerners. The Fourteenth and Fifteenth Amendments would be dead letters in the South until well into the twentieth century. On the two great issues confronting the nation at the end of the Civil War, reunion and freedom, the white South had won.

THE MEMORY OF RECONSTRUCTION

Southern Democrats used the memory of Reconstruction to help maintain themselves in power. As white Southerners elevated Civil War heroes into saints, and battles into holy struggles, Reconstruction became the Redemption. Whenever Southern Democrats felt threatened over the next century, they reminded their white constituents of the "horrors of Reconstruction," the menace of black rule, and the cruelty of Yankee occupiers. The Southern view of Reconstruction permeated textbooks, films, and standard accounts of the period. By the early 1900s, professional historians at the nation's finest institutions concurred in this view, and most Americans believed that the policies of Reconstruction had been misguided and had brought great suffering to the white South. This view allowed the South to maintain its system of racial segregation and exclusion without interference from the federal government.

The national historical consensus grew out of a growing national reconciliation concerning the war, a mutual agreement that it was time to move on. Lost in all the good will was the tacit agreement among both Southern and Northern whites that the South was free to work out its own resolution to race relations.

There is much to be said in favor of sectional reconciliation as opposed to persistent animosity. There are enough examples in the world today of antagonists in the same country never forgetting or never forgiving their bloody histories. Ideally, Americans could have had *both* healing and justice, but instead, they settled for the former. Frederick Douglass worried about what the peace that followed the Civil War would mean for race relations: "If war among the whites brought peace and liberty to the blacks, what will peace among the whites bring?" But white Americans seemed intent on shaking hands and getting on with their lives.

The Failed Promise of Reconstruction

Most black people and white people in 1877 would have agreed on one point: Reconstruction had failed. If the demise of Reconstruction elicited a sigh of relief from most white Americans, black Americans greeted it with frustration. Their dreams of land ownership faded as a new labor system relegated them to a lowly position in Southern agriculture. Redemption reversed their economic and political gains and deprived them of most of the civil rights they had enjoyed under Congressional Reconstruction.

The former slaves were certainly better off in 1877 than in 1865. They were free, however limited their freedom. Some owned land; some held jobs in cities. But by 1877, the "golden moment"—an unprecedented opportunity for the nation to live up to its ideals by extending equal rights to all its citizens, black and white alike—had passed.

SHARECROPPING

When they lost political power, black Southerners also lost economic independence. As the Freedmen's Bureau retreated from supervising farm labor contracts and opportunities for black people to possess their own land dried up, the bargaining power of black farm laborers decreased, and the power of white landlords increased.

The upshot was that by the late 1870s, most former slaves in the rural South had been drawn into a subservient position in a new labor system called *sharecropping*. The premise of this system was relatively simple: The landlord furnished the sharecroppers a house, a plot of land to work, seed, some farm animals and farm implements and advanced them credit at a store the landlord typically owned. In exchange, the sharecroppers promised the landlord a share of their crop, usually one-half. The croppers kept the proceeds from the sale of the other half to pay off their debts at the store and save or spend as they and their families saw fit. In theory, a sharecropper could save enough to secure economic independence.

With landlords holding the accounts at the store, black sharecroppers found that the proceeds from their share of the crop never left them very far ahead. In exchange for extending credit to sharecroppers, store owners felt justified in requiring collateral. But sharecroppers had no assets other than the cotton they grew. So Southern states passed crop lien laws, which gave the store owner the right to the next year's crop in exchange for this year's credit. The sharecropper sank deeper into dependence.

Sharecropping represented a significant step down from tenancy. Tenants owned their own draft animals, farm implements, and seed. Once they negotiated with a land owner for a fixed rent, they kept whatever profits they earned. Eventually, they could hope to purchase some land and move into the landlord class themselves.

Historians have often depicted the sharecropping system as a compromise between white landlord and black laborer. But compromise implies a give-and-take between relatively equal negotiators. As Northern and federal support for Reconstruction waned after 1870 and Southern Democrats regained political control, white power over black labor increased. Black people had no recourse to federal and state authorities or, increasingly, to the polls as a white reign of terror stripped them of their political rights.

MODEST GAINS AND FUTURE VICTORIES

Black Southerners experienced some advances in the decade after the Civil War, but these owed little to Reconstruction. Black families functioned as economic and psychological buffers against unemployment and prejudice. Black churches played crucial roles in their communities. Self-help and labor organizations offered mutual friendship and financial assistance. All of these institutions had existed in the slavery era, although on a smaller scale. And some of them, such as black labor groups, schools, and social welfare associations, endured because comparable white institutions excluded black people. Black people also scored some modest economic successes during the Reconstruction era, mainly from their own pluck.

The Fourteenth and Fifteenth Amendments to the Constitution are among the few bright spots in Reconstruction's otherwise dismal legacy. The Fourteenth Amendment guaranteed former slaves equality before the law; the Fifteenth Amendment protected their right to vote. Both amendments elevated the federal government over the states by protecting freedmen from state attempts to deny them their rights. But the benefits of these two landmark amendments did not accrue to African Americans until well into the twentieth century. In the *Slaughterhouse cases* (1873), the Supreme Court contradicted the intent of the Fourteenth Amendment by decreeing that most citizenship rights remained under state, not federal, control. In *United States* **v.** *Cruikshank* (1876), the Court overturned the convictions of some of those responsible for the Colfax Massacre, ruling that the Enforcement Act applied only to violations of black rights by states, not individuals. Within the next two decades, the Supreme Court would uphold the legality of racial segregation and black disfranchisement, in effect declaring that the Fourteenth and Fifteenth Amendments did not apply to African Americans. The Civil War had killed secession forever, but states' rights enjoyed a remarkable revival.

Conclusion

Formerly enslaved black Southerners had entered freedom with many hopes, among the most prominent of which was to be let alone. White Southerners, after four bloody years of unwanted attention from the federal government, also longed to be left alone. But they did not include their ex-slaves as equal partners in their vision of solitude. Northerners, too, began to seek escape from the issues and consequences of the war, eventually abandoning their commitment to secure civil and voting rights for black Southerners.

White Southerners robbed blacks of their gains and sought to reduce them again to servitude and dependence, if not to slavery. But in the process, the majority of white people lost as well. Yeoman farmers missed an opportunity to break cleanly from the Old South and establish a more equitable society. Instead, they allowed the old elites to regain power and gradually ignore their needs. They preserved the social benefit of a white skin at the cost of almost everything else. Many lost their farms and sank into tenancy, leasing land from others. Fewer had a voice in state legislatures or Congress. A new South, rid of slavery and sectional antagonism, had indeed emerged, redeemed, regenerated, and disenthralled. But the old South lingered on in the new like Spanish moss on live oaks.

As Federal troops left the South to be redeployed restraining striking workers in the North and suppressing Native Americans on the Great Plains, an era of possibility for American society ended and a new era began. "The southern question is dead," a Charleston newspaper proclaimed in 1877. "The question of labor and capital, work and wages" had moved to the forefront. The chance to redeem the sacrifice of a bloody civil war with a society that fulfilled the promise of the Declaration of Independence and the Constitution for all citizens slipped away. It would take a new generation of African Americans a long century later to revive it.

REVIEW QUESTIONS

1. Do you think white Southerners should have supported black people's aspirations for civil rights, land, and suffrage? How differently would things have turned out if they had?

2. Is it fair to blame Reconstruction's failures on Southern Republicans? Explain your response.

3. What gains did black people achieve during Reconstruction, despite its overall failure?

4. In T. Thomas Fortune's recollection of a boyhood incident, why was it important for him and his friends to fight back?

APPENDIX

The Declaration of Independence

When in the course of human events it becomes necessary for one people to dissolve the political bands which have connected them with another and to assume, among the powers of the earth, the separate and equal station to which the laws of nature and of nature's God entitle them, a decent respect to the opinions of mankind requires that they should declare the causes which impel them to the separation.

We hold these truths to be self-evident, that all men are created equal; that they are endowed by their Creator with certain unalienable rights; that among these are life, liberty, and the pursuit of happiness. That, to secure these rights, governments are instituted among men, deriving their just powers from the consent of the governed; that, whenever any form of government becomes destructive of these ends, it is the right of the people to alter or to abolish it, and to institute a new government, laying its foundation on such principles, and organizing its powers in such form, as to them shall seem most likely to effect their safety and happiness. Prudence, indeed, will dictate that governments long established should not be changed for light and transient causes; and, accordingly, all experience hath shown that mankind are more disposed to suffer, while evils are sufferable, than to right themselves by abolishing the forms to which they are accustomed. But when a long train of abuses and usurpations, pursuing invariably the same object, evinces a design to reduce them under absolute despotism, it is their right, it is their duty, to throw off such government and to provide new guards for their future security. Such has been the patient sufferance of these colonies, and such is now the necessity which constrains them to alter their former systems of government. The history of the present King of Great Britain is a history of repeated injuries and usurpations, all having, in direct object, the establishment of an absolute tyranny over these States. To prove this, let facts be submitted to a candid world:

He has refused his assent to laws the most wholesome and necessary for the public good.

He has forbidden his governors to pass laws of immediate and pressing importance, unless suspended in their operation till his assent should be obtained; and, when so suspended, he has utterly neglected to attend to them.

He has refused to pass other laws for the accommodation of large districts of people, unless those people would relinquish the right of representation in the legislature, a right inestimable to them and formidable to tyrants only.

He has called together legislative bodies at places unusual, uncomfortable, and distant from the depository of their public records, for the sole purpose of fatiguing them into compliance with his measures.

He has dissolved representative houses, repeatedly for opposing, with manly firmness, his invasions on the rights of the people.

He has refused, for a long time after such dissolutions, to cause others to be elected; whereby the legislative powers, incapable of annihilation, have returned to the people at large for their exercise; the state remaining, in the meantime, exposed to all the danger of invasion from without and convulsions within.

He has endeavored to prevent the population of these States; for that purpose, obstructing the laws for naturalization of foreigners, refusing to pass others to encourage their migration hither, and raising the conditions of new appropriations of lands.

He has obstructed the administration of justice by refusing his assent to laws for establishing judiciary powers.

He has made judges dependent on his will alone for the tenure of their offices and the amount and payment of their salaries.

He has erected a multitude of new offices and sent hither swarms of officers to harass our people and eat out their substance.

He has kept among us, in time of peace, standing armies, without the consent of our legislatures.

He has affected to render the military independent of, and superior to, the civil power.

He has combined with others to subject us to a jurisdiction foreign to our Constitution and unacknowledged by our laws, giving his assent to their acts of pretended legislation—

For quartering large bodies of armed troops among us;

For protecting them by mock trial, from punishment for any murders which they should commit on the inhabitants of these States;

For cutting off our trade with all parts of the world;

For imposing taxes on us without our consent;

For depriving us, in many cases, of the benefit of trial by jury;

For transporting us beyond seas to be tried for pretended offences;

For abolishing the free system of English laws in a neighboring province, establishing therein an arbitrary government, and enlarging its boundaries, so as to render it at once an example and fit instrument for introducing the same absolute rule into these colonies;

For taking away our charters, abolishing our most valuable laws, and altering, fundamentally, the powers of our governments.

For suspending our own legislatures and declaring themselves invested with power to legislate for us in all cases whatsoever.

He has abdicated government here by declaring us out of his protection and waging war against us.

He has plundered our seas, ravaged our coasts, burnt our towns, and destroyed the lives of our people.

He is, at this time, transporting large armies of foreign mercenaries to complete the works of death, desolation, and tyranny already begun with circumstances of cruelty and perfidy scarcely paralleled in the most barbarous ages, and totally unworthy the head of a civilized nation.

He has constrained our fellow citizens, taken captive on the high seas, to bear arms against their country, to become the executioners of their friends and brethren, or to fall themselves by their hands.

He has excited domestic insurrections amongst us and has endeavored to bring on the inhabitants of our frontiers, the merciless Indian savages, whose known rule of warfare is an undistinguished destruction of all ages, sexes, and conditions.

In every stage of these oppressions, we have petitioned for redress in the most humble terms; our repeated petitions have been answered only by repeated injury. A prince whose character is thus marked by every act which may define a tyrant is unfit to be the ruler of a free people.

Nor have we been wanting in attention to our British brethren. We have warned them, from time to time, of attempts made by their legislature to extend an unwarrantable jurisdiction over us. We have reminded them of the circumstances of our emigration and settlement here. We have appealed to their native justice and magnanimity, and we have conjured them, by the ties of our common kindred, to disavow these usurpations, which would inevitably interrupt our connections and correspondence. They, too, have been deaf to the voice of justice and consanguinity. We must, therefore, acquiesce in the necessity which denounces our separation, and hold them, as we hold the rest of mankind, enemies in war, in peace, friends.

We, therefore, the representatives of the United States of America, in general Congress assembled, appealing to the Supreme Judge of the world for the rectitude of our intentions, do, in the name and by the authority of the good people of these colonies, solemnly publish and declare, that these united colonies are, and of right ought to be, free and independent states: that they are absolved from all allegiance to the British Crown, and that all political connection between them and the state of Great Britain is, and ought to be, totally dissolved; and that, as free and independent states, they have full power to levy war, conclude peace, contract alliances, establish commerce, and to do all other acts and things which independent states may of right do. And, for the support of this declaration, with a firm reliance on the protection of Divine Providence, we mutually pledge to each other our lives, our fortunes, and our sacred honor.

The Articles of Confederation and Perpetual Union*

Between the states of New Hampshire, Massachusetts bay, Rhode Island and Providence Plantations, Connecticut, New York, New Jersey, Pennsylvania, Delaware, Maryland, Virginia, North Carolina, South Carolina, and Georgia.

ARTICLE 1

The Stile of this Confederacy shall be "The United States of America."

ARTICLE 2

Each state retains its sovereignty, freedom, and independence, and every power, jurisdiction, and right, which is not by this Confederation expressly delegated to the United States, in Congress assembled.

ARTICLE 3

The said States hereby severally enter into a firm league of friendship with each other, for their common defense, the security of their liberties, and their mutual and general welfare, binding themselves to assist each other, against all force offered to, or attacks made upon them, or any of them, on account of religion, sovereignty, trade, or any other pretense whatever.

ARTICLE 4

The better to secure and perpetuate mutual friendship and intercourse among the people of the different States in this Union, the free inhabitants of each of these States, paupers, vagabonds, and fugitives from justice excepted, shall be entitled to all privileges and immunities of free citizens in the several States; and the people of each State shall have free ingress and regress to and from any other State, and shall enjoy therein all the privileges of trade and commerce, subject to the same duties, impositions, and restrictions as the inhabitants thereof respectively, provided that such restrictions shall not extend so far as to prevent the removal of property imported into any State, to any other State of which the owner is an inhabitant; provided also that no imposition, duties or restriction shall be laid by any State, on the property of the United States, or either of them.

If any person guilty of, or charged with, treason, felony, or other high misdemeanor in any State, shall flee from justice, and be found in any of the United States, he shall, upon demand of the Governor or executive power of the State from which he fled, be delivered up and removed to the State having jurisdiction of his offense.

Full faith and credit shall be given in each of these States to the records, acts, and judicial proceedings of the courts and magistrates of every other State.

ARTICLE 5

For the most convenient management of the general interests of the United States, delegates shall be annually appointed in such manner as the legislatures of each State shall direct, to meet in Congress on the first Monday in November, in every year, with a power reserved to each State to recall its delegates, or any of them, at any time within the year, and to send others in their stead for the remainder of the year.

---

*Agreed to in Congress November 15, 1777; ratified March 1781.

No State shall be represented in Congress by less than two, nor by more than seven members; and no person shall be capable of being a delegate for more than three years in any term of six years; nor shall any person, being a delegate, be capable of holding any office under the United States, for which he, or another for his benefit, receives any salary, fees or emolument of any kind.

Each State shall maintain its own delegates in a meeting of the States, and while they act as members of the committee of the States.

In determining questions in the United States in Congress assembled, each State shall have one vote.

Freedom of speech and debate in Congress shall not be impeached or questioned in any court or place out of Congress, and the members of Congress shall be protected in their persons from arrests or imprisonments, during the time of their going to and from, and attendence on Congress, except for treason, felony, or breach of the peace.

ARTICLE 6

No State, without the consent of the United States in Congress assembled, shall send any embassy to, or receive any embassy from, or enter into any conference, agreement, alliance or treaty with any King, Prince or State; nor shall any person holding any office of profit or trust under the United States, or any of them, accept any present, emolument, office or title of any kind whatever from any King, Prince or foreign State; nor shall the United States in Congress assembled, or any of them, grant any title of nobility.

No two or more States shall enter into any treaty, confederation or alliance whatever between them, without the consent of the United States in Congress assembled, specifying accurately the purposes for which the same is to be entered into, and how long it shall continue.

No State shall lay any imposts or duties, which may interfere with any stipulations in treaties, entered into by the United States in Congress assembled, with any King, Prince or State, in pursuance of any treaties already proposed by Congress, to the courts of France and Spain.

No vessel of war shall be kept up in time of peace by any State, except such number only, as shall be deemed necessary by the United States in Congress assembled, for the defense of such State, or its trade; nor shall any body of forces be kept up by any State in time of peace, except such number only, as in the judgement of the United States in Congress assembled, shall be deemed requisite to garrison the forts necessary for the defense of such State; but every State shall always keep up a well-regulated and disciplined militia, sufficiently armed and accoutered, and shall provide and constantly have ready for use, in public stores, a due number of filed pieces and tents, and a proper quantity of arms, ammunition and camp equipage.

No State shall engage in any war without the consent of the United States in Congress assembled, unless such State be actually invaded by enemies, or shall have received certain advice of a resolution being formed by some nation of Indians to invade such State, and the danger is so imminent as not to admit of a delay, till the United States in Congress assembled can be consulted; nor shall any State grant commissions to any ships or vessels of war, nor letters of marque or reprisal, except it be after a declaration of war by the United States in Congress assembled, and then only against the Kingdom or State and the subjects thereof, against which war has been so declared, and under such regulations as shall be established by the United States in Congress assembled, unless such State be infested by pirates, in which case vessels of war may be fitted out for that occasion, and kept so long as the danger shall continue, or until the United States in Congress assembled shall determine otherwise.

ARTICLE 7

When land forces are raised by any State for the common defense, all officers of or under the rank of colonel, shall be appointed by the legislature of each State respectively, by whom such forces shall be raised, or in such manner as such State shall direct, and all vacancies shall be filled up by the State which first made the appointment.

ARTICLE 8

All charges of war, and all other expenses that shall be incurred for the common defense or general welfare, and allowed by the United States in Congress assembled, shall be defrayed out of a common treasury, which shall be supplied by the several States in proportion to the value of all land within each State, granted to or surveyed for any person, as such land and the buildings and improvements thereon shall be estimated according to such mode as the United States in Congress assembled, shall from time to time direct and appoint.

The taxes for paying that proportion shall be laid and levied by the authority and direction of the legislatures of the several States within the time agreed upon by the United States in Congress assembled.

ARTICLE 9

The United States in Congress assembled, shall have the sole and exclusive right and power of determining on peace and war, except in the cases mentioned in the sixth article; of sending and receiving ambassadors; entering into treaties and alliances, provided that no treaty of commerce shall be made whereby the legislative power of the respective States shall be restrained from imposing such imposts and duties on foreigners, as their own people are subjected to, or from prohibiting the exportation or importation of any species of goods or commodities whatsoever; of establishing rules for deciding in all cases, what captures on land or water shall be legal, and in what manner prizes taken by land or naval forces in the service of the United States shall be divided or appropriated; of granting letters of marque and reprisal in times of peace; appointing courts for the trial of piracies and felonies committed on the high seas and establishing courts for receiving and determining finally appeals in all cases of captures, provided that no member of Congress shall be appointed a judge of any of the said courts.

The United States in Congress assembled shall also be the last resort on appeal in all disputes and differences now subsisting or that hereafter may arise between two or more States concerning boundary, jurisdiction or any other causes whatever; which authority shall always be exercised in the manner following. Whenever the legislative or executive authority or lawful agent of any State in controversy with another shall present a petition to Congress stating the matter in question and praying for a hearing, notice thereof shall be given by order of Congress to the legislative or executive authority of the other State in controversy, and a day assigned for the appearance of the parties by their lawful agents, who shall then be directed to appoint by joint consent, commissioners or judges to constitute a court for hearing and determining the matter in question: but if they cannot agree, Congress shall name three persons out of each of the United States, and from the list of such persons each party shall alternately strike out one, the petitioners beginning, until the number shall be reduced to thirteen; and from that number not less than seven, nor more than nine names as Congress shall direct, shall in the presence of Congress be drawn out by lot, and the persons whose names shall be so drawn or any five of them, shall be commissioners or judges, to hear and finally determine the controversy, so always as a major part of the judges who shall hear the cause shall agree in the determination: and if either party shall neglect to attend at the day appointed, without showing reasons, which Congress shall judge sufficient, or being present shall refuse to strike, the Congress shall proceed to nominate three persons out of each State, and the secretary of Congress shall strike in behalf of such party absent or refusing; and the judgement and sentence of the court to be appointed, in the manner before prescribed, shall be final and conclusive; and if any of the parties shall refuse to submit to the authority of such court, or to appear or defend their claim or cause, the court shall nevertheless proceed to pronounce sentence, or judgement, which shall in like manner be final and decisive, the judgement or sentence and other proceedings being in either case transmitted to Congress, and lodged among the acts of Congress for the security of the parties concerned: provided that every commissioner, before he sits in judgement, shall take an oath to be administered by one of the judges of the supreme or superior court of the State, where the cause shall be tried, "well and truly to hear and determine the matter in question, according to the best of his judgement, without favor, affection or hope of reward:" provided also, that no State shall be deprived of territory for the benefit of the United States.

All controversies concerning the private right of soil claimed under different grants of two or more States, whose jurisdictions as they may respect such lands, and the States which passed such grants are adjusted, the said grants or either of them being at the same time claimed to have originated antecedent to such settlement of jurisdiction, shall on the petition of either party to the Congress of the United States, be finally determined as near as may be in the same manner as is before prescribed for deciding disputes respecting territorial jurisdiction between different States.

The United States in Congress assembled shall also have the sole and exclusive right and power of regulating the alloy and value of coin struck by their own authority, or by that of the respective States; fixing the standards of weights and measures throughout the United States; regulating the trade and managing all affairs with the Indians not members of any of the States; provided that the legislative right of any State within its own limits be not infringed or violated; establishing or regulating post offices from one State to another, throughout all the United States, and exacting such postage on the papers passing through the same as may be requisite to defray the expenses of the said office; appointing all officers of the land forces in the service of the United States, excepting regimental officers; appointing all the officers of the naval forces, and commissioning all officers whatever in the service of the United States; making rules for the government and regulation of the said land and naval forces, and directing their operations.

The United States in Congress assembled shall have authority to appoint a committee, to sit in the recess of Congress, to be denominated "A Committee of the States," and to consist of one delegate from each State; and to appoint such other committees and civil officers as may be necessary for managing the general affairs of the United States under their direction; to appoint one of their members to preside, provided that no person be allowed to serve in the office of president more than one year in any term of three years; to ascertain the necessary sums of money to be raised for the service of the United States, and to appropriate and apply the same for defraying the public expenses; to borrow money, or emit bills on the credit of the United States, transmitting every half year to the respective States an account of the sums of money so borrowed or emitted; to build and equip a navy; to agree upon the number of land forces, and to make requisitions from each State for its quota, in proportion to the number of white inhabitants in such State; which requisition shall be binding, and thereupon the legislature of each State shall appoint the regimental officers, raise the men and cloath, arm and equip them in a soldierlike manner, at the expense of the United States; and the officers and men so cloathed, armed and equipped shall march to the place appointed, and within the time agreed on by the United States in Congress assembled; but if the United States in Congress assembled shall, on consideration of circumstances judge proper that any State should not raise men, or should raise a smaller number of men than the quota thereof, such extra number shall be raised, officered, cloathed, armed and equipped in the same manner as the quota of each State, unless the legislature of such State shall judge that such extra number cannot be safely spared out in the same, in which case they shall raise, officer, cloath, arm and equip as many of such extra number as they judge can be safely spared. And the officers and men so cloathed, armed, and equipped, shall march to the place appointed, and within the time agreed on by the United States in Congress assembled.

The United States in Congress assembled shall never engage in a war, nor grant letters of marque or reprisal in time of peace, nor enter into any treaties or alliances, nor coin money, nor regulate the value thereof, nor ascertain the sums and expenses necessary for the defense and welfare of the United States, or any of them, nor emit bills, nor borrow money on the credit of the United States, nor appropriate money, nor agree upon the number of vessels of war, to be built or purchased, or the number of land or sea forces to be raised, nor appoint a commander in chief of the army or navy, unless nine States assent to the same: nor shall a question on any other point, except for adjourning from day to day be determined, unless by the votes of the majority of the United States in Congress assembled.

The Congress of the United States shall have power to adjourn to any time within the year, and to any place within the United States, so that no period of adjournment be for a longer duration than the space of six months, and shall publish the journal of their proceedings monthly, except such parts thereof relating to treaties, alliances or military operations, as in their judgement require secrecy; and the yeas and nays of the delegates of each State on any question shall be entered on the journal, when it is desired by any delegates of a State, or any of them, at his or their request shall be furnished with a transcript of the said journal, except such parts as are above excepted, to lay before the legislatures of the several States.

ARTICLE 10

The Committee of the States, or any nine of them, shall be authorized to execute, in the recess of Congress, such of the powers of Congress as the United States in Congress assembled, by the consent of the nine States, shall from time to time think expedient to vest them with; provided that no power be delegated to the said Committee, for the exercise of which, by the Articles of Confederation, the voice of nine States in the Congress of the United States assembled is requisite.

ARTICLE 11

Canada acceding to this confederation, and adjoining in the measures of the United States, shall be admitted into, and entitled to all the advantages of this Union; but no other colony shall be admitted into the same, unless such admission be agreed to by nine States.

ARTICLE 12

All bills of credit emitted, monies borrowed, and debts contracted by, or under the authority of Congress, before the assembling of the United States, in pursuance of the present confederation, shall be deemed and considered as a charge against the United States, for payment and satisfaction whereof the said United States, and the public faith are hereby solemnly pledged.

ARTICLE 13

Every State shall abide by the determination of the United States in Congress assembled, on all questions which by this confederation are submitted to them. And the Articles of this Confederation shall be inviolably observed by every State, and the Union shall be perpetual; nor shall any alteration at any time hereafter be made in any of them; unless such alteration be agreed to in a Congress of the United States, and be afterwards confirmed by the legislatures of every State.

These articles shall be proposed to the legislatures of all the United States, to be considered, and if approved of by them, they are advised to authorize their delegates to ratify the same in the Congress of the United States; which being done, the same shall become conclusive.

The Constitution of the United States of America

We the people of the United States, in order to form a more perfect union, establish justice, insure domestic tranquillity, provide for the common defense, promote the general welfare, and secure the blessings of liberty to ourselves and our posterity, do ordain and establish this Constitution for the United States of America.

ARTICLE I

SECTION 1. All legislative powers herein granted shall be vested in a Congress of the United States, which shall consist of a Senate and House of Representatives.

SECTION 2.

1. The House of Representatives shall be composed of members chosen every second year by the people of the several States, and the electors in each State shall have the qualifications requisite for electors of the most numerous branch of the State legislature.

2. No person shall be a representative who shall not have attained to the age of twenty-five years, and been seven years a citizen of the United States, and who shall not, when elected, be an inhabitant of that State in which he shall be chosen.

3. Representatives and direct taxes[1] shall be apportioned among the several States which may be included within this Union, according to their respective numbers, which shall be determined by adding to the whole number of free persons, including those bound to service for a term of years, and excluding Indians not taxed, three fifths of all other persons.[2] The actual enumeration shall be made within three years after the first meeting of the Congress of the United States, and within every sub-sequent term of ten years, in such manner as they shall by law direct. The number of representatives shall not exceed one for every thirty thousand, but each State shall have at least one representative; and until such enumeration shall be made, the State of New Hampshire shall be entitled to choose three, Massachusetts eight, Rhode Island and Providence Plantations one, Connecticut five, New York six, New Jersey four, Pennsylvania eight, Delaware one, Maryland six, Virginia ten, North Carolina five, South Carolina five, and Georgia three.

4. When vacancies happen in the representation from any State, the executive authority thereof shall issue writs of election to fill such vacancies.

5. The House of Representatives shall choose their speaker and other officers; and shall have the sole power of impeachment.

SECTION 3.

1. The Senate of the United States shall be composed of two senators from each State, chosen by the legislature thereof,[3] for six years; and each senator shall have one vote.

2. Immediately after they shall be assembled in consequence of the first election, they shall be divided as equally as may be into three classes. The seats of the senators of the first class shall be vacated at the expiration of the second year, of the second class at the expiration of the fourth year, and of the third class at the expiration of the sixth year, so that one third may be chosen every second year; and if vacancies happen by resignation, or otherwise, during the recess of the legislature of any State, the executive thereof may make temporary appointments until the next meeting of the legisla-ture, which shall then fill such vacancies.[4]

3. No person shall be a senator who shall not have attained to the age of thirty years, and been nine years a citizen of the United States, and who shall not, when elected, be an inhabitant of that State for which he shall be chosen.

4. The Vice President of the United States shall be President of the Senate, but shall have no vote, unless they be equally divided.

5. The Senate shall choose their other officers, and also a president pro tempore, in the absence of the Vice President, or when he shall exercise the office of the President of the United States.

6. The Senate shall have the sole power to try all impeachments. When sitting for that purpose, they shall be on oath or affirmation. When the President of the United States is tried, the chief justice shall preside: and no person shall be convicted without the concurrence of two thirds of the members present.

7. Judgment in cases of impeachment shall not extend further than to removal from office, and disqualification to hold and enjoy any office of honor, trust or profit under the United States: but the

---

[1] See the Sixteenth Amendment.
[2] See the Fourteenth Amendment.
[3] See the Seventeenth Amendment.
[4] See the Seventeenth Amendment.

party convicted shall nevertheless be liable and subject to indictment, trial, judgment and punishment, according to law.

SECTION 4.

1. The times, places, and manner of holding elections for senators and representatives, shall be prescribed in each State by the legislature thereof; but the Congress may at any time by law make or alter such regulations, except as to the places of choosing senators.

2. The Congress shall assemble at least once in every year, and such meeting shall be on the first Monday in December, unless they shall by law appoint a different day.

SECTION 5.

1. Each House shall be the judge of the elections, returns and qualifications of its own members, and a majority of each shall constitute a quorum to do business; but a smaller number may adjourn from day to day, and may be authorized to compel the attendance of absent members, in such manner, and under such penalties as each House may provide.

2. Each House may determine the rules of its proceedings, punish its members for disorderly behavior, and, with the concurrence of two thirds, expel a member.

3. Each House shall keep a journal of its proceedings, and from time to time publish the same, excepting such parts as may in their judgment require secrecy; and the yeas and nays of the members of either House on any question shall, at the desire of one fifth of those present, be entered on the journal.

4. Neither House, during the session of Congress, shall, without the consent of the other, adjourn for more than three days, nor to any other place than that in which the two Houses shall be sitting.

SECTION 6.

1. The senators and representatives shall receive a compensation for their services, to be ascertained by law, and paid out of the Treasury of the United States. They shall in all cases, except treason, felony, and breach of the peace, be privileged from arrest during their attendance at the session of their respective Houses, and in going to and returning from the same; and for any speech or debate in either House, they shall not be questioned in any other place.

2. No senator or representative shall, during the time for which he was elected, be appointed to any civil office under the authority of the United States, which shall have been created, or the emoluments whereof shall have been increased, during such time; and no person holding any office under the United States shall be a member of either House during his continuance in office.

SECTION 7.

1. All bills for raising revenue shall originate in the House of Representatives; but the Senate may propose or concur with amendments as on other bills.

2. Every bill which shall have passed the House of Representatives and the Senate, shall, before it become a law, be presented to the President of the United States; If he approves he shall sign it, but if not he shall return it, with his objections, to that House in which it shall have originated, who shall enter the objections at large on their journal, and proceed to reconsider it. If after such reconsideration two thirds of that House shall agree to pass the bill, it shall be sent, together with the objections, to the other House, by which it shall likewise be reconsidered, and if approved by two thirds of that House, it shall become a law. But in all such cases the votes of both Houses shall be determined by yeas and nays, and the names of the persons voting for and against the bill shall be entered on the journal of each House respectively. If any bill shall not be returned by the President within ten days (Sundays excepted) after it shall have been presented to him, the same shall be a law, in like manner as if he had signed it, unless the Congress by their adjournment prevent its return, in which case it shall not be a law.

3. Every order, resolution, or vote to which the concurrence of the Senate and the House of Representatives may be necessary (except on a question of adjournment) shall be presented to the

President of the United States; and before the same shall take effect, shall be approved by him, or being disapproved by him, shall be repassed by two thirds of the Senate and House of Representatives, according to the rules and limitations prescribed in the case of a bill.

SECTION 8.

1. The Congress shall have the power

2. To lay and collect taxes, duties, imposts, and excises, to pay the debts and provide for the common defense and general welfare of the United States; but all duties, imposts, and excises shall be uniform throughout the United States.

3. To borrow money on the credit of the United States;

4. To regulate commerce with foreign nations, and among the several States, and with the Indian tribes;

5. To establish a uniform rule of naturalization, and uniform laws on the subject of bankruptcies throughout the United States;

6. To coin money, regulate the value thereof, and of foreign coin, and fix the standard of weights and measures;

7. To provide for the punishment of counterfeiting the securities and current coin of the United States;

8. To establish post offices and post roads;

9. To promote the progress of science and useful arts, by securing for limited times to authors and inventors the exclusive right to their respective writings and discoveries;

10. To constitute tribunals inferior to the Supreme Court;

11. To define and punish piracies and felonies committed on the high seas, and offenses against the law of nations;

12. To declare war, grant letters of marque and reprisal, and make rules concerning captures on land and water;

13. To raise and support armies, but no appropriation of money to that use shall be for a longer term than two years;

14. To provide and maintain a navy;

15. To make rules for the government and regulation of the land and naval forces;

16. To provide for calling forth the militia to execute the laws of the Union, suppress insurrections and repel invasions;

17. To provide for organizing, arming, and disciplining the militia, and for governing such part of them as may be employed in the service of the United States, reserving to the States respectively, the appointment of the officers, and the authority of training the militia according to the discipline prescribed by Congress;

18. To exercise exclusive legislation in all cases whatsoever, over such district (not exceeding ten miles square) as may, by cession of particular States, and the acceptance of Congress, become the seat of the government of the United States, and to exercise like authority over all places purchased by the consent of the legislature of the State in which the same shall be, for the erection of forts, magazines, arsenals, dockyards, and other needful buildings; and

19. To make all laws which shall be necessary and proper for carrying into execution the foregoing powers, and all other powers vested by this Constitution in the government of the United States, or any department or officer thereof.

SECTION 9.

1. The migration or importation of such persons as any of the States now existing shall think proper to admit, shall not be prohibited by the Congress prior to the year one thousand eight hundred and eight, but a tax or duty may be imposed on such importation, not exceeding ten dollars for each person.

2. The privilege of the writ of habeas corpus shall not be suspended, unless when in cases of rebellion or invasion the public safety may require it.

3. No bill of attainder or ex post facto law shall be passed.

4. No capitation, or other direct, tax shall be laid, unless in proportion to the census or enumeration herein before directed to be taken.[5]

5. No tax or duty shall be laid on articles exported from any State.

6. No preference shall be given by any regulation of commerce or revenue to the ports of one State over those of another: nor shall vessels bound to, or from, one State be obliged to enter, clear, or pay duties in another.

7. No money shall be drawn from the treasury, but in consequence of appropriations made by law; and a regular statement and account of the receipts and expenditures of all public money shall be published from time to time.

8. No title of nobility shall be granted by the United States: and no person holding any office of profit or trust under them, shall, without the consent of the Congress, accept of any present, emolument, office, or title, of any kind whatever, from any king, prince, or foreign State.

SECTION 10.

1. No State shall enter into any treaty, alliance, or confederation; grant letters of marque and reprisal; coin money; emit bills of credit; make any thing but gold and silver coin a tender in payment of debts; pass any bill of attainder, ex post facto law, or law impairing the obligation of contracts, or grant, any title of nobility.

2. No State shall, without the consent of the Congress, lay any imposts or duties on imports or exports, except what may be absolutely necessary for executing its inspection laws: and the net produce of all duties and imposts laid by any State on imports or exports, shall be for the use of the treasury of the United States; and all such laws shall be subject to the revision and control of the Congress.

3. No State shall, without the consent of the Congress, lay any duty of tonnage, keep troops, or ships of war in time of peace, enter into any agreement or compact with another State, or with a foreign power, or engage in war, unless actually invaded, or in such imminent danger as will not admit of delay.

ARTICLE II

SECTION 1.

1. The executive power shall be vested in a President of the United States of America. He shall hold his office during the term of four years, and, together with the Vice President, chosen for the same term, be elected, as follows:

2. Each State shall appoint, in such manner as the legislature thereof may direct, a number of electors, equal to the whole number of senators and representatives to which the State may be entitled in the Congress: but no senator or representative, or person holding any office of trust or profit under the United States, shall be appointed an elector.

The electors shall meet in their respective States, and vote by ballot for two persons, of whom one at least shall not be an inhabitant of the same State with themselves. And they shall make a list of all the persons voted for, and of the number of votes for each; which list they shall sign and certify, and transmit sealed to the seat of the government of the United States, directed to the president of the Senate. The president of the Senate shall, in the presence of the Senate and House of Representatives, open all the certificates, and the votes shall then be counted. The person having the greatest number of votes shall be the President, if such number be a majority of the whole number of electors appointed; and if there be more than one who have such majority, and have an equal number of votes, then the House of Representatives shall immediately choose by ballot one of them for President; and if no person have a majority, then from the five highest on the list the said House shall in

---

[5]See the Sixteenth Amendment.

like manner choose the President. But in choosing the President, the votes shall be taken by States, the representation from each State having one vote; a quorum for this purpose shall consist of a member or members from two thirds of the States, and a majority of all the States shall be necessary to a choice. In every case after the choice of the President, the person having the greatest number of votes of the electors shall be the Vice President. But if there should remain two or more who have equal votes, the Senate shall choose from them by ballot the Vice President.[6]

3. The Congress may determine the time of choosing the electors, and the day on which they shall give their votes; which day shall be the same throughout the United States.

4. No person except a natural born citizen, or a citizen of the United States, at the time of the adoption of this Constitution, shall be eligible to the office of President; neither shall any person be eligible to the office who shall not have attained to the age of thirty-five years, and been fourteen years a resident within the United States.

5. In case of the removal of the President from office, or of his death, resignation, or inability to discharge the powers and duties of the said office, the same shall devolve on the Vice President, and the congress may by law provide for the case of removal, death, resignation or inability, both of the President and Vice President, declaring what officer shall then act as President, and such officer shall act accordingly until the disability be removed, or a President shall be elected.

6. The President shall, at stated times, receive for his services a compensation which shall neither be increased nor diminished during the period for which he shall have been elected, and he shall not receive within that period any other emolument from the United States, or any of them.

7. Before he enter on the execution of his office, he shall take the following oath or affirmation:—"I do solemnly swear (or affirm) that I will faithfully execute the office of President of the United States, and will to the best of my ability, preserve, protect and defend the Constitution of the United States."

SECTION 2.

1. The President shall be commander in chief of the army and navy of the United States, and of the militia of the several States, when called into the actual service of the United States; he may require the opinion in writing, of the principal officer in each of the executive departments, upon any subject relating to the duties of their respective offices, and he shall have power to grant reprieves and pardons for offenses against the United States, except in cases of impeachment.

2. He shall have power, by and with the advice and consent of the Senate, to make treaties, provided two thirds of the senators present concur; and he shall nominate, and by and with the advice and consent of the Senate, shall appoint ambassadors, other public ministers and consuls, judges of the Supreme Court, and all other officers of the United States, whose appointments are not herein otherwise provided for, and which shall be established by law; but the Congress may by law vest the appointment of such inferior officers, as they think proper, in the President alone, in the courts of laws, or in the heads of departments.

3. The President shall have power to fill up all vacancies that may happen during the recess of the Senate, by granting commissions which shall expire at the end of their next session.

SECTION 3. He shall from time to time give to the Congress information of the state of the Union, and recommend to their consideration such measures as he shall judge necessary and expedient; he may, on extraordinary occasions, convene both Houses, or either of them, and in case of disagreement between them with respect to the time of adjournment, he may adjourn them to such time as he shall think proper; he shall receive ambassadors and other public ministers; he shall take care that the laws be faithfully executed, and shall commission all the officers of the United States.

SECTION 4. The President, Vice President, and all civil officers of the United States, shall be removed from office on impeachment for, and conviction of, treason, bribery, or other high crimes and misdemeanors.

---

[6]Superseded by the Twelfth Amendment.

ARTICLE III

SECTION 1. The judicial power of the United States shall be vested in one Supreme Court, and in such inferior courts as the Congress may from time to time ordain and establish. The judges, both of the Supreme and inferior courts, shall hold their offices during good behavior, and shall, at stated times, receive for their services, a compensation, which shall not be diminished during their continuance in office.

SECTION 2.

1. The judicial power shall extend to all cases, in law and equity, arising under this Constitution, the laws of the United States, and treaties made, or which shall be made, under their authority;—to all cases of admiralty and maritime jurisdiction;—to controversies to which the United States shall be a party;[7]—to controversies between two or more States;—between a State and citizens of another State;—between citizens of different States;—between citizens of the same State claiming lands under grants of different States, and between a State, or the citizens thereof, and foreign States, citizens or subjects.

2. In all cases affecting ambassadors, other public ministers and consuls, and those in which a State shall be party, the Supreme Court shall have original jurisdiction. In all the other cases before mentioned, the Supreme Court shall have appellate jurisdiction, both as to law and fact, with such exceptions, and under such regulations as the Congress shall make.

3. The trial of all crimes, except in cases of impeachment, shall be by jury; and such trial shall be held in the State where the said crimes shall have been committed; but when not committed within any State, the trial shall be such place or places as the Congress may by law have directed.

SECTION 3.

1. Treason against the United States shall consist only in levying war against them, or in adhering to their enemies, giving them aid and comfort. No person shall be convicted of treason unless on the testimony of two witnesses to the same overt act, or on confession in open court.

2. The Congress shall have power to declare the punishment of treason, but no attainder of treason shall work corruption of blood, or forfeiture except during the life of the person attained.

ARTICLE IV

SECTION 1. Full faith and credit shall be given in each State to the public acts, records, and judicial proceedings of every other State. And the Congress may by general laws prescribe the manner in which such acts, records and proceedings shall be proved, and the effect thereof.

SECTION 2.

1. The citizens of each State shall be entitled to all privileges and immunities of citizens in the several States.[8]

2. A person charged in any State with treason, felony, or other crime, who shall flee from justice, and be found in another State, shall on demand of the executive authority of the State from which he fled, be delivered up to be removed to the State having jurisdiction of the crime.

3. No person held to service or labor in one State under the laws thereof, escaping into another, shall, in consequence of any law or regulation therein, be discharged from such service or labor, but shall be delivered up on claim of the party to whom such service or labor may be due.[9]

---

[7]See the Eleventh Amendment.
[8]See the Fourteenth Amendment, Sec. 1.
[9]See the Thirteenth Amendment.

SECTION 3.

1. New States may be admitted by the Congress into this Union; but no new State shall be formed or erected within the jurisdiction of any other State, nor any State be formed by the junction of two or more States, or parts of States, without the consent of the legislatures of the States concerned as well as of the Congress.

2. The Congress shall have power to dispose of and make all needful rules and regulations respecting the territory or other property belonging to the United States; and nothing in this Constitution shall be so construed as to prejudice any claims of the United States, or of any particular State.

SECTION 4. The United States shall guarantee to every State in this Union a republican form of government, and shall protect each of them against invasion; and on application of the legislature, or of the executive (when the legislature cannot be convened) against domestic violence.

ARTICLE V

The Congress, whenever two thirds of both Houses shall deem it necessary, shall propose amendments to this Constitution, or, on the application of the legislatures of two thirds of the several States, shall call a convention for proposing amendments, which in either case shall be valid to all intents and purposes, as part of this Constitution, when ratified by the legislatures of three fourths of the several States, or by conventions in three fourths thereof, as the one or the other mode of ratification may be proposed by the Congress; Provided that no amendment which may be made prior to the year one thousand eight hundred and eight shall in any manner affect the first and fourth clauses in the ninth section of the first article; and that no State, without its consent, shall be deprived of its equal suffrage in the Senate.

ARTICLE VI

1. All debts contracted and engagements entered into, before the adoption of this Constitution, shall be as valid against the United States under this Constitution, as under the Confederation.[10]

2. This Constitution, and the laws of the United States which shall be made in pursuance thereof; and all treaties made, or which shall be made, under the authority of the United States, shall be the supreme law of the land; and the judges in every State shall be bound thereby, any thing in the Constitution or laws of any State to the contrary notwithstanding.

3. The senators and representatives before mentioned, and the members of the several State legislatures, and all executive and judicial officers, both of the United States and of the several States, shall be bound by oath or affirmation to support this Constitution; but no religious test shall ever be required as a qualification to any office or public trust under the United States.

ARTICLE VII

The ratification of the conventions of nine States shall be sufficient for the establishment of this Constitution between the States so ratifying the same.

Done in Convention by the unanimous consent of the States present the seventeenth day of September in the year of our Lord one thousand seven hundred and eighty-seven, and of the independence of the United States of America the twelfth. In witness whereof we have hereunto subscribed our names.

[Signatories' names omitted]

Articles in addition to, and amendment of, the Constitution of the United States of America, proposed by Congress, and ratified by the legislatures of the several States, pursuant to the fifth article of the original Constitution.

---

[10]See the Fourteenth Amendment, Sec. 4.

Amendment I

[First ten amendments ratified December 15, 1791]
Congress shall make no law respecting an establishment of religion, or prohibiting the free exercise thereof; or abridging the freedom of speech, or of the press; or the right of the people peaceably to assemble, and to petition the government for a redress of grievances.

Amendment II

A well regulated militia, being necessary to the security of a free State, the right of the people to keep and bear arms, shall not be infringed.

Amendment III

No soldier shall, in time of peace be quartered in any house, without the consent of the owner, nor in time of war, but in a manner to be prescribed by law.

Amendment IV

The right of the people to be secure in their persons, houses, papers, and effects, against unreasonable searches and seizures, shall not be violated, and no warrants shall issue, but upon probable cause, supported by oath or affirmation, and particularly describing the place to be searched, and the persons or things to be seized.

Amendment V

No person shall be held to answer for a capital or otherwise infamous crime, unless on a presentment or indictment of a grand jury, except in cases arising in the land or naval forces, or in the militia, when in actual service in time of war or public danger; nor shall any person be subject for the same offense to be twice put in jeopardy of life or limb; nor shall be compelled in any criminal case to be a witness against himself, nor be deprived of life, liberty, or property, without due process of law; nor shall private property be taken for public use, without just compensation.

Amendment VI

In all criminal prosecutions, the accused shall enjoy the right to a speedy and public trial, by an impartial jury of the State and district wherein the crime shall have been committed, which district shall have been previously ascertained by law, and to be informed of the nature and cause of the accusation; to be confronted with the witnesses against him; to have compulsory process for obtaining witnesses in his favor, and to have the assistance of counsel for his defense.

Amendment VII

In suits at common law, where the value in controversy shall exceed twenty dollars, the right of trial by jury shall be preserved, and no fact tried by a jury shall be otherwise reexamined in any court of the United States, than according to the rules of the common law.

Amendment VIII

Excessive bail shall not be required, nor excessive fines imposed, nor cruel and unusual punishments inflicted.

Amendment IX

The enumeration in the Constitution of certain rights shall not be construed to deny or disparage others retained by the people.

Amendment X

The powers not delegated to the United States by the Constitution, nor prohibited by it to the States, are reserved to the States respectively, or to the people.

Amendment XI [January 8, 1798]

The judicial power of the United States shall not be construed to extend to any suit in law or equity, commended or prosecuted against one of the United States by citizens of another State, or by citizens or subjects of any foreign State.

Amendment XII [September 25, 1804]

The electors shall meet in their respective States, and vote by ballot for President and Vice President, one of whom, at least, shall not be an inhabitant of the same State with themselves; they shall name in their ballots the person voted for as President, and in distinct ballots, the person voted for as Vice President, and they shall make distinct lists of all persons voted for as President and of all persons voted for as Vice President, and of the number of votes for each, which lists they shall sign and certify, and transmit sealed to the seat of the government of the United States, directed to the President of the Senate;—The President of the Senate shall, in the presence of the Senate and House of Representatives, open all the certificates and the votes shall then be counted;—The person having the greatest number of votes for President, shall be the President, if such number be a majority of the whole number of electors appointed; and if no person have such majority, then from the persons having the highest numbers not exceeding three on the list of those voted for as President, the House of Representatives shall choose immediately, by ballot, the President. But in choosing the President, the votes shall be taken by States, the representation from each State having one vote; a quorum for this purpose shall consist of a member or members from two thirds of the States, and a majority of all the States shall be necessary to a choice. And if the House of Representatives shall not choose a President whenever the right of choice shall devolve upon them, before the fourth day of March next following, then the Vice President shall act as President, as in the case of the death or other constitutional disability of the President. The person having the greatest number of votes as Vice President shall be the Vice President, if such number be a majority of the whole number of electors appointed, and if no person have a majority, then from the two highest numbers on the list, the Senate shall choose the Vice President; a quorum for the purpose shall consist of two thirds of the whole number of Senators, and a majority of the whole number shall be necessary to a choice. But no person constitutionally ineligible to the office of President shall be eligible to that of Vice President of the United States.

Amendment XIII [December 18, 1865]

SECTION 1. Neither slavery nor involuntary servitude, except as a punishment for crime whereof the party shall have been duly convicted, shall exist within the United States, or any place subject to their jurisdiction.

SECTION 2. Congress shall have power to enforce this article by appropriate legislation.

Amendment XIV [July 28, 1868]

SECTION 1. All persons born or naturalized in the United States, and subject to the jurisdiction thereof, are citizens of the United States and of the State wherein they reside. No State shall make or enforce any law which shall abridge the privileges or immunities of citizens of the United States; nor shall any State deprive any person of life, liberty, or property, without due process of law; nor deny to any person within its jurisdiction the equal protection of the laws.

SECTION 2. Representatives shall be apportioned among the several States according to their respective numbers, counting the whole number of persons in each State, excluding Indians not taxed. But when the right to vote at any election for the choice of electors for President and Vice President of the United States, representatives in Congress, the executive and judicial officers of a State, or the members of the legislature thereof, is denied to any of the male inhabitants of such State, being twenty-one years of age, and citizens of the United States, or in any way abridged, except for participating in rebellion, or other crime, the basis of representation there shall be reduced in the proportion which the number of such male citizens shall bear to the whole number of male citizens twenty-one years of age in such State.

SECTION 3. No person shall be a senator or representative in Congress, or elector of President and Vice President, or hold any office, civil or military, under the United States, or under any State, who having previously taken an oath, as a member of Congress, or as an officer of the United States, or as a member of any State legislature, or as an executive or judicial officer of any State, to support the Constitution of the United States, shall have engaged in insurrection or rebellion against the same, or given aid or comfort to the enemies thereof. But Congress may by a vote of two thirds of each House, remove such disability.

SECTION 4. The validity of the public debt of the United States, authorized by law, including debts incurred for payment of pensions and bounties for services in suppressing insurrection or rebellion; shall not be questioned. But neither the United States nor any State shall assume or pay any debt or obligation incurred in aid of insurrection or rebellion against the United States, or any claim for the loss or emancipation of any slave; but all such debts, obligations, and claims shall be held illegal and void.

SECTION 5. The Congress shall have the power to enforce, by appropriate legislation, the provisions of this article.

Amendment XV [March 30, 1870]

SECTION 1. The right of citizens of the United States to vote shall not be denied or abridged by the United States or by any State on account of race, color, or previous condition of servitude.

SECTION 2. The Congress shall have power to enforce this article by appropriate legislation.

Amendment XVI [February 25, 1913]

The Congress shall have power to lay and collect taxes on incomes, from whatever source derived, without apportionment among the several States, and without regard to any census or enumeration.

Amendment XVII [May 31, 1913]

The Senate of the United States shall be composed of two senators from each State, elected by the people thereof, for six years; and each senator shall have one vote. The electors in each State shall have the qualifications requisite for electors of the most numerous branch of the State legislature.

When vacancies happen in the representation of any State in the Senate, the executive authority of such State shall issue writs of election to fill such vacancies: Provided, That the legislature of any State may empower the executive thereof to make temporary appointments until the people fill the vacancies by election as the legislature may direct.

This amendment shall not be so construed as to affect the election or term of any senator chosen before it becomes valid as part of the Constitution.

Amendment XVIII[11] [January 29, 1919]

After one year from the ratification of this article, the manufacture, sale, or transportation of intoxicating liquors within, the importation thereof into, or the exportation thereof from the United States and all territory subject to the jurisdiction thereof for beverage purposes is thereby prohibited.

The Congress and the several States shall have concurrent power to enforce this article by appropriate legislation.

This article shall be inoperative unless it shall have been ratified as an amendment to the Constitution by the legislatures of the several States, as provided in the Constitution, within seven years from the date of the submission hereof to the States by Congress.

---

[11]Repealed by the Fourteenth Amendment, Sec. 1.

Amendment XIX [August 26, 1920]

The right of citizens of the United States to vote shall not be denied or abridged by the United States or by any State on account of sex.

Congress shall have the power to enforce this article by appropriate legislation.

Amendment XX [January 23, 1933]

SECTION 1. The terms of the President and Vice President shall end at noon on the 20th day of January and the terms of Senators and Representatives at noon on the 3d day of January, of the years in which such terms would have ended if this article had not been ratified; and the terms of their successors shall then begin.

SECTION 2. The Congress shall assemble at least once in every year, and such meeting shall begin at noon on the 3d day of January, unless they shall by law appoint a different day.

SECTION 3. If, at the time fixed for the beginning of the term of President, the President-elect shall have died, the Vice President-elect shall become President. If a President shall not have been chosen before the time fixed for the beginning of his term, or if the President-elect shall have failed to qualify, then the Vice President-elect shall act as President until a President shall have qualified; and the Congress may by law provide for the case wherein neither a President-elect nor a Vice President-elect shall have qualified, declaring who shall then act as President, or the manner in which one who is to act shall be selected, and such person shall act accordingly until a President or Vice President shall have qualified.

SECTION 4. The Congress may by law provide for the case of the death of any of the persons from whom, the House of Representatives may choose a President whenever the right of choice shall have devolved upon them, and for the case of the death of any of the persons from whom the Senate may choose a Vice President whenever the right of choice shall have devolved upon them.

SECTION 5. Sections 1 and 2 shall take effect on the 15th day of October following the ratification of this article.

SECTION 6. This article shall be inoperative unless it shall have been ratified as an amendment to the Constitution by the legislatures of three-fourths of the several States within seven years from the date of its submission.

Amendment XXI [December 5, 1933]

SECTION 1. The Eighteenth Article of amendment to the Constitution of the United States is hereby repealed.

SECTION 2. The transportation or importation into any State, Territory, or possession of the United States for delivery or use therein of intoxicating liquors in violation of the laws thereof, is hereby prohibited.

SECTION 3. This article shall be inoperative unless it shall have been ratified as an amendment to the Constitution by conventions in the several States, as provided in the Constitution, within seven years from the date of the submission thereof to the States by the Congress.

Amendment XXII [March 1, 1951]

No person shall be elected to the office of the President more than twice, and no person who has held the office of President, or acted as President, for more than two years of a term to which some other person was elected President shall be elected to the office of the President more than once.

But this article shall not apply to any person holding the office of President when this article was proposed by the Congress, and shall not prevent any person who may be holding the office of President, or acting as President, during the term within which this article becomes operative from holding the office of President or acting as President during the remainder of such term.

This article shall be inoperative unless it shall have been ratified as an amendment to the Constitution by the legislatures of three-fourths of the several States within seven years from the date of its submission to the States by the Congress.

Amendment XXIII [March 29, 1961]

SECTION 1. The District constituting the seat of Government of the United States shall appoint in such manner as the Congress may direct.

A number of electors of President and Vice President equal to the whole number of Senators and Representatives in Congress to which the District would be entitled if it were a State, but in no event more than the least populous State; they shall be in addition to those appointed by the States, but they shall be considered, for the purposes of the election of President and Vice President, to be electors appointed by a State; and they shall meet in the District and perform such duties as provided by the twelfth article of amendment.

SECTION 2. The Congress shall have power to enforce this article by appropriate legislation.

Amendment XXIV [January 23, 1964]

SECTION 1. The right of citizens of the United States to vote in any primary or other election for President or Vice President, for electors for President or Vice President, or for Senator or Representative in Congress, shall not be denied or abridged by the United States or any State by reason of failure to pay any poll tax or other tax.

SECTION 2. The Congress shall have power to enforce this article by appropriate legislation.

Amendment XXV [February 10, 1967]

SECTION 1. In case of the removal of the President from office or of his death or resignation, the Vice President shall become President.

SECTION 2. Whenever there is a vacancy in the office of the Vice President, the President shall nominate a Vice President who shall take office upon confirmation by a majority of both Houses of Congress.

SECTION 3. Whenever the President transmits to the President pro tempore of the Senate and the Speaker of the House of Representatives his written declaration that he is unable to discharge the powers and duties of his office, and until he transmits to them a written declaration to the contrary, such powers and duties shall be discharged by the Vice President as Acting President.

SECTION 4. Whenever the Vice President and a majority of either the principal officers of the executive departments or of such other body as Congress may by law provide, transmit to the President pro tempore of the Senate and the Speaker of the House of Representatives their written declaration that the President is unable to discharge the powers and duties of his office, the Vice President shall immediately assume the powers and duties of the office as Acting President.

Thereafter, when the President transmits to the President pro tempore of the Senate and the Speaker of the House of Representatives his written declaration that no inability exists, he shall resume the powers and duties of his office unless the Vice President and a majority of either the principal officers of the executive departments or of such other body as Congress may by law provide, transmit within four days to the President pro tempore of the Senate and the Speaker of the House of Representatives their written declaration that the President is unable to discharge the powers and duties of his office. Thereupon Congress shall decide the issue, assembling within forty-eight hours for that purpose if not in session. If the Congress, within twenty-one days after receipt of the latter written declaration, or, if Congress is not in session, within twenty-one days after Congress is required to assemble, determines by two-thirds vote of both Houses that the President is unable to discharge the powers and duties of his office, the Vice President shall continue to discharge the same as Acting President; otherwise, the President shall resume the powers and duties of his office.

Amendment XXVI [June 30, 1971]

SECTION 1. The right of citizens of the United States who are eighteen years of age or older to vote shall not be denied or abridged by the United States or by any State on account of age.

SECTION 2. The Congress shall have power to enforce this article by appropriate legislation.

Amendment XXVII[12] [May 7, 1992]

No law, varying the compensation for services of the Senators and Representatives, shall take effect until an election of Representatives shall have intervened.

Presidential Elections						
Year	Number of States	Candidates	Party	Popular Vote*	Electoral Vote†	Percentage of Popular Vote
1789	11	GEORGE WASHINGTON	No party designations		69	
		John Adams			34	
		Other Candidates			35	
1792	15	GEORGE WASHINGTON	No party designations		132	
		John Adams			77	
		George Clinton			50	
		Other Candidates			5	
1796	16	JOHN ADAMS	Federalist		71	
		Thomas Jefferson	Democratic-Republican		68	
		Thomas Pinckney	Federalist		59	
		Aaron Burr	Democratic-Republican		30	
		Other Candidates			48	
1800	16	THOMAS JEFFERSON	Democratic-Republican		73	
		Aaron Burr	Democratic-Republican		73	
		John Adams	Federalist		65	

*Percentage of popular vote given for any election year may not total 100 percent because candidates receiving less than 1 percent of the popular vote have been omitted.
†Prior to the passage of the Twelfth Amendment in 1904, the electoral college voted for two presidential candidates; the runner-up became vice-president. Data from Historical Statistics of the United States, Colonial Times to 1957 (1961), pp. 682–683, and The World Almanac.

---

[12]James Madison proposed this amendment in 1789 together with the ten amendments that were adopted as the Bill of Rights, but it failed to win ratification at the time. Congress, however, had set no deadline for its ratification, and over the years—particularly in the 1980s and 1990s—many states voted to add it to the Constitution. With the ratification of Michigan in 1992 it passed the threshold of 3/4ths of the states required for adoption, but because the process took more than 200 years, its validity remains in doubt.

Presidential Elections (Continued)

Year	Number of States	Candidates	Party	Popular Vote*	Electoral Vote†	Percentage of Popular Vote
		Charles C. Pinckney	Federalist		64	
		John Jay	Federalist		1	
1804	17	THOMAS JEFFERSON	Democratic-Republican		162	
		Charles C. Pinckney	Federalist		14	
1808	17	JAMES MADISON	Democratic-Republican		122	
		Charles C. Pinckney	Federalist		47	
		George Clinton	Democratic-Republican		6	
1812	18	JAMES MADISON	Democratic-Republican		128	
		DeWitt Clinton	Federalist		89	
1816	19	JAMES MONROE	Democratic-Republican		183	
		Rufus King	Federalist		34	
1820	24	JAMES MONROE	Democratic-Republican		231	
		John Quincy Adams	Independent-Republican		1	
1824	24	JOHN QUINCY ADAMS	Democratic-Republican	108,740	84	30.5
		Andrew Jackson	Democratic-Republican	153,544	99	43.1
		William H. Crawford	Democratic-Republican	46,618	41	13.1
		Henry Clay	Democratic-Republican	47,136	37	13.2
1828	24	ANDREW JACKSON	Democrat	647,286	178	56.0
		John Quincy Adams	National Republican	508,064	83	44.0
1832	24	ANDREW JACKSON	Democrat	687,502	219	55.0
		Henry Clay	National Republican	530,189	49	42.4
		William Wirt	Anti-Masonic	33,108	7	2.6
		John Floyd	National Republican		11	

Presidential Elections (Continued)

Year	Number of States	Candidates	Party	Popular Vote*	Electoral Vote†	Percentage of Popular Vote
1836	26	MARTIN VAN BUREN	Democrat	765,483	170	50.9
		William H. Harrison	Whig		73	
		Hugh L. White	Whig	739,795	26	
		Daniel Webster	Whig		14	49.1
		W. P. Mangum	Whig		11	
1840	26	WILLIAM H. HARRISON	Whig	1,274,624	234	53.1
		Martin Van Buren	Democrat	1,127,781	60	46.9
1844	26	JAMES K. POLK	Democrat	1,338,464	170	49.6
		Henry Clay	Whig	1,300,097	105	48.1
		James G. Birney	Liberty	62,300		2.3
1848	30	ZACHARY TAYLOR	Whig	1,360,967	163	47.4
		Lewis Cass	Democrat	1,222,342	127	42.5
		Martin Van Buren	Free Soil	291,263		10.1
1852	31	FRANKLIN PIERCE	Democrat	1,601,117	254	50.9
		Winfield Scott	Whig	1,385,453	42	44.1
		John P. Hale	Free Soil	155,825		5.0
1856	31	JAMES BUCHANAN	Democrat	1,832,955	174	45.3
		John C. Frémont	Republican	1,339,932	114	33.1
		Millard Fillmore	American ("Know Nothing")	871,731	8	21.6
1860	33	ABRAHAM LINCOLN	Republican	1,865,593	180	39.8
		Stephen A. Douglas	Democrat	1,382,713	12	29.5
		John C. Breckinridge	Democrat	848,356	72	18.1
		John Bell	Constitutional Union	592,906	39	12.6
1864	36	ABRAHAM LINCOLN	Republican	2,206,938	212	55.0
		George B. McClellan	Democrat	1,803,787	21	45.0
1868	37	ULYSSES S. GRANT	Republican	3,013,421	214	52.7
		Horatio Seymour	Democrat	2,706,829	80	47.3

Presidential Elections (Continued)

Year	Number of States	Candidates	Party	Popular Vote*	Electoral Vote†	Percentage of Popular Vote
1872	37	ULYSSES S. GRANT	Republican	3,596,745	286	55.6
		Horace Greeley	Democrat	2,843,446	*	43.9
1876	38	RUTHERFORD B. HAYES	Republican	4,036,572	185	48.0
		Samuel J. Tilden	Democrat	4,284,020	184	51.0
1880	38	JAMES A. GARFIELD	Republican	4,453,295	214	48.5
		Winfield S. Hancock	Democrat	4,414,082	155	48.1
		James B. Weaver	Greenback-Labor	308,578		3.4
1884	38	GROVER CLEVELAND	Democrat	4,879,507	219	48.5
		James G. Blaine	Republican	4,850,293	182	48.2
		Benjamin F. Butler	Greenback-Labor	175,370		1.8
		John P. St. John	Prohibition	150,369		1.5
1888	38	BENJAMIN HARRISON	Republican	5,447,129	233	47.9
		Grover Cleveland	Democrat	5,537,857	168	48.6
		Clinton B. Fisk	Prohibition	249,506		2.2
		Anson J. Streeter	Union Labor	146,935		1.3
1892	44	GROVER CLEVELAND	Democrat	5,555,426	277	46.1
		Benjamin Harrison	Republican	5,182,690	145	43.0
		James B. Weaver	People's	1,029,846	22	8.5
		John Bidwell	Prohibition	264,133		2.2
1896	45	WILLIAM MCKINLEY	Republican	7,102,246	271	51.1
		William J. Bryan	Democrat	6,492,559	176	47.7
1900	45	WILLIAM MCKINLEY	Republican	7,218,491	292	51.7
		William J. Bryan	Democrat; Populist	6,356,734	155	45.5
		John C. Woolley	Prohibition	208,914		1.5
1904	45	THEODORE ROOSEVELT	Republican	7,628,461	336	57.4
		Alton B. Parker	Democrat	5,084,223	140	37.6
		Eugene V. Debs	Socialist	402,283		3.0
		Silas C. Swallow	Prohibition	258,536		1.9

*Because of the death of Greeley, Democratic electors scattered their votes.

Presidential Elections (Continued)

Year	Number of States	Candidates	Party	Popular Vote*	Electoral Vote†	Percentage of Popular Vote
1908	46	WILLIAM H. TAFT	Republican	7,675,320	321	51.6
		William J. Bryan	Democrat	6,412,294	162	43.1
		Eugene V. Debs	Socialist	420,793		2.8
		Eugene W. Chafin	Prohibition	253,840		1.7
1912	48	WOODROW WILSON	Democrat	6,296,547	435	41.9
		Theodore Roosevelt	Progressive	4,118,571	88	27.4
		William H. Taft	Republican	3,486,720	8	23.2
		Eugene V. Debs	Socialist	900,672		6.0
		Eugene W. Chafin	Prohibition	206,275		1.4
1916	48	WOODROW WILSON	Democrat	9,127,695	277	49.4
		Charles E. Hughes	Republican	8,533,507	254	46.2
		A. L. Benson	Socialist	585,113		3.2
		J. Frank Hanly	Prohibition	220,506		1.2
1920	48	WARREN G. HARDING	Republican	16,143,407	404	60.4
		James M. Cox	Democrat	9,130,328	127	34.2
		Eugene V. Debs	Socialist	919,799		3.4
		P. P. Christensen	Farmer-Labor	265,411		1.0
1924	48	CALVIN COOLIDGE	Republican	15,718,211	382	54.0
		John W. Davis	Democrat	8,385,283	136	28.8
		Robert M. La Follette	Progressive	4,831,289	13	16.6
1928	48	HERBERT C. HOOVER	Republican	21,391,993	444	58.2
		Alfred E. Smith	Democrat	15,016,169	87	40.9
1932	48	FRANKLIN D. ROOSEVELT	Democrat	22,809,638	472	57.4
		Herbert C. Hoover	Republican	15,758,901	59	39.7
		Norman Thomas	Socialist	881,951		2.2
1936	48	FRANKLIN D. ROOSEVELT	Democrat	27,752,869	523	60.8
		Alfred M. Landon	Republican	16,674,665	8	36.5
		William Lemke	Union	882,479		1.9
1940	48	FRANKLIN D. ROOSEVELT	Democrat	27,307,819	449	54.8
		Wendell L. Willkie	Republican	22,321,018	82	44.8

Presidential Elections (Continued)

Year	Number of States	Candidates	Party	Popular Vote*	Electoral Vote	Percentage of Popular Vote
1944	48	FRANKLIN D. ROOSEVELT	Democrat	25,606,585	432	53.5
		Thomas E. Dewey	Republican	22,014,745	99	46.0
1948	48	HARRY S TRUMAN	Democrat	24,105,812	303	49.5
		Thomas E. Dewey	Republican	21,970,065	189	45.1
		J. Strom Thurmond	States' Rights	1,169,063	39	2.4
		Henry A. Wallace	Progressive	1,157,172		2.4
1952	48	DWIGHT D. EISENHOWER	Republican	33,936,234	442	55.1
		Adlai E. Stevenson	Democrat	27,314,992	89	44.4
1956	48	DWIGHT D. EISENHOWER	Republican	35,590,472	457*	57.6
		Adlai E. Stevenson	Democrat	26,022,752	73	42.1
1960	50	JOHN F. KENNEDY	Democrat	34,227,096	303†	49.9
		Richard M. Nixon	Republican	34,108,546	219	49.6
1964	50	LYNDON B. JOHNSON	Democrat	42,676,220	486	61.3
		Barry M. Goldwater	Republican	26,860,314	52	38.5
1968	50	RICHARD M. NIXON	Republican	31,785,480	301	43.4
		Hubert H. Humphrey	Democrat	31,275,165	191	42.7
		George C. Wallace	American Independent	9,906,473	46	13.5
1972	50	RICHARD M. NIXON‡	Republican	47,165,234	520	60.6
		George S. McGovern	Democrat	29,168,110	17	37.5
1976	50	JIMMY CARTER	Democrat	40,828,929	297	50.1
		Gerald R. Ford	Republican	39,148,940	240	47.9
		Eugene McCarthy	Independent	739,256		
1980	50	RONALD REAGAN	Republican	43,201,220	489	50.9
		Jimmy Carter	Democrat	34,913,332	49	41.2
		John B. Anderson	Independent	5,581,379		
1984	50	RONALD REAGAN	Republican	53,428,357	525	59.0
		Walter F. Mondale	Democrat	36,930,923	13	41.0

*Walter B. Jones received 1 electoral vote.
†Harry F. Byrd received 15 electoral votes.
‡Resigned August 9, 1974: Vice President Gerald R. Ford became president.

Presidential Elections (Continued)

Year	Number of States	Candidates	Party	Popular Vote*	Electoral Vote	Percentage of Popular Vote
1988	50	GEORGE BUSH	Republican	48,901,046	426	53.4
		Michael Dukakis	Democrat	41,809,030	111	45.6
1992	50	BILL CLINTON	Democrat	43,728,275	370	43.2
		George H.W. Bush	Republican	38,167,416	168	37.7
		H. Ross Perot	United We Stand, America	19,237,247		19.0
1996	50	BILL CLINTON	Democrat	45,590,703	379	49.0
		Robert Dole	Republican	37,816,307	159	41.0
		H. Ross Perot	Reform	7,866,284		8.0
2000	50	GEORGE W. BUSH	Republican	50,459,624	271	47.9
		Albert Gore Jr.	Democrat	51,003,328	266	49.4
		Ralph Nader	Green	2,882,985		2.7

Supreme Court Justices

Name*	Years on Court	Appointing President
JOHN JAY	1789–1795	Washington
James Wilson	1789–1798	Washington
John Rutledge	1790–1791	Washington
William Cushing	1790–1810	Washington
John Blair	1790–1796	Washington
James Iredell	1790–1799	Washington
Thomas Jefferson	1792–1793	Washington
William Paterson	1793–1806	Washington
JOHN RUTLEDGE†	1795	Washington
Samuel Chase	1796–1811	Washington
OLIVER ELLSWORTH	1796–1800	Washington
Bushrod Washington	1799–1829	J. Adams
Alfred Moore	1800–1804	J. Adams
JOHN MARSHALL	1801–1835	J. Adams
William Johnson	1804–1834	Jefferson
Brockholst Livingston	1807–1823	Jefferson
Thomas Todd	1807–1826	Jefferson
Gabriel Duvall	1811–1835	Madison
Joseph Story	1812–1845	Madison
Smith Thompson	1823–1843	Monroe
Robert Trimble	1826–1828	J. Q. Adams
John McLean	1830–1861	Jackson

Capital letters designate chief justices.
†*Never confirmed by the Senate as chief justice.*

Supreme Court Justices (Continued)

Name*	Years on Court	Appointing President
Henry Baldwin	1830–1844	Jackson
James M. Wayne	1835–1867	Jackson
ROGER B. TANEY	1836–1864	Jackson
Philip P. Barbour	1836–1841	Jackson
John Cartron	1837–1865	Van Buren
John McKinley	1838–1852	Van Buren
Peter V. Daniel	1842–1860	Van Buren
Samuel Nelson	1845–1872	Tyler
Levi Woodbury	1845–1851	Polk
Robert C. Grier	1846–1870	Polk
Benjamin R. Curtis	1851–1857	Fillmore
John A. Campbell	1853–1861	Pierce
Nathan Clifford	1858–1881	Buchanan
Noah H. Swayne	1862–1881	Lincoln
Samuel F. Miller	1862–1890	Lincoln
David Davis	1862–1877	Lincoln
Stephen J. Field	1863–1897	Lincoln
SALMON P. CHASE	1864–1873	Lincoln
William Strong	1870–1880	Grant
Joseph P. Bradley	1870–1892	Grant
Ward Hunt	1873–1882	Grant
MORRISON R. WAITE	1874–1888	Grant
John M. Harlan	1877–1911	Hayes
William B. Woods	1881–1887	Hayes
Stanley Matthews	1881–1889	Garfield
Horace Gray	1882–1902	Arthur
Samuel Blatchford	1882–1893	Arthur
Lucious Q. C. Lamar	1888–1893	Cleveland
MELVILLE W. FULLER	1888–1910	Cleveland
David J. Brewer	1890–1910	B. Harrison
Henry B. Brown	1891–1906	B. Harrison
George Shiras Jr.	1892–1903	B. Harrison
Howell E. Jackson	1893–1895	B. Harrison
Edward D. White	1894–1910	Cleveland
Rufus W. Peckham	1896–1909	Cleveland
Joseph McKenna	1898–1925	McKinley
Oliver W. Holmes	1902–1932	T. Roosevelt
William R. Day	1903–1922	T. Roosevelt
William H. Moody	1906–1910	T. Roosevelt
Horace H. Lurton	1910–1914	Taft
Charles E. Hughes	1910–1916	Taft
EDWARD D. WHITE	1910–1921	Taft
Willis Van Devanter	1911–1937	Taft
Joseph R. Lamar	1911–1916	Taft
Mahlon Pitney	1912–1922	Taft
James C. McReynolds	1914–1941	Wilson
Louis D. Brandeis	1916–1939	Wilson

Supreme Court Justices (Continued)

Name*	Years on Court	Appointing President
John H. Clarke	1916–1922	Wilson
WILLIAM H. TAFT	1921–1930	Harding
George Sutherland	1922–1938	Harding
Pierce Butler	1923–1939	Harding
Edward T. Sanford	1923–1930	Harding
Harlan F. Stone	1925–1941	Coolidge
CHARLES E. HUGHES	1930–1941	Hoover
Owen J. Roberts	1930–1945	Hoover
Benjamin N. Cardozo	1932–1938	Hoover
Hugo L. Black	1937–1971	F. Roosevelt
Stanley F. Reed	1938–1957	F. Roosevelt
Felix Frankfurter	1939–1962	F. Roosevelt
William O. Douglas	1939–1975	F. Roosevelt
Frank Murphy	1940–1949	F. Roosevelt
HARLAN F. STONE	1941–1946	F. Roosevelt
James F. Brynes	1941–1942	F. Roosevelt
Robert H. Jackson	1941–1954	F. Roosevelt
Wiley B. Rutledge	1943–1949	F. Roosevelt
Harold H. Burton	1945–1958	Truman
FREDERICK M. VINSON	1946–1953	Truman
Tom C. Clark	1949–1967	Truman
Sherman Minton	1949–1956	Truman
EARL WARREN	1953–1969	Eisenhower
John Marshall Harlan	1955–1971	Eisenhower
William J. Brennan Jr.	1956–1990	Eisenhower
Charles E. Whittaker	1957–1962	Eisenhower
Potter Stewart	1958–1981	Eisenhower
Byron R. White	1962–1993	Kennedy
Arthur J. Goldberg	1962–1965	Kennedy
Abe Fortas	1965–1970	L. Johnson
Thurgood Marshall	1967–1991	L. Johnson
WARREN E. BURGER	1969–1986	Nixon
Harry A. Blackmun	1970–1994	Nixon
Lewis F. Powell Jr.	1971–1987	Nixon
William H. Rehnquist	1971–1986	Nixon
John Paul Stevens	1975–	Ford
Sandra Day O'Connor	1981–	Reagan
WILLIAM H. REHNQUIST	1986–	Reagan
Antonin Scalia	1986–	Reagan
Anthony Kennedy	1988–	Reagan
David Souter	1990–	Bush
Clarence Thomas	1991–	Bush
Ruth Bader Ginsburg	1993–	Clinton
Stephen Breyer	1994–	Clinton

Admission of States into the Union

State	Date of Admission	State	Date of Admission
1. Delaware	December 7, 1787	26. Michigan	January 26, 1837
2. Pennsylvania	December 12, 1787	27. Florida	March 3, 1845
3. New Jersey	December 18, 1787	28. Texas	December 29, 1845
4. Georgia	January 2, 1788	29. Iowa	December 28, 1846
5. Connecticut	January 9, 1788	30. Wisconsin	May 29, 1848
6. Massachusetts	February 6, 1788	31. California	September 9, 1850
7. Maryland	April 28, 1788	32. Minnesota	May 11, 1858
8. South Carolina	May 23, 1788	33. Oregon	February 14, 1859
9. New Hampshire	June 21, 1788	34. Kansas	January 29, 1861
10. Virginia	June 25, 1788	35. West Virginia	June 20, 1863
11. New York	July 26, 1788	36. Nevada	October 31, 1864
12. North Carolina	November 21, 1789	37. Nebraska	March 1, 1867
13. Rhode Island	May 29, 1790	38. Colorado	August 1, 1876
14. Vermont	March 4, 1791	39. North Dakota	November 2, 1889
15. Kentucky	June 1, 1792	40. South Dakota	November 2, 1889
16. Tennessee	June 1, 1796	41. Montana	November 8, 1889
17. Ohio	March 1, 1803	42. Washington	November 11, 1889
18. Louisiana	April 30, 1812	43. Idaho	July 3, 1890
19. Indiana	December 11, 1816	44. Wyoming	July 10, 1890
20. Mississippi	December 10, 1817	45. Utah	January 4, 1896
21. Illinois	December 3, 1818	46. Oklahoma	November 16, 1907
22. Alabama	December 14, 1819	47. New Mexico	January 6, 1912
23. Maine	March 15, 1820	48. Arizona	February 14, 1912
24. Missouri	August 10, 1821	49. Alaska	January 3, 1959
25. Arkansas	June 15, 1836	50. Hawaii	August 21, 1959

Demographics of the United States

Population Growth		
Year	Population	Percent Increase
1630	4,600	
1640	26,600	478.3
1650	50,400	90.8
1660	75,100	49.0
1670	111,900	49.0
1680	151,500	35.4
1690	210,400	38.9
1700	250,900	19.2
1710	331,700	32.2
1720	466,200	40.5
1730	629,400	35.0
1740	905,600	43.9
1750	1,170,800	29.3
1760	1,593,600	36.1
1770	2,148,100	34.8
1780	2,780,400	29.4
1790	3,929,214	41.3
1800	5,308,483	35.1
1810	7,239,881	36.4
1820	9,638,453	33.1
1830	12,866,020	33.5
1840	17,069,453	32.7
1850	23,191,876	35.9
1860	31,443,321	35.6
1870	39,818,449	26.6
1880	50,155,783	26.0
1890	62,947,714	25.5
1900	75,994,575	20.7
1910	91,972,266	21.0
1920	105,710,620	14.9
1930	122,775,046	16.1
1940	131,669,275	7.2
1950	151,325,798	14.5
1960	179,323,175	18.5
1970	203,302,031	13.4
1980	226,542,199	11.4
1990	248,718,301	9.8
2000	281,421,906	13.1

Source: *Historical Statistics of the United States* (1975); *Statistical Abstract by the United States* (2001).
Note: Figures for 1630–1780 include British colonies within limits of present United States only; Native American population included only in 1930 and thereafter.

Work Force

Year	Total Number Workers (1000s)	Farmers as % of Total	Women as % of Total	% Workers in Unions
1810	2,330	84	(NA)	(NA)
1840	5,660	75	(NA)	(NA)
1860	11,110	53	(NA)	(NA)
1870	12,506	53	15	(NA)
1880	17,392	52	15	(NA)
1890	23,318	43	17	(NA)
1900	29,073	40	18	3
1910	38,167	31	21	6
1920	41,614	26	21	12
1930	48,830	22	22	7
1940	53,011	17	24	27
1950	59,643	12	28	25
1960	69,877	8	32	26
1970	82,049	4	37	25
1980	106,940	3	43	23
1990	125,840	3	45	16
2000	140,863	2	47	12

Source: Historical Statistics of the United States (1975); *Statistical Abstract of the United States* (2001).

Vital Statistics (In Thousands)

Year	Births	Deaths	Marriages	Divorces
1800	55	(NA)	(NA)	(NA)
1810	54.3	(NA)	(NA)	(NA)
1820	55.2	(NA)	(NA)	(NA)
1830	51.4	(NA)	(NA)	(NA)
1840	51.8	(NA)	(NA)	(NA)
1850	43.3	(NA)	(NA)	(NA)
1860	44.3	(NA)	(NA)	(NA)
1870	38.3	(NA)	9.6 (1867)	0.3 (1867)
1880	39.8	(NA)	9.1 (1875)	0.3 (1875)
1890	31.5	(NA)	9.0	0.5
1900	32.3	17.2	9.3	0.7
1910	30.1	14.7	10.3	0.9
1920	27.7	13.0	12.0	1.6
1930	21.3	11.3	9.2	1.6
1940	19.4	10.8	12.1	2.0
1950	24.1	9.6	11.1	2.6
1960	23.7	9.5	8.5	2.2
1970	18.4	9.5	10.6	3.5
1980	15.9	8.8	10.6	5.2
1990	16.7	8.6	9.8	4.7
1997	14.6	8.6	8.9	4.3

Source: Historical Statistics of the United States (1975); *Statistical Abstract of the United States* (1999).

Racial Composition of the Population (In Thousands)

Year	White	Black	Indian	Hispanic	Asian/Pacific Islander
1790	3,172	757	(NA)	(NA)	(NA)
1800	4,306	1,002	(NA)	(NA)	(NA)
1820	7,867	1,772	(NA)	(NA)	(NA)
1840	14,196	2,874	(NA)	(NA)	(NA)
1860	26,923	4,442	(NA)	(NA)	(NA)
1880	43,403	6,581	(NA)	(NA)	(NA)
1900	66,809	8,834	(NA)	(NA)	(NA)
1910	81,732	9,828	(NA)	(NA)	(NA)
1920	94,821	10,463	(NA)	(NA)	(NA)
1930	110,287	11,891	(NA)	(NA)	(NA)
1940	118,215	12,866	(NA)	(NA)	(NA)
1950	134,942	15,042	(NA)	(NA)	(NA)
1960	158,832	18,872	(NA)	(NA)	(NA)
1970	178,098	22,581	(NA)	(NA)	(NA)
1980	194,713	26,683	1,420	14,609	3,729
1990	208,727	30,511	2,065	22,372	2,462
2000	211,461	34,658	2,476	35,306	10,642

Source: U.S. Bureau of the Census, U.S. *Census of Population: 1940*, vol. II, part 1, and vol. IV, part 1; *1950*, vol. II, part 1; *1960*, vol. I, part 1; *1970*, vol. I, part B; and *Current Population Reports*, P25-1095 and P25-1104; *Statistical Abstract of the United States* (2001).

The Economy and Federal Spending

Year	Gross National Product (GNP) (in billions)	Foreign Trade (In Millions) Exports	Imports	Balance of Trade	Federal Budget (in billions)	Federal Surplus/ Deficit (in billions)	Federal Debt (in billions)
1790	(NA)	$20	$23	$−3	$0.004	$+0.00015	$0.076
1800	(NA)	71	91	−20	0.011	+0.0006	0.083
1810	(NA)	67	85	−18	0.008	+0.0012	0.053
1820	(NA)	70	74	−4	0.018	−0.0004	0.091
1830	(NA)	74	71	+3	0.015	+0.100	0.049
1840	(NA)	132	107	+25	0.024	−0.005	0.004
1850	(NA)	152	178	−26	0.040	−0.004	0.064
1860	(NA)	400	362	−38	0.063	−0.01	0.065
1870	$7.4	451	462	−11	0.310	+0.10	2.4
1880	11.2	853	761	+92	0.268	+0.07	2.1
1890	13.1	910	823	+87	0.318	+0.09	1.2
1900	18.7	1,499	930	+569	0.521	+0.05	1.2
1910	35.3	1,919	1,646	+273	0.694	−0.02	1.1
1920	91.5	8,664	5,784	+2,880	6.357	+0.3	24.3
1930	90.7	4,013	3,500	+513	3.320	+0.7	16.3
1940	100.0	4,030	7,433	−3,403	9.6	−2.7	43.0

The Economy and Federal Spending (continued)

Year	Gross National Product (GNP) (in billions)	Foreign Trade (In Millions)			Federal Budget (in billions)	Federal Surplus/ Deficit (in billions)	Federal Debt (in billions)
		Exports	Imports	Balance of Trade			
1950	286.5	10,816	9,125	+1,691	43.1	−2.2	257.4
1960	506.5	19,600	15,046	+4,556	92.2	+0.3	286.3
1970	992.7	42,700	40,189	+2,511	195.6	−2.8	371.0
1980	2,631.7	220,783	244,871	+24,088	590.9	−73.8	907.7
1990	5,524.5	394,030	494,042	−101,012	1,251.8	−220.5	3,233.3
2000	9,958.7	1,068,397	1,438,086	−369,689	1,788.8	+236.4	5,629.0

Source: U.S. Office of Management and Budget, Budget of the United States Government, Annual; Statistical Abstract of the United States, 2001.

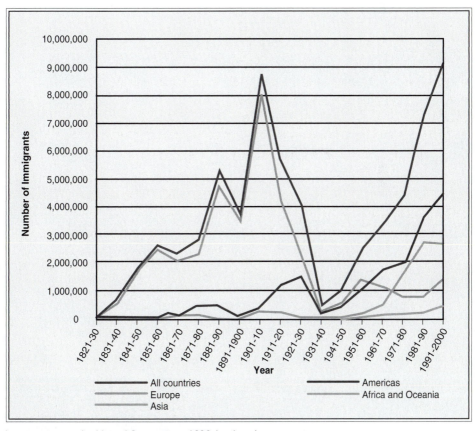

Immigration to the United States since 1820, by decade.

Source: Statistical Yearbook of the Immigration and Naturalization Service, 2001.

GLOSSARY

Acquired Immune Deficiency Syndrome (AIDS) A complex of deadly pathologies resulting from infection with the human immunodeficiency virus (HIV).

Act for Religious Toleration The first law in America to call for freedom of worship for all Christians.

Actual Representation The practice whereby elected representatives normally reside in their districts and are directly responsive to local interests.

Affirmative action A set of policies to open opportunities in business and education for members of minority groups and women by allowing race and gender to be factors included in decisions to hire, award contracts, or admit students to higher education programs.

Age of Enlightenment Major intellectual movement occurring in Western Europe in the late seventeenth and early eighteenth centuries.

Agricultural Wheel One of several farmer organizations that emerged in the South during the 1880s. It sought federal legislation to deal with credit and currency issues.

Alamo Franciscan mission at San Antonio, Texas, that was the site in 1836 of a siege and massacre of Texans by Mexican troops.

Albany Plan of Union Plan put forward in 1754 calling for an intercolonial union to manage defense and Indian affairs. The plan was rejected by participants at the Albany Congress.

Albany Regency The tightly disciplined state political machine built by Martin Van Buren in New York.

Alien and Sedition Acts Collective name given to four acts passed by Congress in 1798 that curtailed freedom of speech and the liberty of foreigners resident in the United States.

Alliance for Progress Program of economic aid to Latin America during the Kennedy administration.

Allies In World War I, Britain, France, Russia, and other belligerent nations fighting against the Central Powers but not including the United States.

American Anti-Slavery Society The first national organization of abolitionists, founded in 1833.

American Colonization Society Organization, founded in 1817 by antislavery reformers, that called for gradual emancipation and the removal of freed blacks to Africa.

American Federation of Labor (AFL) Union formed in 1886 that organized skilled workers along craft lines and emphasized a few workplace issues rather than a broad social program.

American Indian Movement (AIM) Group of Native American political activists who used confrontations with the federal government to publicize their case for Indian rights.

American System of Manufacturing A technique of production pioneered in the United States in the first half of the nineteenth century that relied on precision manufacturing with the use of interchangeable parts.

American System The program of government subsidies favored by Henry Clay and his followers to promote American economic growth and protect domestic manufacturers from foreign competition.

Americans with Disabilities Act Legislation in 1992 that banned discrimination against physically disabled persons in employment, transportation, and public accommodations.

Anarchists Persons who believe that all government interferes with individual liberty and should be abolished by whatever means necessary.

Anglican Of or belonging to the Church of England, a Protestant denomination.

Anglo-American Accords Series of agreements reached in the British-American Conventions of 1818 that fixed the western boundary between the United States and Canada, allowed for joint occupation of Oregon, and restored American fishing rights.

Annapolis Convention Conference of state delegates at Annapolis, Maryland, that issued a call in September 1786 for a convention to meet at Philadelphia to consider fundamental changes.

Antifederalists Opponents of the Constitution in the debate over its ratification.

Anti-Masons Third party formed in 1827 in opposition to the presumed power and influence of the Masonic order.

Appeal to the Colored Citizens of the World Written by David Walker, a published insistence that "America is more our country, than it is the whites'—we have enriched it with our blood and tears."

Articles of Confederation Written document setting up the loose confederation of states that comprised the first national government of the United States.

Atlanta Compromise Booker T. Washington's policy accepting segregation and disenfranchisement for African Americans in exchange for white assistance in education and job training.

Atlantic Charter Statement of common principles and war aims developed by President Franklin Roosevelt and British Prime Minister Winston Churchill at a meeting in August 1941.

Australian ballot Secret voting and the use of official ballots rather than party tickets.

Axis Powers The opponents of the United States and its allies in World War II.

Aztecs A warrior people who dominated the Valley of Mexico from 1100 to 1521.

Bacon's Rebellion Violent conflict in Virginia (1675–1676), beginning with settler attacks on Indians but culminating in a rebellion led by Nathaniel Bacon against Virginia's government.

Baker v. *Carr* U.S. Supreme Court decision in 1962 that allowed federal courts to review the appointment of state legislative districts and established the principle that such districts should have roughly equal populations ("one person, one vote").

Bank War The political struggle between President Andrew Jackson and the supporters of the Second Bank of the United States.

Battle of New Orleans Decisive American War of 1812 victory over British troops in January 1815 that ended any British hopes of gaining control of the lower Mississippi River Valley.

Battle of Put-in-Bay American naval victory on Lake Erie in September 1813 in the War of 1812 that denied the British strategic control over the Great Lakes.

Battle of the Atlantic The long struggle between German submarines and the British and U.S. navies in the North Atlantic from 1940 to 1943.

Battle of the Little Bighorn Battle in which Colonel George A. Custer and the Seventh Cavalry were defeated by the Sioux and Cheyennes under Sitting Bull and Crazy Horse in Montana in 1876.

Battles of Lexington and Concord The first two battles of the American Revolution that resulted in a total of 273 British soldiers dead, wounded, and missing and nearly one hundred Americans dead, wounded, and missing.

Bay of Pigs Site in Cuba of an unsuccessful landing by fourteen hundred anti-Castro Cuban refugees in April 1961.

Beaver Wars Series of bloody conflicts, occurring between 1640s and 1680s, during which the Iroquois fought the French for control of the fur trade in the east and the Great Lakes region.

Benevolent empire Network of reform associations affiliated with Protestant churches in the early nineteenth century dedicated to the restoration of moral order.

Berlin blockade Three-hundred-day Soviet blockade of land access to United States, British, and French occupation zones in Berlin, 1948–1949.

Berlin Wall Wall erected by East Germany in 1961 that isolated West Berlin from the surrounding areas in Communist-controlled East Berlin and East Germany.

Bill of Rights A written summary of inalienable rights and liberties.

Black codes Laws passed by states and municipalities denying many rights of citizenship to free black people before the Civil War.

Black Hawk's War Short 1832 war in which federal troops and Illinois militia units defeated the Sauk and Fox Indians led by Black Hawk.

Black Panthers Political and social movement among black Americans, founded in Oakland, California, in 1966 and emphasizing black economic and political power.

Black Power Philosophy emerging after 1965 that real economic and political gains for African Americans could come only through self-help, self-determination, and organizing for direct political influence.

"Bleeding Kansas" Violence between pro- and antislavery forces in Kansas Territory after the passage of the Kansas-Nebraska Act in 1854.

Blitzkrieg German war tactic in World War II ("lightning war") involving the concentration of air and armored firepower to punch and exploit holes in opposing defensive lines.

Bolshevik Member of the Communist movement in Russia that established the Soviet government after the 1917 Russian Revolution.

Bonus Army Unemployed veterans of World War I gathering in Washington in 1932 demanding payment of service bonuses not due until 1945.

Bosnia A nation in southeast Europe that split off from Yugoslavia and became the site of bitter civil and religious war, requiring NATO and U.S. intervention in the 1990s.

Boston Massacre After months of increasing friction between townspeople and the British troops stationed in the city, on March 5, 1770, British troops fired on American civilians in Boston.

Boston Tea Party Incident that occurred on December 16, 1773, in which Bostonians, disguised as Indians, destroyed £9,000 worth of tea belonging to the British East India Company in order to prevent payment of the duty on it.

British Constitution The principles, procedures, and precedents that governed the operation of the British government.

Brook Farm A utopian community and experimental farm established in 1841 near Boston.

Brown v. *Board of Education of Topeka* Supreme Court decision in 1954 that declared that "separate but equal" schools for children of different races violated the Constitution.

Bureau of Reclamation   Federal agency established in 1902 providing public funds for irrigation projects in arid regions.

Cahokia   One of the largest urban centers created by Mississippian peoples, containing 30,000 residents in 1250.

Californios   Californians of Spanish descent.

Camp David Agreement   Agreement to reduce points of conflict between Israel and Egypt, hammered out in 1977 with the help of U.S. president Jimmy Carter.

Carpetbaggers   Northern transplants to the South, many of whom were Union soldiers who stayed in the South after the war.

Central Intelligence Agency (CIA)   Agency established in 1947 that coordinates the gathering and evaluation of military and economic information on other nations.

Central Powers   Germany and its World War I allies in Austria, Turkey, and Bulgaria.

Chain migration   Process common to many immigrant groups whereby one family member brings over other family members, who in turn bring other relatives and friends and occasionally entire villages.

Charles River Bridge **v.** *Warren Bridge*   Supreme Court decision of 1837 that promised economic competition by ruling that the broader rights of the community took precedence over any presumed right of monopoly granted in a corporate charter.

Cherokee War   Conflict (1759–1761) on the Southern frontier between the Cherokee Indians and colonists from Virginia southward.

Chesapeake **incident**   Attack in 1807 by the British ship *Leopard* on the American ship *Chesapeake* in American territorial waters.

Chisholm Trail   The route followed by Texas cattle raisers driving their herds north to markets at Kansas railheads.

Church of Jesus Christ of Latter-day Saints (Mormon Church)   Church founded in 1830 by Joseph Smith and based on the revelations in a sacred book he called the Book of Mormon.

Civil Rights Act of 1964   Federal legislation that outlawed discrimination in public accommodations and employment on the basis of race, skin color, gender, religion, or national origin.

Claims clubs   Groups of local settlers on the nineteenth-century frontier who banded together to prevent the price of their land claims from being bid up by outsiders at public land auctions.

Coercive Acts   Legislation passed by Parliament in 1774; included the Boston Port Act, the Massachusetts Government Act, the Administration of Justice Act, and the Quartering Act of 1774.

Cold War   The political and economic confrontation between the Soviet Union and the United States that dominated world affairs from 1946 to 1989.

Collective Bargaining   Representatives of a union negotiating with management on behalf of all members.

Colored Farmers' Alliance   An organization of Southern black farmers formed in Texas in 1886 in response to the Southern Farmers' Alliance, which did not accept black people as members.

Columbian Exchange   The transatlantic exchange of plants, animals, and diseases that occurred after the first European contact with the Americas.

Committee of Safety   Any of the extralegal committees that directed the revolutionary movement and carried on the functions of government at the local level in the period between the breakdown of royal authority and the establishment of regular governments.

Committee on Public Information (CPI)   Government agency during World War I that sought to shape public opinion in support of the war effort through newspapers, pamphlets, speeches, films, and other media.

Committees of Correspondence   Committees formed in Massachusetts and other colonies in the pre-Revolutionary period to keep Americans informed about British measures that would affect the colonies.

Communism   A social structure based on the common ownership of property.

Compromise of 1850   The four-step compromise that admitted California as a free state, allowed the residents of the New Mexico and Utah territories to decide the slavery issue for themselves, ended the slave trade in the District of Columbia, and passed a new fugitive slave law to enforce the constitutional provision stating that a slave escaping into a free state shall be delivered back to the owner.

Compromise of 1877   The congressional settling of the 1876 election that installed Republican Rutherford B. Hayes in the White House and gave Democrats control of all state governments in the South.

Conciliatory Proposition   Plan whereby Parliament would "forbear" taxation of Americans in colonies whose assemblies imposed taxes considered satisfactory by the British government.

Confederate States of America   Nation proclaimed in Montgomery, Alabama, in February 1861, after the seven states of the Lower South seceded from the United States.

Confiscation Act Second confiscation law passed by Congress, ordering the seizure of land from disloyal Southerners and the emancipation of their slaves.

Congress of Industrial Organizations An alliance of industrial unions that spurred the 1930s organizational drive among the mass-production industries.

Congress of Racial Equality (CORE) Civil rights group formed in 1942 and committed to nonviolent civil disobedience.

Congressional Reconstruction Name given to the period 1867–1870 when the Republican-dominated Congress controlled Reconstruction era policy.

Conservation The efficient management and use of natural resources, such as forests, grasslands, and rivers, as opposed to preservation or controlled exploitation.

Constitution of the United States The written document providing for a new central government of the United States.

Constitutional Convention Convention that met in Philadelphia in 1787 and drafted the Constitution of the United States.

Constitutional Union Party National party formed in 1860, mainly by former Whigs, that emphasized allegiance to the Union and strict enforcement of all national legislation.

Continental Army The regular or professional army authorized by the Second Continental Congress and commanded by General George Washington during the Revolutionary War.

Continental Association Agreement, adopted by the First Continental Congress in 1774 in response to the Coercive Acts to cut off trade with Britain until the objectionable measures were repealed.

Contract Theory of Government The belief that government is established by human beings to protect certain rights—such as life, liberty, and property—that are theirs by natural, divinely sanctioned law and that when government protects these rights, people are obligated to obey it.

Contract with America Platform proposing a sweeping reduction in the role and activities of the federal government on which many Republican candidates ran for Congress in 1994.

Copperheads A term Republicans applied to Northern war dissenters and those suspected of aiding the Confederate cause during the Civil War.

Council of Economic Advisers Board of three professional economists established in 1946 to advise the president on economic policy.

Counterculture Various alternatives to mainstream values and behaviors that became popular in the 1960s, including experimentation with psychedelic drugs, communal living, a return to the land, Asian religions, and experimental art.

Country (Real Whig) Ideology Strain of thought (focusing on the threat to personal liberty and the taxation of property holders) first appearing in England in the late seventeenth century in response to the growth of governmental power and a national debt.

Coureur de Bois French for "woods runner," an independent fur trader in New France.

Covenant A contract with God, binding settlers to meet their religious obligations in return for God's favor.

Coxey's Army A protest march of unemployed workers, led by Populist businessman Jacob Coxey, demanding inflation and a public works program during the depression of the 1890s.

Cult of domesticity The belief that women, by virtue of their gender, should stay home as the moral guardians of family life.

Currency Act Law passed by Parliament in 1764 to prevent the colonies from issuing legal tender paper money.

Dartmouth College **v.** *Woodward* Supreme Court decision of 1819 that prohibited states from interfering with the privileges granted to a private corporation.

Dawes Act An 1887 law terminating tribal ownership of land and allotting some parcels of land to individual Indians with the remainder opened for white settlement.

D-Day June 6, 1944, the day of the first paratroop drops and amphibious landings on the coast of Normandy, France, in the first stage of Operation OVERLORD during World War II.

Declaration of Independence The document by which the Second Continental Congress announced and justified its decision to renounce the colonies' allegiance to the British government.

Declaration of London Statement drafted by an international conference in 1909 to clarify international law and specify the rights of neutral nations.

Declaration of Rights and Grievances Resolves asserting that the Stamp Act and other taxes imposed on the colonists without their consent were unconstitutional.

Declaration of Sentiments The resolutions passed at the Seneca Falls Convention in 1848 calling for full female equality, including the right to vote.

Deism Religious orientation that rejects divine revelation and holds that the workings of nature alone reveal God's design for the universe.

Democratic Party Political party formed in the 1820s under the leadership of Andrew Jackson;

favored states' rights and a limited role for the federal government.

Denmark Vesey's Conspiracy   The most carefully devised slave revolt in which rebels planned to seize control of Charleston in 1822 and escape to freedom in Haiti, a free black republic, but they were betrayed by other slaves, and seventy-five conspirators were executed.

Deregulation   Reduction or removal of government regulations and encouragement of direct competition in many important industries and economic sectors.

Détente   (French for "easing of tension") Used to describe the new U.S. relations with China and the Soviet Union in 1972.

Disfranchisement   The use of legal means to bar individuals or groups from voting.

Dixiecrats   States' Rights Democrats.

Dollar diplomacy   The U.S. policy of using private investment in other nations to promote American diplomatic goals and business interests.

Dominion of New England   James II's failed plan of 1686 to combine eight Northern colonies into a single large province, to be governed by a royal appointee with no elective assembly.

Dred Scott **Decision**   Supreme Court ruling, in a lawsuit brought by Dred Scott, a slave demanding his freedom based on his residence in a free state, that slaves could not be U.S. citizens and that Congress had no jurisdiction over slavery in the territories.

Eastern Front   The area of military operations in World War II located east of Germany in eastern Europe and the Soviet Union.

Economic Recovery and Tax Act of 1981 (ERTA)   A major revision of the federal income tax system.

Emancipation Proclamation   Decree announced by President Abraham Lincoln in September 1862 and formally issued on January 1, 1863, freeing slaves in all Confederate states still in rebellion.

Embargo Act of 1807   Act passed by Congress in 1807 prohibiting American ships from leaving for any foreign port.

Empresarios   Agents who received a land grant from the Spanish or Mexican government in return for organizing settlements.

Encomienda   In the Spanish colonies, the grant to a Spanish settler of a certain number of Indian subjects, who would pay him tribute in goods and labor.

Enumerated Products   Items produced in the colonies and enumerated in acts of Parliament that could be legally shipped from the colony of origin only to specified locations.

Environmental Protection Agency (EPA)   Federal agency created in 1970 to oversee environmental monitoring and cleanup programs.

Era of Good Feelings   The period from 1817 to 1823 in which the disappearance of the Federalists enabled the Republicans to govern in a spirit of seemingly nonpartisan harmony.

Espionage Act   Law whose vague prohibition against obstructing the nation's war effort was used to crush dissent and criticism during World War I.

Fair Employment Practices Committee (FEPC)   Federal agency established in 1941 to curb racial discrimination in war production jobs and government employment.

Farmers' Alliance   A broad mass movement in the rural South and West during the late nineteenth century, encompassing several organizations and demanding economic and political reforms.

Fascist Government   A government subscribing to a philosophy of dictatorship that merges the interests of the state, armed forces, and big business.

Federal Deposit Insurance Corporation (FDIC)   Government agency that guarantees bank deposits, thereby protecting both depositors and banks.

Federal Highway Act of 1956   Measure that provided federal funding to build a nationwide system of interstate and defense highways.

Federal Reserve Act   The 1913 law that revised banking and currency by extending limited government regulation through the creation of the Federal Reserve System.

Federal Trade Commission   Government agency established in 1914 to provide regulatory oversight of business activity.

Federalism   The sharing of powers between the national government and the states.

Federalists   Supporters of the Constitution who favored its ratification.

Field Order No. 15   Order by General William T. Sherman in January 1865 to set aside abandoned land along the southern Atlantic coast for forty-acre grants to freedmen, rescinded by President Andrew Johnson later that year.

Fifteenth Amendment   Passed by Congress in 1869, guaranteed the right of American men to vote, regardless of race.

Fireside Chats   Speeches broadcast nationally over the radio in which President Franklin D. Roosevelt explained complex issues and programs in plain language, as though his listeners were gathered around the fireside with him.

First Continental Congress   Meeting of delegates from most of the colonies held in 1774 in response to the Coercive Acts. The Congress endorsed the Suffolk Resolves, adopted the Declaration of Rights and Grievances, and agreed to establish the Continental Association.

First Persian Gulf War   War (1991) between Iraq and a U.S.-led coalition that followed Iraq's invasion of Kuwait and resulted in the expulsion of Iraqi forces from that country.

Fletcher **v.** *Peck*   Supreme Court decision of 1810 that overturned a state law by ruling that it violated a legal contract.

Fort Sumter   A fort located in Charleston, South Carolina, where President Lincoln attempted to provision federal troops in 1861, triggering a hostile response from on-shore Confederate forces, opening the Civil War.

Fourteenth Amendment   Passed by Congress in 1866, guaranteed every citizen equality before the law by prohibiting states from violating the civil rights of their citizens, thus outlawing the black codes.

Frame of Government   William Penn's constitution for Pennsylvania that included a provision allowing for religious freedom.

Franco–American Accord of 1800   Settlement reached with France that brought an end to the Quasi-War and released the United Sates from its 1778 alliance with France.

Free Silver   Philosophy that the government should expand the money supply by purchasing and coining all the silver offered to it.

Free Speech Movement (FSM)   Student movement at the University of California, Berkeley, formed in 1964 to protest limitations on political activities on campus.

Freedmen's Bureau   Agency established by Congress in March 1865 to provide social, educational, and economic services, advice, and protection to former slaves and destitute whites; lasted seven years.

Freedom Summer   Voter registration effort in rural Mississippi organized by black and white civil rights workers in 1964.

French and Indian War   The last of the Anglo-French colonial wars (1754–1763) and the first in which fighting began in North America. The war ended with France's defeat.

Fugitive Slave Act   Law, part of the Compromise of 1850, that required the authorities in the North to assist Southern slave catchers and return runaway slaves to their owners.

Fundamental Constitutions of Carolina   A complex plan for organizing the colony of Carolina, drafted in 1669 by Anthony Ashley Cooper and John Locke.

Gabriel Prosser's Rebellion   Slave revolt that failed when Gabriel Prosser, a slave preacher and blacksmith, organized a thousand slaves for an attack on Richmond, Virginia, in 1800.

Gag Rule   A procedural device whereby antislavery petitions were automatically tabled in Congress with no discussion.

Gang System   The organization and supervision of slave field hands into working teams on Southern plantations.

Gentlemen's Agreement   A diplomatic agreement in 1907 between Japan and the United States curtailing but not abolishing Japanese immigration.

GI Bill of Rights   Legislation in June 1944 that eased the return of veterans into American society by providing educational and employment benefits.

Gibbons **v.** *Ogden*   Supreme Court decision of 1824 involving coastal commerce that overturned a steamboat monopoly granted by the state of New York on the grounds that only Congress had the authority to regulate interstate commerce.

Gilded Age   Term applied to late-nineteenth-century America that refers to the shallow display and worship of wealth characteristic of that period.

Glasnost   Russian for "openness" applied to Mikhail Gorbachev's encouragement of new ideas and easing of political repression in the Soviet Union.

Glorious Revolution   Bloodless revolt that occurred in England in 1688 when parliamentary leaders invited William of Orange, a Protestant, to assume the English throne.

Gospel of Wealth   Thesis that hard work and perseverance lead to wealth, implying that poverty is a character flaw.

Grand Settlement of 1701   Separate peace treaties negotiated by Iroquois diplomats at Montreal and Albany that marked the beginning of Iroquois neutrality in conflicts between the French and the British in North America.

Grandfather Clause   Rule that required potential voters to demonstrate that their grandfathers had been eligible to vote; used in some Southern states after 1890 to limit the black electorate.

Grange   The National Grange of the Patrons of Husbandry, a national organization of farm owners formed after the Civil War.

Granger Laws   State laws enacted in the Midwest in the 1870s that regulated rates charged by railroads, grain elevator operators, and other middlemen.

Great Awakening   Tremendous religious revival in colonial America striking first in the Middle Colonies and New England in the 1740s and then spreading to the Southern colonies.

Great Compromise   Plan proposed at the 1787 Constitutional Convention for creating a national bicameral legislature in which all states would be equally represented in the Senate and proportionally represented in the House.

Great Depression   The nation's worst economic crisis, extending through the 1930s, producing unprecedented bank failures, unemployment, and industrial and agricultural collapse.

Great Migration   The mass movement of African Americans from the rural South to the urban North, spurred especially by new job opportunities during World War I and the 1920s.

Great Society   Theme of Lyndon Johnson's administration, focusing on poverty, education, and civil rights.

Great Uprising   Unsuccessful railroad strike of 1877 to protest wage cuts and the use of federal troops against strikers; the first nationwide work stoppage in American history.

Greater East Asia Co-Prosperity Sphere Japanese nationalists believed that Japan should expel the French, British, Dutch, and Americans from Asia and create this sphere in which Japan would give the orders and other Asian peoples would comply.

Greenback Party   A third party of the 1870s and 1880s that garnered temporary support by advocating currency inflation to expand the economy and assist debtors.

Gulf of Tonkin Resolution   Request to Congress from President Lyndon Johnson in response to North Vietnamese torpedo boat attacks in which he sought authorization for "all necessary measures" to protect American forces and stop further aggression.

Halfway Covenant   Plan adopted in 1662 by New England clergy to deal with the problem of declining church membership, allowing children of baptized parents to be baptized whether or not their parents had experienced conversion.

Harlem Renaissance   A new African-American cultural awareness that flourished in literature, art, and music in the 1920s.

Headright System   Instituted by the Virginia Company in 1616, this system gave fifty acres to anyone who paid his own way to Virginia and an additional fifty for each person (or "head") he brought with him.

Helsinki Accords   Agreement in 1975 among NATO and Warsaw Pact members that recognized European national boundaries as set after World War II and included guarantees of human rights.

Holocaust   The systematic murder of millions of European Jews and others deemed undesirable by Nazi Germany.

Homestead Act   Law passed by Congress in May 1862 providing homesteads with 160 acres of free land in exchange for improving the land within five years of the grant.

Hoovervilles   Shantytowns, sarcastically named after President Hoover, in which unemployed and homeless people lived in makeshift shacks, tents, and boxes.

Horizontal Integration   The merger of competitors in the same industry.

House Committee on Un-American Activities (HUAC)   Originally intended to ferret out pro-Fascists, it later investigated "un-American propaganda" that attacked constitutional government.

House of Burgesses   The legislature of colonial Virginia. First organized in 1619, it was the first institution of representative government in the English colonies.

Hull House   Chicago settlement house that became part of a broader neighborhood revitalization project led by Jane Addams.

Immigration and Nationality Act of 1965 Federal legislation that replaced the national quota system for immigration with new limits for each hemisphere.

Imperialism   The policy and practice of exploiting nations and peoples for the benefit of an imperial power either directly through military occupation and colonial rule or indirectly through economic domination of resources and markets.

Indentured servants   Individuals who contracted to serve a master for a period of four to seven years in return for payment of the servant's passage to America.

Independent Treasury System   Fiscal arrangement first instituted by President Martin Van Buren in which the federal government kept its money in regional vaults and transacted its business in hard money.

Indian Removal Act   President Andrew Jackson's measure that allowed state officials to override federal protection of Native Americans.

Initiative   Procedure by which citizens can introduce a subject for legislation, usually through a petition signed by a specific number of voters.

Intermediate Nuclear Force Agreement (INF)   Disarmament agreement between the United States and the Soviet Union under which an entire class of missiles would be removed and destroyed and on-site inspections would be permitted.

International Monetary Fund   International organization established in 1945 to assist nations in maintaining stable currencies.

Internet   The system of interconnected computers and servers that allows the exchange of email, posting of Web sites, and other means of instant communication.

Interstate Commerce Act The 1887 law that expanded federal power over business by prohibiting pooling and discriminatory rates by railroads and establishing the first federal regulatory agency, the Interstate Commerce Commission.

Intolerable Acts American term for the Coercive Acts and the Quebec Act.

Irreconcilables Group of U.S. senators adamantly opposed to ratification of the Treaty of Versailles after World War I.

Island Hopping The Pacific campaigns of 1944 that were the American naval versions of the *Blitzkrieg*.

Jay's Treaty Treaty with Britain negotiated in 1794 in which the United States made major concessions to avert a war over the British seizure of American ships.

Jazz Age The 1920s, so called for the popular music of the day as a symbol of the many changes taking place in the mass culture.

Jim Crow Laws Segregation laws that became widespread in the South during the 1890s.

John Brown's Raid New England abolitionist John Brown's ill-fated attempt to free Virginia's slaves with a raid on the federal arsenal at Harpers Ferry, Virginia, in 1859.

Joint-stock company Business enterprise in which a group of stockholders pooled their money to engage in trade or to fund colonizing expeditions.

Judicial Review A power implied in the Constitution that gives federal courts the right to review and determine the constitutionality of acts passed by Congress and state legislatures.

Judiciary Act of 1789 Act of Congress that implemented the judiciary clause of the Constitution by establishing the Supreme Court and a system of lower federal courts.

Kansas-Nebraska Act Law passed in 1854 creating the Kansas and Nebraska Territories but leaving the question of slavery open to residents, thereby repealing the Missouri Compromise.

King George's War The third Anglo-French war in North America (1744–1748), part of the European conflict known as the War of the Austrian Succession.

King Phillip's War Conflict in New England (1675–1676) between Wampanoags, Narragansetts, and other Indian peoples against English settlers; sparked by English encroachments on native lands.

King William's War The first Anglo-French conflict in North America (1689–1697), the American phase of Europe's War of the League of Augsburg.

Knights of Labor Labor union founded in 1869 that included skilled and unskilled workers irrespective of race or gender.

Know-Nothing Party Anti-immigrant party formed from the wreckage of the Whig Party and some disaffected Northern Democrats in 1854.

Korean War Pacific war started on June 25, 1950, when North Korea, helped by Soviet equipment and Chinese training, attacked South Korea.

Kosovo Province of Yugoslavia where the United States and NATO intervened militarily in 1999 to protect ethnic Albanians from expulsion.

Ku Klux Klan Perhaps the most prominent of the vigilante groups that terrorized black people in the South during Reconstruction era, founded by the Confederate veterans in 1866.

Land Grant College Act Law passed by Congress in July 1862 awarding proceeds from the sale of public lands to the states for the establishment of agricultural and mechanical colleges.

Land Ordinance of 1785 Act passed by Congress under the Articles of Confederation that created the grid system of surveys by which all subsequent public land was made available for sale.

League of Nations International organization created by the Versailles Treaty after World War I to ensure world stability.

League of Women Voters League formed in 1920 advocating for women's rights, among them the right for women to serve on juries and equal pay laws.

Lecompton Constitution Proslavery draft written in 1857 by Kansas territorial delegates elected under questionable circumstances; it was rejected by two governors, supported by President Buchanan, and decisively defeated by Congress.

Levittown Suburban Long Island community of postwar rental houses built by William Levitt for veterans of World War II.

Liberty Bonds Interest-bearing certificates sold by the U.S. government to finance the American World War I effort.

Liberty party The first antislavery political party, formed in 1840.

Limited Test Ban Treaty Treaty, signed by the United States, Britain, and the Soviet Union, outlawing nuclear testing in the atmosphere, in outer space, and under water.

Lincoln-Douglas Debates Series of debates in the 1858 Illinois senatorial campaign during which Douglas and Lincoln staked out their differing opinions on the issue of slavery.

Lost Cause The phrase many white Southerners applied to their Civil War defeat. They viewed the war as a noble cause but only a temporary setback in the South's ultimate vindication.

Lynching   Execution, usually by a mob, without trial.

Mahanism   The ideas advanced by Alfred Thayer Mahan, stressing U.S. naval, economic, and territorial expansion.

Manhattan Project   The effort, using the code name Manhattan Engineer District, to develop an atomic bomb under the management of the U.S. Army Corps of Engineers during World War II.

Manifest Destiny   Doctrine, first expressed in 1845, that the expansion of white Americans across the continent was inevitable and ordained by God.

Marbury v. *Madison*   Supreme Court decision of 1803 that created the precedent of judicial review by ruling as unconstitutional part of the Judiciary Act of 1789.

Marshall Plan   Secretary of State George C. Marshall's European Recovery Plan of June 5, 1947, committing the United States to help in the rebuilding of post–World War II Europe.

McCarthyism   Anti-Communist attitudes and actions associated with Senator Joe McCarthy in the early 1950s, including smear tactics and innuendo.

Medicaid   Supplementary medical insurance for the poor, financed through the federal government; program created in 1965.

Medicare   Basic medical insurance for the elderly, financed through the federal government; program created in 1965.

Mercantilism   Economic system whereby the government intervenes in the economy for the purpose of increasing national wealth.

Mexican Cession of 1848   The addition of half a million square miles to the United States as a result of victory in the 1846 war between the United States and Mexico.

Middle Passage   The voyage between West Africa and the New World slave colonies.

Minute Men   Special companies of militia formed in Massachusetts and elsewhere beginning in late 1744.

Missouri Compromise   Sectional compromise in Congress in 1820 that admitted Missouri to the Union as a slave state and Maine as a free state and prohibited slavery in the northern Louisiana Purchase territory.

Model Cities Program   Effort to target federal funds to upgrade public services and economic opportunity in specifically defined urban neighborhoods between 1966 and 1974.

Monroe Doctrine   Declaration to Congress by President James Monroe in 1823 that the Western Hemisphere was to be closed off to further European colonization and that the United States would not interfere in the internal affairs of European nations. According to Monroe, Americans "are henceforth not to be considered as subjects for future colonization by any European power."

Muckraking   Journalism exposing economic, social, and political evils, so named by Theodore Roosevelt for its "raking the muck" of American society.

Mugwumps   Elitist and conservative reformers who favored sound money and limited government and opposed tariffs and the spoils system.

Multinational corporations   Firms with direct investments, branches, factories, and offices in a number of countries.

Nat Turner's Rebellion   Uprising of slaves in Southampton County, Virginia, in the summer of 1831 led by Nat Turner that resulted in the death of fifty-five white people.

Nation of Islam   Religious movement among black Americans that emphasizes self-sufficiency, self-help, and separation from white society.

National Aeronautics and Space Administration (NASA)   Federal agency created in 1958 to manage American space flights and exploration.

National American Woman Suffrage Association   The organization, formed in 1890, that coordinated the ultimately successful campaign to achieve women's right to vote.

National Association for the Advancement of Colored People (NAACP)   Interracial organization co-founded by W. E. B. Du Bois in 1910 dedicated to restoring African-American political and social rights.

National Origins Act of 1924   Law sharply restricting immigration on the basis of immigrants' national origins and discriminating against southern and eastern Europeans and Asians.

National Security Council Paper 68 (NSC-68)   Policy statement that committed the United States to a military approach to the Cold War.

National Security Council   The formal policymaking body for national defense and foreign relations, created in 1947 and consisting of the president, the secretary of defense, the secretary of state, and others appointed by the president.

Nationalists   Group of leaders in the 1780s who spearheaded the drive to replace the Articles of Confederation with a stronger central government.

Nativism   Favoring the interests and culture of native-born inhabitants over those of immigrants.

Nativist Organizations   Joined by American-born artisans in the 1840s who sought to curb mass immigration from Europe and limit the political rights of Catholic immigrants.

Natural Rights Political philosophy that maintains that individuals have an inherent right, found in nature and preceding any government or written law, to life and liberty.

Neoliberal Advocate or participant in the effort to reshape the Democratic party for the 1990s around a policy emphasizing economic growth and competitiveness in the world economy.

New Deal The economic and political policies of the Roosevelt administration in the 1930s.

New Federalism President Richard Nixon's policy to shift responsibilities of government programs from the federal level to the states.

New Freedom Woodrow Wilson's 1912 program for limited government intervention in the economy to restore competition by curtailing the restrictive influences of trusts and protective tariffs, thereby providing opportunities for individual achievement.

New Frontier John F. Kennedy's domestic and foreign policy initiatives, designed to reinvigorate sense of national purpose and energy.

New Harmony Short-lived utopian community established in Indiana in 1825, based on the socialist ideas of Robert Owen, a wealthy Scottish manufacturer.

New Jersey Plan Proposal of the New Jersey delegation for a strengthened national government in which all states would have an equal representation in a unicameral legislature.

New Lights People who experienced conversion during the revivals of the Great Awakening.

New Nationalism Theodore Roosevelt's 1912 program calling for a strong national government to foster, regulate, and protect business, industry, workers, and consumers.

Niagara Movement African-American group organized in 1905 to promote racial integration, civil and political rights, and equal access to economic opportunity.

Nineteenth Amendment Constitutional revision that in 1920 established women citizens' right to vote.

Nisei U.S. citizens born of immigrant Japanese parents.

Nixon Doctrine President Nixon's new American policy (1969) toward Asia in which the United States would honor treaty commitments but would gradually disengage and expect Asian nations to handle military defense on their own.

Nonimportation Movement A tactical means of putting economic pressure on Britain by refusing to buy its exports to the colonies.

North American Free Trade Agreement (NAFTA) Agreement reached in 1993 by Canada, Mexico, and the United States to substantially reduce barriers to trade.

North Atlantic Treaty Organization (NATO) Organization of ten European countries, Canada, and the United States who together formed a mutual defense pact in April 1949.

Northwest Ordinance of 1787 Legislation that prohibited slavery in the Northwest Territories and provided the model for the incorporation of future territories into the union as co-equal states.

Nullification A constitutional doctrine holding that a state has a legal right to declare a national law null and void within its borders.

Nullification Crisis Sectional crisis in the early 1830s in which a states' rights party in South Carolina attempted to nullify federal law.

Office of Economic Opportunity (OEO) Federal agency that coordinated many programs of the War on Poverty between 1964 and 1975.

Olive Branch Petition adopted by the Second Continental Congress as a last effort of peace that avowed America's loyalty to George III and requested that he protect them from further aggressions.

Omaha Platform The 1892 platform of the Populist party repudiating laissez-faire and demanding economic and political reforms to aid distressed farmers and workers.

Oneida Community Utopian community established in upstate New York in 1848 by John Humphrey Noyes and his followers.

Open Door American policy of seeking equal trade and investment opportunities in foreign nations or regions.

Open Shop Factory or business employing workers whether or not they are union members; in practice, such a business usually refuses to hire union members and follows antiunion policies.

Operation Desert Storm Code name for the successful offensive against Iraq by the United States and its allies in the Persian Gulf War (1991).

Operation OVERLORD U.S. and British invasion of France in June 1944 during World War II.

Oregon Trail Overland trail of more than two thousand miles that carried American settlers from the Midwest to new settlements in Oregon, California, and Utah.

Organization of Petroleum Exporting Countries (OPEC) Cartel of oil-producing nations in Asia, Africa, and Latin America that gained substantial power over the world economy in the mid- to late-1970s by controlling the production and price of oil.

Panic of 1857 Banking crisis that caused a credit crunch in the North; it was less severe in the South, where high cotton prices spurred a quick recovery.

Pan-Indian Resistance Movement   Movement calling for the political and cultural unification of Indian tribes in the late eighteenth and early nineteenth centuries.

Parson's Cause   Series of developments (1758–1763) that began when the Virginia legislature modified the salaries of Anglican clergymen, who complained to the crown and sued to recover damages. British authorities responded by imposing additional restrictions on the legislature. Virginians, who saw this as a threat, reacted by strongly reasserting local autonomy.

Patriot Act   Federal legislation adopted in 2001, in response to the terrorist attacks of September 11, intended to facilitate antiterror actions by federal law enforcement and intelligence agencies.

Peace of Paris   Treaties signed in 1783 by Great Britain, the United States, France, Spain, and the Netherlands that ended the Revolutionary War.

Pendleton Civil Service Act   A law of 1883 that reformed the spoils system by prohibiting government workers from making political contributions and creating the Civil Service Commission to oversee their appointment on the basis of merit rather than politics.

Pentagon Papers   Classified Defense Department documents on the history of the United States' involvement in Vietnam, prepared in 1968 and leaked to the press in 1971.

Pequot War   Conflict between English settlers and Pequot Indians over control of land and trade in eastern Connecticut.

Perestroika   Russian for "restructuring," applied to Mikhail Gorbachev's efforts to make the Soviet economic and political systems more modern, flexible, and innovative.

Pilgrims   Settlers of Plymouth Colony, who viewed themselves as spiritual wanderers.

Platt Amendment   A stipulation the United States had inserted into the Cuban constitution in 1901 restricting Cuban autonomy and authorizing U.S. intervention and naval bases.

Plessy **v.** *Ferguson*   Supreme Court decision holding that Louisiana's railroad segregation law did not violate the Constitution as long as the railroads or the state provided equal accommodations.

Pogroms   Government-directed attacks against Jewish citizens, property, and villages in tsarist Russia beginning in the 1880s; a primary reason for Russian Jewish migration to the United States.

Poll Taxes   Taxes imposed on voters as a requirement for voting.

Pontiac's Rebellion   Indian uprising (1763–1766) led by Pontiac of the Ottawas and Neolin of the Delawares.

Popular Sovereignty   A solution to the slavery crisis suggested by Michigan senator Lewis Cass by which territorial residents, not Congress, would decide slavery's fate.

Populist or People's Party   A major third party of the 1890s, formed on the basis of the Southern Farmers' Alliance and other reform organizations, mounting electoral challenges against Democrats in the South and the Republicans in the West.

Potsdam Declaration   Statement issued by the United States during a meeting of U.S. president Harry Truman, British prime minister Winston Churchill, and Soviet premier Joseph Stalin in which the United States declared its intention to democratize the Japanese political system and reintroduce Japan into the international community.

Predestination   The belief that God decided at the moment of Creation which humans would achieve salvation.

Preparedness   Military buildup in preparation for possible U.S. participation in World War I.

Proclamation Line   Boundary, decreed as part of the Proclamation of 1763, that limited British settlements to the eastern side of the Appalachian Mountains.

Proclamation of 1763   Royal proclamation setting the boundary known as the Proclamation Line.

Progressive Era   An era in the United States (roughly between 1900 and 1917) in which important movements challenged traditional relationships and attitudes.

Prohibition   A ban on the production, sale, and consumption of liquor, achieved temporarily through state laws and the Eighteenth Amendment.

Prohibition Party   A venerable third party still in existence that has persistently campaigned for the abolition of alcohol but has also introduced many important reform ideas into American politics.

Proposition 187   California legislation adopted by popular vote in California in 1994, which cuts off state-funded health and education benefits to undocumented or illegal immigrants.

Proprietary Colony   A colony created when the English monarch granted a huge tract of land to an individual or group of individuals, who became "lords proprietor."

Protestant Fundamentalists   Religious conservatives who believe in the literal accuracy and divine inspiration of the Bible.

Protestants   All European supporters of religious reform under Charles V's Holy Roman Empire.

Pueblo Revolt   Rebellion in 1680 of Pueblo Indians in New Mexico against their Spanish overlords, sparked by religious conflict and excessive Spanish demands for tribute.

Puritans Individuals who believed that Queen Elizabeth's reforms of the Church of England had not gone far enough in improving the church. Puritans led the settlement of Massachusetts Bay Colony.

Putting-Out System System of manufacturing in which merchants furnished households with raw materials for processing by family members.

Quakers Members of the Society of Friends, a radical religious group that arose in the mid-seventeenth century. Quakers rejected formal theology, focusing instead on the Holy Spirit that dwelt within them.

Quartering Acts Acts of Parliament requiring colonial legislatures to provide supplies and quarters for the troops stationed in America.

Quasi-War Undeclared naval war of 1797 to 1800 between the United States and France.

Quebec Act Law passed by Parliament in 1774 that provided an appointed government for Canada, enlarged the boundaries of Quebec, and confirmed the privileges of the Catholic Church.

Queen Anne's War American phase (1702–1713) of Europe's War of the Spanish Succession.

Radical Republicans A shifting group of Republican congressmen, usually a substantial minority, who favored the abolition of slavery from the beginning of the Civil War and later advocated harsh treatment of the defeated South.

Recall The process of removing an official from office by popular vote, usually after using petitions to call for such a vote.

Reconquista The long struggle (ending in 1492) during which Spanish Christians reconquered the Iberian peninsula from Muslim occupiers.

Red Scare Post-World War I public hysteria over Bolshevik influence in the United States directed against labor activism, radical dissenters, and some ethnic groups.

Redemptioner Similar to an indentured servant, except that a redemptioner signed a labor contract in America rather than in Europe.

Redlining The withholding of home purchase loans and insurance coverage from inner-city older neighborhoods by federal housing agencies and private industry.

Referendum Submission of a law, proposed or already in effect, to a direct popular vote for approval or rejection.

Reformation Martin Luther's challenge to the Catholic Church, initiated in 1517, calling for a return to what he understood to be the purer practices and beliefs of the early church.

Regulators Vigilante groups active in the 1760s and 1770s in the western parts of North and South Carolina. The South Carolina Regulators attempted to rid the area of outlaws; the North Carolina Regulators were more concerned with high taxes and court costs.

Repartimiento In the Spanish colonies, the assignment of Indian workers to labor on public works projects.

Republican (Jeffersonian) Party Party headed by Thomas Jefferson that formed in opposition to the financial and diplomatic policies of the Federalist party; favored limiting the powers of the national government and placing the interests of farmers over those of financial and commercial groups.

Republican Party Party that emerged in the 1850s in the aftermath of the bitter controversy over the Kansas-Nebraska Act, consisting of former Whigs, some Northern Democrats, and many Know-Nothings.

Republicanism A complex, changing body of ideas, values, and assumptions, closely related to country ideology, that influenced American political behavior during the eighteenth and nineteenth centuries.

Rescate Procedure by which Spanish colonists would pay ransom to free Indians captured by rival natives.

Reservationists Group of U.S. senators favoring approval of the Treaty of Versailles, after amending it to incorporate their reservations.

Roe v. Wade U.S. Supreme Court decision (1973) that disallowed state laws prohibiting abortion during the first three months (trimester) of pregnancy and established guidelines for abortion in the second and third trimesters.

Roosevelt Corollary President Theodore Roosevelt's policy asserting U.S. authority to intervene in the affairs of Latin American nations; an expansion of the Monroe Doctrine.

Rush-Bagot Agreement Treaty of 1817 between the United States and Britain that effectively demilitarized the Great Lakes by sharply limiting the number of ships each power could station on them.

Sabbatarian Movement Reform organization founded in 1828 by Congregationalist and Presbyterian ministers that lobbied for an end to the delivery of mail on Sundays and other Sabbath violations.

Sack of Lawrence Vandalism and arson committed by a group of proslavery men in Lawrence, the free-state capital of Kansas Territory.

Sagebrush Rebellion Political movement in the Western states in the early 1980s that called for easing of regulations on the economic issue of federal lands and the transfer of some or all of those lands to state ownership.

SALT (Strategic Arms Limitation Treaty) Treaty signed in 1972 by the United States and the Soviet Union to slow the nuclear arms race.

Sand Creek Massacre The near annihilation in 1864 of Black Kettle's Cheyenne band by Colorado troops under Colonel John Chivington's orders to "kill and scalp all, big and little."

Santa Fe Trail The 900-mile trail opened by American merchants for trading purposes following Mexico's liberalization of the formerly restrictive trading policies of Spain.

Scalawags Southern whites, mainly small landowning farmers and well-off merchants and planters, who supported the Southern Republican party during Reconstruction.

Search and Destroy U.S. military tactic in South Vietnam, using small detachments to locate enemy units and then massive air, artillery, and ground forces to destroy them.

Second Bank of the United States A national bank chartered by Congress in 1816 with extensive regulatory powers over currency and credit.

Second Great Awakening Series of religious revivals in the first half of the nineteenth century characterized by great emotionalism in large public meetings.

Second Party System The national two-party competition between Democrats and Whigs from the 1830s through the early 1850s.

Second Treaty of Fort Laramie The treaty acknowledging U.S. defeat in the Great Sioux War in 1868 and supposedly guaranteeing the Sioux perpetual land and hunting rights in South Dakota, Wyoming, and Montana.

Securities and Exchange Commission (SEC) Federal agency with authority to regulate trading practices in stocks and bonds.

Sedition Act Broad law restricting criticism of America's involvement in World War I or its government, flag, military, taxes, or officials.

Segregation A system of racial control that separated the races, initially by custom but increasingly by law during and after Reconstruction.

Selective Service Act of 1917 The law establishing the military draft for World War I.

Selective Service System Federal agency that coordinated military conscription before and during the Vietnam War.

Self-determination The right of a people or a nation to decide on its own political allegiance or form of government without external influence.

Seneca Falls Convention The first convention for women's equality in legal rights, held in upstate New York in 1848.

Separatists Members of an offshoot branch of Puritanism. Separatists believed that the Church of England was too corrupt to be reformed and hence were convinced they must "separate" from it to save their souls.

Seventeenth Amendment Constitutional change that in 1913 established the direct popular election of U.S. senators.

Shakers The followers of Mother Ann Lee, who preached a religion of strict celibacy and communal living.

Sharecropping Labor system that evolved during and after Reconstruction whereby landowners furnished laborers with a house, farm animals, and tools and advanced credit in exchange for a share of the laborers' crop.

Shays's Rebellion An armed movement of debt-ridden farmers in western Massachusetts in the winter of 1786–1787. The rebellion created a crisis atmosphere.

Sheppard–Towner Maternity and Infancy Act The first federal social welfare law, passed in 1921, providing federal funds for infant and maternity care.

Sherman Antitrust Act The first federal antitrust measure, passed in 1890; sought to promote economic competition by prohibiting business combinations in restraint of trade or commerce.

Silicon Valley The region of California including San Jose and San Francisco that holds the nation's greatest concentration of electronics firms.

Sixteenth Amendment Constitutional revision that in 1913 authorized a federal income tax.

Slaughterhouse **Cases** Group of cases resulting in one sweeping decision by the U.S. Supreme Court in 1873 that contradicted the intent of the Fourteenth Amendment by decreeing that most citizenship rights remained under state, not federal, control.

Slave Codes A series of laws passed mainly in the Southern colonies in the late seventeenth and early eighteenth centuries to defend the status of slaves and codify the denial of basic civil rights to them.

Social Darwinism The application of Charles Darwin's theory of biological evolution to society, holding that the fittest and wealthiest survive, the weak and the poor perish, and government action is unable to alter this "natural" process.

Social Gospel Movement Movement created by reform-minded Protestant ministers seeking to introduce religious ethics into industrial relations and appealing to churches to meet their social responsibilities.

Socialism Political and economic theory advocating that land, natural resources, and the chief industries should be owned by the community as a whole.

Solid South The one-party (Democratic) political system that dominated the South from the 1890s to the 1950s.

Sons of Liberty   Secret organizations in the colonies formed to oppose the Stamp Act.

Sound Money   Misleading slogan that referred to a conservative policy of restricting the money supply and adhering to the gold standard.

Southeast Asia Treaty Organization (SEATO)   Mutual defense alliance signed in 1954 by the United States, Britain, France, Thailand, Pakistan, the Philippines, Australia, and New Zealand.

Southern Christian Leadership Conference (SCLC)   Black civil rights organization founded in 1957 by Martin Luther King Jr. and other clergy.

Southern Farmers' Alliance   The largest of several organizations that formed in the post-Reconstruction South to advance the interests of beleaguered small farmers.

Southern Homestead Act   Largely unsuccessful law passed in 1866 that gave black people preferential access to public lands in five Southern states.

Southern Manifesto   A document signed by 101 members of Congress from Southern states in 1956 that argued that the Supreme Court's decision in *Brown* v. *Board of Education of Topeka* itself contradicted the Constitution.

Southwest Ordinance of 1790   Legislation passed by Congress that set up a government with no prohibition on slavery in U.S. territory south of the Ohio River.

Specie Circular   Proclamation issued by President Andrew Jackson in 1836 stipulating that only gold or silver could be used as payment for public land.

Spheres of Influence   Regions dominated and controlled by an outside power.

Spoils System   The awarding of government jobs to party loyalists.

Stamp Act Congress   October 1765 meeting of delegates sent by nine colonies, held in New York City, that adopted the Declaration of Rights and Grievances and petitioned against the Stamp Act.

Stamp Act   Law passed by Parliament in 1765 to raise revenue in America by requiring taxed, stamped paper for legal documents, publications, and playing cards.

States' Rights   Favoring the rights of individual states over rights claimed by the national government.

Stonewall Rebellion   On June 27, 1969, patrons fought back when police raided the gay Stonewall Inn in New York.

Stono Rebellion   Uprising in 1739 of South Carolina slaves against whites; inspired in part by Spanish officials' promise of freedom for American slaves who escaped to Florida.

Strategic Defense Initiative (SDI)   President Reagan's program, announced in 1983, to defend the United States against nuclear missile attack with untested weapons systems and sophisticated technologies.

Student Nonviolent Coordinating Committee (SNCC)   Black civil rights organization founded in 1960 and drawing heavily on younger activists and college students.

Students for a Democratic Society (SDS)   The leading student organization of the New Left of the early and mid-1960s.

Subtreasury Plan   A program promoted by the Southern Farmers' Alliance in response to low cotton prices and tight credit. Farmers would store their crop in a warehouse until prices rose, in the meantime borrowing up to 80 percent of the value of the stored crops from the government at a low interest rate.

Suffolk Resolves   Militant resolves adopted in 1774 in response to the Coercive Acts by representatives from the towns in Suffolk County, Massachusetts, including Boston.

Suffrage   The right to vote in a political election.

Sugar Act   Law passed in 1764 to raise revenue in the American colonies. It lowered the duty from 6 pence to 3 pence per gallon on foreign molasses imported into the colonies and increased the restrictions on colonial commerce.

Sunbelt   The states of the American South and Southwest.

Sussex Pledge   Germany's pledge during World War I not to sink merchant ships without warning, on the condition that Britain also observe recognized rules of international laws.

Swann v. Charlotte-Mecklenburg Board of Education   U.S. Supreme Court decision in 1971 that upheld cross-city busing to achieve the racial integration of public schools.

Sweatshops   Small, poorly ventilated shops or apartments crammed with workers, often family members, who pieced together garments.

Taft-Hartley Act   Federal legislation of 1947 that substantially limited the tools available to labor unions in labor-management disputes.

Taos Revolt   Uprising of Pueblo Indians in New Mexico that broke out in January 1847 over the imposition of American rule during the Mexican War; the revolt was crushed within a few weeks.

Tariff Act of 1789   Apart from a few selected industries, this first tariff passed by Congress was intended to raise revenue and not protect American manufacturers from foreign competition.

Tea Act of 1773   Act of Parliament that permitted the East India Company to sell through agents in America without paying the duty customarily collected in Britain, thus reducing the retail price.

Tejanos   Persons of Spanish or Mexican descent born in Texas.

Teller Amendment   A congressional resolution adopted in 1898 renouncing any American intention to annex Cuba.

Temperance   Reform movement originating in the 1820s that sought to eliminate the consumption of alcohol.

Temporary Assistance for Needy Families (TANF)   Federal program, utilizing work requirements for and time limits on benefits, created in 1996 to replace earlier welfare programs to aid families and children.

Tenements   Four- to six-story residential dwellings, once common in New York, built on tiny lots without regard to providing ventilation or light.

Tennessee Valley Authority (TVA)   Federal regional planning agency established to promote conservation, produce electric power, and encourage economic development in seven southern states.

Thirteenth Amendment   Constitutional amendment ratified in 1865 that freed all slaves throughout the United States.

Tonnage Act of 1789   Duty levied on the tonnage of incoming ships to U.S. ports; tax was higher on foreign-owned ships to favor American shippers.

Tories   A derisive term applied to Loyalists in America who supported the king and Parliament just before and during the American Revolution.

Townshend Duty Act   Act of Parliament, passed in 1767, imposing duties on colonial tea, lead, paint, paper, and glass.

Trail of Tears   The forced march in 1838 of the Cherokee Indians from their homelands in Georgia to the Indian Territory in the West.

Transcendentalism   A philosophical and literary movement centered on an idealistic belief in the divinity of individuals and nature.

Trans-Continental Treaty of 1819   Treaty between the United States and Spain in which Spain ceded Florida to the United States, surrendered all claims to the Pacific Northwest, and agreed to a boundary between the Louisiana Purchase territory and the Spanish Southwest.

Transportation Revolution   Dramatic improvements in transportation that stimulated economic growth after 1815 by expanding the range of travel and reducing the time and cost of moving goods and people.

Treaty of Ghent   Treaty signed in December 1814 between the United States and Britain that ended the War of 1812.

Treaty of Greenville   Treaty of 1795 in which Native Americans in the Old Northwest were forced to cede most of the present state of Ohio to the United States.

Treaty of Lancaster   Negotiation in 1744 whereby Iroquois chiefs sold Virginia land speculators the right to trade at the Forks of the Ohio.

Treaty of Paris   The formal end to British hostilities against France and Spain in February 1763.

Treaty of San Lorenzo (Pickney's Treaty)   Treaty with Spain in 1795 in which Spain recognized the 31st parallel as the boundary between the United States and Spanish Florida.

Treaty of Tordesillas   Treaty negotiated by the pope in 1494 to resolve the territorial claims of Spain and Portugal.

Treaty of Versailles   The treaty ending World War I and creating the League of Nations.

Truman Doctrine   President Harry Truman's statement in 1947 that the United States should assist other nations that were facing external pressure or internal revolution.

Underground Railroad   Support system set up by antislavery groups in the Upper South and the North to assist fugitive slaves in escaping the South.

Underwood-Simmons Tariff Act   The 1913 reform law that lowered tariff rates and levied the first regular federal income tax.

Union Leagues   Republican party organizations in Northern cities that became an important organizing device among freedmen in Southern cities after 1865.

United States **v.** *Cruikshank*   Supreme Court ruling of 1876 that overturned the convictions of some of those responsible for the Colfax Massacre, ruling that the Enforcement Act applied only to violations of black rights by states, not individuals.

University of California **v.** *Bakke*   U.S. Supreme Court case in 1978 that allowed race to be used as one of several factors in college and university admission decisions but made rigid quotas unacceptable.

Valley Forge   Area of Pennsylvania approximately 20 miles northwest of Philadelphia where General George Washington's Continental troops were quartered from December 1777 to June 1778 while British forces occupied Philadelphia during the Revolutionary War.

Vertical Integration   The consolidation of numerous production functions, from the extraction of the raw materials to the distribution and marketing of the finished products, under the direction of one firm.

Viet Cong   Communist rebels in South Vietnam who fought the pro-American government established in South Vietnam in 1954.

Virginia Plan   Proposal calling for a national legislature in which the states would be represented according to population.

Virtual Representation   The notion that parliamentary members represented the interests of the nation as a whole, not those of the particular district that elected them.

Volstead Act   The 1920 law defining the liquor forbidden under the Eighteenth Amendment and giving enforcement responsibilities to the Prohibition Bureau of the Department of the Treasury.

Voting Rights Act   Legislation in 1965 that overturned a variety of practices by which states systematically denied voter registration to minorities.

Waltham System   During the industrialization of the early nineteenth century, the recruitment of unmarried young women for employment in factories.

War Hawks   Members of Congress, predominantly from the South and West, who aggressively pushed for a war against Britain after their election in 1810.

War Industries Board (WIB)   The federal agency that reorganized industry for maximum efficiency and productivity during World War I.

War of 1812   War fought between the United States and Britain from June 1812 to January 1815 largely over British restrictions on American shipping.

War on Poverty   Set of programs introduced by Lyndon Johnson between 1963 and 1966 designed to break the cycle of poverty by providing funds for job training, community development, nutrition, and supplementary education.

Watergate   A complex scandal involving attempts to cover up illegal actions taken by administration officials and leading to the resignation of President Richard Nixon in 1974.

Webster-Ashburton Treaty   Treaty signed by the United States and Britain in 1842 that settled a boundary dispute between Maine and Canada.

Welfare Capitalism   A paternalistic system of labor relations emphasizing management responsibility for employee well-being.

Whig Party   Political party, formed in the mid-1830s in opposition to the Jacksonian Democrats, that favored a strong role for the national government for promoting economic growth.

Whigs   The name used by advocates of colonial resistance to British measures during the 1760s and 1770s.

Whiskey Rebellion   Armed uprising in 1794 by farmers in western Pennsylvania who attempted to prevent the collection of the excise tax on whiskey.

Whitewater   Arkansas real estate development in which Bill and Hillary Clinton were investors; several fraud convictions resulted from investigations into Whitewater, but evidence was not found that the Clintons were involved in wrongdoing.

Wilmot Proviso   The amendment offered by Pennsylvania Democrat David Wilmot in 1846 which stipulated that "as an express and fundamental condition to the acquisition of any territory from the Republic of Mexico . . . neither slavery nor involuntary servitude shall ever exist in any part of said territory."

Wobblies   Popular name for the members of the Industrial Workers of the World (IWW).

Women's Christian Temperance Union (WCTU)   Women's organization whose members visited schools to educate children about the evils of alcohol, addressed prisoners, and blanketed men's meetings with literature.

World Bank   Designed to revive postwar international trade, it drew on the resources of member nations to make economic development loans to governments for such projects as new dams or agricultural modernization.

World Trade Organization (WTO)   International organization that sets standards and practices for global trade, and the focus of international protests over world economic policy in the late 1990s.

World Wide Web   A part of the Internet designed to allow easier navigation of the network through the use of graphical user interfaces and hypertext links between different addresses.

Wounded Knee Massacre   The U.S. Army's brutal winter massacre in 1890 of at least two hundred Sioux men, women, and children as part of the government's assault on the tribe's Ghost Dance religion.

Writs of Assistance   Documents issued by a court of law that gave British officials in America the power to search for smuggled goods whenever they wished.

XYZ Affair   Diplomatic incident in 1798 in which Americans were outraged by the demand of the French for a bribe as a condition for negotiating with American diplomats.

Yalta Conference   Meeting of U.S. president Franklin Roosevelt, British prime minister Winston Churchill, and Soviet premier Joseph Stalin held in February 1945 to plan the final stages of World War II and postwar arrangements.

Yellow Press   A deliberately sensational journalism of scandal and exposure designed to attract an urban mass audience and increase advertising revenues.

Yellow-Dog Contracts   Employment agreements binding workers not to join a union.

Maverick, Maury, Lt., 482
Maximilian, Archduke of Austria, 302
Maxwell House Hotel, 382
Mayan civilization, 4
Mayflower Compact, 32
Maynard, Lucy, 253
Maysville Road Bill, 191
McAdoo, William, 472, 477, 479
McCall's magazine, 585
McCarran Committee, 574
McCarthy, Eugene, Minnesota senator, 613
McCarthy, Joseph, Wisconsin senator, 575, 613
McCarthyism, 573–576, 579–580
McClellan, George B., general
   at Battle of Antietam, 302
   led Army of Potomac, 299–300, 314
   presidential candidate, 316
   replaced by Lincoln, 304
McClure, Samuel S., 427
McClure's Magazine, 427, 429
McCormick, Cyrus, 254
McCoy, Joseph, 395
McCrae, Jane, 115
McCulloch v. *Maryland* (1819), 179
McDonald's restaurants, 581
McDowell, Calvin, 352
McDowell, Irvin, general, 297
McGovern, George, South Dakota senator, 618
McGuffey Readers, 242
McInerny, Jay, 631
McKinley, William, U.S. president
   assassination, 439
   on Cuban affairs, 456–457, 464
   as governor of Ohio, 419–420
   imperialism debate, 456, 459, 461
   and Panama Canal, 464
McKinley Tariff Act (1890), 412, 416, 419, 454
McLemore, Jeff, 474
McNamara, John, 652–653
McNamara, Robert, 591, 597, 618
McVeigh, Timothy, 656–657
Meade, George, Union general, 305, 314, 315
Measles, 14, 17, 262
Meat Inspection Act (1906), 442
Meatpacking center in Cincinnati, 229
Meatpacking industry, 365, 427
Meatpacking workers, 492
Meat rationed, 542
Mechanics, 230–231, 233
Mechanic's Free Press, 231
Mechanization, 373, 520, 528
Mecklenburg County, North Carolina, 130
Medicaid, 598, 659
Medical care, 113, 330
Medical Care Act, 598
Medicare, 598, 644, 659
Mediterranean, 549
Mediterranean tribute system, 168
Mellon, Andrew, secretary of Treasury, 496, 497
Melting pot, 492
Melville, Herman, 245, 384
Memorial Day Massacre, Chicago (1937), 525–526
Memphis, Tennessee, 297, 299, 352, 375–376, 498

Men
   changing roles in late 19th century, 382
   division of labor
      in Africa, 9
      in Native America, 7
      in New England, 35
      in New South in late 19th century, 344
      on Oregon Trail, 262
      in Western Europe, 10
   employment opportunities in colonial cities, 65–66
   gender segregation during Great Depression, 515
   images as protectors of family, 236
   on Indian reservations, 392
   manufacturing workers, 232
   in military in WWII, 544
   political rights, 127–130
   slave life, 214
   Southern planters, 217
   superiority over household, 241
   as wage earners, 236
Mencken, H. L., 506
Mendes Africans, 8
Menlo Park, New Jersey, 363
Mennonites, 69
Mental hospitals, 243, 634
Mercantilism, 62–63
Merchant marine, 171
Merchant vessels as privateers, 118
Merger mania, 630–631
Merrimack River, 229, 233
Mesoamerica, 3–4
Mestizos, 49, 60, 263
Metacom (King Philip), 50
Methodist Church
   financial ties to state governments, 131
   religious divisions in War of 1812, 175
   settlement houses, 349
   split over slavery in 1844, 221, 284
Methodist clergy, 349, 352
Methodists
   Second Great Awakening, 187
   and social reform, 426
Mexican Americans
   See also Hispanic Americans
   agricultural workers, 611
   attacked by Klan, 505
   in Chavez Ravine, 581
   derogatory stereotypes of, 269
   immigrants, 500, 505, 641, 642
   race riots in WWII, 547
   reestablish city council districts, 664
   workers during WWII, 546
Mexican Borderlands, 262–266
Mexican Cession of 1848, 267
Mexican cowboys, 397
Mexican deportations, 516
Mexican migrant labor, 376, 478, 505, 580
Mexican War, 266, 268–269, 272
Mexico, 1, 3, 4
   California and Southwest lost to U.S., 265–266
   cross-border economy, 643
   during Civil War, 302
   and Germany, Zimmerman note, 476
   slavery in territories, 271–273
   Texas independence, 264–265
   Wilson's actions, 467
Mexico City, 269

Mezzogiorno, Italy, 373
Miami, Florida, 498, 643
Miami Indians, 157, 158
Michigan, 254, 256, 353, 543
Michigan Liberty Party, 249
Michigan University, 641
Micmac Indians, 46
Microsoft Corporation, 659
Mid-Atlantic pluralism in 1800, 150–151
Middle class
   domesticity, 239
   early industrialization in 1800s, 234–236
   in late 19th century, 382–384
   move to suburbs, 382
   and school reform, 242
   support of Nixon, 616–617
   voters in FDR coalition, 524
Middle East, 637
Middle Passage, 54
Midnight, Captain, 545
Midway Island, 452
Midway Island, Battle of, 541
MIG 15s, 571
Migrant labor, 376, 478, 504, 580
Migrations
   of African Americans, 498, 500, 608
   to cities in 1920s, 498–500
   into West, 398
   from New Jersey and Pennsylvania to Old Northwest, 254
   from Old Southwest, 257
   from Upper South to West, 209
   urban crisis in 1970s, 608–609
   of whites going West, 251–252
   of whites on Oregon Trail, 260–262
Milholland, Inez, 424
Militarized society after WWII, 561
Military aid to European governments, 572
Military airplanes, 552, 571, 588, 591, 595
Military bases, 641
Military courts, 544
Military life, 113
Military power
   European *c.*1500, 11
   in Latin America, 463–467
   subjugating Indians, 389–391
Military practices in Europe, 81
Military Reconstruction Acts, 328
Military spending. *See* Defense spending
Military supply depots, 546
Militia. *See* State militias
Millenarian folk movement, 399
Milling machines, 233
Mills, C. Wright, 585
Milwaukee, Wisconsin, 229, 353, 426
Mine inspectors, 395
Minerals, 441, 630
Miners' Union Library, 394
Mingo Indians, 151
Minimum wages, 526
   law for women, 497
Mining, 214
   bonanza in American West, 392–395
   camps, 392–394
   safety legislation, 394
Mining industry, 394–395
Mink brigade, 429
Minneapolis, Minnesota, 611
Minnesota, 286, 398, 410, 415, 416, 481

SINGLE PC LICENSE AGREEMENT AND LIMITED WARRANTY

READ THIS LICENSE CAREFULLY BEFORE OPENING THIS PACKAGE. BY OPENING THIS PACKAGE, YOU ARE AGREEING TO THE TERMS AND CONDITIONS OF THIS LICENSE. IF YOU DO NOT AGREE, DO NOT OPEN THE PACKAGE, PROMPTLY RETURN THE UNOPENED PACKAGE AND ALL ACCOMPANYING ITEMS TO THE PLACE YOU OBTAINED THEM.

1. GRANT OF LICENSE AND OWNERSHIP: THE ENCLOSED COMPUTER PROGRAMS <<AND DATA>> ("SOFTWARE") ARE LICENSED, NOT SOLD, TO YOU BY PEARSON EDUCATION, INC. PUBLISHING AS PEARSON PRENTICE HALL ("WE" OR THE "COMPANY") AND IN CONSIDERATION OF YOUR PURCHASE OR ADOPTION OF THE ACCOMPANYING COMPANY TEXTBOOKS AND/OR OTHER MATERIALS, AND YOUR AGREEMENT TO THESE TERMS. WE RESERVE ANY RIGHTS NOT GRANTED TO YOU. YOU OWN ONLY THE DISK(S) BUT WE AND/OR OUR LICENSORS OWN THE SOFTWARE ITSELF. THIS LICENSE ALLOWS YOU TO USE AND DISPLAY YOUR COPY OF THE SOFTWARE ON A SINGLE COMPUTER (I.E., WITH A SINGLE CPU) AT A SINGLE LOCATION FOR ACADEMIC USE ONLY, SO LONG AS YOU COMPLY WITH THE TERMS OF THIS AGREEMENT. YOU MAY MAKE ONE COPY FOR BACK UP, OR TRANSFER YOUR COPY TO ANOTHER CPU, PROVIDED THAT THE SOFTWARE IS USABLE ON ONLY ONE COMPUTER.

2. RESTRICTIONS: YOU MAY NOT TRANSFER OR DISTRIBUTE THE SOFTWARE OR DOCUMENTATION TO ANYONE ELSE. EXCEPT FOR BACKUP, YOU MAY NOT COPY THE DOCUMENTATION OR THE SOFTWARE. YOU MAY NOT NETWORK THE SOFTWARE OR OTHERWISE USE IT ON MORE THAN ONE COMPUTER OR COMPUTER TERMINAL AT THE SAME TIME. YOU MAY NOT REVERSE ENGINEER, DISASSEMBLE, DECOMPILE, MODIFY, ADAPT, TRANSLATE, OR CREATE DERIVATIVE WORKS BASED ON THE SOFTWARE OR THE DOCUMENTATION. YOU MAY BE HELD LEGALLY RESPONSIBLE FOR ANY COPYING OR COPYRIGHT INFRINGEMENT THAT IS CAUSED BY YOUR FAILURE TO ABIDE BY THE TERMS OF THESE RESTRICTIONS.

3. TERMINATION: THIS LICENSE IS EFFECTIVE UNTIL TERMINATED. THIS LICENSE WILL TERMINATE AUTOMATICALLY WITHOUT NOTICE FROM THE COMPANY IF YOU FAIL TO COMPLY WITH ANY PROVISIONS OR LIMITATIONS OF THIS LICENSE. UPON TERMINATION, YOU SHALL DESTROY THE DOCUMENTATION AND ALL COPIES OF THE SOFTWARE. ALL PROVISIONS OF THIS AGREEMENT AS TO LIMITATION AND DISCLAIMER OF WARRANTIES, LIMITATION OF LIABILITY, REMEDIES OR DAMAGES, AND OUR OWNERSHIP RIGHTS SHALL SURVIVE TERMINATION.

4. LIMITED WARRANTY AND DISCLAIMER OF WARRANTY: COMPANY WARRANTS THAT FOR A PERIOD OF 60 DAYS FROM THE DATE YOU PURCHASE THIS SOFTWARE (OR PURCHASE OR ADOPT THE ACCOMPANYING TEXTBOOK), THE SOFTWARE, WHEN PROPERLY INSTALLED AND USED IN ACCORDANCE WITH THE DOCUMENTATION, WILL OPERATE IN SUBSTANTIAL CONFORMITY WITH THE DESCRIPTION OF THE SOFTWARE SET FORTH IN THE DOCUMENTATION, AND THAT FOR A PERIOD OF 30 DAYS THE DISK(S) ON WHICH THE SOFTWARE IS DELIVERED SHALL BE FREE FROM DEFECTS IN MATERIALS AND WORKMANSHIP UNDER NORMAL USE. THE COMPANY DOES NOT WARRANT THAT THE SOFTWARE WILL MEET YOUR REQUIREMENTS OR THAT THE OPERATION OF THE SOFTWARE WILL BE UNINTERRUPTED OR ERROR-FREE. YOUR ONLY REMEDY AND THE COMPANY'S ONLY OBLIGATION UNDER THESE LIMITED WARRANTIES IS, AT THE COMPANY'S OPTION, RETURN OF THE DISK FOR A REFUND OF ANY AMOUNTS PAID FOR IT BY YOU OR REPLACEMENT OF THE DISK. THIS LIMITED WARRANTY IS THE ONLY WARRANTY PROVIDED BY THE COMPANY AND ITS LICENSORS, AND THE COMPANY AND ITS LICENSORS DISCLAIM ALL OTHER WARRANTIES, EXPRESS OR IMPLIED, INCLUDING WITHOUT LIMITATION, THE IMPLIED WARRANTIES OF MERCHANTABILITY AND FITNESS FOR A PARTICULAR PURPOSE. THE COMPANY DOES NOT WARRANT, GUARANTEE OR MAKE ANY REPRESENTATION REGARDING THE ACCURACY, RELIABILITY, CURRENTNESS, USE, OR RESULTS OF USE, OF THE SOFTWARE.

5. LIMITATION OF REMEDIES AND DAMAGES: IN NO EVENT, SHALL THE COMPANY OR ITS EMPLOYEES, AGENTS, LICENSORS, OR CONTRACTORS BE LIABLE FOR ANY INCIDENTAL, INDIRECT, SPECIAL, OR CONSEQUENTIAL DAMAGES ARISING OUT OF OR IN CONNECTION WITH THIS LICENSE OR THE SOFTWARE, INCLUDING FOR LOSS OF USE, LOSS OF DATA, LOSS OF INCOME OR PROFIT, OR OTHER LOSSES, SUSTAINED AS A RESULT OF INJURY TO ANY PERSON, OR LOSS OF OR DAMAGE TO PROPERTY, OR CLAIMS OF THIRD PARTIES, EVEN IF THE COMPANY OR AN AUTHORIZED REPRESENTATIVE OF THE COMPANY HAS BEEN ADVISED OF THE POSSIBILITY OF SUCH DAMAGES. IN NO EVENT SHALL THE LIABILITY OF THE COMPANY FOR DAMAGES WITH RESPECT TO THE SOFTWARE EXCEED THE AMOUNTS ACTUALLY PAID BY YOU, IF ANY, FOR THE SOFTWARE OR THE ACCOMPANYING TEXTBOOK. BECAUSE SOME JURISDICTIONS DO NOT ALLOW THE LIMITATION OF LIABILITY IN CERTAIN CIRCUMSTANCES, THE ABOVE LIMITATIONS MAY NOT ALWAYS APPLY TO YOU.

6. GENERAL: THIS AGREEMENT SHALL BE CONSTRUED IN ACCORDANCE WITH THE LAWS OF THE UNITED STATES OF AMERICA AND THE STATE OF NEW YORK, APPLICABLE TO CONTRACTS MADE IN NEW YORK, EXCLUDING THE STATE'S LAWS AND POLICIES ON CONFLICTS OF LAW, AND SHALL BENEFIT THE COMPANY, ITS AFFILIATES AND ASSIGNEES. THIS AGREEMENT IS THE COMPLETE AND EXCLUSIVE STATEMENT OF THE AGREEMENT BETWEEN YOU AND THE COMPANY AND SUPERSEDES ALL PROPOSALS OR PRIOR AGREEMENTS, ORAL, OR WRITTEN, AND ANY OTHER COMMUNICATIONS BETWEEN YOU AND THE COMPANY OR ANY REPRESENTATIVE OF THE COMPANY RELATING TO THE SUBJECT MATTER OF THIS AGREEMENT. IF YOU ARE A U.S. GOVERNMENT USER, THIS SOFTWARE IS LICENSED WITH "RESTRICTED RIGHTS" AS SET FORTH IN SUBPARAGRAPHS (A)-(D) OF THE COMMERCIAL COMPUTER-RESTRICTED RIGHTS CLAUSE AT FAR 52.227-19 OR IN SUBPARAGRAPHS (C)(1)(II) OF THE RIGHTS IN TECHNICAL DATA AND COMPUTER SOFTWARE CLAUSE AT DFARS 252.227-7013, AND SIMILAR CLAUSES, AS APPLICABLE.

SHOULD YOU HAVE ANY QUESTIONS CONCERNING THIS AGREEMENT OR IF YOU WISH TO CONTACT THE COMPANY FOR ANY REASON, PLEASE CONTACT IN WRITING LEGAL DEPARTMENT. PRENTICE HALL. I LAKE STREET, UPPER SADDLE RIVER, NJ 07450 OR CALL PEARSON EDUCATION PRODUCT SUPPORT AT 1-800-677-6337